European Union Politics

European Union Politics

FOURTH EDITION

Michelle Cini

Nieves Pérez-Solórzano Borragán

OXFORD

UNIVERSITY PRESS

OXFORD
UNIVERSITY PRESS

Great Clarendon Street, Oxford OX2 6DP,
United Kingdom

Oxford University Press is a department of the University of Oxford.
It furthers the University's objective of excellence in research, scholarship,
and education by publishing worldwide. Oxford is a registered trade mark of
Oxford University Press in the UK and in certain other countries

First edition published in 2003
Second edition published in 2007
Third edition published in 2010

Impression: 1

British Library Cataloguing in Publication Data
Data available

ISBN 978-0-19-969475-4

Printed in Italy by
L.E.G.O. S.p.A—Lavis TN

Preface

This fourth edition of *European Union Politics* builds on the success of the previous three editions by retaining and updating many of the chapters published in earlier versions of the book, whilst bringing in a small number of new contributors and co-authors. In particular, where relevant, chapters now include reflections on the post-Lisbon Treaty context—and one new chapter deals explicitly with the post-2008 economic crisis from an EU perspective.

This edited book remains true to its earlier ambition, which was to offer students of EU politics an introductory text that would be both accessible and challenging, written by authors who are experts in their field. It was designed with undergraduates in mind, particularly those coming to the topic of the EU for the first time; but we know that it has also proven a useful basic text for more advanced students. As in previous editions, we aim to make the study of the European Union an appealing prospect for students. All students should, however, be reading beyond this book, and we provide some guidance on reading at the end of each chapter with that recommendation in mind.

The large number of chapters in this volume (twenty-seven in this edition) should not be taken to imply that the book is comprehensive; rather, it aims to provide a solid overview of a range of topics falling loosely under the rubric of EU politics. Other textbooks focus more specifically on history, theories, institutions, or policies. This book aims to give a taste of all of these areas of EU study. We thank our contributors, without whom this book really would not have been possible. We also owe a debt of gratitude to Catherine Page at Oxford University Press for her efficient handling of the early stages of the project, and Kirsty Reade, and later Jo Hardern and Martha Bailes who took over from Catherine. Kirsty, Jo, and Martha have been engaged and helpful, quick to respond to our queries, as we worked towards the submission of the typescript. We would also like to thank Rachel Minto for taking on the task of updating the *European Union Politics* online resources pages. Rachel has provided readers of this book (both students and teachers) with an excellent supplementary resource. We very much hope that you will take advantage of it.

Michelle Cini

Nieves Pérez-Solórzano Borragán

May 2012

New to this edition

- Extensive revision taking account of the economic crisis in the EU, including a new chapter dedicated to this topic.
- New chapters including governance in the EU, and democracy and legitimacy in the EU.
- Analysis of the effects of the Lisbon Treaty.

Contents

PART 5   Issues and Debates

Detailed Contents

PART I   The Historical Context

PART 2   Theories and Conceptual Approaches

PART 3   Institutions and Actors

PART 4   Policies and Policy-making

PART 5   Issues and Debates

List of Figures

List of Boxes

List of Tables

List of Contributors

David Benson is a Lecturer in Environmental Politics at the School of Environmental Sciences, University of East Anglia, UK.

Tanja A. Börzel is Professor of Political Science and holds the Chair of European Integration, Free University of Berlin, Germany.

Charlotte Burns is a Lecturer in Environmental Policy in the Environment Department at the University of York, UK.

Thomas Christiansen is Jean Monnet Professor of European Institutional Politics at the Faculty of Arts and Social Sciences, Maastricht University, Netherlands.

Clive H. Church is Emeritus Professor in the Department of Politics and International Relations, University of Kent, UK and visiting Professor in the European Institute, University of Sussex, UK.

Michelle Cini is Professor of European Politics in the School of Sociology, Politics and International Studies (SPAIS) at the University of Bristol, UK.

Robert Dover is a Senior Lecturer in International Relations in the Department of Politics, History and International Relations at Loughborough University, UK.

Ralf Drachenberg is currently Policy Manager at FIGIEFA, the International Federation of Independent Wholesalers and Retailers of Automotive Replacement Parts.

Michelle Egan is Associate Professor in the School of International Service at the American University, Washington DC, US.

Morten Egeberg is Professor of Public Policy and Administration in the Department of Political Science and at ARENA, University of Oslo, Norway.

Rainer Eising is Professor of Political Science in the Faculty of Social Science, Ruhr University, Bochum, Germany.

Gerda Falkner is Director of the Institute for European Integration Research and Professor at the University of Vienna, Austria.

Eve Fouilleux is a CNRS Director of Research at CIRAD and CEPEL, University of Montpellier, France.

Simona Guerra is a Lecturer in Politics in the Department of Politics and International Relations, University of Leicester, UK.

Dermot Hodson is a Senior Lecturer in Political Economy in the Department of Politics, Birkbeck College, University of London, UK.

Andrew Jordan is Professor of Environmental Politics in the School of Environmental Sciences, University of East Anglia, Norwich, UK.

Ana E. Juncos is a Lecturer in European Politics in the School of Sociology, Politics, and International Studies at the University of Bristol, UK.

Ilias Kapsis is a Lecturer in Law in the Bradford University School of Management, Bradford, UK.

Sonja Lehringer is a Researcher in the Faculty of Social Science, Ruhr University, Bochum, Germany.

Jeffrey Lewis is Associate Professor in the Department of Political Science at Cleveland State University, US.

Lauren M. McLaren is Associate Professor in the School of Politics and International Relations, University of Nottingham, UK.

Diana Panke is Professor of Political Science at the Albert-Ludwigs University, Freiburg, Germany.

Nieves Pérez-Solórzano Borragán is a Senior Lecturer in European Politics at the School of Sociology, Politics and International Studies, University of Bristol, UK.

David Phinnemore is Professor of Politics in the School of Politics, International Studies and Philosophy, Queen's University Belfast, Northern Ireland and Visiting Professor at the College of Europe, Bruges, Belgium.

Uwe Puetter is Jean Monnet Chair in European Public Policy and Governance, and Director of the Centre for European Union Research, at the Central European University, Budapest, Hungary.

Ben Rosamond is EURECO Professor and Deputy Director of the Centre for European Politics, Department of Political Science, University of Copenhagen, Denmark.

Stijn Smismans is Professor in Law, Jean Monnet Chair in European Law and Governance, and Director of the Jean Monnet Centre of Excellence at the Cardiff Law School, Cardiff University, UK.

Michael Smith is Jean Monnet Professor of European Politics at the Department of Politics, History and International Relations, Loughborough University, UK.

Carsten Strøby Jensen is Professor and Head of the Department of Sociology at Copenhagen University, Denmark.

Emek M. Uçarer is Associate Professor of International Relations in the Department of International Relations at Bucknell University, Pennsylvania, US.

Derek W. Urwin was, until his death, Emeritus Professor of Politics and International Relations at the University of Aberdeen, UK.

Amy Verdun is Professor and Chair of Political Science, Jean Monnet Chair 'Ad Personam' and Director of the Jean Monnet Centre of Excellence at the University of Victoria, Canada.

Alex Warleigh-Lack is Professor of EU Politics, and Jean Monnet Chair in Comparative Regional Integration Studies in the School of Politics, Surrey University, UK, and Associate Fellow, United Nations University (UNU-CRIS), Bruges, Belgium.

List of Abbreviations

ACP	African, Caribbean, and Pacific
AER	Assembly of European Regions
AFSJ	Area of Freedom, Security, and Justice
AG	Advocate-General
AGFISH	Council for Agriculture and Fisheries
ALDE	Alliance of Liberals and Democrats for Europe
AmCham	American Chamber of Commerce
AoA	Agreement on Agriculture
APEC	Asia Pacific Economic Co-operation
ARNE	Antiracist Network for Equality in Europe
ASEAN	Association of Southeast Asian Nations
BDI	Federation of German Industries
BEUC	*Bureau Européen des Unions des Consommateurs* [European Consumer Union Bureau]
BLEU	Belgium Luxembourg Economic Union
BSE	bovine spongiform encephalopathy ('mad cow disease')
BTO	Brussels Treaty Organization
BUAV	British Union for the Abolition of Vivisection
BUSINESSEUROPE	Confederation of European Business
CALRE	Conference of European Regional Legislative Parliaments
CAP	Common Agricultural Policy
CARDS	Community Assistance for Reconstruction, Development and Stabilization
CCP	Common Commercial Policy
CdT	Translation Centre for the Bodies of the European Union
CDU	Christian Democratic Union (Germany)
CEAS	Common European Asylum System
CEB	Council of Europe Development Bank
CEDEC	European Federation of Local Public Energy Distribution Companies
CEDEFOP	European Centre for the Development of Vocational Training
CEE	Central and Eastern Europe
CEEP	*Centre Européen des Entreprises Publics* [European Association for Public Sector Firms]
CEFIC	European Chemical Industry Council
CEMR	Council for European Municipalities and Regions
CEN	European Committee for Standardization
CENELEC	European Committee for Electro-technical Standardization
CEPOL	European Police College
CFCs	chlorofluorocarbon
CFCA	Common Fisheries Control Agency
CFI	Court of First Instance
CFP	Common Fisheries Policy
CFR	Charter of Fundamental Rights
CFSP	Common Foreign and Security Policy
CGS	Council General Secretariat
CIREA	Centre for Information, Discussion and Exchange on Asylum
CIREFI	Centre for Information, Discussion and Exchange on the Crossing of Frontiers and Immigration
CIVAM	Network of French Alternative Farmers
CJEU	Court of Justice of the European Union
CLRA	Congress of Local and Regional Authorities
CMO	common market organization
CNJA	*Centre National des Jeunes Agriculteurs* [French Young Farmers' Association]
CO_2	carbon dioxide
CoA	Court of Auditors
CoE	Council of Europe
COGECA	General Committee for Agricultural Cooperation in the European Union
CONECCS	Consultation, the European Commission and Civil Society database
COPA	Committee of Professional Agricultural Organizations
COPS	*See* PSC
CoR	Committee of the Regions
Coreper	Committee of Permanent Representatives
CPMR	Conference of Peripheral Maritime Regions
CPVO	Community Plant Variety Office
CSDP	Common Security and Defence Policy

CSG	Council Secretariat General	EFC	Economic and Financial Committee (of ECOFIN)
CSO	civil society organization		
CSU	Christian Social Union (Germany)	EFD	Europe of Freedom and Democracy
CT	Constitutional Treaty	EFSA	European Food Safety Authority
DCFTA	deep and comprehensive free trade area	EFSF	European Financial Stability Facility
DG	Directorate-General	EFSM	European Financial Stabilization Mechanism
E&T	education and training		
EACEA	Education, Audiovisual and Culture Executive Agency	EFTA	European Free Trade Association
		EGC	European General Court
EACI	Executive Agency for Competitiveness and Innovation	EGF	European Globalization Adjustment Fund
		EIA	environmental impact assessment
EAEC	European Atomic Energy Community	EIB	European Investment Bank
EAGGF	European Agricultural Guidance and Guarantee Fund	EIoP	*European Integration Online Papers*
		EJA	European Judicial Area
EAHC	Executive Agency for Health and Consumers	EMCDDA	European Monitoring Centre for Drugs and Drug Addiction
EAP	Environmental Action Plan	EMEA	European Medicines Agency
EASA	European Aviation Safety Agency	EMS	European Monetary System
EAW	European arrest warrant	EMSA	European Maritime Safety Authority
EBRD	European Bank for Reconstruction and Development	EMU	economic and monetary union
		ENDS	Environmental Data Services Ltd
EC	European Community; European Communities	ENISA	European Network and Information Security Agency
ECA	European Court of Auditors	ENP	European Neighbourhood Policy
ECB	European Central Bank	ENPI	European Neighbourhood Partnership Instruments
ECDC	European Centre for Disease Prevention and Control		
		EONIA	European Overnight Index Average
ECHA	European Chemicals Agency	EP	European Parliament
ECHO	European Community Humanitarian Office	EPA	economic partnership agreement
		EPC	European Political Community; European political cooperation
ECHR	European Convention on Human Rights		
ECJ	European Court of Justice	EPERN	European Parties Elections and Referendums Network
ECOFIN	Council of Economics and Finance Ministers		
		EPI	environmental policy integration; European policy integration
Ecosoc	*See* EESC		
ECR	European Conservative Reform Group	EPP	European People's Party
ECSC	European Coal and Steel Community	EPSCO	Council for Employment, Social Policy, Health and Consumer Affairs
ecu	European currency unit		
EDA	European Defence Agency	ERA	European Railway Agency
EDC	European Defence Community	ERC	European Research Council Executive Agency
EdF	Électricité de France		
EDP	excessive deficit procedure	ERDF	European Regional Development Fund
EDU	European Drug Unit	ERM	Exchange Rate Mechanism
EEA	European Economic Area; European Environment Agency	ERPA	European Research Papers Archive
		ERRF	European Rapid Reaction Force
EEAS	European External Action Service	ERT	European Round Table of Industrialists
EEB	European Environmental Bureau	ESC	Economic and Social Committee
EEC	European Economic Community	ESCB	European System of Central Banks
EES	European Employment Strategy	ESDP	European Security and Defence Policy
EESC	European Economic and Social Committee	ESF	European Social Fund
EFA	European Free Alliance	ESM	European Stability Mechanism

ETCG	Education and Training 2010 Coordination Group	FYR	former Yugoslav Republic
ETF	European Training Foundation	GAC	General Affairs Council
ETI	European Transparency Initiative	GAERC	General Affairs and External Relations Council
ETS	Emissions Trading Scheme	GATT	General Agreement on Tariffs and Trade
ETSI	European Telecommunications Standards Institute	GDP	gross domestic product
ETSO	European Association of Transmission Systems Operators	GDR	German Democratic Republic
		GEODE	*Groupement Européen de Sociétés et Organismes de Distribution d'Énergie* [European Group of Societies for the Distribution of Energy]
ETUC	European Trade Union Congress		
EU	European Union		
EUDO	European Union Democracy Observatory	GMO	genetically modified organism
EUL	European United Left	GNI	gross national income
EUMC	European Union Military Committee	GNP	gross national product
EUMM	European Union Monitoring Mission	GNSS	Global Navigation Satellite System
EUMS	European Union Military Staff	GSA	European GNSS Supervisory Authority
EU-OSHA	European Agency for Safety and Health at Work	GSC	General Secretariat of the Council
		HLWG	High-Level Working Group on Asylum and Immigration
EUPM	European Union Police Mission	ICJ	International Court of Justice
Euratom	*See* EAEC	ICTY	International Criminal Tribunal of former Yugoslavia
EURELECTRIC	Union of the Electricity Industry		
EUROCHAMBRES	Federation of the Chambers of Commerce in the European Union	IEEP	Institute for European Environmental Policy
EURO-COOP	European Consumer Co-operatives Association	IFIEC	International Federation of Industrial Energy Consumers
EURODAC	European dactyloscopy	IFOAM	International Federation of Organic Agricultural Movements
EUROFOUND	European Foundation for the Improvement of Living and Working Conditions		
		IGC	intergovernmental conference
Eurojust	European Union's Judicial Cooperation Unit	ILO	International Labour Organization
		IMF	International Monetary Fund
Europol	European Police Office	IMP	Integrated Mediterranean Programmes
Eurostat	European Statistical Office	IMPEL	Network for Implementation and Enforcement of Environmental Law
EUSA	European Union Studies Association		
EUSC	European Union Satellite Centre	IPA	Instrument for Pre-Accession Assistance
EWL	European Women's Lobby	IPE	international political economy
FDI	foreign direct investment	IR	international relations
FDP	Free Democratic Party (Germany)	ISAF	International Security Assistance Force
FEU	full economic union	ISPA	Instrument for Structural Policies for Pre-accession
FIFG	Financial Instrument for Fisheries Guidance		
		ISS	European Union Institute for Security Studies
FNSEA	*Fédération Nationale des Syndicats d'Exploitants Agricoles* [French National Federation of Famers' Unions]		
		JAC	*Jeunesse Agricole Chrétienne* [Young Christian Farmers]
FoodSovCAP	European Movement for Food Sovereignty and another Common Agricultural Policy	JASPER	Joint Assistance in Supporting Projects in Europena Regions
FPU	full political union		
FRA	European Fundamental Rights Agency	JEREMIE	Joint European Resources for Micro and Medium Enterprises
Frontex	European Agency for the Management of Operational Cooperation at the External Borders of the Member States of the European Union	JESSICA	Joint European Support for Sustainable Investment in City Areas
		JHA	Justice and Home Affairs
FTA	free trade area	JNA	Joint National Army (of Serbia)

LI	liberal intergovernmentalism	PNR	passenger name record
LMU	Latin monetary union	PNV	*El Partido Nacionalist Vasco* [Basque Nationalist Party]
MBS	mortgage-backed security		
MC	Monetary Committee	PPP	purchasing power parity
MDG	Millennium Development Goals (UN)	PR	proportional representation; public relations
MEP	member of the European Parliament		
MEQR	measures having equivalent effect	PSC	Political and Security Committee (also COPS)
Mercosur	*Mercado Común del Sur* [Southern Common Market]		
		PTCF	(European) Police Chiefs Task Force
MFA	Minister of Foreign Affairs; Multi-Fibre Arrangement	QMV	qualified majority voting
		R&D	research and development
MGQ	maximum guaranteed quantity	R&T	research and technology
MINEX	System for the Promotion of Mineral Production and Exports	RABIT	rapid border intervention teams (Frontex)
		REA	Research Executive Agency
MLG	multilevel governance	REGLEG	Conference of European Regions with Legislative Powers
MP	member of Parliament		
MTR	mid-term review (CAP)	RIA	regulatory impact assessment
NAFTA	North Atlantic Free Trade Agreement	S&D	Social and Democratic Alliance
NAP	national action plan	SAA	stabilization and association agreement
NATO	North Atlantic Treaty Organization	SAP	Stabilization and Association Process
		SAPARD	Special Accession Programme for Agriculture and Rural Development
NEPI	new environmental policy instrument		
NGO	non-governmental organization	SCA	Special Committee on Agriculture (of AGFISH)
NLG	Nordic Green Left		
NMGs	new modes of governance	SDR	special drawing right
NUTS	Nomenclature of Units for Territorial Statistics	SEA	Single European Act
		SEM	Single European Market
OCA	optimum currency area	SFP	Single Farm Payment
ODA	overseas development assistance	SGP	Stability and Growth Pact
OECD	Organisation for Economic Co-operation and Development	SIS	Schengen Information System
		SitCen	Situation Centre (GSC)
OEEC	Organization for European Economic Cooperation	SLIM	Simpler Legislation for the Internal Market
		SMEs	small and medium-sized enterprises
OHIM	Office for the Harmonization of the Single Market (Trade Marks and Designs)	SMP	Securities Markets Programme
		SSC	Scientific Steering Committee
OJ	Official Journal (of the European Union)	STABEX	System for the Stabilisation of ACP and OCT Export Earnings
OLP	ordinary legislative procedure		
OMC	open method of coordination	TA	Treaty of Amsterdam
OSCE	Organization for Security and Cooperation in Europe	TACIS	Programme for Technical Assistance to the Independent States of the Former Soviet Union and Mongolia
PDB	preliminary draft Budget		
PES	Party of European Socialists	TCN	third-country national
PHARE	Poland and Hungary Aid for Economic Reconstruction	TEC	Treaty on the European Community
		TEN-TEA	Trans-European Transport Network Executive Agency
PIREDEU	Providing an Infrastructure for Research on Electoral Democracy in the European Union		
		TEU	Treaty on European Union
		TFEU	Treaty on the Functioning of the European Union
PJCCM	Policy and Judicial Cooperation in Criminal Matters		
		UEAPME	European Association of Craft, Small and Medium Sized Enterprises
plc	public limited company		
PLO	Palestine Liberation Organization	UK	United Kingdom
PM	Prime Minister	UN	United Nations

UNFCCC	UN Framework Convention on Climate Change	VCI	*Verband Chemischer Industrie* [(German) Chemical Industry Association]
UNHCR	Office of the United Nations High Commissioner for Refugees	VIS	Visa Information System
		VOC	volatile organic compound
UNICE	*See* BUSINESS EUROPE	WEU	Western European Union
UNIPEDE	International Union of Producers and Distributors of Electrical Energy	WPEG	White Paper on European Governance
		WTO	World Trade Organization
UNMIK	UN Mission in Kosovo	WWF	World Wildlife Fund for Nature
UNSC	UN Security Council	YES	Young Workers' Exchange Scheme
US	United States		
VAT	value added tax		

Guided Tour of Learning Features

This book is enriched with a range of learning tools to help you navigate the text and reinforce your knowledge of the European Union. This guided tour shows you how to get the most out of your textbook package.

Reader's Guides

Reader's Guides at the beginning of every chapter set the scene for upcoming themes and issues to be discussed, and indicate the scope of coverage within each chapter.

Reader's Guide

This chapter discusses the European Union's response to the economic crisis that began in mid-2007. The chapter covers the period up to the middle of 2012. It identifies what challenges this crisis poses to the existing institutional set-up of economic and monetary union (EMU) and the EU as a whole. A timeline of the crisis thus far is provided and the main changes to the institutional framework of European economic governance are reviewed. It is considered whether the crisis can be understood as a catalyst for further integration or rather uncertainly over the fate of the euro constitutes an existential threat to the process of European integration itself. Mention is also made here of the potential impact of the crisis on relations between euro area members and the rest of the EU, and on the Union's role as an actor in the international arena. The chapter concludes by discussing how the crisis might unfold.

Boxes

BOX 9.3 Explaining 'uploading' and 'shaping'

The bottom-up Europeanization literature uses two concepts interchangeably in order to describe how states influence policies, politics, or institutions of the European Union: 'uploading' and 'shaping'. An EU member state is a successful shaper (or uploader) if it manages to make its preferences heard, so that an EU policy, political process, or institution reflects its interests.

Throughout the book, boxes provide you with extra information on particular topics that complement your understanding of the main chapter text.

sion, European Central Bank (ECB), and International
Monetary Fund (IMF) in negotiating and monitoring
the conditionality of national bailouts—appear as a further evidence of the significant role that technocrats are
playing in the response to the crisis. At the same time
this shift towards technocracy at the European level
frequently clashes with the operation of representative
democracy at the national level. The 'governance turn'
has certainly made its mark on the European Union.

Glossary Terms

Key terms appear in blue in the text and are defined in a glossary
at the end of the book to aid you in exam revision.

KEY POINTS

- The concept of governance has successfully described
  the transformation of policy-making in many parts of t
  world over the past few decades.
- Using the governance concept has been particularly us
  ful in the context of the EU given the difficulty involve
  in categorizing the Euro-polity in terms of the tradition
  distinction between international system and nation st

Key Points

Each section ends with a set of key points that summarize the
most important arguments.

 QUESTIONS

I. Why did the Common Agricultural Policy originally s
2. What were the negative consequences of the CAP's
3. Why did the 1992 reform take place?
4. What do the 1992, 1999, 2003, and 2008 CAP reform
5. To what extent does the current round of internatio

Questions

A set of carefully devised questions has been provided to help you
assess your understanding of core themes, and may also be used
as the basis of seminar discussion or coursework.

 GUIDE TO FURTHER READING

Checkel, J. T. and Katzenstein, P. J. (eds) (2009) *European I*
examines European identity after the latest EU enlargeme

Hooghe, L. and Marks, G. (eds) (2007) *Acta Politica*, 42/2
special issue examines economic interest and identity as
public opinion is cued by the media and political parties.

Leconte, C. (2010) *Understanding Euroscepticism* (Basingstd

Further Reading

Reading lists have been provided as a guide to finding out more
about the issues raised within each chapter and to help you locate
the key academic literature in the field.

 WEBLINKS

http://ec.europa.eu/enlargement/index_en.htm   The E

http://twitter.com/#!/eu_enlargement   The Twitter pa

http://www.cvce.eu/   A detailed online archive on th
enlargement rounds.

http://www.euractiv.com/enlargement   An up-to-date

Important Websites

At the end of every chapter you will find an annotated summary
of useful websites which will guide further research into the
European Union.

Guided Tour of the Online Resource Centre

www.oxfordtextbooks.co.uk/orc/cini4e/

The Online Resource Centre that accompanies this book provides students and instructors with ready-to-use teaching and learning materials. These resources are free of charge and designed to maximize the learning experience.

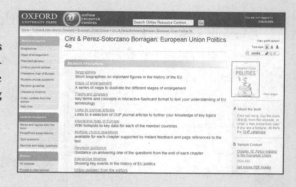

Interactive Timeline

An interactive timeline provides summaries of the key events in the history of European Union politics as you click on each date.

Biographies

Short biographies offer interesting background information on important figures in the history of the EU.

Maps

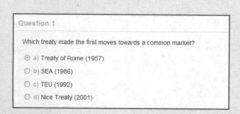

A series of maps has been provided to show you the different stages of EU enlargement and outline vital social and political facts about each member state.

Multiple-choice Questions

A bank of self-marking multiple-choice questions has been provided for each chapter of the text to reinforce your understanding and to act as an aid to revision.

Flashcard Glossary

A series of interactive flashcards containing key terms and concepts allows you to test your understanding of the terminology of the European Union.

Revision Tips

A list of key points to consider in answering the end-of-chapter questions will help keep your revision on track.

Video Updates

Regular updates will be posted to keep you informed of the latest developments in the European Union.

Links to OUP Journal Articles

Links to relevant OUP journal articles allow students and lecturers to explore and research European Union politics in even greater detail.

FOR INSTRUCTORS:

PowerPoint Presentations

These complement each chapter of the book and are a useful resource for preparing lectures and handouts.

Essay, Seminar, and Quiz Questions

Essay, seminar, and quiz questions are provided for each chapter to offer a variety of methods for reinforcing the key themes.

Boxes and Figures from the Text

All boxes and figures from the text have been provided in high resolution format for downloading into presentation software or for use in assignments and exam material.

1

Introduction

Michelle Cini and Nieves Pérez-Solórzano Borragán

Reader's Guide

This chapter comprises a very brief introduction to EU politics. It aims to help those students who are completely new to the European Union by drawing attention to some general (background) information that helps to make sense of the chapters that follow. To that end, this introductory chapter reflects on what the EU is, why it was set up, who can join, who pays, what the EU does, and what role there is in the EU for citizens. The chapter ends by explaining how the book is organized.

Why a European Union?

The economic crisis of 2007–08, and the eurozone (or euro area) crisis that followed from 2010, led many European citizens and elites to question the continued existence of the European Union. Increasingly, the EU is viewed not as a solution to Europe's ills, but as part of the problem. While the impact of the crisis has certainly been, and continues to be, severe, it is also worth remembering that the European integration project has—in the past—coped with crisis; some even see crises as a spur to EU reform, whether leading to further European integration or simply a different kind of European Union. Whether the EU will rise to the challenge of dealing effectively with the post-2010 euro area crisis remains to be seen (as discussed in Chapter 27). But we should not underestimate the resilience of the European integration process and its ability to adapt (if only slowly at times) to changing external circumstances.

Understanding the EU from a historical perspective means stepping back to the post-1945 era. The European integration process was initiated in the 1950s largely as a consequence of the negative experiences of the founding member states during and in the immediate aftermath of the Second World War. Maintaining peace was a primary objective at the time. Even though the idea of a formalized system of European cooperation was not entirely new, the shape that the post-1945 Communities (and later Union) would take was—while drawing on familiar models of government—innovative (see Chapter 2).

From the standpoint of the twenty-first century, it is perhaps easy to forget how potent the anti-war rationale for European integration was in the 1940s and 1950s. But this pacifist ambition went hand-in-hand with a general awareness that (Western) Europe had to get back on its feet economically after the devastation of the war years. Inter-state cooperation was considered an essential step towards a new post-war world. Fundamental to this objective was the reconstruction and rehabilitation of Germany, as the engine of the wider European economy. One might imagine how controversial such an idea would have been at the time. Surely encouraging the re-emergence of a strong Germany would pose a serious threat to the security of Western Europe? Was this not a case of short-term economic objectives trumping long-term geopolitical ones? Ultimately, however, these two ostensibly contradictory objectives of 'peace' and 'economic reconstruction' began to be viewed as mutually reinforcing. European integration—or rather the prospect of it—was the instrument that allowed this change of perspective to occur.

The EU has changed dramatically since the early days of the Community and some argue that the original objectives of the 1950s are no longer relevant. Certainly, the prospect of war between EU member states seems extremely slim now, demonstrating, one might argue, the success of the integration project. However, European integration has been criticized and challenged on a number of fronts—not least for substituting technocratic governance for democracy, and for failing to deliver economic growth and global competitiveness. These criticisms gained a new resonance with the onset of the financial and economic crises in 2007–08.

For the time being, however, it seems that the European Union will continue to exist, even if its future form and trajectory may be unpredictable. Any explanation of why this is the case must rest on an understanding of the importance of the 'security' dimension of the EU's role. It is almost a truism now to state that, since the early 1990s, the discourse around 'old' definitions of security that imply *military* security—closely related to the notion of *defence*—has been subsumed within a more wide-ranging notion of security. Even if the actions of governments do not always live up to the ambitions of this discourse, security issues can now be said to encompass environmental hazard, migration flows, financial crisis, and demographic change—as well as military threats. Two contextual 'events' have been crucial in accounting for the broadening out of the concept: the end of the Cold War in 1989; and the terrorist attacks on the World Trade Center in New York and the Pentagon in Washington DC on 11 September 2001 (known as '9/11'). While the former ended the bipolarity of the post-1945 period, the latter redefined security threats as internal as well as external, as more multi-dimensional and fluid, and as less predictable. Add to this a growing awareness of the threats posed to future generations from climate change and to current populations from environmental pollution, extreme instability in financial markets, and, in the period of global economic crisis from 2008, challenges—however short-lived—to the dominant neoliberal, capitalist paradigm, and it seems in retrospect that the period after 1989 has marked a transition phase during which a new world order has begun to emerge.

The EU is as much a product of this new world order as it is an actor seeking to manage change, or an arena in which other actors attempt to perform a similar function. Thus there is no claim here that the EU alone can address these issues. It is but one response, one that is highly institutionalized, which facilitates agreement through procedural mechanisms such as qualified majority voting (QMV) and norms of consensus, all overseen by a goal-oriented, politically involved bureaucracy, a directly elected co-legislature, and an (at times) activist judicial system. Even though recent events often present the European Union as a 'problem' to be solved, this book demonstrates in many different ways that it also has the potential to provide solutions to the challenges facing Europe in the second decade of the twenty-first century.

The EU is not only about security, however, no matter how broadly we define the concept. It also concerns welfare-related issues. From a normative perspective, which accepts that the state ought to take responsibility for the well-being and social condition of its citizens (rather than leaving them to fend for themselves), the notion of the EU as a neoliberal object accounts for only part of what the EU is or does. In its original form, the welfare state was a European construct, so it should come as no surprise to find that the EU has had ambitions in this direction. But it is important not to overstate the EU's capacity in this respect. Although redistribution and EU-level intervention finds expression in many European policies, when this is compared to the functions performed by its member states, it is clear that the EU performs only a minimal welfare role. While some argue that this is right and proper, others would like to see the EU developing its activities further in this direction.

What is the European Union?

The European Union is a family of liberal-democratic countries, acting collectively through an institutionalized system of decision-making. When joining the EU, members sign up not only to the body of EU treaties, legislation, and norms (the so-called *acquis communautaire*), but also to a set of shared common values, based on democracy, human rights, and principles of social justice. Even so, members, and indeed the European institutions, are keen to stress the diversity of the Union—most obviously in cultural and linguistic terms. By 2012, the EU comprised twenty-seven member states, and over 497 million people, with the promise of a new member state, Croatia, joining on 1 July 2013, bringing the total number of members to twenty-eight and taking the total population of the EU to over 500 million.

Since its establishment in the 1950s, commentators have argued over the kind of body that the European Community (now Union) is. While there is a growing consensus that the EU now sits somewhere between a traditional international organization and a state, the question of whether it resembles one of these 'models' more than the other remains contested. Although it might seem fair to claim that the European Union is unique, or a hybrid body, even this point can be contentious when it prevents researchers from comparing the EU to national systems of government and international organizations.

The common institutions of the EU—that is, the Commission, Parliament, Council, courts, and, since the Lisbon Treaty entered into force, the European Council and the European Central Bank (ECB), along with many other bodies—are perhaps the most visible attributes of the European Union. These institutions are highly interdependent and together they form a nexus for joint decision-making in a now extremely wide range of policy areas. While many argue that the EU Council (comprising the EU's governments and support staff) still predominates as the primary legislator, the importance of the European Parliament has grown substantially since the 1980s, so that it is now generally considered as a co-legislature. Ultimately, however, the member states remain in a privileged position within the EU, because it is they (or rather their governments) who can change the general institutional framework of the Union through treaty reform—or even (potentially) withdraw from the Union, although it seems highly unlikely that any state would take such a dramatic step. The ECB is a unique actor that enjoys a high degree of independence in determining the eurozone's monetary policy, but the response of which to financial crisis is constrained by that very independence, and the failure of the architects of economic and monetary union (EMU) to foresee the necessary interaction between monetary and fiscal policy in the euro area.

Who can join?

From the very beginning of the project, the European Community (EC) was open to new members. The criteria for joining were, however, rather vague. States had to be European, of course, but there was no real definition of what 'European' actually meant. There was also an assumption that member states had to be democratic, but again, this was ill-defined and was not included in any treaty. This changed when, in 1993, the Copenhagen European Council agreed that countries wishing to join the Union had to meet political and economic criteria—in other words, they must have working market economies and liberal democracies, and be able to take on board the *acquis communautaire* (the existing body of EU treaties, legislation, and norms). These conditions of membership became known as the 'Copenhagen criteria' and they have served ever since as the template for assessing a country's readiness to join the European Union.

Although there had been enlargements in the 1970s (with the UK, Ireland, and Denmark joining in 1973) and the 1980s (with Greece joining in 1981, and Spain and Portugal in 1986), the end of the Cold War brought a very different phase in the history of the expansion of the EU. Without the Soviet threat and after a history of more than thirty years of successful cooperation with the EU

under the aegis of the European Free Trade Association (EFTA), Sweden, Finland, and Austria became members in 1995. After gaining independence, the former communist states saw in the EU the anchor supporting their political and economic transitions, and the gateway ensuring their return to Europe. Yet accession would be completed only over a decade later, because both the European Union and the new member states first had to adapt to the challenges of a larger and more diverse Union. It was not until May 2004 that the Czech Republic, Estonia,

Figure 1.1 Map of Europe

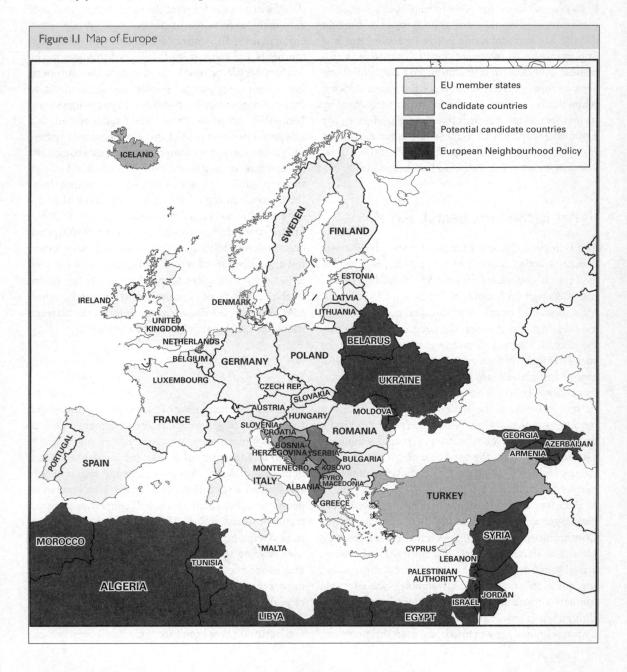

Hungary, Poland, Latvia, Lithuania, Slovakia, and Slovenia joined, along with two small island states, Cyprus and Malta. Bulgaria and Romania joined in 2007. While Croatia is set to join in 2013, Turkey's accession looks unlikely in the short term, even though negotiations began as early as 2004. The prospects of the western Balkans (including Serbia) and Iceland have more promise. In the case of the latter, negotiations began in 2011.

The EU's enlargement experience to date has been extremely successful—one of the great achievements of the European integration project. The prospect of membership pushes reforms in the potential candidates and is a guarantee for stability in the entire region. The EU has been able to accommodate new members remarkably well, notwithstanding certain teething problems. Moreover, each successive enlargement has been accompanied by internal reforms that have, in most cases, strengthened the integration progress. However, the prospect of an EU of thirty or more is controversial in some member states, so it is likely that the question 'Who joins?' will become intrinsically linked to the EU's ability to communicate enlargement effectively to its citizens.

Who pays?

The European Union has its own budget, referred to either as the EU (or, perhaps more accurately, the Community) Budget. Unlike national governments, the Union does not have the capacity to tax European citizens in a direct way, which leads us to ask: from where does this money come? In fact, the Community Budget has more than one source: it comprises receipts from customs duties and sugar levies, contributions at the EU's borders, a percentage of contributions based on value added tax (VAT), and national contributions provided by the member states, amounting to 1 per cent of gross national product (GNP). The EU Budget is, however, relatively small. In 2011, it amounted to just over €140 billion. (Compare that to the annual cost of the UK's National Health Service (NHS) at roughly €130 billion.) To avoid the annual wrangling over the Budget, it was decided in the 1980s that the general framework of the Budget would be decided on a multi-annual basis. Agreement on this framework is always controversial. This is not surprising, because the negotiations establish the amount to be paid by each individual member state and the overall levels of funding, as well as ceilings for particular policy areas such as agriculture or regional policy. For example, in June 2011, when the European Commission presented its proposals for the period 2014–20, the fact that this would increase the Budget by 4.8 per cent caused consternation in national capitals. This was because the average inflation rate for the previous decade had been around 2 per cent—and this came at a time when national governments were themselves going through a period of 'belt-tightening'.

The EU's budgetary process is a complex one. It involves the Commission, the EU Council, and the European Parliament. Negotiations may last several months, if not years (the negotiations for the 2007 Budget started in 2005) and it is always highly technical. The budgetary process provides an excellent illustration of the necessity of inter-institutional cooperation amongst Commission, Parliament, and Council. Although there is a technical dimension to it, the process is highly political. It is not surprising that disputes often leap out of the meeting rooms and corridors of the Brussels institutions and into the newspapers.

What does the European Union do?

The European Union is involved in a wide range of activities, the most high-profile and important of which involve the making and management of European-level policies. These policies, once agreed, must (or should) be implemented across all EU member states. But because implementation is usually the responsibility of national or sub-national governments, the EU-level actors devote most of their attention to coming up with policy ideas and turning those ideas into legislation or actions that have concrete effects. Many of those policy ideas respond to problems that have arisen in Europe as a consequence of increasing transnational (or cross-border) movements. There are exceptions to this; but the EU is most competent to act where the single market is concerned. One example of this has been the EU's recent involvement in the reduction of Europe-wide 'roaming' charges for mobile phone calls.

How, then, is European policy made? It is not easy to summarize the European policy process in just a few paragraphs. One reason for this is that there is no *one* way of making European policy. Some policies, such as foreign policy and policy on judicial cooperation in criminal matters, are very intergovernmental and use a decision-making process that is based largely on government-to-government cooperation. By contrast, there is much more of a supranational quality to policies, such as agricultural policy and policy on, say, Europe-wide mergers. Focusing on policy types, Helen Wallace (2010) sought to group similar types of policy together, identifying five 'modes' of European decision-making: the classical Community method; the EU regulatory mode; the EU distributional mode; the policy coordination mode; and intensive transgovernmentalism. These five modes give some indication of the extent of variation there is across the EU's policy process.

In some of the earliest textbooks on the European Community, the adage that 'the Commission proposes, the Council disposes' was often repeated. As a general statement of how EU policy-making operates today, this is now far from an accurate depiction. It is certainly true that, in the more supranational policy areas, the Commission proposes legislation; however, this does not provide a good summary of the Commission's role across the board.

It is fair to say that policy now emerges as a result of the interaction of a number of actors and institutions. First amongst these is what is sometimes referred to as the 'institutional triangle' of the European Commission, the European Parliament, and the Council of the European Union (the EU Council). However, many other European, national and sub-national bodies, including interest groups, also play an important role. The functions, responsibilities, and obligations of these actors and institutions depend on the particular rules that apply to the policy under consideration. While there are rather different rules that apply to budgetary decisions and to the conclusion of international agreements, and indeed for economic and monetary union (EMU), much of the work of the European Union involves regulatory activities.

Although different procedures still govern the way in which policy is made, this variation is arguably not as extreme as it once was. Most legislation is now made using the ordinary legislative procedure (OLP). This procedure used to be called 'co-decision'; older books and articles will still refer to it as such. The OLP allows both the Parliament and the Council, as co-legislators, two successive readings of legislative proposals drafted by the Commission. Roughly speaking, it means that the Council, comprising national ministers or their representatives, and the European Parliament, made up of elected representatives, together 'co-decide' EU laws. Together, then, they make up the EU's legislature. The Commission, by contrast, is often labelled the EU's executive body (note, however, that the Council also performs some executive functions). The Commission is not a government as such, but has some government-type functions, in that it proposes new laws and has responsibility for managing policies once they have been agreed.

For EU member states sitting in the Council of the European Union, policy is determined on the basis of either unanimity, under which all countries have a potential veto, or a weighted voting system called 'qualified majority voting' (QMV). Most EU policies are now decided upon on the basis of a qualified majority. However, increasingly, other 'modes' of policy-making are being used beyond the formal kinds of decisions that require a vote from the Council and the Parliament. The most discussed of these (by academics, at least) is called the open method of coordination (OMC). This provides a framework for member states to work towards policy convergence in areas of national competence such as employment, social protection, social inclusion, education, and youth and training, through sharing common objectives, policy instruments, best practice, and peer pressure to achieve policy convergence. The Commission, the Parliament, and the European Court of Justice (ECJ) have a limited or no role in the process, which makes this form of policy largely intergovernmental in character.

Focusing solely on the legislative process, then, tells only part of the story of what the EU does. It does not tell us anything about the role that the EU plays in distributing money, through its Structural Funds or by providing research grants to university researchers, nor does it say much about the substance of EU activities, such as the foreign policy actions that take place under the European flag, EU efforts to forge consensus on economic governance, or the environmental initiatives that shape the EU's position in international negotiations on climate change. Neither does it tell us about what the EU means for democracy in Europe and the extent to which the EU is a Union for European citizens. It is to this question that we now turn.

The European Union and its citizens

In the Preamble to the Treaty of Rome, the member states stated their determination to lay the foundations for 'an ever closer union among the peoples of Europe'. As the chapters in this book will show, the process of European integration has deeply affected the lives of all Europeans—from everyday things such as the labelling on packets of crisps and the colour of their passports, to more complex and perhaps non-tangible changes such as the rights bestowed to them by virtue of being citizens of a member state. Yet at the same time the European Union is often said to possess a 'democratic deficit' (see Chapter 25). The Maastricht Treaty established a new citizenship of the Union conceived of as a supplement to, not a substitute for, national citizenship (see Chapter 25). This European citizenship conferred on every citizen of a member state the right to move and reside freely in the Union, the right to vote for and stand as a candidate at municipal and European Parliament elections in whichever member state the EU citizen might reside, the right to petition to the Parliament and the European Ombudsman, and the right to diplomatic and consular protection. Such rights were further extended at Amsterdam, incorporating an anti-discrimination clause and member states' commitment to raise the quality of, and guarantee free access to, education. The Charter of Fundamental Rights, included in the Lisbon Treaty, summarizes the common values of the member states and brings together a set of common civil, political, economic, and social rights.

However, almost since its inception, the EU has struggled to communicate the rationale of integration to the citizens of Europe and to generate some sense of identification with the European project. European citizens tend to conceive of the EU as a remote entity suffering from a permanent democratic deficit: the EU's decision-making mechanisms are considered complex and opaque; it lacks a parliamentary chamber that holds the decisions of government to account; it is run by a set of political elites who have failed to consult citizens on the direction and objectives of the integration process; and more often than not it is portrayed by the media and national political leaders as the source of unpopular political decisions (see Chapter 26). This set of feelings translates into low voter turnout to European Parliament elections. Indeed, a record low was reached in 2009, when only 43 per cent of the EU electorate voted. Similarly, according to a Eurobarometer survey published in December 2011, only 34 per cent said that they

trusted the European Union (Eurobarometer, 2011). That said, trust in national parliaments and national governments was even lower, at 27 and 24 per cent respectively. While this detachment seemed less obvious and perhaps less significant in the early years of the integration process, the so-called 'permissive consensus' ended at Maastricht in 1992, with the negative outcome of the Danish referendum and the French almost-'*non*'. For the first time, the citizens of Europe contested the move towards further integration. Ever since, contestation has become the norm rather than the exception each time the direction of European integration has been put to the vote, as the ratifications of the Nice Treaty, the Constitutional Treaty, and the Lisbon Treaty have shown. Hence, despite attempts to give more powers to the European Parliament, the introduction of the principle of subsidiarity to give more voice to localities and regions, the commitment to a permanent dialogue with civil society, a new citizens' initiative, and a communication policy aimed at 'listening better, explaining better and going local', European integration is still a politicized issue that generates negative mobilization of public opinion with regard to EU policies and institutions. 'We are not forming coalitions of states, we are uniting men', said Jean Monnet. Yet European citizens have different interests, culture, language, and history. Any attempt to forge an ever-closer union among the peoples of Europe needs to account for such a variety of goals, perceptions, and expectations. Such variety of goals and expectations is clearly evident in the public perception of the EU's ability to find solutions to the economic crisis, but also in the perceived fairness of the effects that the crisis is having in different member states. As in the period after the Second World War, the European Union is faced again with an apparent contradiction: how to support countries to address their sovereign debt problems, while ensuring that economic growth and ultimately the well-being of European citizens are not compromised by a focus on austerity-driven measures that have managed to overthrow governments and bring vociferous contestation to the streets.

The organization of the book

The book is organized into five parts.

- Part One covers the historical evolution of the European Community from 1945 to early 2012 (but see also Chapter 27 on the economic crisis).

Chapter 2 focuses on the origins and early years of the European integration process. Chapter 3 covers the period from the Single European Act to the Nice Treaty, and Chapter 4 reviews the period from the Constitutional Treaty's failed ratification to the Lisbon Treaty.

- Part Two deals with theoretical and conceptual approaches that have tried to explain European integration and EU politics. Chapter 5 reviews the fortunes of neo-functionalism, while Chapter 6 summarizes the key elements of the intergovernmental approaches to European integration. Chapter 7 has a wide remit, focusing on a range of relatively new (or more recent) theories of European integration and EU politics. Chapter 8 focuses on governance approaches and Chapter 9 on Europeanization.

- Part Three introduces the European institutions: the Commission (Chapter 10); the EU Council (Chapter 11); the European Parliament (Chapter 12); and the European Courts (Chapter 13). It also includes a chapter on interest intermediation (Chapter 14).

- Part Four covers a sample of European policies, which, while not aiming to be in any way comprehensive, demonstrates the various ways in which such policies have evolved, and—although to a lesser extent—how they operate. It starts in Chapter 15 with an overview of the EU policy process. Thereafter, Chapter 16 tackles external economic policy, Chapter 17 focuses on enlargement, Chapter 18, on foreign, security, and defence policy, and Chapter 19, on the single market. Chapter 20 discusses social policy, and Chapter 21 examines policies on freedom, security, and justice. Chapters 22 and 23 deal, respectively, with economic and monetary union (EMU) and the Common Agricultural Policy (CAP). Finally, Chapter 24 examines the EU's environment policy.

- The final part of the book, Part Five, comprises three chapters, each of which deals with specific issues related to EU politics. The first, Chapter 25, discusses democracy and legitimacy in the EU; the second, Chapter 26, focuses on public opinion; the third and final chapter, Chapter 27, brings us up to date by considering the EU's recent approach to the post-2008 economic crisis.

PART I
The Historical Context

2

The European Community: From 1945 to 1985

Derek W. Urwin

Chapter Contents

Reader's Guide

This chapter reviews the principal developments in the process of European integration from the end of the Second World War through to the mid-1980s. While ideas and arguments in favour of European unity have a much longer history, the war and its aftermath provided greater urgency and a new context. In the mid-1980s, the European Community took a series of decisions that launched it firmly on a trajectory towards intensive political, economic, and monetary integration. Between these two points in time, neither the support for integration nor the institutional and structural forms that it took were preordained or without opposition. The rate and direction of integration depended upon a shifting constellation of forces: the nature of interactions between federalist ideas and their supporters; national governments and their assessments of national self-interest; and the broader international environment. Within these parameters, the chapter looks at the emergence of international organizations in Western Europe in the 1940s, the establishment of the Community idea from the Schuman Plan through to the Treaty of Rome, and the factors that contributed towards the seemingly erratic progress towards ever-closer union made by the European Community after 1958.

Introduction

The institutional structure and operation of the European Union (EU) can trace a direct line of descent back to the establishment of the European Coal and Steel Community (ECSC). Indeed, while the intervening decades may have witnessed extensive embellishment and refinement, the broad outline and principles remain those of 1951. However, the idea and dream of a politically integrated Europe possess a much longer pedigree. Across the centuries, numerous intellectuals and political leaders have argued for, and have attempted to bring order and unity to, the fragmented political mosaic of the European continent. As part of this long-standing dream, an increased intellectual agitation for unity in Europe emerged in the nineteenth century, but almost exclusively among people who were, at best, at the fringes of political decision-making. Their arguments and blueprints held little appeal or relevance for political leaders. However, there did emerge a more widespread recognition that some form of economic cooperation might well contain some potential political advantages for states. Those schemes that did become operative, however, were either short-lived or, like the *Zollverein* established among German states, highly region-specific and protectionist in their external mien.

The peace process after the First World War, by its emphasis upon national self-determination, made the continental political mosaic even more complex, so leading to a greater urgency for, and difficulty surrounding any process of, cooperation. After 1918, the hopes that had been invested in the League of Nations as a world body dedicated to a cooperative peace quickly foundered in a highly charged atmosphere of economic uncertainty and historic political antipathies. The Benelux and the Nordic states explored possibilities of economic cooperation, but with no significant outcome. A few politicians—most notably perhaps Aristide Briand, the French Foreign Minister—did raise the idea of political integration. But in concrete terms this did not advance beyond the 1930 Briand Memorandum, a generalized proposal advocating a kind of intergovernmental union with its own institutional infrastructures within the League of Nations. Outside political circles, a plethora of associations expounded schemes for cooperation and integration, but failed to achieve any positive results. By the 1930s, economic depression and crisis, and the rise of fascism, had led countries to look to

their own defences; the outbreak of war in 1939 simply confirmed the absence of any radical change to the European world of states. The history of European integration, as it is conventionally understood today, essentially begins in 1945. The chapter that follows charts that history, focusing on the period between 1945 and 1985.

The opening moves

The Second World War was a catalyst for a renewed interest in European unity. It contributed to arguments that nationalism and nationalist rivalries, by culminating in war, had discredited and bankrupted the independent state as the foundation of political organization and international order, and that a replacement for the state had to be found in a comprehensive continental community. These ideas were most forcefully expressed in the political vision of Italian federalist Altiero Spinelli, who produced a blueprint for a 'United States of Europe' as the overriding priority for the post-war peace. His arguments found strong favour among the various national Resistance movements. At first, the new European administrations seemed to give European unity a low priority, concentrating more upon issues of national economic reconstruction. But for several reasons the siren voices of federalism were heard by, and swayed, a larger audience than had been the case in the interwar period, so enabling the possibility and dream of union to survive as an item on the European political agenda (see Box 2.1).

One important factor was the increasingly glacial international political climate. This division of Europe between East and West after 1945, and the subsequent Cold War between the world's two superpowers, the US and the USSR, fuelled alarm in Western Europe about its own fragile defences in the light of what it feared were the territorial ambitions of the USSR. This led to a deep involvement of the US in European affairs in the late 1940s. The consequent ideological bipolarization in turn helped to propel Western Europe towards defining itself as an entity with common interests. This changing mood was assisted by a general concern over the parlous state of the national economies, a concern that helped to generate a widespread belief that economic recovery would require both external assistance from the US, and collaboration on development and trade across the Western

BOX 2.1 Issues and debates in the early years of European integration

Why European integration began and the reasons why the subsequent plot developed as it did have been the subject of intense debate. There has been a tendency, especially among those strongly committed to a federal Europe, to see development moving if not smoothly, then nevertheless inexorably along a single plane towards a predetermined goal. Yet the history of integration since the formation of the European Coal and Steel Community (ECSC) in 1951 has not been like that. The rate of integrative progress has been far from consistent, and all arguments and pressures for further advances have had to contend with equally powerful countervailing forces pulling in the opposite direction. Nor was there anything preordained about the structural route taken in 1950 or that future developments would revolve largely around a **Franco-German axis**. There might, both then and later, have been broad agreement about the desirability and principle of a united Europe, but there has rarely been consensus on anything else. As **Robert Schuman**, the French Foreign Minister, commented in May 1950 when he unveiled his plan for a pooling of coal and steel resources: 'Europe will not be made all at once, or according to a single plan.'

In reality, the story of integration is complex, with numerous subplots, varying strategies, and different ambitions. As advocated by the federalists, the role of ideas and beliefs has always been central to the progress of integration. Even so, there has been tension within the federalist camp as to the most appropriate strategy to adopt. Simplifying the complex strands of thought somewhat, there have been two competing strategic schools. On the one hand, there are those who have followed the arguments of people such as Altiero Spinelli, who, in the Ventotene Manifesto of 1940 and his subsequent writings and actions, urged a once-and-for-all 'big bang' solution, an instantaneous and all-embracing transformation into a federal European state. On the other side was a more cautious and pragmatic strategy, encapsulated by the inputs of people such as **Jean Monnet** and Robert Schuman, who envisaged a slower process of steady accretion through a series of limited actions and innovations. But while central and necessary, the force of ideas by itself has not been sufficient. The impact and rate of advance of the federalist impulse has been modified by the input and role of national governments—by their policies and by the degree to which integrative proposals have been seen as fitting with, or at the very least not seeming to threaten, what **regimes** perceive to be the national interests of their own states. The way in which processes of integration have developed over the past half-century, therefore, is the product of a complex interaction of centripetal and centrifugal pressures, of ideas, principles, and realpolitik scepticism. This intricate dance has occurred within a broader and ever-shifting international political and economic environment that itself has affected, sometimes positively and sometimes negatively, the degree of enthusiasm for, commitment to, and rate of progress of integration.

European states. It was widely assumed across Western Europe that the lead in any moves towards closer collaboration, because of its wartime role, would be taken by the UK and that, with Germany prostrate and militarily occupied, a British–French alliance would lie at the core of European organization. However, the initial moves towards enhanced collaboration by governments were limited in scope, an exception being the wartime decision by the governments in exile of Belgium, Netherlands and Luxembourg to establish a Benelux **customs union**. While governments were more typically interested in security arrangements, they did little more than consider mutual aid treaties of the traditional variety. The only formal agreements to emerge were the 1947 **Treaty of Dunkirk** between the UK and France, and its 1948 extension in the fifty-year **Treaty of Brussels** (formally, the Treaty of Economic, Social and Cultural Collaboration and Collective Self-Defence), which incorporated the Benelux states as signatories and which was later to serve as the basis of the **Western European Union (WEU)**. While these treaties listed economic and cultural cooperation as objectives, they were first and foremost mutual security pacts with promises of reciprocal assistance, specifically to guard against possible future German aggression. While other countries and federalists alike looked to the UK to take a lead, the British attitude towards anything more than cooperation between independent states was consistently negative, at best deeply sceptical, and at worst totally hostile.

By 1948, the Cold War was in full swing. Heightened alarm over events in Central and Eastern Europe helped to consolidate the final marriage between Western Europe and the US, with the formation of the North Atlantic Treaty Organization (NATO) in 1949. NATO was the conclusion of a programme of American support first outlined in the Truman Doctrine of March 1947, which pledged American assistance for 'free peoples who are resisting subjugation'. It provided a protective shield behind which Western

BOX 2.2 Key dates in European integration, 1947–57

1947	March	Announcement of the Truman Doctrine by the US
		Signature of the Treaty of Dunkirk by the UK and France
	June	Declaration of the Marshall Plan by the US
1948	January	Start of the Benelux Customs Union
	March	Signature of the Treaty of Brussels by the UK, France, and Benelux
	April	Establishment of the Organization for European Economic Cooperation (OEEC) by sixteen European states, the US, and Canada
	May	The federalist Congress of Europe meets at The Hague, Netherlands
1949	April	Signature of the Atlantic Pact and formation of the North Atlantic Treaty Organization (NATO) by twelve states
	May	Treaty of Westminster establishes the Council of Europe
1950	May	Schuman Plan proposes a pooling of coal and steel resources by France, the Federal Republic of Germany, and any other state wishing to join them
	October	Proposal for a European Defence Community (EDC)
1951	April	Treaty of Paris establishes the European Coal and Steel Community (ECSC)
1952	May	Signature of the EDC Treaty
	July	The ECSC comes into operation
1953	March	Draft Treaty of a European Political Community (EPC)
1954	August	French Parliament rejects the EDC
		The EDC and EPC plans collapse
	October	The Treaty of Brussels is modified to establish the West European Union (WEU)
1955	June	Foreign ministers of the ECSC states meet in Messina, Italy, to consider 'further European integration'
1957	March	Signature of the Treaty of Rome establishes the European Economic Community (EEC) and the European Atomic Energy Community (EAEC, or Euratom)

Europe was free to consider and develop its political and economic options without necessarily having to devote time and scarce resources to military defence. Equally, the US, itself a federation, saw nothing inherently problematic about closer integration in Western Europe; indeed, also partly because of its own strategic interests, the US lent its weight after 1947 to proposals for more intensive collaboration. The American commitment was strongly welcomed by the two leading states, the UK and France. But although they were expected to form the vanguard of the European future, neither saw this as leading to radical reconstruction. French European policy was dominated by the need to keep Germany weak and to control its future, a concern met by the military occupation of the country after 1945. The UK was suspicious of anything beyond close collaboration that

might diminish its own sovereignty and freedom to act independently.

It was against this backdrop that the protagonists of a federal Europe nevertheless began to receive endorsement from a growing number of senior politicians from several countries. Soon, the dominant issue became not whether there should be integration, but rather what form it should take. Governments and political parties took positions on the question of whether this should be only intensive intergovernmental collaboration embedded in formalized treaties and arrangements, or something deeper that would embrace an element of supranationalism and the diminution of national sovereignty. This was the core of the debate at the Congress of Europe in 1948, which led to the establishment of the Council of Europe in 1949 (see Box 2.3).

BOX 2.3 The establishment of the Council of Europe

The Congress of Europe, a gathering of over 700 delegates or representatives of pro-integration or federalist organizations from sixteen countries, along with observers from Canada and the US, was held at The Hague (in the Netherlands) in May 1948. The Congress was too unwieldy to achieve any practical outcome, not least because it did not speak for governments. But in calling for a European federation or union, with its own institutions, a charter of human rights linked to a European court, a **common market**, and **monetary union**, it helped to place integration more firmly and visibly on the agenda. It stimulated a process of discussion and debate that culminated in May 1949 in the establishment by ten states of the intergovernmental Council of Europe, the first post-1945 European political organization. The Council, however, represented a victory for those, especially the UK, who wished to see only cooperation, not integration: decisions would

require the consent of all of its members, and hence it could not enforce any view or policy upon reluctant member states. Federalists accepted the final outcome of the Council only reluctantly, viewing it as a start that would not preclude a search for something better. By contrast, for others it epitomized the totality of what was desirable or necessary. In seeking to accommodate two contrasting positions, the product was very much a dead end. More importantly, however, the Council of Europe represented a watershed. It convinced the protagonists of a united Europe that they would have to narrow their horizons even further. It brought the curtain down on the willingness to compromise in order to keep reluctant states and governments on board. It was, therefore, the point at which the post-war belief that the UK should and would take the lead in radical political reorganization came to an end (Bond, 2011).

Political developments were paralleled by activity on the economic front through the introduction of the European Recovery Programme, or Marshall Plan. The essence of the Plan was an American offer of economic aid to Europe. The aid, however, was contingent upon the administration of the relief programme being collective, in order to maximize its benefits. The US further insisted that the European participants in the programme had to decide themselves how aid was to be distributed across the countries involved. These were the basic tasks of the Organization for European Economic Cooperation (OEEC), established in April 1948. The OEEC was primarily concerned with macroeconomic cooperation and coordination. Like the Council of Europe, it was intergovernmental in nature, only able to operate with the full consent of all of its members. Both organizations, however, had to have some permanent institutions to enable them to perform their allotted functions satisfactorily. While limited in scope and bound very much by the principle of voluntary cooperation, both nevertheless reflected a growing realization in Western Europe of the interdependence of states and that these states, especially against the backdrop of the Cold War, would prosper or fail together. Both contributed significantly to a learning curve among the participants about how collaboration might occur. Yet it remained the case that both organizations, in terms of the degree of integration and limitations on national sovereignty, operated on the basis of the lowest common denominator of

intergovernmental cooperation. While this clearly met the needs of some states and governments, it was a situation that could not satisfy those who believed in the imperative of union (see Hogan, 1987).

KEY POINTS

- The first post-1945 governments, although interested in European cooperation and integration, were more concerned with economic issues than with European integration.

- Federalists and supporters of integration expected the UK, because of its wartime role, to take the lead in reorganizing Europe.

- The Cold War heightened Western European fears of insecurity, and led to a massive American political and economic involvement in Europe.

- European international organizations established in the late 1940s were all intergovernmental in nature.

The Community idea

If a union were to become a political objective, a different path had to be sought, and federalists had to acknowledge that such a path would prove acceptable only to some countries. The radical redirection of effort was provided by then French Foreign Minister Robert Schuman, who, in May 1950, cut through the tangled debate to propose a pooling of coal and steel resources. The Schuman Plan was the blueprint for the European Coal and Steel Community (ECSC), formally established in April 1951 as Western Europe's first organization to involve the yielding of a degree of state sovereignty to a supranational authority (Diebold, 1959).

That such a scheme could be proposed, drafted, and realized was the outcome of a combination of shifting circumstances. It had an immediately identifiable and concrete goal, making it more attractive to senior politicians than an instantaneous federal transformation, no matter how strongly they might favour intensive integration. The drafter of the plan had been Jean Monnet, whose experiences as the supremo of national economic planning in France after 1945 had confirmed his long-held view that economic development and prosperity could best be achieved at a European, rather than a national, level, and that therefore the route to political integration was a long road that inevitably lay through economics. Equally importantly, Monnet had also consistently argued that peace and stability in Europe could be achieved only through a *rapprochement* between the historical rivals, France and Germany; for Monnet, the two states had to form the core of any integrative venture. These were views to which Schuman also strongly subscribed. He was able to persuade his governmental colleagues in Paris of their virtues in part because of further changes in the international environment.

Relations between East and West had reached a nadir in 1948. One consequence was the decision by the US, backed by the UK and a reluctant France, to form a German state out of the western military zones of occupation in the country. This decision and the establishment of an independent Federal Republic of Germany in 1949 destroyed at a stroke the foundation of France's post-1945 European policy. In addition, the compensatory decision to establish an International Ruhr Authority in April 1949 to supervise coal and steel production in West Germany's dominant industrial region failed to satisfy anyone. In 1950, with the Ruhr Authority increasingly ineffectual and on the point of being abandoned, Monnet's ideas offered France a way out of the dilemma, by indicating a strategy by which the new West Germany could be subject to external influence while it was still politically weak. Schuman's proposal proved equally attractive to West German leader Konrad Adenauer, who saw it as a potentially valuable element of his policy of tying the Federal

Republic firmly to Western Europe politically, economically, and militarily. Submerging the country in European ventures, he hoped, would further reassure his neighbours that West Germany had abandoned the aggressive nationalism of the past. It is not insignificant that Schuman's announcement was for a structure enabling the pooling of French and West German coal and steel resources, which other countries were welcome to join if they so wished. He further made it clear that a new structure would be created even if no other state wished to join: '[I]f necessary, we shall go ahead with only two [countries].' Be that as it may, the Schuman Plan was overtly about more than only coal and steel: Schuman emphasized that it would set down 'common bases for economic development as a first step in the federation of Europe'.

Hence the formation of the ECSC was the product of a combination of integrationist impulses and ideas, national self-interest, and international circumstances. Hailed by Jean Monnet as 'the first expression of the Europe that is being born', the ECSC set in motion a groundswell that, some forty years later, was to result in the European Union. While an invitation to join the new body was extended to all Western European states, and especially the UK, only four other countries—Belgium, Italy, Luxembourg, and the Netherlands—felt able to accept the supranational principle of the ECSC. The institutional structure adopted by the ECSC—which included a supreme judicial authority—was to serve as a model for all future developments. The most innovative (and, in the future, highly contentious) feature was the divided executive and decision-making structure: a High Authority vested with significant power to represent and uphold the supranational principle, and a Council of Ministers to represent and protect the interests of the governments of the member states (Poidevin and Spierenberg, 1994).

However, if the ECSC were to be the first step towards deeper union, European integration could not end there. Monnet himself saw the ECSC as the opening phase of a process of sectoral integration, where the ultimate goal of political union would be the long-term culmination of an accretion of integrative efforts, of trust and experience, in a sector-by-sector linkage of specific economic areas and activities that ultimately would result in a common economic market (see Chapter 5). Discussions began more or less immediately on what would and should follow on from coal and steel—for example, transport or agriculture—as the next instances of sectoral economic integration.

The ECSC survived as a separate entity until 1967 when the merged European Communities (EC) was created. Its record of economic success was rather mixed, however. Even though Jean Monnet had been appointed head of the High Authority, the latter failed to bring national coal and steel policies and practices fully under its control, and it had little or no control over or effect on other economic sectors. By themselves, these issues might in time have forced a re-evaluation of the strategy of sectoral integration. In the event, the direction taken by the latter was altogether surprising. The determining factor was a further transformation in the international climate, which had once again changed for the worse as armed conflict broke out in Korea during the ECSC negotiations. Concerned that the Asian war might be a prelude to war in Europe, the US called for a strengthening of the North Atlantic Treaty Organization (NATO), while simultaneously stressing that, because of its global role and commitments, the US itself could not provide the necessary additional resources. When the European members of NATO argued that their economies were too weak to bear substantial additional defence costs, the US proposed a West German military contribution to NATO.

Only a few years after the overthrow of Nazism, the idea of a German army alarmed its neighbours. In France, the possibility of West German rearmament threatened once again to undermine the core of its European policy. Yet, prompted by Jean Monnet, who saw sectoral integration as a solution to the dilemma, the French government proposed a European Defence Community (EDC), modelled upon the ECSC, which would establish a Western European army that would include military units from all of the member states, including West Germany. However, the exercise failed when the French National Assembly refused to take a decision to ratify the Treaty in 1954 (see Box 2.4).

The consequences for integration of the EDC debacle seemed to be severe. It proved to be the high-water mark of the sectoral approach to integration. Only the ECSC survived the damage to the integration cause and there were fears that it too would collapse. A somewhat disillusioned Jean Monnet announced his intention not to seek reappointment as President of the ECSC High Authority, in order to pursue the goal of integration as a private citizen. However, there remained across

Western Europe a substantial degree of institutional cooperation built up over the previous decade: NATO, the Organization for European Economic Cooperation (OEEC), the Council of Europe, and, of course, the ECSC. Within these networks, there had survived in the 'little Europe' of the ECSC Six a strong commitment to further integration. At a meeting of their foreign ministers at Messina in Sicily in June 1955, the six members of the ECSC took a decisive step forward. Taking as their core text the 1952 Dutch proposal for the abolition of quotas and tariffs within, and the introduction of a common external tariff for, the Community area, the foreign ministers agreed to launch 'a fresh advance towards the building of Europe'. This set in motion progress towards plans for a customs union and, ultimately, a common market, plans that culminated in March 1957 with the Treaty of Rome and the formation of the European Economic Community (EEC). Again, however, only the six members of the ECSC were willing to commit themselves to the leap of faith demanded by the Rome Treaty.

KEY POINTS

- The Schuman Plan offered a way for France and the Federal Republic of Germany to become reconciled with each other, and a path towards integration that went beyond intergovernmental cooperation.

- The European Coal and Steel Community (ECSC) was the first step in an anticipated process of sectoral economic integration. The rejection by France of plans for a European Defence Community (EDC) led to its abandonment. The failure of the EDC threatened to destroy the whole process of integration.

- In 1955, the ECSC states launched a rescue operation and committed themselves to further integration, signing the Treaty of Rome two years later.

Rome and the stalling of ambition

Because the new organization was to range over an extremely wide area of activity, the provisions of the Treaty of Rome were necessarily complex. Its Preamble may have been less prescriptive than that of its European Coal and Steel Community (ECSC) predecessor, yet, in referring to the determination 'to lay the foundations of an ever closer union among the peoples of Europe', its implications were far-reaching. More specifically, the Treaty enjoined its signatories

BOX 2.4 The European Defence Community

Under plans for a European Defence Community (EDC), German units would be part of a European army, all falling under an integrated European, rather than an independent West German, command. The other member states would have only a proportion of their armed forces within the EDC framework. The EDC proposal was immediately seen by federalists and others as a significant second step towards integration. However, the question of the desirability or necessity of some form of political control over, and the direction of, an EDC soon led to arguments for a European Political Community (EPC)—something that would short-circuit sectoral integration by an immediate advance towards creating a comprehensive federation. Dutch Foreign Minister Johan Willem Beyen took the argument one step further in 1952, suggesting a parallel drive to economic unity. Arguing that sectoral integration by itself was insufficient for economic development and unity, Beyen proposed that the EDC/EPC nexus be extended to embrace the construction of a customs union and common market.

Only the ECSC countries were willing to explore these possible new ventures. The UK declined a specific invitation to join the EDC, but, because it wished NATO to be strengthened, it indicated support for a European army that would include a West German military contribution. The EPC idea remained at the draft stage and Beyen's ideas were largely put on hold, because it was clear, not least in the minds of supporters of further integration, that any advance down that road was dependent upon the success or failure of **ratification** of the EDC by the national parliaments of the proposed members. Ironically, the stumbling block was France, for which the idea of a rearmed Germany, even within the EDC, remained deeply perturbing. France had

originally wanted, and perhaps had expected, the UK to be part of the new organization as an extra guarantee against any possible resurgence of German militarism, the well-known British hostility to anything that smacked of supranationalism notwithstanding. In a sense, the French proposal for an EDC had been, for many of its politicians, a delaying tactic—perhaps even an idea so outrageous in its audacity that it would become mired in years of debate and argument. The extent to which the notion was embraced both within the ECSC states and beyond, and the speed at which the subsequent talks progressed, placed successive French governments, all short-lived, weak, and concerned more with mere survival than innovation, in a quandary. Confronted by strong political and popular opposition, all were unable or unwilling to make the effort to secure a parliamentary majority for EDC ratification (Aron and Lerner, 1957).

After almost four years of stalemate, France rejected the EDC in 1954 on a technicality (the vote was not on whether the Treaty should be approved, but whether the Parliament wished to discuss the Treaty). With it fell the hopes for an EPC. The vote did not remove the issue of West German rearmament from the agenda. In a frantic search to salvage something from the wreckage, agreement was secured on a British proposal to revamp the 1948 Treaty of Brussels, bringing into it all of the projected members of the EDC. A new body, the Western European Union (WEU), was established, linking together the UK and the ECSC states in a defence arrangement within which West German rearmament would occur. In reality, the WEU remained more or less moribund until the 1980s, and a rearmed West Germany entered NATO as a full and equal member in 1955. The outcome, therefore, was the one result that France had hoped to avoid.

to establish a common market (defined as the free movement of goods, persons, services, and capital), to approximate national economic policies, and to develop common policies, most specifically in agriculture. Although the objectives of the Treaty were expressed in economic terms, a political purpose lay behind them. In aiming to create something more than a common market, the Treaty emphasized the principle that the problems of one member state would be the problems of all.

The institutional structure was modelled on that of the ECSC, with the quasi-executive and supranational European Commission intended to be the driving force of integration (see Chapter 10); its authority was counterbalanced by the Council of Ministers, representing the member states (see Chapter 11). Facing these executive bodies was a much weaker Assembly

with little in the way of significant decision-making powers (see Chapter 12). The Assembly, which quickly adopted for itself the title of European Parliament (EP), was soon engaged in a perpetual struggle to enlarge its own authority, including a demand for implementation of the Treaty provision on direct elections. The final major EEC institution was the European Court of Justice (ECJ), which rapidly, not least by its ruling that EEC law took precedence over national law, asserted itself as a major bonding force (see Chapter 13). The new EEC shared its Assembly and Court with the ECSC and the less significant European Atomic Energy Community (EAEC, or Euratom), also set up in 1957 by a second Treaty of Rome to promote collaboration on the development of nuclear energy for peaceful economic purposes. The three Communities retained separate executive

BOX 2.5 Key dates in European integration, 1958–85

1958	January	Establishment of the EEC and Euratom
1959	January	First tariff cuts made by the EEC
1961	July	The Fouchet Plan for a 'union of states' proposed
1961	July–August	The UK, Denmark, and Ireland apply for EEC membership
1962	January	The EEC develops basic regulations for a Common Agricultural Policy (CAP)
	May	Norway applies for EEC membership
1963	January	President de Gaulle vetoes British membership
		The Franco-German Treaty of Friendship and Reconciliation is signed
1965	April	The Treaty merging the executives of the three Communities is signed in Brussels
	June	France walks out of the Council of Ministers and begins a boycott of the EEC institutions
1966	January	The Luxembourg Compromise ends the French boycott
1967	July	The three Communities merge to form the European Community
	November	President de Gaulle vetoes British membership for the second time
1968	July	The EC establishes a customs union and agrees on a CAP
1969	December	The Hague Summit agrees to consider EC enlargement, and supports greater policy cooperation and economic and monetary union (EMU)
1970	October	The Werner Report on EMU is published
		The Davignon Report on foreign policy cooperation leads to the establishment of European political cooperation (EPC)
1972	March	The currency 'snake' is established, limiting margins of fluctuation between participating currencies
1973	January	Accession of the UK, Denmark, and Ireland
1974	December	The Paris Summit agrees to establish the European Council and accepts the principle of direct elections to the European Parliament
1976	January	The Tindemans Report is published, recommending reform of the EC institutions
1979	March	Establishment of the European Monetary System (EMS)
	June	First direct elections to the European Parliament
1983	June	The Solemn Declaration on European Union is signed by the heads of state and government
1984	February	The European Parliament approves the Draft Treaty Regarding European Union
	June	The Fontainebleau Summit of the European Council agrees to take action on a number of outstanding issues hindering progress on integration
1985	March	The European Council agrees to the establishment of a single market by the end of 1992
	June	The European Council agrees on a reform of the Treaty of Rome

structures until 1967, when they were merged to form the European Communities (EC).

The Treaty of Rome set a target for its objectives. Within specified time limits, the implementation and completion of a customs union, and then a common market, were to be achieved through a three-stage process. The auguries were initially bright. Under the leadership of a proactive Commission, early progress towards the goals of Rome was satisfactory. By 1961, EEC internal tariff barriers had been substantially reduced and quota restrictions on industrial products largely eliminated. Towards the end of the decade, the EEC could proudly claim that the customs union had been implemented ahead of schedule. Internal EEC trade flourished, rates of economic growth were impressive, and work had begun on establishing a

Common Agricultural Policy (CAP). These positive advances raised hopes among those committed to the establishment of a political union that that goal might also be expedited. Indeed, Walter Hallstein, the forceful West German statesman and economist who served as President of the Commission from 1958 to 1967, could inform journalists that perhaps he should be regarded as a kind of Western European prime minister. The optimism, however, proved to be premature. Broadly speaking, the transformation of the EEC into a common market was scheduled to be spread over a period of twelve to fifteen years. By the early 1970s, however, the EEC was seemingly no nearer that goal than it had been a decade earlier. A series of circumstances had led to its derailment.

The issues that the EEC was obliged to confront in the 1960s were issues that have remained central ever since. In simple terms, they related to the deepening and widening of the Community: the extent to which, and the rate at which, more intensive integration should be pursued, and how these aspects of integration should relate to the enlargement of the EEC. The specific context in which these issues emerged in the 1960s had a focal point in French President Charles de Gaulle. While he was generally supportive of the EEC as a means of retaining French influence in Western Europe, forging in particular a close relationship with Konrad Adenauer and the German economic giant across the Rhine in 1963, de Gaulle was suspicious of anything that might affect that influence and undermine French sovereignty. In 1961, he had tried to push the EEC down a somewhat different route, floating the idea of a 'Union of States' that would entail the incorporation of the EEC into a new intergovernmental organization for the coordination of foreign and defence policy. His proposal was given detailed institutional flesh in the subsequent Fouchet Plan. But the idea received, at best, little support outside West Germany and was rejected in 1962 after a series of acrimonious meetings. While the smaller EEC members were concerned about being presented with some kind of Franco-German fait accompli, the episode merely added extra substance to de Gaulle's longstanding suspicions that the EEC, or anything like it, might well act as a brake on his ambitions for France.

Two further episodes heightened the mood of crisis. First, the immediate economic success of the EEC as a trading bloc after 1958 had persuaded other Western European states that had previously rejected involvement to revise their opinion and seek membership. The most important candidate was the UK, which applied for membership in 1961. In 1963, and again in 1967, de Gaulle, against the wishes of his five partners, vetoed the British application on the grounds that the country, because of its Commonwealth links and close relationship with the US, was not sufficiently committed either politically or economically to Europe or to EEC objectives. Although not subject to a veto, the other applicant states declined to proceed without the UK. Second, according to the schedule set by the Treaty of Rome, the EEC was expected to take some decisive decisions in 1966, including a move to an extension of qualified majority voting (QMV) in the Council of Ministers. At the same time, the EEC was faced with approving financial arrangements for the CAP (see Chapter 23) and a Commission proposal for enhancing supranational authority, by giving more powers to itself and the EP. The latter proposal clearly involved a diminution of national sovereignty, as would any extension of QMV, which would reduce the number of areas in which unanimity across the member states was necessary. Instead, for many decisions, a two-thirds majority would suffice, with the result that a state could be outvoted, but not block the decision by exercising a veto. While the Treaty of Rome had envisaged a steady diminution of the right of a member state to exercise a veto, de Gaulle was not prepared to accept the increased risk of France being outvoted in key decisions. In 1965, he provoked a crisis (known as the 'empty chair' crisis) by withdrawing all French participation in Council of Ministers' business except for that dealing with low-level and routine technicalities. The EEC almost ground to a halt. The crisis was resolved only by the Luxembourg Compromise of 1966 (Palayret et al., 2006) (see Box 2.6).

Overall, the results of de Gaulle's actions seemed to indicate that political integration, as advocated by the federalists, was off the agenda and that the future development of the EC would be more as an intergovernmental grouping of independent states. This shift of emphasis and mood seemed to be symbolized by the 1967 resignation of Hallstein as Commission President. To some extent, the early rapid progress after 1958 had been possible not only because of favourable internal and external economic conditions, but also because, apart from the furore over the Fouchet Plan, national leaders had remained relatively uninvolved in EEC business, being content to allow the Commission to push things forward. If, however, future progress was to be governed by the Luxembourg

> ### BOX 2.6 The Luxembourg Compromise
>
> The Luxembourg Compromise (or Luxembourg Agreement) is the name often given to the agreement among the then six member states of the European Community that concluded the 'empty chair' crisis of 1965. The agreement stated that, in cases of the vital national interest of one of the member states, the Council would aim to find a consensus solution, thus creating a de facto veto right.
>
> The Compromise had practical effects for both the Council and the Commission. In the case of the Council, member states were more willing to accept an extension of QMV, knowing that, in the final instance, they could invoke the Luxembourg Compromise and veto unwanted legislation. In the case of the Commission, it meant that this institution had to make more of an effort to ensure that its proposals would not impact upon the vital interests of any member state. In so doing, it made the Commission much more cautious in its policy proposals. These effects were felt despite the fact that the Luxembourg Compromise was never recognized by the ECJ as legally binding.

Compromise, a more positive national governmental input would be required. But even that might be insufficient as long as Charles de Gaulle remained in power. Hence any way forward had to await the French President's retirement in 1969 (Ludlow, 2007).

> ### KEY POINTS
>
> - The Treaty of Rome (1957) set out a plan and schedule for a customs union and common market as a prelude to some form of political union.
>
> - In the 1960s, the European Economic Community (EEC) witnessed tensions over the deepening and widening the Community structure.
>
> - A division of opinion emerged between France and its five partners over the course of the 1960s.
>
> - In 1965, a serious dispute between France and the other member states over institutional change crippled the EEC. It was resolved by the Luxembourg Compromise.

The emergence of summits

In 1969, at a summit meeting in The Hague in the Netherlands intended to discuss the options open to the EC, the six heads of state and government attempted to restore some momentum to the stalled integration process. The Hague Summit opened the way for the enlargement of the EC, especially for the British. It agreed to extend the budgetary competence of the European Parliament (EP) and argued for more common policy. It also called for a move towards economic and monetary union (EMU), initially through an exchange rate system for the EC, as an important step towards the ultimate goal of political union (see Chapter 22). In practice, the Hague meeting inaugurated summitry as a new style of EC decision-making, recognizing that integration could develop further only if it were able to reconcile itself with national concerns. Summitry—that is, the use of European summits to set the political agenda of the Community—was to be formalized and placed on a regular footing with the establishment of the European Council in 1974 as a meeting place for the leaders of national governments (see Chapter 11).

Achievement of the objectives declaimed at The Hague was only partially successful. The first enlargement of the EC duly occurred in 1973, with the accession of the UK, Denmark, and Ireland (Nicholson and East, 1987). The other candidate for membership in the 1960s, Norway, had already withdrawn from the final negotiations as a result of a referendum in 1972, which, against government advice, had rejected EC membership. Equally, the EC began to be able to assert a more positive and united presence in international affairs. Represented by the Commission, it spoke with one voice in international trade negotiations and, after the 1970 Davignon Report on policy cooperation, the member states, through European political cooperation (EPC), developed an impressive and (on balance) quite successful structure and pattern of collaboration on, and coordination of, foreign policy (see Chapter 18). After the mid-1970s, two Structural Funds, the European Regional Development Fund (ERDF) and the European Social Fund (ESF), began to play an important role in providing aid for economic and employment restructuring. The Common Agricultural Policy (CAP) had also come fully on stream in 1972, although in its final form it developed as a protectionist device that shielded European farmers from the full impact of market forces, and from the necessity of taking markets and demand into account when planning production (see Chapter 23).

However, while the balance sheet around the end of the 1970s did feature many positive aspects, there was also a debit side. The achievements gained could not disguise the fact that, on the broader front of the ambitions of the Treaty of Rome, the EC still seemed to be marking time. A common market seemed to be as far away as ever, with the prospect of political union even more remote. The major integrative impetus propounded at the Hague Summit had been EMU. The leaders had set up a committee under Luxembourg premier Pierre Werner to put some flesh on the proposal. The Werner Report of 1970 outlined a three-stage process for the full implementation of EMU by 1980 (see Chapter 22).

The decade, however, had not progressed very far before this rekindling of ambition was thwarted. In 1972, the EC did attempt to establish a European zone of stability by imposing limits on how far EC currencies would be permitted to float against each other (the so-called 'snake'), but this barely got off the ground. Undermined not least by the quadrupling of oil prices in 1973—the consequence of war in the Middle East—the 'snake' structure was already dead when it was abandoned in 1976. In addition, the EC experienced both rapidly growing unemployment and inflation in the 1970s. The consequent political and electoral pressures forced governments to turn more to national issues and national defence. Some stabilization was eventually achieved after 1979 with the relaunch—sponsored by the European Council—of a monetary policy. The European Monetary System (EMS) did, through an exchange rate mechanism (ERM), have currency stabilization as an objective. However, by itself, the EMS could not achieve monetary union. It was a more modest design and could be only a first step on the road back to EMU. In the 1980s, the EMS was deemed, perhaps because of its modesty, to have had some success in curbing currency fluctuations, inflation, and unemployment, thereby contributing to the return of EMU to the central EC agenda in 1989 (Marsh, 2009; see also Chapter 22).

On the broader integrative front, the initiative had passed firmly to the European Council. Its formation in 1974 confirmed the central role that had to be adopted by the heads of government in determining the future path of the EC. More specifically, it brought to an apogee the Franco-German axis that lay at the core of the EC and which had been, two decades earlier, an essential sub-theme for people such as Monnet and Schuman. Formalized in a Treaty of Friendship and Reconciliation in 1963, the relationship and its significance for the EC were to become far more overt in the 1970s. While the two states might not always be able to impose their will upon their partners, their active consent was vital for any progress to be made. Although the leaders of the two states, Valéry Giscard d'Estaing and Helmut Schmidt, accepted the need to utilize and develop the EC as an instrument of pragmatic integration, both tended to evaluate ideas in terms of national interest and were seemingly reluctant to pursue an advanced federalist route. That Franco-German drive had to await the leadership of François Mitterrand and Helmut Kohl, who came into power in 1981 and 1982 respectively (Simonian, 1985). With the Commission seemingly downgraded and kept on a short leash, the real achievements that were gained could not conceal the fact that the EC was not progressing, or at least was doing so only minimally, towards the aims of the Treaty of Rome.

Nevertheless, the EC, and the European Council in particular, continued to pay lip service to the ideal of full economic and political union. From its commissioning of the 1976 Tindemans Report, which recommended strengthening the EC institutions and the adoption of more common policies, through to its 1983 Solemn Declaration on European Union, the European Council sponsored studies on how to advance the cause of union or rhetorically reasserted its faith in the ultimate goal. In 1974, the Council of Ministers had eventually agreed to implement the Rome requirement that the European Parliament should be elected directly by the national electorates. The first direct elections were held in 1979. They gave the EP a sense of greater legitimacy, a feeling that it now had a mandate to review existing structures, and to urge the EC to progress to a more cohesive and genuine union. With its moves coordinated by veteran federalist Altiero Spinelli, who had been elected to the Parliament, the EP produced a Draft Treaty Establishing the European Union. While the European Council took no immediate action on the EP proposals, the Treaty nevertheless provided a working basis for, and contributed towards, the developments that, within a decade, led to the establishment of the European Union (EU).

At the end of the day, however, initiative and commitment had to come from the European Council. For this to happen, it needed to take on board a growing number of issues that it had earlier sought to shelve or avoid: the EC's Budget and how national contributions to it were determined; the burgeoning costs, problems, and distorting consequences of the CAP; the need to consider and develop further common policies; future enlargements; and a more detailed and positive response to how the EC should fit into a rapidly changing international world. Indeed, adapting to the international environment seemed to increase in urgency in the 1980s. European leaders began to worry that, in a new economic era of high technology, which required massive investment, Western Europe was already lagging far behind the market leaders of the US and Japan, Increasingly, the argument was heard that European survival and competitiveness in this brave new world could be achieved only through cooperation and a common front.

Moreover, the EC states had become alarmed in the late 1970s by an increasingly bellicose Soviet foreign policy that they feared might destabilize the Western European status quo. After 1980, they became equally alarmed at the aggressive American response, fearing that they might be dragged into conflict by an American policy over which they had no influence. After 1985 and the arrival of Mikhail Gorbachev as leader of the USSR, the two superpowers began to talk to each other about means of reducing tension and accommodating each other's interests. Almost predictably, the EC states began to express concerns that the two superpowers might reach an agreement that would not take their interests into account.

This international background provided, as it often had done in previous decades, a necessary stimulus for more visible activity on the domestic Western European front. Partly by choice and partly by necessity, European Council sessions turned to internal matters. At the core of this new activity was French President Mitterrand. After the failure of his initial attempts to reflate the French economy after 1981, Mitterrand concluded that recuperation could more readily be achieved by means of European integration, especially when working in close harness with West Germany. With the encouragement of Mitterrand and others, there emerged, in short, a new sense of direction and purpose. In 1984, the Fontainebleau Summit meeting of the European Council reached agreement on tackling a backlog of issues that had hitherto stalled the integration progress. With these agreements behind them, members of the European Council were able to take a series of decisions intended to advance the cause of union. They agreed to the establishment of a single internal market by the end of 1992 and to a major revision of the Treaty of Rome. In so doing, they pushed the EC decisively towards a more intense economic integration, the Treaty on European Union (TEU), and the establishment of the EU (see Chapter 3).

KEY POINTS

- The Hague Summit of 1969 opened the way for the admission of new members to the EC and agreed to seek new initiatives in policy cooperation, especially economic and monetary union (EMU).

- The practice of summitry was institutionalized by the establishment of the European Council in 1974.

- In 1984, the European Council reached agreement on several important outstanding issues. This permitted it, in the following year, to consider future developments. It committed the EC to a single internal market and a major overhaul of the Treaty of Rome.

- These initiatives were helped by concerns that Western Europe's international status, both political and economic, had declined.

Conclusion

The story of the events that led to the Treaty of Rome, and then to its reform in the 1980s, do not portray an inevitable and steady progression towards European union. Behind the rhetoric of inexorable progress towards the goal of 'an ever closer union', there lies a rather more complex reality. Thus it might be more appropriate to liken the story of integration to a rollercoaster ride, during which the uphill and downhill gradients that determined the speed of the ride were the product of a multitude of factors.

The history of the formative decades of European integration was the product of an array of complex interactions. The world of ideas and the agitation of committed federalists had to contend with and were counterbalanced by the roles played by national leaders and governments, and their assessment of how developments and proposals might impinge upon national self-interest. No matter how intricate the consequent dance, the steps and routines were influenced by and contained within parameters set by the broader flows of the international political and economic environment. At the heart of this complex product lay the health of the relationship between France and West Germany. When all, or perhaps only most, of these factors were in positive conjunction with each other, progress could be rapid, significant, and impressive. When they were not, the process of integration was more likely merely to mark time.

? QUESTIONS

1. Why did it prove difficult to establish a momentum for integration in the years immediately following the end of the Second World War?

2. How important was the development of international European organizations between 1945 and 1950 as a necessary condition for European integration?

3. What lessons for the future could be adduced from the strategy of sectoral integration in the 1950s?

4. To what extent does the failure of the European Defence Community (EDC) suggest that there are some areas of policy that are not amenable to integration?

5. How important were the crises of the 1960s in shaping the future development of the European Community?

6. How important was the establishment of the European Council as a mechanism for promoting further integration in the European Community?

7. To what extent was cooperation between France and West Germany necessary for a process of integration to begin?

8. To what extent has the international political and economic environment stimulated or hindered processes of integration?

GUIDE TO FURTHER READING

Dedman, M. (2009) *The Origins and Development of the European Union: A History of European Integration* (London: Routledge)   A good concise introduction to the broad sweep of European integration history that is useful for the beginner.

Dinan, D. (2004) *Europe Recast* (Basingstoke: Palgrave)   An excellent textbook that moves beyond the range of concise introductions, whilst not assuming any prior knowledge of the history of the European Union.

Gilbert, M. F. (2011) *European Integration: A Concise History* (Lanham, MD: AltaMira Press)   A concise introduction to the history of the EU, which aims to escape from the perspectives of both 'Euroscepticism' and 'Eurofanaticism'.

Gillingham, J. (2003) *European Integration 1950–2003: Superstate or New Market Economy* (Cambridge: Cambridge University Press)   A thorough analysis of European integration history from an author who is not afraid to challenge conventional wisdoms about the EU.

Urwin, D. W. (1995) *The Community of Europe* (London: Longman)   A broad introductory survey of the post-1945 history of European cooperation and integration.

⊕ WEBLINKS

http://europa.eu/about-eu/eu-history/index_en.htm   The European Union's summary history of the European integration process.

http://europa.eu/50/index_en.htm   The European Union site celebrating the fiftieth anniversary of the Treaty of Rome.

http://www.cvce.eu   A detailed online archive on the development of European integration.

http://www.eu-historians.eu/Journal   The website of the *Journal of European Integration History*.

http://www.eui.eu/Research/HistoricalArchivesOfEU/Index.aspx   The European University Institute's Historical Archives of the European Union.

3

The European Union: Establishment and Development

David Phinnemore

Reader's Guide

The focus of this chapter is the emergence and development of the European Union. Key issues include the significance for the idea of union of the Single European Act (SEA) (1986), the Treaty on European Union (TEU) (1992), and the structure of the EU. The chapter also examines the origins and impact on the EU of the Treaty of Amsterdam (1997) and the Treaty of Nice (2000), presenting their key reforms and assessing the extent to which they contribute to the idea of the EU as a union. The chapter also introduces the 'Future of Europe' debate launched in 2001, which led to the adoption of the Treaty establishing a Constitution for Europe (2004) and subsequently the Treaty of Lisbon (2007).

Introduction

To what extent is the European Union a union? This may seem an odd question to ask, but an examination of what the EU was when it was formally established on 1 November 1993 and how it has since evolved, at least in terms of its formal structures, reveals that it remains less than its name implies. Indeed, whereas 'union' might conjure up ideas of coherence and uniformity, the EU today continues to be characterized as much by variation in its structure and exceptions for certain of its member states. Hence voices are often heard calling for change. It is in part the desire to ensure that the EU behaves and acts as a union that has been behind the various reform attempts—successful or otherwise—that have dominated the EU's agenda ever since its creation. Indeed, in the initial ten years after the EU was formally established, two major sets of treaty amendments were introduced. There were also various other adjustments resulting from three enlargements (see Chapter 17). Each set of amendments introduced reforms to the EU (see Box 3.1). More recently, the Treaty of Lisbon has introduced further reforms (see Chapter 4).

This chapter discusses the original structure of the EU and how this was affected by certain key developments during its first decade or so. The chapter examines not only the origins of the EU, but also the background to, and content of, the Treaty of Amsterdam (1997) and the Treaty of Nice (2000). In between discussing how these changed the EU and impacted on the idea of union, consideration is given to the significance of the launch of economic and monetary

union (EMU), a process that simultaneously promoted closer union and differentiated integration within the EU, thus showing that member states may integrate in different ways or at different speeds. A similar argument can be made of cooperation in the Schengen area (see Chapter 21). The chapter concludes by introducing the issues that the EU and its member states sought to address as part of the 'Future of Europe' debate that eventually led to the Treaty of Lisbon (see Chapter 4). Before then, however, the EU as a union and the Treaty on European Union (TEU) need to be considered.

The European Union as a European union

The idea of creating a European union has long been a goal of states committed to European integration. This was made clear in the 1950s when the six original members of the European Economic Community (EEC) expressed their determination in the first recital

BOX 3.1 Key dates in European integration, 1986–2004

1986	February	Single European Act (SEA) signed
1987	July	SEA enters into force
1991	December	Maastricht European Council agrees Treaty on European Union (TEU)
1992	February	TEU signed
1993	November	European Union established
1995	January	EU enlarges to fifteen member states
1996	March	1996 Intergovernmental Conference (IGC) launched
1997	June	Amsterdam European Council agrees Treaty of Amsterdam
	July	Agenda 2000 published
	October	Treaty of Amsterdam signed
1999	January	Stage III of economic and monetary union (EMU) launched
	May	Treaty of Amsterdam enters into force
2000	February	2000 IGC launched
	December	Nice European Council agrees Treaty of Nice
2001	February	Treaty of Nice signed
	December	Laeken European Council adopts Declaration on the Future of the Union
2002	January	Introduction of the euro
	March	Launch of the European Convention
2003	February	Treaty of Nice enters into force

of the Preamble to the Treaty of Rome 'to lay the foundations of an ever closer union among the peoples of Europe' (see Box 3.2). They reaffirmed this in 1972 when they expressed their intention to convert 'their entire relationship into a European Union before the end of the decade'. In joining them in the European Communities (EC), new members from 1973 (Denmark, Ireland, and the UK), 1981 (Greece), and 1986 (Portugal and Spain) also signed up to this goal. Reaffirmation of the commitment was central to the Solemn Declaration on European Union proclaimed at the Stuttgart European Council in June 1983 and, in part, inspired the Single European Act (SEA) of 1986. This, as its Preamble noted, was adopted in response to the member states' desire to 'transform' their relations into 'a European Union', to 'implement' this new entity, and to invest it 'with the necessary means of action'.

The Single European Act

In adopting the SEA, the member states agreed some significant reforms to the Treaty of Rome. In terms of policies, the SEA introduced a range of formally new competences (environment, research and development, and economic and social cohesion), established a deadline for the completion of the internal market and facilitated the adoption of harmonized legislation to achieve this, committed the member states to cooperate on the convergence of economic and monetary policy, and expanded social policy competences to include health and safety in the workplace and dialogue between management and labour (see Chapter 19). As regards the institutions, it expanded the decision-making role of the European Parliament (EP) through the introduction of the cooperation procedure to cover mainly internal market issues, and the assent procedure governing association agreements

and accession. It also extended the use of qualified majority voting (QMV) in the Council, allowed the Council to confer implementation powers on the Commission, and established a Court of First Instance (CFI) to assist the European Court of Justice (ECJ) in its work. In addition, it gave formal recognition to the European Council and European Political Cooperation (EPC), the latter being the forerunner of the Common Foreign and Security Policy (CFSP). The fact that neither the European Council nor EPC were technically part of the EC was reflective of member states' differences on how much supranational integration they were willing to pursue (see Chapter 1). For some, there was a clear preference for intergovernmental cooperation. Evidently, the desire for a European union was not universal.

Agreement on establishing a European Union was not, however, far off. Despite being a very brief document and one that failed in many respects to meet the aspirations of integrationists, the SEA and the launch of the initiative to complete the internal market by the end of 1992 ushered in a period of renewed dynamism for the EC during the second half of the 1980s. At the time, calls for further steps towards European union were being made by senior European leaders such as French President François Mitterrand and German Chancellor Helmut Kohl, as well as by Commission President Jacques Delors. Others—most notably, UK Prime Minister Margaret Thatcher—resisted. With momentum for economic and monetary union (EMU) building among its supporters, however, a new intergovernmental conference (IGC) of the member states would soon be launched in 1991; so too would a second IGC—on political union—following the collapse of communist regimes in Central and Eastern Europe (CEE) in 1989, the end of the Cold War, and the prospect of German unification (see Box 3.3). Out of these emerged the Treaty on European Union (TEU).

BOX 3.3 From intergovernmental conference (IGC) to treaty

The European Union and the European Community were both established by constitutive treaties concluded between their founding member states. If the current member states wish to reform the EU or the EC, they need to amend the constitutive treaties. This is formally done via an intergovernmental conference (IGC) in which the member states negotiate amendments. Agreed amendments are then brought together in an **amending treaty** that all member states must sign and ratify. **Ratification** normally involves each member state's parliament approving the treaty by vote. In some member states, for either procedural or political reasons, treaties are also put to a referendum.

BOX 3.4 The Treaty on European Union

The impact of the TEU on the process of achieving 'ever-closer union' was considerable. Most significantly, it formally established the EU. In addition, it promoted European integration in a whole variety of ways, whether through the promotion of cooperation in the two new CFSP and JHA intergovernmental pillars or through the expansion of EC activities. Indeed, thanks to the TEU, the EC was given new competences in the fields of education, culture, public health, consumer protection, trans-European networks, industry, and development cooperation. Citizenship of the EU was also established and, of course, the TEU set out the timetable for EMU by 1999. As for existing competences, some were expanded—notably in the areas of social policy, the environment, and economic and social cohesion—although, in an attempt to assuage concerns about the over-centralization of power, the principle of **subsidiarity** was introduced. Moreover, the TEU saw the establishment of new institutions and bodies, including the **European Central Bank (ECB)**, the **Committee of the Regions (CoR)**, and the **Ombudsman**. As for existing institutions, the powers of the European Parliament were increased (not least through the introduction of the new **co-decision** procedure), greater use of qualified majority voting (QMV) in the Council was agreed, the Court of Auditors was upgraded to an institution, and the European Court of Justice (ECJ) gained the power to fine member states.

The Treaty on European Union

Agreed at Maastricht in December 1991 and entering into force on 1 November 1993, the TEU—often referred to as the 'Maastricht Treaty'—was designed to expand the scope of European integration, to reform the EC's institutions and decision-making procedures, and to bring about EMU (see Box 3.4). Moreover, the goal of ever-closer union was to be furthered by bringing together the EEC—now renamed the European Community—the European Coal and Steel Community (ECSC), and the European Atomic Energy Community (EAEC, or Euratom) as part of an entirely new entity, to be called the 'European Union'. This was to be more than simply the existing supranational Communities. Established in 1993, it comprised not only their supranational activities, but also intergovernmental cooperation in foreign and security policy matters (CFSP) and justice and home affairs (JHA).

This mix of supranational integration and intergovernmental cooperation on which the member states had agreed meant that the new EU fell short of what might normally be considered a union: a political and legal entity with a coherent and uniform structure. Indeed, in an early assessment of the EU, Curtin (1993) referred to its constitutional structure as a 'Europe of bits and pieces'. Depending, for example, on the policy area, the roles of the relevant institutions involved in decision-making differed. In the early years of the EC, there was essentially one approach, the so-called 'Community method'—that is, the use of supranational institutions and decision-making procedures to develop, adopt, and police policy. This would no longer be the case.

That the EU lacked uniformity in terms of its structures and policy-making procedures was evident from the terminology widely used to describe it. For many, whether practitioners, academics, or others, the EU prior to the Treaty of Lisbon was structurally akin to a Greek temple consisting of three pillars. The first comprised the original Communities (the EC, EAEC/ Euratom, prior to mid-2002, the ECSC—see Box 3.5), while the second and third consisted of essentially intergovernmental cooperation in the areas of CFSP and, originally, JHA (see Figure 3.1). Changes in the relationship between the pillars after 1993 meant that the boundaries between them became blurred.

BOX 3.5 The European Communities: from three to two to one

Originally, there were three European Communities: the European Coal and Steel Community (ECSC); the European Atomic Energy Community (EAEC, or Euratom); and the European Economic Community (EEC), which was formally renamed the European Community in 1993 thanks to the TEU (although that name had often been used informally as shorthand for the EEC before that date). The ECSC was disbanded in July 2002, its founding treaty having expired, as envisaged, after fifty years. Since then, through the Treaty of Lisbon, the EC has been merged into the EU, leaving only the EAEC/Euratom as a discrete 'Community'.

Figure 3.1 The pillar structure from Maastricht to Amsterdam

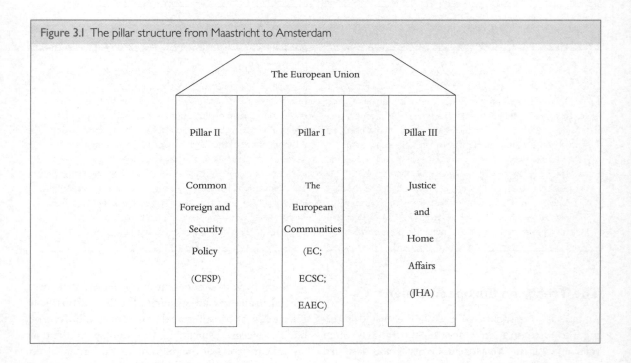

Indeed, with the entry into force of the Treaty of Lisbon on 1 December 2009, the pillars disappeared (see Chapter 4).

To supporters of supranational integration, the establishment of the EU in 1993 on the basis of three pillars represented a clear setback. This was because the intergovernmental pillars threatened to undermine the supremacy of the Community method. For others, adopting a mix of supranational and intergovernmental pillars merely formalized existing practice. Even prior to the TEU, the member states were pursuing intergovernmental cooperation outside the framework of the EC. The most obvious examples were EPC and Schengen activities relating to the removal of border controls (see Chapter 21). These had been taking place since the early 1970s and mid-1980s respectively. All the same, the mix of supranationalism and intergovernmentalism—particularly given that the Community institutions, with the exception of the Council, were at best marginal players in pillars I and II—meant that the EU, when established, was less of a union than many had either hoped or feared.

The idea of the new EU as a union was also undermined by other features of the TEU. First, plans for EMU—the most important new area of EC activity—were set to create a three-tier EU, with member states divided between those that would become full participants, those that would fail to get in (that is, those that would fail to meet the convergence criteria), and those—the UK and Denmark—that either had availed or could avail themselves of opt-outs (see Chapter 22). Semi-permanent differentiation between member states in a major policy area would characterize the new EU. Second, it was agreed that closer integration in the area of social policy would be pursued only by eleven of the then twelve member states. Resolute opposition to increased EU competences meant that new legislation resulting from the so-called 'Social Chapter' would not apply to the UK. Third, Denmark was later granted a de facto opt-out from involvement in the elaboration and implementation of foreign policy decisions and actions having defence implications. All of this created the image of a partially fragmented EU.

That the TEU's provisions did not all apply to the same extent to all member states was significant, because such differentiation had never been enshrined in the EU's treaty base before. This is not to say that differentiation between member states had never existed, but it had been temporary, with new member states given strict time limits for fulfilling the requirements and obligations of membership. Hence there were fears that the Maastricht opt-outs would set a precedent leading, at worst, to an à la carte EU, with member states picking and choosing the areas in which they were willing to pursue closer integration. Such fears were initially assuaged when, at the time of the 1995 enlargement, the EU refused to consider any permanent exemptions or opt-outs from the existing *acquis communautaire* for the new member states. Austria, Finland, and Sweden had to, and indeed did, accept all of the obligations of membership, including those concerning social policy, EMU, and the CFSP, the latter being significant because each of the three countries was still notionally neutral.

KEY POINTS

- Despite 'ever-closer union' being a long-established goal of the EC member states, the EU was not created until 1993.

- The new EU lacked a uniform structure, consisting of one supranational and two intergovernmental pillars.

- The TEU introduced opt-outs from certain policy areas for some member states.

Reviewing the Union: the 1996 Intergovernmental Conference and the Treaty of Amsterdam

That the European Union, when it was created, was less than its title implied was recognized not only by those studying the EU, but also those working in its institutions and representing its member states. Even

those who drafted the TEU acknowledged that what they were creating was not the final product, but part of an ongoing process. In the TEU's very first Article, the member states proclaimed that the establishment of the EU 'marks *a new stage* in the process of creating an ever closer union among the peoples of Europe' (emphasis added). They then proceeded to facilitate the process by scheduling an intergovernmental conference (IGC) for 1996 at which the TEU would be revised in line with its objectives.

The 1996 IGC

Views on the purpose of the 1996 IGC differed. For the less integrationist member states, notably the UK, it would provide an opportunity to review and fine-tune the functioning of the EU and its structures. It was too soon to consider anything radical. Other member states did not want to rule out a more substantial overhaul. The IGC would provide an opportunity to push ahead with the goal of creating 'ever-closer union', something that the European Parliament was particularly keen to see, as its draft Constitution of February 1994 demonstrated. Ever-closer union, it was argued, was necessary if the EU wished to rectify the shortcomings of the structures created at Maastricht and prepare itself, having enlarged in 1995 to fifteen member states, to admit the large number of mainly Central and Eastern European (CEE) applicants (see Chapter 17). Enlargement was now on the agenda: at Copenhagen in June 1993, the European Council had committed the EU to admit CEE countries once they met the accession criteria. Moreover, several member states were growing increasingly impatient with the reluctance of the less integrationist member states to countenance closer integration and there was also the need to bring the EU closer to its citizens. Popular reaction to the TEU had shown that more needed to be done to convince people of the value of union. Not only had the Danish people initially rejected the TEU in June 1992, but also the French people had only narrowly approved it three months later.

The shortcomings of the EU's structures were highlighted in reports produced by the Council, Commission, and EP in 1995. They all agreed that the pillar structure was not functioning well and that the intergovernmental nature of decision-making in Pillar III was a significant constraint on the development of cooperation in JHA areas. As for Pillar II, its inherent weaknesses had been highlighted by the

EU's ineffective foreign policy response to the disintegration of Yugoslavia. Such shortcomings, it was argued, needed to be addressed, particularly given that enlargement was now firmly on the EU's agenda. Preparations would have to be made, notably where the size and composition of the institutions were concerned. In addition, there was the matter of qualified majority voting (QMV). Its extension to replace unanimity would be necessary if the EU were to survive enlargement and avoid decision-making paralysis. Also needed within an enlarged EU, at least in the eyes of supporters of closer integration, were mechanisms that would allow those member states keen on closer integration to proceed without the need for unanimous agreement of the others. There was consequently much discussion of ideas concerning a 'core Europe', variable geometry, and a multi-speed EU. It was against this background that preparations for reforming the EU took place.

These began in earnest in 1995 with the formation of a 'Reflection Group'. Its report suggested three key aims for the 1996 IGC: bringing the EU closer to its citizens; improving its functioning in preparation for enlargement; and providing it with greater external capacity. In doing so, the report also promoted the idea of 'flexibility' mechanisms that would facilitate 'closer cooperation' among groups of willing member states.

The IGC was then launched in March 1996, with the early stages of the negotiations confirming expectations that any agreement on reform would not be easily reached. A draft treaty was produced for the Dublin European Council in December 1996, but this left many issues unresolved. Eventually, following the Labour Party's victory in the UK general election in May 1997, the Dutch council presidency was able to draw the IGC to a close more easily and secure agreement on what would become the Treaty of Amsterdam.

The Treaty of Amsterdam

Signed on 2 October 1997, this latest amending treaty attracted far less popular attention than the TEU had. This does not mean that it was an insignificant treaty. It certainly caught the attention of lawyers and practitioners, renumbering as it did all but four Articles in the Treaty of Rome and TEU. Moreover, in terms of substantive changes, it added the establishment of an 'area of freedom, security and justice' (AFSJ) to the EU's objectives and shifted much of JHA activity from Pillar III into Pillar I—in what is often referred to as Communitarization. In doing so, the thrust of cooperation in Pillar III was refocused on police and judicial cooperation in criminal matters (PJCCM), and the pillar renamed accordingly (see Figure 3.2). At the

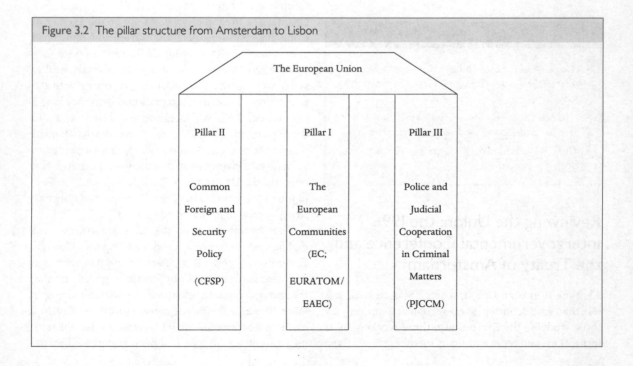

Figure 3.2 The pillar structure from Amsterdam to Lisbon

The European Union

Pillar II	Pillar I	Pillar III
Common Foreign and Security Policy (CFSP)	The European Communities (EC; EURATOM/ EAEC)	Police and Judicial Cooperation in Criminal Matters (PJCCM)

same time, provision was made for Schengen cooperation to be incorporated into the EU. These developments meant greater coherence in EU activity. Yet the changes were also accompanied by increased differentiation. The UK, Ireland, and Denmark gained various opt-outs from both the new AFSJ and Schengen cooperation (see Chapter 21).

There was also the potential for further differentiation, with the introduction of mechanisms for 'closer cooperation'. Under these, member states that wished to could use the EC framework to pursue enhanced cooperation among themselves. This was possible provided that the mechanisms were only used as a last resort, that a majority of member states would be participating, and that the cooperation would be open to all other member states. Moreover, closer cooperation could not detract from either the principles of the EU and the *acquis* nor from the rights of member states, nor could it be pursued for CFSP matters. Such restrictions, as well as the de facto veto that each member state had over closer cooperation, meant that the provisions would be difficult to use. In fact, the first formal request to use them was not made until 2008, when nine member states proposed closer cooperation to pursue common rules on cross-border divorce. All the same, the possibility of increasing differentiation within the EU was being established.

Where the Treaty of Amsterdam lessened differentiation within the EU was in its repeal of the UK opt-out from social policy. There was a bolstering of the EC's social policy competences too (see Chapter 20). Moreover, an employment policy chapter was introduced, in part as an attempt to assuage popular concerns that the EU did not have its citizens' interests at heart. The need to make the EU more citizen-friendly was also behind other new emphases—notably, the enhanced EC competences concerning consumer and environmental protection, greater efforts to promote transparency and subsidiarity, and a reassertion that EU citizenship does not undermine national citizenship (see Chapter 25).

In terms of addressing the shortcomings of Pillar II, the IGC resisted calls for a communitarization of the CFSP, preferring to maintain existing intergovernmental arrangements. Reforms were, however, introduced in an attempt to improve the consistency of EU action by involving the European Council more, by creating the post of High Representative, by establishing a policy planning and early warning

unit, by seeking to develop long-term strategies, by clarifying the nature of the different instruments available, by defining more precisely the EU's concept of security (the so-called 'Petersberg tasks' of humanitarian and rescue tasks, peacekeeping, and crisis management, including peacemaking), and by allowing for 'constructive abstention' so that member states abstaining would not block CFSP initiatives (see Chapter 18). The commitment to deeper integration was evident in the renewed references to a common defence policy and a common defence.

Finally, the Treaty of Amsterdam was supposed to prepare the EU institutionally for enlargement. In this regard, it failed. Rather than agreeing reforms, it simply deferred to a later date the resolution of key questions, such as the size of the Commission, the redistribution of votes in the Council, and the nature of majority voting. Unanimity was replaced by QMV in some nineteen instances, but even here, thanks to German insistence, progress was far less than anticipated or desired by many member states. This was underlined in a declaration issued by Belgium, France, and Italy to the effect that further treaty reform should be a precondition for the signing of the first accession treaties with applicant countries. The Treaty of Amsterdam did not fail totally, however, regarding institutional reform. The size of the European Parliament (EP) was capped at 700 members, and use of the assent and co-decision procedures was extended, thus enhancing the legislative role of the EP. The EP's hand in the appointment of the Commission was also increased, as was its right to set its own rules for its elected members (see Chapter 12).

KEY POINTS

- Early experiences of the EU raised concerns about the functioning of the pillar structure.

- The desire not to be held back by more recalcitrant member states led to mechanisms for closer cooperation between interested and willing member states.

- Despite the acknowledged need to introduce institutional reforms in preparation for enlargement, the Treaty of Amsterdam failed to prepare the EU sufficiently to admit more than a handful of new members.

Preparing for enlargement: the 2000 Intergovernmental Conference, the Treaty of Nice, and the 'Future of Europe' debate

With momentum in the late 1990s building towards enlargement to include the ten Central and Eastern European (CEE) countries as well as Cyprus and potentially Malta, the need to introduce institutional reform remained on the European Union's agenda. Without such reform it was feared that policy-making could grind to a halt. Moreover, there were concerns that enlargement could challenge the whole idea of union. Admitting ten CEE countries, most of which had been undergoing processes of wholesale transformation from command economies to fully functioning market economies, was something that the EU had never done before. How to accommodate and integrate the new members became a major question. At the same time, integrationists were determined to ensure that the EU's *acquis* and the notion of union would be neither impaired nor undermined by enlargement, and that its institutions could continue to function as decision-making and decision-shaping bodies. Moreover, confronted with the prospect of what amounted to almost a doubling of the EU's membership, integrationists were faced with the challenge of ensuring that the commitment towards 'ever-closer union' would be maintained. By contrast, opponents of 'ever-closer union' often welcomed enlargement for precisely such reasons.

Enlargement moves centre-stage

Preparing the EU institutionally for enlargement had been a key objective of the 1996 Intergovernmental Conference (IGC). However, as noted at 'The Treaty of Amsterdam', the resulting Treaty of Amsterdam failed to deliver enlargement. Instead, reform was postponed. A Protocol envisaged that, at the time of the next enlargement, the Commission would consist of one national representative per member state provided, by then, the weighting of votes within the Council had been modified either via a reweighting or through the adoption of a dual majority system of voting (see Chapter 11). The idea behind the reweighting was to compensate the larger member states for giving up 'their' second Commissioner. The Protocol also provided for an IGC to carry out a 'comprehensive

review of . . . the composition and functioning of the institutions' at least one year before the membership of the EU exceeds twenty member states.

In reality, the provisions of the Protocol were mainly ignored. Even before the Treaty of Amsterdam entered into force on 1 May 1999, the European Council in 1998 had identified institutional reform as an issue of primary concern. Then, in June 1999, it agreed to hold an IGC in 2000 to address the key institutional questions. The issues—the size and composition of the Commission, the weighting of votes in the Council, and the possible extension of qualified majority voting (QMV) in the Council—became known as the 'Amsterdam leftovers'.

What pushed the European Council into calling an IGC for 2000 were changes in the EU's handling of the enlargement process. In July 1997, a matter of weeks after the Amsterdam European Council, the Commission had published *Agenda 2000*, its blueprint for enlargement. Following its recommendations, the Luxembourg European Council in December 1997 agreed to launch an inclusive accession process with all applicant states (except Turkey), but to open accession negotiations proper with only six of the applicants. It was felt at the time that six new members could be squeezed into the EU without necessarily holding an IGC. Within eighteen months, however, attitudes towards enlargement had changed and, in the aftermath of the 1999 Kosovo conflict, the decision was taken to open accession negotiations with six more applicants and to recognize all applicants, including Turkey, as 'candidate countries'. Opening up the possibility of large-scale enlargement made the need to address the Amsterdam leftovers more urgent. Hence an IGC was called.

The 2000 IGC

The 2000 IGC opened in February 2000 with a limited agenda. This reflected the preferences of most member states for an IGC focused on the Amsterdam leftovers. Others, including the Commission and the European Parliament, favoured a broader agenda. In a Commission-inspired Wise Men's Report published in October 1999, strong support was voiced for a reorganization of the treaties and the integration of the Western European Union (WEU) into the EU as a step towards a common defence policy. A Commission report in January 2000 also reminded the member states that it was incumbent on them to ensure that the IGC reformed the EU in such a way that it would remain flexible enough 'to allow continued progress towards our goal of European integration. What the Conference decides will set the framework for the political Europe of tomorrow'. The EU, it warned, 'will be profoundly changed by enlargement, but must not be weakened by it'. As for the EP, it came out strongly in favour of a wider agenda, dismissing the 'excessively narrow agenda' adopted by the Helsinki European Council in December 1999 as one that 'might well jeopardize the process of integration'.

Such calls were initially overlooked by the IGC, although 'closer cooperation' was added to its agenda by the Feira European Council in June 2000. By this time, however, certain member states were beginning to think more openly about the future of the EU. Hence negotiations were soon taking place against a backdrop of speeches from German Foreign Minister Joschka Fischer, advocating in a personal capacity 'a European federation' (see Box 3.6), and French President Jacques Chirac, championing proposals for a

European constitution. Other proposals on the future shape of the EU from, among others, UK Prime Minister Tony Blair and his Spanish counterpart, José María Aznar, soon followed.

Many of the proposals were too ambitious for the IGC, in which progress was already proving to be slow, not least owing to major differences on how best to deal with the Amsterdam leftovers. This was evident from the harsh words exchanged at the Biarritz European Council in October 2000. The situation was not helped by the heavy-handed manner in which France, holding the Council presidency, was managing the IGC. Accusations abounded that the French were abusing their position as chair by promoting what was essentially a French agenda rather than seeking to broker compromises between the member states. At no point were the accusations louder than at the Nice European Council, which, after more than four days, eventually agreed a treaty. Once tidied up, the Treaty of Nice was signed on 26 February 2001.

BOX 3.6 From confederacy to federation: thoughts on the finality of European integration

Excerpts from speech by Joschka Fischer at the Humboldt University in Berlin, 12 May 2000:

'Quo vadis Europa?' is the question posed once again by the history of our continent. And for many reasons the answer Europeans will have to give, if they want to do well by themselves and their children, can only be this: onwards to the completion of European integration. A step backwards, even just standstill or contentment with what has been achieved, would demand a fatal price of all EU member states and of all those who want to become members; it would demand a fatal price above all of our people . . .

The task ahead of us will be anything but easy and will require all our strength; in the coming decade we will have to enlarge the EU to the east and south-east, and this will in the end mean a doubling in the number of members. And at the same time, if we are to be able to meet this historic challenge and integrate the new member states without substantially denting the EU's capacity for action, we must put into place the last brick in the building of European integration, namely political integration . . .

Permit me therefore to remove my Foreign Minister's hat altogether in order to suggest a few ideas both on the nature of this so-called finality of Europe and on how we can approach and eventually achieve this goal . . .

Enlargement will render imperative a fundamental reform of the European institutions. Just what would a European

Council with 30 heads of state and government be like? Thirty presidencies? How long will Council meetings actually last? Days, maybe even weeks? How, with the system of institutions that exists today, are 30 states supposed to balance interests, take decisions and then actually act? How can one prevent the EU from becoming utterly intransparent, compromises from becoming stranger and more incomprehensible, and the citizens' acceptance of the EU from eventually hitting rock bottom?

Question upon question, but there is a very simple answer: the transition from a union of states to full parliamentarization as a European Federation, something Robert Schuman demanded 50 years ago. And that means nothing less than a European Parliament and a European government which really do exercise legislative and executive power within the Federation. This Federation will have to be based on a constituent treaty.

I am well aware of the procedural and substantive problems that will have to be resolved before this goal can be attained. For me, however, it is entirely clear that Europe will only be able to play its due role in global economic and political competition if we move forward courageously. The problems of the twenty-first century cannot be solved with the fears and formulae of the nineteenth and twentieth centuries . . .

Source: The text can be accessed via the extensive online depository of documents relating to European integration and the development of the EU hosted by the Centre Virtuel de la Connaissance sur l'Europe (http://www.cvce.eu).

The Treaty of Nice

What the member states agreed at Nice attracted much criticism. Although it was rightly heralded as paving the way for enlargement, for many it produced suboptimal solutions to the institutional challenges raised by the prospect of an enlarged membership. All the same, the new Treaty did equip the EU better to accept new members and to avoid decision-making and institutional paralysis. For example, QMV was extended to nearly forty more Treaty provisions, albeit in many instances ones concerned with the nomination of officials rather than policy-making, although some ten policy areas did see increased use of QMV. Reaching a decision using QMV did not, though, become any easier. Despite a reweighting of votes—each member state saw its number of votes increase, with the larger member states enjoying roughly a trebling and the smaller member states roughly a doubling—the proportion of votes required to obtain a qualified majority remained at almost the same level as before and was actually set to increase. Moreover, a new criterion was introduced: any decision could, at the behest of any member state, be required to have the support of member states representing 62 per cent of the EU's total population.

The Treaty of Nice also provided for a staged reduction in the size of the Commission. From 2005, each member state would have one Commissioner. Then, once the EU admitted its twenty-seventh member, the next Commission would comprise a number of members less than the total number of member states. There was, however, a proviso: an equitable rotation system would have to be agreed. Staying with the institutions, the cap on the size of the EP was revised upward to 732 and maximum sizes were agreed for the Committee of the Regions (CoR) and the European Economic and Social Committee (EESC, or Ecosoc). Reforms were also introduced to the competences and organization of the ECJ and the CFI (see Chapter 13).

The imminence of enlargement to fairly young democracies in CEE, coupled with an awareness of existing institutional difficulties, also accounted for an enhanced stress on democracy and rights. Hence a 'yellow card' procedure was introduced for member states deemed to be at risk of breaching the principles on which the EU is founded. Thanks to the Treaty of Amsterdam, it had already been agreed that the voting and other rights of such member states could be

suspended. Moreover, the Treaty of Nice revised the mechanisms for closer cooperation—now referred to as 'enhanced cooperation'. These become notionally easier to use mainly because the number of member states needed to start a project and the opportunities to block such a project were reduced. Enhanced cooperation could also now be used for non-military aspects of the Common Foreign and Security Policy (CFSP). All of this opened up the possibility of the EU becoming a less uniform entity.

At the same time, however, the Treaty of Nice gave the EU a greater sense of coherence. In the area of CFSP and following the development of the European Rapid Reaction Force (ERRF), it made the EU rather than the WEU responsible for implementing the defence-related aspects of policy (see Chapter 18). It also increased the focus on Brussels as the de facto capital of the EU. With enlargement, all European Council meetings would be held in Brussels.

Yet although the Treaty of Nice paved the way for a more 'European' EU by introducing the institutional reforms necessary for enlargement, it did little in terms of furthering the avowed goal of 'ever-closer union'. Integration-minded members of the European Parliament (MEPs) were quick to express their concerns, voicing particular criticism of the perceived drift towards intergovernmentalism and the consequent weakening of the Community method (Leinen and Méndez de Vigo, 2001). The new Treaty did, however, set in motion a process that drew on the speeches made by Fischer, Chirac, and others, in 2000 and after, to promote a debate on the future of the EU. To some, the Commission especially, this would provide an opportunity to create a stronger, more integrated EU with a less fragmented structure. Others, however, envisaged greater flexibility, a clear delimitation of competences, and a weakening of commitments to 'ever-closer union'.

Beyond Nice: the 'Future of Europe' debate

The initial terms of reference for the 'Future of Europe' debate were outlined in a declaration adopted by the 2000 IGC in which the member states called for 'a deeper and wider debate about the future of the European Union'. This would focus, inter alia, on four issues: how to establish and monitor a more precise delimitation of powers between the EU and its member states; the status of the Charter of Fundamental Rights proclaimed at the Nice European Council; a simplification of the treaties, with a view to making them clearer and better understood; and the role of national parliaments in the European architecture. In addition, ways of improving and monitoring the democratic legitimacy and transparency of the EU and its institutions would be sought. The aim was to bring them closer to the citizens. A further IGC and treaty would follow.

The agenda for the debate appeared quite limited. However, by the time the debate was formally launched by the Laeken European Council in December 2001, the reference to 'inter alia' had been seized on and a whole raft of often wide-ranging questions had been tabled for discussion. In all, the resulting 'Laeken Declaration' contained more than fifty questions. These dealt with matters ranging from the democratic legitimacy of the EU to the future of the pillar structure and cooperation in the area of social exclusion (see Box 3.7). Also, it had been agreed that the debate would not feed directly into an IGC. Instead, a Convention comprising representatives of member state governments, members of national parliaments,

---

BOX 3.7 Laeken Declaration on the future of the European Union, December 2001 (excerpts)

[T]he Union stands at a crossroads, a defining moment in its existence. The unification of Europe is near. The Union is about to expand to bring in more than ten new Member States . . . At long last, Europe is on its way to becoming one big family, without bloodshed, a real transformation clearly calling for a different approach from 50 years ago, when six countries first took the lead . . .

The European Union needs to become more democratic, more transparent and more efficient. It has to resolve three basic challenges: how to bring citizens, and primarily the young, closer to the European design and the European institutions, how to organize politics and the European political area in an enlarged Union and how to develop the Union as a stabilizing factor and a model in the new multipolar world . . .

Citizens often hold expectations of the European Union that are not always fulfilled . . . Thus the important thing is to clarify, simplify and adjust the division of competences between the Union and the Member States in the light of the new challenges facing the Union . . .

A first series of questions that needs to be put concerns how the division of competence can be made more transparent. Can we thus make a clearer distinction between three types of competence: the exclusive competence of the Union, the competence of the Member States and the shared competence of the Union and the Member States? At what level is competence exercised in the most efficient way? How is the principle of subsidiarity to be applied here? And should we not make it clear that any powers not assigned by the Treaties to the Union fall within the exclusive sphere of competence of the Member States? And what would be the consequences of this?

The next series of questions should aim, within this new framework and while respecting the 'acquis communautaire', to determine whether there needs to be any reorganization of competence. How can citizens' expectations be taken as a guide here? What missions would this produce for the Union?

And, vice versa, what tasks could better be left to the Member States? What amendments should be made to the Treaty on the various policies? How, for example, should a more coherent common foreign policy and defence policy be developed? Should the Petersberg Tasks be updated? Do we want to adopt a more integrated approach to police and criminal law cooperation? How can economic policy coordination be stepped up? How can we intensify cooperation in the field of social inclusion, the environment, health and food safety? But then, should not the day-to-day administration and implementation of the Union's policy be left more emphatically to the Member States and, where their constitutions so provide, to the regions? Should they not be provided with guarantees that their spheres of competence will not be affected?

Lastly, there is the question of how to ensure that a redefined division of competence does not lead to a creeping expansion of the competence of the Union or to encroachment upon the exclusive areas of competence of the Member States and, where there is provision for this, regions. How are we to ensure at the same time that the European dynamic does not come to a halt? In the future as well the Union must continue to be able to react to fresh challenges and developments and must be able to explore new policy areas. Should Articles 95 and 308 of the Treaty be reviewed for this purpose in the light of the 'acquis jurisprudentiel'? . . .

Who does what is not the only important question; the nature of the Union's action and what instruments it should use are equally important. Successive amendments to the Treaty have on each occasion resulted in a proliferation of instruments, and directives have gradually evolved towards more and more detailed legislation. The key question is therefore whether the Union's various instruments should not be better defined and whether their number should not be reduced.

In other words, should a distinction be introduced between legislative and executive measures? Should the number of legislative instruments be reduced: directly applicable rules, framework legislation and non-enforceable instruments (opinions, recommendations, open coordination)? Is it or is it not desirable to have more frequent recourse to framework legislation, which affords the Member States more room for manoeuvre in achieving policy objectives? For which areas of competence are open coordination and mutual recognition the most appropriate instruments? Is the principle of proportionality to remain the point of departure? . . .

[H]ow can we increase the democratic legitimacy and transparency of the present institutions . . . ?

How can the authority and efficiency of the European Commission be enhanced? How should the President of the Commission be appointed: by the European Council, by the European Parliament, or should he be directly elected by the citizens? Should the role of the European Parliament be strengthened? Should we extend the right of codecision or not? Should the way in which we elect the members of the European Parliament be reviewed? Should a European electoral constituency be created, or should constituencies continue to be determined nationally? Can the two systems be combined? Should the role of the Council be strengthened? Should the Council act in the same manner in its legislative and its executive capacities? With a view to greater transparency, should the meetings of the Council, at least in its legislative capacity, be public? Should citizens have more access to Council documents? How, finally, should the balance and reciprocal control between the institutions be ensured?

A second question, which also relates to democratic legitimacy, involves the role of national parliaments. Should they be represented in a new institution, alongside the Council and the European Parliament? Should they have a role in areas of European action in which the European Parliament has no competence? Should they focus on the division of competence between Union and Member States, for example through preliminary checking of compliance with the principle of subsidiarity?

[A] third question concerns how we can improve the efficiency of decision making and the workings of the institutions in a Union of some 30 Member States. How could the Union set its objectives and priorities more effectively and ensure better implementation? Is there a need for more decisions by a qualified majority? How is the codecision procedure between the Council and the European Parliament to be simplified and speeded up? What of the six-monthly rotation of the Presidency of the Union? What is the future role of the European Parliament? What of the future role and structure of the various Council formations? How should the coherence of European foreign policy be enhanced? How is synergy between the High Representative and the competent Commissioner to be reinforced? Should the external representation of the Union in international fora be extended further? . . .

[A further question] concerns simplifying the existing Treaties without changing their content. Should the distinction between the Union and the Communities be reviewed? What of the division into three pillars?

Questions then arise as to the possible reorganization of the Treaties. Should a distinction be made between a basic treaty and the other treaty provisions? Should this distinction involve separating the texts? Could this lead to a distinction between the amendment and ratification procedures for the basic treaty and for the other treaty provisions? . . .

The question ultimately arises as to whether this simplification and reorganization might not lead in the long run to the adoption of a constitutional text in the Union. What might the basic features of such a constitution be? The values which the Union cherishes, the fundamental rights and obligations of its citizens, the relationship between Member States in the Union?

Source: European Council, 'Laeken Declaration on the Future of Europe', 15 December 2001. The text can be accessed via the extensive online depository of documents relating to European integration and the development of the EU hosted by the Centre Virtuel de la Connaissance sur l'Europe (**http://www.cvce.eu**).

MEPs, and Commission representatives, as well as governmental representatives and members of Parliament (MPs) from the thirteen candidate countries would be established to explore how the questions raised in the Laeken Declaration could be answered. Only after the Convention had completed its work would the IGC meet (see Chapter 4).

For supporters of integration disappointed by the Treaty of Amsterdam and the Treaty of Nice, this 'Future of Europe' debate was welcomed as providing a further opportunity to promote the idea of 'ever-closer union'. Eurosceptics were, initially at least, also enthused. At last, a major opportunity existed to make the case for less integration. However, the debate soon became dominated by advocates of more, not less, integration. Before long, they were advancing the case for a European constitution—something that the EP in particular had long been championing, and which the French and German governments had publicly endorsed. The EP was also keen to see the Communitarization of a strengthened foreign policy and remaining Pillar III matters, formal recognition of the EU's legal personality, election of the Commission president, simplification of decision-making procedures, and an extension of its own powers (Leinen and Méndez de Vigo, 2001). Many of these ideas were shared by the Commission, which also proposed removing existing opt-outs (European Commission, 2002c). They would also be fed, along with a range of other ideas from various sources, into the work of the Convention. The challenge that it faced would be to come up with acceptable answers. Whether these would result in a further step along the road to 'ever-closer union', and whether they would be accepted by national governments and electorates, remained to be seen.

KEY POINTS

- Changes in the approach that the EU was adopting towards enlargement in 1999 gave greater urgency to the need to address the 'Amsterdam leftovers' and to agree institutional reform.

- The Treaty of Nice may have paved the way for enlargement, but to many it provided suboptimal solutions to the institutional challenges posed by a significantly larger EU.

- While criticized for potentially weakening the EU, the Treaty of Nice initiated a process designed to respond to calls for a European Federation and a European Constitution.

Conclusion

In the history of the European Union and its predecessors, there has rarely been a point at which ideas for increased integration have not been aired. This has been particularly true of the period from the mid-1980s under discussion here, during which treaty reform and intergovernmental conferences (ICGs) became almost permanent items on the agenda of the EU. As a result, the EU that was established in 1993 evolved in a variety of ways: the member states agreed to expand the range of policies in which the EU has a competence to act; they adjusted the decision-making powers of the institutions; and they embarked on some major integration projects—notably, economic and monetary union (EMU) and the adoption of the euro in 2002, and enlargement that brought the membership to twenty-seven.

Consequently, the EU assumed, during its first ten years, many of the characteristics of a union. For some, it soon resembled, or was deemed to be becoming, a superstate. Yet for many, particularly supporters of political union, it had always been a much looser and more fluid organization than its name suggests. Its pillar structure embodied a complex mix of intergovernmental cooperation and supranational integration that brought together, in various combinations, a range of supranational institutions and the member states to further a variety of policy agendas. Adding to the complexity were the various opt-outs that Denmark, Ireland, and the UK introduced, notably regarding certain Justice and Home Affairs (JHA) matters and in particular Schengen, as well as the differentiated integration created by EMU and the emergence of the eurozone. Moreover, successive rounds of treaty reform sought to facilitate a more multi-speed EU through the introduction and refinement of mechanisms for enhanced cooperation. All of this raised questions about how uniform the EU was and would be in the future.

What the various rounds of treaty reform also reveal, however, is that the EU and its member states were aware of the challenges raised by its complex structure and procedures, particularly in the light of enlargement. This is not to say that its member states ever really warmed to the challenges, introduced appropriate reforms, streamlined the EU, or decided what its *finalité politique* should be. There was, and there remains, considerable difference of opinion. This was evident in the subsequent negotiation of the Constitutional Treaty (2004), its rejection, and the adoption of the replacement Treaty of Lisbon (2007). As the next chapter shows, several reforms have made the EU more like the union that its name implies. On balance, however, they have done little to transform the EU. It has been since its establishment in 1993, and remains, a complex—indeed messy—mix of supranationalism, intergovernmentalism, and differentiated forms of integration.

QUESTIONS

1. Is it appropriate to describe the European Union in terms of 'pillars'?

2. What is meant by 'ever-closer union'?

3. Do opt-outs and mechanisms for enhanced cooperation undermine the EU as a union?

4. What impact did the Treaty of Amsterdam have on the pillar structure of the EU?

5. Why did the 1996 Intergovernmental Conference fail to adopt the institutional reforms necessary to prepare the EU for enlargement?

6. Did the Treaty of Nice prepare the EU adequately for enlargement?

7. Why was the agenda for the 'Future of Europe' debate expanded between Nice and Laeken?

8. To what extent has the EU been characterized structurally by a complex mix of supranationalism, intergovernmentalism, and differentiated forms of integration?

 GUIDE TO FURTHER READING

Church, C. H. and Phinnemore, D. (2002) *The Penguin Guide to the European Treaties: From Rome to Maastricht, Amsterdam, Nice and Beyond* (London: Penguin)   A comprehensive guide to the treaty base of the EU prior to the Treaty of Lisbon.

Galloway, D. (2001) *The Treaty of Nice and Beyond* (Sheffield: Sheffield Academic Press)   A detailed analysis of key reforms introduced by the Treaty of Nice.

Laursen, F. (ed) (2006) *The Treaty of Nice: actor preferences, bargaining and institutional choice* (Leiden: Martinus Nijhoff)   An analysis of the making of the Treaty of Nice, paying particular attention to member states and key issues on the agenda of the IGC.

Lynch, P., Neuwahl, N., and Rees, W. (eds) (2000) *Reforming the European Union from Maastricht to Amsterdam* (London: Longman)   A volume assessing developments in the EU during the 1990s, paying particular attention to the reforms introduced by the Treaty of Amsterdam.

Monar, J. and Wessels, W. (eds) (2001) *The European Union after the Treaty of Amsterdam* (London: Continuum)   An informative collection of studies explaining the significance for the EU of the institutional and policy reforms introduced by the Treaty of Amsterdam.

 WEBLINKS

http://ec.europa.eu/archives/igc2000/index_en.htm   The archives of the 2000 IGC.

http://europa.eu/about-eu/basic-information/decision-making/treaties/index_en.htm   The EU's treaties.

http://europa.eu/about-eu/eu-history/index_en.htm   The European Union's summary history of the European integration process.

http://www.cvce.eu   A detailed online archive on the development of European integration.

http://www.eui.eu/Research/HistoricalArchivesOfEU/Index.aspx   The European University Institute's Historical Archives of the European Union.

4

From the Constitutional Treaty to the Treaty of Lisbon and Beyond

Clive Church and David Phinnemore

Reader's Guide

This chapter primarily explores the origins and evolution of the Treaty of Lisbon. The origins lie in the Constitutional Treaty of 2004, and in the French and Dutch referendum defeats of May and June 2005, which led to a period of so-called reflection. Then, mainly under the German Council presidency of early 2007, there was an emphatic drive to resolve underlying political disagreements amongst the European Union's member states and produce not a constitution, but an orthodox amending treaty to carry forward the basic reforms of the Constitutional Treaty. This process succeeded in getting a deal by October 2007 with a text acceptable to all member states, embedding most of the changes negotiated in 2002–04 into consolidated treaties. However, while parliamentary ratification went successfully, an initial referendum rejection in Ireland in June 2008 cast doubt on the new Treaty's future. In part, this symbolized a rejection of some elements of the Treaty, but it also owed much to a deeper unease about the EU, which an active opposition was able to exploit. Hence the Union again found itself in crisis. However, once Irish concerns had been assuaged, a second referendum produced the necessary 'yes' to ratification and, following some last-minute concessions to the Czech Republic, the Treaty of Lisbon entered into force on I December 2009. As responses to the eurozone crisis have shown, this did not mean the end of treaty reform.

Introduction

Given the political difficulties that the process of treaty amendment has caused, it is perhaps surprising that the European Union has pursued it so doggedly over the last decade, especially after the two resounding 'no' votes to the Constitutional Treaty (CT) in 2005. Opponents put this down to an unholy lust for power on the part of a basically anti-democratic European elite seeking to replace national and popular sovereignty by a centralized, and probably neoliberal, superstate. The truth is less dramatic. Many European decision-makers believed the enlarging Union needed substantial institutional reform to develop effectively. This had to take precedence over the opposition of those who queried the EU project because their countries had held a referendum, but who offered no alternative text. The opposition overlooked the fact that the reforms had been more democratically devised and directed than in previous treaty reforms. In other words, it was not a Manichean war between good and evil, but a normal political conflict over the governance and direction of the Union.

In fact, the EU had set out in the early years of the new century to try to get better institutional arrangements than those provided by the much-criticized Treaty of Nice. This grew out of an awareness of the latter's weaknesses: the existing proliferation of treaties; pressures from the German Länder for a clarification of their rights vis-à-vis the EU; and elite desires for making the Union more democratic and effective through a process of constitutionalization. After a sketchy debate, the Laeken Declaration was adopted in December 2001 (see Chapter 3) and a representative Convention launched to consider a large number of questions about the future of the Union. Meeting from February 2002 until July 2003, the Convention produced a 'Draft Treaty Establishing a Constitution for Europe', which was then revised by an intergovernmental conference (IGC) and signed in October 2004. Ratification proceeded smoothly at first, with a positive referendum in Spain. However, in May and June 2005, referenda in France and the Netherlands rejected the CT.

Many observers thought that the CT was dead, but, during a so-called 'period of reflection', other states continued to ratify it. Although little serious reflection took place, eventually the German Council presidency led a push for a new deal, securing agreement among the member states on a detailed mandate for a new IGC that would preserve many of the innovations of the CT, but within an orthodox treaty that would have nothing of the 'constitutional' about it.

A rapid and technical IGC followed, and the new Treaty was signed in Lisbon in December 2007. The thought behind this strategy was that it was the constitutional element that had alarmed people; removing this would therefore permit easy parliamentary ratification.

To begin with, this was the case. However, on 12 June 2008, the Irish rejected the Treaty of Lisbon, just as they had initially rejected the Treaty of Nice. The reasons for this were partly related to the text itself, but also to specific Irish issues and an underlying popular angst. The rejection nevertheless threw the Union into a new crisis. This time, there was no reflection period, the ball being quickly and firmly left in the Irish court. By the end of the year, with all except three other member states having completed ratification, the Irish government, having secured various clarifications and concessions, committed itself to hold a second referendum. This it won and ratification of the new Treaty was soon completed, despite the obstructionism of Czech President Vaclav Klaus.

Although many expected—and hoped—that the entry into force of the Treaty of Lisbon on 1 December 2009 would usher in a period in which the EU might cease tinkering with its treaty base, treaty reform was soon back on the agenda. This was essentially driven by the financial and debt crises in the euro area. Initial attempts at solution failing, attention turned to treaty amendment to enforce fiscal discipline (see Chapter 27).

Hence this chapter looks initially at the background of the CT and, in particular, the reasons for the 'no' votes. It then traces the emergence and adoption of the Treaty of Lisbon, and explains and assesses its main points. Next, it describes the ratification process, before moving to an assessment of the significance for the EU of the Treaty and the experience of securing its ratification. Finally, the chapter traces the changes that have followed Lisbon's entry into force as the EU seeks to address its latest crisis—that of the eurozone.

The European Convention, the 2004 Intergovernmental Conference, and the Constitutional Treaty

The origins of the Constitutional Treaty (CT) are manifold, but owe much to the 'Future of Europe' debate started by the Nice European Council in 2000 and furthered by the Laeken Declaration adopted a year later (see Box 4.1 and Chapter 3). Although the 'debate' attracted little popular input and few governments

BOX 4.1 Key dates in European integration, from Nice to Lisbon

2001	26 February	Treaty of Nice signed
	7 March	'Future of Europe' debate launched
	15 December	Laeken Declaration
2002	28 February	Inaugural plenary session of the European Convention
2003	20 June	Parts I and II of the Draft Treaty establishing a Constitution for Europe presented to the Thessaloniki European Council
	18 July	Complete Draft Treaty presented to the President of the European Council
	29 September	IGC opens
2004	18 June	European Council agrees a Treaty establishing a Constitution for Europe
	29 October	Treaty establishing a Constitution for Europe signed
2005	29 May	French electorate reject the Constitutional Treaty (CT) in a referendum
	1 June	Dutch electorate reject the CT in a referendum
	16–17 June	European Council announces a 'pause' in ratification
2006	15–16 June	European Council agrees extension to the 'period of reflection'
2007	1 January	Germany assumes presidency of the Council
	25 March	Berlin Declaration adopted on fiftieth anniversary of the signing of the Treaties of Rome
	21–22 June	European Council adopts IGC mandate for new 'reform treaty'
	23 July	IGC opens
	18–19 October	Informal European Council adopts Treaty of Lisbon
	13 December	Treaty of Lisbon signed
2008	12 June	Irish electorate reject Treaty of Lisbon in a referendum
	11–12 December	European Council agrees concessions to Irish government in exchange for commitment to complete ratificaton before 1 November 2009
2009	1 January	Original scheduled date for the entry into force of the Treaty of Lisbon
	18–19 June	European Council finalizes Irish 'guarantees'
	30 June	German Constitutional Court ruling on Lisbon
	2 October	Irish accept Treaty of Lisbon in a second referendum
	29 October	European Council agrees 'Czech Protocol'
	1 December	Treaty of Lisbon enters into force
2010	23 June	'Fifteen-minute' IGC adopts 'MEP Protocol'
2011	25 March	European Council adopts treaty amendment to enable the creation of the European Stability Mechanism (ESM)
	11 July	Seventeen euro area member states sign Treaty establishing the ESM (TESM)
	1 December	MEP Protocol enters into force
	9 December	Croatian Accession Treaty signed
2012	2 February	Seventeen euro area member states sign modified TESM
	1–2 March	Twenty-five EU member states sign Treaty on Stability, Coordination and Governance in the Economic and Monetary Union

tried to promote discussion, there was sufficient political support to move towards a further round of treaty reform. This time, in recognition of the need to engage citizens more in the process, the question of how to reform the EU would not be left simply to an intergovernmental conference (IGC). Instead, and drawing on the approach for the Charter of Fundamental Rights in 1999–2000, a 'Convention on the Future of Europe' was established to debate options and to make proposals. This 'European Convention' comprised representatives of national governments, and members of the European Parliament (MEPs) and of national parliaments, as well as representatives from the Commission and the thirteen candidate countries, along with observers from other EU institutions and bodies. It was chaired by a Praesidium, led by former French President and MEP Valéry Giscard d'Estaing.

Although there were doubts about the potential of the Convention, it proved itself an active and, up to a point, an open forum. It responded positively to Giscard's observation at the inaugural plenary that the best option was to produce a single text rather than a set of possibilities. Through a mixture of plenary sessions, working groups, study circles, and Praesidium meetings, it began to move towards a European constitution and not just a new treaty. In a spirit of openness and transparency, all of its papers were posted on the Internet and its plenary sessions were opened to the public. Yet the Convention failed to attract media or popular attention. It remained anonymous and restricted to an essentially self-selecting EU elite, skilfully steered by Giscard.

The Convention was only just able to meet its deadline and present its draft to the European Council in June 2003. Although a minority of Eurosceptics sketched an alternative vision, the vast majority of *conventionnels* accepted it, which made it hard to ignore. This was acknowledged by the Thessaloniki European Council, which declared that the draft was a 'good basis' for further negotiations. The IGC began surprisingly soon afterwards, in September 2003. However, no member state was willing to adopt the draft without amendment, several having serious reservations about some of its contents. In particular, Spain and Poland objected to a proposed new double majority voting system in the Council. Others had doubts about provisions on the Commission, the proposed Union Minister for Foreign Affairs, the reformed presidency, the respective powers of the EP and the Council, the extension of qualified majority voting (QMV), and the revision processes envisaged. Given this, along with poor preparation and chairing by the Italian presidency, it proved impossible to get agreement at the European Council in December.

The sense of crisis then whipped up by the media and opposition politicians had a partly beneficial effect, since it focused minds on the outstanding issues. It also led to a cooling-off period that allowed the incoming Irish Council presidency some time to consider how various problems with the draft could be resolved. Its task was made easier by a change of government in Spain in March 2004 and the adoption by the Polish government of a more accommodating position on the double majority issue. Negotiations resumed and, within little more than a month, agreement was reached. The European Council in Brussels in June 2004 duly adopted the Treaty establishing a Constitution for Europe. The text—90 per cent of which had come from the Convention draft, despite the IGC's eighty amendments—was subsequently tidied up and authentic versions produced in each of the twenty-one official languages of the enlarged EU. The complete version of the CT was then signed on 29 October 2004 at a ceremony in Rome, in the same building where representatives of the original six member states had signed the 1957 Treaty of Rome.

The document that they approved was a lengthy one, divided into four parts. These were supplemented by annexes, protocols, declarations, and a final act (see Box 4.2). It was designed to replace all of the existing treaties and become the single constitutional document of the Union. Yet, although it was all in one volume, for many of those who had hoped, or feared, that the Convention and IGC would produce

---

BOX 4.2 Structure of the Constitutional Treaty

Preamble

Part I

Part II: The Charter of Fundamental Rights

Part III: The Policies and Functioning of the European Union

Part IV: General and Final Provisions

Protocols (36)

Annexes (2)

Final Act

Declarations (50)

a short, succinct constitution, it was a disappointing text—482 pages in length, complex and sometimes impenetrable, and doing little to promote transparency and accountability. This was despite a concise Part I, clear headings, and a single numeration.

The document began with a Preamble, setting out the purpose of the EU. This was followed by a core Part I outlining the fundamentals of the EU. This included everything that one needs to know about what the EU does and how it does this, making it the most innovative and constitutional of the four parts. Part II contained the Charter of Fundamental Rights. The longest element was Part III, which contained detailed rules expanding on the provisions of Part I by bringing much of the existing Treaty on European Union (TEU) and Treaty establishing the European Community (TEC) into line with them. Part IV and the Final Act contained legal provisions common to international treaties, such as revision and ratification procedures. The protocols and declarations provided more detailed specifications and interpretations of what was found in the four parts.

In terms of content, not much was new. The vast bulk of the document came from the existing treaties, albeit slightly altered. The innovations, alongside the replacing of all of the existing treaties, lay mainly in the overall structure of the Union, the style of its operation, changes to the institutions, the addition of the Charter, and alterations to the revision process. Policy and powers changed rather less. The CT abolished the European Community and the pillars, replacing it with the single Union normally recognized by public opinion. This inherited the legal personality of the Community, along with its symbols and the primacy of its law. However, the Union committed itself to respecting its member states, which were recognized as conferring powers on it, and member states were given the right to leave.

The Union's style also changed, with the simplification and unification of the way in which it made rules through the 'ordinary legislative procedure' (OLP) involving joint decision-making by the Council and the EP. Its directives and regulations were rechristened 'laws'. There was also a new focus on values and rights, along with democratic improvements, including new powers for both the EP and national parliaments. The CT also envisaged citizens' initiatives (see Chapter 25). Accompanying all of this was an extended use of QMV, although unanimity would still be required for a range of sensitive and constitutional issues, such as measures relating to tax harmonization, the accession of new members, and revisions of the CT. A change to what constitutes a qualified majority was also planned, with a double majority consisting of 55 per cent of member states representing 65 per cent of the EU's population generally becoming necessary.

The CT also maintained the existing institutions. However, it upgraded the European Council (giving it a permanent president), limited the size of both the EP and the Commission, formalized the use of team presidencies in the Council, and established a new post of Union Minister for Foreign Affairs. The holder was to be at the same time a member of the Commission and the Chair of the Foreign Affairs Council, while being assisted by an External Action Service (see Chapters 11, 16, and 18). The constitutional nature of the document was intensified by the addition of the Charter of Fundamental Rights. This was made binding on the member states, but only when they were applying EU law. Further guarantees were given to the UK that the Charter did not increase EU powers (see Chapter 20). Part IV also introduced a number of easier revision procedures, to avoid the Union being forced to call an IGC for all alterations to its treaties.

As to what the EU could do, the CT specified that its rationalizing changes did not mean any accretion of power. It also clarified the Union's policy competences. It explained what the EU's exclusive competences are—customs union, competition, monetary policy for the euro area, and common commercial policy—and identified those areas in which competence is 'shared' with the member states, including the internal market, social policy, the environment, and the area of freedom, security and justice (AFSJ). In other areas, the EU's role was restricted to supporting and coordinating complementary actions—that is, powers that are explicitly conferred by the member states and are not the EU's by right. Few new competences were conferred. A number of areas—tourism, civil protection, administrative cooperation, and energy—were specifically mentioned for the first time in any detail, but each of these is an area in which the EU has already been active.

Generally speaking, the CT simplified the structure, terminology, and operation of the Union, as well as attempted to make it more comprehensible, democratic, and efficient. Unfortunately, people rarely recognized the simplification and restructuring that it brought. Moreover, the Convention and the IGC, despite producing a single consolidated document, failed to involve the people and to increase the EU's legitimacy in the desired way.

The 'no' votes: crisis and reflection

With little popular and, in many cases, political understanding or appreciation of the CT, ratification by all twenty-five member states was always going to be a challenge. At first, it proceeded relatively smoothly even if not in a uniform or coordinated manner, since some member states, as was their right, chose to have referenda along with parliamentary consideration. In the event, the Lithuanian Parliament ratified first, in November 2004. It was followed by Hungary and Slovenia, before Spain held the first referendum in February 2005. The outcome was, as expected, positive, although low turnout and scant knowledge of the Treaty meant that the vote was essentially an expression of support for EU membership. The same could also be said for several, if not most, of the subsequent positive votes in national parliaments. It was not true, however, of the French referendum on 29 May, when 53.3 per cent of voters—mainly rural, low-income, and public-sector based—rejected the CT. It was equally untrue of the Dutch referendum three days later, which saw an even larger majority (61.07 per cent) say 'nee'. Both defeats attracted a high turnout (see Chapter 26). The far-from-overwhelming endorsement in the Luxembourg referendum in July did little to create a sense that the CT was a text that commanded popular support, even if, by then, the Cypriot, Latvian, and Maltese parliaments had also voted in favour. Not surprisingly, the UK government, after some hesitation, postponed its planned referendum, as did the Irish and Danes.

It was clear that the CT itself was only one element of the problem. Certainly, the text was problematic and, as a complicated compromise document, it was hard for supporters of integration to sell. The issues

that it addressed were also poorly appreciated, thus making room for other concerns, few of which originated in the Treaty. So while a significant proportion of those who voted against it in the Netherlands did so for reasons associated with the CT, detailed studies of the French referendum made little reference to the text. French worries were essentially national and social, seeing the EU as becoming too liberal. Paradoxically, the portions of the Treaty that seem to have motivated this were in Part III, which actually came straight from the existing treaties. This was possibly—as with the TEU in Denmark in 1992—the result of people coming to realize what had been agreed in the past treaties, which previously were rarely, if ever, read.

Therefore it has widely, and rightly, been assumed that popular rejection of the CT was part of a broader malaise that had at its roots a general dissatisfaction with national governments and, especially, a basic alienation from the EU (see Chapter 25). The former had much to do with domestic political frustration over government strategy, unemployment, threats from globalization, and social welfare difficulties. However, some 'European' issues—albeit unconnected to the CT—such as the Bolkestein Directive on services, Turkey's potential membership, and the orientations of the first Barroso Commission—did feature. Beyond this, the increasing pace of treaty reform and the unsettling implications of enlargement in 2004 seemed to have intensified the underlying malaise. Yet little had been done to address it, with national and EU-level efforts to communicate 'Europe' being generally half-hearted and, for the most part, failing abysmally. This had both allowed the gap to widen and questioned the commitment of political elites to making the process of European integration inclusive. So although ratification continued well after the two 'no' votes, the CT was effectively dead, leaving the EU with a constitutional crisis.

'Negotiating' the Treaty of Lisbon

For much of 2005 and 2006, EU leaders were at a loss as to what to do to extricate the Union from its latest crisis. Indeed, the European Union never tried to carry out any kind of enquiry into what the opposition wanted. Moreover, the UK government deliberately sought to avoid discussion of the subject during its Council presidency in late 2005. There were no formal statements of what the French and Dutch wanted in place of the rejected Constitutional Treaty (CT). Despite bright ideas from academics and others about how to get the EU out of its current bind, and the Commission's work on Plan D to improve its communication efforts, there was neither political resolve to find a solution to the 'no' votes nor leadership.

In 2006, the Austrian Council presidency talked bravely of resuscitation, but was unable to overcome national disagreements. Equally, the European Parliament (EP) tried to stimulate debate. However, the issue soon began to slip down the public agenda even though Belgium and Estonia completed ratification. The best that the Commission could come up with was the idea of a declaration for the fiftieth anniversary of the Treaty of Rome. Yet many in Germany, including Chancellor Angela Merkel, made it clear that they supported the revival of the Treaty at the right time. Others, however, felt otherwise. Not surprisingly, in June 2006, the reflection period was extended for a further year.

During the autumn of 2006, new ideas did emerge, prominently France's soon-to-be President Nicolas Sarkozy's idea of a *'mini-traité'*. Enquiries were also carried out into the cost of not having a constitution, and the Spaniards and Luxembourgers were beginning to rally ratifiers in the umbrella movement known as the 'Friends of the Constitution'. More significantly, the Germans were preparing for their Council presidency during the first half of 2007. Chancellor Merkel was a believer in the CT. She felt it absolutely necessary for the EU, especially as there was no realistic alternative. In October 2006, Merkel declared that it would be the German presidency's intention to produce a road map for action by June 2007. Her underlying assumption seems to have been that the real problems lay with the member states and that these had to be settled confidentially. The process would therefore be very tightly controlled, with discussions being limited to a very small group of nationally appointed 'focal points'

and followed by a short 'technical' intergovernmental conference (IGC).

Not everybody shared Merkel's enthusiasm. The UK government was very cautious and the Poles and Czechs wished that the question of what to do would simply go away. However, a Berlin Declaration commemorating the fiftieth anniversary of the signing of the Treaty of Rome, which was designed to reassure people about the EU's ambitions and achievements, was adopted in March 2007, providing an opportunity for the Germans to begin discussions on how to proceed. A questionnaire on issues to be addressed was soon being circulated and in May there were contacts with various European leaders. The election of Sarkozy to the French presidency added political weight to Merkel's plans. By 14 June, when a list of outstanding issues was circulated, much progress had been achieved. Less than a week later, an unprecedentedly detailed mandate for an IGC was produced. This was then approved, along with a decision to launch an IGC, by the European Council on 21 June 2007 after last-minute concessions, notably to the UK and Poland.

The incoming Portuguese Council presidency made completing the negotiations on a new amending treaty its overriding objective. The IGC commenced work on 23 July. Foreign ministers, assisted by MEPs, considered progress at Viano de Castelo on 7–8 September and a final draft was produced in early October. Various loose ends were sorted, notably offering concessions to Bulgaria, Czech Republic, Poland, and Italy, which threatened to veto a deal over its allocation of EP seats. An informal European Council in Lisbon on 18–19 October brought the negotiations to a close. Following legal refinements to the text, a replacement to the CT was signed in Lisbon on 13 December.

KEY POINTS

- The reflection period failed to produce any clear answer to the ongoing constitutional crisis.

- The German presidency followed a tightly controlled strategy to secure member state agreement on an IGC mandate to transfer much of the CT into a conventional amending treaty.

- Under the Portuguese presidency, a technical IGC produced the Treaty of Lisbon.

The main elements of the Treaty of Lisbon

The Treaty of Lisbon was an amending treaty. With its entry into force on 1 December 2009, it altered the existing TEU and TEC—renaming the latter the Treaty on the Functioning of the European Union (TFEU)—and then, in effect, disappeared from view, although commentators still mistakenly assume that it replaced existing treaties. It did not. In one sense, the Treaty was a simple document with only seven Articles (see Box 4.3). However, the first two were extremely long, because they contained a whole series of amendments to the existing treaties. Article 1, dealing with the TEU, contained sixty-one instructions on amending the Treaty, while the second, amending the renamed TEC—now TFEU—contained eight horizontal changes and 286 individual amendments. The remaining Articles made it clear that the Treaty of Lisbon has unlimited temporal effect, that accompanying Protocols are also valid, and that the TEU and TFEU would be renumbered (which they were). In addition to the Treaty text proper, there were thirteen legally binding Protocols, an Annex, a Final Act, and sixty-five numbered Declarations. Five of the Protocols—covering the role of national parliaments, subsidiarity and proportionality, the Eurogroup, permanent structured cooperation, and the EU's planned accession to the European Convention on Human Rights (ECHR)—were originally part of the Constitutional Treaty (CT). The remaining eight were new, including some dealing with the continuing significance of competition, the application of the Charter in the UK and Poland, or interpreting shared competences, values, and public services. There were also various transitional institutional arrangements.

The final two Protocols repealed or adapted existing Protocols to reflect changes brought about by the new Treaty. These amendments and changes meant that the TEU and TFEU in force from 1 December 2009 were significantly revised versions of their immediate predecessors. Thankfully, consolidated versions of these, including the new numbering, were made available well in advance.

The reworking and reshaping of the TEU resulted in a treaty that provides a fairly succinct outline of the purpose and structure of the EU, notably in terms of aims, objectives, principles, and institutions (see Box 4.4). It also includes a good deal of detail on enhanced cooperation and, especially, on external action. If it now has a more constitutional feel about it, since it deals with major facets of the Union, it has exactly the same legal status as the TFEU and cannot be used to override it. The TFEU is still much longer, with seven Parts and 358 Articles, and many Declarations (see Box 4.5). It now starts with a set of common provisions and rules on citizenship, which are followed by the longest section, Part III, which deals with policies. External relations, institutional, and budgetary provisions make up the bulk of the rest. The order is perhaps slightly more logical than in the past.

Together, the TEU and TFEU provide for a simplified and somewhat more efficient Union. First, in structural terms, the key change is that Lisbon brought matters into line with common practice. Hence the Community disappeared and the Union became the sole structure of integration. The latter inherited all of the powers of the Community, including legal personality, institutions, and policy mix. Apart from the Common Foreign and Security Policy (CFSP), everything functions according to the basic Community method. Equally, there are still many opt-outs from

---

BOX 4.3 Structure of the Treaty of Lisbon

Article I: Amendments to the Treaty on European Union (TEU)

Article 2: Amendments to the Treaty on the Functioning of the European Union (TFEU), formerly the Treaty establishing the European Communities (TEC)

Article 3: Duration

Article 4: Amendments to existing protocols and the Treaty establishing the European Atomic Energy Community

Article 5: Renumbering

Article 6: Ratification

Article 7: Languages

Protocols (13)

Annex (1)

Final Act

Declarations (65)

BOX 4.4 Structure of the Consolidated Treaty on European Union (TEU)

Preamble

Title I: Common Provisions

Title II: Provisions on Democratic Principles

Title III: Provisions on the Institutions

Title IV: Provisions on Enhanced Cooperation

Title V: General Provisions on the Union's External Action and Specific Provisions on the Common Foreign and Security Policy

Title VI: Final Provisions

BOX 4.5 Structure of the Treaty on the Functioning of the European Union (TFEU)

Preamble

Part One: Principles

Title I: Categories and Areas of Union Competence

Title II: Provisions having General Application

Part Two: Non-Discrimination and Citizenship of the Union

Part Three: Union Policies and Internal Actions

Title I: The Internal Market

Title II: Free Movement of Goods

Title III: Agriculture and Fisheries

Title IV: Free Movement of Persons, Services and Capital

Title V: Area of Freedom, Security and Justice

Title VI: Transport

Title VII: Common Rules on Competition, Taxation and Approximation of Laws

Title VIII: Economic and Monetary Policy

Title IX: Employment

Title X: Social Policy

Title XI: The European Social Fund

Title XII: Education, Vocational Training, Youth and Sport

Title XIII: Culture

Title XIV: Public Health

Title XV: Consumer Protection

Title XVI: Trans-European Networks

Title XVII: Industry

Title XVIII: Economic, Social and Territorial Cohesion

Title XIX: Research and Technological Development and Space

Title XX: Environment

Title XXI: Energy

Title XXII: Tourism

Title XXIII: Civil Protection

Title XXIV: Administrative Cooperation

Part Four: Association of the Overseas Countries and Territories

Part Five: External Action by the Union

Title I: General Provisions on the Union's External Action

Title II: Common Commercial Policy

Title III: Cooperation with Third Countries and Humanitarian Aid

Title IV: Restrictive Measures

Title V: International Agreements

Title VI: The Union's Relations with International Organizations and Third Countries and Union Delegations

Title VII: Solidarity Clause

Part Six: Institutional and Financial Provisions

Title I: Provisions governing the Institutions

Title II: Financial Provisions

Title III: Enhanced Cooperation

Part Seven: General and Financial Provisions

---

parts of the system, while the facilities for enhanced cooperation have been increased.

Second, despite the talk of a 'superstate', the Treaty of Lisbon made it abundantly clear that the EU is a body based on powers conferred by the member states, enshrined in the treaties, and subject to subsidiarity and proportionality. Member states have rights of action, consultation, recognition, support, and, now, secession. The EU can also give up competences and legal harmonization is subject to clear limits. Equally, the institutions can operate only within defined boundaries. The EU's powers are categorized as exclusive, shared, or supportive, which makes it clear that they are not all-embracing or self-generated.

Third, EU policies were not greatly expanded by Lisbon. Energy, tourism, and civil protection were written more clearly into the TFEU, while space, humanitarian aid, sport, and administrative operation were added for the first time. In energy, there is now specific reference to combating climate change and providing for energy solidarity. The main change was the way in which rules on justice and home affairs (JHA) matters were brought into the mainstream. Since Lisbon was ratified, these have been governed by normal Union procedures and not subject to special, largely intergovernmental, procedures. This is a significant development.

Fourth, in terms of decision-making, the Treaty of Lisbon made co-decision the basic legislative process. The procedure—now referred to as the ordinary legislative procedure (OLP)—was extended to some fifty new areas. Inside the Council, QMV was extended to some sixty new instances—and, from 2014, QMV will be based not on the current complicated formula, but on a double majority of the member states (55 per cent) and the populations that they represent (65 per cent). In doing so, the proportional weight of larger member states such as the UK increases. Member states have also retained unanimity or emergency brakes in areas such as tax harmonization, the CFSP, criminal matters, and social security—and, to satisfy the Poles, old-style QMV can be invoked until 2017, after which a form of the Ioannina Compromise will apply.

Fifth, Lisbon introduced significant changes to institutional arrangements. The EP received extra powers, notably over the Budget and treaty changes. It also now has a virtual veto on the appointment of the President of the Commission. The European Council also emerged strengthened and formalized as an 'institution', now meeting every three months, and given a new role in external relations and overall strategy, which points to the continuing influence of member states. Special arrangements for the Eurogroup were also provided (see Chapter 11). The Commission gained an expanded role in the area of freedom, security, and justice (AFSJ) and in foreign affairs. Thus the High Representative of the Union for Foreign Affairs and Security Policy is now a Vice-President of the Commission, as well as chair of the Foreign Affairs Council. The High Representative is assisted by an External Action Service (see Chapters 16 and 18). The General Affairs Council (GAC) continues to be chaired by the rotating Council presidency. The Courts' jurisdiction was extended, albeit not to the CFSP and police matters. Other institutions were largely unchanged.

A sixth facet was a new emphasis on values and rights. The former were expanded and given more prominence, while the latter were given a dual boost. Hence the Charter of Fundamental Rights was given legal status, subject to safeguards for national jurisdictions insisted on by the UK. Additionally, the Union can now sign up to the wider, independent, ECHR (see Chapter 20).

Lastly, Lisbon tried to make the Union more democratic. Thus democracy now has a separate Title in the TEU. This includes provision for a citizens' initiative. National parliaments have also gained new rights to query proposed EU legislation on subsidiarity grounds, although these are not as extensive as some wished (see Chapter 25).

It is also worth noting briefly what from the CT did not make its way via Lisbon into the revised treaties. The constitutional language and references were dropped, along with the treaty-based mention of the Union's symbols. Thus acts of the Union are no longer to be called 'laws'. Equally, the term 'Minister for Foreign Affairs' was abandoned. This abandonment of 'constitutional' language marked a significant change from the CT, but many critics preferred to ignore this.

> ### KEY POINTS
>
> - The Treaty of Lisbon was not designed to have a lasting existence of its own, since its function was to amend the two treaties—the TEU and TEC—on which the Union is based.
>
> - The TEU and TEC were extensively altered and modernized, and, in the case of the latter, renamed as the TFEU.
>
> - Together, the TEU and TFEU create one structure, the Union, with characteristics fairly close to those of the past.

An appraisal

The first question to be asked is whether the Treaty of Lisbon improved on the much-criticized Constitutional Treaty (CT). It was certainly much more obviously a treaty, since, as well as leaving out constitutional language and symbols, it no longer proposed to abolish all of the other treaties and took typical amending treaty form. Hence any claims that it was still 'a constitution' had to rest on the contents or the style. At worst, it was constitutionalization without a constitution. Moreover, it could hardly be regarded as simpler to understand and read than its predecessor. As an amending treaty, it contained long lists of changes that were not easy to follow. Critics claim that this was a deliberate attempt to make the Treaty unreadable, but this falls down in the face of the demands of legal continuity, and the facts that the existing treaties are all like this and that consolidated versions of the treaties were made available earlier than ever before.

Perhaps the more important question is whether the Treaty succeeded in its intention of increasing the democratic legitimacy and the efficiency of the Union. On the first point, many would claim that the initial Irish rejection shows that it failed. However, this ignores the clear democratic improvements giving more powers to parliaments, both national and European, introducing the citizens' initiative, and signing up to the European Convention on Human Rights (ECHR) and the EU's own Charter. The more precise delimitation of EU powers and the insistence that these are 'conferred' by the member states underlines the role of national democracy in the EU. This is reinforced by the elevation of the European Council's role, equal status among member states, and their right to secede. The expansion of the Courts' jurisdiction can also be seen as reinforcing the legal and democratic nature of the Union, even if critics see this as an example of competence creep. Conversely, some believe that the changes in the Common Foreign and Security Policy (CFSP) downgrade the Commission to the benefit of the member states. As to efficiency, the introduction of a European Council President, the linking of the High Representative with membership of the Commission, the use of simpler voting procedures, and the extension of co-decision involving the European Parliament (EP) and the EU Council should make the Union more efficient. However, such changes have hardly wholly transformed the EU. At best, the improvements have been and will continue to be incremental. Moreover, the reinforcement of the powers of national governments and parliaments could well militate against faster and less contentious decision-making.

Thus Lisbon introduced a wide-ranging series of changes, the actual importance of which cannot yet be determined. Merkel and others certainly intended the Treaty to shake things up. However, the new Union has remained remarkably like the old one and failed to turn the EU world upside down.

KEY POINTS

- The Treaty of Lisbon was much more obviously and deliberately a treaty than the CT; hence it remained complex and difficult to understand.

- The Lisbon Treaty sought to make the EU more democratic and efficient, but this has not always been acknowledged.

- Despite the range of changes introduced, its effects have not been revolutionary.

Ratification

Although the Treaty of Lisbon entered into force, it did so almost a year later than planned thanks to a protracted and contested ratification process. Initially, prospects looked good, with a majority of member states completing the process relatively easily via parliamentary endorsements. This was interrupted by rejection in an Irish referendum in June 2008. However, ratification did not grind to a halt and, by the end of the year, very few approvals remained outstanding. That ratification proceeded so quickly and seemingly free of problems was in no small part owing to the nature of the Treaty of Lisbon. As a reworked version of the Constitutional Treaty (CT), minus its constitutional and other symbolic trappings, the Treaty was deemed to be sufficiently far removed from its predecessor for member states previously committed to ratification via referendum to obviate the need for popular endorsement.

Hungary won the race to be first to ratify on 17 December 2007. Malta and Slovenia quickly followed suit, with the Romanian, French, and European parliaments approving in February 2008. A second wave of approvals came in March and April, beginning with Bulgaria and followed by Slovakia, Austria, Portugal, and Denmark. Germany and Belgium also made progress. By the end of May, Germany had successfully completed parliamentary approval, as had Luxembourg. Three more emphatic ratifications then followed on 11 June, the day before the Irish referendum, in Estonia, Finland, and Greece.

Much to the relief of Eurosceptic groups and other opponents of the Treaty, Ireland had to hold a referendum. Its result was very much to their liking. On a turnout of 53.1 per cent, a clear majority of 53.4 per cent voted against ratification. The arguments against Lisbon varied. To begin with, there was the general lack of knowledge and understanding of the text and its significance. This was a great encouragement to abstention. This gave the impression that the text was ultra-complex and had little meaning for ordinary people, who, in any case, were not really interested in it. In other words, many Irish voters returned to the 'If you don't know, vote no' stance of 2000. However, there were a number of points at which specific elements of the Treaty did attract attention, notably the likely recurring loss of an Irish commissioner, the perceived threat to neutrality (which was seen in some quarters as being replaced by obligatory conscription in a European army), and the threat to the Irish ban on abortion (which was coupled with talk of enforced recognition of same-sex marriages). Governmental inability to counter arguments against the Treaty when levelled by a highly organized and effective opposition also played a part in the rejection.

Although the Irish rejection was a bitter blow to Lisbon's supporters, it did not bring the process of ratification to an end. Various non-ratifiers made a point of pushing ahead. Notable among these was the UK government, which completed parliamentary ratification the week after the Irish referendum. In July 2008, final parliamentary votes followed in the Netherlands, Cyprus, Spain, and Italy. Finland deposited its 'instruments of ratification' with the Italian government in early autumn and the Swedish Parliament approved the Treaty in late November. This left only three countries, apart from Ireland, still to complete ratification: Germany and Poland, where the respective presidents had yet to sign off the ratification bill; and the Czech Republic, where, following a positive ruling by the Constitutional Court and with the threat of the President refusing to sign, MPs decided to postpone their vote until early 2009.

EU leaders decided to leave it to Dublin to come up with a solution. A general assumption was that if all other member states were to ratify, it would increase the pressure on Ireland and oblige voters to consider the possible threat to Irish membership when they voted again. Lisbon was neither dead nor up for revision. However, there could be concessions. Hence the European Council in December 2008 agreed that, assuming that Lisbon entered into force, the size of the Commission would not be reduced, allowing Ireland to retain 'its' Commissioner. Moreover, provided that the Irish government committed itself to completing ratification before 1 November 2009, legal guarantees, acknowledging popular Irish concerns, would be given—namely, that Lisbon does not alter EU competences on taxation, that nothing in the Treaty affects Irish neutrality, and that the Irish Constitution's provisions on the right to life would not be affected by Lisbon, its Justice and Home Affairs (JHA) provisions, or the Charter of Fundamental Rights. The wording of the guarantees was duly negotiated during the first half of 2009, and it was agreed that they would be given legal force via an 'Irish' protocol to be added to the TEU and TFEU after the Treaty of Lisbon's entry into force. Also agreed was a declaration asserting the 'high importance' the EU attaches, inter alia, to social progress and the protection of workers' rights, public services, education, and the family.

All of this paved the way for a second Irish referendum on 2 October 2009. The outcome was a clear 'yes'. On a turnout of 59 per cent, more than two thirds (67.1 per cent) of the 1,816,098 voters who cast their vote voted in favour of ratification. With the German Constitutional Court having ruled the previous week that there were 'no decisive constitutional objections' to ratification, provided that improvements were made to the Bundestag's rights of scrutiny, all that stood in the way of the Treaty of Lisbon's entry into force was ratification in Poland and the Czech Republic. Whereas Polish President Lech Kaczyński soon penned his signature to Poland's Ratification Act, his counterpart in Prague had contrived a further judicial review. He then demanded an 'exemption' from the Charter of Fundamental Rights similar to that already granted to the UK. The European Council grudgingly obliged in order to secure ratification and a 'Czech' protocol was agreed. With the Czech Constitutional Court holding, on 3 November, that the Treaty of Lisbon did not contravene the Czech Constitution, Klaus finally signed off on Czech ratification. The Treaty of Lisbon duly entered into force on 1 December 2009.

KEY POINTS

- Parliamentary ratification proceeded without undue difficulty into summer 2008.

- The main causes of the 'no' vote in Ireland were a lack of knowledge and understanding of the Treaty of Lisbon, together with specific national concerns.

- Ratification of the Treaty of Lisbon continued despite the 'no' vote in Ireland, with the Irish government committing itself to holding a second referendum before 31 October 2009.

- Irish voters' concerns were addressed through 'guarantees' and a dedicated 'Irish' protocol, thus paving the way for a 'yes' vote in a second Irish referendum.

The significance of the Treaty of Lisbon

The Treaty of Lisbon was a second attempt to realize reforms that many European leaders thought necessary to make the EU fit for the world into which it is moving, but in a format more acceptable to European opinion. Critics have suggested that the determination to press on with reforms apparently rejected in 2005 was a piece of arrogance that was either mindless, or a deliberate attempt to foist a superstate on the nations and peoples of Europe. There may be something to this argument, but it was mostly a more pragmatic matter of ensuring that the EU changed in line with its expanding membership and contemporary policy challenges. That the idea was endorsed by those who actually have to work the system deserves to be remembered.

The Treaty of Lisbon substantively repeated that the Constitutional Treaty (CT) was its starting point and not something that need be concealed. Pretending that this was not so was a peculiarly British phenomenon produced by the sulphurous nature of UK anti-Europeanism. It was also an argument that placed too much stress both on understanding the difference between a 'constitution' and a 'treaty', and on the importance attributed by opponents to the CT's constitutional status. Stripping off the constitutional element was seen as the way in which to defuse opposition. This overlooked the fact that opposition to the CT was based on a whole range of often contradictory

stances and beliefs, many of them related more to the EU in general and the way in which Western European society has been developing than to the Treaty's terms. More important were the depth and organization of opposition to treaty reform mobilized by the 2005 'no' votes. Hence the ratification crisis was again seen as symbolizing an underlying alienation from the Union, which was decreasingly being accepted as a wholly good thing. The crisis was also revelatory of governments' failure to give real attention to dealing with the opposition—a failure most egregiously demonstrated in the one country where there was least room for it: Ireland.

So is there a crisis of legitimacy? It is quite clear that there is a major problem in the old member states of Western Europe, the populations of which are now much less inclined to identify with the EU than they used to be. This is because of their economic unease, their lack of confidence in the future, and their feeling that their interests are not being taken into account by 'Brussels' (see Chapter 25). Yet much of the opposition to Lisbon, as with the CT, came from people who described themselves as 'good Europeans'. Their objections were not to integration as such, but to the EU's style and strategy over the previous fifteen years. Lisbon served as a symbolic surrogate for such doubts. While the Irish 'no' in 2008 was certainly a hammer blow for EU elites, it was not a death warrant for Lisbon. As in 2005, it opened a tense period of crisis, thanks in part to the way in which it revived anti-EU and Eurosceptic forces across Europe, which did well in the 2009 European Parliament elections, and the way in which this conflicted with member state governments' commitments to the reforms that it contained. The Irish 'no' also forced the Danes to postpone a referendum on ending their opt-outs. European markets and the EU's standing in the world were also affected. It certainly forced the EU to give more attention to institutional questions at the expense of the policy issues that both friends and foes alike believe should be its main concern. However, talk of the demise of the EU remained, and remains, much exaggerated. While there is clearly vocal and active opposition, this needs something special, such as a referendum, to make an impact (see Chapter 26). Since the ratification crisis, apathy and lack of interest have reasserted themselves. Moreover, and despite the crisis in the euro area, the Union continues to function fairly normally and has not lost confidence, even though some would see this as arrogance.

Beyond Lisbon

When the Treaty of Lisbon was agreed, and later when it eventually entered into force, EU leaders appeared eager to call time on more than twenty years of seemingly interminable discussions about institutional reform and treaty change. As one seasoned observer of European Councils and intergovernmental conferences (IGCs), noted in October 2007 (Ludlow, 2007: 9): 'Everybody wanted an agreement, if only to put this wretched business behind them . . . Most of the heads of state and government were quite simply "fed up with", "sick and tired of" and "bored stiff" with the business.' Two months later, on the day after the signing ceremony in Lisbon, EU leaders declared that the new Treaty provided the Union with 'a stable and lasting institutional framework'. Furthermore, they expected 'no change in the foreseeable future' (Council of the European Union, 2008: point 6). Such sentiments were widely shared. The mood was that the days of treaty reform were now over. Ideally, there would be no major treaty for the next twenty-five years.

However, the Treaty of Lisbon was never conceived as a definitive text establishing the *finalité politique* of the EU. In fact, rather than limiting the options for treaty change and primarily in order to facilitate further treaty revision, it introduced two generally applicable 'simplified revision procedures', and increased the number of provision-specific simplified revision procedures and so-called 'passerelle' clauses in the TEU and TFEU. It would not be long before these, as well as existing provisions, were being put to use. An initial change followed Lisbon's delayed entry into force and the Spanish-led demand for the

reallocation of seats originally planned for the 2009 European Parliament elections to be brought into effect post-haste. On 23 June 2010, a brief '15-minute' IGC was held to adopt the so-called 'MEP Protocol', allowing for a temporary raising of the cap on the size of the EP to 754 MEPS to accommodate twelve additional members. The Protocol entered into force on 1 December 2010.

By then, two European Council Decisions amending the TFEU had also been introduced. The first—altering the status of Saint-Barthélemy, a French overseas collectivity—barely attracted any attention. The second provoked far more debate. This was the amendment to Article 136 TFEU to enable the creation of a European Stability Mechanism (ESM) to help to resolve the looming financial crisis in the euro area. Adopted on 25 March 2011, this was scheduled to enter into force on 1 January 2013. Four months later, a Treaty Establishing the European Stability Mechanism (TESM) was signed by the seventeen members of the eurozone on 11 July 2011. With eurozone leaders adopting additional decisions to strengthen the ESM in July and December 2011, this Treaty soon required modifications, which were contained in a revised TESM signed on 2 February 2012. The scale of the eurozone crisis demanded swift ratification. Entry into force was scheduled for July 2012 (see Chapter 27).

The TESM was not the only new treaty undergoing ratification. At Germany's insistence, a Treaty on Stability, Coordination and Governance in the Economic and Monetary Union had been drawn up following a fractious European Council in December 2011. Signed on 1 March 2012, its core purpose was to create between EU member states a Fiscal Compact fostering budgetary discipline, greater coordination of economic policies, and improved governance of the euro area. However, in what was widely regarded as a portentous move, the Treaty creates, thanks to the UK's obstinate refusal to countenance an agreement signed by all twenty-seven member states, an intergovernmental, extra-EU arrangement that excludes the UK and Czech governments. This not only threatens to further marginalize the UK within the EU, but also raises questions about the position of the EU's supranational institutions within EMU, their influence over national economic policy, and general economic policy coordination. Such fears may prove unfounded if, as the new Treaty envisages, within no more than five years of its operation, its substance will be incorporated into the TEU and TFEU. By then, resistance to the emphasis on austerity means that there could also be more substantial treaty reforms if the calls for closer union from Merkel, Barroso, and others are heeded.

Further treaty changes are likely. Before these materialize, other alterations are anticipated as the 'Czech' and 'Irish' protocols, to which EU leaders agreed to clear the path for Lisbon's eventual ratification, have to be formally adopted. Texts were being considered in early 2012. They are expected to enter into force at the same time as Croatia accedes to the EU, an event scheduled for 1 July 2013, although accession will see only a few minor adjustments to the TFEU (see Chapter 17). By this time too, the European Council is expected to have adopted a decision negating the

reduction in the size of the Commission introduced by Lisbon and reinstating the principle of one Commissioner per member state (see Chapter 10).

> **KEY POINTS**
>
> - The Treaty of Lisbon was never intended to provide closure on EU treaty reform.
> - Ratification and the euro area crisis have forced the EU into adopting further, albeit piecemeal, ad hoc, treaty changes.
> - The UK and Czech governments' refusal to contemplate a new treaty forced twenty-five other member states to adopt an extra-EU 'Fiscal Compact' treaty.

Conclusion

Despite all of the talk of the Constitutional Treaty (CT) and the Treaty of Lisbon creating a superstate, what comes out of all of this is the fact that the European Union is a body dependent on its member states and defined by its treaties. There is no underlying 'Europe' on which to fall back as there is a Denmark, a Netherlands, or a Slovakia. It is because of this dependence on the treaties that amendments to them are so sensitive and controversial. They raise the questions of what the EU is, what it should be, and where it might go. Given this, it should come as no surprise that the existing treaties have already been revised and supplemented as the EU seeks to deal with the euro area crisis. Further occasional revisions are to be expected as the EU keeps its treaty base up to date. Many states revise their constitutions fairly regularly. There is often a pragmatic need for change, as well as idealists pushing for more integration. Moreover, opponents of Lisbon argued for change too—in some cases, even for clearer, shorter, more constitution-like documents. So pressure for reform has not, and will not, go away.

The problem with Lisbon was that EU leaders bet heavily that dropping the constitutional element and

going for a mainly parliamentary ratification would head off the kind of opposition that emerged in 2005. To an extent, the bet paid off, but because Ireland at least felt a referendum was necessary, ratification was never going to be a dead cert. It rather looks as though the Irish government behaved like most others, and made little attempt to devise a convincing case and campaign strategy. This allowed an opposition to mobilize to good effect, even if some of the more persuasive arguments deployed presented Lisbon and the EU decidedly inaccurately.

This all points, and certainly not for the first time, to the need for the EU's institutions and, more importantly, its member states to engage citizens in meaningful and informed debate on what the EU is, and can and should be. It needs to be recognized that the EU is far from static; it remains a work-in-progress and therefore subject to, and often in need of, revision. Moreover, as the formal abandonment of the CT showed, non-ratification of a treaty neither reduces the need for change nor precludes either the EU's development or further attempts to reform it. As events have shown, the Treaty of Lisbon was always unlikely to be the last chapter in the history of EU treaty reform.

? QUESTIONS

1. Why did the European Union in 2001 embark on a process of institutional reform?

2. Why was the Constitutional Treaty rejected in France and the Netherlands?

3. Why did the member states decide to continue with the reform process after 2005?

4. What kind of a document is the Treaty of Lisbon?

5. How does the Treaty of Lisbon compare with the Constitutional Treaty?

6. What enabled the Irish government to commit to, and win, a second referendum in 2009?

7. Why has treaty change continued beyond the adoption of the Treaty of Lisbon?

8. What is the significance of the latest treaty changes for the future of the EU and of European integration?

 GUIDE TO FURTHER READING

Church, C. H. and Phinnemore, D. (2006) *Understanding the European Constitution: An Introduction to the EU Constitutional Treaty* (London: Routledge)   An accessible discussion of the origins, key themes, and content of the Constitutional Treaty, which reprints Part I of the Treaty.

Craig, P. (2010) *The Lisbon Treaty: Law, Politics, and Treaty Reform* (Oxford: Oxford University Press)   A comprehensive legal analysis of the Treaty of Lisbon.

Eriksen, E. O., Fossum, J. E., and Menéndez, A. J. (eds) (2005) *Developing a Constitution for Europe* (London: Routledge)   An academic study of the rationale for a European constitution and the process that led to the adoption of the Constitutional Treaty.

Laursen, F. (ed) (2012) *The Making of the EU's Lisbon Treaty: The Role of Member States* (Bern: Peter Lang)   A collection of analyses exploring the role of those member states most prominent in the negotiation and ratification of the Treaty of Lisbon.

Piris, J.-C. (2010) *The Lisbon Treaty: A Legal and Political Analysis* (Cambridge: Cambridge University Press)   An analysis of the Treaty of Lisbon's negotiation and content from one of its principal architects.

 WEBLINKS

http://europa.eu/lisbon_treaty/index_en.htm   The EU's own Treaty of Lisbon website.

http://europa.eu/scadplus/cig2004/   The archives of the 2003 Intergovernmental Conference.

http://european-convention.eu.int   The European Convention website.

http://www.consilium.europa.eu/documents/treaty-of-lisbon/igc-2007?lang=en   The official site of the 2007 Intergovernmental Conference.

http://www.lisbon-treaty.org/wcm/index.php   A source of documentation on the Lisbon Treaty, including a news feed.

PART 2
Theories and Conceptual Approaches

5

Neo-functionalism

Carsten Strøby Jensen

Chapter Contents

Reader's Guide

This chapter reviews a theoretical position, neo-functionalism, which was developed in the mid-1950s by scholars based in the United States. The fundamental argument of the theory is that states are not the only important actors on the international scene. As a consequence, neo-functionalists focus their attention on the role of supranational institutions and non-state actors, such as interest groups and political parties, who, they argue, are the real driving force behind integration efforts. The chapter that follows provides an introduction to the main features of neo-functionalist theory and to its historical development since the 1950s. It focuses, more specifically, on three hypotheses advanced by neo-functionalists: the spillover hypothesis; the elite socialization hypothesis; and the supranational interest group hypothesis. The chapter also considers the main critiques of the theory to explain why it went out of fashion in the 1970s. The final section scrutinizes the revival of interest in neo-functionalism beginning in the late 1980s and 1990s, and provides some examples of how today's neo-functionalists differ from those of the 1950s.

Introduction

Neo-functionalism is often the first theory of European integration studied by students of the European Union. This is largely for historical reasons, because neo-functionalism was the first attempt at theorizing the new form of regional cooperation that emerged at the end of the Second World War. The chapter begins by asking: 'What is neo-functionalism?' The purpose of this first section is to outline the general characteristics of the theory. The second section then summarizes the rise and fall from grace of neo-functionalism between the 1950s and the 1970s. The third section examines three hypotheses that form the core of neo-functionalist thinking:

1. the spillover hypothesis;
2. the elite socialization hypothesis; and
3. the supranational interest group hypothesis.

These three arguments help to expose neo-functionalist beliefs about the dynamics of the European integration process. The fourth section reviews the main criticisms of the neo-functionalist school, while the final section turns to more recent adaptations of neo-functionalist ideas, accounting for the renewal of interest in this approach to the study of regional integration at the beginning of the 1990s and in the 2000s. The chapter concludes that neo-functionalism remains part of the mainstream theorizing of EU developments, even though there have been some major changes in the way in which neo-functionalism is used today compared with its original application in the 1950s.

What is neo-functionalism?

The story of neo-functionalism began in 1958 with the publication by Ernst B. Haas (1924–2003) of *The Uniting of Europe: Political, Social, and Economic Forces 1950–1957* (Haas, 1958). In this seminal book, Haas explained how six Western European countries came to initiate a new form of supranational cooperation after the Second World War. Originally, Haas's main aim in formulating a theoretical account of the European Coal and Steel Community (ECSC) was to provide a scientific and objective explanation of regional cooperation, a grand theory that would explain similar processes elsewhere in the world (in Latin America,

for example). However, neo-functionalism soon became very closely associated with the European Community (EC) case and, moreover, with a particular path of European integration.

Three characteristics of the theory help to explain what neo-functionalism is. First, neo-functionalism's core concept is spillover. This is covered in more detail in 'Supranationalism and spillover'. It is important to note at this point, however, that neo-functionalism was mainly concerned with the process of integration and had little to say about end goals—that is, about how an integrated Europe would look. As a consequence, the theory sought to explain the dynamics of change to which states were subject when they cooperated. Haas's theory was based on the assumption that cooperation in one policy area would create pressures in a neighbouring policy area, placing it on the political agenda, and ultimately leading to further integration. Thus 'spillover' refers to a situation in which cooperation in one field necessitates cooperation in another (Hooghe and Marks, 2007). This might suggest that the process is automatic or beyond the control of political leaders, but when we look at the various forms of spillover identified by Haas, we will see how this 'automatic' process might be guided or manipulated by actors and institutions, the motives of which are unequivocally political.

A second, albeit related, point that helps to explain neo-functionalism concerns the role of societal groups in the process of integration. Haas argued that interest groups and political parties would be key actors in driving integration forward. While governments might be reluctant to engage in integration, groups would see it as in their interest to push for further integration. This is because groups would see integration as a way of resolving the problems that they faced. Although groups would invariably have different problems and, indeed, different ideological positions, they would all, according to neo-functionalists, see regional integration as a means to their desired ends. Thus one might see integration as a process driven by the self-interest of groups, rather than by any ideological vision of a united Europe or shared sense of identity.

Finally, neo-functionalism is often characterized as a rather elitist approach to European integration. Although it sees a role for groups in the integration process, integration tends to be driven by functional and technocratic needs. Although not apolitical, it sees little role for democratic and accountable governance at the level of the region. Rather, the 'benign elitism'

> **BOX 5.1** Features of neo-functionalism
>
> - Neo-functionalism is a theory of integration that seeks to explain the process of (European) integration. It is a theory that focuses on the supranational institutions of the EU.
> - The theory was particularly influential in the 1950s and 1960s, but is still widely used as a theoretical point of reference.
> - Its main focus is on the 'factors' that drive integration: interest group activity at the European and national levels; political party activity; and the role of governments and supranational institutions.
> - The driving force of integration is the self-interest of groups and institutions. They may well have different goals in mind, but the actions that they choose to achieve their goals drive forward the integration process.
> - European integration is mostly seen as an elite-driven process—that is, as driven by national and international political and economic elites.
> - The concept of 'spillover' is the key concept within neo-functionalism.

of neo-functionalists tends to assume the tacit support of the European peoples—a 'permissive consensus'—upon which experts and executives rely when pushing for further European integration (see Box 5.1).

A brief history of neo-functionalism

Neo-functionalism is very much connected to the case of European integration. Indeed, most neo-functionalist writers have focused their attention on Europe (Lindberg, 1963; Lindberg and Scheingold, 1970, 1971). This was not their original intention. Rather, an early objective was to formulate a general or grand theory of international relations, based on observations of regional integration processes. Political and economic cooperation in Latin America was one of the cases investigated (Haas and Schmitter, 1964). It was in Europe, however, that political and economic integration was best developed, and most suited to theoretical and empirical study. Therefore Europe and European integration became the major focus of neo-functionalism during the 1960s and 1970s.

With the benefit of hindsight, the success of neo-functionalism is understandable, because it seemed that the theory explained well the reality of the European integration process at that time. Until the 1970s, neo-functionalism had wide support in academic circles, although after that it lost much of its appeal. Indeed, it almost disappeared as a theoretical and empirical position in the study of European integration. One reason for this was that neo-functionalism lacked a theoretically solid base for its observations. Another reason was that the kind of incremental political integration that neo-functionalism predicted did not take place. From the mid-1970s, political cooperation seemed less compelling, and researchers became more interested in other kinds of theories, especially those that stressed the importance of the nation state. Even Haas was among those who recognized the limitations of neo-functionalism. On this point, he wrote that 'the prognoses often do not match the diagnostic sophistication, and patients die when they should recover, while others recover even though all the vital signs look bad' (Haas, 1975: 5).

After the early 1990s, neo-functionalism underwent a revival. The new dynamism of the EC/EU, a consequence of the single market programme (see Chapter 19), made relevant once again theories focusing on processes of political integration (Tranholm-Mikkelsen, 1991). Even traditional critics of neo-functionalism, such as Paul Taylor, accepted the need to examine this approach more closely. On this point, Taylor wrote:

The student of the European Community . . . needs to return to . . . the neo-functionalists—whose writings for many years have been unfashionable. They provide the essential context of theory in which to place the practice of diplomacy and even the speeches of Prime Ministers so that they might be better understood.

(Taylor, 1993: 77)

Since this revival of interest in neo-functionalism, a number of scholars have sought to adapt the theory to their own research agendas—whether on the European integration process writ large, on specific policy areas, or on the role of the supranational institutions. Correspondingly, there were, following Haas's death in 2003, a number of attempts to evaluate and re-evaluate the importance of the neo-functionalist contribution to our understanding of the development of the European Union (for example, in a special issue of the *Journal of European Public Policy* in 2005). These new approaches and evaluations will be reviewed under 'The revival of neo-functionalism'.

Supranationalism and spillover

The key questions asked by neo-functionalists are whether and how economic integration leads to political integration, and if it does so, what kind of political unity will result? In this respect, neo-functionalism differs from other traditional approaches to international relations. Realist positions, in particular, stress the power games that occur between states. By contrast, neo-functionalists believed that economic integration would strengthen all of the states involved and that this would lead to further political integration. The fundamental idea was that international relations should not be seen as a zero-sum game, and that everybody wins when countries become involved in processes of economic and political integration.

Another important aspect of neo-functionalist theory is related to the development of supranational institutions and organizations. Supranational institutions are likely to have their own political agendas. Over time, neo-functionalists predict, this supranational agenda will tend to triumph over interests formulated by member states. As an example, one might look at how the European Parliament (EP) operates. Members of the European Parliament (MEPs) are directly elected within the member states. One would therefore expect it to be an institution influenced very much by national interests. In the Parliament, however, MEPs are not divided into groups relating to their national origin; rather, they are organized along party-political and ideological lines (see Chapter 12).

In other words, Social Democrats from Germany work together with Labour members from the UK, and Liberals from Spain work with Liberals from Denmark. According to neo-functionalist theory, MEPs will tend to become more European in their outlook as a consequence of these working practices, although this may be disputed empirically. This is often referred to as 'elite socialization'. The fact that MEPs work together across borders makes it difficult for them to focus solely on national interests. This also makes the EP a natural ally for the European Commission in its discussions with the EU Council, even if the institutions do not always agree on matters of policy.

Political integration is therefore a key concept for neo-functionalists, although it is possible to identify a number of different understandings of this concept in neo-functionalist writings. Lindberg and Scheingold (1971: 59), for example, stressed that political integration involves governments doing together what they used to do individually. It is about setting up supranational and collective decision-making processes. By contrast, Haas saw political integration in terms of shifts in attitudes and loyalties among political actors. In 1958, he famously wrote:

Political integration is the process whereby political actors in several distinct national settings are persuaded to shift their loyalties, expectations and political activities toward a new center, whose institutions possess or demand jurisdiction over the pre-existing national states. The end result of a process of political integration is a new political community, superimposed over the pre-existing ones.

(Haas, 1958: 16)

Neo-functionalist writers developed at least three different arguments about the dynamics of the integration processes:

1. the spillover hypothesis;

2. the elite socialization hypothesis; and

3. the hypothesis on supranational interest groups.

The following subsections set out the content of these hypotheses, after which the next section presents critiques of these arguments.

Spillover

Spillover is neo-functionalism's best-known concept, one that has been widely used both by social scientists and practitioners. The concept of 'spillover' refers to a process in which political cooperation conducted with a specific goal in mind leads to the formulation of new goals in order to assure the achievement of the original goal. What this means is that political cooperation, once initiated, is extended over time in a way that was not necessarily intended at the outset.

In order to fulfil certain goals, states cooperate on a specific issue. For example, the original aim may be the free movement of workers across EU borders—but it may soon become obvious that different national rules on certification prevent workers from gaining employment in other EU states. For example, nurses educated in one member state may not be allowed to work in another because of differences in national educational systems. As a consequence, new political goals in the field of education policy may be formulated so as to overcome this obstacle to the free movement of labour. This process of generating new political goals is the very essence of the neo-functionalist concept of spillover.

Spillover refers . . . to the process whereby members of an integration scheme—agreed on some collective goals for a variety of motives but unequally satisfied with their attainment of these goals—attempt to resolve their dissatisfaction by resorting to collaboration in another, related sector (expanding the scope of mutual commitment) or by intensifying their commitment to the original sector (increasing the level of mutual commitment), or both.

(Schmitter, 1969: 162)

Functional (or technical), political, and cultivated spillover constitute three different kinds of spillover process.

- An example of *functional spillover*—where one step towards cooperation functionally leads to another—can be seen in the case of the single market (see Chapter 19). The single market was functionally related to common rules governing the working environment. This meant that some of the trade barriers to be removed under the single market programme took the form of national regulations on health and safety, because the existence of different standards across the Community prevented free movement. The functional consequence of establishing a single market was, then, that the member states ended up accepting the regulation of certain aspects of the working environment at European level, even though this had not been their original objective (Jensen, 2000).

- *Political spillover* occurs in situations characterized by a more deliberated political process, in which national political elites or interest groups argue that supranational cooperation is needed in order to solve specific problems. National interest groups focus more on European than on national solutions and tend to shift their loyalty toward the supranational level. Interest groups understand that their chances of success increase when they support European rather than national solutions. This type of spillover is closely related to a theory that argues that European integration promotes shifts of loyalty among civil servants and other elite actors.

- *Cultivated spillover* refers to situations in which supranational actors—the European Commission in particular—push the process of political integration forward when they mediate between the member states (Tranholm-Mikkelsen, 1991; Niemann, 2006; Stephenson, 2010). For example, the Commission may take heed only of arguments that point toward further political integration ('more' Europe) during the negotiation process, while ignoring or rejecting arguments that are primarily based on national interests.

Supranational institutions may use special interests as a means of driving forward the integration process. These special interests may be promoted through so-called 'package deals', in which steps are taken to treat apparently discrete issues as a single (composite) item, enabling all (or the majority of) actors to safeguard their interests. For example, if one member state has an interest in a certain policy area, such as preventing cuts in agricultural spending, while another has interests in industrial policy, these member states may agree, formally or informally, to support each other in negotiations. As a result, the two policy areas can be easily linked within the bargaining process, particularly when an entrepreneurial actor such as the Commission takes the initiative.

Thus spillover processes may be seen partly as the result of unintended consequences. Member states might deliberately accept political integration and the delegation of authority to supranational institutions on a particular issue. However, as a result of that decision, they may suddenly find themselves in a position in which there is a need for even more delegation. As a result, Lindberg and Scheingold (1970) are right to stress that political integration need not be the declared

BOX 5.2 Functional spillover: From the Single Market to the Treaty on Stability, Coordination, and Governance

The establishment of the single market increased the possibilities for companies in Europe to trade across borders. This generally implied a growth in trade among the countries of the European Community. However, the increased level of transnational trade in the EC made companies and countries more exposed to exchange rate fluctuations, which demonstrated the functional advantages inherent in a common European currency. From that perspective, **economic and monetary union (EMU)** can be seen as a consequence of a functional logic connecting growth in trade across borders in the EU with the functional need for a common currency to reduce risks related to expanding trade. However, the 2008 financial crisis demonstrated the weakness of the EMU. When the member states agreed to set up a monetary union, they chose not to give the EU the possibility of directly influencing national **fiscal policies**. When the financial crisis hit Europe, this became a serious institutional weakness. In that respect, the agreement of the Treaty on Stability, Coordination and Governance can also be seen as an unintended consequence of functional spillover. The financial crisis revealed that if a group of countries has a common currency, there is a fundamental functional need to have a coordinated **fiscal policy**, even if it was not the original intention of the member states of the **euro area** when the common currency was first set up.

BOX 5.3 'Elite socialization' and 'loyalty transfer'

Neo-functionalism stresses the process of socialization and 'loyalty transfer'. In an analysis of political integration in the educational sector, Warleigh-Lack and Drachenberg (2011: 1006) quote a Director General in the Commission who made the following observation: '[T]he typical socialization process would begin with the Member States' representatives being very hesitant at first. Then they call each other by first names, and then they want to change the world together.' (See also Chapter 15, of which Warleigh-Lack and Drachenberg are the authors.) Socialization leads actors to look beyond their own roles, allowing them to leave behind them the attitude that their own system is the best.

end goal for member states engaging in this process. The latter have their own respective goals, which are likely to have more to do with policy issues than with integration. As Lindberg and Scheingold write:

> We do not assume that actors will be primarily or even at all interested in increasing the scope and capacities of the system per se. Some will be, but by and large most are concerned with achieving concrete economic and welfare goals and will view integration only as a means to these ends.

(Lindberg and Scheingold, 1970: 117)

In this sense, the establishment of supranational institutions such as the EU may be seen to be the result of unintended consequences of actions among the actors involved in decision-making.

Elite socialization

The second aspect of neo-functionalist theory concerns the development of supranational loyalties by participants such as officials and politicians in the decision-making process. The theory here is that, over time, people involved on a regular basis in the supranational policy process will tend to develop European loyalties and preferences. For example, Commission officials are expected to hold a European perspective on problem-solving so that their loyalty may no longer be to any one national polity, but rather to the supranational level of governance.

We can well imagine how participants engaged in an intensive ongoing decision-making process, which may extend over several years and bring them into frequent and close personal contact, and which engages them in a joint problem-solving and policy-generating exercise, might develop a special orientation to that process and to those interactions, especially if they are rewarding. They may come to value the system and their role within it, either for itself, or for the concrete rewards and benefits it has produced or that it promises.

Thus neo-functionalists predicted that the European integration process would lead to the establishment of elite groups loyal to the supranational institutions, and holding pan-European norms and ideas. These elites would try to convince national elites of the advantages of supranational cooperation. At the same time, neo-functionalists also predicted that international negotiations would become less politicized and more technocratic. The institutionalization of the interactions between national actors, and the continued negotiations between different member states, would make it more and more difficult for states to adhere to their political arguments and retain their credibility (Haas, 1958: 291). As a result, it was expected that the agenda would tend to shift towards more technical problems upon which it was possible to forge agreement.

The formation of supranational interest groups

According to neo-functionalist theory, civil servants are not the only groups that develop a supranational orientation; organized interest groups are also expected to become more European, as corporations and business groups formulate their own interests with an eye to the supranational institutions (see Chapter 14). As economic and political integration in a given region develops, interest groups will try to match this development by reorganizing at the supranational level. For example, national industrial and employers' organizations established a common European organization, the *Union des Industries de la Communauté européenne*, or UNICE (now the Confederation of European Business, or BUSINESS-EUROPE), in 1958, at much the same time as the European Community was established. In so doing, their intention was to influence future Community policy. Early neo-functionalists also foresaw a similar role for political parties.

Furthermore, neo-functionalists believed that interest groups would put pressure on governments to force them to speed up the integration process. These groups were expected to develop their own supranational interest in political and economic integration, which would ally them to supranational institutions, such as the European Commission. Thus, 'in the process of reformulating expectations and demands, the interest groups in question approach one another supranationally while their erstwhile ties with national friends undergo deterioration' (Haas, 1958: 313).

Transnational organized interests can also be observed in policy areas such as climate policy. Environmental organizations such as Greenpeace often try to influence policy-making, whilst cutting across national boundaries and national interests. They act as transnational organized interests in the way in which neo-functionalist predicted and argue that it is necessary to increase the competences of the EU in relation to climate issues to push forward the climate agenda.

KEY POINTS

- Neo-functionalists believe that there are different types of spillover.

- Functional, political, and cultivated spillover account for different dynamics in the integration process.

- Elite socialization implies that, over time, people involved in European affairs shift their loyalties to the European institutions and away from their nation state.

- Neo-functionalists believe that interest groups also become **Europeanized**, placing demands on their national governments for more integration.

BOX 5.4 Neo-functionalist expectations about the European institutions

Neo-functionalists have formulated theories that they have used to predict the behaviour of the European institutions.

- The European Commission is expected to act as a 'political entrepreneur' or a 'policy entrepreneur', as well as a mediator. The Commission will, according to neo-functionalist theory, try to push for greater cooperation between the member states in a direction that leads to more and more supranational decision-making.

- The European Court of Justice (ECJ) is expected not only to rule on the basis of legal arguments, but also to favour political integration. In this way, the Court will seek to expand the logic of Community law to new areas.

- The European Parliament is expected to have a supranational orientation and to be the natural ally of the European Commission. Although MEPs are elected by the nationals of their home country, they are divided politically and ideologically in their daily work. Neo-functionalists expect MEPs to develop loyalties towards the EU and the 'European idea', so that they will often (although not always) defend European interests against national interests.

- The EU Council is expected to be the institution in which national interests are defended. However, neo-functionalists would also expect member states to be influenced by the logic of spillover, which would lead them to argue for greater economic and political integration, despite their national interests. The member states are also expected to be influenced by the fact that they are involved in ongoing negotiations in a supranational context. This makes it difficult for a member state to resist proposals that lead to further political integration.

Critiques of neo-functionalism

Neo-functionalism has been criticized on both empirical and theoretical grounds. At an empirical level, the criticism focuses on the absence (or slow pace) of political integration in Western Europe during the 1970s and early 1980s. Neo-functionalism had predicted a pattern of development characterized by a gradual intensification of political integration—a development that, by the 1970s, had clearly not taken place. The French boycott of the European institutions in the mid-1960s had led to a more cautious phase in the evolution of the Community, and recognition of the importance of political leaders as constraints on the process of integration. Indeed, with the European Community having suffered numerous crises, it could even be argued that the integration process had reversed. Moravcsik writes that:

Despite the richness of its insights, neo-functionalism is today widely regarded as having offered an unsatisfactory account of European integration . . . The most widely cited reason is empirical: neo-functionalism appears to mispredict both the trajectory and the process of EC evolution. Insofar as neo-functionalism advances a clear precondition about the trajectory in the EC over time, it was that the technocratic imperative would lead to a 'gradual', 'automatic' and 'incremental' progression toward deeper integration and greater supranational influence.

(Moravcsik, 1993: 476)

Haas even talked about the possibility that there might be a disintegrative equivalent to spillover: 'spillback'!

The second set of objections was based on criticism of the theories formulated by Haas himself. By the late 1960s, Haas had accepted that his prediction—that regional organizations such as the European Union would develop incrementally, propelled forward by various dynamics such as spillover—had failed to encapsulate the reality of European cooperation (Haas, 1975, 1976). He recommended a different approach to regional integration, based on theories of interdependence that were being developed in the mid-1970s by Keohane and Nye (1975, 1976), amongst others. This approach argued that institutions such as the EC/EU should be analysed against the background of the growth in international interdependence, rather than as regional political organizations. Referring to European integration, Haas (1975: 6) wrote that '[w]hat once appeared to be a distinctive

'supranational' style now looks more like a huge regional bureaucratic appendage to an intergovernmental conference in permanent session'. In so arguing, Haas abandoned the theory that he had been so instrumental in developing.

In some later writings, Haas argued that neo-functionalism had a common ground with constructivist thinking (see Chapter 7). Constructivists argued that institutions, discourses, and intersubjectivity are important factors when international relations are analysed (Haas and Haas, 2002), and that these were also areas that attracted major attention among neo-functionalists (although the vocabulary was different), especially with regard to how political elites are socialized. Socialization can be viewed as a process in which certain views are constructed. Haas (2001: 22) writes: 'A case can easily be made that the Neo-functionalist approach, developed in order to give the study of European regional integration a theoretical basis, is a precursor of what has lately been called Constructivism.'

In the third group of objections to the theory, it was said that neo-functionalism had placed undue emphasis on the supranational component of regional integration. Critics suggested that greater importance should be attached to the nation state and that regional forms of cooperation should be analysed as intergovernmental organizations. This line of attack was adopted by Moravcsik (1993, 1998, 2005), amongst others, under the rubric of liberal intergovernmentalism (see Chapter 6): 'Whereas neo-functionalism stresses the autonomy of supranational officials, liberal intergovernmentalism stresses the autonomy of national leaders' (Moravcsik, 1993: 491).

This can be read as a claim that the nation state remains the core element in understanding international relations, including interpretations of the development of cooperation within the EU framework. If we accept this hypothesis, it obviously imposes limits on the opportunities for political integration. The assumption appears to be that political integration is based exclusively on the aggregate interests of the single nation state and on its determination to survive. Nation states are thus prepared to cede formal competence to supranational institutions only if, by so doing, they ensure, or possibly regain, control of specific areas of policy.

Neo-functionalism first and foremost focused on political and administrative elites, and on the processes that developed the cooperation between national elites (Risse, 2005: 297). The assumption was that if the elites started to cooperate, then the populations would follow. The experience of 'no' votes in national referenda on the EU treaties points to the fact that this focus on political elites is a major weakness in neo-functionalist theory. Although the political and administrative elites at the national and European level agreed, for example, on the Lisbon Treaty, this did not mean that the voters followed them. In this respect, one could say that neo-functionalism as a theoretical tradition has a blind spot in its lack of understanding of the need for the EU to establish legitimacy among the peoples of Europe (see Chapter 25).

As we can see, therefore, the original neo-functionalist project has been subject—from many different angles—to critical reappraisal at both the theoretical and empirical levels. Yet this did not mean that neo-functionalism died as a theoretical project. As we shall see under 'The revival of neo-functionalist theory', the theory experienced a renaissance at the beginning of the 1990s and in the 2000s, as neo-functionalist concepts such as 'spillover' were used again to explain contemporary developments in European integration.

KEY POINTS

- Neo-functionalism is criticized on both empirical and theoretical grounds.
- On empirical grounds, neo-functionalism was criticized for no longer living up to the reality of the EC.
- On theoretical grounds, critics denied the existence of elite socialization and stressed the importance of the international dimension of integration.
- Critiques of neo-functionalism have also sought to reposition the nation state at the heart of the study of the European integration process.

The revival of neo-functionalism

After years of obsolescence, there was a revival in interest in neo-functionalism at the beginning of the 1990s. There are a number of reasons for the theory's renewed popularity. The first has to do with general developments in the European Community. The Single European Act (SEA) and the creation of the single market (see Chapter 19) marked a new phase of economic and political cooperation in Western Europe in the mid-1980s. The processes of integration associated with these developments seemed very much in line with the sort of spillover predicted by neo-functionalist theory (Tranholm-Mikkelsen, 1991).

However, this renewed interest in neo-functionalism involved much more than just a step back to the 1960s. Rather than simply adopting the traditional or classical model, many of those who sought to reuse neo-functionalist theory accepted it only as a partial theory—that is, as a theory that would explain some, but not all, of the European integration process. This contrasts with the earlier ambition of the neo-functionalists—to create a grand theory of European integration.

An important contribution to this new approach was made by Stone Sweet and Sandholtz (1998; see also Stone Sweet, 2010). Although these authors are not neo-functionalists in any traditional sense, they do claim that their theoretical considerations have 'important affinities with neo-functionalism' (Stone Sweet and Sandholtz, 1998: 5). They argue that the traditional distinction made in the theoretical literature on European integration—that it is either supranational or intergovernmental—is no longer sufficient. While both tendencies are represented in the real world of European politics, they appear differently in different policy areas within the Union, so that some are characterized by intergovernmentalism, others by supranationalism. However, Stone Sweet and Sandholtz do not use the spillover concept when they seek to explain processes of political integration and the formation of supranational institutions. Instead, they develop what they call a 'transaction-based' theory of integration. This draws attention to the increasing levels of transactions (such as in the field of trade, communications, and travel) across EU borders, which in turn increase demands for European-level regulation. In time, these demands generate a process of institutionalization, leading to the establishment of what the authors call 'supranational governance'.

One of the supranational institutions analysed using this approach was the European Court of Justice (ECJ) (Phelan, 2011; see also Chapter 13). Stone Sweet and Caporaso (1998) observed how the Court interprets the Treaty expansively within its rulings. In doing so, they confirmed their hypotheses about the autonomy of the EU's supranational institutions, about supranational governance, and about the way in which they relate theoretically to neo-functionalism. Elsewhere, Stone Sweet and Brunell explain the extent to which their analysis is similar to that formulated by Haas:

Our results provide broad support for some of the core claims of 'neo-functionalist' theory, first developed by Ernst Haas . . . Haas . . . tried to show that market expansion and political development could be connected to one another through positive feedback loops that would push steadily for more of both. We formalized these insights as hypotheses, gathered data on the processes commonly associated with European integration, and tested our hypotheses in different ways. The evidence supports Haas's basic intuitions.

(Stone Sweet and Brunell, 2004: 52)

Others have also used the ECJ to provide evidence of the existence of neo-functionalist dynamics in the EC. Burley and Mattli (1993) argue that the Court has been a very important institution in the building of a supranational community, because it has played an active role in the creation of Community authority in legal matters. They stress that the founding member states of the Community had no intention of giving the Court supremacy over national legal systems. However, the ECJ was able to develop its doctrine over the course of the 1960s and 1970s. According to Burley and Mattli, the Court has also been able to advance political integration by using technical and apolitical arguments in the legal arena, a process that is close to the type of integration mechanisms proposed by neo-functionalist theory.

Along similar lines, references to neo-functionalist theory have increased dramatically since the beginning of the 1990s. In policy areas such as defence (Guay, 1996), social policy (Jensen, 2000), and telecommunications (Sandholtz, 1998), attitudes among European civil servants (Hooghe, 2001, 2012), competition policy (McGowan, 2007), enlargement (Macmillan, 2009), and transnational liberties (Newman, 2008), authors have discussed neo-functionalism as a possible frame for explaining specific forms of integration. During the 2000s, there have also been some important attempts at further developing the original neo-functionalist framework. Arne Niemann (2006), for example, argues that the process of integration should not be seen as an inevitable process. Integration is no longer viewed as an automatic and exclusively dynamic process, but rather occurs under certain conditions and is better characterized as a dialectic process—that is, the product of both dynamics and countervailing forces. In addition, instead of a grand theory, the revisited approach is understood as a wide-ranging, but partial, theory. Thus, '[w]hile elites are still attributed a primary role for decision outcomes, the wider publics are assumed to impact on the evolution of the European integration process, too' (Niemann, 2006: 5). Niemann discusses the original neo-functionalist concepts of spillover and argues for the relevance of a new form of spillover: 'social spillover' (Niemann, 2006: 37ff). Through this concept, he tries to combine the traditional spillover concept with the socialization theory discussed under 'Elite socialization', arguing that this new concept of social spillover can capture processes that lead to a low level of European integration: 'In contrast to early neo-functionalism, which assumed constant learning and socialization, the revisited framework departs from the presumption and is concerned with delimiting the scope of social spillover' (Niemann, 2006: 42).

Conclusion

Since the first writings of Haas in the 1950s, theories of regional integration, or 'neo-functionalism' as it is more popularly called, have had their ups and downs. As a means of explaining cooperation among states in the 1960s, neo-functionalism became very popular. New forms of cooperation developed after the Second World War, especially in Europe, and these demanded new research perspectives. Neo-functionalism was able to describe and explain these developments in a way that was novel and of its time. In the period after 1945, the fashion was for grand theorizing—that is, the construction of scientific theories that would explain the 'big picture'. Nowadays, most theorists (and particularly those working on the European Union) are content to devote their energies to the generation of less ambitious middle-range theories (see Chapters 7 and 8) that explain only part of the process.

Focusing on the supranational aspects of the new international organizations, neo-functionalism explained cooperation using concepts such as spillover and loyalty transfer. States were expected to cooperate on economic matters in order to realize the economic advantages that come with increased levels of trade. This would lead to demands for political coordination across state borders and, in some cases, to the establishment of supranational institutions. Cooperation in one policy area would involve cooperation in new areas, thereby initiating an incremental process of political integration. Over time, the supranational institutions would become more and more independent and better able to formulate their own agendas, forcing the national states to delegate further competences to the supranational level. Yet, by the mid-1970s, neo-functionalism was no longer a credible position to hold. States remained key actors and it became hard to distinguish supranational institutions from more traditional international organizations.

Supranationalism did experience a revival at the beginning of the 1990s, however. The establishment of the single market and the creation of the EU at Maastricht opened the door to new interest in supranational developments and institutions. The EU suddenly began to look much more like the kind of institution that Haas and others had predicted would emerge as a result of regional economic and political integration. But although there was some interest in neo-functionalism at this time, most of the 'new' neo-functionalists felt free to pick and choose from those elements of the theory that best suited their research agendas. Today, neo-functionalism is not the most frequently used theoretical framework in studies of process of the European integration. It is, however, still an approach that contributes to the understanding of how EU institutions develop and of how political integration in the EU might be explained as a result of the unintended consequence of cooperation among countries.

 QUESTIONS

1.   What do neo-functionalists mean by 'political integration'?

2.   How can private interest groups influence the processes of political integration?

3.   How convincing is Moravcsik's critique of neo-functionalism?

4.   According to neo-functionalist theory, what role do the supranational institutions play in the European integration process?

5.   What evidence is there that 'loyalty-transfer' among the civil servants in the supranational institutions actually occurs?

6.   Does the conduct of the European Court of Justice support neo-functionalist theory?

7.   Why is it very difficult for neo-functionalism to analyse and explain: (a) the rejection of the constitution by the French and Dutch voters in the 2005 referenda; or (b) the 2008 rejection of the Lisbon Treaty by Irish voters?

8.   Can neo-functionalism be used to explain the Treaty on Stability, Coordination and Governance?

 GUIDE TO FURTHER READING

Journal of European Public Policy (2005) 'Special issue: the disparity of European integration: revisiting neo-functionalism in honour of Ernst Haas', 12/2   A special issue of this journal with contributions from Phillip C. Schmitter, Andrew Moravcsik, Ben Rosamond, Thomas Risse, and others. This is the best recent evaluation of neo-functionalism and its contribution to the study of European integration.

Macmillan, C. (2009) 'The application of neofunctionalism to the enlargement process: the case of Turkey', *Journal of Common Market Studies*, 47/4: 789–809   This article uses neo-functionalism to explain how the Turkish **accession** process has progressed so far despite the reluctance of many member states.

Niemann, A. (2006) *Explaining Decisions in the European Union* (Cambridge: Cambridge University Press)   Niemann uses neo-functionalism to explain decision-making processes in the European Union. This is one of the most interesting recent attempts to apply and develop neo-functionalism.

Sandholtz, W. and Stone Sweet, A. (eds) (1998) *European Integration and Supranational Governance* (Oxford: Oxford University Press)   An edited volume that develops the notion of supranational governance, drawing on aspects of neo-functionalist theory.

Tranholm-Mikkelsen, J. (1991) 'Neo-functionalism: obstinate or obsolete? A reappraisal in the light of the new dynamism of the EC', *Millennium: Journal of International Studies*, 20/1: 1–22   The key reference for examining the application of neo-functionalism to the post-1985 period.

 **WEBLINKS**

http://eiop.or.at/erpa/   The European Research Papers Archive: an online collection of working papers relating to EU studies, among which much innovative theoretical work is showcased for the first time.

http://europeangovernance.livingreviews.org/   *Living Reviews in European Governance* is an e-journal, publishing solicited state-of-the-art articles in the field of European integration and governance research.

http://globetrotter.berkeley.edu/people/Haas/haas-con0.html   An interview with Ernst Haas a few years before his death.

http://www.eui.eu/DepartmentsAndCentres/PoliticalAndSocialSciences/People/Professors/Schmitter.aspx
Philippe Schmitter's website at the European University Institute, which includes online access to published papers.

6

Intergovernmentalism

Michelle Cini

Chapter Contents

Reader's Guide

This chapter provides an overview of intergovernmentalist integration theory, focusing particularly on the classical and liberal variants of intergovernmentalism. It first introduces the basic premises and assumptions of intergovernmentalism, identifying its realist underpinnings and the state-centrism that provides the core of the approach, before examining in more detail the specific characteristics of the classical approach associated with the work of Stanley Hoffmann. The subsequent section also examines some of the ways in which intergovernmentalist thinking has contributed to different conceptualizations of European integration. The topics covered in this section are: confederalism; the domestic politics approach; and institutional analyses that emphasize the 'locked-in' nature of nation states within the integration process. Finally, the chapter provides an introduction to liberal intergovernmentalism, as developed by Andrew Moravcsik, which, since the mid-1990s, has become the main focal point for intergovernmentalist research. The chapter concludes by raising some of the criticisms of the liberal intergovernmentalist approach.

Introduction

From the mid-1960s to the present day, intergovernmentalism has continued to provide a useful conceptual account of the European integration process. For many years, students of European integration learnt about the two competing approaches that explained (and, in some cases, predicted) the course of European integration: neo-functionalism (covered in Chapter 5); and intergovernmentalism (the focus of this chapter). Although this dichotomy has been supplemented by newer approaches (see Chapters 7 and 8), intergovernmentalism—or rather contemporary variants of intergovernmentalism—have not been supplanted; to this day, this approach continues to resonate within the mainstream academic discourse on European integration. It is in this sense that one might see it still as a dominant paradigm for explaining European integration at the start of the twenty-first century.

This chapter provides a general introduction to the arguments and critiques of intergovernmentalist theory. It does so by focusing on the works of Stanley Hoffmann, whose early writings date from the 1960s, and Andrew Moravcsik, who began to make an impact on the field in the early 1990s. It also unpacks some of the premises and assumptions underpinning intergovernmentalist thinking. The chapter begins by addressing the question, 'What is intergovernmentalism?' This section outlines the general characteristics of the approach. The section that follows introduces classical intergovernmentalism and its main criticisms. Hoffmann's groundbreaking insights into the phenomenon of European integration, together with critiques of his work, led to new developments in European integration theory from the 1970s onwards. Although these might not always be termed 'intergovernmentalist' in any narrow sense of the word, they are premised upon a 'state-centrism' that owes much to Hoffmann's work. Important examples of these 'variants' of intergovernmentalism are dealt with in the remainder of the chapter: the first highlights the confederal characteristics of the European Union; the second draws attention to the importance of domestic politics; the third groups together a more institutionalist kind of research that shows how states, still central actors, become 'locked into' the European integration process. The final section looks at the work of Andrew Moravcsik and, more specifically, at his 'liberal intergovernmentalist' (LI) theory of European integration. Although this is an extremely rich and influential theory, LI has been widely criticized. Some of these criticisms are addressed at the end of the chapter.

What is intergovernmentalism?

Intergovernmentalism provides a conceptual explanation of the European integration process (see Box 6.1). It is characterized by state-centrism. In other words, intergovernmentalism privileges the role of (national) states within European integration.

Intergovernmentalism is drawn from classical theories of international relations and, most notably, from realist or neo-realist accounts of inter-state bargaining, albeit at only a very general level (Pollack, 2012). Realism views international politics as the interaction of self-interested states in an anarchic environment, in which no global authority is capable of securing order (Morganthau, 1985). States are rational, unitary actors that define their interests based on an evaluation of their position in the system of states (Dunne and Schmidt, 2011). State interest is therefore primarily about survival, with other concerns, such as economic growth, of secondary importance.

Neo-realism, like realism, sees states as self-regarding actors coexisting in an anarchical system (Waltz, 1979). According to neo-realists, regimes are arenas for the negotiation of zero-sum agreements, with the outcomes of those negotiations shaped by the distribution of state power within the regime. However, neo-realists also accept that there is some potential for order through international cooperation, if only as a rational means to state survival (see Axelrod, 1984; Keohane, 1988). However, policy preferences

---

BOX 6.1 Intergovernmentalism as theory and method

In this chapter, intergovernmentalism is defined as a theory of European integration. This means that intergovernmentalism provides a plausible explanation of European integration (or European **cooperation**). Intergovernmentalism may also serve, however, as a *model* of European integration. This understanding of intergovernmentalism is prescriptive, in that it *advocates* a more central role for national governments and a reduction in the role of the **supranational institutions** (the European Commission, the European Parliament, and the Courts). It might also imply the repatriation of European policies to the EU's member states.

(or interests) will often fail to converge, meaning that any attempt to build a community *beyond the state* is likely to be fraught with difficulties and may even intensify the sense of difference felt across state borders. Neo-realists accept that international institutions of all kinds are established to reduce the level of anarchy within the states system and see the European Union as just another of these institutions, albeit within a highly institutionalized setting (de Grieco, 1995, 1996). Their influence on intergovernmentalism is clear, even if intergovernmentalism and (neo-)realism are not one and the same thing (Church, 1996: 25).

Intergovernmentalism is not only associated with EU politics, but also refers to a type of decision-making that occurs within all international organizations. International organizations are intergovernmental bodies, in that they serve as arenas in which states meet to discuss common issues, to share ideas, and to negotiate agreements. They are usually based on international treaties and membership is voluntary. They tend not to have powers of taxation and rely therefore on member state contributions for their operation. Generally, they do not have independent powers and usually find it difficult to enforce decisions when individual members are recalcitrant (Reinalda and Verbeek, 2004). At a general level, intergovernmentalists apply this kind of framework to their understanding of the EU, albeit with some modification.

According to intergovernmentalists, there are costs and benefits attached to involvement in European integration. (Note, however, that intergovernmentalists may prefer to talk of European 'cooperation', rather than of 'integration'.) Participation in cooperation of this kind will rest on a weighing up of the pros and cons of membership, and on the extent to which European integration improves the efficiency of bargains struck among its member states. The main aim in engaging in this qualitative cost–benefit analysis is to protect national interests.

Cooperation within the EU, then, is essentially conservative and pragmatic. It rests on the premise that common solutions are often needed to resolve common problems. To put it another way, cooperation has nothing to do with ideology or idealism, but is founded on the rational conduct of governments as they seek to deal with the policy issues that confront them in the modern world. For intergovernmentalists, European integration is normal or even 'mundane' (O'Neill, 1996: 57) behaviour on the part of state actors. There is nothing particularly special about it, other than it has taken a highly institutionalized form since the 1950s. Because international cooperation always occurs simultaneously on a variety of levels and taking many different forms, cooperation within the EU is deemed to be only one example of a more general phenomenon. This is why intergovernmentalists are reluctant to admit that there is a European integration *process*, as such. Rather, they see cooperation occurring in fits and starts, and not as a trend heading inexorably in one direction towards some sort of European political community or federal state.

As an institutionalized form of inter-state cooperation, European integration facilitated the survival of the Western European state during the Cold War (see Box 6.2). It is perhaps not surprising to find, therefore, that in the early 1990s some intergovernmentalists supported the view that European integration would probably not survive the end of communism in Central and Eastern Europe (CEE) (Mearsheimer, 1990). This prediction has proved inaccurate, yet there is no disputing that the nation state has survived.

At the heart of the intergovernmental hypothesis lies a particular conception of the sovereignty of

---

BOX 6.2 The European rescue of the nation state

In his seminal book *The European Rescue of the Nation State* (1992), the economic historian Alan Milward analysed European integration in the 1940s and 1950s. He argued that the European integration process 'saved', rather than undermined, the nation state. Governments at this time had a number of difficult problems to resolve, arising out of increasing **interdependence** and increased disaffection from social actors. The successful delivery of policy programmes was a matter of survival for the states of Western Europe. European integration became a means to this end. As Rosamond (2000: 139) notes: 'The idea of integration as a progressive transfer of power away from the state managed by emerging supranational elites is given little credence by this hypothesis.' Rather, the key actors are governmental elites.

However, read in a particular way, Milward's work can be seen as challenging the standard polarization of intergovernmentalism and **supranationalism**. Integration does not necessarily entail the drift toward supranational **statehood** and states can be seen as controlling agents with an interest in the promotion of degrees of integration.

national states. 'Sovereignty' remains a very emotive word, particularly when used in the context of EU politics. It has various meanings, holding associations with notions of power, authority, independence, and the exercise of will. One useful definition states that sovereignty implies 'the legal capacity of national decision-makers to take decisions without being subject to external restraints'; another claims that sovereignty is 'the right to hold and exercise authority'. However, many use the word 'sovereignty' as little more than a synonym for 'independence', and this is particularly the case in public discourse (for example, when journalists or politicians discuss sovereignty).

According to intergovernmentalism, not only are the member states deemed to be the most important actors by far, but they also manage to involve themselves in European integration without ceding sovereignty. This implies that states remain very much in control of the process. Accordingly, European cooperation implies at most a pooling or sharing of sovereignty, as opposed to a transfer of sovereignty from the national to the supranational level (Keohane and Hoffmann, 1991: 277).

Intergovernmental cooperation can also involve a delegation of sovereignty (Pollack, 2002; Maher et al., 2009). Intergovernmentalists accept that European integration can involve a transfer of functions from the state executive and, to a lesser extent, from the parliaments of the member states, to the European institutions—to the Commission and the European Court of Justice (ECJ) in particular. The argument is that national governments find it in their interest to hand over certain (regulatory) functions in order to make cooperation work more effectively—that is, to make the commitments into which they have entered more credible. This emphasis on delegation colours how intergovernmentalists understand the role of the EU's institutions. Rather than assuming that these institutions are capable of playing an independent or autonomous role within the European integration process, intergovernmentalists tend to stress that the so-called supranational actors, the Commission in particular, are little more than the servants of the member states. While these institutions may be permitted a more important role in less controversial areas of policy, the functions that they perform in more sensitive policy domains is severely circumscribed. The European institutions that really matter, then, are the EU Council (of national ministers) and the European Council (of heads of state and government), while the role of the other European institutions is considered much more peripheral.

KEY POINTS

- Intergovernmentalism has been influenced by realist and neo-realist assumptions that privilege the role of the state and national interest in explaining European integration or cooperation.

- Intergovernmentalists believe that sovereignty rests with the EU's member states.

- It may be in states' interests to share/pool sovereignty and to delegate it to European-level institutions.

- The supranational institutions are considered agents of the member states.

Classical intergovernmentalism and its critics

Intergovernmentalism, as a theory of or approach to the study of European integration, emerged in the mid-1960s, from a critique of neo-functionalist theory (see Chapter 5) and as a reaction to federalist assumptions that the European Community (EC) would eventually transform itself into a fully fledged state. By the end of the 1960s, it had become the dominant paradigm used to explain European integration, replacing the earlier neo-functionalist orthodoxy and reflecting more accurately, it seemed, the practice of European integration by that time. After then French President General Charles de Gaulle's 'boycott' of the European institutions in mid-1965, the so-called 'empty chair' crisis, and the signing of the Accord that came to be known as the Luxembourg Compromise in early 1966 (see Chapter 2), a tide turned in the history of European integration. The persistence of the national veto after 1966, instability in the international political economy, and institutional changes that privileged the Council of Ministers (now the EU Council) and institutionalized the European Council as key decision-makers within the Community all suggested the limits of supranationalism, and the continued primacy of state actors in European politics. That the Commission began to play a more cautious role after 1966 was also an important factor supporting the intergovernmental hypothesis.

It was Stanley Hoffmann who laid the foundations of the intergovernmentalist approach to European integration. Most of the state-centric variants of integration theory of the 1970s and afterwards drew on his work. Hoffmann's intergovernmentalism, which is called 'classical intergovernmentalism' here, began by rejecting neo-functionalist theory, claiming that, in concentrating on the *process* of European integration, neo-functionalists had forgotten the *context* within which it was taking place. More specifically, intergovernmentalism rejected neo-functionalist claims that European integration was driven by a sort of snowball effect known as 'spillover' (see Chapter 5), arguing that this was more an 'act of faith' than a proven fact.

There was nothing inevitable about the path of European integration from this perspective and neither was there evidence of any political will to create a federal state in Europe (O'Neill, 1996: 63). If anything, the federalist rhetoric did little more than highlight the enduring qualities of the nation state, in that it sought to replicate it on a European scale. As for neo-functionalism, not only did it ignore the global context within which European integration was occurring, but it also missed the importance of cultural differences that were continuing to influence how states perceived their interests. Thus the neo-functionalist idea of 'the logic of integration' was contrasted with a more intergovernmentalist 'logic of diversity', which saw European integration as a dialectic of fragmentation and unity (Hoffmann, 1966). This diversity was a consequence of the unique context of internal domestic politics and of global factors (that is, the situation of the state in the international system), both of which contributed to inexorable centrifugal forces placing limits on European integration (Rosamond, 2000: 76).

Intergovernmentalism therefore offered a 'systematic contextualization' (Rosamond, 2000: 75) of the events of the mid-1960s, drawing on empirical studies of French presidential politics under President Charles de Gaulle. In this sense, it was much more than just an application of realist theory to the European Community case. In the post-1945 period, nation states were dealing with regional issues in very different ways than had earlier been the case. Whilst traditional, exclusive notions of sovereignty were now obsolete, and there was a blurring of the boundaries between the national state and international organizations (Hoffmann, 1966: 908), this did not mean that nation states and national governments had lost their significance. National sovereignty and the nation state were

being tamed and altered, but the latter was not being superseded (Hoffmann, 1966: 910–11). And while the national dimension may well have seemed less important in the immediate post-1945 period than it had in earlier times, it had not taken long for states to reassert themselves (Hoffmann, 1995: 867–9). Indeed, national states had proven themselves extremely resilient actors in international politics: 'The nation-state is still here, and the new Jerusalem has been postponed because the nations in Western Europe have not been able to stop time and to fragment space' (Hoffmann, 1966: 863). The nation state was said to be 'obstinate' not 'obsolete' (Hoffmann, 1966). Despite the fact that societal changes posed real challenges for the nation state, state governments remained powerful for two reasons: first, because they held legal sovereignty over their own territory; and second, because they possessed political legitimacy, because they were democratically elected (George and Bache, 2011).

Although the successes of European cooperation, its distinctive characteristics, and the possibility that it may produce more than zero-sum outcomes were not to be underestimated (Hoffmann, 1995: 4), the events of the 1960s highlighted the *differences* between member states as much as pointed to their *common interests*. This was an important argument, since 'preference convergence' was deemed a prerequisite for European integration. Thus, where states met with uncertainty and as supranational institutions began to develop agendas of their own, national governments would respond by going their own way.

The starting point for explaining European integration was the political rather than the technocratic. Whereas high politics (the political sphere) touched on national sovereignty and issues of national identity, low politics (the economic sphere) was more technocratic and much less controversial. There were clear boundaries between the more dramatic economic integration possible in areas of low politics and the 'impermeable' and very 'political' domain of high politics (O'Neill, 1996: 61), in which integration would not occur. While functional spillover might occur in the former, there could be no assumption that states would allow it to be transferred to the latter.

Although classical intergovernmentalism was based upon realist assumptions, it differed in its concept of the state. In this conception, states are more than just 'black boxes', containing no clear substantive content; rather, they represent communities of identity and belonging. They 'are constructs in which ideas and ideals, precedents and political experiences and domestic forces and rulers all play a role' (Hoffmann, 1995: 5). Hoffmann was particularly critical of the early theorists of European integration who had adopted a simplistic and unrealistic view of how governments defined their interests: interests were not reducible to power and place alone (Hoffmann, 1995: 5), but were calculated on the basis of various historical, cultural, and indeed political concerns.

However, this early form of intergovernmentalism has been subject to a number of critiques. Many of these involved a rejection of Hoffman's rigid demarcation between high and low politics. Even in the 1970s, there were claims that the existence of European political cooperation (EPC), the forerunner to today's European foreign policy (see Chapter 15) and an area of 'high politics', seemed to disprove this particular aspect of his theory. More recent events—most notably, the establishment of the single currency and the Common Foreign and Security Policy (CFSP)—point in that direction as well. Indeed, since the 1960s, Hoffmann himself has softened his position on this issue, accepting that there are limits to the usefulness of the traditional distinction between low and high politics.

Classical intergovernmentalism has also been criticized for playing down the constraints imposed on states as a consequence of their increasing 'interdependence' (see Box 6.3). Moreover, it was argued that he failed to take into consideration the novelty and the complexity of the European integration project. European integration was about more than just the creation of a regional regime and bargains struck at the European level could not simply be reduced to a set of national interests (Rosamond, 2000: 79).

At this stage, intergovernmentalism was not a theory in any systematic sense (Church, 1996: 26), but was rather part of an approach that dealt with the wider phenomenon of regional cooperation. As such, it was extremely influential in shaping the way in which scholars of European integration thought about the (then) European Community and set the agenda for future research undertaken in the field of integration theory from the 1970s onwards. Thus accepting the limits of intergovernmentalism as it was constructed in the 1960s did not mean opting for a supranational theory of integration; rather, it allowed the door to be opened to new variants of intergovernmentalism, some of which are dealt with in the section that follows.

KEY POINTS

- Stanley Hoffmann was the key proponent of intergovernmentalism in the mid-1960s. His work on French, European, and international politics led him to critique the work of the neo-functionalists.

- Hoffmann distinguished between high and low politics, arguing that, while functional integration might be possible in less controversial areas (the economic sphere), states would resist any incursion into areas of high politics (the political sphere).

- Critics have questioned Hoffmann's use of the high/low politics distinction, based on empirical evidence (such as recent moves towards foreign policy integration), and for not taking into consideration the novelty and the complexity of the European integration project. However, his approach has been extremely influential.

Beyond classical intergovernmentalism

This section presents some examples of how classical intergovernmentalism has been supplemented and adapted since the 1960s. While setting aside for the moment the most important example of this adaptation, liberal intergovernmentalism, which is dealt with under 'Liberal intergovernmentalism and its critics', this section deals first with confederalism, second, with the 'domestic politics approach' to European integration, and finally, with analyses that have sought to explain how states become 'locked into' the European integration process.

Confederalism

As a model or framework for European integration, the idea of 'confederation' seems closely allied to intergovernmentalism. A confederation may be viewed as a particular type of intergovernmental arrangement, in which national sovereignty remains intact despite the establishment of a common institutional framework. This could be understood as a concert of sovereign states (O'Neill, 1996: 71; Laursen, 2012). However, there can be no assumption that confederation will lead ultimately to greater unity, even if some authors talk of a 'confederal phase' within the integration process (Taylor, 1975; Chryssochoou, 2009). Rather, confederalism implies that the 'Community is stuck, between sovereignty and integration' (Wallace, 1982: 65).

Confederal approaches draw attention to the institutionalized nature of the European integration process, recognizing (in contrast to intergovernmentalism) its distinctiveness. Confederalism is a helpful supplement to intergovernmentalism, moving it beyond its inherent constraints, while retaining its state-centric core. There are many different ways of differentiating between confederalism and intergovernmentalism, however. Confederalism may be more likely to involve supranational or international law. Alternatively, 'a confederalist approach may be said to apply where the scope of integration is extensive . . . but the level of integration is low' (Taylor, 1975: 343). It may also be characterized by a defensive posture from national governments against the further extension of the powers of supranational actors, by an interpenetration of European politics into the domestic sphere, and by an oscillation between advanced proposals for integration and retreats into national

independence. Much of this argument is state-centric, assuming that the nation state is likely to be strengthened through confederation. At the same time, it adds to intergovernmentalist understandings of European integration by defining the framework within which cooperation and integration take place.

The domestic politics approach

In the 1970s and 1980s, an approach that focused on domestic politics and policy-making became fashionable in the field of European integration studies. Although not a theory of European integration per se, the approach was critical of intergovernmentalism's failure to capture the transnational nature of the European policy process (Church, 1996: 26) and sought, as a consequence, to focus attention on the impact of domestic politics on EC policy-making (Bulmer, 1983). In this, we can identify the origins of what today would be called the 'Europeanization' literature (see Chapter 9). We might also see this approach as one that links classical intergovernmentalism to later state-centric approaches—and particularly to liberal intergovernmentalism (Rosamond, 2000: 76).

The domestic politics approach argued that it was impossible to understand the European Community without taking domestic politics into consideration. It was therefore important to identify the domestic determinants of preference formation through undertaking in-depth case studies of the European policy process. This allowed researchers to identify variations in patterns of policy-making, emphasizing the linkages between the national and supranational dimensions of European politics. Two dimensions of domestic politics were of particular interest: policy-making structures; and attitudes towards the EC (Bulmer, 1983).

There are a number of elements involved in this approach, which, when taken together, provide a framework for analysing the behaviour of member states. First, the national polity is considered the basic unit of the EC/EU. Second, each national polity is different in terms of its unique socio-economic characteristics, and it is these differences that shape national interests. Third, European policy is only one facet of national political activity. Fourth, the national polity lies at the juncture of national and European politics. And finally, an important lens through which one might understand these elements was that of the 'policy style' concept (Bulmer, 1983: 360).

The importance of the domestic politics approach is that it demonstrated how intergovernmentalists had failed to look in any coherent way *within* the member states when analysing the European integration process. Although it was stated earlier in this chapter that intergovernmentalism is closely related to (neo-)realism in international relations, newer variants of intergovernmentalism have also been greatly influenced by neoliberal ideas. Neoliberalism, as an approach to the study of international relations, is concerned with the *formation* of state preferences or 'national interests'. It therefore places the national polity, rather than only national executives, or governments, at the heart of the European integration project. This is a point that will be picked up again when we come to look at the liberal intergovernmentalist approach.

The 'locking-in' of states

As a more recent example of how intergovernmentalism has evolved, a number of analyses explain how states have become *locked into* the European integration process. These draw heavily on a particularly German approach to the study of federalism, in which 'interlocking politics' (*Politikverflectung*) characterizes interactions between different levels of government (Risse-Kappen, 1996). While these approaches rest on state-centric premises, they move quite far beyond classical intergovernmentalism and show how European integration is about much more than interstate bargains. In the process, they emphasize the importance of institutional factors (see Chapter 7), and show how intergovernmentalist ideas may provide a starting point from which new arguments about and analyses of the European integration process develop.

An example of this kind of approach has been labelled the 'fusion hypothesis' (Wessels, 1997). This rests soundly on state-centric premises in that it sees national interests as the primary driving force of integration, but it also links integration processes to the evolution of the state. The argument is that, after 1945, Western European states became increasingly responsible for the welfare of their citizens, enhancing their legitimacy as a consequence. For the welfare state to persist, however, national economies had to be strong. In order to maintain economic growth, states recognized the need to open up their markets, which led governments to rely more and more on the joint management of shared policy problems. This amounted to much more than just a pooling of sovereignties. As states became more interdependent, they lost the ability to act autonomously, blurring the lines of accountability and

responsibility that connect citizens to the state. These trends are increasingly difficult to reverse.

Also grounded in state-centrism is an approach that draws an analogy between German federalism and the European Union. This explains how European integration has become almost irreversible because of the intense institutionalization to which it has been subject. European decision-making offers states the ability to solve problems jointly; yet the outcomes of these decisions are likely to be suboptimal, in that they do not emerge from any assessment of the best available solutions, but are reached through a process of bargaining that inevitably leads to the striking of compromises. In other words, as national interests determine policy positions, creative (and rational) problem-solving is not possible (Scharpf, 1988: 255). As such, no member state is likely to be entirely satisfied by what European integration has to offer. This is something that, over time, will contribute to the slowing down of the integration process. However, the institutionalization of the decision-making process means that retreating from integration is not an option. As such, states are trapped in a European Union from which they cannot escape, in a paradox characterized as 'frustration without disintegration and resilience without progress' (Scharpf, 1988: 256)—that is, a 'joint decision trap'.

More recently still, historical institutionalists have sought to explain how states become locked into the European integration process through a process of path dependence. One element in this argument is that the more states integrate, the more future options become constrained by past decisions (Pierson, 2004; see Chapter 7). The only way of escaping this integration path is through a 'critical juncture'—a dramatic break with past practice.

KEY POINTS

- Confederalism complements and extends intergovernmentalism, by acknowledging the institutionalized character of the European Union.

- The domestic politics approach claims that it is impossible to study European integration without looking at policy-making within the member states.

- Wessels's fusion hypothesis, Scharpf's joint decision trap, and Pierson's path dependence explain how states have, over time, become locked into the European integration process.

Liberal intergovernmentalism and its critics

In 1988, Robert Putnam published an influential article in which he explored the dynamics of domestic and international politics using the metaphor of 'two-level games' (Putnam, 1988). The first game deals with how states define their policy preferences (or national interest) at home within the domestic environment; the second is played on the international stage and involves the striking of inter-state bargains. This insight provides a framework for analysing the myriad entanglements involved in domestic–international interactions, as well as offering a starting point for understanding liberal intergovernmentalism.

Liberal intergovernmentalism

Since the early 1990s, liberal intergovernmentalism (LI) has become one of the most important theories of European integration (Moravcsik, 1998). It has become a touchstone against which all integration theory is now judged, even for those who do not agree with its assumptions, its methods, or its conclusions (Moravcsik and Schimmelfennig, 2009). Drawing on and developing earlier intergovernmentalist insights, it offers a 'grand theory' approach that is much more rigorous than those of its antecedents, incorporating within it both realist and neoliberal elements, and dealing explicitly with the interface between domestic and international politics.

From this perspective, the European Union is a successful intergovernmental regime designed to manage economic interdependence through negotiated policy coordination. The theory assumes that states behave rationally, while emphasizing the importance of both the *preferences* and the *power* of states. While national politicians advance state interests that reflect domestic policy preferences, all decisions made by the EU are ultimately the result of bargaining amongst states. Agreements are usually reached on a 'lowest common denominator' basis, with clear limits placed on the transfer of sovereignty to supranational agents. Thus '[t]he broad lines of European integration since 1955 reflect three factors: patterns of commercial advantage, the relative bargaining power of important governments, and the incentives to enhance the credibility of inter-state commitment' (Moravcsik, 1998: 3). When economic or commercial concerns converge, integration takes place.

There are two separate dimensions to LI: the supply side and the demand side. The argument is that both the *demand* for cooperation, which derives from the national polity, and the *supply* of integration, arising out of inter-state negotiations, are important in understanding European integration. To explain the link between demand and supply in this context, the theory is composed of three steps, each of which is explained by a different set of factors and each of which draws on complementary theories of economic interest, relative power, and credible commitments (Moravcsik, 1998: 4).

First, deriving from liberal theories of *national preference formation*, the theory shows how state goals can be shaped by domestic pressures and interactions, which, in turn, are often conditioned by the constraints and opportunities that derive from economic interdependence (Nugent, 2010). Thus underlying societal factors provoke an international demand for cooperation. National political institutions are subject to myriad pressures from nationally based interests, leading to a process of preference formation. State preferences are formed as groups compete with each other for the attention of government elites and these feed into inter-state negotiations. To put it another way, national policy preferences are constrained by the interests of dominant, usually economic, groups within society. Resting on a pluralistic understanding of state–society relations, national governments represent these interests in international forums. Thus national interests are derived from the domestic politics of the member states and not the state's perception of its relative position in the states system—that is, from geo-political concerns. Thus 'the vital interest behind General de Gaulle's opposition to British membership in the EC . . . was not the pursuit of French *grandeur* but the price of French wheat' (Moravcsik, 1998: 7 and Box 6.4).

Second, the supply side in LI rests on *intergovernmentalist theories of inter-state relations*, with European integration supplied by intergovernmental bargains, such as revisions to the Treaty (Moravcsik, 1998: 7). More specifically, this 'draws on general theories of bargaining and negotiation to argue that relative power among states is shaped above all by asymmetrical interdependence, which dictates the relative value of agreement to different governments' (Moravcsik, 1998: 7). It emphasizes the centrality of strategic bargaining among states and the importance of governmental elites in shaping inter-state relations. States are now considered to be unitary actors and supranational institutions are

---

BOX 6.4 Moravcsik's five case studies

In his 1998 book *The Choice for Europe*, Andrew Moravcsik applies his theory of LI to five cases in the history of the European integration process, as follows.

1. The negotiation of the **Treaty of Rome** (1955–58)

2. The consolidation of the **common market** and the Common Agricultural Policy (CAP) (1958–69)

3. Monetary cooperation and the setting up of the **European Monetary System (EMS)** (1969–83)

4. The negotiation of the **Single European Act (SEA)** (1984–88)

5. The negotiation of the Treaty on European Union (TEU) (1988–91)

In each case, Moravcsik—drawing on secondary historical and some documentary sources—argues that what was important in driving elite support for European integration was national economic interest. This line of argument was contrary to the conventional wisdom usually put forward by historians at the time that geopolitical factors were what mattered most in explaining European integration. Moravcsik makes the case that geopolitics, such as France's pursuit of a policy of *grandeur*, although not irrelevant, were merely a secondary consideration as national governments established their bargaining positions on history-making decisions.

---

deemed to have a very limited impact on outcomes. This generally involves a two-stage process of negotiation: first, governments must resolve the policy problems that confront them; they do this by taking decisions, and only then do they try to reach agreement on institutional mechanisms that would allow them to implement those decisions. Various bargaining strategies and techniques, such as 'coalitional alternatives to agreement'—that is, the linking of issues and threats of exclusion and inclusion—shape outcomes. A bargaining space, a sort of window of opportunity, is formed out of the amalgamation of national interests, with the final agreement determining the distribution of gains and losses. This implies a restrictive range of possible integration outcomes, although inter-state bargains can lead on occasion to positive-sum outcomes. Governments bargain hard to gain the upper hand. The power of individual states is crucial in determining whose interests win out in the end. This means that LI focuses most of its attention on the preferences of the largest and most powerful EU states: the UK, France, and Germany. In stressing the points that integration *benefits* states, that states face few constraints in the Council, and that inter-state negotiations enhance their domestic autonomy, the question of why governments engage in European integration when it might otherwise seem like an irrational thing to do is addressed by this part of the theory (Rosamond, 2000: 138).

The third element within LI is that of *institutional delegation*. The argument here is that international (European) institutions are set up to improve the efficiency of inter-state bargaining. Governments delegate

and pool sovereignty in such institutions to secure the substantive bargains that they have made by ensuring that all parties commit to cooperation (Moravcsik, 1998: 3–4). Thus, in the case of the EU, the European institutions create linkages and compromises across issues regarding which decisions have been made under conditions of uncertainty and in instances in which non-compliance would be a temptation. In other words, institutional delegation reflects the desire for 'credible commitments'.

In this respect, LI has been influenced by liberal institutionalism (Keohane, 1989). This sees institutions as ways of facilitating positive-sum bargaining ('upgrading the common interest') among states, whilst denying that they undermine in any way the longer-term self-interest of the member states. From this perspective, then, '[t]he entrepreneurship of supranational officials . . . tends to be futile and redundant, even sometimes counterproductive' (Moravcsik, 1998: 8).

Critiques of liberal intergovernmentalism

Although LI has been much criticized, it remains an extremely useful way in which to organize data and to construct empirical studies. At the same time, it offers a framework that can be hard, if not impossible, to reconcile with alternative interpretations of European integration and EU politics (albeit that LI theorists would disagree with this claim).

Perhaps the most commonly repeated criticism of LI is that it simply does not fit the facts. One perspective on this is that LI may have explained the earlier treaty changes, but as the EU increasingly came to focus on non-economic issues, this was much less the case (Finke, 2009). In other words, LI has too narrow a focus to be called a theory of European integration, because it is too selective with its empirical references (Nugent, 2010: 433). Liberal intergovernmentalism is applied only to those cases that will result in proving the theory correct. It has been claimed by Scharpf (1999: 165), for example, that applying the theory to cases of *intergovernmental negotiation*, in which economic integration is the main concern and in which decisions were taken on the basis of unanimous voting in the Council, will invariably confirm the theory; 'Given this focus for his attention, it is hardly surprising that Moravcsik comes to the view that the EC is primarily motivated by the aggregation and conciliation of national interests' (Wincott, 1995: 602). The assumption is, then, that, in 'harder' cases, in which international negotiations are not the primary form of decision taking and in which majority voting applies, LI may not produce such clear-cut results. The critique is often articulated in the following way: that liberal intergovernmentalism may explain the majority of 'history-making' decisions—that is, high-profile changes of constitutional significance, which often involve treaty change and which occur through inter-state negotiations—but it is much less able to explain how the EU works in matters of day-to-day politics.

The second criticism often directed at LI is that its conception of the state is too narrow. Liberal intergovernmentalism pays little attention to the way in which the state may be broken down into its component parts. Critics argue that, in order to understand fully how governmental positions (or preferences) are determined, a more nuanced analysis of domestic politics is required. Indeed, ' . . . in some ways it [LI] was less sophisticated in its account of domestic politics than Hoffmann's' (George and Bache, 2011: 13). Thus, in this pluralist or liberal view, the primary determinant of government preferences is the balance between *economic* interests. In practice, however, there are diverse influences likely to impinge on national preference formation. For example, domestic structures may be important. On this basis, the LI account is too simplistic, because it focuses solely on economic and (to a lesser extent) geopolitical concerns (Wincott, 1995: 600–1). Moreover, the 'two-level

game' metaphor does not depict the reality of EU politics today if one accepts the premises of multilevel governance theorists that the EU is a multilevel polity (see Chapter 8).

A third critique of LI is that the theory understates the constraints faced by key policy-makers. The case of the single market programme is often used to back up this argument. It is frequently argued that LI plays down to too great an extent the role of supranational actors within the European integration process. In other words, it does not provide a full enough account of the supply side of the model when focusing solely on inter-state negotiations. As the roles of the European Commission and the ECJ are deemed relatively unimportant, if not entirely irrelevant, in terms of policy outcomes, their interests and strategies do not figure particularly strongly in LI explanations. This view of the supranational institutions' potential influence over integration outcomes has frequently been contested.

The LI depiction of the Commission as little more than a facilitator in respect of significant decision-making has attracted particular criticism, with numerous empirically based studies claiming to show that the Commission does exercise an independent and influential decision-making role, be it as *animateur*, a policy entrepreneur, or a motor force (Nugent, 2010: 135–7). For example, there is empirical evidence of how the Commission has been able to influence policy outcomes, by means of its policy entrepreneurship, and how it is able to exploit the differences between the preferences of member states to promote its own independent agenda (Sandholtz and Stone Sweet, 1998). There is also some evidence that the ECJ has been able to have an independent influence on European integration through its innovative legal rulings in cases such as those pertaining to human rights (Burley and Mattli, 1993; Wincott, 1995; see also Chapter 13). A similar point also applies to non-state 'transnational' actors, such as European firms and European interest groups. Business groups in the 1980s, for example, were particularly important in influencing the single market project (Cowles, 1995; Armstrong and Bulmer, 1998; see also Chapter 14). Although these groups were not the sole cause of the '1992' programme:

[I]ntergovernmental theory cannot explain the activities of the key non-state actors in the 1992 process. The single market programme was not merely the result

In Forster's interesting 1998 study, the LI hypothesis was applied to three policy cases, each of which covers one aspect of the UK's role in the negotiation of the **Maastricht Treaty**: (a) social policy; (b) foreign and security policy; and (c) the powers of the European Parliament (Forster, 1998). The research casts doubt on LI's explanation of national preference formation; it questions the extent to which governments always act as purposive and instrumental actors; and it challenges the LI understanding of bargaining.

The article can conclude only by expressing serious doubts about LI's ambitious claim to provide a parsimonious predictive and explanatory theory. From a methodological perspective, the theoretical approach is simply too complex, often requiring unknowable or non-existent information, to provide a 'toolkit' for explaining and predicting the actions of governments (Anderson,

1995). Above all, however, LI's empirical foundations are weak. In particular, its inadequate conceptualization of the state raises very large question marks over the value of an approach consciously 'derived independently of the matter being studied', rather than based on empirical evidence (Moravcsik, 1993: 477).

In the final analysis, LI is thus perhaps best regarded less as a theory of intergovernmental bargaining than as pre-theory or analytical framework. It provides some very useful insights, but, as empirical testing proves, it must be supplemented by other models in order to explain fully how and why a government chooses among various outcomes. Similarly, other models are needed to explain the determinants of politicians' choices among competing alternatives. The irony is that, like neo-functionalism, LI's aspiration to generality ultimately renders it 'oddly apolitical'.

of conventional statecraft. Nor were Member States' actions predicated solely on the basis of domestically defined interest group activity, as suggested by a recent version of intergovernmentalism [LI] . . . Indeed, the story of the ERT [European Round Table of Industrialists] points to the fact that non-state actors—and in particular, multinational enterprises—also play two-level games in EC policy-making.

(Cowles, 1995: 521–2)

This is not just about which actors and institutions matter in the process of European decision-making; it is also about how much weight can be placed on the more formal aspects of European decision-making, at the expense of the informal, 'behind the scenes' dimension. If informal politics matter in shaping policy outcomes, this may mean that actors who appear on the surface to be responsible for decision-taking may not really be in control. As such, the substance of inter-state negotiations may already have been framed well before **intergovernmental conferences** (ICGs) and European summits meet to take their formal decisions (see also Box 6.5).

Finally, LI has been criticized for not really being a theory at all (Wincott, 1995). This assumes that a rigorous theory ought to spell out the conditions under which it might be refuted or disproved. Liberal intergovernmentalism does not do this, but engages in an act of closure on certain types of argument about European integration. As such, LI should be considered an 'approach' rather than

a theory—one that brings together three existing theories (preference formation, intergovernmental bargaining, and institutional delegation) to provide a 'pre-theory' or 'analytical framework' that can be applied to the European integration process (Forster, 1998: 365). Not surprisingly, many of these criticisms about LI are contested by the proponents of the theory—not least by Andrew Moravcsik himself (see, for example, Moravcsik and Schimmelfennig, 2009).

KEY POINTS

- Liberal intergovernmentalism provides an explanation of European integration based on national preference formation, inter-state bargaining, and institutional delegation.

- Liberal intergovernmentalism supplements a rich account of bargaining inside the European and EU Councils, with a concern for how national interests (or preferences) are formed from the pressures placed on governments by domestic economic interests.

- Liberal intergovernmentalism is criticized for focusing only on 'history-making decisions' (treaty change in particular), and for ignoring day-to-day politics and the multilevel character of the European Union.

- Liberal intergovernmentalism is criticized for not being a theory of European integration, but rather an approach to studying European integration.

Conclusion

This chapter has reviewed the theory of European integration known as 'intergovernmentalism'. It has shown how intergovernmentalist premises (and, more specifically, state-centrism) have provided the foundations for a range of theories and models that have sought to explain the nature of decision-making and the 'locking in' of states within the European integration process. A particularly important variant, liberal intergovernmentalism, became dominant in the mid-1990s, and remains a touchstone for all researchers and students of European integration to this day (Pollack, 2012).

While intergovernmentalist approaches continue to provide inspiration for many scholars of European integration, new theories have tested the resilience of intergovernmentalist arguments, both old and new. Intergovernmentalism has been flexible enough to adapt, however. It has increasingly be allied to rational institutionalist approaches (Puchala, 1999; Pollack, 2009; see Chapter 7), with the latter more able to account for day-to-day policy-making, whilst based on many of the same premises. Moravcsik and Schimmelfennig (2009) also say that it is in line with recent research on Europeanization (see Chapter 9). Even though there are many scholars who contest the (liberal) intergovernmentalist account of European integration, no student of the integration process can claim to be well informed without an understanding of the contribution that it makes to current thinking on the European Union.

QUESTIONS

1. How convincing are intergovernmentalist accounts of European integration?

2. Why has liberal intergovernmentalism been so influential?

3. What value does the 'domestic politics' approach add to classical intergovernmenalism?

4. How useful a model for explaining the EU is confederalism?

5. What are the main elements of classical intergovernmentalism?

6. How central is the nation state within the process of European integration?

7. In what sense and to what extent is European integration a 'mundane' affair?

8. How justified are the most common critiques of liberal intergovernmentalism?

GUIDE TO FURTHER READING

Hoffmann, S. (1995) *The European Sisyphus: Essays on Europe 1964–1994* (Oxford: Westview Press)   An excellent collection of Stanley Hoffmann's work, showing how his ideas have changed (or not) over the years. Includes seminal articles published in the 1960s, which set the scene for future intergovernmentalist writings.

Moravcsik, A. (1998) *The Choice for Europe: Social Purpose and State Power from Messina to Maastricht* (London: UCL Press)   The seminal liberal intergovernmentalist book, by the founder of the approach. Chapter 1, 'Theorizing European integration', both covers a critique of neo-functionalism and sets out the characteristics of LI in some detail.

Moravcsik, A. and Schimmelfennig, F. (2009) 'Liberal intergovernmentalism' in A. Wiener and T. Diez (eds) *European Integration Theory*, 2nd edn (Oxford: Oxford University Press), pp. 67–87   An interesting chapter on liberal intergovernmentalism, which uses agriculture and **enlargement** as case studies to show how LI might be applied to contemporary European issues (see Chapter 7).

O'Neill, M. (1996) *The Politics of European Integration: A Reader* (London: Routledge), ch. 4   Ostensibly a 'reader', but also includes a useful chapter on state-centric approaches to European integration.

Rosamond, B. (2000) *Theories of European Integration* (Basingstoke: Macmillan), ch. 6   The most recent, overarching text on European integration theory, with numerous references to intergovernmentalism and a specific chapter devoted to 'Intergovernmental Europe'. A new, up-to-date edition is planned for 2013.

WEBLINKS

http://eiop.or.at/erpa/   The European Research Papers Archive is an online collection of working papers relating to EU studies, in which much innovative theoretical work is showcased for the first time.

http://europeangovernance.livingreviews.org/   *Living Reviews in European Governance* is an e-journal, publishing solicited state-of-the-art articles in the field of European integration and governance research

http://www.princeton.edu/~amoravcs   Andrew Moravcsik's home page, this includes access to published and forthcoming papers.

http://www.oup.com/uk/orc/bin/9780199569090/   The open-access Online Resources Centre for Bayliss, Smith, and Owens' 2010 book *The Globalization of World Politics* (5th edn, Oxford: Oxford University Press) provides information on the realist, neo-realist, and liberal theories that have influenced intergovernmentalism.

7

Theorizing the European Union after Integration Theory

Ben Rosamond

Chapter Contents

Reader's Guide

This chapter deals with recent theoretical work on the European Union. Three analytical pathways that depart from the classical debate are discussed in this chapter: comparative political science; a revitalized international relations (IR); and 'critical theory'. Two additional pathways—governance and normative political theory—are considered in other chapters (see Chapters 8 and 25). This chapter discusses in turn the contribution to EU studies of comparative political science in general and new institutionalist political science in particular, the emergence of social constructivist approaches to the EU, IR's contribution to the theorization of EU external action, together with approaches from the subfield of international political economy (IPE), and a variety of critical theoretical readings of the EU. The chapter also explores how IR theories might be brought back into EU studies. The purpose of the chapter is to show how the EU raises significant questions about the nature of authority, statehood, and the organization of the international system in the contemporary period.

Introduction

It is still commonplace to introduce theoretical discussion of the European Union in terms of the classical debate between neo-functionalism and intergovernmentalism (see Chapters 5 and 6). There is a rationale for continuing to explore the opposition between these two schools. Thinking in this way forces us to address key issues of continuity versus change in European politics.

However, recent years have witnessed concerted attempts to 'think otherwise' about the EU. This chapter deals with some of these new approaches (see also Chapters 8 and 25). It is worth pausing for thought to consider what 'new' might mean in this context. The term implies, after all, that some theories are old—or perhaps redundant. In particular, many academics who offer new theoretical prospectuses tend to begin with the proposition that the classical terms of debate—as represented by the rivalry between neo-functionalism and intergovernmentalism—fail to capture adequately what is going on in the contemporary EU. This chapter is attentive to this premise and begins with a deeper discussion of its soundness as a proposition for theoretical departure.

This discussion alerts us to the importance of thinking carefully about theoretical work. Theory is not simply a self-indulgent exercise, nor can it be side-stepped by any serious student of the EU. Being conscious about the theoretical propositions chosen by authors is important because alternative readings of the EU and European integration follow from alternative theoretical premises. That said, writers rarely (these days at least) attempt to construct 'grand theories' of integration. Instead, since the 1970s, they have tended to build theories to aid the understanding and explanation of elements of: (a) the integration process; and (b) EU governance (so-called 'mid-range' theorizing). Even the direct descendants of neo-functionalism and intergovernmentalism have limited ambitions. For example, Sandholtz and Stone Sweet's (1998) theory of supranational governance explicitly 'brackets' (that is, sets aside) the origins of the EU, because the theory has no way of explaining this (see Chapter 5). By implication, that job can be left to other theories. This suggests, in turn, an approach to the analysis of politics premised on the idea that different theories can explain different parts of the same phenomenon. Moreover, Moravcsik (2001) has emphasized that his liberal intergovernmentalism is not intended to be a comprehensive theory of European integration, but rather a theory of intergovernmental bargaining only (see Chapter 6).

These caveats still do not bypass the objection that the old neo-functionalist–intergovernmentalist debate fails to capture highly significant attributes of the present EU. The principal objection is that 'old' theories are rooted in an outdated conception of what the EU is. However, we need to be aware that the study of the EU is not something that simply ebbs and flows with the real-world development of European integration and the evolution of the European Union—what we might call the 'external drivers' of theoretical work (Rosamond, 2007). It is also—and perhaps more predominantly—bound up with developments in social scientific fashion, or 'internal drivers'. Many scholars think about this issue in terms of theoretical 'progress'—that is, as social science in general and political science in particular 'improve' their techniques and refine their theories, so we can expect objects of study such as the European Union to be treated more rigorously than previously. The alleged consequence is that theoretical advancement delivers more robust and reliable results, thereby advancing our empirical knowledge of the EU. In contrast to this upbeat account of theoretical progress, scholars approaching the history of academic fields via the sociology of knowledge / science tend to see theoretical choices as altogether more contingent and bound up with disciplinary power structures, and institutional practices and norms.

In short, there are two overlapping meta-debates that help us to think about the development of theory in EU studies. The first discusses whether internal (academic) or external (real world) drivers account for the changing shape of theoretical work over time. The second involves a disagreement about whether theory development follows a progressive logic of scientific progress or whether instead it reflects the operation of disciplinary structures that enable some kinds of work, while marginalizing others. It is worth keeping these distinctions in mind as we examine the contemporary theoretical landscape of EU studies in this chapter.

The limits of the classical debate and five ways forward

The legacies of neo-functionalism and intergovernmentalism remain intact in much current writing about integration and the European Union. Even when analysts of the EU attempt to offer an alternative point of theoretical departure, they often set their co-ordinates with reference to the established neo-functionalist and intergovernmentalist positions. There is always a danger that the histories and trajectories of neo-functionalism and intergovernmentalism can end up being caricatured in such accounts; suffice to say that the early texts of integration theory repay careful reading by present-day students. This is not only because of the obviously useful legacies of ideas such as 'spillover', but also because it is true to say that the ways in which these 'old' theories are criticized is open to contest. Indeed, the idea that there is a convenient and rigid division between 'new' and 'old' theories is open to considerable critical scrutiny (see Haas, 2001, 2004; Rosamond, 2005; Börzel, 2006; Niemann and Schmitter, 2009).

The 'old' debate has been criticized on at least three interrelated counts (discussed in Chapters 5 and 6): its alleged inability to capture the reality of integration and the EU; its supposed entrapment in the disciplinary wilderness of international relations; and its so-called 'scientific' limitations.

It would be a mistake to think that these criticisms have been completely decisive and have ushered EU studies into a new theoretical age. Each is contested and, even where scholars agree that there is some substance in the above argument, many argue that the theoretical landscape is more nuanced and complex than many of the critics of classical theory suggest. Yet not all critiques would take the failures of neo-functionalism and intergovernmentalism to match 'reality' as a legitimate starting point. Theorists working in what is sometimes called the 'constitutive' tradition regard the relationship between theory and reality as intimate and problematic, and would choose altogether different criteria for evaluating theories than their ability to correspond to and/or predict the 'real' world (see Jackson, 2011).

Moreover, the dismissal of international relations (IR) as a parent discipline has been taken to task by those who suggest that what goes on within IR departments and journals bears little resemblance to the grand theorizing and state-fixated area of study depicted by the critics. In any case, it is a bold claim that overstates the extent to which the study of European integration was ever cordoned off as a sub-field of IR. The likes of Ernst Haas, Karl Deutsch, Leon Lindberg, and Philippe Schmitter studied the early

communities as self-conscious (and often pioneering) exponents of the latest political science (Haas, 2001, 2004; Ruggie et al., 2005). Integration theory's most obvious connection to IR was its contribution to the emergence of international political economy (IPE), a sub-area that explicitly emphasizes the fuzziness of the boundaries between domestic politics and international relations (Katzenstein et al., 1998b). Others suggest that IR theories retain a valuable place in EU studies because they act as valuable tools for understanding the global environment within which the EU operates (Hurrell and Menon, 1996; Peterson and Bomberg, 2009).

The third point—the type of theorizing involved in the 'old' debate—is less a criticism than an observation about how the study of a phenomenon (in our case, the EU) is bound up with the ebbs and flows of social science, as much as it is related to the context supplied by that phenomenon. Markus Jachtenfuchs (2001) draws a distinction between a classical phase of integration theory, during which the 'Euro-polity' was the dependent variable, and the contemporary 'governance' phase, in which the 'Euro-polity' becomes the independent variable. In the other words, the EU has shifted from being a phenomenon that analysts seek to explain to become a factor that contributes to the explanation of other phenomena. This amounts to moving from asking 'Why does integration occur?' to posing the question 'What effect does integration have?'

Dissatisfaction with established modes of theorizing the EU and European integration can be the starting premise for a number of alternative theoretical projects. Within conventional political science, research has tended to go in one of two broad directions. First, those who think of the EU as a conventional political system have tended to use EU studies as a space for the application and development of some of the tools of comparative political science (see Hix, 2007). Some of the key themes from this literature are discussed in this chapter. Second, those who prefer to see the EU as a newer type of political form are more inclined to align with the burgeoning literature on governance (see Jachtenfuchs, 2007; see also Chapter 8). A further trend has been the very significant expansion of work that brings the concerns of normative political theory to bear upon the analysis of the European Union (Føllesdal, 2007). Normative political theory is the consideration, using abstract philosophical techniques, of how political systems *should* be organized.

Such questions have become especially urgent in the EU context with the decline of the so-called 'permissive consensus' on integration. Until the early 1990s, runs the argument, European integration was a project that was driven and settled by elites. European mass publics were compliant with, if not overly supportive of, the process. The troubled ratification of the Maastricht Treaty (1992) set the pattern for all subsequent treaty revisions as governments across the member states encountered intense societal and parliamentary opposition to the Treaty. The emerging disconnect between elites and masses was an obvious source of interest for those interested in questions of legitimacy and democracy. In addition, Maastricht deepened integration significantly, with explicit moves into areas of 'high' politics such as foreign and security policy and monetary union. The Treaty also created the legal category of EU citizenship (see Chapter 25). In other words, fundamental questions of sovereignty came to the fore, together with intriguing questions of how 'post-national' citizenship might work. In short, issues of direct concern to normative political theorists were now of core concern in EU studies (see also

Bellamy and Attuci, 2009; Neyer and Wiener, 2011; Eriksen and Fossum, 2012).

There has also been, as this chapter will note, something of a revival in IR work on the EU. Internal and external drivers have been equally prominent. The growth of EU external action generally, and the evolution of the Common Foreign and Security Policy (CFSP) in particular, mean that the EU is an actor in world politics, while IR itself has brought forth approaches such as constructivism, which in turn have been exported to other subfields. We will discuss some of the most prominent themes in this new IR literature in this chapter.

Finally, beyond conventional analyses of politics and IR sit a range of self-consciously 'critical' approaches. In so far as the growing body of feminist, Foucauldian, post-structuralist, and neo-Marxist work has a unifying theme, then it is a commitment to using social science as a force for critique, social change, and human emancipation. Again, this chapter will address some of the ideas about the EU contained in such work.

There are several points of departure for such newer theories. Among the most important are the

Table 7.1 Five pathways beyond integration theory

Approach	External drivers	Internal drivers
Comparative political science (this chapter)	EU as a source of authoritative policy outputs	Rise of **rational choice** theory
	EU as a political system with identifiable **executive**, legislative, and judicial features	The '**new institutionalism**(s)'
Governance (Chapter 8)	EU as a source of **regulation**	Theories of governance
	Hybrid/incomplete EU political system Multilevel character of the EU	New theories of public policy-making
Normative political theory (Chapter 25)	End of the 'permissive consensus'	Revival of political philosophy
	Emergence of EU citizenship	Development of international political theory
	Attempts to **constitutionalize** the EU	
International relations (this chapter)	Growth of EU foreign and security policy **competence**	Emergence of constructivist IR theory
	Growth of EU external action	Growth of international political economy (IPE) as a subfield of IR
	Reappearance of 'regionalism' as a feature of world politics	Appearance of scholarship on the 'new regionalism'
Critical theories (this chapter)	End of the 'permissive consensus'	Feminism
	Rise of **neoliberalism** as the EU's dominant policy mode	Development of neo-Gramscian political economy
		Critical and Habermasian political theory Post-structuralism

literatures on comparative political science, govern-ance, and normative political theory. In addition, a re-vival of IR scholarship in the EU and a growing body of critical theoretical work has added to the very substan-tial body of contemporary theoretical work on the EU.

Political science, the 'new institutionalism', and the European Union

'Integration' fails to capture a great deal of what actu-ally matters in the European Union. This is because the EU is a source of authoritative policy outputs. A range of demands and supports are fed into that policy sys-tem, which means that the EU would seem to conform to a political system as defined in the classic work of David Easton (1965). The system that produces those policy outputs is institutionalized and those well-estab-lished institutions are assigned functions—executive, legislative, bureaucratic, and judicial—that resemble the classical design of all political systems. Moreover, the EU political system is full of interested actors pur-suing their interests and looking to secure a close corre-spondence between their policy preferences and policy outputs. Interest groups and even political parties are visible to the academic observer of this system. The long and the short of it is that institutions and processes studied by political scientists are all in place within the EU system. If this is *empirically* valid, then it would seem to be *analytically* valid to draw upon the theoreti-cal toolkit developed to study political systems.

The analytical case for moving towards the concep-tual reservoir of political science is bolstered further by the claim that treating the EU as a political system solves the notorious $n = 1$ problem. This describes a situation in which the object under scholarly scrutiny cannot be compared to other cases. This renders gen-eralization beyond the case impossible (because there are no other instances of what is being studied). For many scholars, this is a point at which social science is no longer possible and, for some critics of integration theory, this is precisely the situation in which EU stud-ies found itself by the 1980s. The European Communi-ties had developed in such a distinctive way that it was meaningless to talk about the European case as and instance of a more general phenomenon ('regional integration') (Hix, 1994). However, by redefining the EC/EU as a political system, a move that seemed to have some prima facie empirical credibility, the analyst had available not only the 200 or so functioning con-temporary political systems, but also every political system in recorded human history as comparators.

The move to comparative political science as EU studies' 'feeder' discipline has spawned much research and, naturally, draws upon a wide range of political science theories (see Hix, 2007; Hix and Høyland, 2011). By the standards of regional integration schemes worldwide, the EU is heavily institutionalized. It pos-sesses a distinctive set of supranational institutions, as well as a number of intergovernmental bodies. The treaties define the roles of these various institutions, as well as the ways in which they are supposed to inter-act. Four points are worthy of note. First, the founders of the European Communities sought to capture their desired balance between national and supranational forces through careful institutional design. Most ac-cept that the balance has altered over time, but the for-mal institutional structure of European integration has remained remarkably resilient for half a century. Sec-ond, close observers of the EU often note the growth of distinct cultures within the various institutions. It is not only that there is a particular modus operandi within the Commission, but also that individual Di-rectorates General (DGs) of the Commission possess distinct institutional cultures. The same is true of dif-ferent Council formations. Third, scholarship has re-vealed the existence of various informalities within the formal institutional shape of the EU. This work sug-gests that much that is decisive within the policy proc-ess is the consequence of regularized practices that do not have formal status within the treaties. In spite of that, these established routines are frequently defined as institutions. Fourth, much recent scholarly effort has been directed at understanding the *multilevel* character of the EU's institutionalized polity (see Chapter 8). So much of the corpus of EU studies involves the analysis of formal and informal institutions, and the impact that institutionalized practices have upon policy outcomes. At the same time as studies of the EU have multiplied in recent years, so the wider world of political science has become infused with the so-called 'new institutionalism' (Hall and Taylor, 1996).

It would be a mistake to regard the new institutionalism as a single theoretical perspective. Institutionalists agree, more or less, that 'institutions matter' (see Box 7.1). Institutions contain the bias that individual agents have built into their society over time, which in turn leads to important distributional consequences. They structure political actions and outcomes rather than simply mirror social activity and rational competition among disaggregated units (Aspinwall and Schneider, 2001: 2).

Importantly, institutionalists of different hues have alternative accounts of just *how much* institutions matter. Aspinwall and Schneider (2001) think about institutional political science as a spectrum. At one end of this spectrum sits an economistic-rationalist position that sees institutions as the consequence of long-run patterns of behaviour by self-seeking agents. Institutions in this account are both modifiers of the pursuit of self-interest and a medium through which actors may conduct their transactions with greater efficiency. At the opposite end of the spectrum is a sociological position where actors' interests are actually constructed through processes of institutional interaction. Hall and Taylor's (1996) landmark discussion

identifies three subspecies of institutionalism: rational choice; historical; and sociological. Each of these has a presence in EU studies (see Table 7.2).

Rational choice institutionalism is the most obvious way in which rational choice approaches to politics have infiltrated EU studies (Dowding, 2000; Pollack, 2007). This is a close relative—in terms of foundational theoretical premises—of Moravcsik's liberal intergovernmentalism. Rational choice theory—perhaps the dominant (although much criticized) strand in contemporary American political science—is based on the idea that human beings are self-seeking and behave rationally and strategically. The goals of political actors are organized hierarchically. They form their preferences on the basis of their interests. Institutions are important because they act as intervening variables. This means that institutions do not alter preference functions, but will have an impact upon the ways in which actors pursue those preferences. Consequently, changes in the institutional rules of the game, such as the introduction of the codecision procedure (now known as the ordinary legislative procedure, or OLP), which gave the Council and the European Parliament co-legislative power in certain areas, or alterations to the voting rules within the EU Council (from unanimity to qualified majority) will induce actors to recalculate the ways in which they need to behave in order to realize their preferences.

By and large, rational choice institutionalists have been interested in how their theory develops

---

BOX 7.1   Institutions and the new institutionalism

For most students of politics, 'institution' brings to mind phenomena such as the legislative, executive, and judicial branches of government—what we might think of as ongoing or embedded sets of formalities, often underwritten or codified by constitutional prescription. Early political science dealt with the study of this sort of institution. Scholars explored how such bodies operated, how they interacted, and how they supplied sets of rules that helped to account for the ways in which political systems operated. Often, such studies concluded that institutional patterns reflected the character of a country's politics. This 'old' institutionalism was criticized—especially by behaviouralists—for an overemphasis on the formal, codified aspects of politics at the expense of looking at the nitty-gritty of politics: the interaction of groups in pursuit of their interests and the basis, form, and consequences of individual and collective political behaviour. However, classical institutional studies

did bequeath a concern with the impact of rules upon the behaviour of actors and thus upon political outcomes more generally. 'New' institutionalism proceeds from the axiom that 'institutions matter' as shapers of, and influences upon, actor behaviour (rather than as mere expressions of political culture). This is combined with a broader definition of 'institution' to embrace not only formal rules, but also forms of ongoing social interaction that together make up the 'compliance procedures and standard operating practices' in the political economy, to borrow Peter Hall's well-established definition (Hall, 1986: 19). Thus, from the new institutionalist vantage point, we may be talking about anything from written constitutional rules through to norms, or even collectively recognized symbols, when we speak of 'institutions'. With this in mind, it is hardly surprising that the EU has become a favoured venue for the practice of new institutionalist political science.

Table 7.2 The 'new institutionalisms'	
Type of institutionalism	Research objective
Rational choice institutionalism	The changing relative power of institutions
Historical institutionalism	The long-term effects of institutions
Sociological institutionalism	The role of culture OR persuasion and communicative action

Source: Hall and Taylor (1996)

propositions about the changing relative power of institutional actors in the policy process. Scholars of this persuasion assume that institutional actors seek policy outcomes that correspond as closely as possible to their preferences. This is why institutions are created in the first place (the so-called 'functionalist' theory of institutional design). The construction of formal models, often deploying the type of reasoning found in economic analysis, allows for empirical research on specific cases to be mapped against formal decisions. Thus EU studies have developed lively debate about matters such as the agenda-setting power of the various institutions. Another key component of the rationalist argument has been the application of 'principal–agent analysis' to EU politics. Here, self-regarding actors ('principals') find that their preferences are best served by the delegation of certain authoritative tasks to common institutions ('agents'). In the EU case, this approach provides powerful explanations for member states' decisions to create and assign tasks to supranational institutions such as the Commission and the European Court of Justice (ECJ) (Pollack, 2002).

For their proponents, rational choice perspectives offer rigorous foundations for the development and testing of falsifiable hypotheses around a series of core shared propositions. This improves knowledge in a progressive and cumulative way. Scholars work from a set of (admittedly stylized) assumptions to produce progressively improved understandings of how the EU works. For their opponents, rational choice institutionalists miss the point: their focus on formal rules leads them to ignore the various informal processes that grow up around the codified practices, but it is these informalities that better explain policy outcomes. Moreover, rational choice accounts of actor preferences tend to leave these fixed rather than recognize the ways in which processes of socialization can mould interests and identities.

Historical institutionalists are interested in how institutional choices have long-term effects. Institutions are designed for particular purposes, at particular times, in particular sets of circumstances. They are assigned tasks, and in this process acquire interests and ongoing agendas. If institutions interact with one another in a decision-making process, then patterns that are constitutionally prescribed or evolve in the early lifetime of the institutions concerned may 'lock in' and also become ongoing. This lock-in means that a 'path-dependent' logic may set in. The ongoing nature of institutional interests (their continuing bureau-shaping agendas and their preference for self-preservation) means that institutions become robust and may well outlive their creators. This also means that institutions may have an impact that their creators could not have foreseen, not least because they survive to confront new circumstances and new challenges. But these new challenges are met through the prism provided by pre-existing institutions; thus the range of possible action and policy choice is constrained. Policy entrepreneurs may attempt to redesign institutions to meet current needs, but they do so in the face of institutional agendas that are locked in and which are therefore potentially difficult to reform.

Like the other two variants of institutionalism, historical institutionalism is not exclusive to EU studies. But its applications are obvious. That said, scholars use this basic template in various ways. Paul Pierson's well-known discussion of path dependency (Pierson, 1998) looks at the problem of unintended consequences. He argues that the immediate concerns of the architects of the European Communities led them, at a critical juncture, into acts of institutional design that ultimately helped to erode the capacity of national governments to control the governance of their economies. So while the intention of Western European governments of the 1950s may have been to rescue the nation state (Milward, 1992), Pierson's work suggests

Supporters of rational choice institutionalism believe that this approach to the EU is able to build knowledge in a systematic way. Scholars working under the auspices of rational choice subscribe to particular methods of theory-building. This usually involves the development of models capable of generating hypotheses, which can then be subjected to confirmation or disconfirmation through exposure to hard empirical evidence. Such work relies on the deployment of assumptions and the use of **game theory** as a tool of analysis. The substantial work of Geoffrey Garrett and George Tsebelis (for example, Tsebelis, 1994; Garrett and Tsebelis, 1996) yields the counter-intuitive claim that the codecision/OLP procedure has strengthened the EU Council at the expense of the Commission and the European Parliament. The analysis is sophisticated, but relies on the assumption that institutions' preferences are arranged along a continuum according to the amount of integration that they favour. For critics, this type of work may produce intriguing results, but it relies too much on unrealistic assumptions and describes games that bear no relation to the complex interactions that take place between EU institutions on a day-to-day basis. Another dimension to this debate is that rational choice institutionalists often advance the view that theirs is a more rigorous form of political science than that offered by either EU studies 'traditionalists' or those of a more constructivist persuasion.

that the long-term consequence of their deliberations may have been to engineer precisely the reverse. The implications for research from this theoretical insight are quite interesting. It pushes students of the EU to think about policy pathways—that is, how particular EU-level competences emerge over time as a result of specific decisions. We are asked to think about how rational acts at one point in time influence rational action in the future.

Less wedded to rational actor assumptions is other historical institutionalist work such as that of Kenneth Armstrong and Simon Bulmer (1998) in their extensive study of the single market. Armstrong and Bulmer are more interested in the way in which institutions can become carriers of certain ideas, values, and norms over time. Once again, we are directed to think about how such normative and ideational 'matter' is loaded into institutions at their inception. But students of the EU are also invited to explore how institutional cultures (say, of the Commission generally, or of specific DGs) impact upon all stages of the policy process, influence action and policy choice, and (perhaps) assist in the conditioning of the interests of actors.

This last comment provides a link to sociological institutionalism, a strand of literature that is closely bound up with the constructivist 'turn' in international and European studies (discussed under 'Social constructivist approaches to the European Union'; see also Wiener, 2006; Checkel, 2007; Risse, 2009). It is important to note that sociological institutionalists tend to reject the other institutionalisms because of their inherent 'rationalism'. The meaning of this term is discussed under 'Social constructivist approaches to

the European Union', but for now it is worth remembering that sociological institutionalists/constructivists operate with a quite distinct **ontology** (that is, an underlying conception of the world). This boils down to a very particular take on the nature of actors' interests. While rational choice and (most) historical institutionalists see interests as exogenous (external) to interaction, so sociological institutionalists see them as endogenous (internal). In other words, interests are not pre-set, but rather the product of social interaction between actors.

This leads sociological institutionalists towards a concern with two broad issues: the 'culture' of institutions; and the role of persuasion and communicative action within institutional settings (Börzel and Risse, 2000). 'Culture' is used to mean the emergence of common frames of reference, norms governing behaviour, and 'cognitive filters'. In this account, 'institutions do not simply affect the strategic calculations of individuals, as rational choice institutionalists contend, but also their most basic preferences and very identity' (Hall and Taylor, 1996: 948). With this in mind, sociological institutionalist analysis of the EU looks at the ways in which ongoing patterns of interaction and 'normal' forms of behaviour emerge within institutional settings. As one writer puts it, 'institutions have theories about themselves' (Jachtenfuchs, 1997: 47). Thus institutions contribute to actors' understandings of who they are, what their context is, and what might be the motivations of other actors. This sort of work aims to add substance to often-heard claims such as the idea that different DGs of the European Commission function in quite distinct ways.

Another area in which the application of this sort of thinking seems appropriate is the investigation of whether formally intergovernmental processes such as those associated with the Common Foreign and Security Policy (CFSP) conform to established patterns of inter-state interaction, or whether they bring about new norms of exchange between the envoys of member states, thereby transforming long-established norms of inter-state politics.

The roles of communication, argument, and persuasion are seen as particularly important in these contexts. This is likely to occur in settings in which norms have been established, but these deliberative processes also contribute to the establishment of common understandings. Thus sociological institutionalists often embark upon empirical quests for so-called 'norm entrepreneurs'—'well placed individual actors . . . [who] . . . can often turn their individual beliefs into broader, shared understandings' (Checkel, 2001: 31). Sociological institutionalism is not simply interested in the EU level of analysis. A lot of work is being done on the interaction of national and European-level norms, and in particular the ways in which 'European' norms filter into the existing political cultures of the member states.

KEY POINTS

- The EU has become a major venue for the application of 'new institutionalist' political science and for debates between its main strands.

- Rational choice institutionalists are interested in how the relative power of actors shifts in accordance with changes in institutional rules.

- Historical institutionalists focus on the long-term implications of institutional choices made at specific points in time.

- Sociological institutionalists pay attention to the 'culture' of institutions, and the ways in which patterns of communication and persuasion operate in institutional settings.

Social constructivist approaches to the European Union

The rise of constructivism has been the big news in international relations (IR) theory over the past two decades. The work of constructivist scholars such as Alexander Wendt (1999) has come to pose a serious challenge to the established schools of IR theory. Constructivists attack formalized, *rationalist* versions of IR—that is, the **neo-realist** and neoliberal approaches that operate with a view of the world that sees interests as materially given, which adhere to a positivistic conception of how knowledge should be gathered, and which involve a commitment to 'scientific' method, the neutrality of facts, and the existence of observable realities (S. Smith, 2001: 227). Ranged against rationalism is a range of **reflectivist** and **interpretivist** approaches—such as postmodernism and critical theory—that begin from wholly different premises.

The appeal of constructivism—or at least the type of constructivism that has entered the IR mainstream in the last decade—is that it claims to offer a middle way between rationalism and reflectivism. Constructivists such as Wendt see interests as socially constructed rather than pre-given, which means that regularities in the international system are the consequence of collective (or 'intersubjective') meanings. Constructivists are interested in how collective understandings emerge, and how institutions constitute the interests and identities of actors. However, some authors believe that constructivism can and should share the rationalist commitment to developing knowledge through clear research programmes, refutable hypotheses, and the specification of causal mechanisms that produce regularities (see Checkel, 2007). Many—although certainly not all—IR constructivists aspire to this ambition.

Various authors occupy different positions along the continuum between rationalism and reflectivism (Christiansen et al., 2001). Moreover, the commitment to 'break bread' with rationalist theories such as liberal intergovernmentalism varies from author to author. That said, constructivists argue that they are best placed to study integration as a *process*. While intergovernmentalists recommend that the European Union be studied as an instance of inter-state bargaining and comparativists think about the EU as a political system, constructivists purport to investigate the character of the move from a bargaining regime to a polity. Thus if we think about European integration as a process bound up with change, then it makes sense to draw on a meta-theoretical position that treats reality as contested and problematic. This means that constructivist-inspired work should focus on 'social ontologies and social institutions, directing research at the origin and reconstruction of identities, the impact of rules and norms, the role of language and political discourse' (Christiansen et al., 2001: 12).

More concretely, as Risse (2009) notes, constructivists are predisposed to think about how human agents interact in ways that produce structures (be they norms, institutions, shared cultural understandings, or discourses) that simultaneously shape and influence social interaction, and the possibilities for action that follow. Constructivists endeavour to understand the constitution of interests and (thus) identities. Moreover, they are interested in the ways in which institutions act as arenas for communication, deliberation, argumentation, persuasion, and socialization. Constructivists also touch base with discourse analysts (Wæver, 2009) to emphasize the power resident in the capacity to create meaning and so to frame policy choices in often non-negotiable ways.

Perhaps the best way in which to present constructivism in EU studies is to mention a few examples of what constructivists actually work on. Many are interested in how European identities emerge. So the idea of a 'European economy', a 'European security community', or 'European citizenship' should not be read as a consequence of actors' interests changing rationally in response to external material changes such as the onset of globalization or the end of the Cold War. Rather, constructivists insist that we need to investigate the ways in which these identities are constructed through the use of language, the deployment of ideas, and the establishment of norms. We also need to pay attention to the ways in which these norms and ideas are communicated, and to the processes of learning and socialization that take place among actors. 'Norms' are particularly important in the constructivist vocabulary. These are defined as 'collective expectations for the proper behaviour of actors with a given identity' (Katzenstein, 1996: 5). It is through the internalization of norms that actors acquire their identities and establish what their interests are. This is what constructivists mean when they talk about the 'constitutive effects' of norms.

The constructivist research agenda in EU studies (which has much in common with that of sociological institutionalism) also pays attention to the ways in which European-level norms, ideas, and discourses penetrate into the various national polities that make up the EU (Börzel, 2002).

KEY POINTS

- Constructivism is not a theory of integration, but a position on the nature of social reality (that is, an ontology).

- There are many constructivist approaches and significant disagreement about the compatibility of constructivism with rationalist theories.

- Constructivists are interested in European integration as a process. They focus in particular on questions of identity, and the ways in which European norms are established and play out within the EU institutions and the member states.

International relations and international political economy revisited

In recent years, attempts have been made to 'bring international relations (IR) back in' to the study of the European Union, of which three in particular stand out:

1. the possibility that the EU can be studied as an instance of the so-called 'new regionalism' that has emerged in recent years across the world as (perhaps) a response to globalization;

2. the growing significance of the EU as an actor on the world stage; and

3. the attempt to locate the analysis of the EU within burgeoning debates in international political economy (IPE).

The EU and the 'new' regionalism

Regional integration—especially in the form of free trade areas (FTAs) and customs unions—is not a new phenomenon. However, the period since the mid-1980s has been characterized by the growth of many regional economic blocs in the global political economy. Among the most conspicuous are the North American Free Trade Agreement (NAFTA), Asia Pacific Economic Co-operation (APEC), and the *Mercado Común del Sur* [Southern Common Market], or Mercosur, in South America.

The most obvious explanation for the revival of regional integration is the development of globalization. Globalization is a deeply contentious topic, but is usually thought of as a combination of things such as heightened capital mobility, intensified cross-border transactions, the multinationalization of production, and the spread of neoliberal economic policy norms—in short, the growth of market authority at the expense of formal political authority. This debate is very complex, but one line of argument is that regionalism (as represented by NAFTA or Mercosur) is the primary way in which states have responded to globalization. The move to regionalism suggests that states have seen fit to pool resources in order to recapture some of the authority that globalization has taken away—a type of collective insurance against globalization.

Debate exists over the extent to which states actually and effectively lead the creation of regional integration schemes. This is where a distinction between regionalism and regionalization is important in the literature. While regionalism describes state-led projects of institution-building among groups of countries, regionalization is a term used to capture the emergence of a de facto regional economy, propelled by the cross-border activities of economic actors, particularly firms. The question here is whether the formal institutions of regional integration are created to deal with and regulate this emergent transnational economic space, or whether the growth of cross-border activity is stimulated by the decisions of governments. These are empirical questions at one level, but the two positions in this particular debate emerge from two different theoretical accounts of the world—one largely state-centric and one not.

There is also a debate in international economics about the impact of regional agreements on the global economy. All of the foregoing instances mentioned are actual or aspirant FTAs. The question is whether the creation of regional FTAs creates or diverts trade on a global scale. Put another way, it asks whether we are heading for a regionalized world (of competing regional blocs) or a globalized world. Again, such matters can be measured empirically, but theoretical intervention is needed if we are to fully understand the meaning of a term such as 'globalization'. Notice also how much of the foregoing implies a particular type of relationship between globalization and statehood, and, it should be said, between structure and agency. Alternative accounts place differential emphasis upon the structural qualities of globalization—its ability to set imperatives and to shape the behaviour of actors.

The theoretical relevance of the questions raised in the preceding paragraphs becomes especially apparent when we think about their application to the EU. Thinking theoretically, as James Rosenau and Mary Durfee (1995) point out, involves asking 'Of what is this an instance?' The 'new regionalism' literature forces us to ask whether the EU is a comparable case with, say, NAFTA. If the answer is 'yes', then the study of comparative regional *integration* is brought back into play, with the EU as one of the primary cases.

Of course, the EU is at best a deviant case of regionalism. Its longevity rules out any claim that the EU was *created* as a response to global economic upheavals in the late 1970s and early 1980s. Moreover, compared with other cases of regionalism, the EU is considerably more institutionalized and much more deeply integrated. To use the EU as a benchmark case against which other regional projects should be measured is clearly a fallacy. Yet at the same time the acceleration of economic integration through the single market programme and progress towards monetary union has coincided with the growth of regional projects elsewhere.

There are two suggestions as to how the field of EU studies might be reunited with the study of comparative regional integration without the EU becoming the paradigm case. The first follows Warleigh-Lack's (2006) argument that EU studies offer a rich and fertile range of ideas for scholars interested in questions of governance beyond the nation state, the interplay between domestic politics and collective institutions, and the possibilities for post-national democracy and legitimacy. The second suggested strategy involves the rediscovery of some of the neglected themes of classical integration theory, particularly neo-functionalism, in which there was an overt emphasis on the study of the requisite material and cognitive background conditions for the formation and consolidation of regional projects (see Warleigh-Lack and Rosamond, 2010).

The EU as an international actor

What does the EU's maturing external policy competence mean for the ways in which we might conceptualize and theorize the EU's role in world politics? In addressing this question, it is important to consider whether we can conceptualize the EU as an *actor*—that is, is the EU a discernible entity with its own capacity to act on the basis of its own interests? Certainly, the EU possesses certain formal roles in world politics and in the management of the global economy. It speaks with a common voice in international trade negotiations, and has the makings of an embryonic foreign and security policy (Smith, 2008). On the other hand, it consists of twenty-seven member states, all of which operate as actors within the current international system (which very phrase—'inter-national system'—connotes an order founded on the interaction of authoritative national states).

That the EU is not a state (at least in the conventional modern sense of the term) is not really in dispute (Caporaso, 1996)—but is it becoming one? If this is the case, then we might want to argue that the EU is an embryonic state writ large, formed through the gradual merger of its component member states. This might then allow us to slot the EU—as a constituent unit of the international system—into long-established theories of IR, such as realism. This would construe the EU as an entity seeking to advance its own interests and, particularly, to render itself secure from external threat.

However, we might be reluctant to arrive at this conclusion. The EU might appear to be a unique entity, lacking those decisive authoritative attributes normally associated with modern (supposedly sovereign) nation states. If we think about the image of the EU that is described by the literature on multilevel governance (see Chapter 8) and then project outwards, students of integration will be confronted with something that seems to fit very badly with conventional theories of IR (Ruggie, 1998: 173–4). Indeed, rather than trying to fit the EU into IR theory, perhaps

IR theorists need to look carefully at their established theoretical toolkits if they are to properly comprehend the EU. Theories such as neo-realism and neoliberal institutionalism (which dominate theoretical discourse in IR, especially in the US) are built around the idea of states as the dominant units of analysis in the world system. The EU might be a freak occurrence, specific to the peculiarities of Europe, but the ways in which the boundaries between domestic and international politics have become blurred, along with the styles of governance that have evolved, may well have a much wider application.

One caveat to this is that the EU's external action takes place, whether in terms of foreign policy or commercial policy, in conditions that still respond to the rules of state-centred international politics. Thus, for the EU to acquire legitimacy and recognition as a valid actor in the system, we might hypothesize that it has to conform to the rules of that system; this, in turn, would create pressures for the EU to become state-like. Therefore the paradox is that while the EU may appear to transcend the international system, it is still in meaningful ways constituted (as constructivists would put it) by the norms of that very system.

The EU and international political economy

International political economy (IPE) is a well-established field of inquiry that explores the relationship between political and economic processes, and between states, markets, and international institutions in the

---

BOX 7.3   The EU and statehood

Much of the routine political discourse surrounding European integration bothers itself with the question of whether the EU is becoming a 'federal **superstate**', which, by definition, is supplanting the powers of its constituent member states. Without doubt, the EU lacks some of the classical indices of 'statehood', as it has come to be understood (not least in Europe) over the past 350 years. For example, the EU lacks fixed territorial boundaries and does not possess monopolistic control over the legitimate means of violence. It does not engage in extensive programmes of redistribution, yet it does exercise meaningful and emphatic authority over the governance of its constituent economies, and by extension over the lives of hundreds of millions of Europeans. Moreover, the presumption of many current theorists is that the EU is sufficiently

similar to national political systems to allow the deployment of the tools of normal political science and policy analysis. But statehood also has external dimensions. Thus world politics has developed into a game played between states with the notion of 'sovereignty' as the ultimate rule. Much contemporary IR literature debates the extent to which processes such as globalization have begun to transform this system. Yet the language of statehood, international politics, sovereignty, and diplomacy remains central to world politics. We might argue that the condition for admission to the world polity remains the achievement of statehood. So the question becomes whether the EU is being constituted and shaped by the existing world system, or whether it is contributing to a radical reshaping of world politics.

establishment, maintenance, and transformation of world order. International political economy has been the venue for intense debate about the conditions under which liberal economic orders rise and fall. Economic order over the past 200 years is often depicted as vacillating between periods of economic openness (during which free trade ideology is underpinned by functioning international monetary institutions) and periods of growing protectionism, rising economic nationalism, and the spawning of international economic rivalries. Within IPE, several explanations are offered for the rise and decline of open liberal orders. The most popular focuses on state power, with the argument that liberal international trading and monetary orders are possible only when sponsored and underwritten by a hegemonic state. A second explanation focuses on the presence or absence of international institutions to create systems of rules for a market-based order. Neo-realists acknowledge that states will create cooperative institutions from time to time, but point out that some states will benefit more than others from the existence of the institution. So even if every state is benefitting from the arrangements, the fact that some states are accumulating more power means that those states losing out in this pattern of 'relative gains' have a substantial incentive to defect from the institution. Neoliberals, on the other hand, countenance the possibility that institutions can deliver 'absolute gains', which means that institutionalized cooperation will not exaggerate power asymmetries. Moreover, neoliberals see institutions as places where relations of trust between states can be augmented and where the transaction costs associated with international interaction can be minimized. Neo-realists see a world in which the structural condition of 'anarchy' (the absence of authority beyond the state) cannot be overcome, whereas neoliberals imagine the gradual replacement of anarchy by a rule-bound and (increasingly pacific) market order overseen by established institutions.

A third type of explanation emphasizes the power of ideas. From this vantage point, liberal orders emerge and consolidate because of the widespread acceptance of liberal narratives of how to organize the relationship between state, society, and market both domestically and internationally. For example, states come to believe in the technical and normative propriety of liberal free trade ideas. This means that both (a) the claim that allocative efficiency is best achieved by countries minimizing tariff barriers and special-izing production in areas of comparative advantage, *and* (b) the moral case that free trade is ethically superior to other economic doctrines, become more or less commonsensical. The fall of liberal orders is associated with the increasing persuasiveness of other sets of ideas—in the twentieth century, left-wing and right-wing variants of the idea that national economic welfare should prevail over liberal notions of the universality of the market.

A fourth type of IPE explanation examines the relationship between economic order and domestic social purpose. In his famous account of the nineteenth and twentieth centuries written in 1944, Polanyi (2001) held that the successful rise of the doctrine of the 'self-regulating market' in the 1800s had created a situation in which society was increasingly subordinate to the market (rather than the market serving domestically negotiated social purposes). Polanyi saw such a situation as unsustainable and insisted that society would react in a counter-movement to the rise of the self-regulating market. Thus he was able to explain increasing protectionism in the latter part of the nineteenth century and concrete governing projects—such as social democracy, communism, and fascism—in the twentieth century as instances of such societal counter-movements. This type of analysis inspired Ruggie's (1982) description of the interwar international order as one of 'embedded liberalism'—a compromise under which the (desirable) goal of global economic liberalization was tempered by allowing governments very significant domestic policy autonomy. The product of this compromise was a regime known as the Keynesian welfare state, which was able to service domestic social purposes much more effectively.

How do these debates relate to the EU? The key to understanding the relevance of these IPE debates to European integration is to recognize that one of the main ways in which to read the EU is as a sustained project of liberal market-making. This means that the four IPE discussions just outlined can be applied to the EU in two broad ways. The first simply tries to understand the origins and sustainability of a pan-European liberal market order sitting above, yet feeding from and also shaping, the national economies of European states. The second revisits the question about the relationship between the creation of a distinctively European economic order, on the one hand, and the project of global market liberalization ('globalization'), on the other.

So if we begin with the question of hegemony, IPE debates immediately force scholars to think about whether the construction of the European single market is dependent on a particular configuration of state power—both internally and globally. The status and importance of Germany as an internal hegemon and the US as an external hegemon are obvious follow-up questions here, but the key from this perspective is to understand how much European market integration relies upon a permissive environment in which the most powerful states are prepared to bear the costs of maintaining liberal order.

In terms of debates about institutions, there are at least two lines of enquiry suggested by IPE debates. The first is to understand whether the EU is a durable institutional order. This, of course, is an especially pertinent question in times of economic crisis during which states might be expected to draw back from international commitments to liberalize markets and during which relative, rather than absolute, gains might become more visible. The second (following also from some strands of the new institutionalism) is to assess the degree to which institutions shape the conditions of possibility for addressing new challenges. A good example here is the financial crisis that has been affecting the EU in general and the euro area in particular since 2008. Have the eurozone's intergovernmental decision rules hampered the search for effective solutions to the crisis? To what extent are solutions premised on austerity budgeting and the installation of technocratic governments direct consequences of prior institutional design? To what extent has the institutional design of both EU decision-making in general and eurozone governance in particular facilitated the pursuit of neoliberal policies? (See Chapter 27.)

This last point bridges to questions about the relationship between the EU and the influence of certain economic ideas and particular conceptions of the economy. As we will note under 'Critical theories and the European Union', a number of critical political economists have suggested that the EU represents a quasi-state form that is particularly useful for the 'constitutionalization' of neoliberal policy frameworks (Gill, 1998). This position would suggest that the institutionalization of European integration has been closely related to, if not fundamentally determined by, the growing legitimacy of neoliberal ideas about the technical propriety and normative appropriateness of a free market order with minimal capacity for public authority to develop either welfare institutions or social policies to compensate for the effects of markets (Scharpf, 2002). This raises an interesting debate regarding whether the EU is ineluctably neoliberal in character or whether it contains the potential for both market-making and market correction (see Jabko, 2006).

This type of debate is directly related to the final IPE debate mentioned here: the relationship between the construction of market orders and social purpose. Over the past twenty-five years, much official EU policy discourse has asserted that there is a 'social dimension' to market integration, that the EU embodies something called the 'European social model', and that the EU, both internally and externally, exists for the purpose of 'managing globalization'. While some analysts have broadly endorsed the idea that the EU is more than a crude institutional device for promoting the subordination of European society to the market (for example, Caporaso and Tarrow, 2009), there are interesting questions to be asked about how precisely the EU manages to 'embed' itself within European social purpose, especially given the problem of the democratic deficit (see Chapter 25). At the same time, there is an influential line of argument that insists that the EU should do no more than create the conditions for a free market order. This normative position is central to claims about the EU's status as a 'regulatory state' (Majone, 2009). Moreover, it is the EU's status as a market regulator that spills over most conspicuously into the global political economy beyond Europe (Damro, 2012). So the question of whether the EU represents a counterweight to the spread of neoliberal

---

KEY POINTS

- Much recent conceptual thinking in IR has been directed towards the analysis of the growth of regionalism in the global political economy, of which the EU may be a (peculiar) instance.

- Also important is recent thinking that challenges the state-centric vision of the world that has characterized much mainstream IR theory.

- The particular character of the EU as a presence in the global system confronts this traditional imagery by pointing to a number of ways in which structures of authority and patterns of politics may be changing.

- The important subfield of IPE raises a series of question about the politics of international market orders which are of direct relevance for discussions of the EU.

market discipline is not only localized to Europe. If the EU is a major source of global market rules, or at least a major player in the negotiation of those rules, then it is difficult to study IPE and think about the world though the conceptual frames that it provides without bringing the EU squarely into the analytical frame.

Critical theories and the European Union

The term 'critical theories' is used here as an umbrella term to gather together some important reflections about 'alternative' or non-mainstream approaches to the European Union. We need to use the term with caution, since it does have a precise meaning in the history of ideas. The term is most associated with the neo-Marxist Frankfurt School of social theory. In one of the key founding texts of the Frankfurt School originally published in 1937, Max Horkheimer (1982) talked about 'critical theory' as a self-conscious attempt to theorize, in a non-dogmatic way, the conditions for human emancipation. Built into critical theory from the start, then, is a very clear commitment to unravelling the contradictions and injustices of present social order, combined with a very clear commitment to the pursuit of human freedom. This, of course, yields a distinctive understanding of the nature and purpose of social science, and one that is very different from most of the approaches to political analysis discussed in this and the previous two chapters. The critical theoretical position tends to see conventional social science as bound up with the object that it seeks to analyse and demystify. Modern economic theory, for example, is held to be complicit in the perpetuation of power structures. Robert Cox makes this point very effectively in a much-cited essay in which he writes that '[t]heory is always for someone and some purpose . . . there is no such thing as a theory in itself, divorced from a standpoint in time and space' (Cox, 1981: 128). Cox goes on to distinguish between two types of theory: 'problem-solving'; and 'critical'. The former is the everyday matter of most social science. It consists of finding solutions to puzzles that are set by overarching and largely unquestioned frameworks for understanding social reality and social order. Such work, at a fundamental level, does not think about the possibilities for social transformation. It thereby contributes to the reproduction of existing social order. Thinking about EU studies in light of Cox's discussion, then, it is very likely that neo-functionalism, intergovernmentalism, comparative political science, a good portion of governance theory, much contemporary international relations (IR) and international political economy (IPE), and even a good chunk of normative political theory would be placed in the 'problem-solving' category.

In contrast, for Cox, 'critical theory' does not take for granted the prevailing social order as if it were fixed. Indeed, the task of critical theory is to theorize the possibilities for change. A key step towards that goal is the realization that all social theories—even those purporting to be value-free and 'scientific'—emerge from and seek to reinforce particular perspectives, and, as such, can be tools of the powerful. One of the things to look for from a broadly critical theoretical perspective is silences in conventional academic work: what is *not* discussed, and why is it not discussed? An additional point, noted by Manners (2007), is the question of where to look for non-mainstream or critical work. If EU studies journals and book series are responsible for establishing, policing, and reproducing orthodox 'problem-solving' work, then we should hardly expect to find heterodox, critical work routinely showing up in such outlets.

In so far as it is possible to classify non-orthodox or critical work in EU studies, it seems to cluster around four broad approaches, all of which tend to begin by noting a missing component of the standard debate in EU studies. First, feminists have drawn attention to the highly gendered nature of EU theoretical and policy discourses. Kronsell's (2005) critique of integration theory provides a very good illustration of the extent to which standard political science approaches screen out gender relations from their analysis. The point is not simply to examine things such as the policy implications of European integration for gender equality (although that is very important); a feminist-inspired reconstruction of EU studies must also think about the ways in which gendered practices are sustained and reproduced within both EU policy discourses and the academic analysis of EU politics (see also Locher and Prügl, 2009). The conception of politics that underpins most accounts of integration reduces the political to what happens in the public domain of the state. As such, it excludes most of those often private sites that feminists have identified as crucial to the practice of power relations. Moreover, most conventional political science theories rest upon heavily masculinist conceptions of rationality. As such, political science theories are actually affirming the gendered self-narrative of public institutions by assuming that they operate according to this very particular conception of rationality.

Second, there have been long-standing Marxist analyses of the EU. Marxists of various kinds insist on locating the EU's development within a broader analysis of the dynamics of capitalism. The earliest Marxist analyses from the 1960s understood the evolution of supranational institutions as a redesign of the capitalist state to take account of the changing nature of European relations of production. Thus Mandel (1970) saw European-level institutions as central to the process of capital concentration in Europe. Likewise, Cocks (1980) understood integration as crucial to the dynamic development of capitalist productive forces. More recently, neo-Gramscians (inspired by the Italian Marxist Antonio Gramsci) have been interested in the ways in which the EU has drifted towards treaty commitments and policy regimes (such as in corporate governance or competition policy) in which neoliberal frameworks prevail and in which popular **accountability** is weak. Gill (1998) sees the EU as part and parcel of a global trend to lock in and constitutionalize neoliberal conceptions of market society.

Third, writers inspired by Michel Foucault tend to think about the EU as a particular expression of liberal rationalities of government that seek to define the human subject in particular ways. This is interesting in the European context because the development of the single market regime requires the definition of the typical transnational human agent that inhabits and moves across that market space. Parker (2012) suggests that there are two potentially contradictory versions of the liberal European subject imagined in the treaties: one is a pure market actor—a 'subject of interest'—using European transnational space as an arena for economic transaction; the other is a political actor, a transnational citizen—a 'subject of right'—whose **cosmopolitanism** extends well beyond the arena of market transaction. Foucauldians

are also interested in how governing actors, as part of the governing process, contribute to the statistical and discursive construction of the space over which they exercise authority. From this point of view, the outputs of **Eurostat** and **Eurobarometer** are not simply neutral data, but active constructions of Europe and Europeans designed to render the EU space governable from the European level.

Finally, post-structuralists (a category that usually embraces Foucauldians as well) have focused on the importance of linguistic constructions of Europe and its others, and the ways in which the supposed removal of borders of one kind is often accompanied by the imposition of bordering practices of other kinds. Diez (1999), for example, shows how the academic efforts trying to define the EU are not merely analytical moves, but active interventions in developing widespread understandings of Europe in wider political debates. Walters (2004) engages in a radical rethink of the EU's external borders—which we might think of straightforwardly as the point at which the EU ends and other jurisdictions begin—as objects of different types of governing strategy. As with all post-structuralist work, the emphasis is on problematizing a facet of the social world that may appear to be unambiguous and perhaps of little academic interest, and on showing how that facet (in this case, borders) can be rendered intelligible in different ways.

KEY POINTS

- A wide range of so-called critical theoretical traditions have been applied to the study of the EU.

- These include feminist, Marxist, Foucauldian, and post-structuralist perspectives.

- Critical theories of this kind point to the limited problem-solving qualities of conventional theory.

- They see a close relationship between orthodox academic work and the reproduction of power relations.

Conclusion

The revival of interest in theory in EU studies has occurred within the context of some serious thinking about the role of theory in political science. Some of the 'new' theories discussed in this chapter have emerged from a concern to render theoretical work

more rigorously 'scientific'. Other newer approaches have emerged from positions that explicitly challenge the positivist mainstream in social science. Other theorists still—notably certain constructivists—try to occupy a middle position between positivism and reflectivism. These debates have begun to intrude into EU studies and have been played out more extensively in the broader international relations (IR) literature.

Theoretical reflection and debate simply bring out into the open assumptions that reside in any empirical discussion of the European Union. Alternative theories have different accounts of social reality and sometimes lead to quite different strategies for acquiring valid knowledge about that world (Jackson, 2011). This translates eventually into a set of disagreements about fundamental matters: what sort of entity is the EU and how should it be studied?

Much of the 'new' theoretical work introduced in this chapter represents a self-conscious departure from thinking about the EU in terms of 'integration'. Its status as a supplier of authoritative policy outputs suggests that the toolkit of political science and policy analysis might be useful. At the same time, however, the fact that the EU is not a state as conventionally understood poses all sorts of challenges to those seeking to understand not only European integration, but also the nature of world order in the early twenty-first century. The EU may offer a clear indication of what a 'denationalized' world order might look like. It sits between nation states and the international system, and arguably transforms both through its very existence.

The facts that the EU is multidimensional, that integration is uneven, and that EU governance is composed of multiple, coexisting policy modes all force us to think carefully about how the nature of authority is changing. The trick—as employers of the 'multilevel governance' metaphor remind us (Chapter 8)—is to think about the EU as part and parcel of this changing pattern of governance. To treat the EU as a political system 'above' national political systems ignores the complex interpenetration of the domestic and the supranational in contemporary Europe. The task of theories—whether drawn from the formal disciplinary domains of 'international relations' or 'political science'—is to offer ways of organizing our thoughts about what is going on in this context. We might continue to be confused about the complexity of the EU, but the present vibrant theoretical culture in EU studies at least gives us a chance of being confused in a reasonably sophisticated way.

? QUESTIONS

1. Is it fair to say that comparative politics provides a better disciplinary homeland for EU studies than international relations?

2. Can there be a single institutionalist research agenda in EU studies?

3. How helpful is the idea of 'multilevel governance' for organising the way in which we think about the EU?

4. What added value do social constructivists bring to the study of the EU?

5. How might we go about theorizing the EU's role in the world?

6. To what extent is it possible to compare the EU with other instances of 'regionalism' in the global political economy?

7. Evaluate the claim that the EU is nothing more than an institutionalized expression of neoliberal ideology.

8. How can we explain conventional integration theory's silence about gender?

GUIDE TO FURTHER READING

Christiansen, T., Jørgensen, K. E., and Wiener, A. (eds) (2001) *The Social Construction of Europe* (London: Sage)   A collection of constructivist-inspired readings of aspects of European integration, this contains critical responses and a notable late essay by Ernst Haas, the founder of neo-functionalism.

Cini, M. and Bourne, A. K. (eds) (2006) *Palgrave Advances in European Union Studies* (Basingstoke: Palgrave Macmillan)   A collection on the state of the art in EU studies, with numerous theoretical insights.

Jørgenson, K. E., Pollack, M. A., and Rosamond, B. (eds) (2007) *Handbook of European Union Politics* (London: Sage)   A wide-ranging survey of the EU literature that includes a helpful section on EU theories— including the new theories addressed in this chapter.

Rosamond, B. (2000) *Theories of European Integration* (Basingstoke: Palgrave)   A critical discussion of past and present theories of integration.

Wiener, A. and Diez, T. (eds) (2009) *European Integration Theory*, 2nd edn (Oxford: Oxford University Press)   Practitioners of a wide variety of theoretical perspectives discuss and apply their approaches to the EU.

 WEBLINKS

http://eiop.or.at/erpa/   The European Research Papers Archive is an online collection of working papers relating to EU studies, in which much innovative theoretical work is showcased for the first time.

http://europeangovernance.livingreviews.org/   *Living Reviews in European Governance* is an e-journal, publishing solicited state-of-the-art articles in the field of European integration and governance research.

http://www.reconproject.eu/projectweb/portalproject/Publications.html/   An impressive archive of publications associated with a major Europe-wide research project ('Reconstituting Democracy in Europe'); much of the work available is theoretically cutting-edge.

8
Governance in the European Union

Thomas Christiansen

Reader's Guide

This chapter provides an overview of the 'governance turn' in the study of European integration. Opening with a discussion of the reasons why governance as a concept and as a practice has become so prevalent in Europe, the chapter goes on to discuss the various ways in which the governance approach has evolved. Two strands of this literature—'multilevel governance' and the 'regulatory state'—are examined in greater detail here (but see Chapter 15 for a discussion of the open method of coordination, or OMC). The chapter then introduces some of the important normative debates to which the 'governance turn' has given rise, before concluding with some observations about the relevance of the governance approach in the current phase of European integration.

Introduction

The concept of 'governance' has become ubiquitous over the past couple of decades. Looking at EU politics, in particular, in terms of *governance*—that is, as a way of governing that does not assume the presence of a traditional, hierarchical *government* at the helm of the polity—is attractive from a conceptual point of view, not least because it promises a systematic way of studying the European Union that recognizes the particularities of the European construction. At the same time, as a concept, governance has shown itself to be rather open and flexible, facilitating a wide variety of usages. Taking as its starting point a rather vague agreement on what governance is *not*, it has been possible for scholars to find numerous applications for the governance concept in empirical research.

Beyond the academic community, the idea of governance also has political appeal in allowing policy-makers to talk about EU decision-making without invoking the idea that Europe is in the process of becoming a state (if not a 'super-state'). Even if statehood at the European level has never been a possibility, or indeed desirable, there was nevertheless a period in the early 2000s when the linguistic taboo of discussing the EU using the nation-state analogy was broken. Romano Prodi, the former Commission President, spoke of the European Commission as a 'European government'; Joschka Fischer, then German Foreign Minister, called for the '*finalité politique*' of the integration process, and the Constitutional Convention that was in part inspired by these ambitions drafted a treaty that foresaw an EU Foreign Minister, EU laws, and a 'constitution for Europe'.

However, as we now know, these ambitions were buried when the Constitutional Treaty failed to be ratified. The Lisbon Treaty, while largely preserving the substance of the constitutional project, changed the language of statehood, because this was considered to be highly problematic in terms of popular acceptance. In this context, the concept of governance has offered an appealing alternative to the conception of the EU as a nascent state.

As a result, talk about 'European governance' and the use of the governance concept have become extremely widespread, spawning a vast literature of policy papers, scholarly articles, books, and even an online journal dedicated specifically to European governance (*Living Reviews in European Governance*—see 'Weblinks'). But the extensive and somewhat inflationary application of the concept has itself become a problem. It is applied to an increasingly broad range of phenomena and its diverse usage across different communities of scholars makes it difficult to identify what 'governance' seeks to describe (Kohler-Koch and Rittberger, 2009).

Conceptualizing governance in the European Union

In his seminal article, Jachtenfuchs (2001: 245) discussed the 'governance approach to European integration' in juxtaposition to 'classical integration theory'. The

governance approach, in this perspective, is distinctive because it treats the Euro-polity as an independent, not (as 'classical' theories have done) as a dependent variable. In other words, those studying governance are more interested in what the European Union does, rather than how the EU has come about. In charting the conceptual roots of the approach, Jachtenfuchs identified, inter alia, network governance, regulatory politics, and Europeanization research (see Chapter 9) as influential contributions to the governance literature.

Other authors have helped to clarify what governance is (see Box 8.1). Rhodes (1996: 652) defined governance as 'self-organising, inter-organisational networks [which] complement markets and hierarchies as governing structures for authoritatively allocating resources and exercising control and coordination'. Stoker (1998: 17) reminded us that while governance is seen increasingly in opposition to government, it does actually perform the same functions, 'creating the conditions for ordered rule and collective action'. This implies that its distinctive focus is not on outputs, as such, but on the *process* of achieving those outputs. Hix (1998: 343), in his important contribution to the debate, pointed out that the 'new governance conception of the EU emphasises the informal nature of the policy process, the non-hierarchical structure of the institutions and the non-redistributive nature of policy outputs'.

From this, we can see that most authors identify as important the role of non-hierarchical networks; regulation rather than redistribution in policy-making; and the use of new instruments and procedures. However, contributors to the governance debate often privilege one of these aspects over the others and, as a result, the governance literature has mushroomed in a number of different directions. The reliance on, and relation to, research on policy networks and epistemic communities has been particularly strong (see, for example, Börzel, 1997; Zito, 2001; Knill and Tosun, 2009; Faleg, 2012).

Building on such insights, the governance approach has also been used to explore the way in which policy networks in the EU have become institutionalized, whether through committee structures (Christiansen and Kirchner, 2000) or through the growing number of regulatory agencies (Coen and Thatcher, 2007; Trondal and Jeppesen, 2008; Dehousse et al., 2010; Groenleer et al., 2010; Wonka and Rittberger, 2011). Others have focused on the informal dimension of governance (Christiansen and Piattoni, 2004).

As the same time, governance research has also increasingly 'drilled down' into the specifics of particular

BOX 8.1 | Definitions of 'governance'

(European) Governance	'Self-organising, inter-organisational networks [which] complement markets and hierarchies as governing structures for authoritatively allocating resources and exercising control and coordination' (Rhodes, 1996: 652)
	'The development of governing styles in which boundaries between and within public and private sectors have become blurred [and a] focus on governing mechanisms which do not rest on recourse to the authority and sanctions of government' (Stoker, 1998: 17)
	'The intentional regulation of social relationships and the underlying conflicts by reliable and durable means and institutions, instead of the direct use of power and violence' (Jachtenfuchs, 2001: 246)
	'A process and a state whereby public and private actors engage in the intentional regulation of societal relationships and conflicts [and which] denotes the participation of public and private actors, as well as non-hierarchical forms of decision making' (Kohler-Koch and Rittberger, 2006: 28)
Multilevel governance	'The dispersion of authority to multi-task, territorially mutually exclusive jurisdictions in a relatively stable system with limited jurisdictional levels and a limited number of units [as well as the presence of] specialized, territorially overlapping jurisdictions in a relatively flexible, non-tiered system with a large number of jurisdictions' (Hooghe and Marks, 2001a: 000)
Regulatory state	'Reliance on regulation—rather than public ownership, planning or centralised administration—characterizes the methods of the regulatory state' (Majone, 1994: 77)
	'Relies on extensive delegation of powers to independent institutions: regulatory agencies or commissions, but also the judiciary' (Majone, 1999:1)

sectors or policy fields. See, for example, the work done on European environmental governance (Lenschow, 1999; von Homeyer, 2004), on EU economic governance (Puetter, 2012), or on EU external governance (Lavenex, 2004; Schimmelfennig and Wagner, 2004). While this proliferation of sector-specific applications demonstrates the value of a governance perspective in guiding research in a multitude of different arenas, it contradicts the expectations of Jachtenfuchs (2001), for whom the governance approach was a welcome departure from the fragmentation of policy studies that had characterized EU research in the 1970s and 1980s.

Matters are somewhat complicated by the fact that one of the first and most important contributions on 'supranational governance' (Sandholtz and Stone Sweet, 1997, 1999) did not depart from the use of traditional concepts and debates. Indeed, Sandholtz and Stone Sweet's theory positioned itself within the established theoretical arena of intergovernmentalism and neo-functionalism. Their main contribution was to re-evaluate the role of supranational institutions in the integration process, and in particular to emphasize the importance of judicial rule-making as one of the key drivers of this process.

What this example demonstrates is that, with respect to the expanding field of governance research, it is becoming increasingly difficult to identify it as a single, coherent approach. Beyond agreement on the basic elements of what constitutes governance (and what it is not), the selective focus of individual authors means that governance denotes rather different things to different people. Arguably, this suggests that the different strands of governance research deserve, or even require, their own distinctive label in order to maintain analytical clarity. An exercise in coming to grips with the way in which the concept of governance has been used to study the EU therefore needs to start by distinguishing some of the different usages of this concept.

It is possible to identify three approaches that have been especially important:

- the *multilevel governance approach*, which emphasizes the nature of EU policy-making as involving a multiplicity of actors on a variety of territorial levels beyond the nation state;

- the *new governance approach (or agenda)*, which views the EU as a 'regulatory state' using non-majoritarian decision-making to engage in problem-solving; and

- the study of *new modes of governance*, drawing on the use of non-binding instruments to make policies at the European level (with the open method of coordination, or OMC, as a prime example—see Chapter 15).

Each of these understandings of governance takes the view that there is something fundamentally 'new' in the way in which the EU operates that requires a departure from traditional approaches. As such, their application in the study of European integration has mainly been driven by external factors—that is, by perceived changes in the empirical object of study, rather than (internal) developments within integration theory (see Chapter 7). A common feature of these governance approaches is their emphasis on non-hierarchical networks as a key aspect of EU policy-making and of the EU as a whole. The presence of such policy networks, bringing together EU officials, national administrators and regulators, business interests, non-governmental organization (NGO) representatives, and other stakeholders, is analytically relevant, because networks 'cut across' the formal boundaries that exist between institutions, territorial levels, and the public and the private spheres.

However, despite such commonalities, there are also important differences within this field; these, however, are in danger of being overlooked. One difference lies in which 'classical' theory is being critiqued. For example, multilevel governance is best seen as part of the more established integration theory debate, and in particular as a response to the dominance of liberal intergovernmentalism in the 1990s. By contrast, the new governance agenda can be seen in opposition to the comparative politics approach to the EU. In other words, 'governance' is sometimes presented as an alternative to the view that the EU is an intergovernmental arrangement among sovereign states; it is sometimes juxtaposed with the view that the EU itself should be studied as an emerging state, with its institutions and procedures comparable to those of nation states.

From this opposition to both (liberal) intergovernmentalist and comparative politics perspectives to European integration resulted a perception that governance approaches could constitute some sort of 'third way' to the study of the EU, one that eschews the reliance on the Westphalian state as the underlying paradigm of EU politics (Pollack, 2005). This not only justified the original designation of governance as 'new' when it was first introduced during the 1990s, but it also underpinned its perception of the EU as a *sui generis* kind of polity—a new kind of political construct that departs from the way in which both international and domestic politics have operated in the past, or are operating elsewhere.

This presentation of governance as one corner of a triangular debate about integration theories involving international relations and comparative politics approaches might have helped to group together a variety of perspectives, presenting these as an 'approach'. But this has become more difficult in view of the way in which governance has also become widely used in the study of international and domestic politics. In this sense, governance, be it global, regional, or national, appears to be a universal phenomenon, albeit one that has a strong and distinctive presence in the context of the EU. There is, for example, a expanding literature on 'global governance'. The extent to which similar approaches and assumptions can be employed to study global politics *and* EU politics raises questions over the uniqueness of the EU as a political system (see Rosenau and Cziempiel, 1992, for an early discussion of global governance, and Reilly, 2004, for a comparison of national, sub-national, and European understandings of the concept).

What this discussion shows is that, even though the governance approach has been seen by some as an argument for treating the EU as *sui generis* (see Hix, 1998), it has at the same time helped others to make a connection, if not a comparison, between research on the EU and on phenomena elsewhere. This has helped to overcome the $n = 1$ problem that arises when European integration is treated as unique (Krahmann, 2003). In this vein, research on European governance can draw on insights from research in other areas, or on other territorial levels, while in turn work on the EU can inspire governance research elsewhere.

KEY POINTS

- The concept of governance has successfully described the transformation of policy-making in many parts of the world over the past few decades.

- Using the governance concept has been particularly useful in the context of the EU, given the difficulty involved in categorizing the Euro-polity in terms of the traditional distinction between international system and nation state.

- The governance approach is a broad concept, capturing a variety of different perspectives and applications. At its core, it involves the understanding that policy is made through non-hierarchical networks of both public and private actors located across different territorial levels.

- Multilevel governance, the regulatory state approach, and the study of new modes of governance are the main expressions of the 'governance turn' in EU studies.

Multilevel governance

Multilevel governance (MLG) was advanced in the 1990s as a particular take on governance in the European Union, challenging the state-centric nature view of the EU prevalent up to that point (Marks et al., 1996). In their account of European integration, the founders of MLG emphasized the independent role of supranational institutions, such as the Commission and the European Court of Justice (ECJ), whilst also pointing out the internal differences that exist within member states and the inability of national executives to control how interests within individual states are represented. 'Multilevel' here referred primarily to the influence of EU-level actors and regional actors alongside the representatives of national executives (see also Marks, 1992). Whereas the former was very much in the mould of earlier neo-functionalist and more recent supranational governance accounts of integration, the addition of the regional level as part of the analytical frame was new and innovative. This aspect of MLG struck a chord with many researchers at the time, especially because it connected to the analysis of the EU conducted in federal systems such as Germany (Conzelmann, 1998; Benz and Eberlein, 1999; Eising and Kohler-Koch, 1999).

From the mid-1990s onwards, MLG quickly established itself as one of the main rivals to liberal intergovernmentalism. It starts from the observation that much of EU policy-making relies on networks of actors, but goes beyond this by emphasizing the significance of different territorial levels in this process. On the back of a critique of the liberal intergovernmentalist assumption that central governments aggregate national preferences, MLG points to the direct relations that have developed between EU actors and regional and local representatives within states. These relations bypass central governments and thereby prevent national executives maintaining a monopoly over the representation of territorial interests. Consequently, regions and municipalities become recognizable as actors independent of their central state. Moreover, their networking with the European Commission and amongst each other creates regional and local levels of interest representation within the EU. From this perspective, then, EU politics transforms itself from a 'two-level game' (Putnam, 1988) to one that involves multiple levels of government. Together with the incorporation of insights from the study of policy networks, this perspective constituted the basis of the MLG concept.

A number of interrelated developments in the late 1980s and early 1990s—the reform of the Structural Funds, the growth of regional lobbying, and the creation of the Committee of the Regions (CoR)—all brought home the fact that territorial entities within the member states did have meaningful, two-way contact with supranational institutions. This in turn fuelled interest in MLG.

The appeal of this approach meant that its application, initially centred around the study of EU regional policy (Sutcliffe, 2000; Bache, 2008), eventually expanded to cover numerous other policy domains. Through the lens of MLG, authors have analysed the influence of regional actors in areas such as employment policy (Goetschy, 2003), research policy (Kaiser and Prange, 2002), environmental policy (Bulkeley et al., 2003), and even foreign policy (Smith, 2004; see also the expansive collection of sectoral case studies in Tömmel and Verdun, 2008).

What these policy studies have shown is that there is added value to incorporating actors beyond national executives and EU officials in accounts of EU policy-making. At the same time, these studies demonstrate the variation of such influence across different policy sectors and over different points in time (Schultze, 2003). Subsequently, MLG has also been applied to the implementation stage of the policy process, a logical move in view of the decentralized nature of the EU's administrative system (Thielemann, 1998; O'Toole and Hanf, 2003).

Multilevel governance has therefore succeeded not only as an effective critique of 'state-centric' integration theories, but also in framing a growing body of research on various aspects of the EU policy process; it addresses deeper questions about the potential for transformation in the Euro-polity (Eising and Kohler Koch, 1999; Piattoni, 2009). However, while MLG has effectively exposed the weaknesses of liberal intergovernmentalism, it has not developed systematic and explicit statements about cause and effect, about dependent and independent variables, or about the scope conditions governing its explanatory power. In other words, it lacks the credentials of a theory such as liberal intergovernmentalism. As it stands, then, MLG constitutes an approach that has added valuable insights, which allow for a more comprehensive understanding of EU politics and policy-making, but it has not developed as a fully fledged theory.

Recent advances in the literature have nevertheless sought to advance MLG beyond the early claims that

EU level and sub-state level actors matter in the European policy process. These aim to enhance its explanatory power and theoretical potential. Piattoni (2009), for example, building on the earlier work of Hooghe and Marks (2001a) and Skelcher (2005), has pointed out that territory in the emerging Euro-polity is not neatly separated into European, national, regional, and local levels, but that policies are often made within or for overlapping, interstitial, or loosely defined spaces that do not necessarily correspond to pre-existing territorial jurisdictions. This distinction between the older 'type I' form of MLG and a more recently identified 'type II' approach helps scholars to engage with the tensions between different forms of MLG, whilst also bringing new normative dilemmas to light.

Although the initial statement of MLG was rationalist in its emphasis on cost–benefit calculations, informational asymmetries, and institutional self-interests, other contributions to the field have sought to demonstrate the constructivist potential of MLG (Christiansen, 1997). For example, in an interesting departure from the usual application of MLG, Aalberts (2004) employs a constructivist reading of the concept that seeks to reconcile the empirical observation that the significance of sovereignty in the Euro-polity has been declining with the apparent resilience of the nation state.

KEY POINTS

- Multilevel governance emphasizes the involvement and potential influence of actors from different territorial levels in the making of EU policy.

- Much of the literature making use of the insights of MLG has focused on the role of regions in the politics of the EU.

- Multilevel governance has demonstrated its usefulness above all in research on the **agenda-setting** and implementation phases of the EU policy process.

- Beyond the study of EU policy-making, MLG has also informed research on constitutive politics and the transformation of governance in the EU.

'New governance' and the European regulatory state

A rather different perspective on governance has been taken by authors who have conceptualized the European Union as a regulatory state. Rather than focusing on multiple levels of governance or on networks of actors, here the focus is on the kind of decisions being taken at the European level and the instruments that are being employed in order to achieve outcomes. The 'regulatory state' is seen in contrast to the traditional welfare state, interchangeably labelled also as the 'interventionist', 'positive', or *'dirigiste'* state—that is, one that is heavily involved in the allocation of goods and the redistribution of wealth. The regulatory state, by contrast, does not involve classic decisions about spending and taxation, but is essentially concerned with socio-economic regulation (Majone, 1994, 1996; Caporaso, 1996; McGowan and Wallace, 1996).

While the rise of the regulatory function of the state has been part of a wider phenomenon both within states as well as globally (Moran, 2002), the argument about the EU as a regulatory state built on a number of factors that were specific to the EU. First, the EU's Budget, in relation to the combined gross domestic product (GDP) of the member states' economies, is comparatively small and does not permit the kind of social expenditure that welfare states have at their disposal. At the same time, the EU has no practically no tax-raising powers and cannot use taxes as an instrument of redistribution.

As a result, the EU has no choice but to intervene in the economy and in society through regulation. While regulatory activity at the European level was modest until the mid-1980s, hampered by the need for unanimous decision-making, a step-change occurred with the Single European Act (SEA) and the roll-out of the 1992 Programme. The move to qualified majority voting (QMV) made the passage of European legislation much easier. Re-regulation at the European level, combined with the mutual recognition of technical and product standards at the national level, opened up member states' markets, and created the conditions for regulatory competition among national and regional jurisdictions (Young, 2006).

In terms of institutional foundations, scholars have focused on a number of particular arrangements in the EU through which regulatory activity takes place. Among these are the delegation of powers to the European Commission, the creation of a large number of decentralized agencies, and the growth of regulatory networks. What these mechanisms have in common, and what has been identified as a hallmark of the European regulatory state, is that decision-making through these institutional arrangements is both non-majoritarian and removed from the electoral process. This means that regulatory decisions are not taken through the 'normal' channels used by liberal democratic systems—majority votes by elected representatives in parliament or decisions by national executives accountable to voters—but by non-elected technocrats.

This departure from standard norms of parliamentary democracy has led to debate among scholars (see 'Normative debates about governance' for a discussion). For proponents of regulatory governance, the immediate justification for this independence from politics has centred on the following argument: the kind of regulatory decisions that are taken in the EU are about the search for the best solution to a given regulatory problem. As such, they are about identifying what is called the 'Pareto optimal' outcome among a range of possible solutions—a Pareto optimum being the outcome at which the greatest possible collective gain is reached. Setting technical standards for industrial goods, regulating financial services, preventing monopolistic tendencies and other forms of market abuse, or supervising safety standards and procedures for air travel and maritime transport, are all examples of the kind of activities that should, from this perspective, better be left to independent European regulators.

In the same vein, it is argued that it is not only right, but indeed imperative to entrust technocrats and experts with the search for the best possible solutions. Equipped with access to information, possessing expertise in the particular area in which regulatory decisions are required, and insulated from political pressures, technocrats will have the best chances of identifying the right solution. Indeed, from the vantage point of the search for the Pareto-optimal outcome, **majoritarian** institutions, which tend to decide through voting on different options, cannot be trusted to come up with the *best* solutions. Consequently, regulatory governance arrangements involve the setting up of *independent* agencies that are removed from political interference so that they can do their work objectively.

The logic of non-majoritarian decision-making is most entrenched in the area of monetary policy in which the independence of **central banks** has become an article of faith. As long as the goal of stable money and low inflation is accepted as beneficial to society as a whole, it follows that the setting of **interest rates** and decisions about **money supply** should not be subject to the shifting preferences of electoral competition and party politics. Independent central bankers can ignore the short-term pressures of elections and instead can take decisions based on the long-term interests of monetary stability.

In line with the central bank analogy, the 'regulatory state' school of thought has identified a growing number of regulatory decisions as 'outsourced' to independent agencies. This has affected areas such as competition policy, utilities regulation, financial services oversight, and the implementation of public services more generally. The resulting rise of the regulatory state is seen as a global phenomenon, driven by competitive pressures in **globalized** markets, with the EU as a particular expression of this trend. In the EU, **negative integration**—the removal of domestic **non-tariff barriers**—has been accompanied, albeit to a more limited extent by **positive integration**—the setting of minimum standards at the European level. Re-regulation—the creation of new standards applicable to the **single market**—has largely been left to networks of national regulators meeting at the European level, either informally through networks or in the more formalized settings of agencies and committees.

In addition, the European Commission has been entrusted with the centralized implementation of much of EU legislation, through the delegation of powers (see also Chapter 25). This leads to the European Commission adopting thousands of implementing measures each year, with many of these being of a regulatory nature. Given that the Commission is exercising these delegated powers in the place of national administrations, member states have insisted on the setting up of a large number of advisory, management, and regulatory committees composed of national representatives. These committees oversee the adoption of implementing measures (Blom-Hansen, 2011). The resultant system is known as 'comitology' and not only provides a framework for member state control over the Commission's use of delegated powers, but also can be seen as a site for the systematic cooperation—indeed the 'fusion'—of national and EU-level administrations (Wessels, 1998).

A number of issues have been highlighted in the new governance literature. For example, the fact that European regulatory networks tend to be only loosely coupled, and essentially rely on national agencies to implement regulatory decisions agreed at the European level, has led Eberlein and Grande (2005) and others to point out that potential 'supranational regulatory gaps' may arise. The relative weakness of regulatory networks, lacking formal powers to sanction the uniform implementation of decisions, means that agreements might either fall victim to distributive conflict, or otherwise not be subject to democratic accountability (see also McGowan and Wallace, 1996).

This dilemma between effectiveness and accountability has been a common debating point among those studying the regulatory state. Indeed, Majone (1994) himself has been quick to point to the need for strong accountability structures that can go hand in hand with the empowerment of independent regulators. However, accountability is not understood in terms of political control in this case—something that, from the new governance perspective, carries the 'danger' of politicization—but rather relies on judicial review. In an accountability structure compatible with the tenets of the regulatory state, judicial control through courts, acting on behalf of political institutions, and enforcing established standards constitutes the best way of ensuring compliance with agreed standards (Majone, 1999). Courts therefore, together with central banks and independent regulatory agencies, are the non-majoritarian backbone of the regulatory state.

KEY POINTS

- The literature on the 'European regulatory state' has developed from a wider recognition of the changing role of the state in society in the neoliberal era.

- This variant of the new governance literature sees the EU as important in the shift from redistributive to regulatory politics in Europe.

- The regulatory state model advocates a de-politicization of regulatory decision-making through the setting up and strengthening of independent and non-majoritarian institutions.

- The proposition that regulatory decision-making constitutes the search for Pareto-optimal solutions that can be best left to technocrats has given rise to normative debates about the accountability of decision-makers.

Normative debates about governance

The previous sections have already alluded to the normative challenges that the governance turn has to confront. The main debate in this regard has concerned the difficulties in reconciling the governance approach with the traditional form of liberal democracy, which is generally taken as the benchmark in this kind of normative assessment. This debate can be broken down into two distinct arguments in which scholars have engaged: first, do new forms of governance actually require legitimation in terms of traditional representative democracy; and second, does governance constitute a move towards an alternative kind of democracy, distinct from traditional models?

In terms of the first of these debates, the case 'against democracy' has already been presented under '"New governance" and the European regulatory state'. Advocates of the regulatory state approach argue that what matters here is not democratic legitimacy as expressed through the electoral process, but judicial means of holding independent regulators to account. The essence here is procedural control: ensuring that policy-makers have followed the required steps in the regulatory process (Majone, 1999). As long as that is ensured, the normatively desirable outcome of the policy process will be reached. While this initial argument has been applied to the delegation of power to the European Commission or the further 'outsourcing' of particular decisions from the Commission to independent agencies, others have taken this further, arguing that the European Union deals only with technocratic decisions and that, since it is not involved in 'high politics' kind of a kind that matters to citizens, there is no reason to worry about the putative 'democratic deficit' (Moravcsik, 2002).

This argument is in part based on the assumption that decision-making does not involve controversial choices and that, as such, there is no need for the politicization of decision-making. Against this assumption, critics have pointed to many regulatory decisions that have had significant societal implications and which have the potential to favour certain groups, sectors, or member states over others. Decisions of this kind, it has been argued, require legitimation in terms of representative democracy (Føllesdal and Hix, 2006). Take, for example, the regulation of genetically modified organisms (GMOs), which, in the EU, has been a highly contentious issue that has divided both societies and member states (see Box 8.2). The question of whether or not to permit the cultivation and use of GMOs in foodstuffs has shown itself to be more than a technocratic challenge to find the 'right' solution, and has been overlaid with ethical, emotional, and economic arguments that the EU's regulatory system has found difficult to integrate (Skogstad, 2003). The

BOX 8.2   The authorization of GMOs: a case study of European regulatory governance

The authorization of GMOs in the EU can be seen as good example of the challenges and difficulties of the European regulatory state. The need to regulate GMOs has arisen fairly recently and, within the EU's single market, requires the involvement of supranational institiutions in order to ensure that such goods can be freely traded. In response to this challenge, the European Parliament and Council have adopted a number of regulations concerning both the cultivation of GMOs in Europe, and the bringing into the market of food and animal feed containing GMO ingredients.

Such legislation adopted under the ordinary legislative procedure, or OLP (formerly the **co-decision** procedure), however, does not in itself permit or prohibit the use of GMOs. Instead, these regulations delegate powers to the European Commission, which then has the responsibility of ruling on individual authorization applications from industry. The Commission itself is then obliged, under the procedural rules that have been adopted, to consult a number of other institutions before taking its decision. This includes primarily the scientific assessment of the proposed product by the European Food Safety Authority (EFSA) in Parma, as well as the approval of the Commission's intended decision by a comitology committee composed of representatives of member state administrations. In addition, the examination process also involves networks of national laboratories and committees of experts in bio-ethics. It is an exhaustive process that has frequently taken more than a year until the Commission was in a position to adopt its decision. In fact, on several occasions the process took so long that applicants have taken the Commission to court for inaction.

Three particular issues have been identified that have caused delays or created problems in this field. First, the examination of the safety of new products conducted by EFSA relies, owing to the Authority's limited resources, to a large extent on the scientific evidence provided by the applicant—evidence that has, on occasion, been shown to be biased in favour of the safety of the product. It must therefore be questioned whether there is actually the possibility of a neutral assessment of such applications.

Second, the comitology committee overseeing the Commission's use of delegated powers is required, under the rules, to give its approval with a qualified majority. However, member states are almost evenly divided among themselves between supporters and opponents of authorizing GMOs, meaning that it has proven difficult for the Commission to achieve the necessary majority for approval. The absence of qualified majority voting (QMV) in favour of authorization has meant that applications are regularly referred to the Council, which can in theory overrule the Commission by QMV. But given the foregoing situation, no such majority can be found here either, which means that, in the face of 'no decision' in the Council, the Commission has the final say after all. At the end of this process, the Commission has regularly found itself faced with (a) a favourable scientific report from EFSA, (b) no opinion either way emerging from internally divided comitology committees and Council meetings, and (c) threats of court cases for inaction looming. The usual end result has been the authorization of such GMO applications by the Commission, albeit in the face of strong opposition from a number of national governments (not to mention protests from NGOs and political parties), leading in some cases to domestic bans for GMOs in certain member states.

Third, opponents of GMOs have complained that the process lacks **transparency** and is biased in favour of GMOs, whereas industry has bemoaned the long delays in reaching a final decision, which is seen to leave Europe uncompetitive in the application of this new technology. By the early 2010s, the difficulties experienced with the delegation of these regulatory powers to the European Commission and EFSA led to the search for a new legislative framework that would allow for greater political input.

In sum, the case of GMO authorization demonstrates amply the challenges to the delegation of regulatory powers to independent agencies when issues at stake are contested and carry the potential for politicization.

result is not only a perceived lack of legitimacy in this area of EU policy-making, but also problems with the effective regulation of this sector (Christiansen and Polak, 2009).

Authors have advanced many other examples of such 'loaded' decisions that, from a democratic theory point of view, would require legitimation through representative rather than non-majoritarian institutions. The EU's response to the 2008 banking crisis and the eurozone's subsequent sovereign debt crisis have been further triggers for debates about the

legitimacy of European governance in this field. One observation made in this context has been that the alleged flexibility and adaptability of regulatory networks has been lacking (Mügge, 2011). In this reading, close cooperation among financial market regulators sharing a neoliberal outlook has meant that financial regulations were devised by an epistemic community based on a dogmatic worldview—a regulatory paradigm that was not adaptable to the changing requirements of the current crisis. This diagnosis echoes the earlier critique by Gill (1998) of the bias in what he called the 'new constitutionalism' of European economic governance.

From this perspective, regulatory decisions require democratic legitimation—if not through representative institutions, then at the very least through deliberative mechanisms. The presence of, or the need for, deliberation in the policy process takes us to the second of the normative debates. Some authors, focusing either on multilevel governance (MLG) or **new modes of governance (NMGs)** have explored the degree to which these forms of governance might meet the expectations of deliberative democracy (Steffek et al., 2007).

While research has demonstrated that such opportunities exist, it has also pointed out the limitations of such deliberation (Eriksen, 2011). The involvement of 'European **civil society**' is generally translated into the **consultation** of Brussels-based NGOs, casting doubts over the representativeness of such cooperation (Kohler-Koch, 2010). Furthermore, observers have pointed out that many of the organizations representing civil society are, in fact, dependent on financial support from the European Commission, possibly resulting in their co-option within a sphere of 'approved' participants in the policy process (Bellamy and Castiglione, 2011). Authors have also pointed to the normative problems inherent in the way in which technocratic

'**good governance**' has been 'exported' to third countries outside the EU (Karppi, 2005; Hout, 2010; Knio, 2010). At the extreme, critics have argued that 'far from laying the grounds for a more inclusive, participatory and democratic political order, the [European] Commission's model to governance represents a form of neoliberal governmentality that is actually undermining democratic government and promoting a politics of exclusion' (Shore, 2011: 287).

KEY POINTS

- The governance approach, as a departure from traditional liberal democratic procedures of decision-making, raises important normative questions.

- Some authors point to the normative benefits of governance, such as greater opportunities for deliberation, the potential of greater inclusiveness in the policy process, and the advantages of depoliticized regulatory activity producing the best result.

- Critics of the governance approach have pointed to the way in which theoretical advantages do not materialize in practice, and have warned of the rigidity and dogmatism that may arise if policy-making is left to an exclusive community of experts.

Conclusion

In summarizing the main arguments advanced in this chapter, four points need to be emphasized. First, the 'governance turn' has been an important development in the literature on the European Union, signifying the changing nature of the integration process since the **Maastricht Treaty** and demonstrating the desire of scholars to adapt their research tools accordingly. Second, the study of European governance centres on the role of non-hierarchical networks in the policy process, emphasizing their relevance in a shift away from classic state-centric theories as developed in the subfields of international relations and comparative politics. Third, governance has become a broad and internally highly diverse orientation, involving a range of different applications, based on a variety of underlying assumptions, making it increasingly difficult to talk of a single 'governance approach'. Fourth, the governance turn has raised, both explicitly and implicitly, a number of normative questions, leading to debates about the limitations of,

and the need for, the democratic legitimation of EU governance arrangements.

These normative debates are ongoing and would seem all the more important as the study of governance has become part of the mainstream of approaches analysing EU politics. An interesting site of debate, driving home this point, is the discussion about the future of economic governance in the EU. In view of the existential crisis that the eurozone has been facing since 2010, the criticism levied at the weaknesses in both the financial services sector and the management of single currency, and the calls for a tighter and more comprehensive *gouvernement economique*, the early 2010s have been an opportunity for the reassessment of governance.

In fact, the **Stability and Growth Pact (SGP)**, which sets targets for member states in terms of permissible levels of **public debt** and budget deficits, is the most prominent example of the failure of the soft mode of governance, given that the non-compliance of member states with the SGP targets contributed to (if not caused) the crisis. Nevertheless, negative experiences of this kind do not mean that the EU will abandon this form of governance. Indeed, future plans with regards to economic governance include the tightening of the supranational oversight of **fiscal policies** through the introduction of a '**European semester**', which permits the European Commission to monitor national budget plans more closely before their domestic adoption (Hacker and van Treeck, 2010). Other aspects of the response to the sovereign debt crisis—in particular the close cooperation between the European Commis-

sion, **European Central Bank (ECB)**, and **International Monetary Fund (IMF)** in negotiating and monitoring the **conditionality** of national bailouts—appear as a further evidence of the significant role that technocrats are playing in the response to the crisis. At the same time, this shift towards technocracy at the European level frequently clashes with the operation of representative democracy at the national level. The 'governance turn' has certainly made its mark on the European Union, but the debate about the way in which such governance can be legitimated remains as relevant as ever.

QUESTIONS

1. How do you explain the success of the governance approach?

2. How is European governance distinguished from traditional forms of governing?

3. What are the main elements of the 'governance turn' in EU studies?

4. Does the governance approach constitute a convincing critique of liberal intergovernmentalism?

5. What is distinctive about multilevel governance?

6. What are the strengths and weaknesses of multilevel governance in analysing the process of European integration?

7. How is decision-making by unelected technocrats legitmized in the European regulatory state?

8. What are the main criticisms on normative grounds that can be advanced against new governance?

GUIDE TO FURTHER READING

Eising, R. and Kohler-Koch, B. (eds) (1999) *The Transformation of Governance in the European Union* (London: Routledge)   Presenting the findings of a large-scale research project, this volume includes chapters on governance in a range of different sectors and member states.

Hooghe, L. and Marks, G. (2001a) *Multi-Level Governance and European Integration* (London: Rowman & Littlefield)   This is the definitive statement of the key elements and findings of the multilevel governance approach by its founders.

Majone, G. (ed.) (1996) *Regulating Europe* (London: Routledge)   A collection of contributions from the founder of the European regulatory state approach and others.

Marks, G., Scharpf, F. W., Schmitter, P. C., and Streeck, W. (1996) *Governance in the European Union* (London: Sage Publications)   A collection of essays by senior scholars exploring different dimensions of the governance approach.

Scharpf, F. W. (1999) *Governing in Europe: Effective and Democratic?* (Oxford: Oxford University Press)   A collection of essays exploring both the empirical and normative dimensions of governance in the EU.

WEBLINKS

http://ec.europa.eu/governance/index_en.htm   The official website of the European Commission, developed alongside the launch of the Commission's *White Paper on European Governance* in 2001.

http://eiop.or.at/erpa/   The European Research Papers Archive is an online collection of working papers relating to EU studies, in which much innovative theoretical work is showcased for the first time.

http://europeangovernance.livingreviews.org/   *Living Reviews in European Governance* is an e-journal, publishing solicited state-of-the-art articles in the field of European integration and governance research.

http://www.unc.edu/~gwmarks/   Gary Marks' home page, which includes access to published and forthcoming papers.

http://www.unc.edu/~hooghe/   Liesbet Hooghe's home page, which includes access to published and forthcoming papers.

9

Europeanization

Tanja A. Börzel and Diana Panke

Chapter Contents

Reader's Guide

The first section of the chapter explains what Europeanization means and outlines the main approaches to studying this phenomenon. The second section describes why this concept has become so prominent in research on the European Union and its member states. In the third section, the chapter reviews the state of the art with particular reference to how the EU affects states ('top-down' Europeanization). It illustrates the theoretical arguments with empirical examples. Similarly, the fourth section examines how states can influence the EU ('bottom-up' Europeanization) and provides some theoretical explanations for the empirical patterns observed. This is followed by a section that presents an overview of research that looks at linkages between bottom-up and top-down Europeanization, and considers the future of Europeanization research. The conclusion argues that Europeanization will continue to be an important field of EU research for the foreseeable future.

Introduction: what is Europeanization?

Europeanization has become a prominent concept in the study of the European Union and **European integration** (see Box 9.1). While Europeanization generally refers to interactions between the EU and its member states or third countries, there is no consensus on the definition of the term. Broadly, one can distinguish between two different notions of Europeanization: 'bottom-up' and 'top-down' Europeanization.

The bottom-up perspective analyses how member states and other domestic actors shape EU policies, EU politics, and the European polity. For bottom-up Europeanization approaches, the phenomenon to be explained is the EU itself. This research analyses whether and how member states are able to upload their preferences to the EU institutions by, for example, giving the European Parliament (EP) more **powers**, by extending policy content and scope (as is the case in the **liberalization of services**), or by focusing on political processes, such as in increasing the areas in which the **ordinary legislative procedure (OLP)** (formerly **co-decision**) applies. European **integration** theories, such as **neo-functionalism, liberal intergovernmentalism**, and **supranationalism**, address such uploading efforts by member state governments (see Chapters 5, 6, and 7). They conceptualize the EU as a political arena in which actors from multiple levels of government compete and cooperate over the making of EU policies and the shaping of the European integration process (Hooghe and Marks, 2001a; see also Chapter 8).

In the top-down perspective, the phenomenon to be explained and the causes are reversed. Here, the focus is on how the EU shapes institutions, processes, and political outcomes in both member states and third countries (Ladrech, 1994; Sanders and Bellucci,

2012). The phenomenon to be explained is whether and how states download EU policies and institutions that subsequently give rise to domestic change. In other words, how does the EU impact on domestic institutions, policies, or political processes? To what extent, for example, has the shift of policy **competences** from the domestic to the EU level undermined the powers of national parliaments by reducing their function to that of merely transposing EU **directives** into national law? Is the EU responsible for a decline of public services by forcing France or Germany to liberalize telecommunications, postal services, or their energy markets? And to what extent has European integration empowered populist parties, such as the **Front National, Die Linke**, or **Sinn Féin**, which seek to mobilize those who feel that they have lost out because of the **single European market**?

Top-down Europeanization approaches search for causes at the EU level that explain domestic change. They share the assumption that the EU can (but does not always) cause adaptations of domestic policies, institutions, and political processes if there is a misfit between European and domestic ideas and institutions (Börzel et al., 2010). The incompatibility of European and domestic norms facilitates top-down changes only if it creates material costs or if it challenges collectively shared knowledge or beliefs about how to address societal problems. For example, it raises the question of whether it is more appropriate to protect the environment by preventing pollution (the German approach) or by fighting environmental pollution where it becomes too damaging (the British approach).

In addition to analyzing separately bottom-up and top-down Europeanization, some scholars put forward a sequential perspective by analysing policy cycles or long-term interactions between the EU and its members (Kohler-Koch and Eising, 1999; Radaelli, 2003). Member states are not merely passive takers of EU demands for domestic change; they proactively shape European policies, institutions, and processes, which they have to download and to which they later have to adapt. Moreover, the need to adapt domestically to European pressure may also have significant effects at the European level, where member states seek to reduce the misfit between European and domestic arrangements by shaping EU decisions. For example, when Germany succeeded in turning its air pollution **regulations** into the Large Combustion Plant Directive adopted by the EU in 1988 (Directive 88/609/EEC), it did not have to introduce any major

---

BOX 9.1 Europeanization

Europeanization captures the interactions between the European Union and member states or third countries (including **accession** and neighbourhood). One strand of Europeanization research analyses how member states shape EU policies, politics, and **polity**, while the other focuses on how the EU triggers domestic change.

legal and administrative changes, and German industry had little difficulty in complying with EU air pollution standards. The UK, by contrast, was forced to overhaul its entire regulatory structure and British industry had to buy new abatement technologies for which German companies were the market leaders.

The sequential approach is not a new research avenue, but rather synthesizes the top-down and bottom-up Europeanization approaches. It analyses how member states shape the EU (uploading), how the EU feeds back into member states (downloading), and how the latter react in changing properties of the EU (uploading) (see Börzel and Risse, 2007).

KEY POINTS

- Europeanization has become a key but disputed term in research on European integration.

- Top-down Europeanization seeks to explain how the European Union induces domestic change in member states or third countries.

- Bottom-up Europeanization analyses how member states and other domestic actors shape EU policies, EU politics, and the European polity.

- The sequential approach to Europeanization synthesizes the merits of top-down and bottom-up Europeanization.

Why does Europeanization matter?

A search of any university library catalogue or research database shows that Europeanization is a very active research field. Why is it that Europeanization has attracted so much attention from scholars?

For a start, the European Union has become ever more important for the daily lives of its citizens. The EU has gained more and more policy competences, which now range from market creation and trade liberalization policies, health, environmental research, and social policies, to cooperation in the fight against crime and foreign policy. As a consequence, it is very important to explain how the EU has obtained these competences and how its policies have been formulated. Which actors and which coalitions are active in shaping the EU? Why is it that we observe a general broadening and widening of integration where the member states have been willing

to give the EU ever more power on fighting crime and illegal immigration, while resisting any significant sovereignty loss with regard to conflict prevention and conflict resolution? Are the 'big three' (the UK, France, and Germany) in a better position to make their interests heard in the EU than Luxembourg, Ireland, Latvia, or Malta?

Likewise, it is very important to examine how the EU affects the domestic structures of its member states. Europe has hit virtually all policy areas. What kind of domestic change (of policies, institutions, or political processes) does the EU trigger? Do Greece, the UK, Poland, Luxembourg, France, or Denmark all download EU policies in a similar way, or do national and regional differences remain even after Europeanization?

A second reason why research on Europeanization has been thriving is that European integration does not only affect member states, but can also have intended or unintended side effects on third countries. The EU is actively seeking to change the domestic structures of its neighbours and other third countries by exporting its own governance model. Examples of what is often referred to as 'external Europeanization' are the EU's enlargement policy with the famous Copenhagen criteria, which prescribe liberal democracy and market economy for any country that seeks to join the club (see Chapter 17), and the EU's neighbourhood policy that stipulates similar requirements. Both seek to induce third countries to implement parts of the *acquis communautaire*. Thus the EU has not only talked France, Germany, Spain, Greece, and the Central and Eastern European (CEE) countries into granting their citizens general access to environmental information, but has also asked Ukraine, Georgia, Armenia, and Azerbaijan to make data on the environmental impact of planned projects accessible to the public. Conditionality and capacity-building provide a major incentive for accession and for neighbourhood countries to adapt to Europe. Finally, Europeanization can have unintended effects on member states and third countries. Domestic actors can use the EU for their own ends and can induce domestic changes in the name of Europe (Lavenex, 2001). For example, gay and lesbian groups in Poland have used the EU to push for the rights of sexual minorities in the absence of any specific EU legislation. Countries that are not current or would-be members of the EU are subject to the indirect influence of the EU too. Norway, for example, became part of the Schengen Agreement because it forms a passport union with the Scandinavian EU member states. Outside Europe, farmers in developing countries in Latin America and Africa suffer from consequences of the Common Agricultural Policy (CAP), which effectively shuts their products out of the single market (see Chapter 23).

The EU has penetrated the lives of its citizens in many respects. It not only regulates the quality of their drinking water, the length of parental leave, or roaming fees for mobile phones, but Europeanization has also fundamentally affected core institutions of the member states and accession countries by, for example, disempowering national parliaments (Schmidt, 2006; see also Chapter 25). At the same time, the EU is a multilevel system of governance, in which the member states shape the policies made in Brussels (see Chapter 8). A good illustration of this is the Bolkestein Directive, which seeks to open up certain domestic markets to foreign service providers (see Chapter 19).

KEY POINTS

- Europeanization has become a key concept in the study of European integration.

- Europeanization research examines how the EU has obtained a broad array of policy competences over the course of more than fifty years of integration and also how this triggers changes in member states affecting various aspects of the daily lives of EU citizens.

- Students of Europeanization also investigate how the EU affects third countries, which may or may not want to become members, by pushing for market liberalization, democracy, human rights, and **good governance**.

- Europeanization research shows that European integration has had unintended effects on states both within and outside the EU.

Explaining top-down Europeanization

Top-down Europeanization seeks to explain the conditions and causal mechanisms through which the European Union triggers domestic change in its member states and in third countries. It starts from the empirical puzzle that European norms facilitate domestic change, but do not provoke the convergence of national polities, politics, or policies. It also posits that EU policies and institutions are a constant impetus of domestic change for all states (Cowles et al., 2001; Sanders and Bellucci, 2012). To solve the puzzle, the literature has drawn on two different strands of neo-institutionalism (see Chapter 7). While both assume that institutions mediate or filter the domestic impact of Europe, rationalist and constructivist approaches to top-down Europeanization differ in their assumptions about exactly how institutions matter.

Rational choice institutionalism argues that the EU facilitates domestic adaptation by changing opportunity structures for domestic actors. In a first step, a misfit between the EU and domestic norms creates demands for domestic adaptation. In a second step, the downloading of EU policies and institutions by the member states is shaped by cost–benefit calculations of the strategic actors whose interests are at stake. Institutions constrain or enable certain actions by strategic rational actors by rendering some options more costly than others (Tsebelis, 1990; Scharpf, 1997). From this perspective, Europeanization is largely conceived of as an emerging political opportunity structure that offers some actors additional resources with which to exert influence, while severely constraining the ability of others to pursue their goals. Domestic change is facilitated where the institutions of the member states empower domestic actors to block change at veto points or to facilitate it through supporting formal institutions (Börzel and Risse, 2007). For example, the liberalization of the European transport sector (Regulations 96/1191 and 1893/91) empowered internationally operating road hauliers and liberal parties in highly regulated member states, such as Germany or the Netherlands, which had been unsuccessfully pushing for privatization and deregulation at home. But while the German reform coalition was able to exploit European policies to overcome domestic opposition to liberalization, Italian trade unions and sectoral associations successfully vetoed any reform attempt (Héritier et al., 2001). Likewise, public agencies in the UK supported the appeal of women's organizations in support of the Equal Pay and Equal Treatment Directives (Directives 75/117/EEC and 76/107/EEC, respectively) to further gender equality by providing them with legal expertise and funding to take employers to court. In the absence of such formal institutions, French women were not able to overcome domestic resistance by employers and trade unions to implement EU equal pay and equal treatment policies (Caporaso and Jupille, 2001; Cowles et al., 2001).

Other research in the Europeanization literature draws on *sociological institutionalism* (see Chapter 7). This specifies change mechanisms based on the ideational and normative processes involved in top-down Europeanization. Sociological institutionalism draws on the 'logic of appropriateness' (March and Olsen, 1989), which argues that actors are guided by collectively shared understandings of what constitutes proper, socially accepted behaviour. These norms influence the way in which actors define their goals and what they perceive as rational action. Rather than maximizing egoistic self-interest, actors seek to meet social expectations. From this perspective, Europeanization is understood as the emergence of new rules, norms, practices, and structures of meaning to which member states are exposed and which they have to incorporate into their domestic structures. For example, consider a normative or cognitive misfit between what the British believe or know about protecting the environment best and what EU policies prescribe is a necessary, but not sufficient, condition for domestic change in response to top-down Europeanization. If there is such a misfit, norm entrepreneurs, such as epistemic communities or advocacy networks, socialize domestic actors into new norms and rules of appropriateness through persuasion and social learning. Domestic actors then redefine their interests and identities accordingly (Börzel and Risse, 2007). The more active norm entrepreneurs are and the more they succeed in making EU policies resonate with domestic norms and beliefs, the more successful they will be in bringing about domestic change.

Moreover, collective understandings of appropriate behaviour strongly influence the ways in which domestic actors download EU requirements (see Box 9.2). First, a consensus-oriented or cooperative decision-making culture helps to overcome multiple veto

---

BOX 9.2 Explaining 'downloading' and 'taking'

The top-down Europeanization literature uses the concepts 'downloading' and 'taking' as synonyms. Both terms capture the response of member and third states to the European Union. States are good in taking or downloading policies if they are able to respond swiftly to impetuses for change coming, for example from the EU in the form of EU law, EU neighbourhood policy, or EU development policy.

---

points by rendering their use for actors inappropriate. Cooperative federalism prevented the German Länder from vetoing any of the Treaty revisions that deprived them of core decision powers. Obstructing the deepening and widening of European integration would have not been acceptable to the political class (Börzel, 2002). Likewise, the litigious German culture encouraged German citizens to appeal to national courts against the deficient application of EU law, while such a culture was absent in France, where litigation is less common (Conant, 2002).

Second, a consensus-orientated political culture allows for a sharing of adaptational costs, which facilitates the accommodation of pressure for adaptation. Rather than shifting adaptational costs onto a social or political minority, the 'winners' of domestic change compensate the 'losers'. For example, the German government shared its decision powers in European policy-making with the Länder to make up for their EU-induced power losses. Likewise, the consensual corporatist decision-making culture in the Netherlands and Germany facilitated the liberalization of the transport sector by offering compensation to employees as the potential losers of domestic changes (Héritier et al., 2001). In short, the stronger informal cooperative institutions are in a member state, the more likely domestic change will be.

While Europeanization has affected the policy, polity, and politics of all member states, the degree of change differs significantly. If we consider the example of environmental policy, the EU has promoted change towards a more precautionary problem-solving approach, particularly in the area of air and water pollution control. It also introduced procedural policy instruments such as the Access to Environmental Information and the Environmental Impact Directive (Directive 90/313/EEC). Equally, EU policies have led to tighter standards in virtually all areas of environmental policy. While the EU has affected the policy content of all member states, the environmental latecomers (Spain, Portugal, Greece, Ireland, the UK, and more recently the CEE countries) have been much more Europeanized than the environmentally progressive 'leader' states (Denmark, Sweden, Finland, the Netherlands, Germany, and Austria) (see Chapter 17).

The Europeanization of administrative structures paints a similar picture, although domestic change has been more modest. In old and new member states, the domestic impact of Europe has fostered the centralization of environmental policy-making competences in the hands of central government departments and agencies at the expense of subordinate levels of government. While regional governments in highly decentralized states have, to some extent, been compensated by co-decision rights in the formulation and implementation of EU environmental policies, the main losers of Europeanization are the national and regional parliaments. While the Europeanization of environmental policy-making has created new political opportunities, particularly for citizens and environmental groups, it has reinforced existing consensual and adversarial styles rather than changed them. The only exceptions are the three northern countries that joined the EU in 1995. In Austria, Sweden, and to a lesser extent Finland, the need to implement EU environmental policies in a timely fashion has reduced the scope for extensive consultation with affected interests thus undermining the traditionally consensual patterns of interest intermediation. Moreover, the legalistic approach of the Commission in the monitoring of compliance with EU law has constrained the discretion public authorities used to exercise in the implementation of environmental regulations in the UK, Ireland, and France.

External Europeanization also corroborates the differential impact of Europe. Europeanization has had a more similar effect on accession and neighbourhood countries than it has on member states when it comes to the strengthening of core executives and the increase in their autonomy from domestic political and societal pressures. It has also led to the development of a less politicized civil service and to a degree of decentralization and regionalization, at least when compared with the Communist legacy (Schimmelfennig and Sedelmeier, 2005a). At the same time, however, Europeanization effects on institutions and politics vary considerably. EU political conditionality was successful only in cases of unstable democracy, in which it strengthened liberal politics (as in Slovakia or Serbia), while being irrelevant in those countries that already had strong democratic constituencies (most of the CEE countries) or in autocratically ruled states such as Belarus or Azerbaijan (Schimmelfennig et al., 2006). In general, there has been little institutional convergence around a single European model of governance.

In sum, the top-down impact of Europeanization is differential. EU policies and institutions are not downloaded in a uniform manner. Denmark, the UK, and Sweden are better takers than France, Italy, and Greece, because they have more efficient administrations (Börzel et al., 2010). Thus we should not be too surprised to find hardly any evidence of convergence towards an EU policy or institutional model: convergence is not synonymous with Europeanization. Member states can undergo significant domestic change without necessarily becoming more similar.

By focusing on 'goodness of fit' and mediating factors, such as veto players, facilitating formal institutions, or norm entrepreneurs, we can therefore account for the differential impact of Europe. These factors increasingly point to complementary rather than competing explanations of Europeanization. As such, students of Europeanization primarily seek to identify scope conditions under which specific factors are more likely to influence the downloading of EU policies and institutions by the member states.

KEY POINTS

- Top-down Europeanization explains how the EU triggers domestic change. A central concept in this regard is 'misfit'. Only if domestic policies, processes, or institutions are not already in line with what is required by the EU can the latter causally induce domestic change.

- If misfit is present, the impact of the European Union can be explained through different theoretical approaches—namely, sociological or rational choice institutionalism.

- A frequent question of top-down Europeanization research is whether the policies, politics, and polity of states converge over time as an effect of membership, or whether states maintain distinct features.

Explaining bottom-up Europeanization

Bottom-up Europeanization research analyses how states upload their domestic preferences to the EU level. These preferences may involve EU policies, such as environmental standards; they may relate to European political processes, such as how far day-to-day decision-making should involve the European Parliament; or they can touch on issues of institutional design regarding, for example, whether the European Commission should get additional competences in Justice and Home Affairs (JHA) matters (see Box 9.3). Bottom-up Europeanization studies can be

BOX 9.3 Explaining 'uploading' and 'shaping'

The bottom-up Europeanization literature uses two concepts interchangeably in order to describe how states influence policies, politics, or institutions of the European Union: 'uploading' and 'shaping'. An EU member state is a successful shaper (or uploader) if it manages to make its preferences heard, so that an EU policy, political process, or institution reflects its interests.

divided into those that analyse intergovernmental conferences (IGCs) (Moravcsik, 1998) and those that examine the daily decision-making process (Thomson et al., 2006; Thomson, 2011). In order to conceptualize how bottom-up Europeanization works and how states are able to upload their preferences, students of the European Union have drawn on rationalist and constructivist approaches. Rationalist approaches assume that actors have fixed and predefined interests, and pursue them through recourse to their power resources (often economic strength or votes in the EU Council) in strategically calculating the costs and benefits of different options. Constructivist approaches assume that actors are open to persuasion and change their flexible interests in the wake of good arguments.

One of the most prominent rationalist decision-making approaches is intergovernmentalism (Hoffmann, 1966, 1989) and its newer version, liberal intergovernmentalism (Moravcsik, 1998; see also Chapter 6). Intergovernmentalism assumes that states with many votes in the EU Council and high bargaining power are in a better position to shape outcomes in EU negotiations than states with fewer votes. Moreover, powerful states are more likely to influence successfully the content of EU law if the policy at stake is very important for them and if they manage to form winning coalitions through concessions (package deals or side payments) or through threats, such as the disruption of further cooperation, stopping support in other issues, or reducing side payments. Hence the higher the bargaining power of a state and the higher the issue salience for that state, the more likely it is that this state will shape the content of the European policy (successful bottom-up Europeanization).

Quantitative studies of European decision-making attribute different causal weight to formal rules,

ranging from traditionally power-based studies to more institutionalist approaches. The former assume that political and material power is the crucial explanatory factor governing EU negotiations (Widgren, 1994), whereas the latter put more emphasis on formal rules such as decision-making procedures or the share of votes (Tsebelis and Garrett, 1997). The collaborative research project 'The European Union Decides', investigating eleven different EU decision-making models, showed that 'powerful actors who attach most salience to the issues receive the largest concessions from other negotiators' (Schneider et al., 2006: 305; see also Thomson et al., 2006). Hence the share of votes that a member state has in the EU Council is an important negotiation resource, but does not determine outcomes. This is the result of an informally institutionalized consensus norm, according to which 'powerful and intense actors are conciliates, even when they might be legally ignored' (Achen, 2006: 297). Moreover, in order to influence policies successfully, states have to create coalitions. While there is evidence of the rationalist account of bottom-up Europeanization, a considerable amount of empirical variation is left unexplained.

Qualitative studies also demonstrate that bargaining and voting power are very important for bottom-up Europeanization, because power influences the opportunities that states have to upload national preferences to the EU level (Liefferink and Andersen, 1998). Thus a study by Eugénia da Conceição-Heldt (2004) on the Common Fisheries Policy (CFP) highlights that power, preferences, and preference intensity influence the outcomes of complex, iterated negotiations under conditions of uncertainty (Box 9.4). Another example of the importance of bargaining power in the shadow of votes is the Working Time Directive (Directive 2003/88/EC). During the two years of negotiations in the Committee of Permanent Representatives (Coreper) prior to an agreement, a potential compromise shifted the outcome towards the UK as a strong veto player. A majority of states favoured the Directive. Although member states could have voted according to qualified majority voting (QMV), they abstained from proceeding in this way, seeking instead to bring the UK on board as well. As a result, the UK achieved key concessions before the Directive was passed (Lewis, 2003: 115–19). In line with the findings of the 'The European Union Decides' project, the bargaining power of a big state with high preference intensity

---

BOX 9.4 Bottom-up Europeanization: the Common Fisheries Policy

The CFP case is a good illustration of how states make use of their voting power and the threat of a negative vote in order to obtain better deals for themselves. Back in 1976, the European Commission proposed rules on fishing quotas and member states' access to fishing areas. This policy required **unanimity** among the member states. Everyone agreed to the proposal, with Ireland and the UK opting for higher quotas and limitations of the equal access principle. Ireland and the UK had high bargaining power, because their agreement was required to pass the policy. In the course of several years of bargaining, the Irish government accepted the Commission's modified proposal because it achieved concessions in the form of quota increases.

The UK, however, maintained its opposition and was brought back into the 'boat' only later, when the CFP was linked to the UK's budget contribution in a comprehensive package deal. At that point, however, Denmark turned into a veto player, because it became dissatisfied with the quota system. Denmark demanded higher and more flexible fishing quotas, and created a stalemate by evoking the **Luxembourg Compromise**. To the threat of continued blockade, the Community responded with higher offers. Only after Denmark received higher quotas as side payments could the CFP finally come into existence in 1983.

Source: da Conceição-Heldt (2006)

---

mattered in the case of the Working Time Directive. Even though proceeding to vote could have secured support for the Directive against British interests, all large states' interests were accommodated. Therefore it is clear that qualitative studies lend support to major quantitative findings in showing that, when it comes to hard bargaining in the shadow of votes, the size of a member state matters in shaping its likely influence.

Constructivist approaches assume that the preferences of state and non-state actors are not completely fixed during interactions, but can change in the wake of good arguments (Risse, 2000). Actors have an idea of what they want when they start negotiating in the EU, but can change their preferences if another actor makes a convincing statement, for example, should new scientific insights be made available (Panke, 2011). According to this approach, policy outcomes and integration dynamics are shaped by processes of arguing among member states, typically involving supranational institutions such as the Commission, or policy experts and epistemic communities (Haas, 1970; Sandholtz and Zysman, 1989). Good arguments are the ones that resonate well with all interests. If an argument wins the competition of ideas, it influences outcomes. States are more successful in shaping policy outcomes (successful bottom-up Europeanization) the better their arguments resonate with the beliefs and norms of other actors.

While quantitative studies do not (yet) test the power of ideas and good arguments, qualitative studies can trace ideational processes. They demonstrate that the power of argument is highly important in influencing the opportunity that a member state has to influence the content of European laws, European institutions, or EU political processes. Concerning market creating and regulating policies, fewer than 15 per cent of all Council positions on a Commission proposal are actually decided at the level of the EU Council. Coreper and, especially, the working groups of the Council are the forums in which the vast majority of political decisions are taken (see Chapter 11). In both lower-level arenas, hard political bargaining, in which states resort to the threat of hierarchical delegation and voting, is rare. The usual way of doing business is based on the exchange of arguments (Beyers and Dierrickx, 1998; Elgström and Jönsson, 2000). A comprehensive study of negotiations within the EU Council shows, for example, that high-quality arguments can convince others even if the point is put forward by a small state with limited bargaining and voting power (Panke, 2010). The possibility of persuading others with a convincing argument and norms of mutual responsiveness both work as great equalizers in Coreper negotiations. As a result, smaller member states can sometimes punch above their weight (Lewis, 2005b; Panke, 2010). This case lends support to the constructivist hypothesis on bottom-up Europeanization.

The two theoretical accounts of the shaping of European policies are compatible rather than mutually exclusive. We know empirically that, in EU institutions, actors sometimes engage in bargaining (as expected by the rationalist intergovernmental approach) and sometimes argue (as expected by the constructivist supranational approach). Therefore both explanations of bottom-up Europeanization can account for different parts of social reality (Panke, 2006).

KEY POINTS

- Bottom-up Europeanization explains how states can trigger changes in the EU.

- Misfit is a necessary condition for EU-induced changes. If states' preferences are not already in accordance with EU policies, politics, or polity, states can induce European-level changes.

- Different theories focus on different means available to states to make their voices heard, such as economic and voting power, or argumentative and moral power.

- Two prominent questions of bottom-up Europeanization research ask whether large states, such as Germany, France, the UK, or Poland, are more successful in influencing European policies than smaller states and under which conditions small states can punch above their weight.

Towards a sequential perspective on Europeanization?

As explained under 'Introduction: what is Europeanization?', the sequential perspective on Europeanization seeks to explain both the shaping and taking of EU and state-level policies, procedures, and institutions. Few students of Europeanization have made an attempt to bring the two approaches together, although some studies consider 'shaping' as the cause of 'taking' or vice versa (Andersen and Liefferink, 1997; van Keulen, 1999). Member states that have the power and capacity to upload successfully their preferences, and to shape EU policies accordingly, have fewer difficulties in taking and downloading them. This explains why southern European member states are laggards in implementing EU environmental policies (Börzel, 2003). Portugal and Greece simply lack capacities and power to strongly shape EU policy, and consequently face a higher 'misfit', incurring significant implementation costs. Problems in taking EU policies can provide member states

with important incentives to engage in (re-)shaping in order to reduce the 'misfit'. France, for example, which had already deregulated its transport sector when it met the EU demands for liberalization, pushed for re-regulating the impact of liberalization in order to safeguard public interest goals (Héritier et al., 2001).

The more successful member states are in shaping EU policies, the fewer problems they are likely to face in taking these policies. For example, if a state with high regulatory standards in the environmental policy field, such as Denmark, manages to upload its environmental policy preferences to the European level, it has to invest fewer resources in implementing EU policies later on, which in turn reduces the risk of Denmark violating EU environmental law (Börzel, 2003). But are successful shaping and taking explained by the same factors, or do the two stages of the policy process require different explanations? Some factors might be more important to shaping than to taking, or vice versa; they could also have contradictory effects. However, so far only a small number of Europeanization studies have systematically combined and compared the causal influence of different factors in the two stages of the EU policy process.

KEY POINTS

- The bulk of Europeanization research focuses either on top-down or on bottom-up processes.

- Sequential approaches analyse interactions between the shaping and the taking of European policies.

- There is limited research that identifies the interaction between unsuccessful uploading of preferences to the EU level and implementation problems at the national level.

- There is great potential for future research that seeks to integrate sequentially top-down and bottom-up Europeanization approaches.

Conclusion

The chapter has introduced the concept of Europeanization and has reviewed the research that has been undertaken thus far on this topic. The chapter has focused attention on the theoretical literature around the

concepts of top-down and bottom-up Europeanization by identifying their explanatory quality and by contextualizing them in the wider political science literature. The empirical examples have shown how the European

Union has contributed to changing structures, processes, and behaviour in national arenas, but also under what conditions member states are able to incorporate their preferences into EU policies, politics, and processes. Moreover, the chapter has addressed the external dimension of Europeanization as the EU is able to affect third countries by pushing for socio-economic and political reform. The chapter has also presented a sequential understanding of Europeanization that brings together the merits of top-down and bottom-up Europeanization approaches, and has outlined possible avenues for future research. Ultimately, the chapter concludes that Europeanization research will continue to be an important field of EU research for the foreseeable future.

 QUESTIONS

1. What is Europeanization, and what are the differences between bottom-up and top-down Europeanization?

2. Why is Europeanization an important research field?

3. What is 'misfit'?

4. How can we explain why member states respond differently to Europeanization?

5. How can we explain member states' ability to shape EU policies and institutions successfully?

6. Are some states better equipped to shape EU policies than others?

7. What do the terms 'uploading' and 'downloading' mean?

8. Can states be subject to Europeanization without being members of the EU?

 GUIDE TO FURTHER READING

Cowles, M. G., Caporaso, J. A., and Risse, T. (eds) (2011) *Transforming Europe: Europeanization and Domestic Change* (Ithaca, NY: Cornell University Press)   This edited volume gives a good overview of empirical studies on top-down Europeanization in the pre-accession EU 15.

Featherstone, K. and Radaelli, C. (eds) (2003) *The Politics of Europeanisation* (Oxford: Oxford University Press)   This book gives a comprehensive overview of the various theoretical approaches and dimensions of top-down Europeanization.

Sanders, D. and Bellucci, P. (eds) (2012) *The Europeanization of National Polities? Citizenship and Support in a Post-Enlargement Union* (Oxford: Oxford University Press)   This book offers interesting insights into top-down Europeanization.

Schimmelfennig, F. and Sedelmeier, U. (eds) (2005a) *The Europeanization of Central and Eastern Europe* (Ithaca, NY: Cornell University Press)   This book provides an excellent account of top-down Europeanization in accession countries and new member states.

Thomson, R. (2011) *Resolving Controversy in the European Union: Legislative Decision-Making Before and After Enlargement* (Cambridge, Cambridge University Press)   This book provides insights into bottom-up Europeanization with and without the new member states.

 WEBLINKS

http://ec.europa.eu/eu_law/infringements/infringements_annual_report_en.htm   This website contains the European Commission's Annual Reports on the application of European law in its member states (top-down Europeanization).

http://ec.europa.eu/prelex   The European Union hosts a website on decision-making and the preparation of EU policies. This provides insights into bottom-up Europeanization.

http://eiop.or.at/erpa/   The European Research Papers Archive is an online collection of working papers relating to EU studies, in which much innovative theoretical work is showcased for the first time.

http://europeangovernance.livingreviews.org/   *Living Reviews in European Governance* is an e-journal, publishing solicited state-of-the-art articles in the field of European integration and governance research. The main focus of the articles is on European integration and European governance, and it reflects the whole spectrum of Europeanization research.

http://www.qub.ac.uk/schools/SchoolofPoliticsInternationalStudiesandPhilosophy/Research/PaperSeries/EuropeanisationPapers/   The Queen's Papers on Europeanisation contribute to the theoretical development and empirical exploration of 'Europeanization' in a way that straddles disciplines and facilitates a dialogue between contending perspectives.

PART 3
Institutions and Actors

10

The European Commission

Morten Egeberg

Chapter Contents

Reader's Guide

This chapter provides a general introduction to the European Commission. It argues that it is more productive to compare the Commission to national **executives** or to a government than to a secretariat of a traditional international organization. It begins with a summary of the Commission's functions within the European Union's policy process. It then considers the question of Commission influence and autonomy, before moving on to look at the structure, demography, and decision behaviour within the organization—that is, at the role of the President of the Commission and the Commissioners, at the Commissioners' personal staffs, and at the Commission administration. It then looks at committees and administrative networks that link the Commission to national administrations and **interest groups**, and also deals with the recent growth of EU agencies. The chapter concludes by emphasizing that the Commission is moving away from its **intergovernmentalist** roots towards becoming much more of a European(ized) institution than it was at its inception.

Introduction

To many observers, the Commission is a unique institution. It is much more than an international secretariat, but not quite a government, although it has many governmental characteristics, as we shall see. The Commission encompasses elements of both intergovernmentalism (a national dimension) and supranationalism (a European dimension). It is the opposing pull of these two elements that forms the focal point of this chapter. By exploring the national and supranational features of the Commission's organization, the chapter restates the question: what sort of institution is the European Commission?

The Commission dates back to the High Authority of the European Coal and Steel Community (ECSC). It represented a considerable institutional innovation, and it still does, if we compare the institutional arrangement of the European Union with international organizations around the world. What constitutes its most innovative aspect is that, for the first time in the history of international organizations, a separate executive body, with its own political leadership, had been set up *outside* the Ministers' Council. The concept of an Assembly, later the European Parliament (EP), was already known from the United Nations, the North Atlantic Treaty Organization (NATO), and the Council of Europe. An International Court of Justice (ICJ) had been in place in The Hague since the early twentieth century. An independent executive, on the other hand, was something quite new.

The chapter begins with a brief review of the Commission's main functions, which revolve around its role in the EU policy process. These involve the Commission in agenda-setting and, more specifically, in the drafting of legislation, in the implementation of policies (albeit at arm's length) and the management of programmes, and in the formulation and negotiation of certain aspects of the EU's external relations. Moreover, the Commission also has a role to play in mediating between the Parliament and Council, and amongst national government and non-state actors involved in European policy-making, and in presenting its own, or a European, perspective on issues and events. The second section focuses on the question of Commission influence and autonomy, viewing this matter through the lens of integration theorists (see Chapters 5, 6, 7, 8, and 9). In the sections that follow, attention turns to organizational features and their behavioural consequences, with the focus first on the Commission President and College of Commissioners, second, on the Commissioners' cabinets (their personal staffs), third, on the Commission administration, and finally on the role of committees, external administrative networks, and the more recent EU agencies. The conclusions to the chapter are that, even though some commentators on the Commission argue that it is becoming a more intergovernmental organization, the Commission is in many respects a more European institution than it ever was in the past.

The functions of the Commission

The European Commission is, like governments, composed of a political executive wing (the Commissioners and their staffs) and an administrative wing (the departments and 'services'). It has a wide range of functions within the EU system: policy initiation, the monitoring of policy implementation, the management of European programmes, an important external relations role, and other functions that involve it as a mediator amongst the twenty-seven member states, and between the EU Council and the European Parliament (EP), as well as asserting its own European identity. The Commission is clearly involved in the EU's policy process from start to finish. In much the same way as are national executives, the Commission is responsible for the initiation and formulation of policies, usually in the form of legislative, budgetary, or programme proposals. To put it bluntly, the Commission drafts the legislation that is to be passed on to the two legislative bodies, the EP and the Council. It is in this sense that, in the majority of policy areas, such as the single market (see Chapter 19) and Justice and Home Affairs (JHA—see Chapter 21), the Commission performs an important agenda-setting role. Other actors, such as the European Council (the heads of state and government), the EP, national officials, and interest groups, may also take initiatives and advance policy proposals, but it is generally up to the Commission to decide whether these ideas will be picked up and sub-. sequently passed on to the legislature in the form of a formal legislative proposal, even if in practice these sorts of policy initiative quite often originate from outside the Commission. By contrast, the Commission does not enjoy such a privileged agenda-setting role in relation to the Common Foreign and Security Policy (CFSP), although it may still be active in developing policy programmes. Arguably, however, the Lisbon

Treaty brought the High Representative for Foreign Affairs and Security Policy closer to the Commission in the sense that he or she is no longer the Secretary General of the Council, but rather a Vice-President of the Commission (see Chapter 18). However, in CFSP matters, the High Representative is still to be mandated by the Council.

Also very much in line with the functions performed by national executives, the Commission has an important role to play in the implementation of European policies. What this means in an EU context is that the Commission is responsible for the *monitoring* of implementation within the EU's member states. In much the same way as occurs in Germany, the execution or putting into effect of policy remains largely the responsibility of the constituent states. However, before implementation can occur at the national or sub-national levels, it may be necessary for secondary (or administrative) legislation to be agreed. This is because laws adopted by the Council and the EP may take the form of broad policy guidelines or frameworks rather than detailed steering instruments. Thus it is up to the Commission, in close cooperation with the member states, to detail and fill in EP/Council legislation by agreeing more specific rules, often in the form of Commission directives or regulations, in what is called 'delegated legislation'. Only in very few policy areas, such as competition policy, is the Commission responsible for implementation in the sense of handling individual cases. Finally, the Commission has an external representation role, such as when it acts as the main negotiator for the Union in trade and cooperation negotiations, and within international bodies such as the World Trade Organization (WTO) (see Chapter 16).

The Commission also performs other less tangible and more diffuse functions within the EU. Important amongst these is its role as a mediator between the EU's member states, and between the EP and the EU Council. Thus the Commission does its best, once it has produced a proposal, to ensure that agreement is reached within the Union's legislative bodies. After having agreed a policy proposal internally (see 'The President and the Commissioners' for more on the internal functioning of the Commission), the officials who drafted the proposal may attend meetings of the relevant EP committee and Plenary sessions (see Chapter 12), the relevant Council working party, the Council Committee of Permanent Representatives (Coreper), and the relevant Council ministerial meeting (see Chapter 11), in order to defend their line and, if necessary, to mediate between conflicting parties. The Commission also presents policy documents to heads of state and government at European Council (summit) meetings and at intergovernmental conferences (IGCs). The Commission not only helps in the process of achieving a final agreement, but also has its own institutional position to advance, one that may involve the presentation of a more European picture of events than emerges from national quarters.

KEY POINTS

- The European Commission has a variety of functions to perform in the EU system, including policy initiation, implementation, management, and external relations.

- The Commission is involved in almost all stages of the European policy process.

- The Commission plays a more limited role in foreign and security policy.

Commission influence

It is all very well to state that the Commission is involved at almost all stages of the EU policy process, but to what extent does the Commission have any real influence? In studies of the European Commission, there is a great deal of dispute over whether Commission initiatives make a significant difference or not to EU outcomes.

On the one hand, intergovernmentalists believe that national governments are the real driving forces in the European project. In the *liberal* intergovernmentalist version of this theoretical stance (see Chapter 6), it is accepted that the Commission has an important role to play. However, liberal intergovernmentalists claim that the authority that the Commission exercises as an agenda-setter and overseer of implementation at the national level is merely a derived and delegated authority. According to this view, the Commission may facilitate intergovernmental cooperation, but it has no real power basis of its own, because the Commission's powers are decided upon and framed by the member states within treaty negotiations.

Intergovernmentalist thinking on the role of the Commission is countered by those whose approach might be labelled 'neo-functionalist' (see Chapter 5) or 'institutionalist' (see Chapter 7). Most of these institutionalists would argue that there is ample evidence that the Commission has displayed strong leadership and, on a number of occasions, has even had a profound effect on the outcomes of 'history-shaping' and frame-setting intergovernmental conferences (IGCs), and European Council meetings. For example, Armstrong and Bulmer (1998) assign a highly significant role to the Commission (and indeed to other EU institutions) in the process that led to the creation of the single market. The single market programme is one of the important frameworks within which the Commission operates. Institutionalists argue that treaty-based frameworks, which are the main focus of intergovernmentalists, are quite often vague and ambiguous constructions that need to be translated into practical politics through day-to-day policy-making. And when it comes to this sort of crucial follow-up work, the Commission is one of the key actors.

Another related scholarly dispute questions the extent to which the Commission is able to affect significantly decisions even within its own organizational boundaries. Not surprisingly perhaps, to many intergovernmentalists, the Commission appears very much as an arena permeated by national interests. From this perspective, Commissioners, their personal staffs ('cabinets'), as well as officials in the Commission's departments (services), are primarily pursuing the interests of their respective nation states. By contrast, institutionalists tend to emphasize that the Commission, like other institutions, furnishes individual actors with particular interests and beliefs, and that it may even be able to resocialize participants so that they gradually come to assume supranational identities.

KEY POINTS

- Intergovernmentalists see the Commission as relatively insignificant.

- Neo-functionalists and institutionalists view the Commission as having an independent impact on policy outcomes.

- Intergovernmentalists and institutionalists hold different views on the extent to which the Commission is permeated by national interests.

The President and the Commissioners

The European Commission has both a political and an administrative dimension. While there is no doubt that the actions of the administrative branch also have political significance, for example in providing expertise and capacity for policy development, there is still a useful distinction to be made between the Commission's political leaders—the College of Commissioners—and the officials who sit in the Commission's departments and services.

The 'College' consists of twenty-seven Commissioners, including the President of the Commission. Within the Commission's internal decision-making process, contentious issues that have not been resolved at the lower echelons of the Commission are lifted to this formally political level in the last instance. The College strives to achieve consensus through arguing and bargaining. If this does not result in a consensus, voting may take place, although this seems to be relatively rare. When it does happen, all Commissioners, including the President, carry the same weight—one vote each—and an absolute majority is necessary for a final decision to be reached. Since the College operates on the basis of the principle of collegiality—in other words, all Commissioners are collectively responsible for all decisions taken—it would be reasonable to assume that a relatively large proportion of all controversial decisions is referred to the College. However, as a result of the present size of the College, more issues seem to be dealt with through direct interaction between the President and the particularly affected Commissioner(s). Thus one asks whether 'presidentialization' is taking place, meaning that the President changes from being a *primus inter pares* ('first among equals') to becoming a *primus super pares* ('first above equals') (Kurpas et al., 2008). It is now accepted that the work of the College is subject to the President's political leadership. And, like a national prime minister, the President also has at his (or her) disposal a permanent secretariat, the Secretariat-General (or General Secretariat, as it is sometimes called), which has been strengthened over the last few years.

Commissioners have policy responsibilities (portfolios), which involve oversight of one or more Commission department. These departments are known as Directorates-General (DGs) (see Box 10.3 under 'The Commission administration'). Because DGs tend to be organized sectorally (for example, DG Agriculture)

Although much media focus during autumn 2011 was on the euro crisis and thus on the Economic and Monetary Affairs Commissioner as well as the Commission President, this does not mean that other Commission activities were in general put on ice. During two critical weeks (from 24 November to 7 December 2011), the weekly *European Voice* reported, inter alia, that the Home Affairs Commissioner called on members of the European Parliament (MEPs) to embrace an EU–US deal on passenger data, that the Transport Commissioner asked member states to speed up on implementing 'single European sky'

legislation, that the Commissioner for Climate Action was trying to push others in the EU direction at the climate summit in Durban, that the Research and Science Commissioner unveiled a €80 billion research programme, that the Internal Market Commissioner expected a deal on the single EU patent, that the Home Affairs Commissioner launched a new border-control proposal, and that the Commissioner for Health wanted the Commission to lead EU responses to health crises. All of these 'business as usual' activities illustrate very well the complex and compound nature of the Commission organization.

or functionally (for example, DG Budget), one might expect this to trigger conflicts amongst Commissioners more often along sectoral or functional lines than along territorial (national) lines (see Box 10.1).

Although Commissioners are supposed not to take instruction from outside the Commission and do not represent national governments in any formal sense, they are nevertheless nominated by them. Previously, larger countries had two Commissioners each, while the other member states had to make do with one each. From 2004 onwards, all governments nominate only one Commissioner each. A major concern has been to avoid the College becoming too large, since this could threaten its decision-making capacity. With too many Commissioners, one also faces difficulties finding meaningful portfolios of a reasonable size. For example, in 2007, the new Commissioner from Romania became Commissioner for multilingualism—not a particularly broad or meaningful policy responsibility. Before appointing Commissioners, however, the national governments must first agree on a candidate for the Commission presidency. This is necessary if the new President is to be given an opportunity to influence the composition of the College. Over time, the President's role in selecting his (or her) colleagues has grown. In the treaty revisions agreed at Amsterdam in 1997, the President is able, for the first time, to reject candidates nominated by member governments. The President also has the final say in how portfolios are allocated and even has the right to reshuffle the team during the Commission's five-year term of office by redistributing dossiers or portfolios.

National governments have increasingly seen their role in the make-up of the College of Commissioners diminish. By contrast, the European Parliament has gradually gained more of a stake in the process in a number of different ways, indicating that the EU

has taken some steps in the direction of a parliamentary system. First, from the very start, the EP has been able to dismiss the entire College by taking a vote of no confidence. Second, the term of office of the Commissioners has been extended from four to five years, so as to bring it into close alignment with the term of the EP. This means that the appointment of a new College takes place after the EP elections, to allow MEPs to have a say on the matter. Not only is the EP consulted on the choice of President, but it also has the right to approve their appointment. In fact, the outcome of the 2004 European elections was probably decisive for the choice of a candidate close to the European Peoples' Party (EPP), since this party formed the largest group in the EP. Moreover, the EPP had a say as regards the person nominated as Commission President. José-Manuel Barroso, former prime minister of Portugal, had been a vice-president of the EPP and was this party's candidate. Steps have also been taken to render the Commission more directly accountable to the Parliament, as illustrated by the fact that the EP committees now scrutinize nominated Commissioners and the political programme of the Commission (see Box 10.2).

What kind of College does this inspire? First, it means that the political leadership of the Commission always has a fixed mix of nationals. Second, it tends to bring people into the College who have the same political party background as the national government nominating them. Over time, nominations to Commission posts have included people with impressive political experience and it is now quite usual to see prominent national ministers in the list of nominees. Such a recruitment pattern obviously furnishes the College with political capital, although probably not so much in a strict party-political sense. A coherent party platform for the College is almost unthinkable under the current appointment

> **BOX 10.2** Growing party-politicization of the College of Commissioners?
>
> The weekly Brussels newspaper *European Voice* (27 January 2005: 6) reported that socialist members of the European Parliament were challenging the Commission's five-year work plan over what they saw as a lack of concern for social rights and the environment. The Commission President had told the Parliament that his team's main objective was to stimulate economic growth. Paul Nyrup Rasmussen, President of the European
>
> Socialist Party, criticized the Commission's plan for being old-fashioned. But Hans-Gert Pöttering, leader of the centre-right European Peoples' Party, described the Commission's programme as realistic and ambitious: 'Anyone who neglects the nurturing of European competitiveness will be responsible for the fact that in the future we will have no European social model to preserve.'

procedure; instead, Commissioners' nationality is likely to be a more crucial background factor to take into account in explaining their conduct (Wonka, 2008). This is so since national governments, lobbyists, and the like tend to contact 'their' Commissioner as a first port of call when they want to obtain information or have a say at the very highest level of the Commission. And Commissioners may also become involved in social networks with their compatriots—for example, in gatherings at their respective **permanent representations** (their national embassies to the EU) in Brussels.

It should not be concluded from this, however, that Commissioners act primarily as agents of the national government that nominated them. In fact, a Commissioner's portfolio, or DG affiliation, is also quite important in order to explain his or her behaviour with regard to a particular decision. Like national ministers, Commissioners see multiple and often conflicting role expectations imposed upon them: at one and the same time, they are supposed to feel some allegiance, albeit informal, to the geographical area from which they originate, to champion Commission interests, to advance their own portfolio, and to assume a party-political role (Egeberg, 2006a). Balancing these diverse pressures is not always an easy task.

> **KEY POINTS**
>
> • The European Commission is composed of a political leadership in the form of the College of Commissioners.
>
> • Commissioners are nominated by national governments, but they are expected to act independently and seem to do so to a considerable extent.
>
> • The Commission President has gained more powers since the 1980s, so that the current President is no longer simply 'first among equals'.

Commissioners' cabinets

Like many national ministers in Europe, Commissioners have their own political secretariat or private office. The Commissioner's *cabinet* (note that the French pronunciation is sometimes used), as it is called, is organizationally separate from the administration of the Commission. It is composed of people trusted by the Commissioner in question, who may be hired and fired at the Commissioner's discretion. Consequently, their tenure can last only as long as the Commissioner's. A cabinet consists of about six or seven advisers, plus a number of clerical staff. Their role is to help to push Commissioners' ideas down to the departments (Directorates-General), on the one hand, and, on the other, to edit and filter policy proposals coming up from the DGs before they are referred to the Commissioner and the College. As an integral part of this 'editorial work', a Commissioner's cabinet frequently interacts with other cabinets in order to register disagreements and to pre-empt objections that might be raised at the level of the College. Because of the principle of collegiality, in essence a form of mutual responsibility, each of the twenty-seven cabinets covers all Commission portfolios. Thus a Commissioner's cabinet is vital as a source of information about issues beyond his or her own remit. Ahead of the weekly meeting of the College, the *chefs de cabinet* (cabinet heads) convene to ensure that the Commission acts as coherently and cohesively as possible. These inter-cabinet gatherings are chaired by the Secretary-General, the administration's top official.

In addition to the role played by cabinets in coordinating, both vertically and horizontally, the flow of information within the Commission, they also have important functions at the interface between the Commission and the outside world. Cabinets are crucial points of access for governments, lobbyists, and other actors and institutions keen to influence the

Commission (see Chapter 14). Their role is to assist Commissioners in this respect, with cabinet members responsible, amongst other things, for writing Commissioners' speeches, standing in for them, and representing them at conferences and meetings. Cabinets have also acted as a kind of liaison office between the Commissioners and 'their' respective governments, particularly via 'their' permanent representations. Thus they are able to inform the national governments about forthcoming Commission proposals that might become politically interesting from a national point of view, whilst at the same time acting as a conduit for information about national positions on policy initiatives under consideration in the Commission.

Cabinets have often been portrayed as national enclaves. This description was appropriate given that, in the past, the nationality of cabinet personnel almost directly reflected the nationality of the lead Commissioner. Since the Prodi Commission, however, at least three different nationalities have to be represented in each cabinet and the head or the deputy head of the cabinet should be of a different nationality from that of the Commissioner. In 2004, at the start of the Barroso Commission, the formal requirements were clearly overfulfilled: 96 per cent of the cabinets contained more nationalities than formally prescribed and 57 per cent of the personnel were non-compatriots of their respective Commissioners (Egeberg and Heskestad, 2010). Moreover, at least half of cabinet members should be recruited from within the Commission services. This may also have interesting implications for the role of nationality in the cabinets since those coming from the Commission administration may have weaker ties to any particular national constituency (see 'The Commission administration'). Those who have come to the cabinets from outside the Commission have, for the most part, served in national administrations, but some have also come from other kinds of organizations, such as from the political party to which the Commissioner belongs.

Before the Prodi Commission's reforms of the cabinet system in 1999, one would probably have concluded that the structure, as well as the demography, of these bodies would tend to foster kinds of intergovernmental patterns of behaviour within the Commission. However, the structure and demography of the cabinets have changed. As a consequence of these reforms, it would seem very likely that the role of cabinets as the interface between national governments and the Commission will be profoundly redefined.

The Commission administration

As is the case in national executives, the political leadership of the Commission is served by an administrative staff. Key components of the Commission's administration are the Directorates-General, which are roughly equivalent to the administrative components of national government departments and which now cover almost all possible policy fields (see Box 10.3). The basic principles of organizational specialization are also quite similar to those of national ministries. While DG Agriculture and DG Justice reflect a sectorally structured Commission, DG Budget and DG Human Resources (personnel and administration) are organized around the functions that they perform. Precisely because they are functionally oriented, DG Budget and DG Human Resources are also said to be the Commission's horizontal services—that is, the administrative units that are assigned coordination tasks, or which deal with issues cutting across sectoral departments. The Secretariat-General is the most important of these horizontal services. As the permanent office of the Commission President, it plays an important role in shaping a coherent policy profile for the Commission as a whole, and also has a crucial part to play in managing relationships between the Commission and other key institutions inside and outside the Union. The role of Secretary-General, the head of the secretariat, very much parallels that of a permanent secretary within national prime ministers' offices, so that he or she may be identified as the first among equals of the administrative heads. Examples of other horizontal services are the European Statistical Office (Eurostat) and the Legal Service. The Legal Service provides much of the Commission's legal expertise, although lawyers are also found in large numbers in other parts of the Commission. Thus the Legal Service primarily serves as an expert body that

---

BOX 10.3   Commission departments/Directorates-General (DGs)

Agriculture and Rural Development (AGRI)	Joint Research Centre (JRC)
Budget (BUDG)	Justice (JUST)
Climate Action (CLIMA)	Maritime Affairs and Fisheries (MARE)
Communication (COMM)	Mobility and Transport (MOVE)
Competition (COMP)	Regional Policy (REGIO)
Economic and Financial Affairs (ECFIN)	Research and Innovation ((RTD)
Education and Culture (EAC)	Secretariat General (SG)
Employment, Social Affairs and Inclusion (EMPL)	Taxation and Customs Union (TAXUD)
Energy (ENER)	Trade (TRADE)
Enlargement (ELARG)	Translation (DGT)
Enterprise and Industry (ENTR)	**Services**
Environment (ENV)	Bureau of European Policy Advisers (BEPA)
EuropeAid Development and Cooperation (DEVCO)	Central Library
Eurostat (ESTAT)	European Anti-Fraud Office (OLAF)
Foreign Policy Instruments Service (in EEAS)	European Commission Data Protection Officer
Health and Consumers (SANCO)	Historical archives
Home Affairs (HOME)	Infrastructures and Logistics—Brussels (OIB)
Humanitarian Aid (ECHO)	Infrastructures and Logistics—Luxembourg (OIL)
Human Resources and Security (HR)	Internal Audit Service (IAS)
Informatics (DIGIT)	Legal Service (SJ)
Information Society and Media (INFSO)	Office for Administration and Payment of Individual Entitlements (PMO)
Internal Market and Services (MARKT)	
Interpretation (SCIC)	Publications Office (OP)

---

other departments consult. It makes sure that legislative proposals drafted within the DGs comply with the technical and linguistic standards that are deemed appropriate for EU legislation, thereby pre-empting future challenges to European legislation in the European or domestic courts (see Chapter 13).

Headed by a Director-General, DGs usually consist of several directorates, with each of these headed by a director. Each directorate is further split into units. Obviously, some tasks and new policy initiatives do not fit well into this strictly specialized hierarchical structure. To meet such needs, special task forces or interdepartmental working groups are created. Sometimes, these temporary or ad hoc bodies become institutionalized and end up as new DGs or departments. The DGs usually have a total permanent and full-time staff of about 300–700 each, but their size varies considerably. The

Commission employs approximately 24,000 officials. In addition, there are about 6,000 people on temporary contracts. The most prestigious posts belong to the so-called 'AD' category, which consists of around 12,500 officials mainly engaged in policy-making and policy management. When the scholarly literature deals with 'Commission officials', it is referring to staff in this category (rather than those performing executive, clerical, and manual tasks).

In addition to staff paid by the Commission, the services also include approximately 1,000 AD-category officials seconded from member governments. These seconded officials, or 'detached national experts', have their salaries paid by their national employer. In the early days of the High Authority of the European Coal and Steel Community (ECSC), the forerunner of the Commission (see Chapter 2), most officials were appointed on temporary contracts or seconded from the member states. Over time, this has changed. As we have seen, an overwhelming majority of the posts are now permanent, while temporary jobs might be used for hiring personnel who might provide additional expertise on particular policy issues.

Recruitment of new AD-category candidates for a career in the Commission administration is based largely on the meritocratic principle. What this means is that appointments should be made based on what a person has achieved in his or her educational and professional career so far, rather than on any other criteria, such as a candidate's social or geographical background, or the extent to which he or she has 'good contacts'. This principle is inherently linked to an understanding of what a modern and well-functioning bureaucracy should look like if it is to avoid nepotism, favouritism, and corruption. Thus, in accordance with this principle, those who want to embark on a Commission career are normally required to hold a university degree. Subsequently, they have to pass a competitive exam called the *concours*. The *concours* is modelled on the French standard entry route into the higher civil service, which means in practice that all applicants have to pass written, as well as oral, tests. These tests are arranged in the member states on a regular basis and may involve thousands of applicants. A loose quota system (in the form of 'targets') regulates more or less the intake of new recruits on a geographical basis. As a result, those hired should be drawn proportionately from all member states, so that larger countries provide more candidates than smaller ones. In a way, this sort of quota arrangement is at odds with the meritocratic principle, but the huge number of qualified applicants should nevertheless provide for a highly professional staff. This system does ensure that the Commission—or rather, the AD category—is not overpopulated by staff from only a few of the EU's member states.

Once in post, seniority matters for promotion at the lower levels of the AD category. In addition to an official's immediate superior, the staff unions also play a significant role in decisions about promotion at this level. For appointments as head of unit and above, achievements in earlier positions matter more than seniority as a criterion for promotion. The role of staff unions is also considerably reduced at these senior levels. Instead, nationality has traditionally been a crucial factor, and increasingly so the more senior the level of the appointment. Obviously, the narrower the pyramid, the more complicated it has become to manage the national quota system in a fair manner, while at the same time paying heed to merit as the basic norm for promotion. In these cases, national governments are often keen to look after 'their share' of jobs, and it has conventionally been up to Commissioners and their cabinets to intervene if the 'balance' is deemed to be threatened. In addition to concerns about proportionality, a top official's immediate subordinate and superior should be of a different nationality. The argument goes that a multinational chain of command will prevent policy proposals from reflecting narrow national concerns.

It would seem that, while the administration should continue to maintain a broad geographical balance, nationality is, subsequent to Prodi Commission reforms, no longer allowed to be the determining factor in appointing a new person to a particular post. The aim was clearly to abolish the convention of attaching national flags to senior positions. New and strict procedures seem in fact to have effectively encapsulated processes in which top officials are appointed: senior Commission officials themselves seem to orchestrate such processes and Commissioners, who take the final decision, usually adhere to the shortlist of candidates presented to them (Fusacchia, 2009). New member states may claim a reasonable share of posts at all levels of the hierarchy and this has meant that highly experienced national officials have had to be brought into the senior ranks of the Commission administration. However, these officials also have to compete for vacant jobs and are subject to the same strict appointment procedures (see Box 10.4).

In accounting for the behaviour of Commission officials, how important is their national background? Given the enduring interest that national governments have shown towards recruitment and appointments, we are led to think that nationality matters very much indeed. However, the attention devoted to the issue does not necessarily correspond to the impact that national origins might have. There is little doubt that officials bring to the Commission administrative styles and *general attitudes* that can be linked to their country of origin. For example, officials stemming from federal or decentralized states such as Germany or Belgium seem to view the prospect of a federal Europe more favourably than do those from unitary states, probably because the former are already more familiar with that kind of system (Hooghe, 2001; Kassim et al., 2012). A common language and nationality facilitate interaction, so that Commission officials become points of access for

The weekly newspaper *European Voice* (12 October 2006: 2) reported that the Commissioner for Enterprise, Gunther Verheugen, when launching a document that set out ways in which to reduce the burden of red tape on EU businesses, had criticized top officials in the Commission for obstructing his 'better regulation' proposal. He suggested that Commissioners should have more power to pick their Directors-General to ensure that they do their political masters' bidding. Verheugen's suggestions were rejected by Personnel and Administration Commissioner Siim Kallas, who argued that the whole point of Commission staff reforms had been to 'oppose political appointments based on criteria other than merit'. But, according to *European Voice*, 'Verheugen's comments echoed recent criticism of the Commission by German Chancellor Angela Merkel who said in a speech in Berlin that Commissioners' lack of control over their directors-general was "unthinkable" for a German minister'.

those keen to know what is going on in the Commission. Moreover, officials of the same nationality often socialize together in Brussels and this may be enough to sustain a sense of national belonging. However, there is virtually no evidence of a clear link between officials' nationality, on the one hand, and their *decision behaviour* in the Commission, on the other hand, because organizational roles and decision-making procedures tend to diminish this sort of variation in conduct. In fact, the attachment of officials to their DGs seems far more important than their national background as an explanation for the preferences and choices that they make in their daily work (Suvarierol, 2008; Trondal et al., 2008; Kassim et al., 2012).

Certain organizational characteristics suggest that the behaviour of Commission officials may be susceptible to national interests and influence (cf. intergovernmentalism). These include the system of seconded national experts and, in the past, the national quotas. Strict quotas might have served to legitimate national identities and consequently national policy orientations, while seconded personnel may have an incentive to pursue not only the interests of their respective DGs, but also the interests of their employer back home—usually their national government. However, there are also a number of organizational features that suggest that the institutionalist perspective is more accurate. Examples include the facts that specialization in the Commission occurs according to sector or function rather than geography, that there is a clear majority of permanent posts, that recruitment is basically on merit, that the Commission comprises multinational units and chains of command, and that there are lifelong career patterns, which facilitate the resocialization of personnel. Over time, these institutional factors have gained in importance: the proportion of officials on temporary contracts or secondments has declined; and recruitment on merit and internal promotion to senior levels in the Commission has gained ever increasing support, particularly from the European courts, the staff unions, and indeed the College of Commissioners.

KEY POINTS

- The Commission's administration comprises sectoral and functional (horizontal) departments, called Directorates-General (DGs).

- Officials' actual decision behaviour is probably best explained by their DG affiliation.

- Officials within the administration are recruited on a merit basis, with a view to an appropriate geographical balance among member countries.

Committees, networks, and agencies

In order to assist the Commission in its preparatory work on new legislation and in other forms of policy-making, approximately 1,200 expert committees have been established. The practical work on a policy initiative often starts in such a committee, which is usually composed of national officials and other experts. Committees of this sort are supposed to provide additional expertise on a particular subject and thus complement the work of the Commission's permanent staff. They may also serve as an arena for floating policy ideas and anticipating future reactions to them. Involving interest organizations that might ultimately be affected by a new proposal might make political support and legitimacy more likely. The Commission particularly welcomes European-level interest groups (see Chapter 14). In policy areas in which these sorts of interest organization have been lacking, the Commission has actively tried to encourage their formation. This is understandable, since it is far more convenient to communicate with one group representing a particular interest than with twenty-seven or more, all representing different national, sectional interests. Encouraging the establishment of transnational interest groups may serve other purposes as well, though. Like the Commission itself, interest-group systems structure themselves primarily along functional and sectoral lines, rather than territorially. Thus the Commission may see transnational interest groups as future partners in an evolving EU polity.

Commission officials chair expert committees and advisory groups, calling officials from member governments to participate. The Commission covers their travel expenses, and they are expected to behave like independent experts and not as government representatives. In general, national officials participating in Commission committees assign considerably less weight to their role as government representative than those attending Council committee meetings (Egeberg et al., 2003).

When committee work comes to an end, the policy proposal is processed in the administrative and political ranks of the Commission before it is submitted to the Council and the European Parliament for final decision. As mentioned earlier, some directives may need to be supplemented by rules of a more technical nature. This kind of legislative work is delegated to the Commission in the same way as national legislatures may let governments hammer out specific regulations. In order to monitor the Commission's legislative activity, however, the Council has set up about 250 so-called 'comitology committees' (also sometimes known as 'implementation committees'). The membership of these committees are formal representatives of national governments, although it is the Commission that calls and chairs the meetings, sets the agenda, submits the proposals requiring discussion, and writes the protocols. Some comitology committees are entitled only to advise the Commission; others have competence to overrule the Commission's proposals under certain conditions. In practice, however, the Commission usually gets its own way, although this is not to

say that national representatives have no influence. It is, of course, also quite possible that the Commission deliberately chooses proposals that national governments are likely to endorse (see Christiansen and Larsson, 2007).

When it comes to the implementation of EU policies at the national level, the Commission has to rely on member-state administrations, since the Commission does not itself possess agencies at this level. This may result in considerable variation in administrative practices across countries. However, there are signs that national regulatory authorities that often work at arm's length from ministries become kind of 'partners' of the Commission in practical implementation, as well as in policy preparation, processes. As a result of these authorities' 'semi-detached' status, they seem to be in a position in which they might be able to serve two masters simultaneously: both the national ministry *and* the Commission. Within a range of policy sectors (such as competition, telecommunications, environment, or food safety), we observe transnational networks of national agencies in which the Commission constitutes the hub (Egeberg, 2006b). Do we then see a multilevel genuine *Union* administration emerging?

Such Commission-led networks of national agencies within various policy fields may contribute to more harmonized application of EU law across member countries. One might interpret the advent of EU agencies from the 1990s on as one further step in the direction of ensuring more uniform practising of EU policies. There are now about forty such administrative bodies, with a staff of about 5,000 in total spread around the EU. Although all of them are located outside Brussels, they are EU-level agencies, meaning that their activities relate to all member states. While member states might agree in general that more even application of EU legislation across countries could be desirable, several have nevertheless been hesitant to transfer more power to the Commission in this respect. A possible compromise was to establish EU-level executive bodies outside the Commission—bodies that were planned to be under considerable member-state control and which were, at the outset, assigned mainly 'soft regulatory power'. The first constraint (member-state control) meant that such agencies became formally subordinated to management boards numerically dominated by government representatives. The second constraint ('soft power') meant that agencies should primarily deal with, for example, information on 'best (implementation) practice', the facilitation of transnational agency networks, and the like. In practice, however, governments' control over EU agencies seems more modest and the Commission constitutes a particularly pivotal partner of EU agencies. EU agencies tend to relate to their respective Commission DGs (that is, within the same issue area) in much the same way as national agencies connect to their 'parent ministries'. Moreover, over time, EU agencies have taken on fewer soft instruments, such as issuing guidelines for EU-law application at the national level and even involvement in individual decisions handled by national agencies. Such 'quasi-regulatory' tasks have been complemented by assigning some agencies the right to make authoritative decisions in individual cases, such as the European Aviation Safety Agency (EASA). In addition to the Commission, national agencies make up the closest interlocutors in the

---

KEY POINTS

- Expert committees have an important role to play in the preparatory work of the Commission.

- Comitology committees monitor the Commission when it is issuing delegated legislation.

- National officials behave less 'intergovernmentally' in Commission committees than in Council committees and comitology.

- Issue-specific networks are emerging among the Commission, EU agencies, and semi-detached national agencies.

---

daily life of EU agencies, indicating how EU agencies might become building blocks in a multilevel Union administration, partly bypassing national ministries (Busuioc et al., 2012).

Conclusion

The Commission has often been portrayed as a hybrid and unique organization because of its mix of political and administrative functions. This is understandable if the Commission is compared with the secretariat of a traditional international organization, since such secretariats are not expected to have a political will of their own. However, the Commission is probably better compared to a national executive. Like governments, the Commission is headed by executive politicians who are responsible for various administrative services. In a similar way to national executives, the Commission is authorized to initiate and formulate policy proposals, and to monitor the implementation of policies. The Commission has not, however, achieved full control of all executive tasks at the EU level, sharing its executive function in foreign relations with the European External Action Service (EEAS).

This chapter has focused on how the various parts of the Commission are organized and staffed, and how these structural and demographic features might be related to the way in which decision-makers

actually behave. Are these features mainly conducive to intergovernmental ways of behaving, or do they instead evoke patterns of decision-making that are more in line with what institutionalists would predict? At all levels—the College, the cabinets, the administration, and the committees—there are components that may be more in line with intergovernmental decision processes than with other kinds of processes. However, those organizational components that work in the opposite direction are becoming more and more important. These components tend to focus attention along sectoral, functional, partisan, or institutional cleavages—that is, on lines of conflict and cooperation that cut *across* national boundaries, and which evoke non-national feelings of belonging among Commissioners and their officials. If these trends persist, the Commission is set to become much more of a genuine European institution than it has been in the past, although one that will inevitably continue to exhibit a mix (albeit a different mix) of both intergovernmental and supranational characteristics.

QUESTIONS

1. To what extent can the Commission be compared to national governments?

2. How influential is the Commission within the EU policy process?

3. How important is the national background of Commissioners in shaping their preferences and decisions?

4. What is the role of the Commissioners' cabinets?

5. How is the Commission administration organized and what are the possible implications for patterns of conflict within the Commission?

6. How might nationality affect decision-making within the administration?

7. What is 'comitology'?

8. Which roles do national officials evoke in EU committees?

GUIDE TO FURTHER READING

Cini, M. (2007) *From Integration to Integrity: Administrative Ethics and Reform in the European Commission* (Manchester: Manchester University Press)   This book is the first to examine how the European Commission has addressed concerns about its ethical standards since 1999.

Egeberg, M. (ed.) (2006b) *Multilevel Union Administration: The Transformation of Executive Politics in Europe* (Basingstoke: Palgrave)   This book deals with decision processes within the Commission, as well as between the Commission and other institutions, in particular national administrations, from an organization theory perspective.

Kassim, H., Peterson, J., Bauer, M. W., Connolly, S. J., Dehousse, R., Hooghe, L., and Thompson, A. (2012) *The European Commission of the Twenty-First Century* (Oxford: Oxford University Press)   This book, based on extensive survey data, analyses Commission officials' backgrounds, careers, and attitudes.

Spence, D. and Edwards, G. (eds) (2006) *The European Commission* (London: John Harper Publishing)   This anthology is particularly detailed and informative on the structure and personnel of the Commission.

Trondal, J. (2010) *An Emergent European Executive Order* (Oxford: Oxford University Press)   This book analyses the EU executive as a compound order.

WEBLINKS

http://ec.europa.eu   The official website of the European Commission features links to its work programme, documents, calendar, the Commissioners, and the administration.

http://www.cec.org.uk   The website of the European Commission representation in the UK.

http://www.eurunion.org   The website of the EU delegation based in the US.

II

The Council of the European Union and the European Council

Jeffrey Lewis

Chapter Contents

Reader's Guide

This chapter examines the heart of decision-making in the European Union, the Council of the European Union (or EU Council) and the **European Council**. The Council is the part of the EU that unabashedly represents national interests in the **European integration** process. Because of this, the Council is a site of intense negotiation, compromise-building, and at times acrimonious disagreement amongst the member states. The Council is not a single body, however, but more a composite of national officials working at different levels of specialization and political seniority—think of it as a system of decision-making. From the heads of state and government, to the ministers, and all the way down the ladder to the expert-level *fonctionnaires* (officials), the Council system embeds governments of the EU into a complex collective decision-making process that deeply penetrates into the national capitals and domestic politics of the member states. In authority, scope, and procedural methods the Council system represents the most advanced, intensive forum of international **cooperation** between sovereign nation states in the modern world. The system also continues to evolve, as exemplified in the **Lisbon Treaty**'s designation of the European Council as a separate institution of the EU with its own President. Overall, this chapter spotlights the organization of the EU Council and European Council, as well as key components that help the system to function, including the **Committee of Permanent Representatives (Coreper)**, the working groups, and the General Secretariat.

Introduction

The focus of this chapter is the Council of the European Union, also known as the EU Council and the antiquated (but still preferred by some) 'Council of Ministers'. The chapter also includes detail on the European Council's role in establishing the Union's 'general political directions and priorities' (Article 15 TEU). The Lisbon Treaty makes the European Council a free-standing EU institution in its own right (Article 13(1) TEU), although substantively, as before, the heads of state and government meetings (or 'summits') serve as an agenda-setting forum for the Council system as a whole. Taken together, the Council system is the epicentre of EU decision-making and plays a pivotal role in making Union policy. While ostensibly representing the interests of the EU's twenty-seven member states, the EU Council and European Council are also European institutions and not merely intergovernmental (de Schoutheete, 2011: 3).

The remainder of the chapter is organized as follows. The next section examines the central role of the EU Council, including the ministerial 'pecking order' amongst different Council formations and the scale of national officials geared to the Council's day-to-day work. This is followed by a section on the layers of the Council system, including European Council summits, the ministers' Council meetings, the work of the Committee of Permanent Representatives (Coreper), involving senior national civil servants, and the technical-minded working groups. This section also considers the increasingly important role of the Council's own officials in the General Secretariat of the Council (GSC). Next, the chapter turns attention to how the Council system works, including voting patterns, the rotating presidency, the 'closed door' nature of deliberations, and current challenges such as the wider implications of enlargement and enhanced cooperation. This is followed by sections on, first, the executive-like role of the European Council, and second, the Union's new foreign policy chief and bureaucracy for external diplomacy. A final concluding section will tie the main themes together, and argue that the Council system is best seen as a hybrid of intergovernmental and supranational elements.

The Council of the European Union: the heart of EU decision-making

The Council of the European Union is the institutional heart of decision-making in the EU. The central legislative function is that all EU proposals (originating from the Commission) must be approved by the Council before becoming EU law. Developments such as the European Parliament's right to more equal decision-making power, known as the ordinary legislative procedure (OLP) (formerly co-decision), has not changed the basic fact that the Council remains at the core of the EU's legislative process.

Legally speaking, there is only one Council, but this is misleading since, in reality, there are numerous formations organized by policy specialization (see Box 11.1). Each Council formation manages a specialized policy sector and the participants authorized to adopt legislative acts are the national ministers from each of the member states who hold domestic responsibility for that sector. Hence the twenty-seven EU ministers of agriculture preside over the Agricultural and Fisheries Council (AGFISH), the environmental ministers over the Environment Council, and so on.

Historically, the 'senior' Council actors with general institutional responsibilities and overall policy coordination were the foreign affairs ministers, who met as the General Affairs Council (GAC). However, general affairs and foreign affairs have become increasingly differentiated, with the latter Council now chaired by the High Representative for Foreign Affairs and Security Policy (see Box 11.2 and 'The High Representative of the Union for Foreign Affairs and Security Policy'). Today, the EU's GAC mirrors the

---

BOX 11.1 EU Council formations

General Affairs

Foreign Affairs

Economic and Financial Affairs (ECOFIN)

Justice and Home Affairs (JHA)

Employment, Social Policy, Health and Consumer Affairs (EPSCO)

Competitiveness (including Internal Market, Industry, and Research)

Transport, Telecommunications, and Energy

Agriculture and Fisheries (AGFISH)

Environment

Education, Youth, Culture

Source: Annex I, Council Decision of 1 December 2009 adopting the Council's Rules of Procedure, OJ L 325/35, 11.12.2009.

domestic-level bureaucratic balance of power, which has generally seen a relative decline in the authority of foreign affairs ministries over EU policy. This is visible in the increasingly heterogeneous mix of job titles among participants in the GAC, which include foreign ministers as well as 'European affairs' ministers, who are often more closely attached to the office of the head of state or government. A further symbol of the decline in foreign ministries' seniority is the pattern that EU foreign ministers are no longer regularly invited to participate in the meetings of the European Council.

Since the dawn of the euro and, some argue, earlier, the finance and economics ministers have increased in stature through their work on the Economic and Financial Affairs Council, otherwise known as ECOFIN. A subset of ECOFIN, made up of those member states that subscribe to the euro, meets additionally in a Council formation known as the Eurogroup, which internally selects its own permanent chair (see Chapter 27). The newest Council additions include the interior/home affairs ministers, who meet in the Justice and Home Affairs (JHA) Council, and the defence ministers, who meet in a 'jumbo' Council format with the foreign ministers to discuss the Common Security and Defence Policy (CSDP).

The policy segmentation of the Council's work into distinct, compartmentalized formations is a hallmark of how the EU works. Each formation has its own pace and legislative agenda, with some meeting monthly (such as the GAC) and some barely twice per year (such as Education, Youth, Culture). Each Council also has its own organizational culture, often including a set of informal (unwritten) rules and distinctive working habits. For example, some, such as Foreign Affairs, rely on highly restricted lunchtime sessions to discuss issues of particular importance or sensitivity. The GAC has institutionalized the right to meet on the day before European Council summits to conduct final preparatory negotiations and to adopt a definitive agenda for the heads of state and government (see Box 11.2). Another informal rule is for the eurozone finance ministers to avoid substantive macroeconomic policy discussions in the Eurogroup meetings that affect non-eurozone EU members without also holding those discussions in the ECOFIN Council. This courtesy has been interpreted by observers as a norm that safeguards against 'us versus them' attitudes between the euro and non-euro members. Thus 'the Council' is a multifaceted decision-making system operating across a wide range of policy domains, with negotiations taking place concurrently. In one guise or

---

BOX 11.2 Renovating the General Affairs Council

Following widespread agreement in the latter half of the 1990s that the Council's premier ministerial body—the General Affairs Council (GAC)—was impossibly over-tasked and increasingly dysfunctional, the European Council decided at the 2002 Seville meeting to split the GAC's work into two tracks:

• General Affairs; and

• Foreign Affairs.

The 'new' General Affairs portion is tasked to 'ensure consistency in the work of the different Council configurations'. This includes the preparatory and follow-up work for European Council meetings. In addition, 'it shall be responsible for overall coordination of policies, institutional and administrative questions, horizontal dossiers which affect several of the European Union's policies, such as the multiannual financial framework and enlargement, and any dossier entrusted to it by the European Council' (Article 2(2), Rules of Procedure).

The Foreign Policy portion is assigned 'the whole of the European Union's external action, namely common foreign and

security policy, common security and defence policy, common commercial policy, development cooperation and humanitarian aid' (Article 2(5), Rules of Procedure).

Technically, the two strands operate independently, with their own meetings and agendas, but in practice General Affairs and Foreign Affairs tend to meet on consecutive days or even back-to-back, with the foreign affairs ministers often attending both. The big difference is who chairs each grouping: the new foreign policy chief is the 'permanent' chair of the Foreign Affairs portion, while the member state holding the rotating presidency continues to chair the General Affairs portion (see also 'The role of the rotating presidency'). Whether this new arrangement imparts greater coherence to the work of the foreign ministers and renews the leadership role of 'General Affairs' is an open question.

Sources: Presidency Conclusions, Seville European Council, 21–22 June 2002; Council Decision of 1 December 2009 adopting the Council's Rules of Procedure, OJ L 325/35, 11.12.2009; Consolidated Versions of the Treaty on European Union(TEU) and the Treaty on the Functioning of the European Union (TFEU), OJ C 83/53, 30.3.2010.

another, the Council is almost continually in session (see Table 11.1).

The ministers are but the tip of the iceberg, however. If it were only a matter of the ministers meeting a few days per month, the EU would be an inchoate and chaotic decision-making system. The work of the Council involves a much larger contingent of national officials. First, there are the EU permanent representatives who staff Coreper. Coreper is responsible for preparing forthcoming Council meetings and this often involves intensive discussions to pave the way for agreement by the ministers. The EU permanent representatives (two per member state, each of which appoints its own EU ambassador and a deputy) live in Brussels, meet weekly, and 'eat, drink, and breathe EU issues seven days a week' (Barber, 1995). Each member state also maintains a **permanent representation** in Brussels run by the EU ambassador and deputy, and staffed by policy specialists from different national ministries.

But that is still not all. The bulk of day-to-day Council activity takes place at the expert working-group level. At any point in time, the Council maintains approximately 200 working groups. Working group officials are tasked with examining proposals in the early stages of negotiation, and the groups serve as a clearing house in which less controversial and/or more technical issues are settled. The working groups also act as an early warning system for complications or political issues that need addressing at the level of Coreper or the ministers.

In total, the Council involves thousands of national officials meeting in dozens of working groups, Coreper, or ministerial settings each week to negotiate and decide on EU proposals. If one adds up all of the national officials involved, earlier estimates put the total number working on EU affairs at around 25,000 (Wessels and Rometsch, 1996: 331). Taking into account a dozen newcomers since then, and the growth of policy activity in the foreign, security, military, and justice fields, this number today must be closer to 40,000 plus. At base, this figure neatly captures the classic **neo-functionalist** term *engrenage* (meaning 'caught up in the gears') and what Ernst Haas insightfully forecast as the Council's 'concept of engagement' (Haas, 1958: 522–3).

Of all of the EU institutions, the Council is perhaps the least documented. Part of this stems from inaccessibility, but more important is the Council's enigmatic appearance. It is the 'chameleon' of EU institutions (Wallace, 2002), because it blurs intergovernmental and supranational organizational traits and behaviours. The standard, glossary image of the Council is one of a stronghold of individualistically oriented national actors who focus more or less exclusively on their own self-interests rather than on the welfare of others or the group as a whole. This interpretation of the Council also forms a basic theoretical foundation for **intergovernmentalist** approaches. But the Council is a more complex and variegated institutional construct. The Council, as an institution, equals more than the sum of its parts (the member states).

Table 11.1 Number of meetings in the EU Council system, 2003–10

Format	2003	2004	2005	2006	2007	2008	2009	2010
Institutional meetings								
Summits	6	5	3	3	3	5	7	7
Councils	77	76	80	76	68	81	74	78
Coreper	134	128	123	120	106	144	130	122
Working groups	4,333	3,971	3,918	4,037	4,183	4,480	4,272	4,127
Total	4,550	4,180	4,124	4,236	4,360	4,710	4,483	4,334
Other meetings*	2,209	2,392	2,791	2,713	1,735	2,051	2,021	1,996
Grand total	6,759	6,572	6,915	6,949	6,095	6,761	6,504	6,330

*Other meetings include training sessions, seminars, information sessions and briefings, and meetings with third countries.

Source: Council of the European Union (2011)

National actors in the Council also act collectively, and many develop a shared sense of responsibility that the work of the Council should move forward and that the legislative output of the Council (even if in only one specialized policy area) should be a success. As a chamber of continuous negotiation across a wide range of issues, national actors often develop long-term relations of trust, mutual understanding, and obligations to try to help out colleagues with domestic political difficulties or requests for special consideration. Council participants can also develop collective interests in the process of joint decision-making itself. This can become a kind of 'global, permanent interest' in addition to the specific national interest on a given subject or proposal. In short, the member states that participate in the system also become socialized into a collective decision-making system.

KEY POINTS

- The Council system represents the member states, and has both executive and legislative functions in the EU system of **governance**.

- The work of the EU Council is compartmentalized into ten sectoral formations.

- The Council system involves 40,000 or more national officials who meet at the ministerial, Coreper, and working-group levels, as well as coordinate EU policy positions back home.

- As an institution, the Council is enigmatic: it is both defender of the national interest and a collective system of decision-making, blurring the theoretical distinctions between intergovernmentalism and **supranationalism**.

The layers of the Council system

This section offers a synopsis of the main elements of the Council system and the division of labour between them.

European Council summitry

As the grouping that brings together the heads of state and government, no other EU body can match the political authority of the European Council. The prime ministers, chancellors, and presidents meeting in the high-profile summits practise executive leadership and supply overall strategic guidance for the Union.

Frequently, issues such as the Budget or enlargement have proven too politically charged for the ministers to settle and the European Council is needed to break deadlocks, to overcome inter-ministerial discord (especially between finance and foreign affairs), and to broker the big, interlocking package deals for which the EU's 'history-making' moments are famous.

The European Council meets formally at least twice a year (in June and December), and at least twice more as 'informal' gatherings organized around a specific topic or theme (such as economic growth and competitiveness). One outgrowth of the eurozone crisis (which spans some two dozen summits since 2008) is the decision to regularize a special 'Euro Summit' among the eurozone leaders at least twice a year (see Chapter 27). The European Council can also convene on an emergency basis, such as the March 2011 'extraordinary meeting' on the Libya crisis and 'Southern Neighborhood' region. European Council summits attract intense public scrutiny, covered by some 1,200 journalists and increasingly accompanied by large turnouts of protesters (ranging from farmers to anti-globalization groups). Given the newest treaty revisions, which recast the European Council as a separate EU institution with its own president, a closer examination will take place under 'The European Council'.

The ministers' Council(s)

In terms of formal decision-making authority, the ministers are the national representatives empowered to vote and commit member states to new EU legislation (Article 16(2) TEU). As we shall see, a lot of informal decision-making takes place in Coreper and the working groups, but the distinction between formal (juridical) and informal (de facto) decision-making authority is important to understand, since the ministers are the elected officials who are accountable to their domestic constituencies for the policies adopted in Brussels.

Some EU Council formations have more work and meet more frequently than others. These include General Affairs, Foreign Affairs, ECOFIN/Eurogroup, and AGFISH. Each meets monthly, usually for one or two days. The workload is particularly intense during certain periods, such as at the end of a presidency when there is a final push to complete a legislative calendar.

The types of legislative acts adopted by the ministers vary by policy area. In traditional 'Community pillar' affairs, legislation is typically in the form of directives, regulations, or decisions. For Justice and Home Affairs (JHA) and Common Foreign and Security Policy (CFSP), most legislative acts are made in the form of a joint action or a common position.

There are also rules for voting. Voting rules divide into two main categories—unanimity and qualified majority voting (QMV)—although some procedural issues are passed by a simple majority vote. Under the unanimity decision rule, any member state can block a proposal with a 'no' vote. Unanimity, in effect, gives each member state a veto right. If a delegation wants to signal disagreement with some aspect of a proposal, but not block adoption by the others, he or she can abstain. Abstentions do not count as 'no' votes. Many policy areas are no longer subject to unanimity, although key areas that still are include CFSP, JHA, taxation, and institutional reform. Qualified majority voting is now the default decision rule, which essentially means that most negotiations take place in the 'shadow of the vote'. How QMV works is tackled under 'How does the Council system work?', but for now it is important to note that majority voting is one of the more distinctive traits of EU decision-making. Some scholars note that only the most advanced and deeply integrated types of regional club operate by majority voting, since an outvoted minority is legally obligated to adopt a law against which it voted (Choi and Caporaso, 2002: 483). Qualified majority voting practices in the EU are all the more distinctive, since the EU does not impart a 'voting/veto' culture, but a normative environment of mutual accommodation and consensus-seeking (a point to which we return under 'How does the Council system work?').

The ministers' meetings take place in Brussels (except during April, June, and October, when they are held in Luxembourg as part of an agreement dating from the 1960s over how to divide where the European institutions would be located). The official residence of the Council is currently the Justus Lipsius building, inaugurated in 1995 and named after the sixteenth-century philosopher. The meetings take place in large rooms equipped with rectangular tables and surrounded by interpreters' booths to provide simultaneous translation into the official EU languages. The meetings are far from intimate: typically, each delegation (and the Commission) will have three seats at the table (minister, permanent representative, assistant) and up to another half dozen who are waiting in the margins for a specific agenda point to be discussed. Normally, there are more than 100 people in the room at any one point, with lots of bilateral conversations, note passing, and strategizing going on at the same time as the individual who has the floor is speaking. But, following the Nice Treaty decision to host all future European Council summits in Brussels coupled with the imminent Eastern expansion of the Union, it was obvious that Justus Lipsius could not handle the demand for meeting space. In 2004, the European Council decided to transform the neighboring Résidence Palace, an art deco luxury apartment complex from the 1920s owned by the Belgian government, into a future headquarters for Council and European Council meetings. The new building will be named 'Europa', and will combine historic and high-tech features such as solar roof panels with a massive urn-shaped meeting space that will light up at night to resemble a giant lantern. The largest meeting room is said to hold up to 250 people and construction is expected to be completed during 2013.

Coreper

Coreper is the preparatory body of the Council, making it one of the most intense sites of negotiation in the EU. Whereas the ministers meet monthly at best, Coreper meets weekly. Officially, Coreper is charged with 'preparing the work of the Council', which reveals remarkably little about how important the Committee has become in making the Council run smoothly. Whereas any particular ministerial Council will be focused on a particular sectoral issue or set of policies, the members of Coreper negotiate across the entire gamut of EU affairs and thus hold the unique responsibility for maintaining the performance of the Council as a whole. In short, Coreper acts as a process manager in the Council system between the ministers and the experts in the working groups. While there are other Council preparatory bodies with a specialized purpose, such as the Special Committee on Agriculture (SCA) for AGFISH or the Economic and Finance Committee (EFC) for ECOFIN, none have the same seniority or density of issues as Coreper. As an institution, Coreper has a unique vantage point because it is vertically placed between the experts and the ministers, and horizontally situated with cross-sectoral policy responsibilities.

Because of the heavy workload in preparing upcoming Councils, since 1962 Coreper has split into two groups: Coreper I and Coreper II (see Box 11.3).

BOX 11.3 Division of labour between Coreper I and II

Coreper I

Single European Market (Internal Market, Competitiveness)

Conciliation in areas of OLP (formerly co-decision)

Environment

Employment, Social Policy, Health and Consumer Affairs

Transport, Telecommunications, and Energy

Fisheries

Agriculture (veterinary and plant-health questions)

Education, Youth, and Culture

Coreper II

General Affairs

Foreign Affairs

Justice and Home Affairs

Multiannual Budget negotiations

Structural and Cohesion Funds

Institutional and horizontal questions

Development and association agreements

Accession

Intergovernmental conference (IGC) personal representatives (varies by member state and IGC)

Coreper I is made up of the deputy permanent representatives, responsible for preparing the so-called 'technical' Councils. The ambassadors (who hold the title of 'EU permanent representative') preside over Coreper II, and primarily work to prepare the monthly General and Foreign Affairs meetings, as well as issues with horizontal, institutional, or financial implications.

Coreper I and II are functionally independent bodies (responsible for different formations of the Council), although the EU ambassadors in Coreper II have a more senior status with the national capitals. The permanent representatives live in Brussels and hold their positions for several years; some stay for a decade or longer, often outliving their political masters (ministers, prime ministers) and providing crucial continuity in the representation of national interests.

The most critical feature of Coreper is not discernible in the treaties—namely, the intensity of the negotiations that take place to prepare the ministers' meetings. Aside from the weekly meetings, Coreper also holds restricted lunch sessions (during which not even the translators are allowed in the room) to sort out the most sensitive and tricky problems. The permanent representatives also sit beside their minister at Council meetings and are often 'on call' in the wings of European Council summits. Putting a finger on the precise value added by Coreper is tricky, however, since the permanent representatives have no formal decision-making authority. It is clear that Coreper is an important de facto decision-making body, evident in the steady stream of pre-cooked agreements that are sent to the ministers for formal adoption. Over the years, Coreper has functioned under a fairly heavy cloak of confidentiality and insulation from domestic politics and domestic constituent pressures. This insulation enables the level of frankness in Coreper discussions that is essential to reaching compromise across so many different subject areas.

Because of the intensity of negotiations and the long periods of tenure, Coreper officials often develop close personal relations with one another, based on mutual trust and a willingness to try to help each other. In this kind of normative environment and under the pressures to keep the Council moving forward, the permanent representatives are always on the lookout for ways in which to reach compromise. At times, the search for collective solutions can border on collusion and the permanent representatives will sometimes 'go out on a limb' to sell the results of an agreement back home to the relevant authorities. The permanent representatives also exemplify the enigmatic identity of the Council: in order to succeed, they must at the same time represent a national set of interests and share a responsibility for finding collective solutions. Coreper illustrates how the Council does not only defend national interests, but is also a collective decision-making process embedded in social relations and informal norms of mutual responsiveness, empathy, and self-restraint.

Working groups

The expert group is the workhorse of the Council. Currently numbering 170, the working groups are a vast network of national officials who specialize in specific areas (such as food safety, the Middle East, olive oil, and financial services) and form the initial starting point for negotiations on any new proposal or issue. The working group is also used in the later stages of negotiation to contemplate specific points of disagreement and can serve as a convenient way in which to place a proposal in 'cold storage' until the political climate is more favourable for an agreement. Some working groups are permanent, while others are ad hoc and disappear after tackling a specific question or issue. The working groups are staffed with officials travelling from the capitals or from the Brussels-based permanent representations, depending on the issue area involved. The purpose of the working group is to pre-solve as much technical and fine detail as possible, while leaving areas in which there is disagreement or the need for political consideration to the permanent representatives or the ministers who have neither the time, nor, in many cases, the substantive knowledge to hold such finely grained discussions.

It is easy to assume that the working-group level is well catalogued, orderly, and coherent, but the reality is much the opposite. The working-group level suffers from bureaucratic sprawl in the Council system and, because it covers such a wide range of issues and policy sectors, it is on the whole very difficult to monitor. For example, in 2012, twenty-two groups reported to General Affairs (on matters including enlargement, drugs, nuclear security, asylum, and migration) and thirty-eight different groups reported to Foreign Affairs (on matters such as Africa, transatlantic relations, European arms policy, and the Middle East peace process).

The working group 'expert', although a vital part of the Council's performance, is not always appreciated at other levels of the Council. The permanent representatives meeting in Coreper, for example, can view their own national experts with some disdain for what one described as their 'bloody single-mindedness' over technical merits without an appreciation of political realities or the broader picture. Likewise, an expert will sometimes feel undermined when a permanent representative or a minister concedes a point that he or she spent five months defending as absolutely essential at the working-group level.

The General Secretariat of the Council

The Council employs a bureaucracy of approximately 3,300 officials known as the General Secretariat of the Council (GSC). Jobs are carefully allotted to all twenty-seven member states, with the majority being linguistic and clerical positions. For example, the GSC Legal Service numbers around 200 employees, of whom nearly half are linguistic experts. The GSC has over 1,200 staff devoted to translation and document production. The top jobs are the 'A grade' (policy-making) positions, which number about 300 in total. At the very top is the highly prestigious position of Secretary-General, a posting decided by the heads of state and government. The GSC is the administrative backbone and institutional memory of the Council. Organizationally, it is divided into the Private Office of the Secretary-General, the Legal Service, the Press Office, and eight Directorates-General (DGs) for different policy areas (see Box 11.4).

The Secretariat is officially charged with keeping a record of all meetings, including note taking (and producing the minutes of the meeting), and translating all documents into the EU's twenty-three official languages. The GSC is also an important asset and ally of the presidency, providing logistical assistance, offering advice, and helping to find constructive solutions (the famous 'presidency compromise'). Over the years, the

---

BOX 11.4 Organization of the General Secretariat of the Council

Office of the Secretary-General

Private Office (Top advisers to the Secretary-General and the Deputy Secretary-General)

Services attached to the Secretary-General (including Inter-institutional Relations, Counter-Terrorism Coordination, and Internal Audit)

Chair of the Eurogroup Working Group

Legal Service

Directorate-General A: Personnel and Administration

Directorate-General B: Agriculture and Fisheries

Directorate-General C: Competitiveness, Innovation and Research, Industry and Information Society, Internal Market

Directorate-General F: Press, Communication, Protocol

Directorate-General G: Economic and Social Affairs

Directorate-General H: Justice and Home Affairs

Directorate-General I: Climate Change, Environment, Health, Consumers, Foodstuffs, Education, Youth, Culture, Audiovisual, and Sport

Directorate-General K: Foreign Affairs Council, Enlargement, Humanitarian Aid, and Civil Protection

GSC has earned the reputation of being a dedicated, highly professional team. The commitment of Secretariat personnel to the Council's work has also earned them the reputation of being 'honest brokers'.

Perhaps the key factor in the ascendance of the Secretariat in EU politics is the office of the Council Secretary-General. In the history of the EU, the position has changed hands only six times. Historically, the long tenure of the position helped the Council to impart a degree of continuity and leadership amidst the thousands of annual meetings. Under Niels Ersbøll, the long-serving Secretary-General (1980–94) from Denmark, the GSC was transformed from relative obscurity to a central position in Council negotiations—albeit a behind-the-scenes role that is not often credited in public (Hayes-Renshaw and Wallace, 2006: 103). The position of Secretary-General was granted new authority following the decision by the heads of state and government at the 1999 Cologne European Council to upgrade the office to include the title of 'High Representative of Common Foreign and Security Policy', although the Lisbon Treaty hives off the chief foreign policy job (and the European External Action Service, or EEAS) and leaves coordination of European Council summits to the new European Council President (see 'The role of the rotating presidency'). Following these changes, the current Secretary-General of the Council performs duties similar to the old (and now defunct) Deputy Secretary-General in overseeing the day-to-day operations of the Council.

KEY POINTS

- The ministerial Councils are divided by policy. The General Affairs, Foreign Affairs, ECOFIN/Eurogroup, and AGFISH Councils stand out for the volume of work and frequency of meetings.

- Coreper is the official preparatory body for the Council, which gives the EU ambassadors and deputies the primary responsibility of pre-negotiating and discussing the agendas of upcoming Council sessions.

- The working groups are the biggest single dimension of the Council's work, involving thousands of national experts, and handling the technical and fine-grained detail of specific proposals.

- The Council has a bureaucracy, the General Secretariat (GSC), which helps to facilitate meetings, takes notes, translates documents, and serves as an 'honest broker'.

How does the Council system work?

Having established the hierarchical layers of how the Council system functions, it is now possible to delve more deeply into how the Council works in practice. We begin by examining voting and consensus practices, including the Lisbon Treaty revisions to how qualified majority voting (QMV) is calculated. Next, we look at the rotating presidency, as well as Council–Commission and Council–Parliament relations. Finally, the 'closed door' nature of the Council is considered, along with the implications of enlargement and enhanced cooperation.

Voting and consensus patterns

A key procedural method for EU decision-making is the possibility of QMV. But under the long shadow cast by the 1966 Luxembourg Compromise, QMV remained circumscribed. This changed with the reintroduction of QMV in the Single European Act (SEA), which was considered a crucial precondition for establishing a single market by the 1992 deadline (see Chapter 19). Qualified majority voting has since gone from being the virtual exception to the rule; the Lisbon Treaty designates QMV as the Council's default decision rule (Article 16(3) TEU). Under QMV rules, each member state has a 'weighted' vote based crudely on population size. But in anticipation of Eastern enlargement, the Nice Treaty revised voting weights, introducing a controversial reweighting and a complicated 'triple majority' system of adopting legislation (see Box 11.5). The French, for example, insisted on keeping a parity weighting with Germany, despite having 23 million or so fewer national citizens. Spain and Poland also came out disproportionately ahead in the weightings, while Belgium actually gave up some relative voting power.

However, one of the most substantively important changes for the Council contained in the Lisbon Treaty is a revision of QMV after 1 November 2014, which simplifies the procedure by dropping weighted votes entirely, and revising the thresholds for population and member state majorities. Thus the anticipated 'new' system for QMV in 2014 will still be based on a 'supermajoritarian' decision-making rule, but on a 'double majority' calculation that is arguably easier to understand and fairer to all.

The post-Nice QMV is based on a 'triple majority' system. The Lisbon Treaty mandates that this system will be phased out in 2014, but under current rules, there must first be a majority of votes in favour (currently 255 votes out of 345), based on the following member state weightings.

	Weighted votes
Germany, France, Italy, UK	29
Spain, Poland	27
Romania	14
Netherlands	13
Belgium, Czech Republic, Greece, Hungary, Portugal	12
Austria, Sweden, Bulgaria	10
Denmark, Ireland, Lithuania, Slovakia, Finland	7
Cyprus, Estonia, Latvia, Luxembourg, Slovenia	4
Malta	3
EU 27 total	345

Second, two-thirds of all member states must vote in favour (at least eighteen in an EU 27). Third, the qualified majority should represent at least 62 per cent of the EU's total population (for 2011, that equals 311,541,800 out of a total EU 27 population of 502,486,700).

Sources: Nice Treaty; Council Decision 17116/11 of 8 December 2011 amending the Council's Rules of Procedure.

The new QMV system is based on two threshold requirements:

- at least 55 per cent of the member states (that is, at least fifteen in an EU27);
- representing at least 65 per cent of the total EU population.

An additional clause requires at least four member states to form a 'blocking minority'. This provides safeguards against hypothetical big-state coalitions that could be used to block legislation. (Any three of the big four—Germany, France, the UK, Italy—represent more than 35 per cent of the EU's population.)

But even where QMV applies, voting is a relatively uncommon occurrence. Rarely is there ever a show of hands; typically, the presidency summarizes discussion and announces that a sufficient majority has been reached, or asks whether anyone remains op-

posed and, if not, notes the matter as closed. Voting is also unpopular in the EU because there is a highly ingrained culture of consensus and it is simply considered inappropriate to 'push for a vote' where there are one or more delegations with remaining objections or difficulties. As a result, actual voting and the use of votes to signal protest are fairly rare. We can see this empirically by looking at the low incidence of contested votes (that is, 'no' votes or abstentions) (see Table 11.2).

Using data from 2004–06 as a reference, we can see that contested votes occur in fewer than 15 per cent of all legislative acts and barely 10 per cent of all Council actions. This affirms the deep-seated 'consensus-seeking' assumption in everyday Council negotiations. At the same time the potential recourse to the vote (the so-called 'shadow of the vote') is a powerful reminder to delegations to avoid becoming isolated by simply saying 'no' and being unwilling to compromise. For this reason, Council participants claim that the fastest way in which to reach consensus is with the QMV decision rule.

But the speed of reaching agreements is not necessarily fast at all. Despite accolades about the Council's ability to forge compromise among sovereign states with divergent interests, few claim it to be an efficient decision-making system. It takes about eighteen months on average for a new proposal to work its way through the stages of negotiation in the Council and with the Parliament, although there are some cases that take much longer. A few notorious examples include the Directive on Lawnmower Noise (Directive 84/538/EEC), negotiated over a dozen years to harmonize the maximum decibel level that mowers can make, or the Chocolate Directive (Directive 2000/36/EC), which took twenty-six years to reach agreement on a common definition for 'chocolate products'!

The role of the rotating presidency

Aside from the 'permanent' leadership jobs (which now include the European Council President, and chairs for the Eurogroup and Foreign Affairs Council), the Council presidency rotates equally between member states every six months. This rotating presidency is responsible for planning, scheduling, and chairing meetings of the Council, Coreper, and the working groups. The true genius of the rotating presidency is how it acts as a power equalizer between big and small states, giving tiny Luxembourg the same chance to run things as, say, Germany, France, or the UK. The

Table 11.2 Contestation and consensus in Council negotiations, May 2004–December 2006

	Legislative acts	Other acts	Total
Uncontested	85.8% (357)	91.1% (858)	89.5% (1,215)
'No' votes	8.9% (37)	6.2% (58)	7.0% (95)
Abstentions	5.3% (22)	2.8% (26)	3.5% (48)
Total	100% (416)	100% (942)	100% (1,358)

Note: Absolute number of acts in parentheses.

Source: Mattila (2008: 27, Table 2.1)

BOX 11.6   Council presidency rotations, 2011–20

Hungary	January–June 2011
Poland	July–December 2011
Denmark	January–June 2012
Cyprus	July–December 2012
Ireland	January–June 2013
Lithuania	July–December 2013
Greece	January–June 2014
Italy	July–December 2014
Latvia	January–June 2015
Luxembourg	July–December 2015
Netherlands	January–June 2016
Slovakia	July–December 2016
Malta	January–June 2017
United Kingdom	July–December 2017
Estonia	January–June 2018
Bulgaria	July–December 2018
Austria	January–June 2019
Romania	July–December 2019
Finland	January–June 2020

Source: Council of the European Union (2007)

rotation is set to give variation between big and small, and newer and older member states (see Box 11.6).

Ideally, the rotating presidency affords opportunity to privilege issues of national interest and priority; this is balanced by stakeholder interests in brokering a raft of successful legislative outcomes during the six months in the limelight, which participants claim carry significant reputation and status concerns. Even the British, long considered an 'awkward partner' (George, 1998), have a reputation for running effective and highly productive EU presidencies. Holding the chair carries formidable logistical duties, because the Council's work is organized into a six-month calendar. Planning for the presidency typically begins eighteen months prior to its start date. Poland, the inaugural presidency of which was the second half of 2011, began active planning in 2008. The staff at the permanent representation is also ramped up to handle presidency duties, such as Denmark's increase from fifty officials in 2010 to eighty-six in 2012, an increase of 58 per cent. Despite the workload, the presidency is highly coveted, since that member state not only organizes meetings, but has a close involvement in setting the agenda—what issues are covered and in what order—and in finding solutions: brokering deals, suggesting compromises, and drafting conclusions. A newer innovation, since 2007, is the institutionalization of greater coordination between presidencies into an eighteen-month work programme organized by a 'presidency trio'. The idea behind the eighteen-month programme is to enhance continuity and to formalize greater coordination in the Council's work. The 'trio's' programme is scrutinized, debated as necessary, and approved by the General Affairs Council (Article 2(6), Rules of Procedure).

The EU presidency involves much quiet diplomacy, behind the scenes and often in bilateral conversations at the margins of meetings (known as 'confessionals') in order to make progress on new proposals, as well as to deal with the inevitable unexpected developments and crises as they arise. Running the presidency involves subtle diplomatic skills, such as knowing in what order to call on member states during discussions to ensure the best chances of success (or failure), when to call for coffee breaks, and how to time the right moment for suggesting a 'presidency compromise'.

The presidency is a great example of the Council's enigmatic identity, since the country holding the position must simultaneously work to advance collective European solutions and be on the lookout for a particular set of national interests. This can be a delicate balancing act, especially in policy areas in which there are highly mobilized domestic constituencies and costly economic issues at stake. Member states that handle this balancing act with a deft touch can accumulate a great deal of political capital and respect. The Finnish presidency of 1999 helped to earn that country a reputation for being very communitarian and skilful at compromise-building despite being relative a newcomer to the EU game. Likewise, it is possible to be seen to be using the presidency to pursue a narrower national agenda or to push through new policies without widespread support, as the French found out during their rotation in 2000 when smaller states accused the presidency of trying to force through new voting weights that advantaged the big states.

Relations with other EU institutions

From the earliest days of the Union, interactions between the Council and Commission have constituted the main pulse and dynamic of European integration. But because the two institutions were created with a certain degree of inbuilt tension, with the Council representing individual member states and the Commission representing the 'European' interest, relations have at times been quite strained. The worst crisis in the history of the Union, the 'empty chair' crisis of 1965, was prompted when French President de Gaulle felt that the Commission had overstepped its authority in seeking to obtain its own sources of revenue (see Chapter 2). During other periods, relations between the Council and the Commission have been smoother, such as the period in the late 1980s when the bulk of legislation to create the single market was adopted in a steady stream by the Council (see Chapter 19). More recently, signs of strain have shown up again in areas of foreign policy, especially over who should represent the EU internationally (see 'The High Representative of the Union for Foreign Affairs and Security Policy' and Chapter 18).

In contrast to the Commission, relations with the European Parliament (EP) for most of the Union's history were very much at arm's length and mostly one-sided. Prior to the Maastricht Treaty, the Council merely had to consult the EP before adopting legislation and proposed EP amendments were not binding (see Chapter 12). This all changed when the co-decision procedure was introduced to selected issue areas, the essential feature of this procedure being that the EP is a co-legislator with the Council, since it is now much more difficult for the Council to ignore or overrule EP amendments. Since the 1990s, with each new treaty (Maastricht, Amsterdam, Nice, Lisbon), co-decision has been introduced or extended to more issue areas. The Lisbon Treaty goes further, codifying co-decision as the EU's 'ordinary legislative procedure' (OLP) rather than something exceptional (Article 289 TFEU). Under OLP rules, where the Council disagrees with EP amendments, there is a procedure known as 'conciliation' in which the two sides meet to reach compromise on a final text. Conciliation meetings, and compromise-seeking negotiations to stave off conciliation with an 'early' (first or second reading) agreement, have dramatically intensified Council–EP relations since the mid-1990s. Working relations between the Council and EP have improved to the point at which the number of OLP files that are concluded by compromise (during the first or second reading) without the need for lengthy conciliation negotiations has steadily increased. Today, 85 per cent of all OLP agreements are reached without the need for conciliation. The growth of co-decision / OLP represents a new dynamic of inter-institutional networking in the EU and shows how the legislative process has evolved to become more like that of other bicameral federal political systems (Lewis, 2005a).

Transparency and accountability

Since the 1990s, the issue of the 'democratic deficit' has been at the top of the EU's agenda. But the inner workings of the Council have largely avoided scrutiny. Reducing the democratic deficit has centred on reforming the EU's decision-making procedures, increasing involvement by the European Parliament, and introducing the subsidiarity principle to keep decisional authority as close to the citizen as possible. Every member government pays lip service to the need for the Union to be more transparent, more accessible, and more connected to EU citizens, but there is less agreement among them on how best to accomplish this task within Council deliberations.

One innovation is to hold 'public debates' by broadcasting select Council meetings on television and the Internet, but this has the perverse effect of stifling real dialogue, since the ministers start reading from set speeches. The Council's Rules of Procedure have become more detailed on requirements for deliberations 'open to the public' (via television and the Internet). Specifically, this is to include open sessions on the adoption of co-decision / OLP acts, the 'first deliberation on important new legislative proposals' that do not involve co-decision/ OLP, and, within the GAC, an open 'public policy debate' on the eighteen-month presidency 'trio' programme (Article 8, Rules of Procedure). But researchers have shown that transparency has its limits in Council negotiations, such as the finding that more open deliberations can lead to bargaining breakdowns as national officials stick to positions that 'posture' and 'pander' for domestic audiences (Stasavage, 2004; Naurin, 2007).

Current challenges: 'absorption capacity' and 'enhanced cooperation'

There are two current challenges in how the Council system works that create institutional uncertainty and could have future unintended consequences. The first issue is enlargement (see Chapter 17) and the ever-expanding size of the Council's negotiating table. Some believe that, through enlargement, the Council will become such an unwieldy and heterogeneous body that it will be little more than a 'talking shop' of ministers. An EU of twenty-seven places strain on the Council's decision-making structures—originally built for six members—by increasing 'transaction costs', which will likely slow the pace and output of new legislation (Hertz and Leuffen, 2011).

Enlargement also increases the workload on Coreper and the expert groups, which hold greater responsibilities for discussing substantive issues and finding agreements at their levels. Ultimately, how easily the Council system can consolidate its new members will depend on how quickly and extensively they become socialized to the EU's normative environment. If, for example, new members are slow to absorb the established norms of compromise and accommodation, the Council could develop a more rigid 'veto culture' or even divide into different voting blocks along geographic or gross domestic product (GDP) lines. Of particular concern is the future admission of Turkey, which could alter the balance of national voting power in the Council in dramatic and unpredictable ways (see Box 11.7).

The second current challenge is known as variable geometry: how will the Council change as the EU becomes more polycentric and differentiated? 'Enhanced' forms of cooperation, which were first legalized by the Nice Treaty, risk altering the very finely tuned mechanisms of exchange and consensus-seeking that has become a reflexive habit among Council participants. Treaty-based rights for enhanced cooperation are interpreted by many as the formalization and legitimation of an à la carte (or pick and choose) Europe. This was packaged as

BOX 11.7 How Turkey might imbalance the 'big state' club of voting power in the Council

The eventual membership of Turkey is one of the EU's most politicized issues. In the press, the issue is often presented as whether Turkey is part of 'Europe', touching on the identity politics of Islam and Christianity stretching back over the centuries. Academics tend to focus more on the high hurdles that Turkey faces in meeting the *acquis communautaire* or passing the constitutionally required referendum on the subject in France. Less attention is paid to how radically Turkey could shake up the delicate balancing of national power within the Council. The problem, in a nutshell, is this: overnight, Turkey would become the first or second most powerful vote on the Council, leapfrogging the French, the British, the Italians, the Spanish, the Polish, and eventually overtaking the Germans. By current demographic projections, Turkey would be the most populous state in a future hypothetical EU sometime around 2015 and hence the most powerful vote on the Council.

Thus it is likely that behind the more vocal worries of smaller members such as Austria and Greece lie deep reservations by many of the founding and big-state members, who are concerned about the institutional and decision-making implications of 'absorbing' such a large and heterogeneous newcomer.

Country	Population/ projections (m)			
	2010	2015	2025	2035
Turkey	77.8	82.5	90.5	96.5
Germany	81.6	80.9	79.2	76.6
France	64.8	66.3	68.5	69.8
United Kingdom	62.4	64.1	67.2	69.4
Italy	60.8	61.9	62.6	62.5
Spain	46.5	48.2	51.4	53.1
Poland	38.5	38.3	37.4	35.6

Source: Summary demographic data, US Census Bureau (2012) International Data Base (IDB), available online at http://www.census.gov/population/international/data/idb/informationGateway.php

a way in which to 'further the objectives of the Union, protect its interests and reinforce its integration process', but a more cynical interpretation is a vanguard of core members can no longer be held back in sensitive policy areas by the most reluctant integrationists. Enhanced cooperation is currently considered 'a last resort' when 'cooperation cannot be attained . . . by the Union as a whole' (Article 10(2) TEU). Outsiders may still participate in deliberations, but they have no voting rights. Adopted acts bind only participating members and do not become part of the EU *acquis*. While many view differentiation as a method of promoting diversity and preventing the blockage of integration by reluctant members, others see differentiation as setting a dangerous precedent for different 'classes' of membership that challenge the principle of equality.

KEY POINTS

• Leadership of the EU Council is supplied by a rotating presidency, which alternates every six months and is coordinated by the eighteen-month work programme of the 'presidency trio'.

• Council decision-making remains remote, opaque, and mysterious to EU citizens despite more formal efforts at deliberation 'open to the public'.

• Enlargement to twenty-seven members and beyond presents ongoing challenges to prevent negotiations from becoming too unwieldy, depersonalized, and unreceptive to compromise-building and consensus-based decision-making.

• Enhanced cooperation is a mechanism for more advanced integration among subsets of member states, but it can also lead to legal and institutional fragmentation, and different tiers of 'club-like' membership.

The European Council

No portrait of the Council system would be complete without including the role of the European Council. The European Council is the pre-eminent political authority for the European Union because it is composed of the heads of state and government of all of the member states. The European Commission President also attends the meetings, as does the High Representative for Foreign Affairs and Security Policy (see 'The High Representative of the Union for Foreign Affairs and Security Policy'). The meetings are chaired by a president whom the European Council selects by qualified majority to serve for a two-and-a-half-year term (renewable once) (Article 15(5) TEU). To give the Council President credible objectivity, the treaties expressly forbid him or her from wearing a 'double hat'—that is, he or she must not simultaneously hold a national office.

The European Council was created in the early 1970s and, by 1974, was informally institutionalized. Many EU scholars credit the European Council with holding the Union together during the nearly two decades of Eurosclerosis. This includes the creation of the European Monetary System (EMS) in the late 1970s, the resolution of major budgetary disputes in the early 1980s, and the launching of new intergovernmental conferences (IGCs) to revise the treaties. But the European Council was not acknowledged in the treaties until 1986 with the Single European Act (SEA). The Lisbon Treaty goes further by officially recognizing the European Council as an institution of the EU. In practical effect, this means that funding for European Council meetings (approximately €12.1 million in 2010) now comes from the central EU Budget, whereas before summits were hosted (and paid for) by the member state holding the rotating presidency. While the European Council rarely makes a decision on a specific proposal, the summits supply the EU with critical navigation and the usual output for a meeting is a lengthy *communiqué* (known as 'Conclusions'), which summarizes positions on issues and sets priorities for future EU policy-making that are then incorporated at the ministerial, Coreper, and working-group levels. The Lisbon Treaty significantly revamped the European Council's leadership capabilities by removing summitry from the regular presidency rotation, and creating a new permanent President to chair meetings and represent the EU externally at forums such as the G8/G20 (see Box 11.8). But the overlapping leadership and representation responsibilities for the European Council and Commission presidents, despite good working relations that include a weekly Monday morning breakfast together, suggest that ambiguities still remain.

The High Representative of the Union for Foreign Affairs and Security Policy

One of the most significant internal Council developments in recent decades has been the consolidation of foreign policy authority in the Union's High Representative. Upgrading the role and resources of the foreign policy post was an early consensus of the proposed 2002–03 Constitutional Convention. While some members, such as the British, could not ultimately swallow the proposed title change— to 'EU Foreign Minister'—the agreed title, 'High Representative of the Union for Foreign Affairs and Security Policy', still carries with it a substantial enhancement of institutional clout. It is the area in which, practically speaking, the European Union gains the most visible international legal personality.

BOX 11.8 Herman Van Rompuy, President of the European Council

Less than one year after becoming Belgium's prime minister, Herman Van Rompuy was unanimously chosen by the EU heads of state and government in November 2009 to serve as the first permanent President of the European Council. Known as a former debt-reducing budget minister and leader who adroitly defused eighteen months of internecine coalition politics between the Dutch-speaking Flemish and French-speaking Walloon parties over how to form a new Belgian government (2007–08), Van Rompuy was considered an ideal compromise-builder. In March 2012, he was reappointed by the European Council to serve through until November 2014. While some see the selection of a small state leader as an unthreatening safeguard to big-state egos, others argue a Belgian leader's instinct for **consultation** and compromise is just what the job requires most. According to a senior member of his cabinet, President Van Rompuy speaks directly to each of the twenty-seven EU leaders before meetings, either by telephone or in person, and as a result, when the European Council begins:

. . . he is the only one in the room that knows everything. And this President has a remarkable memory. It is not a very visible role, in finding agreement, cajoling, and pressuring, but it is essential to getting the European Council to function.

(Author's interview, 2 December 2011)

While the treaties detail the presidency job in generally ambiguous language (Article 15(6) TEU), it is clear that President Van Rompuy's inaugural term has significant precedent-setting implications. The European Council President is expected to:

- chair meetings of the European Council and the newer Euro summits, and drive forward its work;
- ensure the preparation and continuity of the work of the European Council;
- endeavour to facilitate cohesion and consensus; and
- issue a report to the Parliament after each summit.

In his reappointment speech of March 2012, President Van Rompuy explained his job as being to serve as the 'guardian of trust' by 'fostering mutual understanding' among the heads of state and government.

Lauded as Europe's answer to Henry Kissinger's famous quip back in 1973, 'I wouldn't know who to call if I wanted to talk to Europe', the political significance is to enhance the policy-making coherence of the Common Foreign and Security Policy (CFSP) and the European Security and Defence Policy (ESDP) (see Chapter 18).

For EU scholars, the new post is intriguing, because it explicitly blurs the institutional boundaries between the Council and Commission in ways previously unheard of. To avoid organizational chaos in EU external relations, the new foreign policy 'supremo' is not only a top Council actor, but also a vice-president of the Commission in charge of the sizable external relations budget.

The European Council appoints the High Representative by qualified majority for a five-year term. The primary duties include:

- chairing the Foreign Policy Council;
- attending European Council meetings;
- serving as a Vice-President of the Commission and running the External Relations DG; and
- representing the EU externally and conducting high-level diplomacy through the European External Action Service (EEAS).

KEY POINTS

- The European Council brings the heads of state and government together.
- The European Council meets in multi-annual summits to discuss the most pressing business and to provide strategic guidance.
- Since the 1970s, European Council summits have been the source of most 'history-making' decisions for the European integration process.
- The Lisbon Treaty acknowledges the central role of the European Council by formally establishing it as an independent institution with its own permanent President.

The first High Representative to hold this position, Catherine Aston, found herself in the difficult position of sorting out these institutional allegiances (as a key Council official, as well as a member of the college of Commissioners) at the same time as managing a peripatetic travel schedule and creating an external diplomacy corps (the EEAS) *de novo*. A large contingent of officials from the GSC (over 400 in total) were transferred to the EEAS in 2010, which has new responsibilities in preparing Foreign

Policy Councils and managing over 120 EU delegations spread across the world. While it is still too early to tell whether these developments represent a move to create a more federal-like foreign policy in the Union, the recent changes have been interpreted as an effort to increase the coherence of CFSP and to make the EU a more credible global actor.

Conclusion

The Council is the main decision-making body of the European Union. It is the premier EU institution for representing national interests and power. But it is also a collective system of governance that locks member states into permanent negotiations with one another. National officials who participate in this system have developed their own 'rules of the game', which include a culture of behaving consensually through compromise and mutual accommodation. Thus, strictly speaking, the Council is both an institution that represents national interests and a body at the supranational level that makes collective decisions. When examined closely, researchers often find evidence that the Council blurs the traditional distinctions between the national and European levels, between intergovernmentalism and supranationalism.

The most common way in which to portray the Council is as a hierarchy of levels. The reality is a more labyrinthine and nuanced decision-making system, with significant variation by issue area. In some policy areas and with issues that are of a highly technical nature, the specialists in the working group may forge substantive agreement on important issues. In other cases, the permanent representatives who meet in Coreper conduct the detailed negotiations over substance, perhaps because of their legal expertise in applying treaty Articles, or institutional memory in a specific policy area, or sometimes to 'keep the lid' on a controversial subject that risks becoming hamstrung by the ministers. It is also not uncommon, particularly when the rotating presidency is not run efficiently, for a ministerial meeting or even a European Council summit to have the detailed, technical minutiae of a proposal on its agenda for discussion. In organizational imagery, the actual operation of the Council is perhaps closer to a network relationship of inter-organizational authority than a corporate hierarchy, which is the typical portrayal.

Whether the Council can continue to operate as it did for the first fifty years remains open to debate.

There are signs of strain on decision-makers, as agendas continue to balloon and the lines of coordination and coherence between Councils atrophy. Enlargement of the EU to twenty-seven members (or more) risks stretching the system to the point of paralysis; even at fifteen, following the 'Nordic Round' of enlargement in 1995, many Brussels insiders characterized the Council as operating 'over capacity'. In pragmatic terms, the decision-making system originally made for six cannot function the same at nearly thirty; Council participants claim that such a large table is now needed for meetings that many rely on small-screen televisions strategically placed in front of each delegation to see the face of the person talking.

There are also serious questions of democratic accountability that remain unanswered, as Council deliberations continue to be obscure and mysterious to EU citizens. Reshuffling the formations of the ministers' meetings or splitting the work of 'general affairs' into an internal institutional and external foreign policy format is no substantive remedy. Council reform faces sharp trade-offs between greater transparency that is ineffective (public debates leading to set speeches) and more effective decision-making that takes place behind closed doors and out of the public spotlight (lunches, restricted sessions).

Finally, the new focus on differentiated integration could have perverse effects on Council decision-making because some member states may find themselves excluded from certain discussions altogether, as we already see in areas of eurozone policy-making (see Chapters 22 and 27). This would have the unprecedented effect of creating different tiers or classes of membership. On the other hand, the EU has shown a remarkable capacity over the years to cope with crises and to innovate new solutions. The issue of 'institutional reform' is thus likely to be unresolved for some time and, in a governance system as advanced as the EU is, may even be an endemic feature of the EU's agenda.

QUESTIONS

1. In what manner does the Council of the European Union perform both legislative and executive functions in the EU?

2. What kind of institution is the Council? Is it intergovernmental or supranational?

3. How does the Council resemble a hierarchy? How and why can it also resemble a 'network'?

4. Do big states outweigh smaller states in power resources and influence in the Council?

5. How do the member states coordinate the representation of national interests in Council negotiations?

6. What role does the rotating presidency play in EU governance?

7. How does the General Secretariat of the Council act as a 'neutral umpire' and facilitator of meetings?

8. How have Council–Parliament relations changed since the 1990s?

GUIDE TO FURTHER READING

Hayes-Renshaw, F. and Wallace, H. (2006) *The Council of Ministers*, 2nd edn (New York: St. Martin's Press)   The definitive study of the Council as a decision-making institution, newly updated to reflect changes since the mid-1990s.

Naurin, D. and Wallace, H. (eds) (2008) *Unveiling the Council of the European Union: Games Governments Play in Brussels* (London and New York: Palgrave Macmillan)   An edited volume that presents new data and contrasts different approaches to theorizing Council decision-making.

Palayret, J.-M., Wallace, H., and Winand, P. (eds) (2006) *Visions, Votes, and Vetoes: The Empty Chair Crisis and the Luxembourg Compromise Forty Years On* (Brussels: P.I.E.-Peter Lang)   A unique retrospective on the Council's most infamous crisis, blending new analysis by academics with first-hand accounts from close participants.

Puetter, U. (2006) *The Eurogroup: How a Secretive Group of Finance Ministers Shape European Economic Governance* (Manchester: Manchester University Press)   A much-needed study of a powerful Council formation, which emphasizes the insulated and deliberative qualities of the decision-making process.

Tallberg, J. (2006) *Leadership and Negotiation in the European Union* (Cambridge: Cambridge University Press)   A systematic account of how the rotating presidency matters, informed by a sophisticated model in the 'new institutionalism' tradition.

WEBLINKS

http://consilium.europa.eu   The home page of the Council's official website.

http://consilium.europa.eu/council/presidency-websites?lang=en   The listing of the websites of current and former EU presidencies.

http://video.consilium.europa.eu/   Select webcasts from Council meetings.

http://www.consilium.europa.eu/policies/council-configurations/foreign-affairs/high-representative-of-the-union-for-foreign-affairs-and-security-policy?lang=en   The website of the High Representative of the Union for Foreign Affairs and Security Policy.

http://www.european-council.europa.eu/the-president/   The website of the European Council President.

12

The European Parliament

Charlotte Burns

Chapter Contents

Reader's Guide

This chapter focuses upon the European Parliament (EP), an institution that has seen its power dramatically increase in recent times. The EP has been transformed from being a relatively powerless institution into one that is able to have a genuine say in the legislative process and hold the European Union's executive bodies (the Commission and Council, introduced in Chapters 10 and 11) to account in a range of policy areas. However, increases in the Parliament's formal powers have not been matched by an increase in popular legitimacy: turnout in European elections is falling. Thus whilst the EP's legislative power is comparable to that enjoyed by many national parliaments, it has struggled to connect with the wider European public. The chapter explores these issues in detail. In the first section, the EP's evolution from talking shop to co-legislator is reviewed; its powers and influence are explained in the next section; the EP's internal structure and organization are discussed next, with a focus upon the role and behaviour of the political groups; and finally, the European Parliament's representative function as the EU's only directly elected institution is discussed.

Introduction

The European Parliament (EP) is the only directly elected European Union institution. Until 1979, it was an unelected, weak, and marginalized institution. However, the EP has gradually extended its legislative prerogatives so that today, under the terms of the Treaty of Lisbon, it enjoys a range of powers comparable to those enjoyed by national legislatures. This chapter examines the development of the EP and its role within the European Union's political system. In order to understand the function and operation of the Parliament, it examines three key areas of importance:

- the legislative work of the Parliament—namely, its role in shaping EU policies and laws;
- its internal politics, both in relation to the organization of the chamber, and the nature of cooperation and competition between the political groups; and
- the representative role of the Parliament, as a link between the electorate and EU decision-making processes.

As will be shown below, while the EP has developed considerably as an institution, it still faces significant challenges in relation to its representative function, which weaken its claims to be the standard bearer for democracy within the EU's governance structures.

The evolving European Parliament

The European Parliament started life as the Common Assembly of the European Coal and Steel Community (ECSC), and was introduced by the founding fathers to lend some democratic legitimacy to a set of institutions dominated by the unelected High Authority (later to become the European Commission) and national governments. The Assembly's original seventy-eight members were appointed from national legislatures, thereby providing a link with national parliaments, and an avenue for their input to and oversight of the ECSC's activities. The Assembly's powers were limited to dismissing the High Authority. Under the Treaty of Rome, the Assembly became common to all three Communities and was awarded the further right to be consulted upon Commission proposals before they were adopted by the Council. Member state representatives were not, however, obliged to take the Assembly's position into account. Also, members of the early Assembly were national parliamentarians; therefore they were effectively part-time because they had a range of domestic responsibilities. This dual mandate circumscribed the ability of the chamber to fulfil its limited legislative prerogatives. Thus, from its early days, the European Parliament gained the reputation of being little more than an ineffectual talking shop.

The Treaty of Rome included, however, the right for the Assembly to draw up proposals on elections by direct suffrage. This right was subject to unanimity in the Council and, because the member states were reluctant to support an elected Parliament, fearing a challenge to their own autonomy, the first direct elections were not held until 1979. Since those first elections, the Parliament has, as anticipated by the Council, used its status as the only directly elected EU institution to push for increases to its powers. The Parliament has exercised this strategy so effectively that, today, its members are regarded as equal legislative and budgetary partners with the Council, and can scrutinize and hold the Commission to account (see Box 12.1).

The powers and influence of the European Parliament

The European Parliament's powers fall into three key areas: it enjoys considerable influence in relation to the EU Budget; it has the right to scrutinize, appoint, and dismiss the Commission; and, in the context of EU law-making, the EP also has the right to amend and reject Commission proposals for legislation. These powers have expanded enormously in recent years largely as a result of the EP's proactive engagement with the process of treaty reform.

Budgetary powers

The first major increase in the EP's power came with the Budget Treaties of 1970 and 1975, under which the Parliament was accorded the right to amend the Community Budget within certain limits, to reject the Budget, to grant a discharge to the Commission for its execution of the Budget (to sign off the books and agree that the Commission has spent money appropriately), and be consulted on appointments to the Court

BOX 12.1 The evolving Parliament

Year	Event	Parliamentary powers
1952	ECSC Common Assembly created	Seventy-eight nominated members take office
		Right to dismiss High Authority
1958	Becomes EC Common Assembly	142 nominated members take office
		Right to be consulted on legislative proposals.
1975	Treaty changes on Budget	Greater budgetary powers for EP
		Parliament given considerable influence over non-Common Agricultural Policy (CAP) spending
1979	First direct elections	410 elected members
		EP uses status as elected institution to push for greater powers
1980	*Isoglucose* rulings by the European Court of Justice (ECJ) (see 'Legislative powers')	EP's right of **consultation** reinforced
1987	**Single European Act (SEA)** enters into force	**Cooperation procedure** introduced for some legislation, giving EP greater scope to delay, amend, and block laws
		Assent powers granted on some matters
1993	Treaty of Maastricht enters into force	**Co-decision** procedure introduced for some areas
		EP given approval power over nominated Commission
1999	Treaty of Amsterdam enters into force	Co-decision procedure extended and amended in the EP's favour
		EP given formal right to veto Commission President
2003	Treaty of Nice enters into force	Further extension of co-decision
2009	Treaty of Lisbon enters into force	Co-decision renamed 'ordinary legislative procedure' (OLP) and extended to eighty-five policy areas
		EP given equal budgetary status with the Council, and division between compulsory and **non-compulsory spending** removed
		EP political group leaders to be consulted on Commission President nominations and EP to elect Commission President
		EP allowed to request treaty change
2011	**Treaty on Stability, Coordination and Governance in Economic and Monetary Union** agreed	Four members of the European Parliament (MEPs) are included in the negotiations leading to the draft Treaty
2012	**Citizens' initiative** is launched	EU citizens have the right to call for new legislation
2014	Eighth European Elections	751 MEPs elected.

of Auditors (see Corbett et al., 2011). These powers were subject to some important limitations. For example, the EP could request modifications to compulsory spending (largely agricultural policy), but could only insist on changes to non-compulsory spending, which, in the 1970s and early 1980s, made up only about 20 per cent of the overall Budget. Thus the EP's capacity to shape the Budget was limited. In order to extend its budgetary prerogative, the Parliament engaged in a series of battles with the Commission and Council in the early 1980s over spending levels and the allocation of funds between compulsory and non-compulsory expenditure. This period saw the EP reject the draft Budgets of 1979 and 1984; in 1985, it adopted a Budget that went over the limit that had been agreed by the Council and Commission; in 1987, the Commission and EP took the Council to court for failing to bring forward a draft Budget by the deadline required (see Corbett et al., 2011). In 1988, the persistent budgetary conflict between the Council and EP was resolved by a series of inter-institutional agreements that provided for annual Budgets within limits established by a multi-annual financial perspective that typically runs over six years (the next running from 2014 to 2020).

Moreover, under the Treaty of Lisbon the distinction between compulsory and non-compulsory expenditure has been removed, thus extending the EP's scope to amend the Budget across all areas, thereby rendering it an equal partner within the budgetary realm. Today, the EP and Council act as a genuine bicameral budgetary authority, sharing a relationship based upon mutual respect and recognition of the need for stability and certainty when determining the EU's overall expenditure. Hence the EP has won a

key democratic right to decide Europe's budgets and a long-standing cause of inter-institutional conflict has now been removed. However, the EP's new powers come into force at a time when Europe is looking to cut spending, so the negotiation of the 2014–20 multi-annual financial framework will see the Parliament trying to exercise its new powers in an era of austerity.

Scrutiny, appointment, and dismissal

The EP has always enjoyed the right to dismiss the whole Commission. The Parliament has never exercised that right, but it has come close—most spectacularly in 1999, when the whole Santer Commission resigned (over a corruption scandal) in order to avoid a vote of censure from the Parliament. The EP had no powers of appointment under the original treaties, but carved them out over time using its role as an elected institution to pressurize new Commission Presidents to submit themselves to a vote of approval by the Parliament. Formal recognition of the EP's right to appoint the Commission came in the Treaties of Maastricht and Amsterdam, which gave the EP a right to veto the Commission President-designate and the whole team of Commissioners. The Treaty of Lisbon went further by requiring the Council to take into account the outcome of the elections to the European Parliament and to consult the party leaders within the EP before nominating a candidate who is then elected by an absolute majority of all MEPs. If the MEPs reject that candidate, then the Council must propose a new one. Thus the EP now has a direct say in who becomes Commission President and the political balance of the Parliament may play a role in determining that candidate.

In the 2009–14 session, the EP and the Council both had centre-right majorities; thus, when Barroso was appointed for a second term in 2009, it was relatively uncontroversial. The appointment of the Commission is likely to be far more divisive if the ideological balance within the two institutions is different. Moreover, whilst the EP's right to approve the wider Commission does not allow for the dismissal of individuals, the Parliament has successfully used its rights of appointment to force individual candidates to step aside (see Box 12.2). However, an interesting anomaly has emerged under the terms of the Treaty of Lisbon in relation to the EP's rights of appointment. Under Article 17(8) TEU, if the Parliament decides to veto the appointment of the European Commission,

In 2004, the EP used its powers of appointment to force Rocco Buttiglione, the Italian nominee for the post of Commissioner on Justice, Freedom and Security, to stand down after he made a series of disparaging comments about homosexuals and women. Initially, Commission President Barroso and the Italian prime minister refused to withdraw Buttiglione from the list of nominees. However, it soon became clear the Parliament was prepared to reject the entire team of Commissioners rather than accept Buttiglione. After a delay of several weeks, a new Italian candidate, Franco Frattini, was proposed and the

Commission team went on to win the support of a majority of MEPs. By 2009, Barroso and the Council had clearly learned their lesson: when Rumiana Jeleva came under pressure in her parliamentary hearing over irregularities in her declarations of financial interest, she rapidly tendered her resignation and was replaced by alternative candidate Kristalina Georgieva. Thus, whilst on paper the EP is limited to endorsing the whole Commission team, by being prepared to veto the entire team rather than accept an inappropriate candidate, the EP has carved out a de facto right to veto individuals.

the candidate for High Representative for Foreign Affairs, who sits as a vice-president in the Commission, can simply resign from the Commission, yet carry on with his or her duties as High Representative, thereby potentially sowing the seeds for future inter-institutional battles. That said, it seems unlikely that the Council would insist on keeping a candidate in the post of High Representative who did not enjoy the support of the majority of the EP.

When it comes to scrutinizing the executive, the EP's scope is more limited. It can invite Commissioners, Commission officials, and Council presidency representatives to Committee meetings to explain and justify decisions. The Commission also submits its annual work programme to the EP. However, the main leverage that the Parliament possesses to hold the Commission to account is via its powers of appointment and dismissal, and members of the Council are held to account by their own national parliaments.

Legislative powers

Perhaps the area in which the Parliament has made the biggest strides since 1979 is in the sphere of its legislative powers. In 1979, the EP was limited to offering its opinions on legislation, which the Council could duly ignore (the consultation procedure). The European Court of Justice (ECJ), in Case 138/79 *Roquette v Council* [1980] ECR 3333 and Case 139/79 *Maizena v Council* [1980] ECR 3393 (the *Isoglucose* cases), gave the EP the opportunity to delay legislation: the Court declared invalid a Council regulation that had been adopted without waiting for the EP's opinion, arguing that the Council had breached Treaty rules. From then on, the EP had some scope to exercise influence if the Council was impatient to adopt a particular

policy, because the EP could simply delay adopting its opinion in order to secure concessions in the final piece of legislation. Nevertheless, the EP's scope to amend legislation remained fairly limited until 1986, when the first major increase in its legislative power came with the introduction of the cooperation procedure in the Single European Act (SEA). Under the cooperation procedure, the EP gained a second reading of legislation and a conditional right of veto, which meant that the Parliament could reject the legislation, but the Council could overturn its rejection if the member states were unanimous. Moreover, if the Commission supported the EP's amendments, the Council could adopt those amendments by qualified majority voting (QMV), but could reject them only by unanimity. Consequently, the introduction of the cooperation procedure heralded the start of an era of closer collaboration between the Commission and Parliament, because if the EP were to increase its chances of amending legislation, it would need to secure the support of the Commission.

The cooperation procedure was repealed by the Lisbon Treaty in 2009, but its introduction was a turning point for the Parliament. For over a decade, the procedure was the major vehicle for the EP to secure its policy preferences and it paved the way for further increases in the EP's powers in the Maastricht Treaty, which introduced the co-decision procedure, renamed in the Treaty of Lisbon as the ordinary legislative procedure (OLP). Initially, the OLP applied to only fifteen treaty Articles, but its scope was extended in the Amsterdam, Nice, and Lisbon Treaty reforms, so that it now covers eighty-five policy areas. The OLP makes the Parliament a genuine co-legislator with the Council, because the agreement of both institutions is necessary for legislation to be adopted. It introduced a third reading, an unconditional right of rejection for the EP, and a conciliation process, which is triggered after the EP's second reading if the Council cannot accept the Parliament's amendments (see Chapter 15). This process involves a committee composed of delegations of equal size from both the Council and EP, who negotiate a compromise that both sides are prepared to accept. The Commission is also present and tries to help both sides to reach agreement. If either the EP or the Council fails to adopt the compromise text negotiated by the conciliation committee, then the proposal falls.

There is no doubt that the OLP has allowed the EP to shape legislation and to exercise genuine policy-making power. In particular, the Parliament has been able to improve environmental standards, to promote civil liberties, and to improve consumer rights (see Box 12.3). The OLP has also had a profound effect upon inter-institutional relations. Whilst the introduction of cooperation increased informal contacts between the Commission and Parliament, the OLP has facilitated the development of direct informal relations between small negotiating teams from the Council and Parliament from the first reading of legislation onwards. Indeed, most agreement is now concluded at first reading following informal negotiations often involving only a handful of people. A key advantage of this arrangement is that it is clearly easier to reach agreement quickly if there are only a few people involved in negotiations. However, this informality raises questions about the transparency of decision-making, which is of particular concern for the Parliament. The EP has long called for increases in its powers on the grounds that it is the only directly elected European institution, and therefore guarantees transparency and accountability within EU decision-making procedures, thereby addressing the EU's democratic deficit (see Chapter 25). However, with *rapporteurs* (MEPs responsible for drafting legislative opinions) increasingly meeting representatives from the Council informally behind closed doors, there is limited opportunity for MEPs drawn from the wider Parliament to feed their views into the negotiations. In response to concerns about the secretive nature of these processes, the Parliament has adopted new internal rules to try to guarantee that the Parliament's negotiating team in inter-institutional negotiations is acting on the basis of a mandate agreed within the relevant parliamentary committee. Nevertheless, the EP has discovered that, with the increase in its powers and responsibility, it faces a trade-off between efficiency and legitimacy: it is easier to negotiate with small groups of people, but doing so reduces the scope for the wider deliberation that transparent decision-making demands.

An advocate for constitutional change

The Parliament has also been proactive in seeking to enhance its power through advocating constitutional reform under which the EP and the wider European citizenry would be given an enhanced role in determining the shape and function of the European Union (Corbett, 1998; see Chapter 25). In the run-up to the SEA, the EP's Institutional Affairs Committee prepared a draft Treaty of European Union, which was part of a wider set of factors promoting treaty change. In subsequent treaty negotiations, the Committee again prepared detailed reports, and advanced the case for further reform with lobbyists, non-governmental organizations (NGOs), and national governments. As a consequence of this activity, MEPs were formally included in the intergovernmental conference (IGC) reflection groups preparing the Amsterdam and Nice Summits, and under Treaty of Lisbon, the EP has gained the formal right to request treaty changes (see Chapter 4). In recognition of this new role, the EP was asked to assent to changes to the Treaty of Lisbon allowing for the creation of the European Stability Mechanism (ESM) in 2011. Later that same year,

---

BOX 12.3   Policy influence under the ordinary legislative procedure

The European Parliament has been able to improve the quality of life for Europe's citizens via the OLP. It has carved out a reputation as an environmental champion by amending legislation to strengthen air and water quality standards. It has bolstered consumer protection with regard to access to the Internet under the telecoms package, insisted on fair treatment for workers under the **Working Time Directive** (Directive 2003/88/EC), and played a key role in ensuring that the Services Directive facilitating the free market in services (Directive 2006/123/EC) did not weaken consumer or workers' rights.

the President of the European Council requested that a delegation from the Parliament be involved in the negotiations and drafting of the new Fiscal Treaty for the euro area. Thus the EP has an increasing role in drafting treaty changes and can therefore bring more democratic accountability to the process. Moreover, the empowerment of the EP in this area allows for greater involvement of supranational actors in what were traditionally intergovernmental arenas.

KEY POINTS

- The European Parliament gained significant budgetary powers in the 1970s and acts as one half of the EU's bicameral budgetary authority.

- The EP can appoint and dismiss the Commission President and College of Commissioners.

- The EP's powers have extended furthest in the legislative realm. It now acts as a co-legislator with the EU Council in eighty-five policy areas. However, the use of informal meetings raises questions about the wider transparency of EU decision-making.

- The EP has long pressed for constitutional change to bring Europe closer to its citizens; many of its goals were realized in the Treaty of Lisbon. The EP itself is now more closely involved in the process of treaty change.

The internal politics of the European Parliament

The European Parliament has been characterized as an institution composed of strong committees and weak parties. The committees have been viewed as a key vehicle through which the EP can exercise its legislative prerogatives and hold the EU executive to account. However, as the Parliament's powers have expanded, the political groups have emerged as ever more important actors, for it is they who hold the power of patronage within the Parliament, and who act as a key conduit between Brussels and national parliamentary parties. The EP's political groups are cross-national—in other words, they are composed of members from different countries who share the same broad ideological convictions. There are currently seven political groupings and a handful of MEPs who have chosen not to affiliate themselves (see Table 12.1). The two largest groups are the European

People's Party (EPP), a centre-right political group, and the Social and Democratic Alliance (S&D), a centre-left political group, both of which are composed of MEPs from all twenty-seven states drawn from more than thirty national political parties.

The groups play a central role within the EP, because they control appointments to positions of responsibility and set the EP's calendar and agenda. Their importance is perhaps best illustrated by 'the powerlessness of those non-attached members who are not in political groups, who are unlikely, for example, to ever hold a powerful post within the Parliament' or to be able to draft an important report (Corbett et al., 2011: 78). In short, it makes sense for MEPs to affiliate themselves with large groups, but doing so can make for some uncomfortable bedfellows. For example, the largely Eurosceptic Czech Civic Democrats and UK Conservatives found membership of the generally pro-European EPP increasingly challenging, because the UK and Czech contingents viewed European integration and the wider European project much more negatively than the rest of the group. Consequently, they broke away to form a separate European Conservative Reform Group (ECR) after the 2009 European elections. Interestingly, whilst the 2004 and 2007 enlargements led to greater diversity within the political groups, as more parties from a wider range of states are accommodated, group behaviour has become increasingly cohesive, with MEPs voting with their groups on a regular basis (Votewatch, 2011).

The allocation of posts within the EP is determined by group size and, within the groups, by the size of each national delegation. Hence allotting posts requires intra- and inter-group negotiation and coordination. The most important positions within the Parliament are:

- the President, who acts as the EP's figurehead, chairing the Plenary and representing the Parliament in external negotiations and meetings;

- the Vice-Presidents who support the President and help to run the Parliament; and

- the committee chairs, who organize and run committee meetings.

Until 1999, the two larger groups (EPP and S&D) rotated the role of presidency (which has a two-and-a-half-year term of office) between them. However, in 1999, the EPP formed a coalition with the liberal grouping (ALDE) and the two groups agreed to rotate

Table 12.1 Composition of the European Parliament, Spring 2012

Political group	Political orientation	Number of MEPs
European People's Party (EPP)	Centre-right Christian Democrat and Conservatives	272
Group of the Progressive Alliance of Socialists and Democrats (S&D)	Centre-left	190
Group of the Alliance of Liberals and Democrats for Europe (ALDE)	Liberal	84
Group of the Greens and European Free Alliance (Greens/EFA)	Environmentalist and regionalist	58
European Conservatives and Reformists Group (ECR)	Centre-right Conservative, Eurosceptic	52
Confederal Group of European United Left/ Nordic Green Left (EUL/NGL)	Left-wing	34
Europe of Freedom and Democracy Group (EFD)	Eurosceptic and right-wing	34
Non-Affiliated Members (NA)	Various	30
Total		754

the post between them in the 1999–2004 parliamentary session. Thus, between 2002 and 2004, the EP had its first liberal President, Pat Cox, and between 2009 and 2011 its first President from an accession state, Polish Christian Democrat member Jerry Buzek. He was succeeded in the post by Martin Schulz (a German S&D member) in 2012 after a deal between the EPP and S&D. However, controversy arose when British Liberal Democrat Diane Wallis also stood as a candidate in 2011, despite not having the backing of the ALDE group, which had agreed not to field a candidate in return for a range of important appointments within the EP. Wallis's candidacy failed and she stood down as an MEP shortly thereafter, but her decision to stand did shine a spotlight upon the way in which the EP allocates positions of power through deals done between party elites behind closed doors rather than through genuinely contested open elections.

A key position within the EP is the role of committee chair, who is responsible for organizing the calendar and agenda of meetings, chairing meetings, and participating in inter-institutional negotiations under the OLP. The role is important because the committees are the locus for the vast majority of parliamentary work, and they play a key role in enabling the Parliament to exercise legislative power and hold the EU's executive to account. In the 2009–14 Parliament, there were twenty-two standing committees divided functionally into different policy areas. The EP also

appoints temporary committees to report on topical or urgent issues. The membership of each committee roughly mirrors the ideological balance of the wider Parliament. The committees are the repositories of policy expertise, and are, amongst other things, responsible for appointing teams of negotiators who can engage in intra- and inter-institutional negotiations.

Within the committees, MEPs are selected as *rapporteurs* to draft reports, and their work is aided by 'shadow' *rapporteurs*, who are drawn from another political group and can feed in alternative political perspectives to the *rapporteur* and committee, as well as keeping their own party and the wider EP informed about the positions being developed. The *rapporteurs* and shadow *rapporteurs* are central members of the team responsible for negotiating with the Council under the OLP. They also play an important role in shaping the position adopted by their political groups as a result of their policy expertise.

Once committees have crafted their reports, they are subject to amendment and adoption by the EP's Plenary (the meeting of all MEPs), which is typically held in Strasbourg (see Box 12.4). During the Plenary, MEPs vote on the various reports and motions for resolution, and adopt amendments to legislation. The MEPs must secure the support of a majority, and because the largest political group, currently the EPP, cannot on its own command a majority, the adoption of amendments and resolutions requires cooperation between the political parties. Thus securing the support of a majority both in the committees and in Plenary requires inter-group negotiation.

It might be expected that MEPs would vote according to national preferences, forming national blocs regardless of ideological differences. Whilst there are occasional instances of such national defections, studies of the Parliament's voting behaviour show that, as a general rule, the MEPs behave ideologically (Hix et al., 2007). In other words, they vote with their political groups, not with their fellow nationals. Even the new cohorts of MEPs from the 2004 and 2007 accession states quickly acclimatized to the norms of voting behaviour in the EP, and vote according to ideological preferences (Hix et al., 2011). Hence whilst the EP is unique as a parliamentary chamber, given its multinational and multilingual composition (see Box 12.5), to all intents and purposes it behaves as an ordinary parliament, organizing and voting along classic left–right ideological lines (Hix et al., 2007). Another prevalent assumption about MEPs is the idea that they 'go native'—that is, that they become socialized into a more pro-European perspective, thanks to their experience of living and working amongst fellow Europeans in an EU decision-making institution. However, evidence shows that becoming an MEP has little impact upon individual preferences and voting behaviour: if they are pro-European, they stay pro-European; if they are Eurosceptic, they stay Eurosceptic (Scully, 2005).

KEY POINTS

- Members of the European Parliament sit and vote in cross-national political groups, which control appointment to important posts.

- Detailed policy work in the EP is carried out by its committees. Committee *rapporteurs* play a key role in shaping group opinions and in representing the Parliament in inter-institutional negotiations under the OLP.

- The Parliament votes along ideological, rather than national, lines and the voting behaviour of MEPs is increasingly cohesive.

- There is limited evidence of MEPs 'going native'.

BOX 12.4 The seats of the European Parliament

The EP was originally located in Strasbourg on the Franco-German border as a symbol of the new European unity. The EP also has offices in Luxembourg, which were originally established there to work alongside the ECSC High Authority. However, the Parliament has increasingly centred its activities upon Brussels, where the other EU institutions are located. Today, the vast majority of parliamentary work is carried out in Brussels; some administrative staff are still located in Luxembourg and, once a month, MEPs, their staff, and representatives from the Commission and EU Council decamp to Strasbourg for the EP's Plenary session. Although the majority of MEPs would far rather conduct all of their business in Brussels, French opposition to losing the Strasbourg EP seat led to a commitment in the Treaty of Lisbon to maintaining it. Thus the monthly adjournment to Strasbourg will continue despite the cost and inconvenience to MEPs and the European taxpayer.

BOX 12.5 Multilingual EP

The EP has twenty-three official languages (seventeen more than the United Nations). Documents are translated into all languages and, during committee meetings and Plenary sessions, a host of interpreters are present to provide running translation of what is being said. A key logistical issue (apart from the space issues associated with providing interpreters' booths) is the number of language combinations required (currently 506). For less common combinations, translation has to run through a relay of interpreters into more common languages (typically German, French, and English) and from there to the next language, so, for example, a relay could go from Czech to English to Swedish. This peculiarity means that debates in the EP are often based upon set-piece speeches, with limited scope for spontaneity or the cut and thrust typically associated with national chambers. It also circumscribes the capacity for joke-telling, both because of cultural differences (Latvians may not share an Italian's sense of humour), and because the need to relay interpretation means that the punchline may be heard at different intervals and the bursts of laughter to a joke made several minutes earlier can be offputting to those speaking later.

Elections, the people, and the European Parliament

Elections to the European Parliament are held every five years. The rules governing European elections are different from those that typically apply to national elections, because EU citizens resident in another EU state (for example, Bulgarians living in Germany) are entitled to vote in local and European elections, but not in national elections. Citizens resident in an EU state can also stand for election even if they are a non-national, thus Danny Cohn-Bendit, a German citizen, has been elected as an MEP in both Germany (1994–99, 2004–09) and France (1999–2004, 2009–14). Since 1999, European elections have been conducted on the basis of proportional representation (PR) across the whole EU, although there are differences between the member states in the systems that they use. For example, in the UK, the European elections are decided by a regionally based list system, but in Italy a national list is used. An inevitable consequence of this disparity is that the number of constituents whom each MEP represents can vary enormously: for example, in the UK, there are about 5 million constituents in each region, whereas in Italy, because a national list is used, each MEP represents approximately 57 million citizens. Where MEPs represent a large constituency, it is challenging to build a relationship between the elected politician and the citizen (see Table 12.2), which may provide a partial explanation for the EP's declining popularity and legitimacy, as indicated by the fall in turnout at successive European elections (see Figure 12.1).

How can we explain this poor turnout at European elections, particularly as public opinion surveys show that the EP is the best known (81 per cent of those polled have heard of it) and the most trusted of the EU institutions (48 per cent of those polled trust the EP) (Eurobarometer, 2011b)? One potential explanation is that European elections are second-order, so they are viewed as less important than national elections and voters may use them to express dissatisfaction with the governing party of the state (Reif and Schmitt, 1980). Parties also contribute to the problem: election campaigns are organized and financed by domestic political parties rather than by the European political groups. Thus candidates do not seek re-election as a member of the S&D or EPP, but as a French Socialist or a German Christian Democrat.

Table 12.2 Seats in the European Parliament, 2009–19

Member state	Population (m)	Seats 2010–14	Seats 2014–19
Germany	82.4	99	96
France	62.9	74	74
United Kingdom	60.4	73	73
Italy	58.8	73	73
Spain	43.8	54	54
Poland	38.2	51	51
Romania	21.6	33	33
Netherlands	16.3	26	26
Greece	11.1	22	22
Portugal	10.6	22	22
Belgium	10.5	22	22
Czech Republic	10.3	22	22
Hungary	10.1	22	22
Sweden	9.0	20	20
Austria	8.3	19	19
Bulgaria	7.7	18	18
Denmark	5.4	13	13
Slovakia	5.4	13	13
Finland	5.3	13	13
Ireland	4.2	12	12
Lithuania	3.4	12	12
Latvia	2.3	9	9
Slovenia	2.0	8	8
Estonia	1.3	6	6
Cyprus	0.8	6	6
Luxembourg	0.5	6	6
Malta	0.4	6	6
Total	493	754	751

Source: Adapted from Dinan (2009: 102)

Moreover, the parties often campaign on national, rather than genuinely European, platforms.

The EP therefore faces a major hurdle: it has predicated its calls for empowerment upon its status as a democratically elected body that can bring the voice of Europe's citizens to the heart of the EU's decision-making processes, but its legitimacy is undermined by the declining turnout for European elections. The

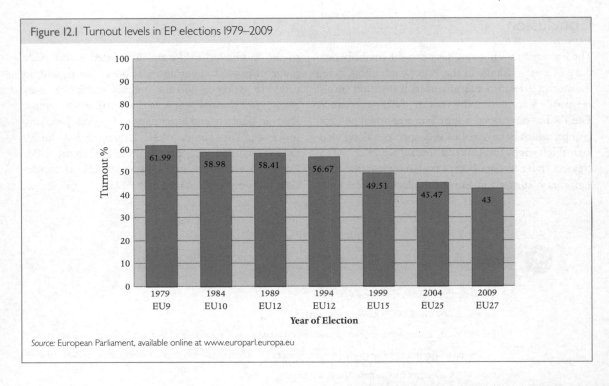

Figure 12.1 Turnout levels in EP elections 1979–2009

Source: European Parliament, available online at www.europarl.europa.eu

Parliament can take some comfort from the fact that it is not suffering alone: turnout is falling in elections across the EU. However, elections legitimate political systems and executives. The EP has argued that it can act as a corrective to the EU's democratic deficit by holding the executive to account and participating in policy-making. Yet if fewer than half of EU citizens vote for the Parliament, not only is the legitimacy of the EP undermined, but so too is that of the wider system of EU governance (see Chapter 25). The Treaty of Lisbon has tried to address these concerns by further extending the EP's powers and by including a greater role for national parliaments in decision-making. Thus, under the 'orange card system' (Protocols 1 and 2 of the Treaty of Lisbon), if a third (or a quarter in relation to freedom, security, and justice) of national parliaments feel that draft legislation could be better achieved by domestic legislation, the Commission must review the act. The Treaty also provides for more cooperation between the EP and national parliaments. It remains to be seen whether these moves to 'parliamentarize' the EU will succeed in connecting EU citizens more closely to EU processes of decision-making. It has also long been suggested that one way in which to improve turnout is to have the choice of Commission President determined by the EP election

KEY POINTS

- The European Parliament is directly elected every five years. The number of constituents represented by each MEP varies widely.

- European elections are typically regarded as being less important than national elections, both by the electorate and by national political parties, which fail to campaign on European issues; this has contributed to the declining turnout.

- Party leaders will be consulted on the choice of candidates for Commission President following European elections and the EP will elect the successful candidate.

- The Lisbon Treaty allows for further involvement of national parliaments in EU decision-making.

results, so that voters feel that their vote makes a difference to the choice of executive. Whilst the Treaty of Lisbon stops short of direct elections for Commission presidency, it does at least link the outcome of the European elections to the choice of Commission President, which may possibly lead to improved turnout in future EP elections.

Conclusion

The European Parliament has been the major beneficiary of treaty change in the European Union, being transformed from a marginalized institution into a key policy actor within the system of EU governance. The EP has developed a set of transnational political groups, which behave cohesively and vote along ideological left–right lines. Whist the EP's power has increased, there has not been a matching increase in its legitimacy: turnout in European elections continues to fall. Moreover, MEPs are now faced with a wide range of powers covering most policy areas, and, in order to enhance decision-making efficiency, they engage in informal practices that further undermine the transparency and legitimacy of EU policy-making processes. Thus the two key challenges that the EP now faces are how to increase its appeal to the wider European electorate, and how to contribute to efficient *and* open governance in the EU.

QUESTIONS

1. Why was the European Parliament created?
2. How and why have the EP's power increased?
3. Do MEPs vote according to nationality or ideology? To what extent are MEPs free from national control?
4. What impact has the empowerment of the European Parliament had upon inter- and intra-institutional relations?
5. How do you account for the poor turnout in European elections?
6. Are the changes in the Treaty of Lisbon likely to increase the EP's profile?
7. What are the principal challenges facing the EP and how should it address them?
8. Is there any point in keeping the European Parliament?

GUIDE TO FURTHER READING

Corbett, R., Jacobs, F., and Shackleton, M. (2011) *The European Parliament*, 8th edn (London: John Harper)   An excellent and comprehensive guide to the history and day-to-day operation of the European Parliament, written by three practitioners.

Hix, S., Noury, A. G., and Roland, G. (2006) *Democratic Politics in the European Parliament* (Cambridge: Cambridge University Press)   A study of the internal politics of the European Parliament that draws upon an extensive dataset of voting behaviour in the Plenary.

Judge, D. and Earnshaw, D. (2009) *The European Parliament*, 2nd edn (Basingstoke: Palgrave)   An excellent textbook, with good reviews of the academic debates and a range of helpful policy case studies.

Rittberger, B. (2005) *Building Europe's Parliament: Democratic Representation Beyond the Nation State* (Oxford: Oxford University Press)   By far the best scholarly study of the historical development of the EP.

Scully, R. (2005) *Becoming Europeans? Attitudes, Behaviour, and Socialization in the European Parliament* (Oxford: Oxford University Press)   A study that refutes widespread conjecture about MEPs 'going native', and draws some important implications from this finding about how we might understand and study the EP.

WEBLINKS

http://www.europarl.europa.eu   The Parliament's own website features plentiful information on the Parliament's activities.

http://www.europarl.europa.eu/code/default_en.htm   The Parliament's OLP page features activity reports and regular updates on the progress of legislation.

http://www.lse.ac.uk/Depts/eprg   The website of the European Parliament Research Group features up-to-date research papers on all aspects of parliamentary behaviour.

http://www.theparliament.com   *The Parliament* is a current affairs journal focusing upon the activities of the European Parliament and the wider EU.

http://www.votewatch.eu   Votewatch is a great resource that tracks and reports on all Plenary votes in the Parliament.

13

The Courts of the European Union

Ilias Kapsis

Reader's Guide

This chapter examines the courts of the European Union, which include the Court of Justice of the European Union (often known as the European Court of Justice, or ECJ), the (European) General Court (EGC), and the Civil Service Tribunal. It focuses on issues of structure and procedure, the extent of the courts' jurisdiction, and their role in the promotion of European integration. The chapter also discusses the criticism directed at the ECJ for the way in which it exercises its judicial powers, which allegedly involve political considerations normally unacceptable for a judicial body. Lastly, the chapter looks at the main challenges facing the courts.

Introduction

The Treaty on European Union (TEU) and the Treaty on the Functioning of European Union (TFEU), which are the supreme laws of the European Union, stipulate that the judicial arm of the EU comprises the European Court of Justice (ECJ), the European General Court (EGC), and specialized courts. The mission of the EU courts has been to ensure that 'in the interpretation and application' of the treaties of the Union, 'the law is observed' (Article 19(1) TEU). In addition to these, there is a **European Court of Auditors** (ECA), the function of which is to control the revenues and expenditure of the EU, but this is not a court in the same way as the others discussed in this chapter.

The role of EU courts is much more limited than that of national courts, because the former have jurisdiction only in specific areas of EU policy, as agreed by member states. However, over time, as European **integration** expanded to new areas of policy and demands increased for more judicial controls over EU operations as a way of enhancing public confidence and democratic legitimacy in the Union, the courts of the EU were gradually granted more powers. The EU courts themselves, especially the ECJ, have been active in the process of expanding their jurisdiction. To that end, they have exploited gaps in legislation and political divisions within the EU. The activities of the ECJ have not been limited to the strengthening of the institutional role of the courts, however. Some of its decisions, although officially focused on **enforcement** of the law, have also conveyed political messages about sensitive issues such as the nature of the EU as an international organization and its relationship with its member states. Through its decisions, the ECJ has emerged as a significant actor in the process of European integration—an actor the role of which has been viewed by many legal scholars and politicians as not only judicial, but also political. This is referred to as the 'judicial activism' of the Court.

This chapter examines in detail the dual role of the EU courts—namely, their judicial functions and their role as actors in the process of political integration. Because the roles of the ECJ and the EGC are more important for EU citizens, this chapter will concentrate on these two courts.

The history of the European courts

The European Court of Justice was created in 1951 by the Treaty establishing the **European Coal and Steel Community** (ECSC). The Court's task was to ensure the lawful interpretation and application of the Treaty. The Court's powers were extended in 1958 by the Treaties of Rome establishing the **European Economic Community** (EEC) and the **European Atomic Energy Community** (EAEC, or Euratom). It would subsequently serve all three Communities, thus

emerging as a **supranational** court with compulsory jurisdiction. The Court's decisions were binding on Community institutions, member states, and individuals. These early European treaties promoted economic integration by abolishing barriers to trade among the Community's member states; this had implications for the jurisdiction of the Court. It meant that its work focused almost exclusively on economic rights (that is, the free movement of goods), placing little emphasis on political rights, such as human rights. Even in 1986, the **Single European Act** (SEA) still excluded foreign policy matters, which had gradually emerged as a political aspect of European integration, from the Court's jurisdiction, although it did establish the Court of First Instance (CFI) (now the General Court) in order to reduce the ECJ's workload and improve its efficiency. The CFI began its work in 1989.

The establishment of the European Union by the **Maastricht Treaty** in 1992 constituted an important step forward for European integration, but, initially at least, it had little impact on the Court's powers. In the EU's new three-pillar structure, only the first pillar (known as the 'Community pillar'), which covered economic integration, remained within the jurisdiction of the Court. Because both the second pillar and third pillar covered sensitive policy areas, such as Common Foreign and Security Policy (CFSP) and Justice and Home Affairs (JHA), which touched upon core aspects of **national sovereignty**, member states preferred to keep them **intergovernmental**, thus preempting any ECJ influence.

Subsequently, the Treaty of Amsterdam gave new powers to the Court by transferring into the Community pillar certain policies previously falling under the third pillar, such as external border control, asylum, and immigration. The Court's powers in the field of police and judicial **cooperation** in criminal matters (PJCCM) were also extended. However, the Court was to have no jurisdiction over operations carried out by national law enforcement agencies, or over acts by member states seeking to maintain law and order, and safeguarding internal security.

Further significant amendments were introduced by the Treaty of Nice, which entered into force in 2003. The CFI was no longer to be attached to the ECJ, but became a court in its own right. The Treaty also provided for the establishment of specialized 'judicial panels' attached to the CFI. These were intended to reduce the CFI's workload by relieving it of insignificant cases in specific areas. The first judicial panel, the Civil Service Tribunal, was established in 2004 to deal with litigation concerning EU staff. Had it been ratified, the Constitutional Treaty (CT) envisaged a significant increase in the powers of the ECJ. The Lisbon Treaty, which entered into force on 1 December 2009, incorporated most of these changes. The Treaty abolished the three-pillar structure and created a single institutional framework for the EU as a whole. The jurisdiction of the courts was extended accordingly to cover acts of all EU institutions except in areas excluded by the treaties. These include human rights in line with the incorporation of the Charter of Fundamental Rights into EU law. In the case of the CFSP, a policy area largely controlled by national governments, the Court now has jurisdiction to rule on the legality of decisions adopted by the Council under CFSP where these impose restrictive measures on natural or legal persons. Lisbon also changed the EU nomenclature for the courts. The term 'Court of Justice of the European Union' (CJEU) that now appears in the treaties includes the (European) Court of Justice, the (European) General Court (EGC), which replaces the CFI, and the specialized courts, the latter being the new name for the judicial panels. This now also covers the Civil Service Tribunal.

The history of the Court demonstrates its increasing involvement in European affairs. This is partly predictable, because the expansion and deepening of European integration requires the existence of a judicial authority with adequate judicial powers to ensure the appropriate interpretation and enforcement of EU law by the Union and its member states, as well as to protect individual rights. However, the jurisdiction of the European Court, compared with that of the courts of sovereign states, is generally more restricted. The Court's jurisdiction is limited legally by the treaties

and politically by the member states. This reflects the political decision of national governments to prevent the Court from closely scrutinizing legal acts across all areas of EU policy. The Court's limited jurisdiction has offered new arguments to those criticizing the EU for its democratic deficit, because full court scrutiny is deemed an essential requirement for a modern democracy and this is something that the EU appears to be lacking. Moreover, as a further constraint, the Court has to share the enforcement of EU law with national courts, because the latter are involved in the enforcement of EU law in national jurisdictions (see 'Jurisdiction').

The Court has attempted over the years to cement and expand its authority within the EU by exploiting the general and rather vague provisions of the treaties, as well as the political disagreements often arising across member states. The EU treaties are generally vague because their provisions are drafted broadly, sometimes as a result of political disagreements among member states about the details. They establish only a general legal framework, giving the EU institutions the power to create the detailed rules and to fill in any gaps in legislation. The Court has made maximum use of this gap-filling opportunity, and has managed over the years to extend its powers and EU competences well beyond their original boundaries, thus fuelling the argument about the Court's judicial activism. One of the techniques used by the Court is the teleological (or purposive) interpretation of the treaties, which involves 'the Court reading the text [of the treaties], and the gaps therein, in such a way as to further what it determines to be the underlying and evolving aims of the [Union] enterprise as a whole' (Craig and de Búrca, 2011: 185). Given that the 'underlying' aims of the Union cannot always be clearly inferred from the treaties, the Court has used the opportunity to advance its own

BOX 13.1 An example of teleological interpretation

The Court used teleological interpretation in Case 26/62 *Van Gend en Loos v Nederlandse Administratie der Belastingen* [1963] ECR I, a groundbreaking decision that shaped the legal order of EU and its relationship with the legal orders of the member states and other international agreements by establishing the principle of direct effect. Relying partly on the text of the treaties existing at the time, and partly on its own vision of the nature and role of the then European

Economic Community (EEC), the Court ruled that member states had an obligation to respect the rights directly granted to their citizens by Community law and to allow individuals to enforce them in their courts. Member states had argued that Community law, as an international agreement between states, did not directly grant rights to individuals unless permitted by the member states. The Court rejected this argument.

vision for the Union by interpreting EU law in ways that are often different from those of the member states (see Box 13.1). The Court has found in teleological interpretation a valuable tool with which to wield influence in the EU and to expand its power, and therefore has used it extensively.

KEY POINTS

- The courts of the European Union include the (European) Court of Justice, the (European) General Court, and the specialized panels, such as the (European) Civil Service Tribunal.

- The jurisdiction of the ECJ, which was originally limited, has expanded over the years as the EU's competences have extended to new policy areas.

- The ECJ has general jurisdiction over all areas of EU activity, except where such jurisdiction is excluded by the treaties.

- Over time, the ECJ has exploited the general and often vague content of the treaties, and the political disagreements amongst member states, to extend its powers and the authority of the EU at the expense of member states.

Composition, structure, and procedure

The European Court of Justice is based in Luxembourg and is made up of twenty-seven judges (one judge per member state) and eight Advocates-General (AGs). The judges hear cases and adopt decisions, whereas AGs deliver impartial and independent opinions prior to the final decision-making stage. Their opinions are not binding on the judges, but have a real impact on the final outcome of a case. The judges and AGs are appointed by the member states in accordance with their national traditions. These are usually individuals 'whose independence is beyond doubt and who possess the qualifications required for appointment to the highest judicial offices in their respective countries or who are juriconsults of recognised competence' (Article 253 TFEU). The appointment of women as judges is very rare and, for a long period, there was none in the ECJ. The first female judge, Fidelma

Macken, was appointed by Ireland in 1999. The secrecy surrounding the appointment procedures and the political nature of the appointments (Barents, 2010: 713) has been addressed by the Lisbon Treaty. The amended appointments procedure requires that an advisory panel comprising members of the Court, members of the national supreme courts, and prominent lawyers, one of whom is proposed by the European Parliament (EP), gives an opinion on the suitability of each candidate. Five of the eight AGs are appointed by the five largest member states and three are appointed on a rotating basis by the remaining members. The Lisbon Treaty allows for an increase in the number of AGs to eleven. Finally, the Court also appoints a Registrar for six years, who is responsible for procedural and administrative matters.

The judges are appointed for staggered terms of six years, which allows for a partial replacement of judges every three years. They are eligible for reappointment and there is no retirement age. The judges and AGs cannot be removed during their term in office, and their duties end only on their death or resignation. A judge or an AG can, however, be dismissed by the unanimous decision of the other judges and AGs if they no longer fulfil the requisite conditions or meet the obligations arising from the office. The judges elect a president by secret ballot. Similarly, the AGs elect the so-called First Advocate-General.

The ECJ sits in chambers of three or five judges or in a Grand Chamber consisting of thirteen judges. Grand Chambers are used in important cases, or if a member state or an EU institution so requests. The Court sits as a full court only in exceptional cases, such as proceedings concerned with the dismissal of a European Commissioner. The Chambers are presided over by their own respective president.

The procedure before the ECJ has a written and an oral stage. The written stage is the most important, comprising the application to the Court, the submission of the documents supporting the application, the defences, the communication to the parties of relevant documents, and the statements of case. In the oral stage, which takes place in open court, the judge assigned to the case presents to the Court a report containing a summary of the facts and the arguments of the parties. At that point, the legal representatives of the parties may make oral submissions to the Court. The oral stage also includes examination of any witnesses or experts, as well as the delivery of the opinion of the AG. The final decision is adopted by a majority where necessary, but no mention of dissenting opinions is made in the judgment, with the latter signed by all judges and delivered in open court. This practice helps to maintain the anonymity, and thereby the independence, of the judges (Chalmers and Tomkins, 2007: 123). The judgment is subsequently published, with a summary, in the EU's *Official Journal* and a more detailed version appears in the official law report. The decisions of the ECJ are final—in other words, there is no appeal process.

The (European) General Court (EGC) consists of 'at least' one judge per member state. The Treaty of Nice gave the EGC an independent status and more cases were transferred to it, such as the right to decide on certain preliminary rulings (see 'Jurisdiction'). To date, the EGC has made a significant contribution to the development of administrative law, especially in the fields of competition and external trade law (Chalmers and Tomkins, 2007: 125). Unlike the ECJ, its cases do not involve sensitive political and constitutional issues. This allows the EGC to focus more on purely legal issues and fact finding. The rules for the appointment of judges at the EGC and their terms of office are similar to those of the ECJ. It does not have AGs, but, when necessary, one of its judges will be appointed to perform this task. The judges of the EGC elect a president and they appoint their own Registrar. Like the ECJ, the EGC usually sits in chambers of three or five judges, but it may also sit in a Grand Chamber of thirteen judges. In special cases, the EGC may sit as a full court. The judgments of the EGC are subject to appeal to the ECJ on points of law—in other words, appeals can be made only on the legal argumentation and never on the assessment of the facts. The EGC delivers its judgments in open court following written and oral proceedings. There are no dissenting or concurring opinions.

Finally, the European Civil Service Tribunal was created in 2004 to reduce the workload of the EGC by relieving it of cases involving the EU's administration (including, for example, Commission officials). The Civil Service Tribunal consists of seven judges. The Tribunal elects its own president, whereas the number of judges sitting to hear cases varies. Its decisions can be appealed on points of law to the EGC.

KEY POINTS

- The European Court of Justice is currently composed of one judge per member state and eight Advocates-General (AGs), whose duty is to perform the tasks assigned to the Court by the treaties.

- The European General Court EGC was created to lessen the workload of the ECJ. It consists of one judge per member state and, unlike the ECJ, it does not have permanent AGs.

- The European Civil Service Tribunal is attached to the EGC and consists of seven judges. It was created to relieve the EGC of its workload by handling disputes involving the civil servants of the Community.

- The procedures before the ECJ have a written and an oral stage.

- The ECJ decisions cannot be appealed, but those of the EGC and the Civil Service Tribunal can be appealed on points of law.

Jurisdiction

The European Court of Justice has often used its jurisdiction to adopt decisions that have a substantial political impact on the operation of the EU and on the EU's relationships with its member states. As far as judicial procedures are concerned, the distinction is often made between direct actions, which are brought directly to the courts of the EU, and are tried and decided by the latter, and references for preliminary rulings, which reach the courts via the intermediation of national courts. In the latter case, national courts will try to decide the case, after consulting the courts of the EU on the interpretation of EU law.

Direct actions

Direct actions can be brought by individuals, 'legal persons' (that is, companies, organizations, etc.), member states, or Union institutions. Actions brought by individuals and legal persons are handled by the General Court, and on appeal by the ECJ. Actions brought by the member states and EU institutions are normally handled by the ECJ. However, since the Treaty of Nice, the EGC has jurisdiction over certain direct actions brought by member states against the EU institutions, such as where an EU institution fails to act in breach of EU law. There are three types of direct action:

infringement proceedings; actions for judicial review (also known as the annulment procedure); and actions for damages. The EU treaties provide the Commission and member states with the power to bring infringement proceedings before the ECJ against member states failing to fulfil their Union obligations. Such a situation could arise, for example, if national law were to be inconsistent with EU law or if the latter were not implemented by member states in a timely or proper fashion. Therefore infringement proceedings aim at securing member state compliance. These proceedings have an administrative stage, at which the Commission and the member state try to resolve the matter through negotiation, and a judicial stage, at which, following the failure of negotiations, the Court is involved. If the ECJ confirms the alleged infringement, the member state will have to comply; otherwise the Commission may bring a new action before the ECJ asking for the imposition of a penalty payment. This penalty may be a lump sum or periodic payment, or both. The provision for a penalty payment was added as a means of making the proceedings more effective in ensuring member state compliance with EU law (see Box 13.2).

Judicial review of Union acts by the Courts is intended to ensure that the EU is subject to judicial scrutiny and control. The Court has jurisdiction to review the legality of acts of the EU institutions intended to produce legal effects. This review covers regulations, directives, and decisions (see Box 13.3), but also any other EU act with binding force or that produces legal effects. If the action taken is successful, the Court will declare void the act concerned. The annulment of an EU act may occur as a result of lack of competence if an EU institution adopts an act that it has no power to adopt under EU law; it may result from an infringement of essential procedural requirements, such as where an EU institution fails to comply with a requirement to explain its decision; it may arise from an infringement of the EU treaties or of any rule of law relating to their application; or it may involve a misuse of powers, such as when an EU institution exercises its powers for an unauthorized purpose.

EU institutions and member states have the right to bring an action of judicial review to the Court, but natural and legal persons—individuals and companies—are able to do so only if they pass a strict admissibility test imposed by EU law. The main reason given by the ECJ

BOX 13.2 Infringement proceedings initiated by the Commission against Greece

In 1991, the Commission initiated infringement proceedings against Greece, alleging its failure to comply with Community law on the disposal of toxic waste in Crete, where a rubbish tip was situated at the mouth of the river Kouroupitos. The tip operated in breach of Community law, which required that toxic and dangerous waste be disposed of without endangering human health and without harming the environment. The Greek government cited popular opposition to its plans to create new waste sites in the area for its failure to close the tip. The Court rejected the argument and, in 1992, issued a judgment declaring that Greece was in breach of its Community obligations. Five years later, after the Greek government failed to comply with the 1992 judgment, the Commission once again brought the case to the ECJ. The ECJ, in its 2000 decision, imposed a payment of €20,000 for each day of delay in implementing the measures necessary to comply with the 1992 judgment. The new ruling proved more effective and, along with pressure exercised on Greece by other Community institutions, the closure of the tip was secured.

Source: Case C-387/97 *Commission v Greece* [2000] ECR I-5047

BOX 13.3 Types of EU legal act

- *Regulations* have general application, and are binding and directly applicable in all member states. 'Directly applicable' means that they do not normally require member states to adopt measures for their implementation.

- *Directives* are addressed to all or some of the member states. Directives lay down specific binding objectives that have to be achieved by specific dates and leave to the discretion of the member states the decision on how best to achieve these objectives.

- *Decisions* are addressed to individuals and are binding in their entirety.

- *Recommendations* and *opinions* have no binding force.

Source: Article 288 TFEU

for the strict test in Case C-50/00 *Unión de Pequeños Agricultores v Council* [2002] ECR I-6677 was that these applicants could use national courts instead. A potentially more convincing reason might be that the Court's aim was to prevent a flood of individual cases that would hamper its work (Arnull, 2006: 93). The Lisbon Treaty amends the admissibility test, giving private applicants more access to the Court. In addition to the review of EU acts, EU law provides a right to legal action in cases in which an EU institution has failed to act in violation of the law. Lastly, EU law allows for compensation to be paid to individuals for damages suffered as a consequence of the illegal activities of Union institutions.

References for preliminary rulings

The enforcement of EU law is not a responsibility of EU courts alone, but also of national courts. The latter will be involved in cases in which EU legislation is applicable in the jurisdiction of member states either directly (for example, regulations are enforced in the member states without their involvement) or indirectly through national agencies (for example, directives are enforced in member states through the enactment of national legislation and with the involvement of national bodies). In these cases, national courts may be called upon to resolve disputes arising from the enforcement of EU law between citizens of the state or between citizens and their government. National courts may also have to resolve conflicts between EU law and their national laws. These instances require a mechanism that involves the ECJ, allowing it to offer authoritative interpretations of EU law and to coordinate action at the national level. Preliminary references provide such a mechanism. Without it, the coherence and application of EU law would be at risk, since different national courts could give contradictory interpretations of EU law provisions. According to Article 267 TFEU, national courts *may*—and where the decision to be adopted is not subject to further appeal *must*—refer questions about the interpretation of EU law arising in the cases examined by them to the ECJ. The ECJ will then provide the relevant interpretation (the preliminary ruling) and the national court will use it to decide the case. The national court is not obliged to make a reference if the meaning of EU provision is clear or if the ECJ has already ruled on the issue in a previous case. The reference to the ECJ does not have the form of an appeal, which would imply reference to a hierarchically higher court, but is aimed

only at clarifying specific issues of interpretation and application of EU law. The relationship between national courts and ECJ in this process is cooperative and non-hierarchical though the Court has over time used the process to enforce EU doctrine in a fashion similar to a hierarchically higher court. The ECJ's jurisdiction concerns preliminary rulings on the interpretation of EU treaties, and on the validity and interpretation of acts of the institutions, bodies, offices, or agencies of the Union.

Preliminary rulings have familiarized national courts with EU law, and have played a central role in shaping the legal order of EU and its relationship with its member states, because the ECJ has used them to issue some very important decisions with great political impact. Indeed, some of the most important legal principles of Community law, such as supremacy, direct effect, and state liability, have been defined by the ECJ in response to preliminary references. In *Van Gend en Loos* (see Box 13.1), the ECJ defined the principle of direct effect for the first time. The political message conveyed by this decision to member states was that EU law will intrude into the domain of national sovereignty in order to achieve adequate enforcement of EU law. In its efforts to ensure member state compliance, the Court was greatly assisted by two powerful allies: national courts, which saw in the enforcement of EU law an opportunity to expand their jurisdiction domestically; and the citizens of the member states, who wanted to take maximum advantage of rights granted to them by the Community and to stop their governments denying them these rights.

In Case 6/64 *Costa v ENEL* [1964] ECR 585, another preliminary rulings case, the Court defined the principle of supremacy of EU law for the first time. It established that EU law, irrespective of its nature (whether it is a treaty provision or a directive), could not be overridden by domestic law, irrespective of the nature of national law. In other words, if there is a conflict between EU law and national law (even a national constitution), EU law must prevail. Further, in its famous ruling in Joined Cases C-6/90 and C-9/90 *Andrea Francovich and ors v Italian Republic* [1991] ECR I-5357, the Court established for the first time the principle of state liability, according to which individuals can seek compensation in national courts for loss suffered as a result of member states' breach of EU law (see Box 13.4).

The adoption of fundamental principles such as direct effect, supremacy, and state liability, which shape the legal order of the EU and its relationship with member states, demonstrate the great value of the preliminary

The applicants in *Francovich* brought proceedings against Italy for failure to implement Directive 80/987, which provided employees with a minimum level of protection in the event of their employer's insolvency. The Directive established that the member states should give specific guarantees for payment of unpaid wage claims. The applicants, who were owed wages by their insolvent employers, sued the Italian government, claiming that the latter had to pay them either the sums payable under the Directive or compensation for the damages suffered as a result of the non-implementation of the Directive. The ECJ rejected the first argument, but accepted the second, concerning the right to compensation. The Court stated that the full effectiveness of Community law would be impaired

and the protection of rights that it grants would be weakened if individuals were unable to obtain compensation when their rights were infringed by a breach of Community law for which a member state was responsible. As a result, the principle of state liability for breaches of Community law is inherent in the Treaty. The Court found further support for its argument in Article 10 TEU (ex 5 EC), which provides that member states are required to take all appropriate measures to ensure fulfilment of their obligations under Community law, including the obligation to nullify the unlawful consequences of a breach of Community law.

Source: Joined Cases C-6/90 and C-9/90 Andrea Francovich and ors v Italian Republic [1991] ECR I-5357

rulings procedure for the development of the Court's jurisprudence and its influence on the political processes in Europe. Moreover, they demonstrate the Court's great success in exploiting the procedure to advance the goals and reach of EU law at the national level. The Court has transformed the EU's relationship with national courts from horizontal to a de facto vertical form of cooperation, under which the Court, operating as a European supreme court, is able to impose its rulings on national courts. Finally, these cases illustrate the application of a teleological approach to the provisions of the Treaty, allowing the Court to adopt important legal doctrines and principles on the basis of a creative interpretation of the treaty texts. This has led to concerns about the Court overstepping its judicial powers and becoming too political. The chapter addresses this issue in the next section.

KEY POINTS

- Direct actions begin and end in EU courts. They can be brought by individuals and 'legal persons', such as companies, member states, and EU institutions.

- There are three types of direct action: infringement proceedings; actions for judicial review; and actions for damages.

- Preliminary rulings provide national courts with the right to refer to the ECJ for guidance on issues of EU law arising in cases brought before them.

- Direct actions and references for preliminary ruling have played a crucial role in the establishment of the legal order of the EU, and have shaped the relationship between the EU and the member states.

'Judicial activism' and the reaction of the member states

The involvement of the European Court of Justice in politically sensitive issues has not been limited to defining the nature of EU or its relationship with the member states; judicial activity has also covered inter-institutional relations within the EU and the promotion of EU policies. The significance of the Court in shaping inter-institutional relations can be seen in a series of important decisions—Case 294/83 *Partie Ecologiste 'Les Verts' v Parliament* [1986] ECR 1339, the *Comitology* Decision 87/373/EEC of 13 July 1987, and *Parliament v Council (Chernobyl)* [1990] ECR 4529—in which the Court ruled that the acts of the European Parliament were subject to judicial review and that the EP should be given the right to stand as an applicant in Court procedures, even though this at the time was not explicitly provided for in the Treaty. These decisions led to the redrafting of the relevant Treaty provisions in the TEU and the Treaty of Nice, giving the European Parliament first limited, and then full, standing rights in the Court in judicial review cases. These decisions by the Court helped to strengthen the position of the EP, the only democratically elected EU institution. On several occasions, the Court has demonstrated its commitment to the promotion of democratic principles within the EU. By way of example, in Case 45/86 *Commission v Council* [1987] ECR 1493, the Court made it clear that the EU institutions had an obligation to give reasons for their acts, which would then be checked by the Court.

With regard to the promotion of EU policies, the free movement of goods is an illustrative example. The then Article 28 EC (now article 34 TFEU) prohibits 'quantitative restrictions on imports and all measures having equivalent effect'. Its aim is to prevent member states from restricting the trade of goods within the Union by placing quotas on the amount of imported goods or adopting measures having equivalent effect (MEQR) to quotas. The Court, in two seminal decisions, Case 8/74 *Procureur du Roi v Dassonville* [1974] ECR 837 and Case 120/78 *Rewe-Zentral AG v Bundesmonopolverwaltung für Branntwein (Cassis de Dijon)* [1978] ECR 649, adopted a very broad interpretation of MEQR, including in the prohibition of Article 28 not only national rules that directly discriminate against imports, but also rules that, without discriminating against imports, have a negative impact on the trade of goods within the EU. Such rules concern, inter alia, the shape, size, or weight of the product. The broad scope that the Court has given to the meaning of MEQR had a very positive impact on the establishment of a single market for goods in the EU by forcing member states to make policy adjustments and to amend considerable parts of their domestic legislation in order to meet the demands of the Court.

More recently, in Case C-438/05 *International Transport Workers' Federation and anor v Viking Line ABP* [2008] IRLR 143, and Case C-341/05 *Laval* [2007] ECR I-11767, the ECJ recognized the workers' right to strike as a fundamental right within the EU, but held that the exercise of this right might infringe employers' rights of freedom of movement and establishment under Articles 49 and 56 TFEU (ex 43 and 49 EC). Industrial action in such cases must be justified and proportionate. The decision was characterized as 'disappointing', because the Court subordinated the right to strike to free movement, showing that its primary concern was the removal of barriers to intra-EU trade rather than the promotion of human rights (Davies, 2008: 147).

Occasionally, national courts express their disagreement with the ECJ's rulings, but finally accept them, thus fostering integration and policy change (Obermaier, 2008: 735). National governments seem to have followed a similar stance (Fennelly, 1998: 198). While they have largely excluded the Court's jurisdiction from politically sensitive areas, such as security, defence, and foreign policy, they have cautiously accepted the expansion of the role of the Court in European affairs and its controversial rulings in other areas. They have even amended their national constitutions to safeguard the unhindered implementation of EU law (Hartley, 2007: 238). There are various possible explanations for the national governments' reaction. One may be that the ECJ's decisions serve the governments' own interests. The Court's rulings have been a useful tool with which to override popular opposition on important issues such as the nature of the EU or the relationship between the EU and member states. Also governments have few reasons to fear the Court's activism, since they are always in a position to retaliate effectively. Governments may be able to amend the EU treaties and their national constitutions, or to insert opt-outs in the treaties that would deprive the Court of jurisdiction. Or they could merely fail to comply. For example, in the Lisbon Treaty, the Irish Republic and the UK have the right to opt in or to opt out of EU policies in the area of Justice and Home Affairs (JHA). The ECJ has no effective responses to those measures. Moreover, the Court's activism is not a zero-sum game. As the history of European integration shows, the Court may not be actually competing against member states, but it may instead be assisting them by offering solutions that advance common interests when political processes fail (Craig and de Búrca, 2011: 64).

KEY POINTS

- The decisions of the European Court of Justice have considerable political impact, not only on the relationship between the EU and member states, but also on both EU inter-institutional relations and the promotion of EU policies.

- National courts and governments appear to support the ECJ's decisions, despite occasional opposition.

- Member states can restrict the Court's power by amending EU treaties, fuelling domestic opposition, or inserting opt-outs in the treaties.

- The Court, with its strong commitment to European integration, could be a useful tool in advancing common values in periods during which political processes fail.

Conclusion

The European Court of Justice has 'no rival as the most effective supranational judicial body in the history of the world' (Stone Sweet, 2004: 1). Its history has been one of great successes and the Court will always have a prominent position amongst the main actors of European integration. The twenty-first century, however, is presenting the courts of the European Union with new challenges. The Eastern enlargement led to the appointment of several new judges to the ECJ from countries with very diverse legal traditions; it also led to a large increase in the courts' workload. So far, the transition seems to have been smooth, but it is still too soon to say how the situation in the enlarged ECJ will develop in the medium and long terms, and how a heavier workload may impact on the Court's activism. However, it should be noted that even before the Eastern enlargement, the Court's activism had shown signs of slowing down. It seems that the deepening of European integration derived from the expansion of the European Parliament's role as co-legislator and the gradual increase of EU competences by agreement of member states helped to 'cool down' the Court's activism. However, the current euro sovereign debt crisis has brought forward significant revisions of EU policies on the economic front that will extend the Court's jurisdiction (see Chapter 27). For example, the signing by twenty-five member states of the Treaty on Stability, Coordination and Governance in the Economic and Monetary Union, which commits EU member states to balanced budgets, envisages a new role for the Court—that of ensuring member state compliance with EU fiscal rules.

Another major challenge for the Court will be the EU's accession to the European Convention on Human Rights (ECHR), as required by the Lisbon Treaty. The protection of human rights has never been the strongest aspect of the EU's work. Thus while the ECJ has developed its own jurisprudence in the area and the Lisbon Treaty, which contains a list of rights that are to be protected, has incorporated into EU law the Charter of Fundamental Rights, an adequate level of protection of human rights in the EU will be achieved only through formal accession to the ECHR (Jacqué, 2011). But the ECHR is a treaty external to the EU that has its own court, the European Court of Human Rights (ECtHR). The EU's accession to the ECHR will subject all EU institutions, including the courts, to the jurisdiction of the ECtHR. Therefore the EU and the courts will see their political and legal autonomy compromised. The process of EU accession to ECHR is still under way. A draft agreement was prepared in July 2011, but it is likely to take years to be completed because it requires approval and ratification by all EU member states, and the member states of the Council of Europe, which is the organization supporting the ECHR. Also the EU is reluctant to accede to all protocols attached to ECHR. It is obvious, however, that despite and beyond these challenges European integration needs the courts' judicial support to offer legitimacy and consistency to the process.

? QUESTIONS

1. What is the role of the European Court of Justice in the process of European integration?

2. Why were the specialized courts established? What function does the European Civil Service Tribunal perform?

3. How does EU law ensure member state compliance with their EU obligations? What is the contribution of the Court?

4. Who can bring an action for judicial review and why does this matter?

5. To what extent and in what ways is the preliminary rulings procedure necessary?

6. What is the political significance of the ECJ's rulings in *Van Gend en Loos*, *Costa*, and *Francovich*?

7. Do you agree with the criticism of the Court's judicial activism?

8. What are the major challenges facing the EU courts?

GUIDE TO FURTHER READING

Arnull, A. (2006) *The European Union and its Court of Justice*, 2nd edn (Oxford: Oxford University Press)   This volume records and analyses the contribution that the European Court of Justice has made to the EU's legal framework.

Arnull, A. and Wincott, D. (eds) (2002) *Accountability and Legitimacy in the European Union* (Oxford: Oxford University Press)   This contains an interdisciplinary collection of essays considering various aspects of accountability and legitimacy in the EU.

Craig, P. and de Búrca, G. (2011) *EU Law: Texts, Cases and Materials*, 5th edn (Oxford: Oxford University Press)   This successful textbook offers an exhaustive analysis of the role of the Court, and the relationship between the EU and national courts.

Dashwood, A., Dougan, M., Rodger, B., Spaventa, E., and Wyatt, D. (2011) *Wyatt and Daswood's European Union Law*, 6th edn, (Oxford: Hart Publishing)   This textbook offers an exhaustive analysis of EU law and institutions.

Lanaerts, K. and Van Nuffel, P. (2011) *European Union Law*, 3rd edn (London: Sweet and Maxwell)   This textbook offers a detailed analysis of EU law and its institutions, including the courts.

 ## WEBLINKS

http://eur-lex.europa.eu/en/index.htm   EUR-Lex provides direct free access to European Union law, specifically the *Official Journal of the European Union*, as well as the treaties, legislation, case law, and legislative proposals.

http://www.curia.eu.int   The official website of the EU courts.

http://www.cvce.eu   A detailed online archive on the development of European integration, which contains a section on the ECJ.

http://www.jeanmonnetprogram.org/index.html   The website of the Jean Monnet Centre for International and Regional Economic Law and Justice at the NYU School of Law. It contains, amongst other things, the Jean Monnet Working Papers, which feature the most current scholarship on EU law.

https://e-justice.europa.eu/home.do?plang=en&action=home   The European e-Justice Portal is electronic 'one-stop shop' that provides information about justice systems in the EU, and general information about case law at the EU and national levels.

14

Interest Groups and the European Union

Rainer Eising and Sonja Lehringer

Reader's Guide

This chapter examines the role of interest groups in EU politics. It also considers the way in which the EU institutions influence interest group structures and activities. The chapter begins with a brief overview of the relationship between the EU institutions and interest groups, and examines the steps taken thus far to regulate that relationship. It then looks at the structure of the interest group system, focusing in particular on two salient aspects: the difference between national and EU organizations; and the difference between business and diffuse interests. Finally, the chapter addresses the Europeanization of interest mediation (see also Chapter 9), to discuss how EU membership may have altered the structure and activities of domestic interest groups.

Introduction

The institutions of the European Union do not make policy in a vacuum and the links that they have with civil society take many different forms. Interest groups (see Box 14.1) have a particularly important role to play in connecting European-level institutions with the citizens of the European Union, as well as in mediating between them. Frequently, they are expected to socialize their members into democratic politics, to give a voice to citizens between elections, to participate in constructing a general will out of the specific concerns of groups, and to serve as 'schools for democracy'.

At first glance, the EU interest group system looks broadly pluralist (see Streeck and Schmitter, 1991). Both the large number of groups and their huge variety suggest that many interests are represented in the EU institutions. Usually, no single interest group enjoys a clear monopoly of representation in any one policy area. Of the EU groups present in the agricultural sector, for example, many reflect particular product specializations. Some of these compete and bargain not only with groups across policy areas, such as with environmental or consumer groups, but also with groups within the agricultural domain. Coalitions are generally fluid and depend on shared interests. Yet examples such as the European Social Dialogue (see 'Business interests') question the notion of free competition between interests, because only certain actors, in this case the social partners, have a guaranteed access to the policy process, thus pointing towards a neo-corporatist practice. The multilevel character of the EU polity that offers interest groups

multiple access points and opportunities, the differing interest representation practices across policy areas and institutions, and the diversity of interests point towards a distinct and dynamic EU system of interest mediation (see Beyers et al., 2008).

The following sections set out the broad terrain of EU interest mediation. The first highlights the impact of the EU institutional setting on interest representation and describes the measures that the EU institutions have implemented to regulate lobbying activities. The second summarizes the structure of the EU interest group system, while the third discusses how the EU may have affected the structure and functions of domestic interest groups, through a process that is now referred to as 'Europeanization' (see also Chapter 9).

The EU institutions and interest groups

Political institutions, such as the European Union, have important effects on interest organizations. They not only form an opportunity structure within

---

BOX 14.1 Lobbies and interest groups

The literature on the European Union's interest groups rests largely on a body of research in the field of comparative politics.

- The term 'lobbyist' originated in the nineteenth century, when individuals waiting in the British parliamentary lobby exerted influence on members of legislatures to pass Bills on behalf of unknown customers. Lobbying was then almost exclusively regarded as a commercial activity. Later, attempts by organizations to influence public bodies were also included in this narrow definition.

- Since the 1920s, the term 'pressure group' has increasingly been used in the political science literature as a term that is considered familiar and which therefore needs little explanation. Its meaning comes close to that of a lobby group, in that it centres on the functions of these groups to influence—or to put pressure on—a parliament or government.

- The term 'interest group' refers to the underlying rationale of these groups. Members join groups because they share common attitudes or interests (Truman, 1951: 34).

- 'Interest organizations' refers to interest groups that are highly formalized. This highlights the continuity of organizations, as well as their ability to cope with complexity via differentiation. It also draws attention away from particular leaders and members, and towards the effects of the organizational form.

- The term 'non-governmental organization' (NGO) connotes a normative outlook and is often used by diffuse interests to avoid the 'interest group' label, which is frequently associated with selfish lobbying for material interests.

- Similarly, the term 'civil society organizations' (CSO) is frequently meant to imply that such organizations act and speak for the citizenry at large, or at least for large segments of society.

Beyers et al. (2008) propose three factors that define an actor as an interest group: organization (which excludes broad movements and waves of public opinion); political interests (also called political advocacy); and informality (no aspiration to public offices and no competition in elections, but the pursuit of goals through frequent informal interactions with politicians and bureaucrats).

which interest groups can pursue their interests, but they also set up committees and bodies to consult regularly with groups (Mazey and Richardson, 2002); they delegate policy-making and implementation powers to such committees and bodies (Falkner et al., 2005); they support a variety of interest groups by providing finance, organizational help, and privileged access (Pollack, 1997; Smismans, 2004); and they pursue their own policy preferences in alliances with groups that are supportive of their case (Eising, 2009). Four characteristics of the EU as a system of governance affect how interest groups seek to influence the European institutions, as well as the ways in which these institutions incorporate interest groups into EU policy-making: first, the EU is a highly dynamic system; second, the EU system is horizontally and vertically differentiated; third, the EU is a system that favours consensus building; and finally, the EU is a system that increasingly attempts to regulate lobbying activities.

Since the mid-1980s, the European Community (and, after 1993, the EU) has significantly extended its competences. This steady accretion of powers gives some indication of the dynamism that characterizes the European political agenda. This has had important consequences for interest groups. From a short-term perspective, it is difficult for interest organizations to forecast the development of the EU's political agenda; therefore they are often uncertain about their political options and stakes, particularly in the early phases of the policy process. This forces interest groups to devote considerable resources to monitoring EU developments. From a long-term perspective, the number of groups operating at the European level has steadily increased in direct response to, or in anticipation of, European institution-building and regulation. At the same time, the formation of European interest groups has triggered responses from competing interests, which has led to even more groups being established. As a result, the interest group system in the EU has become much more diverse over time. Initially, it consisted mostly of economic groups. Groups representing diffuse interests, such as environmental groups or development NGOs, have become more vocal since the 1970s and 1980s. And while only a limited number of groups from the six founding members were initially present in the European arena, nowadays EU policies attract the attention of organizations from the twenty-seven member states and beyond, including from acceding and candidate countries.

The EU's second relevant characteristic with regard to interest groups is its horizontal and vertical differentiation. *Horizontally*, political responsibilities are distributed among the European institutions. The European Commission is the most important point of contact for interest groups at the European level. Since the Commission is dependent on external information when preparing EU policies, interest groups seek not only to be present in the expert committees that advise the Commission, but also to establish and maintain informal contacts with it. The Commission has a monopoly over policy initiation (see Chapter 10), which grants it a crucial role in agenda-setting and policy formulation. As 'guardian of the treaties', it also plays an important role in monitoring member states' and non-state (or private) actors' compliance with Community law. Interest groups rarely approach the Commission as a collegiate body, but tend to maintain relations with one or more Directorates-General (DGs) responsible for specific policy areas and proposals. While the Commission observes general guidelines regulating the relationship between its officials and interest groups, DGs enjoy a large degree of autonomy, which results in different practices of interest mediation.

As the main legislative chamber, the EU Council is a highly relevant contact for interest groups, especially if EU policy proposals are salient to the national actors. The European Council is also an important actor, because it sets the EU's general political direction and priorities, and deals with sensitive issues that cannot be resolved at a lower level of intergovernmental cooperation. Unlike the Commission, the EU Council and the European Council are more difficult targets for interest groups, as both institutions do not tend to be so readily accessible with regard to regular lobbying. Because it is composed of national representatives, the EU Council and its administrative machinery, the Committee of Permanent Representatives (Coreper) and the Council working groups (see Chapter 9), are rarely lobbied directly, although there is some evidence that the Councils are opening up gradually to interest representation (Hayes-Renshaw, 2009: 79). Rather, domestic interest groups tend to address their concerns to politicians and bureaucrats of the national government departments. The European Council is even more removed from interest group pressure.

The co-legislative role of the European Parliament (EP) has been gradually expanded in EU governance since the Maastricht Treaty. The Lisbon Treaty makes the ordinary legislative procedure (OLP) the main procedure for adopting legislation in the European Union, thus making the EP a highly relevant lobbying target for interest groups (see Chapter 12). Within the Parliament, the heads of the standing committees and the *rapporteurs* responsible for particular dossiers are the most important addressees for interest group demands. Since members of the European Parliament (MEPs) are elected by national voters, they are more amenable to national pressures than the Commission; they are also more open to protectionist demands than the Commission and the EU Council, as seen in the debate over service liberalization. Moreover, they seem to be more responsive to diffuse interests, including those representing the environment, consumers, and large groups such as the unemployed and pensioners (Pollack, 1997).

As the EU's judiciary, the Court of Justice of the European Union (CJEU), which, since Lisbon entered into force, includes the European Court of Justice (ECJ) and the General Court, formally interprets EU law and monitors compliance with it. European law takes precedence over national law and grants rights to individual citizens that national courts must uphold. Notably, the preliminary rulings procedure (see Chapter 13) allows national courts to refer questions of European law to the Court, and enables interest groups to challenge the compatibility of domestic and EU law. However, in practice, to take a case to the Court usually demands that a body of EU law already exists. Even when this is the case, the outcome of such an action is uncertain, the financial costs are heavy, and the duration of the case is generally lengthy. This means that this avenue is not available to all citizens and interest groups, and will be worthwhile only when the stakes are perceived to be especially high.

Finally, set up to channel the opinions of organized interests into European politics, the advisory European Economic and Social Committee (EESC) is a tripartite body composed of individual members who are nominated by the EU member states and who represent employers, workers, and other interests such as environmental organizations or farmers. Interest groups consider the EESC to be of much less

importance for the representation of interests within the EU than direct contacts with the EU institutions. Nevertheless, during the debate about the role of civil society in European democracy (see Chapter 25), the EESC sought to establish itself as an important voice of European interests (see EESC, 2004), and has also developed several proposals for strengthening its participation in EU policy formation and institution building (Smismans, 2004).

EU institutions respond differently to lobbying activities and interest groups' preferences in lobbying an institution are shaped by the institution's relative role in the EU policy-making process. However, as the latest treaty revision shows, the EU is committed to ensuring the participation of interest groups in the policy process as a principle of good governance. Title II of the Treaty on European Union (TEU) includes provisions on democratic principles. According to Article 11(2) TEU, the EU institutions 'shall maintain an open, transparent and regular dialogue with representative associations and civil society'. Furthermore, Article 11(3) TEU stipulates that the 'European Commission shall carry out broad consultations with parties concerned in order to ensure that the Union's actions are coherent and transparent'.

Policy-making in the EU is not confined to the European institutions, however. *Vertically*, the EU institutions share powers with the member states, depending on policy areas and on the stages of the policy cycle. Agenda-setting and policy formulation are concentrated at the European level, whereas implementation (excluding competition policy and agricultural policy) is reserved extensively for the member states. The EU is increasingly regarded as a multilevel system (Marks and Hooghe, 2001; see also Chapter 8), implying that multiple points of access are open to interest organizations (Pollack, 1997). Groups must take heed of political developments at the European and the national levels, and need to be present at both levels if they hope to see their interests well represented. They also need to coordinate their strategies across each level. In reality, only a minority of interest groups is able to pursue multilevel strategies in the sense of establishing routine contacts with political institutions at each level. This is because they are tied to their local, regional, national, or European memberships in one form or another, and must also make efficient use of scarce resources.

A third feature of the EU is its preference for consensus-building. This is a consequence of the unpredictability of the EU policy agenda and the complexity of the EU's political system (see Katzenstein, 1997; Kohler-Koch, 1999). For member states, consensual decision-making guarantees some protection against being outvoted in the EU Council when vital interests are at stake. Decision-making by consensus, rather than on the basis of qualified majority voting (QMV), implies that EU institutions and the national governments need to take the opinions of all relevant interest groups into account to prevent groups opposed to the legislation from ultimately blocking the agreement. However, the possibility that the EU Council can use QMV means that national groups are no longer able to rely on a national veto in seeking to defend their interests in the EU Council.

The EU's fourth relevant characteristic is its regulation of interest groups since the 1990s. The contacts between EU institutions and interest groups range from a variety of informal ad hoc consultations to more formal arrangements in EU committees or the EU's Social Dialogue (see 'Business interests'). While these practices differ across EU institutions, there is a common trend to develop better-defined frameworks to institutionalize consultations with interest groups. The European Commission has traditionally preferred not to regulate consultative practices, but to apply administrative rules and to let interest groups operate on the basis of self-regulatory principles. In 1992, it proposed 'an open and structured dialogue' that aimed at making the access of interest groups more transparent (European Commission, 1992b). During the 1990s, the participation of interest groups in EU governance was framed as a mechanism to reduce the EU's assumed democratic deficit. Therefore, in its 2001 White Paper on European Governance (WPEG), the Commission made recommendations on how to enhance democracy in the EU and increase the legitimacy of the institutions (European Commission, 2001a). A series of measures aimed at raising the input legitimacy of the EU by incorporating expert advice into EU policy-making were proposed (see Chapter 25). These measures introduced web-based registers of experts and committees, and a comprehensive code of practice on expert advice, as well as legislative impact assessments (Greenwood, 2011; Quittkat and Kohler-Koch, 2011: 83). Furthermore, the Commission signed protocols with the EESC and the Committee of the Regions (CoR) to involve interest groups earlier in the policy process, and to enhance their function as intermediaries between the EU, on the one hand, and civil society and the regions, on the other. Interest groups could register in the voluntary Consultation, the European Commission and Civil Society (CONECCS) database. In the follow-up to the WPEG, the Commission adopted a set of general principles and minimum standards for consulting interest groups (European Commission, 2002a: 15). These standards expected the Commission to ensure clear and concise communications, to announce open public consultations on a single access point on the Internet, to ensure an adequate coverage of the target groups, and to acknowledge the receipt of comments by reporting on the results of the open public consultations (European Commission, 2002a: 19–22). These measures would enhance the transparency and accountability of consultations, and ensure that all interested parties were being properly consulted. Regarding output legitimacy, the standards aimed at enhancing the effectiveness and coherence of EU policies (see Chapter 25). These standards have been criticized for being insufficient to streamline the consultation patterns, given their non-binding character and the omission of some established modes of consultation. Moreover, some of the initiatives contained in the WPEG and in the 2002 Communication were never properly implemented. To some critics, building linkages with public interests is also an unsuitable strategy to cope with the democratic deficit because EU-level interest groups are rather removed from their domestic constituencies (Warleigh, 2001).

The European Parliament (EP) and the Commission have traditionally differed in their approach to civil society participation. As elected representatives of the European citizens and subject to public scrutiny, MEPs regard interest group influence as potentially problematic in two respects. First, they maintain that 'the European and national parliaments', rather than civil society groups, 'constitute the basis for a European system with democratic legitimacy'. Organized civil society is important, but also 'inevitably sectoral', so that it 'cannot be considered as having its own democratic legitimacy' (European Parliament, 2001: points 8, 11a). In other words, the MEPs do not consider functional representation by interest groups to be equivalent to citizen representation by parliamentarians. Second, concerns about a lack of transparency and a desire to ensure the integrity of its members explain the EP's preference for a stricter lobbying regulation. In 1996, the EP established a register of interest groups. After registration and on acceptance of a code of conduct, interest representatives received a pass that allowed access to the EP for a year. Under the rules of parliamentary procedure, the MEPs and their assistants are also obliged to indicate their paid activities and the donations that they receive, clarifying any relationship that they might have with stakeholders.

In 2005, and in the context of the European Transparency Initiative (ETI), the Commission started a reform of lobbying regulation in the EU that culminated in the creation of the Transparency Register in 2011—that is, a joint register of interest groups for the EP and the European Commission. Commissioner Siim Kallas framed the ETI as an attempt to redress the mistrust of European citizens towards lobbyism and EU institutions. According to the Estonian Commissioner, 'lobbyists can have a considerable influence on legislation, in particular on proposals of a technical nature', but 'their transparency is too deficient in comparison to the impact of their activities' (Kallas, 2005: 6). Thus the ETI sought to enhance the financial accountability of EU funding, to strengthen the integrity and independence of the EU institutions, and to impose stricter controls on lobbying (European Commission, 2006). For this purpose, the Commission proposed the voluntary registration of organizations and optional compliance with a code of conduct, while the EP argued for a single mandatory register of lobbyists for all EU institutions following the United Nations model. After an open consultation with citizens and interest groups, in 2008 the Commission launched a voluntary register for lobbyists seeking to influence EU policy-making. This register replaced the CONECCS database and distinguished three main categories of lobbyist: professional consultancies and law firms; corporate lobbyists and trade associations; and NGOs and think tanks. While requirements for inclusion in the register varied for all three, particularly regarding financial disclosure, inclusion in the register required acceptance of a binding 'Code of Conduct for Interest Representatives' (European Commission, 2008a). In its evaluation of the register in 2009, the Commission highlighted its positive effects in allowing citizens to appreciate the variety of interests active at the EU level. This, it was said, enhanced transparency and provided a reasonable level of financial disclosure. The Commission also noted the relatively high number or registrations despite the voluntary nature of the scheme. By May 2011, 3,923 organizations had registered. In that same month, the EP and the Commission concluded an inter-institutional agreement to establish a common Transparency Register, replacing

the one set up by the Commission in 2008 and the registration system set up by the EP in 1996 (European Parliament, 2011a). This register remains voluntary, although accreditation to access the EP is still compulsory, and the categories of organization have been expanded to reflect the diversity of actors—namely: professional consultancies, law firms, self-employed consultants; in-house lobbyists and trade/professional associations; non-governmental organizations; think tanks, and research and academic institutions; organizations representing churches and religious communities; and organizations representing local, regional, and municipal authorities, and other public or mixed entities. By May 2012, a total of 4,766 lobbyists had registered.

KEY POINTS

- Political institutions, such as the EU, form a **political opportunity structure** that influences the formation and behaviour of interest groups.

- The EU's institutional setting (its dynamic political agenda, its complexity and multilevel character, and its reliance on consensus) shapes the interest group system and interest mediation within the EU.

- There are multiple points of access to the policy process available to interest groups.

- European institutions increasingly regulate interest group behaviour even though there are still significant variations among and within institutions in the handling of interest representation.

European interest groups

The number and variety of interest organizations operating at the EU level are vast, although it is difficult to provide an accurate figure. A number of factors explain this difficulty, including complexities in identifying and classifying actors (Beyers et al., 2008), differing data sources (Berkhout and Lowery, 2008), and the lack of transparency. While different sources do not yield a common figure, they do at least provide consistent indications of growth over time, with the two high-growth periods appearing to be the late 1950s to early 1960s and the mid-1980s to the early 1990s. Also, the mixture of represented interests has changed over time. Currently, not only European interest organizations,

Table 14.1 Interest organizations in the European Union		
Type of interest organization	2007	2011
Corporations	295	313
EU trade associations, associations of the professions, chambers of commerce	843	823
National trade associations, associations of the professions, chambers of commerce	200	–
Non-business EU interest groups	350	372
EU and global trade unions	24	23
Regions	198	226
Think tanks	72	51
Law firms	118	125
Public affairs consultants	153	200

Source: Greenwood (2011) based on Landmarks (2007) and Dod's (2011)

but also national associations, think tanks, professional consultancies, law firms, and organizations representing local, regional, and municipal authorities are active in representing the respective interests involved (see Table 14.1).

One might classify interest groups according to type, number, or the homogeneity of their members, the kind of interests that they represent, or whether they operate at a national or European level, or both. In this chapter, whether groups operate at the national or European level and the type of interest that they represent (business and non-business interests) will be considered in some detail, because these differences have particularly important implications for the EU policy process.

EU and national groups

It is important to distinguish between national and EU interest groups (the latter are sometimes called 'Eurogroups'), because their organizations and constituencies vary and because they tend to pursue different strategies when representing their interests.

Typically, EU interest groups are higher-order associations that are composed of national associations rather than individuals. Many EU interest organizations are federations of national interest groups, while the remaining Eurogroups comprise either the direct membership of other organizations (such as firms), or a combination of these two elements (Aspinwall and Greenwood, 1998). An example of the latter is the European Chemical Industry Council (CEFIC), which brings together both national associations and individual firms. Generally, EU associations perform fewer functions than their national members and, as a consequence, their resources are much smaller. To different degrees, they create links among their memberships, provide and distribute information on EU activities, develop common positions, and promote the interests of their members by presenting expertise and arguments to the EU institutions (Lindberg, 1963: 98). Compared to national associations, they concentrate on the representation of interests rather than on the provision of services to their members. Owing to their multinational membership and the heterogeneity of the national settings represented by these bodies, EU groups often have real difficulty in reaching agreement on important policy questions, as well as in ensuring their members' compliance with these agreements (see Haas, 1958).

National groups are composed of individuals, firms, or non-profit organizations, but can also operate as federations that aggregate other sectoral or regional associations. For example, the Federation of German Industries (BDI) brings together thirty-eight sectoral business associations. Among them is the Association of the German Chemical Industry Association (VCI) that represents 1,650 chemical firms, as well as twenty-one sub-sectoral associations. National associations tend to direct their attention to their national governments, emphasizing the national character of their interests. But some national interest groups now also act as multilevel players, who are present both at the national and the European level.

A fairly elaborate division of labour has evolved between the EU associations and their national counterparts. European interest groups are far more visible at the EU level than are national associations (Eising, 2004), and have become important intermediaries between their national members and the EU institutions. This particularly holds true when the EU political agenda is set and when policies are being formulated by the EU institutions. In contrast, national associations are more vocal than EU associations when EU policies are being transposed into domestic law or being implemented by the national public administration.

Business interests

Business interest organizations make up the largest share of interest groups in the EU. This category of interests was quick to respond to European integration. The Confederation of European Business (BUSINESSEUROPE), formerly the Union of Industrial and Employers' Confederations of Europe (UNICE), which is the primary European employers' association, was set up as early as 1958. The equivalent public sector association, the European Centre for Public Sector Firms (CEEP) followed soon after in 1961. Another body, the Federation of the Chambers of Commerce in the European Union (EUROCHAMBRES), which represents small and medium-sized enterprises (SMEs), was also founded in 1958. Alongside these EU federations, there are a number of cross-sectoral associations that have firms as direct members. For example, the American Chamber of Commerce (AmCham) represents the European Council of American Chambers of Commerce and has a total of 10,000 European and American corporate members. The European Round Table of Industrialists (RTI) is composed of around forty-five executives of leading European firms and was particularly influential in pushing for the single market programme in the mid-1980s (Cowles, 1997; see also Chapter 19).

Along with CEEP and BUSINESSEUROPE, the European Trade Union Congress (ETUC) is the most important cross-industry social partner in the EU. The term 'European social partner' refers to those organizations at EU level that are engaged in the European Social Dialogue as provided for under Articles 151–155 TFEU. The Social Dialogue was set up in the mid-1980s as part of Jacques Delors' strategy to build a social dimension into the single market. In 1991, the Maastricht Treaty included a Social Agreement that provided the legal basis for this mechanism, which was incorporated into the Amsterdam Treaty in 1997. The competences of the social partners in the social field are extensive: they are allowed to provide technical information, to indicate the position of their members, and to suggest alternative courses of action, and they also have the right to formulate and/or implement the policies themselves (see Box 14.2 and Chapter 20).

Large firms have also become increasingly important in the interest group landscape. They lobby EU institutions directly, have formed direct membership organizations (rather than federations), and have also been important in the restructuring of business associations since the 1980s. Within BUSINESSEUROPE, for example, large firms were able to secure top positions in the standing committees, giving them a key role in the formulation of joint policy positions (Cowles, 1997). In sectors such as automobiles, chemicals, and biotechnology, large firms, by acting outside the framework of interest organizations or by forming direct membership organizations, have acquired greater influence than either the national or the EU federations. Individual lobbying by large firms often secures better access to both EU and domestic political institutions than that of the European and national associations—although there is evidence of the contrary, as in the case of *Electricité de France* (EdF), the largest utility company in Europe, which, despite lobbying to protect its monopoly position in France, had to accept the liberalization of the electricity sector as part of the single market programme in the late 1980s. EU institutions in particular may even prefer to cooperate with large firms and direct membership organizations, because these are able to agree on common positions more easily than the EU federations. This has a detrimental effect on European associations, which find it more difficult to aggregate interests along national lines.

BOX 14.2 The role of social partners

- Social partners are procedurally involved in the genesis of any Commission initiative in the social policy field.

- Social partners may decide on how they wish to implement their agreements. Article 155(2) TFEU provides two ways in which to ensure its implementation: the 'voluntary route', relying on national procedures and practices specific to management and labour, and the member states; or the route via 'implementation by Council decision', which leads in practice to implementation by Council **directive**, including all legal consequences specific to the instrument of a directive.

- Social partners may decide on autonomous agreements in all social policy fields—even those not falling under the competences of EU as defined in Article 153 TFEU.

The extent to which the business community is able to pursue its interests effectively varies enormously across time and issues, while, as illustrated, business is far from being a unitary actor. Nonetheless, it remains relevant to ask whether the strong presence of the business community is the result of the greater variety of business interests needing representation, or whether it has more to do with firms being better able to form interest groups based on specific economic interests. Interest group theories have predominantly focused on the latter cause, raising important questions about the democratic implications of interest group activity and leading scholars to characterize EU interest mediation as a form of 'elite pluralism' (Coen, 2009: 160). Elite pluralism may be characterized as a system of interest mediation in which access to the EU consultative institutions is open, but competitive, resulting in biased access patterns.

Non-business interests

Non-business interests include those pursued by religious, social, human rights, consumer, and environmental groups, and are typically recognized under the umbrella level of 'non-governmental organizations' (NGOs) or 'civil society organizations' (CSOs). They are characterized by the broad scope of their policy goals and the absence of a well-defined group membership, which is why they are often also considered to be diffuse interests. Unlike business interests, diffuse interests face two key challenges that constrain their mobilization at the EU level—namely, a relative absence of EU regulation, and collective action problems. As argued under 'Business interests', the expanding policy competences of the European institutions were accompanied by the mobilization of interests at the European level wanting to influence policy outcomes. However, in the early years of the integration process, the absence of regulatory activity in areas such as welfare and social policy resulted in the absence of incentives for diffuse interests to mobilize at the European level, because their key policy concerns were still regulated at the domestic level. Even well into the 1970s, welfare and social policy groups were conspicuously absent from Brussels (Harvey, 1993: 189–90). But the numbers of non-business interests started to significantly increase in the 1980s as a response to new European programmes. Only the EU's increasing regulatory activity has mobilized diffuse interest groups at the European level (see Box

14.3). Thus the growth of anti-poverty groups in the second half of the 1980s was a direct consequence of new EU programmes in this policy area (Harvey, 1993: 190). The foundation of the European Environmental Bureau (EEB) came about as a consequence of the EC's first environmental programme in 1974. Today, the EEB is the most comprehensive European environmental organization, bringing together more than 140 national associations, and is part of the Green 10, a coordinated network of the ten leading environmental NGOs active at EU level, such as Greenpeace, the World Wide Fund for Nature (WWF), and Friends of the Earth, reflecting the new regulatory powers in this policy area. An early example of the impact of the EU institutions on the evolution of diffuse interest groups is the European Consumer Union Bureau (BEUC). Domestic consumer organizations formed the BEUC in 1962, with the support of the European Commission and as a response to market integration (Young, 1997: 157–8).

The second reason for the presence of fewer diffuse interest organizations is their collective action problems. In other words, the broad scope of their policy goals and the absence of a well-defined group membership encourage freeriding and the suboptimal provision of collective goods (Olson, 1965). Moreover, ideological differences, overlapping responsibilities, and competition for scarce EU funds constrain even further the ability of diffuse interests to aggregate the concerns of their constituencies and organize effectively at the European level.

To address this imbalance in interest representation among business and non-business groups, the Commission and the Parliament sponsor the formation of diffuse interest groups. They offer them financial support through EU Budget lines and specific programmes, and enhance their standing in the policy process. While their grants amount only to a small proportion of the EU Budget, to the interest groups concerned they can be of major importance (see Pollack, 1997: 581). However, there are no clear-cut criteria for the distribution of these funds. Some EU Budget lines grant interest groups mid-term financial security, while others provide financial means on a year-by-year basis, endangering the continuity of the organizations' work and even their survival. The information about who receives this financial support is also scarce. Recent research by Mahoney and Beckstrand (2011) shows that, between 2003 and 2007, the Commission made payments amounting to more

BOX 14.3 The European Women's Lobby (EWL) and EU treaty change

Founded in 1990, the European Women's Lobby (EWL) is the largest alliance of women's NGOs in the EU, bringing together thousands of women's organizations throughout Europe. In 2012, the EWL comprised twenty-seven national coordination departments and twenty-one European-wide member organizations. It claims to represent more than 2,500 direct member organizations.

The EWL works for the advancement of equality between women and men, as well as the mainstreaming and monitoring of a feminist gender-equality perspective in all areas of EU policy. Between 1994 and 1997, the EWL worked for the inclusion of a new gender-equality clause into the TEU to overcome the absence of non-work-related issues in the EU's equal opportunity policies at that time. By using a double strategy (at both the European and national levels), the lobby succeeded in having its demands taken up by governmental representatives and, in the end, included in the Treaty's amendments (Helferrich and Kolb, 2001).

After the European Union decided to create a group of experts, the so-called 'Group of Wise Men', to advise member states on what issues should be taken up in the Amsterdam Treaty revision, the EWL assembled a 'Wise Women's' Group' to work on a comprehensive position paper. Several position papers and a survey were followed by a large campaign meant to raise consciousness in the member states, and by Europe-wide petitions, which prompted the European Parliament to

ask members of the EWL to present their position in a hearing. Important aspects of the EWL position were then integrated into the EP's position at the **intergovernmental conference (IGC)**. The following innovations included in the Amsterdam Treaty are said to be at least partly the result of the campaign by the EWL:

- Article 3 of the Treaty incorporates the principle of gender mainstreaming to all policies of the EU; and

- women were added to the new Article on anti-discrimination;

- Article 141 was extended to include equal pay for equal work; and

- the principle of equal treatment was enshrined in the Treaty.

Those contents have been adopted in the Treaties of Nice and Lisbon.

Similar success stories about interest groups are rare. It is important to bear in mind that several external factors enabled the EWL to have such an impact on public policy—namely, the new mandate of the EU for social policy as a result of the northern **enlargement** and the legitimacy crisis of the EU after the signature of the Maastricht Treaty. And the decision to revise the TEU in an IGC created a helpful policy window.

Source: http://www.womenlobby.org/

than €150 million to interest groups. Of the recipients, 29 per cent are EU groups and nearly 64 per cent national or sub-national groups. The former received 61 per cent of the funds and the latter received 28 per cent. EU interest organizations that have a large membership and that have a high visibility in the EU committee system can count on receiving payments. Most of the funding went to groups from the EU-15, while diffuse interest groups constituted a substantial proportion of the beneficiaries. Other research, however, shows that, at least in some EU programmes such as the Life Programme, business interests have received significantly more EU funding than diffuse interest groups (Rozbicka, 2011).

There is a perceived risk that the EU institutions use the diffuse interest groups for window dressing in social policy and that interest organizations become highly dependent on the EU institutions, thus influencing the organizations' political positions and activities. Financial support might allow the EU

institutions to co-opt interest organizations, limiting their opposition to European initiatives. For such reasons, some groups such as Greenpeace do not accept public funding. Yet there is 'no ready evidence of attempts by the Commission to steer networks towards, or for that matter away from, particular policy positions' (Harvey, 1993: 191). A recent study concurs with that finding (Mahoney and Beckstrand, 2011). Recent studies of the Commission's consultations in the areas of employment, social affairs, equal opportunities, and health and consumer policy conclude that the Commission reaches out to a great variety of actors (Quittkat and Kohler-Koch, 2011). In sum, financial support enables diffuse interest organizations to participate in EU decision-making, while simultaneously allowing the Commission to broaden its support base, improve its expertise on the divergent arguments of different groups, and claim that the legitimacy of EU policies has increased. However, even though the degree of bias in the interest group system may have decreased as diffuse interest groups in the EU became more active in the 1990s, the extent of change does not equate to that of the US, where citizen groups constitute a much larger part of the interest group population (Baumgartner and Leech, 1998: 102–6).

KEY POINTS

- Interest groups in the European Union are not a consistent unitary actor. Differences between EU and national groups, and between business and non-business interests, have important implications for the EU policy process.

- The social partners have extensive rights, such as the right to formulate and/or implement European policies themselves. They are co-legislators in EU social policy.

- Business interest organizations still outnumber non-business interests to a significant extent.

- The Commission and the EP provide material and procedural support in order to enable diffuse interest organizations to participate in decision-making.

The Europeanization of interests

European integration affects interest group activity at the European level and also has important consequences for *national* interest groups. These may take a number of different forms.

First, many domestic interests are affected by EU policies. As the European Union extends its remit, more and more issues of concern to interest groups are likely to involve the European institutions. Accordingly, groups need to coordinate interest representation at different levels of governance in the EU multilevel system and decide which roles the Brussels route, the national route, their membership in EU-level interest groups, their own direct lobbying, coalition formation, and the hiring of professional consultants play in their strategies. To cope with these changes in their political environment, domestic interest groups may feel the need to *adapt* to new circumstances through organizational change and through change in their relations with other groups (see Grote and Lang, 2003).

Second, while resourceful actors such as large firms can easily afford to be present in both the domestic and the European arenas (see Coen, 2009), this holds only for a minority of national associations (Eising, 2009). For diffuse interest groups, it is particularly difficult to mobilize their constituencies and supporters in different countries.

Third, the embeddedness of interest groups in the domestic context impacts on the choice of domestic and EU-level strategies. Domestic interest organizations that are situated in an unfavourable domestic opportunity structure have an important incentive to act at the EU level to pursue their interests. The closure of the national route to domestic interests increases the likelihood of EU-level activities (Poloni-Staudinger, 2008). Correspondingly, those interests that are located in a favourable domestic context may feel less need to follow the Brussels route, since the national venue is open to them. However, according to several empirical studies, strong ties with national politicians and bureaucrats enable domestic interests to act also at EU level (Beyers, 2002: 607; Eising, 2009).

Fourth, the impact of the EU on domestic interest mediation is as yet unclear. Relations among domestic groups and domestic institutions need not necessarily weaken because of European integration; rather, European integration may contribute to a strengthening of existing ties among actors (Benz, 1998: 583). For example, when there is some uncertainty over new EU legislation, this can prompt national actors to exchange information or to reinforce domestic alliances. The degree of impact seems to be down to organizational, issue-specific, and systemic factors.

Fifth, the growing importance of EU policy, and the new opportunities and risks that emerge, may even lead national interest groups to redefine their interests. The EU multilevel system may cause groups to look at issues from a European perspective, rather than continue to define problems in purely national terms (Katzenstein, 1997).

Finally, it is as yet unclear whether European integration strengthens the influence of state institutions or allows interest organizations to influence more effectively public policy. On the one hand, it appears that European integration strengthens national executives, because the latter act as gatekeepers between the national and the European arenas. European integration can strengthen the capacity of executives to set the domestic political agenda, to control the flow of policy information, to legitimize political activities, and to contain the ability of opposing actors to veto their political initiatives (Moravcsik, 1998). National executives may also gain autonomy vis-à-vis interest groups by referring to negotiation pressures in the EU Council. This can help them to turn down unwanted interest group demands. Moreover, the complexity of the EU multilevel system may make it difficult for interest organizations to identify 'the' decisive locus of authority in the EU (Grande, 1994). On the other hand, the EU multilevel system offers interest groups multiple venues in which to pursue their interests. Easy access to resources and resource dependencies in their relations with the EU institutions can tip the balance in favour of interest groups.

KEY POINTS

- The increase in European regulation may cause domestic interest groups to redefine or 'Europeanize' their interests.

- Interest groups may change in order to retain some control over public policy as it becomes more Europeanized.

- European integration can strengthen the ties between domestic institutions and interest groups.

- It is unclear whether European integration strengthens national governments at the expense of interest groups or vice versa.

Conclusion

European integration has left its mark on interest representation in Europe. A new multilayered interest group system has emerged to reflect the multi-level institutional set-up of the European Union. While the EU offers interest groups numerous points of access (potentially a source of confusion), it also grants interest groups an important say in the European policy process because of its disposition towards consensual decision-making. The EU institutions actively promote the formation of European-level groups, by providing funds for weaker, more diffuse interests and supporting those involved in implementing European policy. Over time, the view of interest groups has changed. While they are still important contributors to EU policy-making, they are increasingly also regarded as representatives of civil society in the EU.

Some observers even argue that interest groups have the potential to remedy the EU's democratic deficit (see Chapter 25), because they allow for greater political participation. However, this kind of argument has to recognize that there is a potential bias built into the system of EU interest representation. The system is asymmetric, with the large majority of groups representing business interests and only a minority more diffuse social interests. Lacking in organizational capacity, the latter are highly dependent on support from the European institutions. Moreover, interest groups offer a different sort of representation from that of bodies such as national parliaments. It is therefore questionable whether the institutionalization of civil society participation offers an appropriate remedy to the problems of democracy and accountability from which the European Union suffers.

?   QUESTIONS

1. How does the institutional setting of the European Union impact upon interest mediation?

2. How have the European institutions sought to regulate and structure interest group activity?

3. In what way and to what extent does the EU support interest groups? Why does it do this?

4. In what way do interest organizations benefit the EU?

5. How important is each European institution as an addressee of interest group demands?

6. What are the similarities and differences between national and EU groups?

7. Why are there still more business than non-business interests present in the EU?

8. In what sense has there been a Europeanization of interest mediation?

GUIDE TO FURTHER READING

Balme, R. and Chabanet, D. (eds) (2008) *European Governance and Democracy: Power and Protest in the EU* (Lanham, MD: Rowman & Littlefield)   This study explores the interplay between collective action and democracy in the EU and its member states through a wealth of case studies.

Beyers, J., Eising, R., and Maloney, W. (eds) (2008) *West European Politics*, 31/6 (issue entitled 'The politics of organised interests in Europe: lessons from EU studies and comparative politics')   This volume examines the accomplishments of the present interest group literature and identifies potential avenues for future research.

Coen, D. and Richardson, J. (eds) (2009) *Lobbying the European Union: Institutions, Actors, and Issues* (New York: Oxford University Press)   This book follows the role of interest groups in the policy process, from agenda-setting to implementation in the EU.

Greenwood, J. (2011) *Interest Representation in the European Union*, 3rd edition (New York: Palgrave Macmillan)   This textbook provides a useful introduction to the role of interest groups in the EU.

Knodt, M., Greenwood, J., and Quittkat, C. (eds) (2001) *Journal of European Integration*, 33/4 (issue entitled 'Territorial and functional interest representation in EU governance')   This volume compares the lobbying activities of territorial actors (regions, localities) to those of non-territorial interest organizations.

WEBLINKS

http://ec.europa.eu/yourvoice/consultations/index_en.htm   'Your voice in Europe' is the European Commission single online access point for public consultations.

http://ec.europa.eu/transparency/civil_society/index_en.htm   Provides information on the dialogue and consultations of the Commission with civil society.

http://europa.eu/transparency-register/index_en.htm   Provides information on the Commission's and the European Parliament's joint Transparency Register.

http://www.eesc.europa.eu/?i=portal.en.home   The website of the European Economic and Social Committee.

Interest organizations also have their own websites. The following are some examples.

http://www.alter-eu.org   The Alliance for Lobbying Transparency and Ethics Regulation.

http://www.beuc.org   The European Consumer Union Bureau

http://www.businesseurope.eu/Content/Default.asp   BUSINESSEUROPE

http://www.eeb.org   The European Environmental Bureau

http://www.etuc.org   The European Trade Union Congress

http://www.green10.org   A group of leading environmental NGOs active at the EU level

http://www.socialplatform.org   The platform of European social NGOs

PART 4

Policies and Policy-making

15

Policy-making in the European Union

Alex Warleigh-Lack and Ralf Drachenberg

Chapter Contents

Reader's Guide

This chapter discusses how policy decisions are taken in the European Union. The chapter begins with an outline of the ways in which such power was originally exercised in the EU and discusses the evolution of the formal balance between the EU institutions over time, drawing particular attention to the increasing legislative power of the European Parliament (EP). Although the Community method remains the core of the EU policy process, the chapter also outlines the ways in which the EU has begun to complement these formal decision-making channels with a range of 'new governance tools' that act to produce coordinated member state action through iterated processes of standard-setting, best practice identification, and knowledge transfer. Particular attention is paid here to the best known of these processes, the open method of coordination (OMC). The final part of the chapter assesses trends in EU decision-making after the EU enlargements of the 2000s and the coming into force of the Treaty of Lisbon in 2009.

Introduction

Policy-making at the European Union level is complex. All of the member state governments and the EU's supranational political institutions, the European Commission and the European Parliament, play very important roles. In certain policy fields, such as monetary policy, particular specialized institutions have the principal parts; in the case of monetary policy, for example, that institution is the European Central Bank (ECB). A wide range of non-state actors, such as trade unions, interest groups, and non-governmental organizations (NGOs), try to shape policy decisions. Since the 1990s and responding to the expansion of EU policies, numerous agencies with diverse functions (some are quasi-regulatory; others perform specific technical or managerial tasks) have proliferated at the EU level. The delegation of functions to agencies such as the European Food Safety Authority (EFSA), for example, aims to facilitate the independent involvement of experts in highly specialized policy areas, to lighten the workload of key institutions such as the Commission, and to help the coordination with the member states. Always in the background, however, is the balancing act between the various levels of the system that we know as the EU—that is, the 'European' level, the national level, and the sub-national level (local and/or regional governments). Thus it is possible to identify a *horizontal* and a *vertical* separation of powers in the EU.

The elaboration of the classic functions of government in the EU is rather fuzzy (see also Chapter 8). There is clearly a separate judiciary: the Court of Justice of the European Union (CJEU), which includes the European Court of Justice (ECJ) and the (European) General Court (EGC), in conjunction with the national legal systems (see Chapter 13). But the executive and legislative functions of the EU are mixed responsibilities. The EU Council and the Parliament share the legislative function. The task of being the EU's executive—that is, holding responsibility for ensuring

that EU policy is carried out properly—is chiefly performed by the Commission (at times in collaboration with regulatory agencies), with the Court also given powers to rule in cases of alleged non-compliance with EU policy by member states. However, the new modes of governance, such as benchmarking and best practice exchange, allow the member states to coordinate their policies without creating a new common European policy; under these forms of decision-making, the member states are also given an executive role, since they are responsible for their own compliance with the measures agreed at EU level.

On the other hand, the *vertical* separation of powers is shaped by the tensions between member state sovereignty and the incremental involvement of the EU in areas of policy that were not envisaged by the original Treaty of Rome. The principle of subsidiarity, which aims to regulate the exercise of competence (see Box 15.1), and the detailed description of the allocation of competences between the Union and member states in the Treaty aims to clarify and address the tensions inherent in the fluidity of the EU's multilevel system (see Table 15.1). Thus, in some areas of policy, such as tax, the EU has either no or very few powers. In others, such as agriculture or competition, it has essentially replaced the individual member states as the locus of meaningful power. This balance of power between the EU and its member states changes over time; a case in point is environmental policy, in which the EU initially had no formal powers whatever, but in which it is now often seen as the leading actor in the world (see Chapter 24). The original 'Community method' of operating (see 'The evolving Community method') has thus been considerably revised over time.

The structure of this chapter is as follows. First, and briefly, we explore the evolution of the Community method. Next, we investigate the mechanics of EU policy-making through a focus on the ordinary legislative procedure (OLP). The following section focuses on the recent trend towards 'soft policy', and

---

BOX 15.1 The principle of subsidiarity

Under the principle of subsidiarity, in areas which do not fall within its exclusive competence, the Union shall act only if and in so far as the objectives of the proposed action cannot be sufficiently achieved by the member states, either at central level or at regional and local level, but can rather, by reason of the scale or effects of the proposed action, be better achieved at Union level. . . . National Parliaments ensure compliance with the principle of subsidiarity.

(Article 5 TEU)

Table 15.1 Allocation of competences between the EU and the member states

Whose competence?	Policy areas
Exclusive Union competence Only the EU may legislate and adopt legally binding acts, the member states being able to do so themselves only if so empowered by the EU or for the implementation of EU acts.	**Customs union** Establishment of competition rules Monetary policy for the **euro area** Conservation of marine biological resources under the Common Fisheries Policy (CFP) **Common Commercial Policy (CCP)**
Shared **competence** between the Union and member states The member states shall exercise their competence to the extent that the EU has not exercised its competence. The member states shall again exercise their competence to the extent that the EU has decided to cease exercising its competence.	Internal market Aspects of social policy **Cohesion** policy Agriculture and fisheries Environment Consumer protection Transport Energy Area of freedom, security, and justice Research and technology (R&T) development Development policy
Competence to support, coordinate, or supplement the action of the member states The EU shall have competence to carry out actions to support, coordinate, or supplement the actions of the member states, without thereby superseding their competence in these areas.	Human health Industry Culture Tourism Education Civil protection Administrative **cooperation**

Source: Articles 2–6 TFEU

in particular the most well-known instance, the open method of coordination (OMC). In our conclusions, we evaluate the mixture of hard and soft forms of decision-making in the EU, and assess how the system is functioning in the post-Lisbon Treaty period.

The evolving Community method

John Peterson (1995) divides EU decision-making into two basic types: those of 'history-making' proportions, and those of daily law-making. When it comes to the initial category of really major issues—such as setting out a strategy for the European Union as a whole over a period of years, or agreeing changes to the treaties—member state governments have all meaningful power. Meeting at head of state or government level in the European Council, they make complex bargains and ensure that the package of proposals that results from such summits is acceptable to all of them, by means of the unanimity rule. Thus any member state can veto a proposal that it finds unacceptable, even as part of a bigger compromise package. Recent rounds of proposed treaty change have been prepared by Conventions—that is, gatherings of representatives from the EU institutions, member states, and civil society, which have drafted the text of proposed new treaties. These Conventions have been influential in shaping the content of recent treaties, but the power to decide upon what to do with their recommendations remains firmly with the member state governments.

In daily decision-making, Helen Wallace (2010) identifies five policy-making patterns as a heuristic device to describe the diversity that characterizes the EU. Because policy-making in the EU does not take place in a vacuum, these five patterns reflect experimentation and evolution in the EU over time, different degrees of institutional involvement, different treaty bases, changes in national policy-making processes, and the type of decision-making outcome. As shown in Table 15.2, these are: the Community method; the EU regulatory mode; the EU distributional model; intense transgovernmentalism; and policy coordination. The chapter will focus on the Community method (via the ordinary legislative procedure, or OLP) and policy coordination (via the open method of coordination, or OMC).

Thus, in day-to-day decision-making, the standard operating pattern is now a sharing of formal legislative power between the member states (via the EU Council) and the EP, played out against a backdrop of furious network-building. This process, known as the ordinary legislative procedure (OLP—formerly 'co-decision'), has had a fundamental impact on the life and relevance of the EP in particular by increasing its legislative role from marginal to co-legislator with the EU Council (see Chapter 12 and Figure 15.1 under 'The ordinary legislative procedure'). However, this emerging standardization of the legislative process is not the whole story, for it is complemented by the increasing use of the so-called 'new' or 'soft' governance tools such as benchmarking or the OMC. These governance tools give essentially no role to either the CJEU or the EP, although they can involve a range of civil society actors, and produce EU decisions of a rather different kind: not legislation, but recommendations, advice on best practice, and guidelines.

The original Community method was famously analysed by David Coombes (1970). He described a mode of integration that depended upon a two-way separation of political powers, with the Commission and EU Council enjoying a near monopoly on decision-making and agenda-setting (in other words, getting issues onto the legislative agenda). The EP had extremely few powers. Interest groups were encouraged to lobby, but had no formal powers beyond the rather weak European Economic and Social Committee (EESC). The emphasis was clearly upon 'hard' legislation and although progress was often very difficult to obtain, as witnessed by the 'empty chair' crisis of the 1960s and the so-called Eurosclerosis of the 1970s (see Chapter 2), the system was relatively simple. Unanimity in Council was the decision rule in all legislative decisions.

The process of adapting the Community method began in earnest in the mid-1980s, as part of the drive to complete the single market by adopting the Single European Act (SEA). In order to secure this important objective, the member states agreed to give up their veto powers in a specified range of issues, in recognition that the goal of market integration was worth some

sacrifice of national sovereignty (Sandholtz and Zysman, 1989). This introduced qualified majority voting (QMV) to the EU, meaning that only a certain proportion of the member states need to accept a measure for it to obtain the support of the EU Council as a whole. The system allocates a certain number of 'weighted votes' to each member state, roughly in proportion to their population size, and roughly 70 per cent of these weighted votes constitutes a 'qualified majority'. However, from 2014, the calculation of what constitutes a qualified majority will change to a double system: 55 per cent of the votes in Council, so long as the states in the majority group represent at least 65 per cent of the EU population (Article 238 TFEU). Qualified majority voting does not apply to every area of legislation. Nonetheless, it applies to most of it and constitutes a historic departure from the normal practice of international organizations, in which unanimity is required for all decisions. It has contributed enormously to the success of EU decision-making by making it possible to overcome resistance from a small number of member states when consensus cannot be obtained.

The SEA also paid attention to the EP in order to address certain aspects of the democratic deficit (Warleigh, 2003), but also to recognize that, through its canny use of its internal rules and few formal powers, the EP was already becoming a more central player in decision-making. The assent procedure was introduced in certain policy areas and this gave the EP the ability to reject, but not to amend, certain proposals. Over time, for the same underlying reasons and also, perhaps, to drive a wedge between the Commission and the EP (Moravcsik, 1998), the powers of the EP have grown (see Chapter 12).

Thus we can see that the legislative system of the EU is a triangle between EU Council, Parliament, and Commission. Formally speaking, no legislative proposal can be made unless it comes from the Commission, which gives the latter significant power over the EU agenda, although both the EU Council and the EP have been known to make successful 'requests' for a proposal to the Commission. The Lisbon Treaty also makes it possible for citizens to ask the Commission to initiate a legislative proposal via the so-called citizens' initiative (Article 11 TEU) (see Chapter 25). Even under the OLP, the Commission plays a key role in the early stages of the decision-making process, and is able to shape the positions adopted by the EP and the EU Council. At the other end of the process, formal decisions about the content of policy are left to the EU Council and EP.

Table 15.2 Patterns of policy-making in the EU

Policy-making pattern	Key features	Typical policy
The Community method	Legislative function Commission takes policy lead and monopolizes drafting and tabling of legislative proposals European Parliament (EP) usually has joint decision-making powers with Council under the ordinary legislative procedure (OLP); if not, EP must be consulted before any final decision can be taken Court of Justice of the European Union (CJEU) has final jurisdiction over all legislation	Common Agricultural Policy (CAP) Trade policy
Regulatory mode	EU institutions have strong relatively independent decision-making powers Commission acts as agenda-setter, and engages with **stakeholders**, experts, and agencies to develop **regulation** EP and EU Council co-legislate CJEU has a significant role in ensuring implementation	Competition **Single market** Environmental policy
Distributional mode	Commission sets agenda and oversees implementation EU Council is main legislator and decides mainly under unanimity rules EP has key role in deciding the Budget CJEU has marginal role	Budget
Intensive transgovernmentalism	Right of policy initiation not exclusive to Commission, but also held by member states EP in weak consultative position (with regards to consent to international agreements) Focus on cooperation rather than law-making Intensive interaction between governments Decisions made by European Council or Council of Ministers (unanimity) CJEU excluded	Common Foreign and Security Policy (CFSP)
Policy coordination	Open method of communication (OMC) is main policy-making instrument Focus on benchmarking best practices in decentralized approach Commission plays increasingly important monitoring and **agenda-setting** role Policy goals and guidelines set by Council of Ministers (unanimity) Member states submit to Commission and Council annual reports on their progress EP excluded CJEU plays marginal role	Employment Aspects of **fiscal policy**

Source: Wallace (2010: 90–103)

Table 15.3 Types of legal act of the EU (Article 288 TFEU)

Type of legal act	Legally binding?	On whom?
Decision	Yes	The specific group or person concerned, for example a particular member state or firm
Regulation	Yes	All member states, regarding both the substance of the decision and the manner of its implementation
Directive	Yes	All member states regarding substance, but with the manner of implementation at the discretion of the member state
Recommendations and opinions	No	All member states and specific groups concerned

Four types of EU legal act result from this legislative process: regulations; directives; decisions; and recommendations and opinions. These differ in the degree to which they are binding on the member states or the specific legal persons to whom they are applied (see Table 15.3).

Most EU policy is regulated in the form of directives, which gives the member states the maximum leeway on issues of implementation. This is important to note because it allows the different national systems to find their own methods of achieving an agreed common goal. It also means, however, that the EU institutions have fewer powers to oversee implementation of policy than might otherwise be the case.

KEY POINTS

- Decision-making in the European Union is complex. This complexity derives primarily from the vertical and horizontal separation of powers.

- There are five categories of policy-making that describe how decisions are made in the EU: the Community method; the EU regulatory mode; the EU distributional model; intense transgovernmentalism; and policy coordination.

- The Community method began as a two-way separation of powers at EU level, between the Commission and the Council, and with unanimous voting required in the Council.

- Over time, the Community method was adapted to introduce two very significant new components: qualified majority voting (QMV); and what has become a very powerful legislative role for the European Parliament.

The ordinary legislative procedure

Under the Lisbon Treaty, what was formerly known as the co-decision procedure became the ordinary legislative procedure (OLP). To understand the OLP, it helps to remember that it is a *process* and that what happens at one stage of the process has an impact on what happens at the next stage, either by opening up new possibilities or by restricting the scope for action. This is reflected in the idea of the 'policy chain', which is a metaphor for the interlocking stages of the decision-making process as the particular issue moves from conception to implementation amidst complex feedback loops and inter-linkages (Hudson and Lowe, 2004; Versluis et al., 2011). A typical process for a new EU directive would take place roughly as described in Figure 15.1.

Given the fuzzy separation of powers in EU decision-making both horizontally (at EU level) and vertically (between the EU and national/sub-national levels), it is unsurprising that the decision-making process is characterized by a scramble for influence. This process of *hustling* (Warleigh, 2000) begins before the proposal is published, as actors with an interest in the subject of the proposed legislation attempt to shape its content right from the outset if they are aware it is in gestation. The Commission is also often open to input from member states and the European Parliament (EP), in order to avoid making proposals that would not get these other institutions' support. The Commission must also achieve an internal agreement between all of its Directorates-General (DGs) about what should be included in the proposal, reconciling what can often be divergent intra-institutional preferences.

Figure 15.1 The ordinary legislative procedure (OLP)

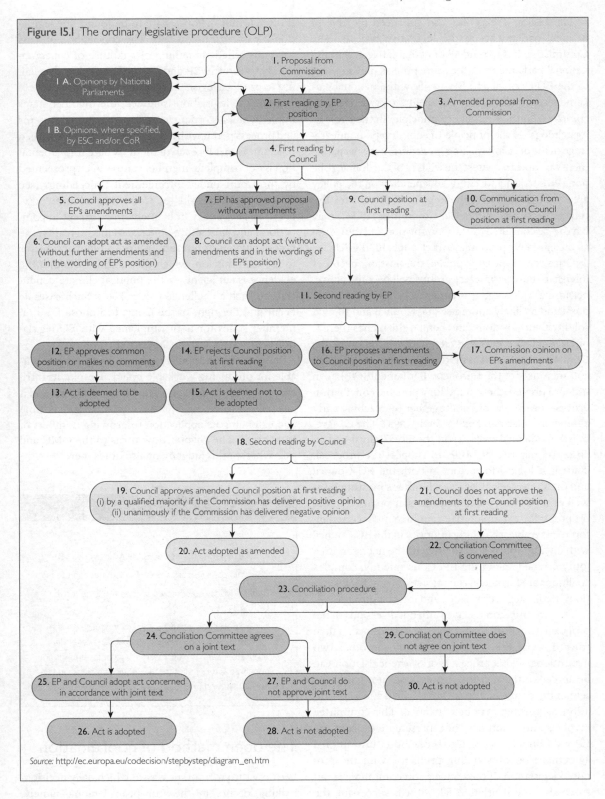

Source: http://ec.europa.eu/codecision/stepbystep/diagram_en.htm

The Lisbon Treaty has also enhanced the role of national parliaments in the legislative process. The Commission has to send all draft legislative acts to the national parliaments at the same time as they are sent to the EU Council and EP, to allow the national parliaments to establish whether the draft legislative texts comply with the subsidiarity principle. In their role as 'watchdogs' of the principle of subsidiarity at an early stage of the decision-making procedure, national parliaments are able to contest the legality of the draft legislation (Protocols 1 and 2 TEU). Depending on the policy area, the Committee of the Regions (CoR) and the European Economic and Social Committee (EESC) may have to be consulted by the Commission and the Council on legislative proposals (Articles 301–307 TFEU).

Once the proposal is public, the hustling becomes intensive. Further interest groups will become active, because at this stage it is easier to be aware of a proposal and its likely contents. The Council and EP will solidify their positions, and behind the scenes there is often regular contact between national ministers, the Committee of Permanent Representatives (Coreper), and members of the European Parliament (MEPs), in order to prepare the ground for a possible conciliation process, or even avoid it altogether by reaching early agreement (Garman and Hilditch, 1998). The OLP requires a qualified majority in the EU Council and an absolute majority of MEPs to support the proposal. Thus it is logical for actors in both the EU Council and the EP to seek allies in each other's institutions as well as their own: a national minister opposed to the proposal, for example, may reinforce a concerted effort to assemble a blocking minority in the EU Council with an attempt to help to prevent the necessary majority crystallizing in the EP. Consequently, complex coalitions are formed involving actors from EU institutions, national governments, and interest groups.

The Commission receives amended versions of the proposal from both the EP and the EU Council. It then tries to revise the proposal to satisfy the other two institutions. If this process works, the legislation can be agreed; if the revision process does not work, the remaining points of dispute are clarified and a conciliation committee may be convened. This committee involves equal numbers of representatives from the EP and Council. Its task is to broker inter-institutional agreement on outstanding problems with the proposed legislation. If the conciliation committee is unsuccessful, the legislation falls; if it is successful, the legislation is put to the vote in the EP and the Council.

If the relevant majorities are to be found, the legislation is passed; if not, it falls. The conciliation process has entrenched something of a culture of collaboration between the EP and Council, meaning that failure to produce legislation is rare (Shackleton, 2012).

Once the legislation is agreed, the member states implement it according to their own national systems and processes, but with a care to ensure that the agreed objective is met by each of them. Where implementation is not complete, member states can be prosecuted by the Court under infringement proceedings (see Chapter 13). That said, the Commission has no powers to inspect policy implementation, except in competition and agriculture policies, so it is, in reality, the task of citizens or interest groups to report problems to the Commission, which then decides whether the evidence is sufficient, or the political climate conducive, to such a challenge (Alter, 2001). Such cases *do* occur and the right of the Court to impose fines on member states for non-compliance with EU legislation was written into the Maastricht Treaty.

In sum, the OLP policy chain is complex, but suitable for producing workable policy. Despite its intricacy, it is able to involve a great array of actors, and it has proven to be capable of both evolving over time and extending its application to growing numbers of issue areas. The chapter now turns to the OMC and asks whether this judgement also holds there.

KEY POINTS

- In the ordinary legislative procedure, the Commission has the right of initiative and is the main agenda-setter.

- The main co-legislators are the EU Council and the EP.

- Other advisory committees, such as the EESC or the CoR, may be consulted.

- In day-to-day policy-making, the key for success is the formulation of a **policy network** that can broker an alliance between the necessary range of institutions and non-state actors to secure the required majority in the EU Council and EP.

The open method of coordination

We now turn to another way in which daily decision-making occurs in the European Union—namely, through 'new modes of governance' (NMGs) and, in particular, the open method of coordination (OMC). The label 'new' might be considered misleading, because while a specific form of governance might be new to the European level, it may have existed for years at national or at international level, such as in the Organisation for Economic Co-operation and Development (OECD). It might be new in a given EU policy area, but not unprecedented in the EU system as a whole; a new mode of governance may be used in combination with other NMGs, or even with the Community method, in a particular issue area. How we study EU governance conceptually has implications for what we see and for what we consider to be 'new' here (Smismans, 2006a).

Moreover, while NMGs can be understood to include any form of policy instrument that deviates from the classical Community method (Scott and Trubek, 2002), others are rather similar to it, so it is right to argue that the distinction between new and old, or hard and soft, modes of governance is one of degree rather than of category (Laffan and Shaw, 2006). Furthermore, these NMGs are not a homogeneous group, because they include a variety of policy-making instruments, such as framework directives, soft law, co-regulation, partnership models, voluntary agreements, and the European Social Dialogue. While these policy instruments differ from each other, they all have certain common characteristics. New modes of governance are essentially voluntary and informal means of cooperation that establish frameworks in which policy issues can be discussed and negotiated. Because they are a form of 'soft law', they do not impose legally binding action or detailed obligations on the member states or national social partners, and they can be easily adapted to national circumstances. They promote flexibility and participation, which can lead to knowledge creation and perhaps to more effective policy, through deliberation. They are often applied in policy areas in which the national situation differs substantially or in which limited competences at EU level exist.

By the 1990s, the EU had reached the point at which the integration process was approaching core areas of national sovereignty for the welfare state, such as employment and social policy. Many actors considered that further EU activity in these areas was necessary to balance the economic integration process, but member states nonetheless remained wary about yielding more sovereignty in these areas (see Chapter 20). Thus an alternative to the Community method was required so that the EU could play a role without threatening what is often highly prized diversity in these issue areas at national level (Borrás and Jacobsson, 2004; see also Box 15.2). In this context, the development and use of the OMC can be seen as a compromise, because it retains member state responsibility for a policy area, while giving the EU a coordinating and possibly policy-shaping role that member states could accept.

The OMC was created as a package by the 2000 European Council meeting in Lisbon on the basis of various existing instruments from previous processes such as the European Employment Strategy (EES) (European Council, 2000). The OMC is a voluntary and informal mode of intergovernmental cooperation, which does not impose policy solutions or proposals on the member states and which can easily be adapted to national circumstances. It is designed to be a method of benchmarking best practices in a decentralized approach in line with the principle of subsidiarity (European Council, 2000). The OMC has now been introduced as a form of policy-making in various policy areas. However, there is no uniform OMC process, because different policy areas apply the method according to their particular circumstances (see Box 15.3). There are several factors explaining the variation in OMC processes, including: whether or not there is a (strong) treaty provision in the area of policy concerned; the role of the different institutions; the extent to which other actors can participate in the process; the existence of benchmarks, indicators, and targets; and the possibility of sanctions.

It is difficult to assess the success or otherwise of the OMC, both because it has been operational for a relatively short time and because it exists in several variants. However, analysis of the literature suggests that there

BOX 15.2 Core features of the open method of coordination

Participation	More and different actors participate in the policy-making process.
Multilevel	Policy coordination involves actors from various levels of the political system.
Subsidiarity	Policy design is decided at the lowest, most appropriate, level.
Deliberation	Policy learning and policy transferability are part of the policy-making process.
Flexibility	The use of soft law ensures the flexibility to adapt policy strategies quickly if needed.
Knowledge creation	Some NMGs use tools such as benchmarking or peer review, which can lead to the creation of new knowledge.

BOX 15.3 The ideal-type OMC, as defined by the Lisbon Strategy

The open method of coordination takes place in areas that fall within the competence of the member states, such as employment, social protection, social inclusion, education, youth, and training. This method has several steps, as follows.

1. Fixing guidelines for the Union, combined with specific timetables for achieving the goals that they set in the short, medium, and long terms.

2. Establishing, where appropriate, quantitative and qualitative indicators and benchmarks against the best in the world,

tailored to the needs of different member states and sectors as a means of comparing best practice.

3. Translating these European guidelines into national and regional policies by setting specific targets and adopting measures, taking into account national and regional differences.

4. Periodic monitoring, evaluation, and peer review, organized as mutual learning processes.

Source: European Council (2000)

---

are a number of areas in which improvements can be made. These include stakeholder participation, learning potential, the role of policy institutions, and transparency. Achieving better stakeholder participation is particularly important, since this is supposed to be a core benefit of the OMC; the recent **Europe 2020** project has recognized this deficit and attempts to correct it, as does the operational practice of several OMC groups.

In order to outline the specificities of an OMC process, the development and functioning of the OMC in the education and training (E&T) policy area will be examined in more detail. Very often, the OMC in employment is used as a case study, because it is the oldest OMC process, with a strong **legal basis** that existed even before the Lisbon Strategy was launched. However, we propose examining the potential of the OMC as a mode of governance in E&T policy because this is more illustrative of OMC in practice; it is an a priori very lightly **Europeanized** policy area, with a very limited legal base for EU action and an almost negligible EU role prior to the Lisbon European Council.

KEY POINTS

- It is important to problematize what is really 'new' about 'new modes of governance'.

- New modes of governance are usually voluntary and informal ways of taking decisions, which provide frameworks for negotiation and deliberation.

- The open method of coordination was an EU compromise, which allowed EU involvement in policy areas over which member states did not want to lose control.

- It is difficult to assess the impact of the OMC, because it is still a relatively new policy instrument.

Exploring the open method of coordination in education and training

Education and training (E&T) is an intriguing policy area, in which a combination of circumstances limits the choice of possible tools and forms of cooperation. First, there is a treaty base (Articles 165 and 166 TFEU) that grants the European Union only supporting competences, excluding legally binding Community initiatives. Second, the enormous diversity of national E&T systems makes **harmonization** particularly difficult even if there is sufficient political will. Consequently, the work of the EU in the field of education and training was limited until the late 1990s to carrying out European education programmes such as **Erasmus**, and no real policy-making took place. At the end of the 1990s, the first attempts were made to improve cooperation in E&T, by adopting the 'rolling agenda', which ensures that the EU Council pays ongoing attention to E&T issues, especially regarding employment, the development of quality standards, and professional mobility, and by establishing networks outside the EU framework, such as the **Bologna Process** in higher education. However, it was not until the European Council in Lisbon in 2000 that policy-making really started. This European Council meeting formulated two imperatives relevant to E&T: first, it set the goal for the EU 'to become the most competitive and dynamic knowledge-based economy in the world', thereby creating an important link between education and employment policies, and making improvements in E&T a necessity for the EU's competitiveness; and second, the European Council required the EU to 'undertake a general reflection on the concrete future objectives of education systems'. This arguably amounts to the member states giving themselves permission to overstep the explicit treaty base in order to realize their new objectives, while avoiding binding legislation (Hingel, 2001).

In general terms, the open method of coordination (OMC) in E&T functions very similarly to the template created at Lisbon. The member states define common objectives and benchmarks, and work on them according to an agreed programme and timetable. Clusters and peer learning activities are carried out in order for participants to identify best practices and to learn from each other; this is supported by continued checking and monitoring on the implementation, which happens through a reporting exercise. The work programme Education and Training 2010 holds all of these elements together by serving as the framework for the OMC in E&T.

Most of the learning about best practice occurs within the so-called 'clusters'. These are expert groups that concentrate on specific aspects of the E&T policy area, organizing the peer learning activities and discussing current developments. Each of the clusters is made up of member state representatives, Commission experts, and, sometimes, social partners. The work of the clusters is coordinated in the Education and Training 2010 Coordination Group (ETCG), which organizes the planning and implementation of the clusters and peer learning activities, and oversees the reporting exercise. Two main documents are published as part of the reporting exercise: an indicator and benchmark document; and a joint document. The indicator and benchmark document is potentially more critical and perhaps negative, because it is purely Commission-driven. The joint document, on the other hand, is based on national reports submitted by the member states, and their representatives are involved in the whole reporting process, both before and after collecting the data. It is this report that is the main 'naming and shaming' instrument used to encourage laggards to catch up.

The Commission and the EU Council are the main actors in the OMC in E&T. At first sight, the Council has by far the most significant role, since it has both the first word, deciding on the objectives, indicators, and benchmarks, *and* the last word, adopting the reports and Council conclusions. However, the role of the Commission should not be overlooked, because the Commission is often the initiator, driver, and main agenda-setter in the OMC process. The role of the

European Parliament in the OMC in E&T, on the other hand, is very limited, because it is only informed of decisions. While the involvement of non-state actors besides government representatives is officially promoted, the practical participation of social partners, regional governments, and civil society at large depends very much on the national traditions and political structures in the member states. For example, federal states usually involve their regions in the OMC processes more fully than more centrally organized member states.

Although it is difficult to quantify the impact of OMC measures in E&T policy, it is fair to say that the OMC in E&T has substantial consequences for policy-making at both European and national levels, albeit with a significant degree of variation between the member states, and with clear limits to the convergence of national policies and systems (Warleigh-Lack and Drachenberg, 2011). Some member states already had policy in keeping with the emerging European consensus and thus needed to change less; in some cases, member states have adopted the new EU standards as their own national equivalents; in other cases, member states have been somewhat cavalier in their approach to the OMC. However, the OMC has shifted the context in which member states make policy on E&T issues and has locked in a new link to competitiveness rather than social policy. Furthermore, national E&T policy-making is increasingly regarded as having joint objectives in a European context: as an illustration, the European qualification framework led, in many member states, to the voluntary creation of national qualification frameworks.

While using the OMC in the E&T policy area has not led to the transfer of any formal competences to the EU, it is also indisputable that the Commission has gained significant influence in this field (Warleigh-Lack and Drachenberg, 2011). There is now a substantial increase of policy output at European level in E&T as a direct consequence of this form of governance (European Commission, 2008b). Moreover, there has been a clear uploading of national issues and approaches via the OMC in this area, such as that by Belgium and France on 'equity' and teacher education.

In sum, while the OMC in E&T is a relatively young and 'weak' way of making policy decisions, it is a successful one. EU cooperation and policy-making in E&T have significantly increased over the last few years, and the Commission has gained an important role for itself. The OMC has led to more political commitment by the member states towards cooperation in E&T at European level—a major change to the situation prior to the 2000 Lisbon European Council. The Commission and EU Council have recently confirmed their support for the continuation of the OMC in this policy area, showing the substantial political momentum that it has gained over the last ten years. Certain changes are proposed, in order to address some of the criticisms and shortcomings. The strategic objectives will be updated and working methods are supposed to be improved, including strengthening of the peer learning activities. Furthermore, the reporting exercise will be improved (making it more visible) and the benchmarks will be updated for the period to 2020 (European Commission, 2008b; Council of the European Union, 2009).

> ## KEY POINTS
>
> - The open method of communication instrument is used differently according to the specific conditions of the policy areas, and thus the OMC template provided by the Lisbon Strategy is not always followed entirely. Consequently, there is not one OMC, but many.
>
> - The Commission has established for itself a significant role as initiator, driver, and agenda-setter in the OMC, at least in the area of education and training (E&T).
>
> - **European integration** in the E&T policy area has increased significantly since using the OMC as a governance form, indicating that the OMC can be a successful means of **deepening** the integration process.
>
> - The policy tools under the original Lisbon Strategy have been updated as part of the recent Europe 2020 strategy.

Conclusion

Recent years have seen several important changes to the EU system, in terms of both its geographical extent (the enlargements of 2004–07, with Croatia set to join in 2013) and its institutions (with the Lisbon Treaty). In this final section of the chapter, we assess how these changes appear to have shaped the EU decision-making process and context so far.

The first point to make is that the European Union continues to make policy decisions in a range of complex ways, and that the difference between 'history-making' and quotidian decision-making remains. New treaties are still agreed by the member states only; the same goes for setting EU strategic directions, which are still established by the European Council. Indeed, in the context of the economic crisis, it has become obvious that the European Council is where the action is regarding the EU's strategic decisions, and that the new 'permanent' President of the European Council—currently Herman van Rompuy—appears to be eclipsing his opposite number in the Commission, politically speaking (Dinan, 2011; see also Chapter 27).

Some policy areas, such as tax, remain almost entirely national competences. That said, the rise in power of the European Parliament is obvious and EU policy decisions are increasingly the source of so-called national policies. Intriguingly, new modes of

governance are often deployed as a *complement* to the Community method, as well as a *substitute* for it, and are often most effective when combined with it. This kind of variation is the result of bargains between the member states when they agree a change to the EU treaties or a new treaty entirely. If the EU is complicated, this is because the member states prefer it that way!

Ideologically, the EU appears to have shifted to the right since the recent enlargements, with less emphasis in the European Council and EU Council on both the regulation of the economy and the integration of new policy areas at European level than in the past. This is, at least to some degree, the result of a north–south/east divide that is discernible on matters of subsidies (Thomson, 2009) or protecting social standards (Crespy and Gajewska, 2010). This trend appears to hold good across a variety of policy areas and institutions, shaping not only the Councils, but also the EP (Burns et al., 2012) and the Commission (Peterson, 2008). Enlargement and the subsequent further diversification of the EU also increased the need for flexible policy tools such as the OMC. In particular in policy areas in which a great variety and diversity exists between the member states and in which competences remain in the medium to long term at national level, the use of these forms of governance remains popular. It remains necessary, however, to hustle frantically in order to shape the content of EU legislation. Indeed, this need to hustle was made more acute by the Lisbon Treaty, which introduced a new role for national parliaments in EU decision-making: an alliance between half of the national parliaments and either the EU Council or the EP can now block a new piece of EU legislation on the grounds of subsidiarity. Such a step may be welcome to boost the EU's legitimacy and to involve national parliamentarians' engagement with EU legislation, but it may make the decision-making process more complex and more obviously multilevel. As ever in the EU, time will tell.

QUESTIONS

1. What was the original Community method and why was it adapted?

2. What is the role of policy networks in EU decision-making?

3. To what extent has the ordinary legislative procedure (formerly co-decision) altered the balance of power between the EP, the Commission, and the EU Council?

4. Why was it considered necessary to use 'new' forms of policy-making such as the open method of communication?

5. To what extent is the OMC a paradigm shift in the way in which the EU makes policy decisions?

6. To what extent, and in which ways, can non-state actors influence policy-making in the EU?

7. What do you consider the main innovations in EU decision-making that were introduced by the Lisbon Treaty and why?

8. Do you think that the EU is more, or less, intergovernmental today than in the past?

GUIDE TO FURTHER READING

Borrás, S. and Radaelli, C. M. (2010) *Recalibrating the Open Method of Coordination: Towards Diverse and More Effective Usages* (Stockholm: Swedish Institute for European Policy Studies)   A very informative piece of research that provides an insight into the successes and shortcoming of the OMC.

Borrás, S. and Radaelli, C. M. (eds) (2011) *Journal of European Public Policy*, 18/4 (special issue entitled 'The politics of the Lisbon Agenda: governance architectures and domestic usages of Europe')   An excellent collection of articles that analyse the creation, evolution, and national impact of the Lisbon Strategy.

Peterson, J. and Bomberg, E. (2009) *Decision-making in the European Union* (Basingstoke: Palgrave Macmillan)   A very useful book on EU decision-making.

Phinnemore, D. and Warleigh-Lack, A. (eds) (2009) *Reflections on European Integration* (Basingstoke: Palgrave)   A collection of essays by leading academics and policy-makers on the development of both the EU system and EU studies.

Versluis, E., van Keulen, M., and Stephenson, P. (2011) *Analysing the European Union Policy Process* (Basingstoke: Palgrave)   An up-to-date guide to understanding the development and usages of the EU political system.

⊕ WEBLINKS

http://ec.europa.eu/prelex/apcnet.cfm?CL=en   The PreLex database on inter-institutional procedures follows the major stages of the decision-making process between the Commission and the other institutions.

http://eucenter.wisc.edu/OMC   The OMC Forum of the University of Wisconsin's European Center of Excellence, which makes recent and forthcoming work on the open method of communication available to researchers, policy-makers, and students.

http://eur-lex.europa.eu/en/index.htm   The Eur-Lex database offers access to EU law and other documents.

http://www.eu-newgov.org   The website of the Integrated Project on New Modes of Governance, coordinated by the Robert Schuman Centre for Advanced Studies at the European University Institute in Florence.

http://www.europarl.europa.eu/code/default_en.htm   The European Parliament's conciliation web page provides information on the progress of conciliation procedures.

16

EU External Relations

Michael Smith

Reader's Guide

This chapter focuses on the external economic relations of the European Union—the longest-established area of international policy-making and action. The chapter begins by examining institutions and policy-making in external economic relations, in which the Commission plays a central role in initiating and conducting policy, and looks especially at the Common Commercial Policy (CCP). It goes on to examine two areas of mixed competence, in which policy responsibility is shared between the EU institutions and national governments: development assistance policy and international monetary policy. The chapter then proceeds to explore the substance and impact of EU external economic policies, and to assess the role of the EU as a global economic power. The conclusions draw attention to a number of tensions and contradictions in EU external economic policies.

Introduction

The European Union is unquestionably one of the largest concentrations of economic power in the global arena. As can be seen from Table 16.1, the Union possesses 'assets' in the form of economic resources, human resources, and territory that put it at least on a par with the United States, Japan, China, Russia, and other leading economic actors, and well ahead of several of them. Equally, in trade, investment, and other forms of international production and exchange, the EU can be seen as a potential economic superpower, not least because it constitutes the largest integrated market in the world. It is rich, it is stable, and it is skilled, and thus it inevitably occupies a prominent position in the handling of global economic issues. This fact of international economic life has only been underlined by the accession of the twelve new member states between 2004 and 2007 (see Chapter 17).

Basic to the conversion of this economic potential into economic power and influence, as in so many other areas of EU policy-making, is the institutional context for the conduct of external economic policy. From the very outset in the 1950s, with the establishment of the customs union, the then European Economic Community (EEC) had to develop a Common Commercial Policy (CCP) with which to handle its relations with partners and rivals in the world economy. During the 1960s, the Community also initiated what was to become a wide-ranging and complex development assistance policy, primarily to manage relations with the ex-colonies of Community members. As early as the 1970s, there was a proposal also to establish a monetary union, with an external monetary policy, but this did not finally become established (and then only for some EU member states) until the twenty-first century. Each of these key areas of external economic policy presents the EU with distinct institutional problems and with distinct opportunities for the exertion of international influence.

The purpose of this chapter is to explore these areas of external economic policy, to link them with the institutions and policy-making processes that they generate within the EU, and to explore the ways in which these create challenges and opportunities for the EU in the global arena. By doing this, the chapter will expose a number of areas in which there are tensions and contradictions within EU policies, as well as linkages between them; it will also enable us to evaluate EU policies towards major partners and rivals in the global arena, and the extent to which the EU has been able to establish itself as a global 'economic power' by converting its potential into action.

Table 16.1 The European Union and its major rivals in the global political economy

	Population (m)	Area (m km^2)	GDP (€ bn)	Share of world trade (%)
China	1,341	9.6	4,434	Imports 11.1 Exports 14.1
India	1,191	3.3	1,231	Imports 3.0 Exports 2.0
Japan	128	0.4	4,118	Imports 5.8 Exports 6.5
Russia	143	17.1	1,116	Imports 1.9 Exports 3.4
United States	310	9.8	10,958	Imports 16.8 Exports 11.4
EU 27 (2005)	501	4.2	12,268	Imports 16.0 Exports 15.0

Note: All figures for 2010.

Source: DG Trade, http://ec.europa.eu/trade/en/; World Trade Organization (WTO), http://www.wto.org/

Institutions and policy-making: the Common Commercial Policy

The core of the European Union's external economic relations is the Common Commercial Policy (CCP). Established by the Treaty of Rome, but not fully implemented until the late 1960s, the CCP is the means by which the EU manages the complex range of partnerships, negotiations, agreements, and disputes that emerge through the operation of the customs union and the single market (see Chapter 19). As we shall see, the definition of 'commercial policy' has broadened considerably since the initiation of the EEC, but it is important to understand the core principles and policy-making procedures of the CCP as the basis for understanding the whole of the Union's external economic policies.

As established in the Treaty of Rome, the CCP was based on Article 113 of the Treaty—since amended to become Article 133 of the consolidated treaties in the late 1990s, and now Article 207 TEU. Article 207 sets out not only the principles on which the CCP is to be pursued, but also the policy-making processes through which it is to be implemented. In terms of principles, as set out in Box 16.1, the CCP embodies not only a set of aims for the external policies of the Union, but also a set of far broader aims in relation to the operation of the world trade system. This key tension is at the heart of the successes registered and the difficulties encountered by the CCP, since it sets up a series of contradictions: is the EU to achieve the aim of prosperity and stability for Europeans at the cost of international stability and development? Or is it to privilege the aim of global prosperity and development at the expense of the EU's citizens and their welfare? The reality, of course, is that there is a complex balancing process for policy-makers as they utilize the instruments of the CCP.

Essentially, these instruments fall into two broad areas. The first deals with what might be called 'trade promotion': the activities that develop the EU's international activities and organize them around certain core practices. These instruments fall partly within the control of the EU itself, but are also to be found in the broader global institutions and rules established in the world arena. Thus the EU has developed a complex range of trade and commercial agreements, covering almost every corner

---

BOX 16.1 The Common Commercial Policy

1 The Common Commercial Policy shall be based on uniform principles, particularly in regard to changes in tariff rates, the conclusion of tariff and trade agreements relating to trade in goods and services, and the commercial aspects of intellectual property, foreign direct investment, the achievement of uniformity in measures of liberalization, export policy and measures to protect trade such as those to be taken in the event of dumping or subsidies. The common commercial policy shall be conducted in the context of the principles and objectives of the Union's external action.

2 The European Parliament and the Council, acting by means of regulations in accordance with the ordinary legislative procedure, shall adopt the measures defining the framework for implementing the common commercial policy.

3 Where agreements with one or more states or international organizations need to be negotiated . . . the Commission shall make recommendations to the Council, which shall authorize the Commission to open the necessary negotiations . . . The Commission shall conduct these negotiations in consultation with a special committee appointed by the Council to assist the Commission in this task and within the framework of such directives as the Council may issue to it. The Commission shall report regularly to the special committee and to the European Parliament on the progress of negotiations.

(Article 207 TFEU)

---

of the globe. Some of these are bilateral, with individual countries such as Russia; others are inter-regional, covering relations with groupings such as the Association of Southeast Asian Nations (ASEAN); others still are multilateral, with the prime example being the World Trade Organization (WTO). In all of these areas of trade promotion, the EU aims to establish stable partnerships and relationships, often with a set of formal rules, which enable trade to develop and diversify.

A second set of CCP instruments are those of 'trade defence'. Here, the EU is concerned to counter perceived unfair trade practices by its key partners, such as the dumping of goods at unrealistically low prices on the EU market, the subsidization of goods, or the creation of barriers to EU exports. To support it in these areas, the Union has developed a battery of trade tools, including anti-dumping and anti-subsidy measures, rules of origin, sanctions, and other punishments. But it does not exercise these powers in isolation; frequently, the Union works through the WTO to counter what are seen as unfair practices, using the WTO dispute settlement procedures to defend itself at the global level. Trade and partnership agreements also include procedures for dealing with trade disputes, as a matter of routine, and sometimes linkages are made with other areas of external policy such as those on human rights and development assistance (see 'Institutions and policy-making: development assistance policy and monetary policy').

In the post-Lisbon Treaty context, the policy processes through which the CCP is implemented still make use of what historically was known as the 'Community method' (see Chapter 15). In practical terms, this means that the Commission has the power of initiative, conduct, and implementation of commercial policy agreements. In many cases, the Commission will propose 'negotiating directives' in which its negotiating mandate is set out; where this is the case, the Council has to approve the mandate as well as any changes in it, and the Commission is monitored by a special Council committee, the Trade Policy Committee of member state representatives. In other areas, the Commission has delegated powers to apply regulations (for example, on anti-dumping cases), subject to monitoring and approval by the Council. The Commission has developed a sophisticated apparatus for the conduct of trade negotiations and the conduct of 'commercial diplomacy' through its delegations and specialist missions, such as that to the WTO in Geneva. It might be argued on this basis that, in this area, the EU has effectively displaced the national trade policies of the member states (in contrast to the position on foreign and security policy, in relation to which the member states remain supreme—see Chapter 18). As a result of the Lisbon Treaty, the European Parliament has also been given a more active role in the CCP, especially in relation to the framework for trade policy-making and to the approval of trade agreements once they have been negotiated.

As time has passed, the Union has also had to respond to the changing nature of world trade and exchange, and the CCP has been reshaped to reflect the key trends. In a number of instances, this has exposed the continuing tension between the national preferences of the member states and the European perspective of the Commission, thus raising questions about the extent to which the EU has really undermined the independence of national commercial policies. A key issue here is that of competence: in the Treaty of Rome and for a long time afterwards, the CCP was assumed to be about trade in manufactured goods, but the changing global economy has given a much more prominent role to trade in services (for example, aviation services or financial services) and to related questions such as that of 'intellectual property' (the trade in ideas, such as those embodied in computer software). In order to cater for these changes, the scope of Article 113 and then 133 had to be expanded during the 1990s, and this was not always a simple process, because member states found reasons to resist the expansion of the Commission's role. The Lisbon Treaty effectively resolved these tensions, and the Union now has competence not only in trade in goods and services, but also in issues relating to intellectual property and foreign investment. Another area of tension, which has existed from the earliest days of the European Community, reflects the linkage (or the gap) between 'internal' EU policies and the Union's external relations. As internal integration reaches new areas, it is inevitably found that these have external policy consequences. Thus, in the early days of the Community, the Common Agricultural Policy (CAP) was recognized to be not only a policy about what went on within the Community, but also a policy about the regulation of food imports, and so it has remained ever since (see Chapter 23). More recently, the completion of the 'single European airline market' during the late 1990s raised questions about who was to negotiate with countries such as the US about the regulation of international air routes. Only after a prolonged struggle was it agreed that the Community (and thus the Commission) could exercise this power. A large number of other 'internal' policy areas, such as competition policy, environmental policy, and industrial policy, are inevitably linked to the global economy, and this will continue to be an issue for the conduct of the CCP and related policies.

As a result of these trends and processes, the CCP has, in a sense, 'spread' to encompass new areas of external commercial policy, especially in the area of regulatory policy. The EU has become engaged with a very large number of international institutions in the conduct of these policies and has developed a complex web of agreements with which to manage them. Not all of the EU's international economic policies fall into this framework. We will now turn to look at two of the most important of these.

Institutions and policy-making: development assistance policy and monetary policy

Historically, there has been pressure for the Community and now the Union to expand the scope of its international economic policies. Thus, from the 1960s onwards, there has been a continuing concern with development assistance policy, stimulated originally by the process of decolonization in the French empire. Since the 1970s, there has been a realization that the process of monetary integration in Europe must be accompanied by some form of international monetary policy. In contrast to the trade and commercial policy area, though, these areas have never been subject to the full Community method and thus to the leading role of the Commission. As a result, they demonstrate distinctive patterns of institutions and policy-making.

Let us first look at Community policies on development assistance. Starting in the early 1960s, a series of increasingly ambitious agreements between the EEC, its member states, and a growing range of ex-colonies created a unique system for the multilateral management of development assistance issues. Box 16.2 summarizes the key phases in this process, especially the progression from the 'Yaoundé system' to the 'Lomé system',

BOX 16.2 Key stages in the evolution of the EU's relations with African, Caribbean, and Pacific (ACP) countries

1963	*First Yaoundé Agreement* (renewed 1969) Reciprocal preferential trade access between EEC member states and associated states (former colonies of member states) European Development Fund Joint Council of Ministers, Joint Parliamentary Assembly, and Committee of Ambassadors
1974	*Lomé Convention* (renewed 1979, 1984, 1990, and 1995) Includes former British colonies ACP group established, with Secretariat in Brussels ACP partners increase from forty-six (1974) to sixty-eight (1995) Non-reciprocal trade preferences Schemes to support ACP agricultural prices (System for the Stabilisation of ACP and OCT Export Earnings, or STABEX, in 1979) and mineral export prices (System for the Promotion of Mineral Production and Exports, or MINEX, in 1984)
2000	*Cotonou Agreement* Twenty-year agreement (entered into force April 2003) Seventy-eight ACP partners (2006) Multilateral agreement to be supplemented by bilateral or minilateral economic partnership agreements (EPAs) by December 2007 (by 2010, only one of seven such EPAs had been concluded) **Conditionality**: aid payments linked to democratic government and human rights provisions

Source: European Commission, http://ec.europa.eu/europeaid/index_en.htm

and then to the present 'Cotonou system' (each taking its name from the place where the agreements were finalized). It can be seen from this summary that the successive conventions have set progressively larger ambitions for the scope of the activities that they cover and also that they have covered an increasing number of partners. As a result, the 'Cotonou system' now covers well over half of all countries in the international system, including some of the very richest and a large number of the very poorest.

The initiation of the Lomé system in the 1970s was widely felt, especially by EC member states, to herald a revolution in development assistance policy by setting up an institutionalized partnership between the EEC and the African, Caribbean, and Pacific (ACP) countries. Processes were established to create and maintain a stable partnership, in which the ACP group would have its own collective voice, and to underpin the development of the poorest economies in the face of an unstable world economy. As time passed, however, there was criticism that the Lomé framework was increasingly irrelevant to the development of a global economy and, as a result, the Cotonou system places a much greater emphasis on what might be called 'bottom-up' processes of development, in which individual ACP countries or groups of them produced their own plans for sustainable development to be negotiated with the EU. The Cotonou system also contains markedly more in the way of what has come to be called 'conditionality'—in other words, provisions that make the granting of EU aid conditional on good governance, observance of human rights, and the introduction of market economics. As such, it parallels broader developments in the provision of aid on the global scale and the United Nations' Millennium Development Goals (MDG). It has also been accompanied by special measures relating to the very poorest countries, especially the Union's 2001 'Everything but Arms' Regulation, which allows free access for all products from the forty poorest countries except those with a military use.

The EU's development assistance policies have thus had to respond to the changing nature of the global economy while taking account of new linkages (for example, between trade and development, environment and development, and so on), and to balance the needs of the developing countries against those of the EU and its member states. The most acute tensions come in the area of agricultural policy: the Common Agricultural Policy (CAP) does demonstrable damage to the economies of some of the poorest countries, by depressing commodity prices, preventing free access to the European market, and subsidizing EU exports. Here, again, we can see that external economic policy is closely connected to internal policy processes, and it is not always a profitable linkage (see Chapter 23).

Central to the problems encountered by the EU's development assistance policies are two factors. The first is an internal institutional problem: the mixture of policy competences between the EU and its member states, and (in the post-Lisbon context) between the new array of EU institutions themselves. The second is an external factor: the ways in which development assistance policies have become increasingly politicized in the contemporary global arena. In terms of the EU's institutional make-up, development assistance policy remains an area of 'mixed competence' in which policies proposed and implemented at the EU level coexist with national policies for international development. Thus, although the EU claims to be the world's largest donor of development aid, the majority of that figure consists of aid given by member states as part of their national programmes (see Table 16.2). The complex programmes that have evolved at the European level are also, unlike the CCP, the result of a complex division of powers between the European institutions and the national governments represented in the Council. As a result, the Commission and the Union cannot claim to speak with one exclusive voice in this area, although their policies and initiatives have had considerable influence on the ways in which development assistance is targeted and allocated. Agreements such as the Lomé and Cotonou conventions are mixed agreements, and the Council collectively and the member states individually have the power to ratify or not to ratify them. As with trade policy, this is also an area in which the European Parliament has a stronger and more assertive voice after the Lisbon Treaty, but the major institutional innovations made by the Treaty lie elsewhere—namely, the establishment of the new **European External Action Service** (EEAS), and the reshaping of the Commission's services into the Directorate-General for Development and Cooperation (DG DEVCO) created significant uncertainties about who controls the policy framework and (perhaps most importantly) the funding for development assistance programmes. At least by early 2012, there remained areas of tension and competition in these policy domains.

In addition to the problems created by internal institutional factors, EU development assistance policies have to contend with the fact that issues of economic and social development have become intensely politicized within the global arena. This means that aid is not simply an economic matter; it has become linked to problems of human rights, of good governance, and of **statehood** in the less developed countries, and the EU has had to develop mechanisms to deal with this. There has been an increasing tendency to concentrate

Table 16.2 EU net bilateral and multilateral overseas development assistance (ODA), 2009

Country	Amount (US$ m)
United Kingdom	13,162
France	12,920
Germany	12,397
Netherlands	6,676
Sweden	5,085
Spain	6,800
Italy	3,334
Denmark	2,923
Belgium	2,670
Finland	1,323
Austria	1,174
Ireland	1,083
Greece	618
Portugal	528
Poland	461
Luxembourg	435
Czech Republic	228
Slovenia	156
Romania	142
Hungary	131
Slovak Republic	76
Cyprus	47
Lithuania	43
Latvia	22
Estonia	19
Bulgaria	17.7
Malta	14
EU 27 total (bilateral and multilateral)	86,277
US	28,700
Japan	9,457

Sources: European Commission/OECD (2010); OECD Development Assistance Committee, http://www.oecd.org/

Cold War, there has also been a series of conflicts, for example in the former Yugoslavia and in Afghanistan, in which the EU has played a key role in coordinating reconstruction and post-conflict economic assistance. As a result, the EU's development assistance policies have moved away from their primary focus on the ACP countries and a far wider range of recipients has been identified. Among these, post-communist regimes and those involved in conflict form a key focus, as do the poorest countries, which are granted additional concessions in terms of free access to the European market for their goods.

Development assistance policy thus represents a long-established, yet continually changing, focus in the EU's external economic relations. Far less well established is the management of the international monetary relations that are an inevitable consequence of the adoption of the euro by seventeen of the EU's member states. It has long been the ambition of enthusiasts for European integration to see the establishment of a 'real' European currency that might rival the US dollar on the world stage. Although there was significant European monetary coordination during the 1980s and 1990s, it was only with the adoption of the euro in 2000 that this became a political and economic reality (and then only for a certain number of EU member states, now in a minority since the enlargement of 2004). The euro experienced a harsh baptism, declining against the dollar continually for two years or more, but it then recovered during 2003–05 as the dollar itself came under pressure. Since then, it has maintained considerable strength not only against the dollar, but also against European non-member currencies such as the British pound sterling, especially after the onset of the global financial crisis in late 2008. This is not the place to discuss the internal workings of the euro (see Chapter 22), but it is important to note that the launching of the euro created at least a partial alternative to the dollar; it has become part of the currency reserves of a wide variety of countries, and it has become a target for those concerned at their overwhelming reliance on the US currency.

The euro is managed through a complex institutional process in which the European Central Bank (ECB) plays a key role. Because it has not been adopted by all of the EU member states, it exists alongside the remaining national currencies such as the pound sterling, the Danish kroner, and the Polish zloty; whilst the governments of the non-euro countries are represented in a number of the bodies overseeing the euro

the EU's development assistance policies, especially through the EuropeAid development office and now through DG DEVCO, and to link them with the operation of agencies such as the European Community Humanitarian Office (ECHO). Since the end of the

and responsible for economic performance in the EU as a whole, there is differential membership, which gives rise to a number of frictions and tensions. The result is a complex picture of overlapping institutions and this has its implications for international monetary management—implications that have been made even more complex and demanding by the global and European financial crises of 2008 and afterwards (see Chapter 27). The euro is a common currency among a number of countries, but it is not managed by a single government: the ECB does not report to a European Finance Minister, and there is no EU system of taxation or macro-economic management. Yet the establishment of the euro has led to calls for adjustment of membership in international financial institutions such as the International Monetary Fund (IMF) to reflect the fact that seventeen governments have merged their currencies into one. Not surprisingly, the United States has been prominent among those who note that the euro area should have only one voice in such bodies as the IMF or the World Bank, and that the persistence of the national representations is an anomaly.

KEY POINTS

- Development assistance and monetary policy are two key areas of 'mixed competence' in EU external relations. Thus the EU has potentially important influence in both areas, but has to contend with complex internal policy processes, as well as international demands.

- Development assistance policy is an area with a long history and one in which the EU can claim global leadership. But there are tensions between the EU's policy framework, global rules, and the needs of developing countries.

- Key problems in development assistance include those caused by the emergence of new issues, such as those concerning the environment or human rights, and the increasing politicization of the area.

- European monetary policy has a shorter history and lacks full coverage of the EU's member states. Nonetheless, the euro area has established a key role in international monetary management.

- There is tension between the internal demands for euro area monetary stability and coordination and the external challenge of a changing global economy. This is particularly clear in the context of global financial crisis.

The European Union's external economic policy objectives

As noted, the European Union is nothing if not explicit about many of its external economic policy objectives. The tone was initially set by the provisions of Article 113 of the Treaty of Rome, in which the Common Commercial Policy (CCP) is established according to explicit principles, applying not only to the EEC and then to the EU, but also to the broader management of international commercial relations. Perhaps significantly, this set of principles has not been absorbed within the general principles and objectives of the EU's external action (see Box 16.1, under 'Institutions and policy-making: the Common Commercial Policy'). This has been backed up over the years by an extremely wide-ranging and sophisticated series of trade agreements with a wide range of partners, which go into great detail about the privileges and concessions to be given to specific partners. This can be seen as establishing an elaborate hierarchy, or 'pyramid of privilege', in which the EU manages and adjusts its relations to individual partners. From time to time, this set of arrangements raises questions about exactly how particular partners should be dealt with: for example, in the case of China, the EU has had to change its approach as the country has developed economically, and as it has increasingly become integrated into the global economy through membership of the World Trade Organization (WTO) and other international bodies.

At the same time, the EU has to balance its external obligations against the internal needs of the member states and of European producers and consumers. We have already noted that the Common Agricultural Policy provides extensive safeguards (often said to be discriminatory) for EU farmers, but this is often at the expense of consumers whose food bills are higher because of the protectionism built into the Common Agricultural Policy (CAP). Likewise, during 2005–06, there was a major crisis in trade between the EU and China because of a surge of Chinese textile and clothing exports; this led to the imposition of quotas on Chinese products, but this in turn brought howls of anguish from EU retailers who had ordered products from China only to see them prevented from entering the European market (see Box 16.3). A large number of the disputes between the EU and the United States (which, between them, account for the majority of

BOX 16.3 The EU, China, and the 'textile wars' of 2005

During the early 2000s, the rapid growth of Chinese exports created a challenging situation for the EU (as it did for other major importers, such as the US). In particular, the phasing out of the Multi-Fibre Arrangement (MFA), an international agreement that allowed importers to impose quotas if they were threatened with a surge of cheap imports, led to a major increase in Chinese penetration of the European market for cheap textiles and clothing. The EU was faced with a dilemma: on the one hand, the remaining European textile producers, concentrated in southern member states such as Italy, Portugal, and Greece, demanded protection; on the other hand, northern member states with rapidly growing markets for cheap T-shirts and other products felt the heat from their consumer and retail lobbies. The Commission was faced with an almost impossible choice: whether to live up to its international obligations and thus offend powerful internal groups, or to impose restrictions and thus potentially renege on its international commitments. The climax of the problem was reached in 2005, when frantic negotiations produced a set of compromise agreements based on voluntary restraints by China, whilst shiploads of clothing products were trapped in European ports. The compromise agreements expired in 2007–08 without an immediate renewal of the crisis—perhaps because of the European economic slowdown and slackening of demand.

disputes brought before the WTO) have been exacerbated by the lobbying of producer groups both in the EU and the US, which has created political problems around disputes that might, in earlier times, have been managed in a technocratic manner by officials and experts.

The net result of these cross-cutting tensions and pressures is a complicated picture in which the EU professes its commitment to the global management of trade issues, but often acts as though it wishes to pursue its own interests in a unilateral manner. Some of the same sorts of tensions emerge in relation to development assistance: the EU trumpets its commitment to international development and claims to be a pioneer of new types of development assistance policy, but there is always a balance to be struck between the broader international aims, those of the EU as a collective, and those of individual member states. This is institutionalized in the EU, thanks to the mixed nature of the institutional framework and the need to get agreement from the member states on major policy initiatives, and also reflects a number of powerful

historical and cultural forces arising from the history of the European empires.

In international monetary policy, we have also noted the tensions between the requirements of internal management of the euro and the pressures of the global economy. The European Central Bank (ECB) has as almost its only major policy objective the achievement of monetary stability and the reduction of inflation, but this has been held responsible for some of the problems experienced by EU economies during the early 2000s and thus for their inability to compete on a global level. Whatever the truth or the final conclusion of that argument, there is no doubt that the major economies of the euro area have often underperformed against their major global rivals and that the need to bed down the eurozone system has contributed to this problem. It can also be argued that the primacy of monetary stability in the eurozone has made it more difficult for its member countries and the ECB to respond rapidly to international financial crises such as those in the late 1990s, during which unfavourable contrasts were drawn between the speed of movement of the US system and the lack of movement from Europe, or that of 2008 and afterwards, during which national measures predominated at some crucial stages (see Chapter 27).

The EU thus has to face up to a number of tensions emerging from its pursuit of external economic policies. These have become more significant as the EU (either as a whole, or through major subgroups such as the euro area countries) has expanded its role in the global economy, and as the linkages between economic, political, and security activities have become

KEY POINTS

- The EU has a general aim of 'organizing' its external environment through commercial agreements and of creating a 'pyramid' of partners in the global economy.

- The demands of external commitments can come into conflict with internal pressures from different interests within the EU.

- This is part of a general problem created by the need for responses to a changing global environment, but can express itself in concentrated disputes and crises for the EU.

- The EU also faces the need to balance between different types of relationship: multilateral; inter-regional; and bilateral. In addition, internal pressures can lead to unilateral behaviour by the Union.

more pronounced. One way of stating these tensions is in terms of the competing demands of multilateralism, inter-regionalism, bilateralism, and unilateralism in EU external economic policies. Each of these patterns can be seen in current EU policies, and they have to be held in a complex and fluctuating balance by a set of collective institutions and individual member states with competing interests.

Obstacles and opportunities: the European Union as a power in the world economy

The European Union has enormous potential for influence and activity in the global economy, but it is equally clear from the argument in this chapter that it faces a number of important constraints on its capacity to turn potential into reality. We have already noted that a series of complex balances have to be struck in the making and implementation of EU external economic policies, between:

- the collective interests of the EU as a whole and those of individual member states or groups of member states;

- the claims and competences of specific institutions and the pressures generated by different sectors of external economic policy;

- the claims of different partners and rivals in the global arena, which demand different patterns of incentives and resources from the EU;

- the economic dimension of the EU's involvement in the global arena and the increasing levels of politicization that accompany international economic transactions; and

- the competing claims of multilateralism, inter-regionalism, bilateralism, and unilateralism in the pursuit of EU policies, often within cross-cutting institutional frameworks with complex patterns of demands.

In some ways, of course, these are no more demanding than the problems confronting any national government in the globalizing world economy. All governments and international institutions are subject to at least some, if not all, of these dilemmas. In the case of the EU, though, they are compounded by the fact that the EU itself is founded on a series of institutional

compromises and a process of continuous negotiation. This makes the competing claims more obvious and, in some ways, less manageable than they might be for a national government, no matter what its size or complexity.

Against this, the EU has considerable assets and opportunities in the global economy. We have already noted that the EU is the world's 'champion trader', with a key position in the exchange of goods, services and ideas, and its position as manager of the world's largest integrated market provides it with opportunities as well as with challenges. In recent years, the Community and then the Union, through the Commission, has sought to exploit a number of these opportunities and to establish itself as a key player in the emerging global economy. Thus it has become increasingly active in leading global trade negotiations, with varying levels of success; it has taken a leading role in the handling of international environmental issues such as those dealt with by the Kyoto Protocol on global warming (see Box 16.4 and Chapter 24); it has pursued its claim to be a leader in the provision of international development assistance,

---

BOX 16.4 The EU and the Kyoto Protocol

The EU has established what many would see as a global leadership role in the implementation of the Kyoto Protocol. This international agreement was reached in 1999 and sets targets for the reduction of greenhouse gas emissions. Whilst the EU was prominent in supporting the Protocol, others, most particularly the US and China, failed to ratify and thus to implement it. The EU spent a lot of time in the early 2000s building a coalition that could bring the Protocol into force despite the absence of the US (to enter into force, it had to be ratified by countries representing a set proportion of global emissions, and since the US is by far the largest 'offender', its absence was a severe handicap). Eventually, with the crucial ratification by Russia, the Protocol entered into force in 2005. Whilst the US is still not part of the Protocol, it has moved towards the EU's position, especially after the coming to office of Barack Obama in 2009, and seems likely to sign up to a successor Protocol to be implemented from 2012. This has had paradoxical implications for the EU: whilst it can still claim to be a leader, there is the possibility that increasing activism on the part of the US and China will lead to a sidelining of the Union as their interests gain leverage. The Copenhagen (2009) and Durban (2011) climate change conferences show contrasting examples of this process and of EU responses.

and increasingly of humanitarian aid and disaster re-lief; and it has begun to exercise material influence, albeit often indirectly and haltingly, on the conduct of international monetary policy.

This means that the EU has increasingly become acknowledged as a power in the global economy. It has acquired the legal and institutional apparatus with which to pursue this ambition, and this legal and insti-tutional framework gives it the capacity to carry out a number of important 'state functions' to preserve and enhance the prosperity of its citizens in a changing world economy. It has been able to establish itself as a key participant in global economic processes, both in formal institutional terms and in less formal terms of engagement in fundamental processes of trade, pro-duction, and exchange. In this, it has had to cope with challenges created by a number of other international economic powers, such as the US, Japan, and (increas-ingly) China and India. It has created an impressive network of international economic partnerships and has, in many cases, been able to link these with in-creasingly political conditions or requirements, for example through the use of economic sanctions. It has also taken an increasing role in global governance through its support for the regulation of international economic conditions through multilateral action.

It remains unclear in some respects what the EU as a global economic power is for or against. As we have

> **KEY POINTS**
>
> • The EU faces a complex balancing act in the global economy. In this, it is constrained by internal complexities and differences of interest.
>
> • But there are considerable opportunities for leadership, especially in new areas such as environment and humani-tarian support.
>
> • The EU is thus a key participant in global governance and its role in this area is expanding.
>
> • Nonetheless, there are still uncertainties about the EU's overall aims and impact within the global arena, and these affect both the EU and its key partners.

seen, this is a reflection of the complex institutional and other forces operating on its external economic policies, and the cross-cutting pressures to which its policy-making processes are subject. The result is a constant disparity between the EU's claims to global economic distinctiveness and the reality of its un-tidy policy-making processes. One thing that is clear, however, is that the enlarged EU of twenty-seven members (and twenty-eight from July 2013 with the expected accession of Croatia) will continue to pursue an ambitious external economic policy and will con-tinue to have a significant global economic impact.

Conclusion

This chapter has dealt with the core elements of the European Union's external economic policies: in-stitutions and policy-making; aims and objectives; constraints and opportunities; and the impact of the EU's activities. It has done so by focusing especially on three areas of policy: external trade and com-mercial policy; development assistance policy; and monetary policy. Each of these areas of policy has its own characteristic history in terms of the evolution of institutions and in terms of the EU's international engagement. We have seen that the Common Com-mercial Policy was almost built into the foundations of the EEC because of the need to manage the cus-toms union, whilst the development assistance policy responded to the need to deal with the ex-colonies of the EU's member states; we have also seen that the EU's international monetary policy emerged directly from the internal integration process expressed in the

establishment of the euro. In each of these cases, the history matters, because it situates the external policy in a certain framework of institutional development and also because it locates the policy in terms of the development of the global economy.

It is also clear that, in each of the policy areas that we have explored, there is a complex and shifting array of pressures and demands to which the EU has more or less successfully responded. The internal pressures—from member state governments, from producer or consumer groups, and from competition between the institutions—intersect with the external pressures cre-ated by globalization, by competition from major es-tablished and emerging economies, and by the pursuit of the EU's sizeable ambitions in a changing world. In these areas, the EU has for a long time had to deal with real and pressing policy dilemmas, which are a natural product of its assumption of major 'state functions'.

Despite these contradictory pressures and the difficulties of constructing policy in a global economy, the EU can claim in its external economic relations to have gone some distance 'beyond the nation state'. This does not mean that the member states are redundant: far from it, they are a major source of policy pressures and challenges for the Union's institutions, and they are a key source of the legitimacy that has been acquired by those institutions in the context of global governance. But there is also the legitimacy that has been acquired by decades of steadily deepening involvement in the global economy, and the acquisition of the knowledge and skills that go with it. These are what give the EU's external economic relations a distinctive significance and impact, and make them a key subject for study.

? QUESTIONS

I. What are the key sources of the European Union's power in the global economy and how have they changed in importance during the course of European integration?

2. What are the key features of the distribution of power between the EU institutions in issues of trade and commercial policy? Has the balance of power between the institutions changed, and if so, how and why?

3. How has the changing nature of world trade affected the EU's Common Commercial Policy?

4. What does it mean to say that development policy and monetary relations are areas of 'mixed competence' in the EU, and how does that affect processes of policy-making?

5. Why is it appropriate to describe the EU's development policies in terms of a 'pyramid of privilege'?

6. What are the key differences between the Lomé and Cotonou systems of EU development policy?

7. Why has the EU not become a 'monetary superpower' since the establishment of the euro? What developments might enable it to become one?

8. What contribution does the EU make to the governance of the global economy? Does this contribution match its potential?

 ## GUIDE TO FURTHER READING

Eeckhout, P. (2004) *External Relations of the European Union: Legal and Constitutional Foundations* (Oxford: Oxford University Press)   This is a detailed legal analysis, best read when one already knows something about the legal and institutional frameworks.

Hill, C. and Smith, M. (eds) (2011) *International Relations and the European Union*, 2nd edn (Oxford: Oxford University Press)   Several chapters deal with various aspects of policy-making and implementation in the EU's external economic relations.

Holland, M. and Doidge, M. (2012) *Development Policy of the European Union* (Basingstoke: Palgrave Macmillan)   The best and most recent general treatment of the aid and development issue, including the negotiation of the Lomé and Cotonou Agreements.

McGuire, S. and Smith, M. (2008) *The European Union and the United States: Competition and Convergence in the Global Arena* (Basingstoke: Palgrave)   Chapters 3–7 cover a number of dimensions of EU–US economic relations.

Verdun, A. (ed.) (2002) *The Euro: European Integration Theory and Economic and Monetary Union* (Lanham, MD: Rowman & Littlefield)   An analysis of the political economy of the euro, including discussion of its international role.

WEBLINKS

http://ec.europa.eu/europeaid/index_en.htm   The Commission's DG DEVCO web page features material on trade, monetary relations, and development policies.

http://www.acpsec.org/   The website of the Secretariat for the African, Caribbean, and Pacific (ACP) states, which are the EU's partners in the Cotonou Convention.

http://www.ecb.eu/   The website of the European Central Bank, which includes studies on the international role and impact of the euro.

http://www.oecd.org/   The website of the Organisation for Economic Co-operation and Development, which includes analysis of EU trade, economic, and development policies among a wide range of other studies.

http://www.wto.org/   The website of the World Trade Organization, which contains analysis and commentary on current trade issues and trade disputes, as well as large amounts of detailed information about trade negotiations.

17

Enlargement

Ana E. Juncos and Nieves Pérez-Solórzano Borragán

Chapter Contents

Reader's Guide

The process of enlargement has transformed the European Union. It has had far-reaching implications for the shape and definition of Europe, and for the institutional set-up and the major policies of the Union. This has been accomplished through a number of enlargement rounds, which the first section of the chapter analyses in detail. This is followed by a review of the enlargement process itself, with a focus on the use of conditionality and the role of the main actors involved. The contributions of neo-functionalism, liberal intergovernmentalism, and social constructivism to explaining the EU's geographical expansion are evaluated in the third section of the chapter. The success and prospect of future enlargement are discussed in the context of wider EU developments, especially the effect of the financial crisis in the euro area, the so-called 'enlargement fatigue', and the domestic challenges in the countries hoping to join the Union.

Introduction

Membership of the European Union has increased over time from the original six to the current twenty-seven. Through a series of enlargement rounds, the territory of the Union has been expanded to stretch from the Mediterranean shores to the Baltic Sea, and from the Atlantic to the Black Sea, in just over four decades. The accession of new member states to the EU is generally considered a success of European integration, because it has proven to promote stability across the continent, while the willingness of countries to join the EU remains undeterred despite the often cumbersome processes attached to adapting to the Union's accession requirements and despite the challenging times faced by the EU as result of the 2008 financial crisis.

EU enlargement is best understood as both a process and a policy. As a process, it involves the gradual and incremental adaptation undertaken by those countries wishing to join the EU in order to meet its membership criteria. This process became more complicated after the end of the Cold War, when the Union had to respond to the accession applications of the newly democratizing countries from Central and Eastern Europe (CEE). With time, the EU's membership requirements have been expanded, and the number and diversity of countries wanting to join the Union have increased, thus intensifying the need for the Union to also adapt its decision-making, policies, and institutional set-up to an ever-increasing membership. As a policy, it refers to the principles, goals, and instruments defined by the EU with the aim of incorporating new member states. Enlargement is a typical intergovernmental policy under which member states retain the monopoly over decision-making, and the Commission plays a delegated role monitoring the suitability of countries to join and acts as a key point of contact. The European Parliament (EP) is involved through the consent procedure.

The accession of new member states poses interesting and challenging questions, such as why do countries want to join the EU? How and why does the EU support the accession of new member states? How has EU enlargement developed over time? How can European integration theories explain enlargement? And what is the future of enlargement? This chapter will address each of these questions in turn. The first part of the chapter briefly traces the evolution of the enlargement since the first round

of accession in 1973 until the latest round (as of 2012) in 2007. The second section outlines the process of enlargement from a country's application for membership to the actual accession and the policy instruments devised by the EU to support applicant countries in their endeavours. The ability of integration theory to explain the EU's geographical expansion is evaluated in the third section of the chapter. The future of enlargement is assessed in the context of wider EU developments, the challenge of the financial crisis, and the characteristics of the countries knocking on the EU's door. The chapter closes with a brief conclusion.

The history of enlargement

The European Union has been involved in four rounds of accession processes adding twenty-one additional members to the original six and bringing the Union's overall population to over 500 million people. These rounds tend to group countries under geographical labels—namely, the 'Northern enlargement', the 'Mediterranean enlargement', the 'EFTA enlargement' (referring to Austria, Finland, and Sweden's membership of the European Free Trade Area), and the 'Eastern enlargement' (see Table 17.1). Each round of enlargements faced the European Community and later Union and the new member states with different sets of challenges; each was informed by different sets of political and economic interests, and had diverse effects on both the Union and the member states. It is widely agreed that the Eastern enlargement was the most challenging for both the EU and the new member states, as it brought about the most extensive change for all parties concerned. What follows is a brief review of each enlargement, explaining key challenges and patterns.

The 1973 Northern enlargement featured the accession to the then European Economic Community (EEC) of Denmark, Ireland, and the UK. Norway had also applied for membership in April 1962, but accession was rejected in a 1972 referendum. The negotiations between the EEC and the applicant countries were characterized by two subsequent French vetoes to the accession of the UK, which affected the destiny of the other two countries. This first enlargement illustrated a characteristic that would define subsequent accession rounds—namely, the asymmetrical relationship between the EU and the applicant countries,

Enlargement rounds		
...ent round	Member states acceding	Accession date
Northern enlargement	Denmark, Ireland, UK	1973
Mediterranean enlargement	Greece	1981
	Portugal, Spain	1986
EFTA enlargement	Austria, Finland, Sweden	1995
Eastern enlargement	Cyprus, Czech Republic, Estonia, Hungary, Latvia, Lithuania, Malta, Poland, Slovakia, Slovenia	2004
	Bulgaria, Romania	2007

which places the latter in a weaker position, meaning that it has to adapt to the accession requirements or risk the negative effect of exclusion. It also illustrated how an enlarging membership brings about more diverse national preferences. The accession of two more Eurosceptic member states, the UK and Denmark, challenged the typically pro-integration approach of the original six, while the UK's political significance unsettled the bargaining influence of the **Franco-German axis**. The institutionalization of the **European Council** in 1974 was, to a large extent, the pragmatic Franco-German response to this challenge (see Chapter 11).

The Mediterranean enlargement took place in two stages: Greece joined in 1981; and Portugal and Spain, in 1986. Turkey had also applied in 1959, but negotiations were suspended in light of the military intervention in 1970. This round of enlargement was characterized by the political and symbolic significance that membership had for three countries that had just completed transitions to democracy. Accession to an organization that required a commitment to democracy was regarded as the guarantee for democratic consolidation. For Spain, it also signified a return to Europe after Franco's self-imposed isolation. While this enlargement round also featured an asymmetric relationship between candidates and member states, and the shifting in bargaining coalitions between member states, which explains the introduction in the **Single European Act (SEA)** of **qualified majority voting (QMV)** in the EU Council (see Chapters 3 and 11), the main effect of the Mediterranean enlargement was financial. Greece, Portugal, and Spain were not **net contributors** to the EU Budget, but rather required financial support to rebuild their lagging economies. The EU's **cohesion** policy was the EU's response to this challenge (see Chapter 20).

The 1995 EFTA enlargement saw the accession of Austria, Finland, and Sweden to the EU. Norway also negotiated accession this time, but, as had occurred in the 1970s, it rejected EU membership in a 1994 referendum. This was perhaps the easiest round of enlargement, because the three countries were wealthy established democracies that became net contributors to the EU Budget. For the EU, the diversity derived from the accession of three new member states affected the formation of coalitions in the EU Council, with the clear emergence of a Nordic pro-environmental block that supported the entrepreneurial role of the Commission in strengthening the EU's environmental policy (see Chapter 24).

The Eastern enlargement took place in two stages: Cyprus, the Czech Republic, Estonia, Hungary, Latvia, Lithuania, Malta, Poland, Slovakia, and Slovenia joined the EU in 2004; and Bulgaria and Romania, in 2007. This round of enlargement was the most complex for the EU. The Union had to respond to the effect of the collapse of communism, the eagerness of the newly established democracies to 'return to Europe', and the new security concerns posed by the end of the Cold War. The symbolic dimension of EU membership was heightened in the early 1990s, as the Union itself regarded enlargement as a tool with which to implement its commitment to democracy and stability promotion to the east of its borders. This, however, did not diminish the strong asymmetrical **power** relationship between the EU and the keen candidates. The EU was prompted to set up a comprehensive list of accession requirements, the so-called 'Copenhagen criteria', and a better-defined staging of the process of accession, as well as a toolkit of policy instruments to support the extensive domestic reforms requested from the **candidate countries** in preparation for EU membership (resulting from the sizeable *acquis communautaire* that they were expected to transpose and implement). The sheer number and variety of new member states, combined with their economic underdevelopment, faced the EU with the challenge of institutional and policy reform to ensure its own readiness for an enlarged membership. This often difficult reform was initiated at Amsterdam and its effects were still felt during the negotiations leading up to the Lisbon Treaty ratification in 2009 (see Chapters 3 and 4). The member states had to agree a new weighting of votes in the EU Council under an extended QMV and a new distribution of seats in the EP, as well as the size of the Commission. Strict transitional arrangements were negotiated to limit the wider effect of this round of enlargement, particularly regarding the free movement of people and direct payments to farmers from the new member states, as well as restrictions to agricultural exports from the new member states. While these are clear evidence of the candidate countries' weak position, it is also evidence of the very diverging opinions and concerns that individual member states had about the Eastern enlargement (see 'Liberal intergovernmentalism'). Suffice to say that while security and economic benefits were obvious to countries such as Germany or the UK, and a sincere Baltic identity explained the Danish, Swedish, and Finnish support, countries such as Spain and Portugal feared the loss of financial support from the EU—that this would shift east to support the struggling economies. Moreover, the accession of Cyprus was a particularly sensitive issue given Greek–Turkish relations at the time (1999), not least because Turkey had finally been awarded candidate country status.

KEY POINTS

- Through successive enlargements, the EU has expanded its membership from the original six to twenty-seven countries.

- Each enlargement round has been characterized by an asymmetrical relationship between member states and the countries wishing to join, the internal adaptation of the EU to cope with a larger membership, and differing national preferences amongst member states.

- The Eastern enlargement has been the most challenging of all enlargements to date.

As it will be explained (see 'Enlargement: the process and actors'), the history of enlargement is not finished yet. In 2012, the negotiation of accession for Croatia, the former Yugoslav Republic (FYR) of Macedonia, Turkey, Iceland, Montenegro, and Serbia was set in motion. The experience of the previous enlargement rounds informs how the EU manages the challenge of further expansion.

Enlargement: the process and actors

Although the main actors have remained the same, the process through which a country becomes a member of the European Union has become more complex over time. This section provides an overview of the changes to the process of accession, the key principles and provisions guiding the enlargement, the role of the different actors involved (member states, the Commission, and the European Parliament), and the main stages in the process. Originally, Article 237 of the Rome Treaty required the applicant country only be a 'European state'. For example, Morocco applied for EU membership in 1987, but its application was turned down because it was not considered to be a European country. By contrast, Turkey, which had applied for membership in the same year as Morocco, was officially recognized as a candidate country by the Helsinki European Council in December 1999, despite the fact that Turkey's European identity had been questioned by some member states. The enlargement procedure was also much more straightforward: the application was dealt with by the Council after receiving an opinion from the Commission and subject to the approval of the member states. But this does not mean that the process was less politicized. For example, French President **Charles de Gaulle** vetoed the British membership application in 1963 and 1967 because of fears that the UK would undermine the EC; the UK would join the EC only in 1973 after the French veto was lifted. Also, despite the Commission's negative *avis* (opinion), the member states decided to start accession negotiations with Greece, with the country joining the EU in 1981. Hence, from the beginning, enlargement has been an intergovernmental policy, strongly in the hands of the member states (see Box 17.1).

The key principle driving the process of enlargement has been that of conditionality. The use of political conditionality and the subsequent establishment of a complex monitoring procedure by the Commission

BOX 17.1 Treaty provision on enlargement

Any European State which respects the values referred to in Article 2 and is committed to promoting them may apply to become a member of the Union. The European Parliament and national Parliaments shall be notified of this application. The applicant State shall address its application to the Council, which shall act unanimously after consulting the Commission and after receiving the consent of the European Parliament, which shall act by a majority of its component members. The conditions of eligibility agreed upon by the European Council shall be taken into account.

The conditions of admission and the adjustments to the Treaties on which the Union is founded, which such admission entails, shall be the subject of an agreement between the Member States and the applicant State. This agreement shall be submitted for ratification by all the contracting States in accordance with their respective constitutional requirements.

(Article 49 TEU)

BOX 17.2 The Copenhagen criteria

To join the European Union, a candidate country must have achieved:

- stability of institutions guaranteeing democracy, the rule of law, human rights, and respect for and protection of minorities;

- the existence of a functioning market economy, as well as the capacity to cope with competitive pressure and market forces within the Union; and

- the ability to take on the obligations of membership, including adherence to the aims of political, economic, and monetary union.

At the 1993 Madrid European Council, an additional administrative criterion was introduced: that the candidate country must have created the conditions for its integration through the adjustment of its administrative structures.

were only introduced with the Eastern enlargement round in the early 1990s. The 1993 Copenhagen European Council adopted a set of political and economic conditions with which countries willing to become EU members had to comply (see Box 17.2). According to the so-called 'Copenhagen criteria', applicant countries must have stable institutions guaranteeing democracy, the rule of law, respect for human rights, and the protection of minorities, a functioning market economy capable of coping with the competitive pressures and market forces within the Union, and the ability to take on the obligations of membership, including adherence to the aims of political, economic, and monetary union, and had to adopt the *acquis communautaire*. The establishment of clear membership conditions satisfied both pro- and anti-enlargement camps. On the one hand, it reassured reluctant member states such as France by increasing the hurdle for enlargement since applicant countries would be admitted to the EU only once these conditions had been met. On the other hand, those in favour of enlargement, such as the UK and Germany, saw the adoption of the Copenhagen criteria as a way in which to provide some certainty about the process, reducing—although not eliminating—the possibilities for politically motivated decisions (Menon and Sedelmeier, 2010: 84–6).

The identification of this set of criteria led to the establishment of a complex monitoring mechanism managed by the Commission's Enlargement Directorate-General (DG Enlargement), which would act as a 'gatekeeper', deciding when countries have fulfilled these criteria and whether they are ready to move to the next stage (Grabbe, 2001: 1020). This monitoring process takes place following the benchmarks set by the Commission in different documents—in the case of the Western Balkans, the stabilization and association agreements (SAAs) and the European partnership agreements (EPAs); and the Europe agreements in the case of the Eastern enlargement. Compliance is also monitored in the regular annual reports produced by the Commission. This monitoring means that the enlargement process follows a merit-based approach (Vachudova, 2005: 112–13), yet political considerations have also played a part in this process.

Linked to the use of conditionality is the principle of differentiation and a preference for bilateralism in the EU's relations with candidate countries. Although enlargement has proceeded in several waves, during the Eastern enlargement, a regional approach was rejected in favour of a meritocratic approach according to which each country would proceed toward membership on its own merits and at its own speed. The expectation was that this approach would spur the adoption of reforms in the candidate countries. The downside was that it could lead to a multi-speed process, with some countries being left behind. For example, the decision made by the Luxembourg Council in December 1997 to distinguish between two groups of applicant countries and to start negotiations with the first group only (Cyprus, the Czech Republic, Estonia, Hungary, Poland, and Slovenia) raised fears among those left out (Slovakia, Lithuania, Latvia, Estonia, Romania, and Bulgaria). The balance between advancing reforms and promoting an inclusive approach was always going to be a difficult one to strike. In the event, accession negotiations were opened with the remaining Central and Eastern European (CEE) applicant countries (in addition to Malta) at the Helsinki European Council in December 1999 and efforts were made to include as many countries as possible in the 'big bang' enlargement of 1 May 2004, which saw the accession of ten new member states (see Table 17.2). Romania

Table 17.2 Applications for EU membership (since 1987)

Applicant country	Date of application	Date of accession
Turkey	14 April 1987	–
Austria	17 July 1989	1 January 1995
Cyprus	3 July 1990	1 May 2004
Malta	16 July 1990	1 May 2004
Sweden	1 July 1991	1 January 1995
Finland	18 March 1992	1 January 1995
Switzerland	26 May 1992	–
Norway	25 November 1992	–
Hungary	31 March 1994	1 May 2004
Poland	5 April 1994	1 May 2004
Romania	22 June 1995	1 January 2007
Slovakia	27 June 1995	1 May 2004
Latvia	13 October 1995	1 May 2004
Estonia	24 November 1995	1 May 2004
Lithuania	8 December 1995	1 May 2004
Bulgaria	14 December 1995	1 January 2007
Czech Republic	17 January 1996	1 May 2004
Slovenia	10 June 1996	1 May 2004
Croatia	21 February 2003	1 July 2013
FYR Macedonia	22 March 2004	–
Montenegro	15 December 2008	–
Albania	28 April 2009	–
Iceland	17 July 2009	–
Serbia	22 December 2009	–

and Bulgaria were not deemed ready to join the EU at that date. At the 2002 Copenhagen European Council, it was agreed that these two countries could join in 2007 provided that they had met the membership criteria. On 1 January 2007, these two countries became EU members despite evidence that they had not fully met their obligations, in particular in the area of rule of law (including judicial reform, corruption, and organized crime). A special 'cooperation and verification mechanism' was thus established by the Commission to monitor progress in these areas and to help the countries to address the outstanding shortcomings.

Conditionality has also been actively used in the EU's enlargement to the Western Balkans as a means to stabilize the region. It involved a realization that it was 'much more effective and cheaper to keep these countries on track by offering them the accession process than to run international protectorates and military occupation in the region' (European Commission, 2002c: 4). This new phase in the EU's intervention also sought to restore the Union's reputation after its failure to stop the war in the former Yugoslavia at the beginning of the 1990s (see Chapter 18). The prospect of future membership for the Western Balkans was first brought to the table during the Kosovo crisis by the German presidency (Friis and Murphy, 2001), and led to the establishment of the Stability Pact and the Stabilization and Association Process (SAP—see Box 17.3). The membership perspective for the Western Balkans was reconfirmed by the European Council in Feira in 2000 and Thessaloniki in June 2003. Since then, most Western Balkan countries have applied for membership; Montenegro, Serbia, and FYR Macedonia have been given candidate status, and Croatia is set to become the twenty-eighth EU member state in July 2013 (see Table 17.2).

The Commission and the Council have repeatedly reminded applicant countries of the meritocratic nature of the process: 'Each country's progress towards the European Union must be based on individual merits and rigorous conditionality, guiding the necessary political and economic reforms' (Presidency of the EU, 2009). However, some candidate and potential candidate countries expressed their disappointment with what seemed like privileged treatment for Iceland. While it took the Council a matter of days to refer Iceland's membership application to the Commission, Montenegro's application was referred only after five months and Albania's application took even longer. As Schimmelfennig and Sedelmeier (2004: 664)

The Stabilization and Association Process (SAP) constitutes the main framework for EU relations with the Western Balkan region (Albania, Bosnia and Herzegovina, Croatia, FYR Macedonia, Montenegro, Serbia, and Kosovo under UN Security Council Resolution 1244). The criteria and the process were established following the strategy used in past accessions in CEE: conditionality and differentiation. In addition to the political, economic, and institutional criteria established at the Copenhagen European Council in 1993, the SAP added four further specific criteria for the Western Balkans: full cooperation with the International Criminal Tribunal for the former Yugoslavia (ICTY); respect for human and minority rights; the creation of real opportunities for refugees and internally displaced persons to return; and a visible commitment to regional cooperation. Those countries complying with the relevant criteria are offered a stabilization and association agreement (SAA) that mirrors the Europe agreements with the CEEs, but are tailored to the particular conditions of the Balkan region. Economic assistance was initially provided under the Community Assistance for Reconstruction, Development and Stabilization (CARDS) programme, replaced by the Instrument for Pre-Accession Assistance (IPA) since 2007.

put it, the effectiveness of EU conditionality depends on the 'credibility of the threats and rewards'. Thus the politicization of enlargement sends the wrong message to the applicant countries, and weakens the Commission's emphasis on a transparent and a merit-based process.

The lessons learned from the 2004 enlargement, and, in particular, problems with the adoption of the *acquis communautaire* in the cases of Bulgaria and Romania, have led to a stricter application of conditionality by the EU. For example, the 'new approach' to enlargement unveiled by the Commission in 2011 is set to pay more attention to issues related to the rule of law. From now on, the first chapters to be opened during accession negotiations will be those dealing with the judiciary, Justice and Home Affairs (JHA), and fundamental rights (European Commission, 2011). The hurdles for accession have also been raised just because of the fact that new legislation has been added to the *acquis*. As a result, the number of chapters has increased from thirty-one to thirty-five. Another concern, that of the 'absorption capacity' of the Union, has also become more salient as new member states have joined the EU, and commitment for enlargement among member states and citizens has waned. Although it was part of the Copenhagen criteria, references to the need to take into account the capacity of the EU to integrate new members increased after the 2004 enlargement and the French and Dutch referenda on the Constitutional Treaty.

In its current version in the Lisbon Treaty, Article 49 outlines the conditions and the main stages in the enlargement process (see Figure 17.1). It states that any European state can apply for membership as long as it respects the foundational values of the EU (freedom, democracy, equality, the rule of law, and respect for human rights). Apart from the role attributed to the Council and the Commission, this Article also requires the consent of the European Parliament and, since the Treaty of Lisbon, that national parliaments be informed of membership applications. Once an application for membership is successful, the Commission is invited to prepare an opinion (*avis*) on the preparedness of applicant countries to meet the membership criteria. The Commission forwards a questionnaire to the concerned government requesting information. Iceland's answers to this questionnaire were sent to the Commission in October 2009, for example, and amounted to more than 8,000 pages! On the basis of the responses to this questionnaire and other information gathered by the Commission in its annual reports about the candidate and potential candidate countries, the Commission might recommend to the European Council the opening of accession negotiations, on which the latter then decides under unanimity. The accession negotiations between the EU and the applicant country begin with the adoption of a negotiating framework and the opening of an intergovernmental conference (IGC). The content of the negotiations is broken down into chapters, each of which covers a policy area of the *acquis* (for example, competition policy, fisheries, or economic and monetary policy). Prior to the negotiation of a specific chapter, the Commission carries out a 'screening' of the *acquis* to familiarize the candidate with its content, as well as to evaluate its degree of preparedness.

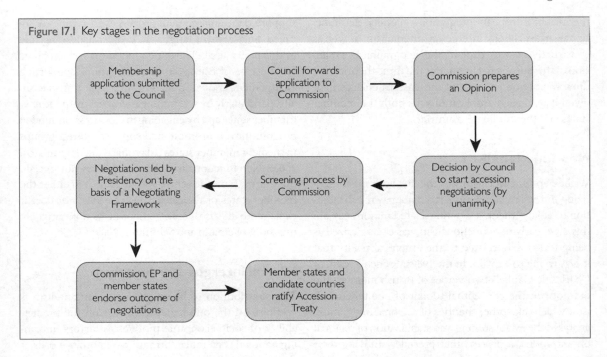

Figure 17.1 Key stages in the negotiation process

The Commission plays a key role during the accession process, in particular through the monitoring of candidate countries' compliance and in drafting the EU's negotiating position. The process remains decidedly intergovernmental, as the opening and closing of each of the negotiating chapters requires the unanimous agreement of the twenty-seven member states. The term 'negotiations' is actually a misnomer: candidate countries cannot affect the substance of the negotiations, but only the timing regarding the implementation of the *acquis*. It is possible for candidate states to negotiate some transition periods, but also for the EU to impose some transitional measures or to withhold some benefits (such as financial disbursements) until a later date. For example, in the Eastern enlargement, a transitional period of up to seven years was agreed during which restrictions on the free movement of workers could be applied to workers from the new member states.

Once all of the chapters have been negotiated, the accession treaty must be approved by the European Parliament and needs to be ratified by each member state and the candidate country in accordance with their respective constitutional requirements. In most cases, candidate countries have held a referendum prior to joining the EU. The most recent referendum was held by Croatia in January 2012, with 66 per cent of the voters supporting EU membership (33 per cent voted against). However, as was the case with the referenda held by the CEEs, the turnout was very low (at 44 per cent).

Explaining enlargement

EU enlargement is a complex process that challenges the explanatory power of European integration. There is a dearth of comparative studies that allow for a systematic analysis of different enlargement rounds. This section summarizes the contributions of traditional theories of European integration—namely, neo-functionalism and liberal intergovernmentalism, as well as constructivism—to explain the geographical expansion of the European Union. For the three theories, we draw mainly on the case of the Eastern enlargement given its extensive implications for both the member states and the candidate countries.

Neo-functionalism

While neo-functionalism was the first attempt at theorizing European integration, it did not pay much attention to enlargement. Two interrelated reasons explain this: first, early neo-functionalism was characterized as being too closely related to the empirical reality that it was trying to explain. In the 1960s, French President Charles de Gaulle's two vetoes of British membership did not suit the conceptual toolkit of neo-functionalism, which, like other theories of regional integration, analysed the establishment and stabilization of regional organizations, a process that precedes studying their territorial expansion (Schimmelfennig and Sedelmeier, 2002: 501). Second, at the time of the first enlargement (1973), neo-functionalism had already lost appeal amongst scholars of European integration (see Chapter 5). In the 1990s, the revived interest in the theory amongst scholars, and the policy and research dynamism surrounding the Eastern enlargement provided the appropriate context for the theory to try to explain the geographical expansion of the EU. Neo-functionalism explains three aspects of enlargement—namely, enlargement as a process, the role of supranational institutions, and functional integration. First, enlargement as a gradual process that involves several incremental stages from the point of membership application, through the association and pre-accession stages, leading to accession, reflects the neo-functionalist logic of the irreversibility of a process in which, as result of successful negotiations, the full *acquis* is imposed upon the new members (Schmitter, 2004: 70). Second, during enlargement, the Commission plays a major role in managing the negotiation process with the countries wishing to join, while providing regular reports to the member states on the progress made by the candidate countries in their road to membership. Its entrepreneurial role is evident in its promotion of the European Social Dialogue in the Central and Eastern European (CEE) countries, which is not strictly a criterion for accession (Pérez-Solórzano Borragán and Smismans, 2012). The Commission has consistently supported the enlargement process even at times of so-called 'enlargement fatigue' to protect its leading role in this policy area. Third, neo-functionalism accounts for the role of European interest groups supporting enlargement and coordinating their role transnationally, particularly by welcoming members from the new member states and by engaging in Commission-funded programmes to promote and support interest groups in the new member states (Blavoukos and Pagoulatos, 2008). Neo-functionalism, however, does not explain the role of domestic actors and structures in either the member states or the candidate countries; nor does it explain the effects of enlargement or its normative dimension (Niemann and Schmitter, 2009: 63).

Liberal intergovernmentalism

The contribution of liberal intergovernmentalism is twofold: on the one hand, it focuses on the predictability of socio-economic motives as factors informing national preference formation—in other words, it shows how 'the costs and benefits of socio-economic interdependence' (Moravcsik and Schimmelfenning, 2009: 80) inform whether member states and candidate countries support enlargement; and on the other hand, it focuses on how states bargain with each other in this typically intergovernmental policy. In the case of the Eastern enlargement, socio-economic factors informed preference formation in the member states to some extent, because countries that benefited the most from market expansion as result of the accession of new member states, such as Germany or the UK, were supportive of a rapid and all-inclusive enlargement, while countries competing for EU funds with the new arrivals had a more conservative approach and thus preferred a more gradual and less inclusive geographical expansion of the EU (Moravcsik and Schimmelfenning, 2009: 83). Similarly, the bargaining process was an asymmetrical relationship between the member states, which could behave as 'an exclusive club dictating the terms of accession to new members' (Risse, 2009: 157), and a set of candidate countries, which accepted such demanding accession criteria in addition to temporary restrictions to the free movements of people, for example, to avoid exclusion from the EU (Vachudova, 2005: 65–79). What liberal intergovernmentalism is unable to explain is why the member states decided to go ahead with negotiating EU accession when, given their stronger position in this asymmetrical relationship, they could have framed their advantageous relationship with their eastern neighbours, plus Malta and Cyprus, in the context of an association/preferential status, thus avoiding the costs resulting from the territorial expansion of the EU such as more qualified majority voting (QMV) in the EU Council or a less cohesive Union.

Social constructivism

Social constructivism turns its attention to two questions unanswered by neo-functionalism and liberal intergovernmentalism: why did member states accept the Eastern enlargement; and why did candidate countries agree to transpose the *acquis communautaire*? The answer to these questions lies in three complementary propositions. First, as Schimmelfennig points out, the constitutive liberal values and norms of the European international community, which are at the basis of the membership criteria, commit member states to the accession of 'states that share the collective identity of an international community and adhere to its constituent values and norms' (Schimmelfennig, 2001: 58–9). In other words, the closer a country is to adhering to these norms, the closer it is to joining the EU. Thus 'rhetorical commitment to community values entrapped EU member states into offering accession negotiations . . . despite the initial preferences against enlargement' (Risse, 2009: 157). Second, Sedelmeier stresses this point by focusing on the discursive creation of a particular identity of the EU towards the new member states, which asserted 'a 'special responsibility' of the EU for the reintegration of the peoples who had been involuntarily excluded from the integration project' (Schimmelfennig and Sedelmeier, 2002: 522). Third, Jacoby (2004) uses the language of social learning and norm diffusion (see Chapter 7) to explain how institutional reform to adapt to EU accession requirements took place in the new member states. He places elites at the core of a process characterized by the emulation of institutional models offered by the EU and the member states in the candidate countries, crucially through twinning projects (see Box 17.4). At a time of profound domestic change following the demise of the communist system, elites wished to 'accelerate their country's embrace of successful Western ways', but also had to cope with very specific norms propagated by the EU (Jacoby, 2004: 35), and a very detailed monitoring process aimed at checking the transposition of an extensive *acquis* and the country's administrative ability to implement it.

> **BOX 17.4** Twinning
>
> Twinning is a horizontal mechanism that involves the secondment of EU member state experts in the implementation of the *acquis* to the candidate country (but also to a new member state or potential candidate country) to facilitate the transposition, enforcement, and implementation of EU legislation through the exchange of expertise and experience. The experts typically come from more than one member state and may be public servants or members of employers' organizations or trade unions. The projects last up to two years and are built around jointly agreed EU policy objectives
>
> *Source:* DG Enlargement (2006: 9–10)

> **KEY POINTS**
>
> - It is possible to explain aspects of enlargement from more than one theoretical perspective.
> - Neo-functionalism explains the entrepreneurial role of the Commission, the role of European interest groups, and the gradual and incremental nature of enlargement.
> - Liberal intergovernmentalism explains the socio-economic preferences behind member states' support for enlargement.
> - Social constructivist approaches explain member states' commitment to enlargement despite the availability of alternative and less demanding options, such as association agreements.

The future of enlargement

The 2004 enlargement was officially heralded as a success, bringing economic prosperity to the new member states and increasing the role of the European Union as a global player in the world economy (European Commission, 2009). New countries have since joined the queue to become EU members, which is testimony that membership continues to be a very attractive incentive for countries in the EU's neighbourhood. After years of negotiations, Croatia is set to become an EU member in 2013. Accession negotiations were opened with Turkey in 2005 and Iceland in 2009. FYR Macedonia is also a candidate country, although no date has been set for the start of accession negotiations. The EU has also

BOX 17.5 The queue to join the EU (as of mid-2012)	
Acceding state	Croatia
Candidate countries	Turkey, Iceland, Montenegro, Serbia, FYR Macedonia
Potential candidate countries	Albania, Bosnia and Herzegovina, Kosovo
Eastern neighbours	Ukraine, Moldova, Georgia

received new applications for membership from Montenegro, Serbia, and Albania, with the first two becoming official candidates. Albania, Bosnia and Herzegovina, and Kosovo have the status of 'potential candidate countries' (see Box 17.5). Furthermore, Ukraine, Moldova, and Georgia have repeatedly expressed their desire to become members of the EU one day.

Despite the continuing attraction of the prospect of membership among the EU's neighbours and the fact that enlargement has been deemed the EU's most successful foreign policy, several problems threaten the enlargement project in the medium and long term. First, almost a decade after the Eastern enlargement, 'enlargement fatigue' is very much evident in EU member states. Support for enlargement within the EU remains low. For example, according to a recent survey, a higher percentage of respondents within the EU is now against further enlargement (47 per cent) than those supporting enlargement (42 per cent) (Eurobarometer, 2011b: 58). More worryingly, support for EU membership is also at a low in the candidate countries. While Macedonian citizens are still largely pro-EU membership (65 per cent considered EU membership a 'good thing'), support for membership has continued to decline in Turkey, where only 41 per cent considered accession to the EU a 'good thing'; in Iceland, too, only a minority of respondents (26 per cent) consider membership to be a positive thing (Eurobarometer, 2011b: 34–5). The accession of Croatia could help to restore some of the credibility, but the challenges ahead remain daunting.

Despite some positive signs, progress in the candidate countries has generally been disappointing. This results from three main factors: high adoption costs; the legacies of the conflicts; and standing bilateral issues. European integration imposes high adoption costs for politicians in the candidate countries. In some cases, EU integration not only threatens the power base of local elites, but also their private economic interests, because many of them profit from weak legal and regulatory frameworks and are involved in organized crime. Thus it is not surprising that the Commission's enlargement strategy papers have identified problems in the candidate and potential candidate countries that have plagued the implementation of reforms in relation to the independence of the judiciary, the fight against corruption and organized crime, a highly confrontational political climate, and ethnic-related tensions. Many of these problems are also linked to the legacies of the conflicts that affected the Western Balkan region in the 1990s and 2000s. The effectiveness of EU conditionality remains low in countries in which the legacies of ethnic conflict make compliance with EU criteria very costly, especially in Serbia and Bosnia and Herzegovina. Political, economic, and social reforms have fallen hostage to recalcitrant nationalist politicians in Bosnia and threaten the European perspective of Serbia, Kosovo, and FYR Macedonia. Bilateral disputes, and in particular the Kosovo issue, remain a significant obstacle to regional cooperation.

In recent years, we have also witnessed a 'creeping nationalization' (Hillion, 2010) or the strengthening of member states' influence over the EU's enlargement policy as they seek to keep tighter control during the intergovernmental stages of the process, insisting on the use of benchmarks before the opening of negotiating chapters and the inclusion of new conditions in every step of the process. For example, in the case of Serbia, the Netherlands managed to include compliance with the International Criminal Tribunal for the former Yugoslavia (ICTY) in the October 2010 European Council Conclusions. The rising number of bilateral disputes holding up the enlargement process constitutes another indication of a stronger role of the member states in the enlargement process. For example, some EU member states have used their privileged position inside the EU to put pressure on candidate countries in the hope that they will make concessions. Thus Turkey's accession has been delayed over the conflict with Cyprus (see Box 17.6), the name dispute between FYR Macedonia and Greece has jeopardized the opening of accession negotiations with the EU, and a long-standing border dispute with Slovenia got in the way

BOX 17.6 The accession of Turkey

A case that illustrates the politicization of enlargement is that of Turkey. The longest-standing candidate, Turkey's membership application was filed in 1987, but the Commission did not recommend the opening of accession negotiations in its opinion. It was not until 1999 that Turkey was granted candidate status, with formal accession negotiations opening in 2005. However, since then, not much progress has been achieved: out of thirty-five, only twelve chapters have been opened, and one chapter has been closed. One of the main reasons for the lack of progress is the continued refusal of Turkey to implement the additional protocol to the association agreement regarding access of Greek Cypriot vessels and planes into Turkish ports and airports. As a consequence, more than half of the negotiating chapters have been blocked by Cyprus, France, or the EU as a whole.

Since its application, Turkish membership has been surrounded by controversy, with member states divided on this matter, and it seems it will remain controversial in the foreseeable future. Among those reasons cited to reject Turkish accession are the size of the country, its geographical and geopolitical situation, the protection of human rights and minority rights, and its predominantly Muslim population, with some questioning Turkey's 'European identity'.

of Croatia's path toward membership. To this long list of bilateral issues can be added another dispute between Iceland, the UK, and the Netherlands over the repayment of billions of deposits lost as a result of the collapse of the Icesave Bank in 2008. Last, but not least, Kosovo's independence remains a divisive issue among EU member states: as of March 2012, five member states still refuse to recognize the breakaway territory on the grounds that it could set an important precedent for other territories seeking independence. Whereas such developments might help increase the credibility of enlargement from the viewpoint of the member states, from the perspective of the candidate countries the enlargement policy is increasingly being perceived as a politicized process, in which the 'rules of the game' change to suit the interests of the member states. This might further undermine the credibility and effectiveness of EU conditionality.

The ratification of the Lisbon Treaty in December 2009 was expected to inject new life into the enlargement process, which had suffered badly in previous years from the uncertainties surrounding institutional reform and issues of absorption capacity. However, the ratification of the Lisbon Treaty, and the appointment of a new Commission and a new **High Representative**, have had little impact on the conduct of the enlargement policy. Given the long-drawn-out ratification process of the Lisbon Treaty, one might expect that future EU institutional reforms will be built into accession agreements rather than take the form of a new treaty—an option that was also considered when the Lisbon Treaty looked in danger of not being ratified.

Finally, the economic crisis has had a major impact on enlargement too. First, it has slowed down the process of economic convergence between the new and old member states, and has had a particularly negative effect on some Central and Eastern European (CEE) states such as Hungary and the Baltics. Second, the economic crisis did not spare the candidate and potential candidate countries, although it affected some countries (Bosnia and Herzegovina, Serbia) more than others (Turkey seems to have escaped the worst of the effects of the economic crisis, on the basis that its economy continued to grow in 2011). The economic crisis resulted in an increase of unemployment, which was already very high in some candidate countries, and worsened the fiscal position of many of these countries. For example, Serbia and Bosnia had to turn to the **International Monetary Fund** (IMF) for financial assistance. Third, the euro area crisis has also increased concerns among EU member states about the financial burdens associated with enlargement. In the current economic climate, EU member states might be more cautious about taking more members on board, especially if that means increasing economic competition and budgetary disbursements. Fourth, the EU's economic malaise is also eroding the EU's attraction power—its so-called 'soft power' in particular—vis-à-vis countries such as Turkey and countries under Russia's sphere of influence. This also raises questions about the effectiveness of enlargement, in particular in terms of sustaining the credibility of membership and the size of rewards. All in all, the prospects for enlargement look rather bleak in the medium and long term.

KEY POINTS

- The prospect of EU membership continues to attract countries in the EU's neighbourhood, with Croatia set to become the twenty-eighth EU member state in 2013.

- Despite the continuing potential of EU membership to promote political and economic reforms in candidate countries, the enlargement project faces significant internal and external challenges going forward.

- Enlargement to the Western Balkans and Turkey faces domestic obstacles in the form of high adoption costs, the legacies of the conflicts, and standing bilateral issues.

- A growing 'enlargement fatigue' and the effects of the 2008 financial crisis risk undermining the credibility and power of EU conditionality.

Conclusion

The enlargement project has remained intrinsically linked to the project of European integration more broadly. Enlargement has both shaped and been shaped by the development of the European Union over time. A more complex EU has meant that the conditions of membership have also become more complex and technical in nature. Different enlargement waves have also been affected by the internal dynamics within the EU, from de Gaulle's veto of UK membership to the impact of the eurozone crisis on the current applicants. As the Union has extended its borders and increased its membership from six to twenty-seven, questions have also been raised about the ability of an enlarged Union to be able to function effectively. Thus each enlargement has required numerous institutional and policy reforms in order to allow the Union to incorporate the new member states. Undoubtedly, the most significant decision for the EU was to expand to Central and Eastern Europe in the 1990s, because of the number and diversity of applicant countries. The Europeanization of the candidate countries has had a significant impact on their institutions, politics, and policies, and has generally been seen as a key incentive in promoting political and economic reforms and fostering stability in those countries (see Chapter 9). Despite significant internal and external challenges currently facing the EU, its territorial expansion is not over yet, with Croatia set to join the EU in 2013 and other countries currently in the process of negotiating accession. How the EU will ensure the incorporation of new members, while continuing to further integrate in new areas such as economic and fiscal governance, will thus remain crucial.

?   QUESTIONS

1. How can we explain the decision of the European Union to enlarge?

2. How similar are the different rounds of enlargement?

3. Has the enlargement process become increasingly politicized over time?

4. What role do the Commission, European Parliament, and member states play in the process of enlargement?

5. What role does conditionality play in the enlargement process?

6. Why did the EU expand the membership criteria after the Eastern enlargement?

7. How successful has EU enlargement been to date?

8. What internal and external challenges does the enlargement process face in the coming years?

 GUIDE TO FURTHER READING

Best, E., Christiansen, T., and Settembri, P. (eds) (2008) *The Institutions of the Enlarged European Union: Continuity and Change* (Cheltenham: Edward Elgar)   This volume examines the impact of the EU's eastward enlargement on the EU's institutions and policy processes.

Grabbe, H. (2006) *The EU's Transformative Power: Europeanization through Conditionality in Central and Eastern Europe* (Basingstoke: Palgrave Macmillan)   An excellent account of the impact of the EU's conditionality on the candidate countries during the Eastern enlargement.

Noutcheva, G. (2012) *European Foreign Policy and the Challenges of Balkan Accession: Conditionality, Legitimacy and Compliance* (London: Routledge)   This offers an in-depth analysis of why western Balkan states have varied so much in their compliance with the EU's accession requirements.

Schimmelfennig, F. and Sedelmeier, U. (eds) (2005a) *The Europeanization of Central and Eastern Europe* (Ithaca, NY: Cornell University Press)   A collection of studies that assess the effect of the Eastern enlargement on the candidate countries.

Schimmelfennig, F. and Sedelmeier, U. (eds) (2005b) *The Politics of European Union Enlargement: Theoretical Approaches* (London: Routledge)   The strength of this volume is its application of theoretical approaches to enlargement.

 WEBLINKS

http://ec.europa.eu/enlargement/index_en.htm   The European Commission's DG Enlargement web page.

http://twitter.com/#!/eu_enlargement   The Twitter page of DG Enlargement.

http://www.cvce.eu/   A detailed online archive on the development of European integration, including earlier enlargement rounds.

http://www.euractiv.com/enlargement   An up-to-date review of news about EU enlargement.

http://www.europarl.europa.eu/committees/en/afet/home.html   The website of the EP's Foreign Affairs Committee (FAC), which deals with the enlargement portfolio.

18

The European Union's Foreign, Security, and Defence Policies

Robert Dover

Chapter Contents

Reader's Guide

This chapter outlines the key historical, institutional, and thematic developments within the European Union's foreign, security, and defence policies. It argues that the EU has been a problematic foreign and security policy actor, unable to formulate a cohesive identity or the credible capabilities with which to project itself on the world stage. This is a consequence of the pre-eminence of the North Atlantic Treaty Organization (NATO) as a security actor binding US political, economic, and military capabilities in the Western European area. Since 1991 and the end of the Cold War, both the EU and NATO have been positioning themselves in the foreign and security policy spheres; a new age of asymmetric military threats typified by terrorist attacks on mass transit systems focused the EU's security efforts on 'homeland security', whilst a resurgent Russia and revolutions in North Africa and the middle east drew Europe's attention in eastern and southerly directions. A lack of coordination and the unilateral actions of member governments remain the hallmarks of this policy, and this looks set to continue into the foreseeable future.

Introduction

Nearly two decades after the Maastricht Intergovernmental Conference (IGC) of 1992 confirmed that 'a common foreign and security policy is hereby established' (Article 21 TEU), the European Union is still a long way from having a supranational foreign policy. As a Union of twenty-seven countries and some 499 million people, and with an economy comparable to that of the United States, the absence of a functioning EU foreign policy suggests that the EU remains a 'civilian power'. Whilst the Maastricht, Amsterdam, and Nice Treaties did little to reduce intergovernmentalism in foreign policy cooperation, member governments managed to create a highly bifurcated system in which the focus of the policy switched to Brussels. However, national ownership of some aspects of foreign affairs (wars of choice, relations with Russia, and intelligence) has increased considerably. This move to a Common Foreign and Security Policy (CFSP) has been a slow and piecemeal process that is now largely taking place outside treaty-making IGCs (see Box 18.1).

The Europeanization of foreign, security, and defence policies runs against many of the preferences held by member governments. The latter have sought to retain their sovereignty over these issues and have allowed integration only in certain areas, such as development (see Chapter 16), procurement, policing, and peacekeeping. These are areas that do not impinge on core national sovereignty, in which there are no requirements to provide additional funding or capabilities and in which there are pre-existing agreements. More 'federalized' security and defence policies have emerged in a piecemeal fashion, and on issues that are at the periphery of NATO's established remit. For example, the Amsterdam Treaty, which came into force in 1997, established political mechanisms through which the EU could remain in regular contact with a large number of non-EU countries through so-called 'troika' meetings. These function to assist the government holding the EU presidency in discharging its responsibilities by bringing into the decision-making process the government that will hold the next EU presidency, the Secretariat of the Council, and the appropriate representative from the Commission. The aim of this policy was to give a global voice and diplomatic leverage to the EU. However, with member governments vigorously pursuing independent foreign policies and some actively seeking to diminish the EU as a foreign policy actor, these efforts have been only moderately successful. International influence has been achieved, however, through the appointment of special representatives and monitoring missions in regions where there are, or have been, particularly acute crises. These have so far covered the Great Lakes (Africa), the Middle East, the former Yugoslav Republic (FYR) of Macedonia, Ethiopia, Afghanistan, the Central African Republic, and Georgia. The special representatives have given the EU a direct role in problem-solving in these areas, as in the case of Bosnia, where the special representative has proved a very high-profile and critically acclaimed symbol of the EU's external relations policy (Toal, 2005).

BOX 18.1 The objectives of the Common Foreign and Security Policy (CFSP)

The five key objectives of the CFSP, as established in Article ll of the Maastricht Treaty and reaffirmed in the Amsterdam, Nice, and Lisbon Treaties are:

- to safeguard the common values, fundamental interests, independence, and integrity of the Union in conformity with the principle of the United Nations Charter;

- to strengthen the security of the Union;

- to preserve peace and to strengthen international security, in accordance with the principles of the United Nations Charter (including those on external borders);

- to promote international cooperation; and

- to develop and consolidate democracy and the rule of law, and respect for human rights and fundamental freedoms.

The Lisbon Treaty (Articles 21–41 TEU) not only identified these core elements, but also described how these objectives should be met.

- The principles behind CFSP and guidelines for implementation should be defined by the European Council.

- Common policies and actions should be established by the European Council to frame the way in which the EU deals with individual countries and regions. These should result in defining and pursuing common policies and actions, and a high degree of coordination.

- Consistency between different areas of external action and other EU policies shall be done by the Council and Commission, assisted by the High Representative.

The overarching aims of this chapter are to provide a guide to historical and institutional developments in EU foreign, security, and defence policy, and to explain why these have occurred (see Box 18.2). The chapter will also analyse some of the main contemporary debates in the CFSP and the European Security and Defence Policy (ESDP), as well as those issues relevant to the medium- and long-term future of the policies.

The changing context of European foreign policy

Despite the absence of an agreed European view about the end of the Cold War, the European Community was well placed to play a leading role in the new economic world order. Organizations such as NATO had, however, lost their *raison d'être* with the fall of communism. What NATO continued to bring to the table was the engagement of the United States in Europe, something that the German, British, and new Central and Eastern European (CEE) governments saw as being particularly important.

The collapse of the Soviet Union removed some significant barriers to the EU's Eastern enlargement, but the forerunner to the CFSP, European political cooperation (EPC) was not up to the task of producing proactive European foreign policy. The collapse of the USSR also allowed members of the European Free Trade Area (EFTA)—that is, Sweden, Finland, Austria, and Norway—to submit applications to join the EU, since the need, from a European perspective, for a 'buffer zone' between Russia and 'the West' was greatly reduced with the cessation of Cold War hostilities. The debate among the EU's governments about whether to enlarge the Union immediately or to add first to its competences was resolved with a very European compromise. This involved an extension of competences, whilst at the same time preparing for enlargement and the challenges of a post-Cold War Europe.

A more developed form of foreign policy cooperation was made possible by the end of the Cold War, as the events of this time created a policy space that avoided American and British accusations that the Community was trying to undermine NATO and US involvement in Europe. Moreover, the new policy arrived at an opportune time for EU–US relations: President Bill Clinton, who took office in 1993, saw an opportunity to reap a 'peace dividend' by limiting US involvement in mainland Europe. This was only possible, however, if EU member governments were able to shoulder more of the security burden in Europe.

The Common Foreign and Security Policy

The sections that follow consider the evolution of the new Common Foreign and Security Policy (CFSP) through its treaty incarnations at Maastricht and Amsterdam.

The Maastricht Treaty

The European Council at Maastricht saw agreement on a Common Foreign and Security Policy (CFSP), which was to form the second pillar (pillar 2) of the new European Union. Pillar 2 was to be intergovernmental, involving very little input from the European Commission and European Parliament. Moreover, the CFSP's decision-making framework was to rest on member state unanimity in the Council, giving each government the ability to veto any policy initiative or operation. As a consequence, EU foreign and security policy was to be a 'lowest common denominator' process, with policy outputs that were extremely conservative.

The CFSP sought to assist EU governments in formulating common foreign policy positions. However, because the CFSP was positioned outside the Community decision-making structures, this was problematic. This is because there were many economic issues within pillar 1—the supranational European Community pillar—that could have had an impact on the EU's external relations (see Chapter 16). Similarly, pillar 3—Justice and Home Affairs (JHA), which dealt with issues such as immigration, asylum, terrorism, and trafficking—used decision-making procedures that varied from those in CFSP and also had obvious external dimensions that made coordination difficult (see Chapter 21). The coordination of European external policy across the three pillars was to be achieved by giving the Commission and the Parliament some formal roles, which were later expanded. The Treaty stated that the Commission should be 'associated with all aspects of the CFSP' and that it had an equal right of initiative on external relations with member governments. In pillar 1, by contrast, the Commission had sole right of initiative. The European Parliament had to be 'kept informed' of policies and initiatives being conducted under CFSP, whilst the European

BOX 18.2   A chronology of the CFSP

1948	The Brussels Treaty Organization (BTO) is formed to promote joint security between the UK, France, Belgium, Netherlands, and Luxembourg.
1949	The North Atlantic Treaty Organization (NATO) is founded by the US, UK, France, Belgium, Netherlands, Denmark, Norway, Italy, and Luxembourg.
1952	The European Defence Community (EDC) Treaty is concluded—and superseded, following its failed French **ratification**, by the creation of the **Western European Union (WEU)** in 1954.
1970	**European political cooperation (EPC)** is instituted; following the 'Luxembourg Report', members agree to cooperate more fully on foreign policy matters.
1992	The Maastricht Treaty establishes the CFSP as the successor to the EPC; it includes the statement that the CFSP would, in time, lead to a common defence policy and common defence.
1996	The Amsterdam Treaty is negotiated, reinforcing the Maastricht proposals and strengthening the position of the Commission in foreign and defence policy-making, but without moving significantly away from an intergovernmental framework.
1999	The Cologne Council puts capabilities at the heart of the ESDP; the **capabilities catalogue** is formulated, but not met with the capabilities required for the EU to operate effectively.
2001	The **Nice Treaty** provides for the development of an EU military capacity, the creation of permanent political and military structures, and the incorporation into the Union of the crisis-management functions of the WEU (which entered into force on 1 February 2003).
2002	An EU delegation begins work in Afghanistan in February to support post-conflict reconstruction.
	In May, the EU carries out its first practice crisis-management exercise under the ESDP banner.
	In December, the EU and NATO formalize the 'Berlin-plus' arrangements that provide the EU with access to NATO assets.
2003	In January, EU ministers approve the first action under the ESDP, sending assistance to FYR Macedonia.
2004	In June, the EU pledges €200 million to support the reconstruction of Afghanistan.
2005	In July, the London public transport system is attacked by four bombers, Madrid having been attacked in March 2004.
	In September, the EU decides by **qualified majority voting (QMV)** to retain email and mobile phone communications for two years.
2007	On 1 January, the EU Operations Centre opens in Brussels; additional operation centres become available in Paris, London, Potsdam, Rome, and Larrisa.
	Throughout the year there are ongoing disputes with Russia about energy security, ballistic missile defence systems, Russian intelligence activity in Europe, and alleged cyber warfare against Estonia.
	In December, the Lisbon Treaty is agreed.
2008	In March, a deployment of 3,000 troops is sent into Chad and the Central African Republic.
	In August, Russia invades Georgia; French President Sarkozy (holding the presidency of the EU) leads the fractured European response.
	In October, the EU Monitoring Mission (EUMM) in Georgia begins.
2009	In December, the Treaty of Lisbon takes full effect: the CFSP is no longer a **pillar** of the EU.
2010	In September, the European Council considers strategic foreign policy partnerships.
	In November, the UK and France sign an agreement to work more closely together on defence matters.
2011	In March, the UK and France lead the diplomatic efforts in the UN over the crisis in Libya, and subsequently lead the military campaign against Gaddafi.
	In June, the WEU is formally dissolved.
	In December, the **European External Action Service (EEAS)** becomes fully operational; well into 2012, the EEAS and Baroness Ashton were still being heavily criticized for an inability to project a unified EU foreign policy strategy and for continued problems within the EEAS itself.

Court of Justice (ECJ) had no role at all. These latter two institutions were kept out of CFSP policy-making to ensure the continuation of member state pre-eminence in the policy.

The Treaty on European Union (TEU) provided three identifiable sources of external relations policy in the EU, binding the states and supranational institutions together. The first was the member states, with their own foreign, defence, and security policies pursued independently of CFSP; the second, the coordinating CFSP framework, which placed a responsibility on member states to 'inform and consult each other [on] matters of foreign and security policy' with the aim of increasing the international leverage that they could exert working together. The Council could establish a 'common position' (see Box 18.3), as it did in the case of the eradication of landmines, and then it fell to national governments to ensure that their policies were in line with these common positions. Thus the EU has played a very strong role in supporting the international norm established by the 1997 Ottawa Treaty to ban the use of and eradicate stocks of anti-personnel landmines (European Commission, 2005a). Alongside common positions, the EU can also adopt joint actions, which require a unanimous vote. Joint actions allow the EU to go beyond mere consultation (as had been the case under the EPC framework), obliging member states to conform to the positions that they adopt. Finally, the Commission, with its extensive responsibilities over trade policy and its large number of overseas representations, provides a third source of foreign policy stimuli in the EU (see Chapter 16).

The Maastricht Treaty also stated that the EU should work towards creating a common defence policy and eventually a common defence. This would later be used as the basis for developing a European Security and Defence Policy (ESDP—see 'The European Security and Defence Policy'). In the meantime, the Treaty established a review procedure for CFSP. This began with the setting up of a reflection group of civil servants in 1996, and culminated in an intergovernmental conference (IGC) and the Amsterdam European Council in June 1997.

The British and French governments disagreed at Amsterdam as to how the policy should develop. The British felt that the Yugoslav experience confirmed that the EU was incapable of formulating a common foreign policy (see Box 18.4), whilst the French government argued that the Yugoslav experience demonstrated why a common policy was required (Howarth, 2000). Very few could argue, however, with the proposition that the CFSP had achieved remarkably little in its first few years. There seemed to be hardly any cooperative and collaborative work of substance on foreign policy amongst national governments. Moreover, common positions were weak, often reflecting disagreements and a lowest-common-denominator style of politics.

The Amsterdam Treaty

At Amsterdam, efforts to give the European Union a defence identity were very slight indeed. Of the changes that were introduced, 'constructive abstention' was notable. This enabled less than a third of member states to opt out of a joint action without vetoing it for the others. This was later replaced by the 'enhanced cooperation'

BOX 18.3 Key instruments of the CFSP

The Maastricht Treaty provided the CFSP with the following key instruments.

- *Common positions*   These require member states to adopt national policies that comply with a stated EU position on a particular issue. For example, the EU has a common position on Zimbabwe. This aims to bring pressure on the Zimbabwean government to change its policies towards the opposition parties. The common position freezes the assets of senior members of the government, military, and security forces, restricts access to the EU for some of these officials, and places a ban on crucial exports.

- *Joint actions*   These operational actions are agreed by the member states and fall under the flag of the EU, and therefore the CFSP. The Balkans provides good examples of the use of these tools: for example, Joint Action 2002/210/CFSP (11 March 2002) established the European Union Police Mission (EUPM) in Bosnia and Herzegovina, which was the first EU civilian crisis-management operation under the CFSP/ESDP. It aimed to establish strong and sustainable policing arrangements by 2005. The EUPM was made up of around 500 seconded policemen, and more than 300 international civilian and local staff.

BOX 18.4 The EU and the Balkans

The Yugoslavian civil war was a wake-up call for the EU, as well as a profound embarrassment. The EU's response to Yugoslavia 1991–95 highlighted the weaknesses within the EU's foreign and security policies. In unilaterally recognizing Slovenian and Croatian independence on 23 December 1991, the German government hastened the crisis; this in turn led to the recognition of independence of Croatia by the EU governments on 15 January 1992 and political moves to establish a sovereign Bosnia following the Dayton Accords in 1995. These attempts to fracture the federation of Yugoslavia prompted a military response from the predominantly Serb Yugoslav National Army (JNA) under the civilian control of Slobodan Milosevic.

The EU's response to the genocide, the displacement of populations, and imperial conquests has been widely condemned as inadequate (Bellamy, 2002). The institutional historical memory of the First and Second World Wars and country allegiances to Croatia and Serbia partially guided EU governments in the early stages of the conflict. There was strong evidence that Croatian forces had been armed by Germany, whilst the French and British governments held historical allegiances with Serbia. This created problems early on in formulating a 'European' response.

These allegiances were less prominent after tipping-point events such as the siege of Sarajevo in 1994, which unified the international community in revulsion over ongoing atrocities.

The United States played a very low-key role in the early stages of the civil war (1992–94), which further exposed the EU's inability to formulate a credible policy towards the conflict. Without being able to deploy a credible threat of military force, international agreements brokered with Milosevic were breached with impunity by the Serbs. It was only when the US began to take an active role in brokering peace that the implied threat of the use of military force saw these agreements honoured.

Furthermore, the EU seemed obsessed with trying to deploy the levers of economic foreign policy to bring the conflict to a close. Economic sanctions and infrastructural aid were policies on which EU governments could agree. Both the sanctions regime and the distribution of aid and infrastructural support were strongly criticized by both practitioners and academics as ineffective; yet economic foreign policy was a policy area in which the EU was more confident and experienced (Keane, 2004). Since the fall of Milosevic, the EU has used the incentive of accession to secure compliance in the Balkans to variable effect.

provisions (see 'The Lisbon Treaty: revising the institutional framework'). Two further significant measures were agreed by the Amsterdam European Council. The first was the creation of the High Representative for CFSP. The holder of this position was also to act as the Secretary-General of the EU Council. The second was the creation of the Policy Planning and Early Warning Unit, which was to reside in the Council Secretariat and which is now known as the 'Policy Unit'. The unit was expanded in 2001, when the European Security and Defence Policy (ESDP) was established by the Treaty of Nice, to incorporate officials from the newly created European Union Military Staff (EUMS). These initiatives served to bring external relations closer to Brussels, with representatives of the Union performing more visible functions than in the past. Even so, the member states have still managed to guarantee the continuation of carefully protected intergovernmentalist working methods and, as a consequence, have maintained their pre-eminence over this policy field.

Finally, the Amsterdam Treaty also introduced, in Article 13(2), the notion of a 'common strategy'. This is decided unanimously by the European Council on the basis of a recommendation by the Council. Strategies on Russia and on the Mediterranean have since been

approved. It is implemented by adopting joint actions and common positions that can be achieved through a qualified majority vote unless a member state argues that the measure runs contrary to its core national interest, in which case it can exercise a veto (Article 210).

KEY POINTS

- Closer political and economic integration (as well as external shocks, such as the Yugoslavian civil war) generated the political desire for closer integration on foreign and security policy—something that has not been matched across the member states following key treaty negotiations.

- Whilst an institutional structure was created around the EU's foreign and security policy, the important competencies remained with individual member states, and a 'Europeanized' policy was mostly the product of 'lowest common denominator' decision-making.

- The introduction of qualified majority voting (QMV) into elements of European foreign and security policy, such as for joint actions and common strategies, and the creation of a High Representative for CFSP, raised the prospect of the EU having a more developed role in global affairs.

The European Security and Defence Policy

As already noted, the Maastricht Treaty did more than just set up the Common Foreign and Security Policy (CFSP); it also looked forward to a time when the European Union would cooperate on matters of defence. However, it was not until 1998 that a window of opportunity opened that would allow convergence on defence to begin.

The Saint Malo Process

A process that began at Saint Malo in France (December 1998) opened the way for a new phase in European foreign policy cooperation, which involved defence issues and which would contribute to a gradual militarization of the European Union. The 'Saint Malo Process' was led by the UK and French governments. For the newly elected Labour government in the UK, the initiative aimed to bring defence cooperation into the heart of the European programme and, as such, became a symbol of the UK government's pro-European leanings. It was also an initiative to prevent the French, Italian, and Spanish governments from forcing military and security policy onto the agenda in a way that disadvantaged British interests (Dover, 2007).

For the French government, the Saint Malo Process was something of an unexpected opportunity. As the least transatlantic of any of the EU governments and the keenest to see NATO scrapped at the end of the Cold War, the French government was surprised to be approached by British officials seeking to advance an EU-based security solution (Howarth, 2000). Getting the French government on board with plans for Europeanizing security was seen as crucial by the British, because the agreement at Saint Malo had to bring together both ends of the security spectrum: the proactive (French) and highly reactive (British). Officials from both sides concluded that any agreement on security and defence policy would result, in the medium or long terms, in a split between the British position, which saw NATO as the security institution of choice in the EU, and the French view that the EU should become a more capable independent security actor.

The Saint Malo meeting and the texts that it produced remained the high-water mark of Anglo-French cooperation until the agreements of December 2010 and February 2012 (see 'The EU's response to the

"Arab Spring"'). It also demonstrated other facets of European policy-making. The influence of the 'big three'—the UK, France, and Germany—over large initiatives was certainly in evidence in this case. The German government was seen as America's closest European ally in the late 1990s and also had a post-war allegiance to NATO, because it was on the front line of a potential clash between NATO and the Warsaw Pact countries. Convinced that European Security and Defence Policy (ESDP) did not aim to undermine the transatlantic alliance, the German government was happy to lend its support to the initiative. Agreement among these governments ensured that the policy would be successful.

After Saint Malo

Through several European Council meetings in Cologne (1999), Helsinki (1999), and Feira (2000), the ESDP proposals were amended and adapted. Of particular note was the inclusion of what would become 'the Petersberg tasks' (see Box 18.5) and a 'headline goal' for the EU: to be able to deploy 60,000 troops, in sixty days, sustainable for up to a year (Rutten, 2002). Proposals such as these were transformed into a 'capabilities catalogue'—a pool of personnel, expertise, and military equipment pledged by member governments that could be used in EU-sponsored military actions. In connecting capabilities explicitly to the Saint Malo Process, its British and French government sponsors aimed to make ESDP more than just a paper policy; indeed, this was a prerequisite for their involvement.

The ESDP is composed of three elements: military crisis management; civilian crisis management; and conflict prevention. In June 1999, the Cologne European Council placed crisis management and the capabilities required to deliver it at the heart of renewed efforts to strengthen the CFSP. Subsequent European Councils refocused efforts on the military assets available to the EU to conduct autonomous operations—including policing and peace enforcement (see Box 18.6).

British and French government negotiators anticipated that the policy would be fully functioning by 2003. However, the member states have been unable to meet the relatively modest targets within the 'capabilities catalogue'. This has been in part because of internal pressures to spend money on more electorally attractive areas such as health and education, whilst foreign and security budgets have been consumed by defence equipment inflation, the conflicts

---

BOX 18.5   The Petersberg Tasks

The Petersberg Declaration announced the readiness of member governments to make available a wide range of conventional military forces for European-led military tasks. The tasks defined by the Declaration include:

- a contribution to the collective defence in accordance with Article 5 of the Washington (NATO) Treaty;*

- humanitarian and rescue tasks;

- peacekeeping tasks; and

- tasks of combat forces in crisis management, including peacemaking.

* Article 5 says 'that an armed attack against one or more of them in Europe or North America shall be considered an attack against them all'. Consequently, they agree that:

if such an armed attack occurs, each of them, in exercise of the right of individual or collective self-defence recognized by Article 51 of the Charter of the United Nations, will assist the Party or Parties so attacked by taking forthwith, individually and in concert with the other Parties, such action as it deems necessary, including the use of armed force, to restore and maintain the security of the North Atlantic area.

BOX 18.6   The ESDP: the military and civilian dimensions

The military side of the ESDP was introduced at Helsinki (1999) and developed at the Nice (2001) European Council. Helsinki resulted in the so-called 'headline goal', whilst Nice provided the institutional structures that support the policy—namely, the Political and Security Committee (PSC), which is assisted by a politico-military working group, and a committee for civilian aspects of crisis management, as well as the European Union Military Committee (EUMC) and the European Union Military Staff (EUMS).

The Feira (2000) and Gothenburg (2001) Councils developed the civilian element of the ESDP which aimed to fill the 'soft' security gaps left by the international community. The Nice Council provided four institutional arrangements to fill these gaps, including a civil–military relations committee, to ensure that interventions run smoothly. The civilian dimension comprises:

- *police cooperation*, creating a capability to deploy 5,000 police officers, including 1,000 within thirty days, for tasks ranging from training local police officers to assisting military forces in restoring order;

- *rule of law*, an ambition to provide up to 200 judges, prosecutors, and other legal experts to areas in crisis;

- *civilian administration*, providing officials to assist in the basic tasks of government administration such as establishing education, infrastructure, and elections;

- *civil protection*, the ability to assist in humanitarian assistance at short notice, with the EU capable, within 3–7 hours, of providing two or three assessment teams, as well as intervention teams consisting of up to 2,000 people; and

- the European Defence Agency (EDA), established in 2004 to identify gaps in the EU's military capability, and then to suggest programmes and assist in conducting efforts to fill these gaps.

---

in Afghanistan and Iraq, recession and the subsequent austerity measures after 2010, and shifting twin priorities in favour of cyber- and homeland security arising out of the ongoing terrorist threat within European countries.

The emphasis on Petersberg-style military tasks reinforces the EU's self-constructed soft security identity and acts as a barrier to military operations, such as the US/UK invasion of Iraq (2003), or engagement in high-end military posturing, such as the deployment of a US anti-ballistic missile system in Poland in 2008. The inclusion of the Petersberg tasks in the ESDP supports the view that the latter is a product of the EU's inability to deal with peacekeeping and peace-enforcement operations such as those presented by the Yugoslavian civil war, and a realization that the threats to the EU come from non-state military actors in the medium-to-long term (Smith, M., 2001).

Civil wars and the consequences of failing states, as in the Balkans in the 1990s, demand the sorts of responses that the Petersberg tasks aim to deliver: humanitarian and rescue tasks; peacekeeping tasks; peacemaking; and crisis management. To give the EU a chance of tackling these scenarios effectively, it was necessary to ensure that the EU had access to NATO assets. The negotiations to secure this access were one of the most important tasks at the periphery of the Nice European Council meeting. The so-called 'Berlin-plus' arrangements were a key marker of whether the ESDP might function as an independent policy area, avoiding duplication with the institutions and assets of NATO and the UN. In this matter, Turkey—a NATO member, but not a member of the EU—was a stumbling block to securing EU rights to these assets, because the Turkish government was keen to tie access to NATO equipment to its efforts to join the EU. Turkish opposition was removed through intensive diplomacy by NATO and the British and American governments in December 2000.

The Nice Treaty

The negotiations for the ESDP were largely conducted outside the formal EU negotiating frameworks to avoid the input of Commission officials and members of the European Parliament (MEPs). These were bilaterally agreed between governments before the final signatures at the Nice European Council. The Cologne, Helsinki, and Feira Councils had meant that, between Saint Malo in December 1998 and the Nice Treaty negotiations in December 2000, much of the detail of the ESDP had been concluded well before it was formally agreed.

The Nice Treaty required the Commission to ensure that the EU's actions were consistent and designed to meet the objectives laid out by national governments. The Nice Treaty also secured further institutional reform. The Treaty entrenched a move towards supranationalism through Article 24, which allowed the Council to use qualified majority voting (QMV) for decisions relating to internal matters— that is, institutional design or the adoption of joint actions. Qualified majority voting was also to be used where the Council appointed a special representative. Moreover, the Treaty replaced the Political Committee with the Political and Security Committee (PSC). Evidence of a drift from the member states can be found in the role of the so-called CFSP 'ambassadors' (foreign relations counsellors) who had previously travelled from capital to capital, but who, after Nice, were to be based in Brussels in semi-permanent session. Despite these changes, the majority of foreign and security activity in the Union remains under the control of national governments.

KEY POINTS

- The Maastricht Treaty established a Common Foreign and Security Policy, which was largely intergovernmental in character. The outcome of the first tests of the CFSP was far from impressive.

- The Amsterdam Treaty revisions sought to rectify some of the institutional problems, but failed to address the question of a European defence policy.

- The British and French governments' agreement in Saint Malo in December 1998 created an overwhelming momentum towards a common European Security and Defence Policy. The negotiations resulted in the production of a capabilities catalogue, which placed an expectation on member states to provide capabilities. As of 2012, they had yet to provide all of these capabilities.

The Lisbon Treaty: revising the institutional framework

Following the failure of the Constitutional Treaty, new security and defence provisions were encapsulated in the Lisbon Treaty (2007). The Lisbon Treaty aimed to develop further the EU's involvement in security issues, particularly those relating to terrorism. The Treaty includes a provision on a common defence response for any EU member subject to a terrorist attack or natural disaster. It also incorporates changes to the institutional framework (see Boxes 18.7 and 18.8).

A High Representative of the Union's Common Foreign and Security Policy (known as 'Mr/Ms CFSP'), who also serves as a vice-president of the Union, is created by the Treaty (Article 18 TEU), reflecting the supposed seriousness with which external relations are now taken. The Commission and the High Representative can submit joint proposals on external action—thus bringing together the economic and military sectors (Article 22 TEU). The first of the High Representatives was the little-known British politician Baroness Catherine Ashton, whose selection for the post was met with some surprise. Her inexperience in foreign affairs and the infancy of the new working arrangements strongly contributed to the sense that she spent excessive amounts of time focusing inwards on the organizational aspects of the job and insufficient time developing the EU's international visibility. The 'Brusselsization' of the CFSP is further deepened by the creation under Article 27 TEU of the European External Action Service (EEAS), which acts as

BOX 18.7 The institutions

The European Council	The European Council lays down the guidelines for CFSP and adopts common strategies.
The Council of the European Union	The EU foreign ministers and the Foreign Policy Commissioner meet at least monthly under the banner of the General Affairs Council (GAC). This body makes decisions on external relations issues, including the CFSP. Its decisions can lead to joint actions and common positions, the implementation of which is mainly the responsibility of the country holding the EU's presidency and of the High Representative, following the ratification of the Lisbon Treaty.
The Council presidency	The country holding the six-monthly Council presidency plays an important role within the CFSP, because it sets the agenda for the political decision-making process. It provides the background administration for all meetings, and is responsible for trying to resolve disagreements and difficulties on all policy issues. This is particularly important in relation to the CFSP because decisions are made unanimously, although the provision for enhanced cooperation does change this dynamic slightly. The presidency is assisted in its work by the Council Secretariat and, since the Amsterdam Treaty, by the Secretary-General/High Representative for CFSP.
The European Commission	The strengthening of the Council with regard to the CFSP has implications for the role of the Commission. The Commission is an important part of the Union, not only because it has such a large role in concluding agreements and managing aid and trade initiatives, but also because it has diplomatic offices (representations) in virtually every country in the world. This is something that the Commission jealously guards. It is, in many respects, the public face of the EU abroad. A declaration added to the Amsterdam Treaty outlined how the Commission proposed to reorganize its Directorates-General (DGs) to bring external relations under the remit of a vice-president, rather than under the control of four Commissioners. However, former Commission President Romano Prodi (1999–2004) did not observe the declaration and appointed four external relations commissioners with functional, rather than geographic, responsibilities (see Box 18.8).
The European Parliament	The Parliament has no formal CFSP role, but is kept informed and consulted on CFSP issues and on the general direction of the policy. MEPs have been very keen to engage in foreign policy issues; they were particularly active through debates and declarations during the Yugoslavian civil war, and the Afghan and Iraqi campaigns, continually pushing their case for an enhanced parliamentary role in external relations.
The Policy Planning and Early Warning Unit	The Early Warning Unit was established within the Council Secretariat and has a responsibility for monitoring and assessing international developments, as well as analysing emerging threats and crises. The Unit's analytical role is important in so far as it provides the member states with the information that they require to formulate a common foreign policy; however evidence from the 2008 Georgian conflict suggests that member states pulled resources back internally at this time of high crisis.
The **Committee of Permanent Representatives (Coreper)**	Coreper meets at least once a week to prepare Council meetings and decisions, including those related to the GAC and the CFSP. Anecdotal evidence from senior officials shows that Coreper plays a crucial role in organizing the work of CFSP and smoothing over policy disagreements.
The Political and Security Committee (PSC)	The PSC (sometimes referred to as COPS) is central to the CFSP and the ESDP. It organizes the EU's response to any crisis. It is composed of national representatives. The PSC prepares recommendations on how the CFSP (and the ESDP) should develop, and also deals with the routine elements of these policies.

The High Representative of the Union for Foreign Affairs and Security Policy

Acting as a vice-president of the Commission and presiding over the Foreign Affairs Council (FAC)—hence the shortened title 'HR/VP'—the High Representative ensures the consistency of the EU's external actions, along with the Council and the Commission. The High Representative has the right to submit joint proposals with the Commission in other areas of external action. The High Representative is assisted by the EEAS.

The European External Action Service (EEAS)

The European External Action Service (EEAS) works with the diplomatic services of member states, comprises officials from relevant departments of the General Secretariat of the Council (GSC) and Commission, and will eventually include officials from national governments. The EEAS manages the EU's response to crises and contains an intelligence function, much like a national foreign service would. The High Representative/Vice-President's first years in office have been spent trying to resolve the political issues concerning the EEAS, particularly between the Commission and the Council, and also with the European Parliament, which wish to fashion themselves a more active foreign policy role. The member states have also been intransigent over the financing of the service and the provision of staff. The EEAS became fully functional in December 2011, but continued to be plagued with staffing and operational difficulties well into 2012.

the diplomatic corps of the EU, and which is made up of seconded staff from the member states, the Commission, and the General Secretariat of the Council (GSC). This is an important move that centralizes foreign policy activity within Brussels, something that is supported by the enhanced cooperation provisions, which allow a group of at least nine member states to agree to deepen their cooperation on foreign and defence policy within a European framework, but without having to get the agreement of the remaining member states. The European Parliament continues to be the junior partner when it comes to foreign and security policy, with MEPs' views being solicited only twice a year.

Articles 77 and 78 TFEU link up internal and external security via policies on border checks and asylum and immigration. This has happened bilaterally or multilaterally across member states that have been affected by terrorism and mass migration, but it is now subject to some level of European cooperation. This cooperation also applies to the policy on organized crime and counter-terrorism, under which member governments are expected to liaise closely on policing issues, operationally, and in the realm of information sharing (Article 87 TFEU).

The Treaty makes it clear that the member governments should make military assets available for common EU activities, but also that member states should actively support the work of the European Defence Agency (EDA), the purpose of which is to identify operational requirements and then stimulate measures and programmes to fill the gaps. In effect, the EDA provides a shorter route into an expanding European defence market for defence-related businesses and, because of the peculiarities of the trade, a boost to the influence of those governments that sponsor successful manufacturers. The reality of the EDA has been somewhat different and partly as a response to this, the British and French governments decided to extend their collaborative work in defence in November 2010. This negotiation resulted in an agreement to create more joint equipment programmes outside of the EDA; in February 2012, the two countries signed a contract jointly to develop unmanned fighter aircraft, effectively undermining the rationale that underpins the EDA.

The most important institutions within the CFSP and the ESDP are the foreign and defence ministries of the member states. Within these institutions, policy initiatives are formulated and agreements struck on whether to accept common positions and joint actions. Neither the Commission nor the High Representative has demonstrated an ability to act with the decisiveness or influence of a domestic ministry. For example, there have been doubts about the quality of internal security in the Commission, with leaked information potentially endangering the safety of officials in the field—something that is particularly sensitive in counter-terrorism operations. There is also concern over the Commission's ability to negotiate as an equal with security partners, such as the US Department for Homeland Security, on security issues such as the passenger name record (PNR) transfers (Bossong, 2012).

- Large-scale initiatives that reformed existing policy and institutional structures gave more weight to the EU's Common Foreign and Security Policy.

- The introduction of bodies such as the European Defence Agency was designed to pump prime military equipment capabilities across Europe, so as to enable the Union to play a more developed role in international affairs.

- The introduction of a full-scale diplomatic structure and the HR/VP aimed to provide the EU with a 'state-like' capability. Whilst this capability is now in place, it remains subject to sustained criticism.

- The euro sovereign debt crisis and austerity policies implemented across Europe in 2010–13 raised the strong prospect of member governments being unable to fulfil their military pledges, instead focusing governmental attention internally on domestic political dissent.

The European Union's response to the 'Arab Spring'

The so-called 'Arab Spring', the series of revolutions and political upheavals in the Middle East and North Africa from December 2010 to the time of writing in 2012, saw established dictatorships crumble in quick succession, and newly freed peoples turning to political blocs such as the EU for assistance and support. Indeed, like the crisis in the Balkans in the 1990s, this was seen as being in 'Europe's backyard', and, as a result, a coherent and strong European response was anticipated, but failed to materialize. The list of criticisms levelled at the High Representative and the European External Action Service (EEAS) as a result have been lengthy and severe.

Whilst the EU makes a strong claim for having responded to the crisis in the Middle East with speed and guile, supporting each country in a differentiated way, the main criticism has concerned the absence of strong leadership by the High Representative/Vice-President (HR/VP), who remained largely invisible during the main months of the crisis. What also became apparent was that very little of the EEAS's activities could be described as classic diplomacy. As a result, the bulk of the diplomatic work was done by individual member states taking their own initiatives (unilaterally or bilaterally), whilst making a claim to be speaking on behalf of the EU as a whole. Thus, in the case of Libya, it was the British and French governments who led the international diplomacy that culminated in the UN-approved airborne military action against Gaddafi's government armed forces (19 March—16 August 2011). By contrast, the EU's institutional response was to ban Libyan government officials from travelling to the EU. In the case of the repression of Syrian protestors, which reached clearly catastrophic levels by early 2012, the HR/VP's response was to coordinate another travel ban and to meet with opposition representatives to offer support. It was again left to individual governments to try to force through stronger measures (against Russian and Chinese opposition) in the United Nations. In the case of Egypt, whilst individual European governments pursued their own intelligence and diplomatic efforts with the transitional movements and the armed forces, the EU deployed €20 million within a civil society fund and negotiated a Deep and Comprehensive Free Trade Area (DCFTA) agreement, something that was easier for the EU to achieve because the Egyptians were reluctant to receive assistance from individual European governments.

The EU's response fell onto tried-and-tested areas, such as mobility (mostly for students via the Erasmus programme), civil society improvement grants (in part via established neighbourhood policy funds), and access to European markets. A much stronger future test of the CFSP will come with the Iranian government's hastening acquisition of nuclear technologies, and the potential militarized response of America and Israel to this development: the EU will need to improve massively on its Arab Spring performance to meet this challenge.

- The Arab Spring represented a key challenge for the EU in its 'backyard', following on from the challenges of the Balkans in the 1990s and the widespread disagreements over the wars in Iraq and Afghanistan during the 2000s. The EU's institutional response was muted, and once again restricted to economic and civil society action. Britain and France effectively spoke and acted on behalf of Europe during the crisis.

- The Arab Spring reinforces the notion that the EUs foreign policy competence can be found in supporting conflict prevention and in post-conflict reconstruction, whilst capable member states carry out the difficult foreign and security functions.

Conclusion

From the European Community's inception more than fifty years ago, defence, foreign, and security policy has been a controversial and contested policy area. Member states' governments have, in the main, been resolute in their desire to retain the unanimity requirement and their veto over all issues that relate to their security and defence. These controls have been relaxed slightly with the introduction of 'enhanced cooperation'. There have been other key successes, such as the formulation of joint actions and common positions, which have helped to create a European approach to important policy issues. These policies have been successful because of the cohesion of member governments on selected issues and because the financing is already in place. Neither joint actions nor common positions have produced radical or ambitious policies; nor have they evolved beyond the EU trait of 'lowest common denominator' policy-making.

Looking into the immediate future, the failures inherent in the early months of the EEAS and the low visibility of the High Representative, coupled with the variable effects of the European Defence Agency, have seen influential member states start to take unilateral foreign policy actions, often claiming to be speaking for Europe. The euro sovereign debt crisis and austerity measures in place across Europe are degrading military capabilities in all European states. This will serve only to reduce the influence that Europe has across the globe in foreign and security terms, whilst the predominant trend (again a response to circumstances) is for EU-level security activity to be focused on homeland security, intelligence, and surveillance, in an attempt to reduce the threat from dissidents and terrorists.

 QUESTIONS

1. What lessons can we learn from the European Union's approach towards the countries affected by the 'Arab Spring' in 2011?

2. Does the presence of the High Representative and the European External Action Service mean that the EU can now be seen as a fully functional foreign policy actor on the world stage? If not, why not?

3. To what extent has foreign and security policy become 'Europeanized'?

4. What do the EU's foreign, security, and defence policies and structures tell us about the EU as a political entity?

5. Is the EU destined to remain a 'soft security' actor?

6. To what extent do the 'big three' (France, Germany, and the UK) speak and act on behalf of Europe in the foreign and security policy domain?

7. Would it be desirable for the European Parliament to have greater influence over European foreign, security, and defence policies?

8. Does the emergence of regional hegemons such as Russia, China, and Iran mean that the EU should revise its security stance away from homeland security?

 GUIDE TO FURTHER READING

Cameron, F. (2012) *An Introduction to European Foreign Policy* (London: Routledge) A comprehensive introduction to the topic.

Menon, A. (2011) 'European defence policy: from Lisbon to Libya', *Survival*, 53/3: 75–90 A strong contribution to our collective understanding of the recent developments in this policy area.

Mérand, F., Foucault, M., and Irondelle, B. (2010) *European Security Since the Fall of the Berlin Wall* (Toronto: University of Toronto Press) A holistic survey of the developments in European security over the post-Cold War period.

Rees, W. (2011) *The US–EU Security Relationship: Tensions between a European and a Global Agenda* (Basingstoke: Palgrave Macmillan)   A well-informed and well-written book tracking the changes in this relationship.

Wong, R. and Hill, C. (eds) (2011) *National and European Foreign Policy: Towards Europeanization* (London: Routledge)   A strong edited collection that is particularly useful for the way in which it can be applied comparatively.

 ## WEBLINKS

http://ecfr.eu/content/archives/publications/   The European Council on Foreign Relations publishes widely on Europe's relationship with the wider world.

http://eeas.europa.eu/   The website of the European External Action Service.

http://eeas.europa.eu/ashton/index_en.htm   The web page of the High Representative, Baroness Ashton.

http://epc.eu/themes.php?theme_id=30   The European Policy Centre (one of the EU's leading think tanks) has a distinct stream of output that focuses on defence and security issues.

http://www.nato.int   The North Atlantic Treaty Organization's website.

19

The Single Market

Michelle Egan

Chapter Contents

Reader's Guide

This chapter charts the evolution of the single market project, from its original conception in the 1950s, beginning with the Treaty of Rome and ending with the Single Market Act. It explores the role of the European Court of Justice (ECJ) in promoting market access, the balance between different economic ideals, and the different regulatory strategies used to foster market integration. The chapter highlights the importance of the single market in promoting competitiveness and growth. It concludes with a review of both traditional international relations theories of integration, and newer approaches in comparative politics and international relations, to understand the governance of the single market.

Introduction

Although the single market is a core element of the European integration process, it has been relatively neglected in recent years. The single market has evolved considerably since its inception in the 1950s, delivering major changes in many policy domains in an effort to liberalize trade, to coordinate economic policies, and to promote competitiveness. It has also become a major political priority in the midst of the euro sovereign debt crisis, as evidenced by the Monti Report (2010) and Single Market Act (2011), which aimed at deepening and widening the internal market. In taking stock of what the European Union has accomplished in terms of internal trade liberalization, regulatory strategies, and legal rulings, this chapter assesses the institutional innovations, ideational rationales, and interests and preferences that shaped single market integration. Although the process has been sharply contested, with deep concerns about socioeconomic rights, the scope of the internal market has continued to widen over the past two decades, both in terms of the external promotion of European norms, rules, and standards, and in response to changes in market transactions and globalization. This chapter reviews the state of the single market, from its historical origins to more recent efforts, recognizing its economic imperatives as well as its political rationale by highlighting different theoretical efforts to understand the dynamics of market integration.

Market integration in historical perspective

In the space of one year, from the Messina Conference in June 1955 to the Venice Conference in May 1956, the idea of economic unification among six Western European states had taken root. After months of lengthy discussion, what became known as the Spaak Report (after its principal author) generated the idea of an entirely new kind of inter-state economic relationship as the basis for treaty negotiations (Bertrand, 1956: 569). This report provided a blueprint for a single market in Western Europe, with three main elements:

- the establishment of normal standards of competition through the elimination of protective barriers;

- the curtailing of state intervention and monopolistic conditions; and

- measures to prevent distortions of competition, including the possible harmonization of legislation at the European level.

The economic intent of such proposals dovetailed with the federalist agenda (Laurent, 1970). Yet turning the single market idea into a political reality has been extremely contentious and protracted.

Based on the Spaak Report, the Treaty of Rome (1957) aimed for a common market by coordinating economic activities, ensuring stability and economic development, and raising living standards. At the core of the proposed European common market was the creation of a customs union (see Box 19.1). This meant that member states would not only abolish all of their customs duties on mutual trade, but also apply a uniform tariff on trade with non-European Community countries. The other measures proposed to promote internal trade liberalization, including free movement of labour, services, and capital, and a limited number of sectoral policies (agriculture, transport, and competition), were to be regulated and managed at the European level.

The transformation of the Community into a common market was to take place over a period of twelve to fifteen years. It began with efforts to address traditional tariffs, starting with the elimination of customs duties and quantitative restrictions in 1958, and by introducing a common external tariff in 1968. Internal tariff reductions were also frequently extended to third countries to limit the discriminatory effects of the customs union, which was politically important in the formative period of the EC (Egan, 2001: 41).

BOX 19.1 Stages in economic integration	
Free trade area (FTA)	Reduces tariffs to zero between members
Customs union	Reduces tariffs to zero between members and establishes a common external tariff
Single market	Establishes a free flow of factors of production (labour and capital, as well as goods and services)
Economic union	Involves an agreement to harmonize economic policies

Membership of the European Community meant more than simply a customs union, however. The Treaty established the 'four freedoms'—the free movement of goods, services, capital, and labour—as central features of the single market. However, the requirements for each freedom varied according to the political exigencies at the time that the Treaty was drafted.

The removal of trade barriers for *goods* focused on the removal of tariffs and quantitative restrictions, and then on the removal of non-tariff barriers. This meant dismantling quotas, subsidies, and voluntary export restraints, and measures such as national product regulations and standards, public purchasing, and licensing practices, which sometimes reflected legitimate public policy concerns, but were often a thinly disguised form of protectionism designed to suppress foreign competition (Egan, 2001: 42).

For the free movement of *capital*, the goal was freedom of investment to enable capital to go where it would be most productive. Yet vivid memories of currency speculation in the interwar period meant that liberalization was subject to particular conditions or 'safeguard clauses', frequently used during recessions.

With regard to free movement of *services*, it meant the freedom of establishment for industrial and commercial activity—that is, the right to set up in business anywhere in the Community. However, the Treaty provisions on services contained virtually no detail on what should be liberalized (Pelkmans, 1997).

For *labour*, the provisions for free movement meant the abolition of restrictions on labour mobility.

National governments were receptive to early efforts to eliminate trade barriers and to create a customs union because they were able to use social policies to compensate for the increased competition stemming from market integration. Favourable starting conditions for the European trade liberalization effort were thus a result of the fact that it occurred against the backdrop of the mixed economy and welfare state, which were central components of the post-war settlement (Tsoukalis, 1997). Yet even with these national policies, it was still felt politically necessary to provide some sort of financial aid at the European level to ease the effects of competition through basic investment in underdeveloped regions, the suppression of large-scale unemployment, and the coordination of economic policies (see Bertrand, 1956; Spaak, 1956). Despite substantial economic growth and increased trade among the member states, the prevalence of domestic barriers to trade resulting from pervasive state regulation of economic activity across all four freedoms signalled the enormity of the task (Tsoukalis, 1997: 78).

A major characteristic of European economies has been their historical and national variation in areas such as industrial relations, social welfare, and financial systems (Zysman, 1994; Berger and Dore, 1996; Rhodes and van Apeldoorn, 1998). There are systematic differences in how national economies are organized, and member states have chosen ways of regulating production, investment, and exchange that constitute different varieties of capitalism (Hall and Soskice, 2001: 15). Thus efforts to create a single market in Europe have sought to unify disparate interests and market ideologies, and the process of market integration has often been deeply contested.

The clash between laissez faire and interventionist ideologies that began in the earliest years of the European Community continues today. The implied commitment to the free market economy, stressing the virtues of competition and greater efficiencies through specialization and economies of scale, was balanced by a widespread acceptance of *dirigisme* and intervention by state agencies and nationalized monopolies, resulting in a tension between 'regulated capitalism' and 'neoliberalism' (Hooghe and Marks, 1997; see Box 19.2). How, then, did the Community tackle such deep-seated differences in rules, standards, and practices as it sought to create a single European market?

KEY POINTS

- The objective of creating a single European market can be traced to the Spaak Report of 1956 and the Treaty of Rome in 1957.

- The Treaty of Rome sought to establish a customs union in Europe.

- The Treaty also sought to dismantle barriers to trade among the six original members of the European Economic Community.

- Distinctive forms of capitalism persist given strong institutionally embedded practices and norms.

BOX 19.2 Characteristics of capitalism

Neoliberalism	Regulated capitalism

Neoliberalism

- Market liberalization—Removes restrictions to trade; provides a regulatory climate attractive to business

- **Regulatory competition** among member states—Leading to competition among different national regulatory policies

- Rejection of greater regulatory **power** for institutions at EU level; insulation of the market from political interference; retention of political authority at the national level

- Supporters include conservative political parties, multinationals, industry associations, and financial institutions

Regulated capitalism

- Market intervention—government intervention in market.

- Social market economy and social solidarity—emphasis on welfare state and distributive politics

- Increased capacity to regulate at European level; mobilization of particular social groups; reform institutions to generate greater use of **qualified majority voting (QMV)**; enhancement of legislative **legitimacy**

- Supporters include social and Christian democratic parties

Source: Adapted from Hooghe and Marks (1997)

Setting the scene for the single market

Two important changes took place that helped to set the scene for the creation of a single market. The first was the emergence of mutual recognition as a key principle; the second, the increasing judicial activism of the European Court of Justice (ECJ).

From harmonization to mutual recognition

In order to tackle those domestic regulations that thwarted the creation of a common or single market, the European Community promoted a policy of harmonization (or standardization) that was to provide a lightning rod for public opposition over efforts to regulate what many felt were long-standing national customs, traditions, and practices (Dashwood, 1983; see Box 19.3). Although the goal of harmonization was a 'barrier-free' single market, the years of fruitless arguments over harmonizing noise limits on lawnmowers, the composition of bread and beer, and tractor rear-view mirrors were a result of unanimity making it extremely difficult to get agreement amongst member states, since it allowed individual governments to exercise a veto on specific legislative proposals.

However, the single market took off with the introduction of a new mode of governance, when the principle of mutual recognition was introduced. Mutual recognition allows member states to recognize regulations as equivalent (Schmidt, 2007). Because member states do not unconditionally accept such mutual equivalence of rules, they reserve the right to enforce their own regulations as a result of 'general interest' considerations. Mutual recognition and harmonization reduce the barriers created by national regulations, but provide the necessary level playing field. Without this, the absence of regulations for product and process standards might lead to a 'race to the bottom' in social and environment standards, as states sought to reduce their domestic measures to attract foreign direct investment (FDI) and to gain significant competitive advantage through social dumping.

The free trade umpire: the European Court of Justice and judicial activism

The problems associated with addressing trade restrictions through harmonization did not go unnoticed by the European Court of Justice (ECJ), which has often used its judicial power for the purposes of fostering an integrated economy (see Chapter 13). Indeed, a large measure of the credit for creating the single market belongs to the judicial activism of the ECJ. Confronted by restrictions on their ability to operate across national borders, firms began to seek redress through the Community legal system. The Court was asked to determine whether the restrictions on imports imposed by member states were legitimate under the Treaty.

Examples of member states' restrictions included Italy's prohibition on the sale of pasta not made with durum wheat, Germany's 'beer purity' regulations prohibiting the sale of any product as 'beer' that was not brewed with specific ingredients, and Belgian regulations that required margarine to be sold only in cube-shaped containers to prevent confusion with butter, which was sold in

---

BOX 19.3 The single market programme

The single market programme involved the removal of three kinds of trade barrier, as follows.

Physical barriers	The removal of internal barriers and frontiers for goods and people
	The simplification of border controls (including the creation of a single administrative document for border entry)
Technical barriers	Coordinating product standards, testing, and certification (under the so-called 'new approach')
	Liberalization of public procurement
	Free movement of capital (by reducing capital exchange controls)
	Free movement of services (covering financial services, such as banking and insurance, to operate under home country control)
	Liberalization of the transport sector (rail, road, and air; rights of *cabotage*; the liberalization of markets and removal of monopolies, state subsidies, and quotas or market-sharing arrangements)
	Free movement of labour and the mutual recognition of professional qualifications (including non-discrimination in employment)
	Europeanization of company law, intellectual property, and company taxation (including the freedom of establishment for enterprises, a **European Company Statute**, and rules on trademarks, copyright, and legal protection)
Fiscal barriers	Harmonization of divergent tax **regimes**, including sales tax
	The agreement of standard rates and special exemptions from sales tax
	Other indirect taxes aimed at reducing restrictions on cross-border sales

---

round-shaped containers. As many of its decisions illustrate, the Court had the task of reconciling the demands of market integration with the pursuit of legitimate regulatory objectives advanced by member states.

Several landmark cases limited the scope and applicability of national legislation. One of the most important in this regard came in Case 8/74 *Procureur du Roi v Dassonville* [1974] ECR 837. Dassonville imported whisky into Belgium purchased from a French supplier. It was prosecuted by Belgian authorities for violating national customs rules that prohibited importation from a third country without the correct documentation. Dassonville argued that the whisky had entered the French market legally, that it must therefore be allowed to circulate freely, and that restrictions on imports within the EC were illegal. In a sweeping judgment, the Court argued that 'all trading rules that hinder trade, whether directly or indirectly, actually or potentially, were inadmissible'.

National measures that negatively impact trade were therefore prohibited (Stone Sweet and Caporaso, 1998: 118). This was softened by the recognition that reasonable regulations made by member states for legitimate public interests such as health, safety, and environment policies were acceptable if there were no European rules in place. The judgment was predicated

on the belief that the European Commission should adopt harmonized standards to allow free movement across markets, while at the same time giving the ECJ the opportunity to monitor member states' behaviour and to scrutinize permissible exceptions.

In what is probably its best-known case, Case 120/78 *Rewe-Zentral AG v Bundesmonopolverwaltung für Branntwein (Cassis de Dijon)* [1978] ECR 649, the Court ruled on a German ban on the sale of a French blackcurrant liqueur because it did not conform to German standards in terms of alcoholic content (see Egan, 2001: 95). The Court rejected German arguments that Cassis, with its lower alcoholic content, posed health risks, but noted that the protection of the consumer could occur by labelling alcohol content. Most importantly, it clearly defined what national measures were deemed permissible. The most-cited part of the ruling suggested that 'there was no valid reason why products produced and marketed in one member state could not be introduced into another member state'.

The notion of equivalence of national regulations, which this ruling introduced, opened up the possibility that harmonization would not always be necessary for the construction of a single market. This was the crucial step in launching a new regulatory strategy, mutual recognition, which would make for an easier circulation of trade and commerce in the Community. Mutual recognition implies that it is only in areas that are not mutually equivalent that member states can invoke national restrictions, practices, and traditions, and restrict free trade in the Community.

In fact, the Court argued that derogations from (or exceptions to) the free trade rule for the purposes of public health, fair competition, and consumer protection were possible, but that they had to be based upon reasonable grounds. Governments, whether national, local, or sub-national, had to demonstrate that any measure restricting trade was not simply disguised protectionism. Anxious to safeguard the Community-wide market, the Court has continued to determine on a case-by-case basis whether specific laws are valid under the Treaty. However, faced with a growing number of cases, the Court, in Joined Cases C-267/91 and 2-268/91 *Keck and Mithouard* [1993] ECR I-6097, reduced the scope of judicial scrutiny in cases that applied to all traders operating in specific national territory, under certain conditions. Thus the Court would not examine issues such as Sunday trading, mandatory closing hours, or other issues that had a limited effect on cross-border trade and which reflected national moral, social, and cultural norms.

Yet despite lagging behind other areas, case law relating to free movement of services and rights of establishment is now at the centre of a wave of recent legal developments, because the 'country of origin' principle is the starting point in assessing restrictions to free movement. In the seminal Case C-438/05 *International Transport Workers' Federation and anor v Viking Line ABP* [2008] IRLR 143, and Case C-341/05 *Laval* [2007] ECR I-11767, and Case C-346/06 *Rüffert v Land Niedersachsen* [2008] IRLR 467, the importance of freedom of establishment and services is prioritized over social and collective labour rights in economic integration. Judicial activism has thus allowed companies the right to choose the least restrictive regulatory environment to allow for more home-country control rules. Scharpf (2010) highlights the constitutional asymmetry that this creates, where these recent court cases and efforts to liberalize services challenge national socio-economic models, as a result of the predominance of market-based treaty obligations promoting economic freedoms and legal obligations to safeguard against protectionism.

The constitutive role of law is crucial in understanding the consolidation of markets in Europe. Market integration involves a substantive legal project

that shapes public and private policies. The ECJ has placed state and local laws under its purview, and has also determined the economic relationship between public intervention and the market, as well as the political relationship between the member states and the Union. European case law has opened up opportunities by reducing much of the cost of innovation and entrepreneurship by shifting the focus towards creating the context for open markets and competition.

KEY POINTS

- Harmonization was initially the main *dirigiste* strategy used to integrate national markets in the 1960s and 1970s, but it achieved limited results.

- Mutual recognition provided a new mechanism for regulatory coordination and the possibility of mutual equivalence of member state rules.

- Legal rulings by the ECJ in cases such as *Dassonville* and *Cassis de Dijon* have played a key role in challenging non-tariff barriers to trade.

- More recent cases, such as *Viking*, *Laval* and *Rüffert*, have raised questions about the balance between economic freedoms and social and labour rights.

The politics of neoliberalism and '1992'

Throughout the 1970s and early 1980s, member state efforts to maintain import restrictions and discriminatory trade practices had thwarted attempts to create a single market. By the mid-1980s, however, things were about to change.

Market-making

Growing recognition of a competitiveness gap vis-à-vis the United States and Japan, on the one hand, and newly industrializing countries, on the other, led to strenuous efforts to maintain overall levels of market activity and provide conditions for viable markets (Pelkmans and Winters, 1988: 6). While past economic policies, notably neo-corporatist class compromises and consensual incomes policies, had successfully promoted growth, these national policies were unable to cope with changes in the international economy as trade deficits soared and stagflation increased.

Assessments were so bleak that, on the twenty-fifth anniversary of the Treaty of Rome, *The Economist* put a tombstone on its cover to proclaim the EC dead and buried. A growing consensus among business and political leaders that a collective strategy was needed to stop an 'escalating trade war' (*Financial Times*, 25 July 1980) led the European Round Table (ERT), the heads of Europe's largest companies, to put forward numerous proposals to improve European competitiveness. It also led the American Chamber of Commerce (AmCham) to flag problems of industry standards, border formalities, and export licences, identifying France and Italy as the worst offenders. Industry began a campaign of proactive lobbying, ambitious proposals, and visible political engagement (*Financial Times*, 20 March 2001). Responding to this groundswell, the European Commission proposed addressing the most problematic barriers in the member states (*Financial Times*, 23 September 1980; *The Economist*, 22 October 1983).

Governments, well aware that their efforts to create national champions, to protect labour markets, and to maintain public spending were not stemming rising trade imbalances and deficits, sought new solutions. Efforts to contain import competition and stabilize industries had failed, shifting strategies from Keynesian demand management towards market liberalization. This did not mean a common consensus around neoliberalism, because different conceptions of the agenda for European integration emerged.

While the British government advocated a genuine common market in goods and services, and promoted a radically neoliberal agenda, the French government argued for the creation of a common industrial space in which trade barriers could be reduced internally, provided that external trade protection would compensate for increased internal competition (Pearce and Sutton, 1983). Major steps taken at the European Council meeting in Fontainebleau in 1984 broke the impasse, as agreement on the long-running disputes over Britain's contribution to the Community Budget and the pending Iberian enlargement were reached. The Dooge Committee was also established to reform the institutional and decision-making structure of the Community.

Agreement at the 1985 Intergovernmental Conference (IGC) in Milan to 'study the institutional conditions under which the internal market could be achieved within a time limit' proved critical for market integration. This built on several earlier developments, including the Spinelli Report, which focused on the need to link national regulations and institutional reform, and the parliamentary draft Treaty on European Union on institutional reform, which included increased parliamentary powers and greater use of qualified majority voting (QMV) in the Council. At the subsequent IGC, the proposed treaty reforms were brought together to become the Single European Act (SEA) (see also Chapter 3).

The SEA endorsed the single market and altered the decision-making rules for single market measures (with exceptions such as taxation and rights of workers) from unanimity to QMV. This linked institutional reforms to substantive goals and made it more difficult for recalcitrant member states simply to veto legislative action, as had been the case under harmonization. The SEA also strengthened the powers of the European Parliament with respect to single market measures by allowing for the rejection or amendment of proposals under the cooperation procedure.

The 1992 Programme: a blueprint for action

By early 1985, the stage was set for an ambitious initiative. Newly appointed Commission President Jacques Delors and Internal Market Commissioner Lord Cockfield, a British former Secretary of State for Industry, put together a package of proposals that aimed to achieve the completion of the single market by 1992. The 300 proposals—subsequently modified and amended to become 283 proposals—became a Commission White Paper entitled *Completing the Internal Market*. The final product became known as the '1992 Programme'.

The White Paper grouped the remaining obstacles to trade in three major categories: physical, technical, and fiscal barriers. Lord Cockfield used this simple categorization to introduce legislative proposals across goods, services, capital, and labour markets to improve market access, and to prevent distortions to competition and restrictive business practices. The European Commission bolstered support by commissioning a series of economic evaluations on the 'costs of non-Europe' (the Cecchini Report, 1988). Although overly optimistic, the estimated trade and welfare gains from removing barriers to trade were compelling. Not only would there be lower trade costs and greater economies of scale as firms exploited increased opportunities, but it was also expected that there would be greater production efficiency achieved through market enlargement, intensified competition, and industrial restructuring.

At the core of the single market project was the concept of mutual recognition, the consequence of which would be increased competition not only among firms within the EU, but also among different national regulatory systems (see Sun and Pelkmans, 1995). Governments sponsoring regulations that restricted market access would be under pressure since firms from other EC member states would not be required to abide by them, putting their own local firms at a disadvantage. The European Commission sought to apply this innovative strategy to the service sector as well. The concept of 'home country control' was to allow banks, insurance companies, and dealers in securities to offer elsewhere in the Community the same services as those that they offered at home. A single licence would operate, so that these sectors would be licensed, regulated, and supervised for the most part by their home country.

Building on the legal decisions outlining the doctrine of mutual recognition as a broad free trade principle and with reference to standard-setting as a more flexible regulatory strategy, the Commission drafted a proposal on harmonization and standards in 1985 (Pelkmans, 1997). This 'new approach' reflected a critical effort to address barriers to trade by sharing regulatory functions between the public and private sectors. Where possible, there was to be mutual recognition of regulations and standards, and Community-level regulation was to be restricted to essential health and safety requirements. The necessary standards are set by the European standards bodies, the European Committee for Standardization (CEN),

the European Committee for Electro-technical Standardization (CENELEC), and the European Telecommunications Standards Institute (ETSI) (Egan, 2001). Such private sector governance allowed states to foster coordination without the agreement costs associated with harmonization, by delegating regulatory authority to private institutions.

The White Paper gained widespread political support by providing a target date for the completion of the single market, emphasizing the merits of economic liberalism. It included measures across the four freedoms, such as the abolition of frontier controls, the mutual recognition of goods and services, rights of establishment for professional workers, and the abolition of capital exchange controls. While most measures in the White Paper focused on market access or negative integration measures, such as removing technical barriers to trade, dismantling quotas, and removing licensing restrictions for cross-border banking and insurance services, they were complemented by a series of market-correcting or positive integration measures, such as health and safety standards, rules for trademarks and deposit insurance, and solvency ratios for banks and insurance (see Box 19.4).

Despite a deadline of 1992, the single market remained incomplete. The White Paper conspicuously avoided a number of issues, such as the social dimension, politically sensitive sectors including textiles and clothing, and the taxation of savings and investment income, despite evident distortions and restrictions in these areas. Completion of the single market meant tackling politically difficult dossiers and ensuring that the legislation was put into effect in all member states; otherwise the confidence of consumers and producers in realizing economic benefits would be

---

BOX 19.4 The frayed edges of the single market: the case of services

The Services Directive (Directive 2005/36/EC) is seen as critical, because liberalization is expected to deliver tangible benefits and serve as the main driver of growth and jobs. Hampered by numerous barriers, the so-called 'Bolkestein Directive', which aimed to do for the trade in services what the '1992 Programme' agenda did for internal market activity in goods, sparked fierce criticism and protest across Europe. Although a key ambition of the Directive was to extend the well-understood EU principle of 'mutual recognition' to the services sector, it stoked fears of a flood of cheap labour from new member states under the 'country of origin' principle. Under this principle, a firm would

be able to operate in a foreign country according to the rules and regulations of its home country, leading to concerns that an influx of cheap labour from Central and Eastern Europe (CEE) would undercut working conditions, wage levels, and welfare benefits in Western Europe, leading to 'social dumping'. 'Polish plumbers'—emblematic job snatchers—came to symbolize concerns about the effects of liberalization among the old member states. European fears that services liberalization reflected the primacy of market liberalization over social protection made this one of the most disputed pieces of European legislation in recent years (Polanyi, 1957; Nicolaïdis and Schmidt, 2007).

undermined. Nationally important sectors such as utilities (gas and postal services, for example) were given special exemptions in the single market on the basis of social and economic arguments that 'universal services' must be provided, resulting in natural monopolies and limited competition. With rapid liberalization and technological changes, the traditional economic rationale for such *dirigiste* policies was being undermined. Pressure to open up telecommunications, electricity, and gas markets resulted in the Commission forcing liberalization of these basic services through its competition powers. The competition policy pursued by the European Commission has reinforced a liberalizing bias to the single market—because the specific features of restrictive practices, monopolies, rules governing state aid to industry, and merger policy have all played a substantial role in reducing market distortions.

Given the transformation of European economies over the past two decades, the traditional means of market integration through the removal of trade barriers and sector harmonization appears outdated in the context of changes in technology and innovation, the growth of tradable services, and changes in production (Hamilton and Quinlan, 2005: 255). While closer economic cooperation has challenged the sovereign capacity of states in terms of their capacity for autonomous action within their own borders, further integration has run into resistance as the irreversible pressures of market liberalization and economic globalization have challenged the European social model. Although high unemployment, low economic growth, and the resulting sense of insecurity in many European states have fuelled pressure for economic reform, they have also triggered anxiety and strong resistance by member states. Efforts to address archaic rules in the service sector, the freedom of services, and rights of establishment through the concept of home-country control sparked a considerable outcry (see Box 19.4). Often forgotten is that the internal market agenda is unfinished. Despite deeper market integration, domestic consumption and investment patterns and labour markets still reveal a distinctive 'home bias' (Delgado, 2006). However, further action is pending in the area of financial services, patents, customs, company law, and taxation. After a period of 'internal market fatigue', these issues re-emerged on the political agenda with the Monti Report, the Europe 2020 strategy, and the Single Market Act all being produced in 2010 and 2011.

KEY POINTS

- In the mid-1980s, business engaged in extensive lobbying for the single market and supported measures to improve European competitiveness

- The White Paper on the single market created a package of measures to liberalize trade that became the 1992 Programme.

- The single market project is a work in progress, with continued efforts to deepen and widen the internal market.

- The Single Market Act is the latest effort to address gaps and to provide new initiatives to complete the single market, engendering renewed awareness of the central role of the single market as a means of promoting growth, innovation, and competitiveness.

Correcting the market: the politics of regulated capitalism

The emphasis on market integration through the '1992 Programme' and subsequently in the Monti Report also brought pressures for ancillary policies along social democratic lines (Scharpf, 1999). Fearful that excessive competition would increase social conflict, proponents of a regulated capitalism approach (see Box 19.2) recommended a variety of inclusive mechanisms to generate broad-based support for the single market. These included structural policy for poorer regions to promote economic and social cohesion, consumer and environmental protection, and rural development. Fiscal transfers spread the burden of adjustment and assisted the adversely affected countries.

Labour representatives also sought to address the impact of market integration through the creation of an ongoing social dialogue (see Chapter 20). These initiatives acknowledged that the domestic political pressures on national welfare states meant that they could no longer compensate for the effects of integration as they had done in the past (Scharpf, 1999). The goal of regulating markets, redistributing resources, and shaping partnership among public and private actors led advocates of regulated capitalism to propose provisions for transport and communications infrastructure, information networks, workforce skills, and research and development (Hooghe and Marks, 1997). The progressive expansion of activities at the European level brought into focus two long-standing opposing views about the economic role of governments.

Some have argued that the single market has progressively increased the level of statism or interventionism in Europe (Messerlin, 2001; Schmidt, 2007). The economic consensus in favour of market forces and neoliberalism under the single market programme in the 1980s has been offset by increased intervention or regulated capitalism in labour markets (minimum wage and working time), and new provisions for culture (broadcast quotas), industry (shipbuilding, textiles, and clothing), and technology (new energy resources, biotechnology, and broadband networks) in the 1990s. Yet these forms of embedded liberalism have, to some degree, been overshadowed by a growing emphasis on competitiveness in the 1990s, in terms of increased market competition and market discipline through the Lisbon Process, a collective strategy across a range of policies in which the single market is a central element to deliver the goals of growth, jobs, innovation, and competition, and to drive European recovery, and more recently Europe 2020. Such market liberalization presents opportunities for mobilization and provides a new context in which opposition can be expressed (Imig and Tarrow, 2001). This is recognized by the recent Monti Report (Monti, 2010) aimed at providing greater awareness of the role of the single market for the European social market economy in an effort to enhance socio-political support and legitimacy.

KEY POINTS

- Proponents of the regulated capitalism approach advocate a number of policies to generate more widespread support for the EU including structural policies and social dialogue.

- The disjuncture between market integration at supranational level and social protection at national level has become a cause for concern.

- Fears about the socio-political legitimacy of market outcomes were echoed in the 2010 Monti Report.

- The Monti Report argued that the social dimensions of a market economy need to be strengthened to create a highly competitive social market economy, as set out in the Preamble to the Treaty of Rome.

The revival of the single market

As Europe faces the challenges of making the single market deliver, greater attention has been given to better governance and compliance, on the one hand, and, on the other hand, to completing the single market to promote growth (Radaelli, 1998; European Council, 2012). The European institutions have promoted regulatory reform and more flexible modes of governance, in part motivated by business requests for an easing of regulatory burdens as a prerequisite for the achievement of a Europe-wide single market (European Commission, 1992a; Molitor, 1995; Mandelkern Group, 2001). Specific initiatives have included 'Simpler Legislation for a Single Market' (SLIM) in 1996, the Action Plan for the Single Market (1997), a scoreboard to generate peer pressure to enhance regulatory compliance (European Report, 28 November 1997), and regulatory impact assessments (RIAs). Yet there remain problems of compliance with single market obligations in both new and old member states, generating a range of formal and informal mechanisms with which to address the situation (Falkner et al., 2004). While the Commission has actively pursued infringement proceedings (under Article 226 of the Treaty), whereby it formally notifies member states of their legal obligations, it has also sought address the slow pace of standardization, as well as misunderstandings with the application of mutual recognition in practice (Nicolaïdis and Schmidt, 2007). This involves out-of-court informal solutions to complaints by consumers and businesses regarding the incorrect application of internal market laws, notification of new national laws and standards to prevent new barriers to trade, and the new goods package, all aimed at better market surveillance. Businesses surveys indicate that firms still face obstacles that prevent them from realizing the full benefits of the single market (Egan and Guimaries, 2011).

Recognizing that the single market constitutes a key driver for European economic growth, Mario Monti, a former Commissioner and current Italian Prime Minister, was commissioned to write a report on how to improve the single market in a time of economic crisis. Facing concerns about 'internal market fatigue' as well as growing nationalist pressures, Monti advocated deepening and widening the single market, using social benefits to generate public support and renewed momentum. On the eve of the twentieth anniversary of the '1992 Programme', the context for the single market had clearly changed, requiring adaptation to new technologies, new business models, and new market practices (Pelkmans, 2010). Seeking to generate a momentum, the timing of the Monti Report, entitled *A New Strategy for the Single Market: At the Service of Europe's Economy and Society*, coincided with the start of the eurozone crisis and was thus largely ignored by the member states. Yet the European Commission persisted, drawing up a list of fifty proposals that would put the report into action. These were then whittled down to twelve key areas that ultimately became the Single Market Act of 2011. Although efforts have been made to address those areas in which economic benefits are still to be had, such as the digital economy, patents, the coordination of tax policies, copyright and electronic commerce, and implementing legislation in the much contested area of services, the goal of delivering on this agenda by the end of 2012 was, from the outset, very ambitious given the economic and political climate in Europe at that time.

KEY POINTS

- Efforts have been made to improve compliance through formal and informal mechanisms.

- Emphasis has been given to the design of better regulatory policies to ease burdens on business and to promote competitiveness.

- The Monti Report and Single Market Act are attempts to address the lack of confidence in the single market using initiatives aimed at enhancing general macroeconomic performance.

Globalization and the single market

Some in Europe argue that European integration contributes to globalization, because the increased flow of goods, services, capital, and people across Europe increases economic opportunities and market openness. Others argue that globalization poses a threat to the European social model, and that the direct impact on national economies requires coordinated action to manage the tensions and challenges created by increased global competition. While much attention within Europe has been focused on the need to manage the consequences of industrial decline, to foster greater productivity, and to ease transaction costs

within Europe, debates about managing economic liberalization have now been transferred to the global level. Yet the single market has also enabled the European Union to exercise its authority in multilateral trade negotiations, and to use market access as an instrument of 'soft power' to promote economic and political reform in Central and Eastern Europe (CEE) and the Balkans through stabilization and association agreements (SAAs) to, in many cases, eventual EU membership.

As the largest single trading area in the world, the European Union has a leading role to play in the context of international trade negotiations and liberalization. Across a broad range of sectors, Europe is increasingly shaping global markets through the transfer of its regulatory rules and standards. The EU, as an international economic regime, has sought to play a leading role by promoting key concepts of its regulatory approach in areas such as competition policy, financial regulations, environmental management standards, and food safety. The EU now seeks to promote its regulatory standards to take advantage of globalization. Yet European integration also takes place in a situation of global sourcing of goods and services, increased tradability of goods and services, and changing patterns of trade and investment. While many studies of globalization have suggested that Europe is moving towards greater levels of economic integration, they have paid much less attention to other parts of the world. Economic integration is continuing, but political integration is either not desired or so limited as to make debates about territoriality, sovereignty, and governance premature.

KEY POINTS

- Opinion is divided on whether globalization is a threat or an opportunity.

- The European Union—as a huge trading bloc—plays an important role in the international economic system, as well as being shaped by it.

- The EU uses its different trading relationships to promote its rules and standards, exporting its single market governance.

- It is unclear whether European integration provides a model for other parts of the world in terms of regional integration.

BOX 19.5 Theorizing the single market

There are different theoretical approaches from a variety of disciplinary perspectives that can explain the causes, content, and consequences of the single market (see Pelkmans et al., 2008).

Intergovernmentalists (see Chapter 6) claim that the institutional dynamics that underpin the single market project were the result of a convergence of policy preferences in the early 1980s between the UK, Germany, and France (Moravcsik, 1991). National interests and policies are expected to constrain integrationist impulses, because state resources, power, and bargaining are the driving factors of economic integration. Garrett (1992) adds to this, arguing that, in important areas of legal activity, the Court was constrained by member states' governments. According to Garrett, the Court anticipates reactions from member states and serves their interests (especially those of the most powerful member states) in rendering its judgments.

By comparison, the *neo-functionalist* account stresses the importance of supranational actors in shaping the single market agenda. Sandholtz and Zysman (1989) point to the Commission as an innovative policy entrepreneur shaping the European agenda, supported by business interests seeking to reap the benefits of an enlarged market. Burley and Mattli (1993) argue that Court rulings have resulted in interactions between national and European courts, creating a distinctive legal regime that shapes rules and procedures governing markets. When political attempts to create a common market stalled, the Court advanced its supranational authority over national courts, expanding its jurisdictional authority in order to make a pivotal contribution to the promotion of free trade (see Shapiro, 1992; Egan, 2001).

Cameron (1992) seeks to blend these different theoretical perspectives by arguing that the 1992 Programme was the result of the complex interaction of different actors and institutions, simultaneously accelerating economic integration and **supranational institution**-building, while also representing intergovernmental bargaining among states. By contrast, van Apeldoorn (1992) argues that market outcomes are the result of struggles between contending transnational forces, and that economic integration reflects the economic interests of transnational capital strengthened by the deepening globalization processes and the rise of neoliberal market ideology within European political economy. Jabko (2006), on the other hand, focuses on the role of ideas in **framing** the single market project, drawing on *constructivist* premises that the market can be strategically used as a political strategy to appeal to various constituencies at different times.

More recently, the single market process has been examined through the lens of *comparative policy analysis*. Empirical studies have shown that European policies are a patchwork of different **policy styles**, instruments, and institutional arrangements (Héritier, 1996). Majone (1996) described such changes in governance,

resulting from the failure of public ownership modes of control and the ensuing turn to privatization policies, as generating an increasing transfer of authority to the EU level to deal with market failures and to ensure credible commitments to a European single market. His argument that the EU as a political system specializes in regulation is based on the notion that regulation is the central instrument of governance at the EU level, since, with limited fiscal resources at its control, the EU has sought to expand its influence through the supply of regulations, the costs of which are borne by the firms and states responsible for complying with them. Thus the single market is an effort to reduce **transaction costs** and to resolve problems of heterogeneity through collective action and coordination. Majone (1995) argues that, in order to achieve such goals, the European Union requires **non-majoritarian** institutions, such as independent banks, regulatory agencies, and courts, to foster collective regulatory outcomes, because they are better suited than traditional political interests, such as parties, legislatures, and **interest groups**, to achieve the independence and credibility necessary to govern the market.

Focusing on issues of *governance*, other scholars have stressed the impact of the single market on regions, sectors, and classes by looking at the relationship between economic development and democratic conditions, seeking to demonstrate that the single market may not be entirely benign in its consequences (Hirst and Thompson, 1996; Scharpf, 1999). While political economists have illustrated how the activism of the European **polity** has increased market competition in sectors hitherto shielded from the discipline of the market (Scharpf, 1999), there has been growing attention in comparative politics to the role of public opinion and party politics in intensifying conflict around European policies. Few subjects have generated more debate than the effects of economic integration and globalization on the policy autonomy of governments. Opponents argue that the increasing constraints on national policy choices, especially the pressures on the welfare states and government-owned monopolies have, in fact, contributed to the growing opposition among the populace towards further European integration. As Hooghe and Marks (2009) have recently argued, as important as economic imperatives are, market integration is also the product of politics—most notably, but not exclusively, tensions and conflicts about **sovereignty**, identity, and governance in a multilevel polity. There is a strong relationship between economic and political developments, as the single market and its ancillary policies require political support and legitimacy, on the one hand, and institutional capabilities and effectiveness, on the other. Market integration generates conflict and bargaining over institutional power and authority, and has resulted in growing economic insecurity among domestic publics about the effects of a broader breakdown of economic barriers on national identity, culture, and values.

Conclusion

While the completion of the single market has suffered a period of relative neglect, its star is once again on the rise (Monti, 2010; Pelkmans, 2010). Although the single market has changed over the past twenty years, the need to enhance productivity and competitiveness across European economies remains. Early efforts to remove obstacles to, and distortions in, goods, services, capital, and labour have transformed the European economic landscape. Yet, in the context of the post-2008 economic crisis, more needs to be done to make the single market function more effectively. The single market needs to enable the European Union to confront the dynamics of increased competition and to respond to the changing global environment by fostering collective coordinated action on a range of regulatory issues. This could help the EU to shape global rules and norms.

Even though the single market is now well entrenched, its feasibility and effectiveness are dependent on two conditions. First, it requires well-defined legal and judicial mechanisms to guarantee enforcement and compliance in single market rules. But it also needs to attend to generating political support and legitimacy for economic integration. In this respect, the relationship between economic rights and social rights needs to be re-examined, since viable and sustainable integration is likely to be more successful if economic growth is fairly distributed. While striking down economic barriers to trade, promoting market liberalization, and freeing up economic access, the European Court of Justice has also created extensive case law that bolsters equity, economic development, and social welfare (Caporaso and Tarrow, 2009). Yet it has increased the asymmetry between economic and social rights, generating public opposition as increased economic divergence within an enlarged EU has made the impact of market integration more salient in domestic politics. Like all internal markets, Europe's single market must balance functional, distributional, and territorial pressures (Anderson, 2012).

 QUESTIONS

1. What policy instruments has the European Union used to address barriers to trade in EU?

2. How successful has the EU been in fostering a single market free of restrictions to trade and commerce?

3. What were the driving forces behind the 'relaunch' of the single market project in the 1980s and 2000s?

4. How have theories and approaches explained the single market programme?

5. What role has the European Court of Justice played in dealing with barriers to trade?

6. What accounts for recent interest in the single market?

7. Is market integration a shield or conduit for the forces of globalization?

8. To what extent are the current problems of market integration a result of its lack of socio-political legitimacy, the economic crisis, or internal 'market fatigue'?

 GUIDE TO FURTHER READING

Anderson, G. (ed.) (2012) *Internal Markets and Multi-level Governance: The Experience of the European Union, Australia, Canada, Switzerland, and the United States* (Oxford: Oxford University Press)   This book considers the concept of the single market in a comparative perspective.

Armstrong, K. and Bulmer, S. (1998) *The Governance of the Single European Market* (Manchester: Manchester University Press)   This study of the single market provides case studies illustrating various legal and regulatory modes of governance.

Egan, M. (2012) 'Single market' in E. Jones, A. Menon, and S. Weatherill (eds) (2012) *Handbook of the European Union* (Oxford: Oxford University Press)   This chapter provides a useful overview of single market issues.

Jabko, N. (2006) *Playing the Market: A Political Strategy for Uniting Europe, 1985–2005* (Ithaca, NY: Cornell University Press)   The author traces the political strategy from the single market of 1986, through the official creation of the European Union in 1992, to the coming of the euro in 1999.

Pelkmans, J., Hanf, D., and Chang, M. (2008) *The EU Internal Market in Comparative Perspective, Economic, Political and Legal Analyses, Vol. 8* (Berlin: Peter Lang Publishers)   This book assesses the state of the internal market through multi-disciplinary lenses.

 **WEBLINKS**

http://ec.europa.eu/bepa/pdf/monti_report_final_10_05_2010_en.pdf   Online access to the Monti Report.

http://ec.europa.eu/citizens_agenda/docs/sec_2007_1519_en.pdf   Online access to EC Commission (2007) *The External Dimension of the Single Market Review*, Commission Staff Working Document, Brussels, which analyses the external dimension of the single market.

http://ec.europa.eu/internal_market/score/index_en.htm   Online access to the *Internal Market Scoreboard*.

http://ec.europa.eu/internal_market/smact/index_en.htm   Online access to the Single Market Act.

http://www.egmontinstitute.be/paperegm/ep43.pdf   Online access to T. Heremans (2011) *The Single Market in Need of a Strategic Relaunch*, Egmont Working Papers, Brussels.

20

The European Union's Social Dimension

Gerda Falkner

Chapter Contents

Reader's Guide

This chapter looks at how European social policy has evolved since the late 1950s. It begins by reflecting on the intergovernmental character of the policy in the early days, and on how the gradual introduction of qualified majority voting (QMV) and the widening scope of the policy allowed the European institutions and European-level interest groups a greater say in the European social dimension. The chapter also looks at the work of the European Social Fund (ESF) and the European Globalization Adjustment Fund (EGF). Focusing on newer developments, later sections chart the arrival of the open method of coordination (OMC), a non-regulatory approach to European policy-making in this field, and the growing importance of social partnership—that is, the involvement of interest groups representing employers and labour in making European-level social policy. The chapter concludes by arguing that social regulation has become more difficult since the accession of a large number of Central and East European (CEE) states, and because of the effects of the financial and economic crisis.

Introduction

What is social policy? In a famous definition, T. H. Marshall (1975) talked of the use of political power to supersede, supplement, or modify operations of the economic system in order to achieve results that it would not achieve on its own. Such a wide definition would include, for example, redistributive EU actions, which provide funding through the European Union's Structural Funds—that is, the social, agricultural, cohesion, and regional funds. This would go far beyond what is usually understood as European social policy and would introduce too vast an array of topics to be covered in this brief chapter. It seems, therefore, more useful to apply a pragmatic understanding of social policy. This involves actions that fall under the so-called 'social dimension of European integration' (that is, any acts carried out under the social policy chapter of the Treaty), policies targeted at facilitating the freedom of movement of workers in the social realm, and, last but not least, action to harmonize the quite diverse social or labour law standards of the member states, whatever the treaty base.

This chapter will first outline the division of social policy competences between the European Union and its member states, the interpretation of these treaty provisions in the day-to-day policy process over time, and the latest formal reforms at Amsterdam, Nice, and in the Lisbon Treaty. It will then analyse the incremental development of European Community or later Union social regulation and activities, including the European Social Fund (ESF) and the so-called open method of coordination (OMC). Since patterns of decision-making are quite distinctive in the social, as opposed to other, fields of EU politics, this chapter will also outline how EU-level interest groups participate therein (see also Chapter 14). The conclusion not only summarizes the results of the chapter, but also discusses the performance of European integration within its 'social dimension'.

The early years of EU social policy

According to the Treaty of Rome (1957), social policy competences were to remain a largely national affair. The Treaty did not provide for the Europeanization of social policies, because too many delegations had opposed this during the negotiations. Some governments (especially the Germans) pleaded for a neoliberal, free market approach to social affairs, even in the realm of labour and social security; others opted for a limited process of harmonization. The French delegation, notably, argued that France's comparatively high social charges, and its constitutional principle of equal pay for men and women, might constitute a competitive disadvantage within the newly formed European market, while Italy feared that the opening up of Community borders might prove costly for the southern part of the country, which was already economically disadvantaged. In the end, a compromise was found, but this did not include explicit European Economic Community (EEC) competences for active social policy harmonization at the European level. The dominant philosophy of the 1957 Treaty was that improvements in welfare would be provided by the economic growth that arose as a consequence of the liberalization of the European market, and not by the regulatory and distributive form of public policy (see Liebfried and Pierson, 1995; Barnard, 2000).

Nevertheless, the Treaty contained a small number of concessions for the more interventionist delegations. These were the provisions on equal pay for both sexes (Article 119 EEC, now 157 TFEU), the maintenance of 'existing equivalence between paid holiday schemes' (Article 120 EEC, now 158 TFEU), and the establishment of a European Social Fund (Articles 123–128 EEC, now 162–164 TFEU). Equal pay and the ESF increased in their importance as the European integration process progressed. There was to be no direct follow-up, however, on the equivalence of paid holiday schemes.

While other provisions of the Treaty's Title III on social policy included some solemn social policy declarations, they failed to empower the EEC to act:

Underwriting this arrangement was the relative feasibility of nation state strategies for economic development in the first decades after World War II. The common market, as it was constructed, was designed to aid and abet such national strategies, not transcend them.

(Ross, 1995: 360)

Yet, in other areas of activity, the Commission was empowered to present legislative proposals to the Council. These proposals would ultimately become binding law. For social policy, however, the Commission was permitted to act only by undertaking relevant studies, delivering opinions, and arranging consultations both on problems arising at national level and on those of concern to international organizations. In legal terms, then, Article 118 EEC (now 156 TFEU) reflected a confirmation of national (as opposed to European) responsibility for social policy.

Paradoxically, the sole explicit Community competence for social policy regulation under the original EEC Treaty was not in the part of the Treaty that dealt explicitly with social policy; rather it belonged to Part II, on the foundations of the Community, which contained provisions on the free movement of goods, labour, services, and capital. Articles 48–51 EEC (now 45–48 TFEU) thus provided for the establishment of the freedom of movement for workers as part of the Treaty's market-making activities. This implied the abolition of all discrimination based on the nationality of workers in the member states in the areas of employment, remuneration, and other conditions of work and employment (Article 48 EEC, now 45 TFEU). In order to 'adopt such measures in the field of social security as are necessary to provide freedom of movement for workers' (Article 51 EEC, now 48 TFEU), the Council was mandated to establish Community-wide rights to benefits, and a way of calculating the amount of those benefits for migrant workers and their dependants.

Yet although there were almost no explicit social policy competences in the Treaty of Rome, an extensive interpretation of the Treaty basis provided, in practice, some room for manoeuvre. This was possible because, where necessary or useful for market integration, intervention in the social policy field was *implicitly* allowed through the so-called 'subsidiary competence' provisions. In other words, laws in the member states that 'directly affect the establishment or functioning of the common market' could be approximated by unanimous Council decision on the basis of a Commission proposal (Article 100 EEC, now 26 TFEU). Moreover, if action by the Community should prove necessary to attain (in the course of the operation of the common market) one of the objectives of the Community and if the Treaty had not provided the necessary powers, the Council was mandated to take the appropriate measures, acting unanimously on a proposal from the Commission and after consulting the European Parliament (Article 235 EEC, now 352 TFEU).

From the 1970s onwards, these provisions provided a loophole for social policy harmonization. However, the unanimous Council vote necessary for this to happen constituted a high threshold for joint action. Each government could veto social measures and, as a result, the EC found itself in what Scharpf (1988) has called a 'joint-decision trap' (see Chapter 6).

In 1987, the Single European Act (SEA) came into force as the first major Community treaty revision (see Chapters 3 and 16). As in the 1950s, an economic enterprise was at the heart of this fresh impetus in favour of European integration. But parallel to the member states' commitment to a single market programme, the Europeanization of social policy remained controversial. In various policy areas touched by market liberalization, notably environmental and research policy, Community competence was formally extended (see Chapter 24). But this was not so for social policy, because the delegations representing the national governments seemed unwilling to give the Community a broader role in this field.

However, one important exception was made. Article 118a EEC on minimum harmonization concerning health and safety of workers provided an escape route out of the unanimity requirement. For the first time in European social policy, it allowed directives to be agreed on the basis of a qualified majority of the Council members (see Chapter 15). The standards adopted following this Article were minimum regulations only. Nevertheless, under this provision, reluctant member states could be forced to align their social legislation with the (large) majority of member states, even against their will. It should be stressed that agreement on this Article was possible only because occupational health and safety issues were closely connected to the single market.

Governments did not expect this 'technical' matter to facilitate social policy integration in the significant way that it would in the decade to follow. An extensive use of this provision was possible mainly because the wording and the definition of key terms in Article 118a were somewhat vague:

Member States shall pay particular attention to encouraging improvements, especially in the working environment, as regards the health and safety of workers, and shall set as their objective the harmonization of conditions in this area, while maintaining the improvements made. In order to help achieve the objective laid down in the first paragraph, the Council, acting by a qualified majority on a proposal from the Commission . . . shall adopt, by means of directives, minimum requirements for gradual implementation . . .

This formulation made it easy to play what has since been called the 'treaty base game' (Rhodes, 1995). It allowed governments to adopt not only measures improving the working environment (for example, a directive on the maximum concentration of airborne pollutants), but also measures that ensured the health and safety of workers by improving working conditions in a more general sense (for example, limiting working time). It was clear that the reason why this treaty basis was frequently chosen was the fact that only this Article allowed for majority voting at the time.

KEY POINTS

- The 1957 EEC Treaty meant that social policy remained largely a national affair.

- However the coordination of social security systems for migrant workers was an exception to this rule. That, as well as some concessions to the more interventionist delegations, provided stepping stones for EU social policy integration in the longer run.

- The Single European Act introduced qualified majority voting to a limited area of social policy. At the time, member state governments did not realize its implications for further policy integration.

From Maastricht to the Lisbon Treaty

The 1991 Intergovernmental Conference (IGC) preceding the Maastricht Treaty negotiated the next reform of the social policy provisions. However, under the requirement of unanimous approval by all (then) twelve member states, the social provisions could not be significantly altered because of the strong opposition from the UK government. At the end of extremely difficult negotiations that threatened all other compromises achieved within the IGC, the UK was granted an opt-out from the social policy measures agreed by the rest of the member states. In the Protocol on Social Policy annexed to the EC Treaty, all members except the UK were authorized to use the institutions, procedures, and mechanisms of the Treaty for the purpose of implementing their 'Agreement on Social Policy' (sometimes called the 'Social Chapter', now incorporated into Articles 151–161 TFEU).

Because of the UK opt-out (or the 'opt-in' of the other member states), the European Union after Maastricht had two different legal bases for the adoption of social policy measures. The EC Treaty's social provisions remained valid for all member states. As introduced in the 1986 Single European Act (SEA), it allowed for minimum harmonization, as well as for qualified majority voting (QMV) in the area of worker health and safety provisions only. By contrast, the innovative social policy provisions of the Social Agreement, applicable to all but the UK, comprised what had been perceived during the IGC as an amendment to the social provisions of the Treaty. These constituted an extension of Community competence into a wide range of social policy issues, including working conditions, the information and consultation of workers, equality between men and women with regard to labour market opportunities and treatment at work (as opposed to formerly only equal pay), and the integration of persons excluded from the labour market. Some issues were, however, explicitly excluded from the scope of minimum harmonization under the Maastricht social policy provisions—namely, pay, the right of association, the right to strike, and the right to impose lock-outs.

Additionally, QMV was extended to many more issue areas than before, including the informing and consultation of workers. Unanimous decisions remained, however, for: social security matters and the social protection of workers; the protection of those whose employment contract is terminated; the representation and collective defence of interests of workers and employers, including co-determination; conditions of employment for third-country nationals (TCNs)—that is, non-EU nationals, legally residing in Community territory; and financial contributions for promotion of employment and job creation.

In contrast to the Maastricht negotiations, in the 1996–97 IGC preceding the Amsterdam Treaty, social policy reform was not a major issue. Because of the fierce resistance to social policy reforms by the UK's Conservative government (in office until May 1997), the IGC decided to postpone discussion of the topic until the very end of the negotiation period, awaiting the result of the 1997 general election. Under the new Labour government, which came into office at this point, the UK's opt-out from the Social Agreement came to an end. Another significant innovation in the Amsterdam Treaty was the new employment policy chapter (now in Articles 145–150 TFEU). While excluding any harmonization of domestic laws, it provides for the coordination of national employment policies on the basis of annual guidelines and national follow-up reports.

The **Charter of Fundamental Rights of the European Union** is the first single document that brings together all of the rights previously found in a variety of legislative instruments, such as national laws and international conventions. At the request of the European Parliament, the 1999 Cologne **European Council** decided to have the rights of European citizens codified, since the 'protection of fundamental rights is a founding principle of the Union and an indispensable prerequisite for her **legitimacy**'. The Charter was drawn up by a convention consisting of the representatives of the heads of state or government of the member states, one representative of the President of the European Commission, members of the European Parliament (MEPs), and members of national parliaments. The Charter was formally adopted in Nice in December 2000. The Lisbon Treaty gives the Charter binding effect, conferring on it the same legal value as the treaties. Poland and the UK negotiated an opt-out.

The Charter contains a Preamble and fifty-four Articles, grouped in seven chapters. The Preamble to the Charter states that the Union is founded on the indivisible universal values of human dignity, freedom, equality, and solidarity, and on the principles of democracy and the rule of law. The Preamble specifies that the EU contributes to the preservation and development of these common values, 'while respecting the diversity of the cultures and traditions of the peoples of Europe as well as the national identities of the Member States'. The rights enshrined in the Charter are enumerated in six chapters on 'Dignity', 'Freedoms', 'Equality', 'Solidarity', 'Citizens' Rights', and 'Justice', and a final seventh chapter on 'General Provisions'.

The final provisions stipulate that 'the provisions of this Charter are addressed to the institutions and bodies of the Union with due regard to the principle of **subsidiarity** and to the Member States only when they are implementing Union law'. They are to apply these provisions 'in accordance with their respective powers'.

Source: Charter of Fundamental Rights of the European Union

Furthermore, a new Article 13 EC (now 19 TFEU) on Community action against discrimination was inserted. On this legal basis, a couple of important new directives on fighting discrimination based on grounds of sex, race, ethnic origin, belief, disability, age, and sexual orientation have been adopted in recent years.

The Nice Treaty of 2001 was not particularly innovative in terms of social policy matters. In some fields, the Council is allowed to decide unanimously upon the use of the then co-decision procedure, now known as the ordinary legislative procedure (OLP) (see Chapter 15). This applies to worker protection where employment contracts have been terminated, to the representation and collective defence of collective interests, and to the interests of TCNs (see Article 153 TFEU). Furthermore, 'measures' (not legislation) to improve transnational cooperation can now be adopted on all social issues, not only those concerning social exclusion and equal opportunities, as was the case after Amsterdam.

Under the Lisbon Treaty, social security provisions for migrant workers are the only new issue to fall within QMV in the EU Council, to the great disappointment of the European Trade Union Congress (ETUC). Furthermore, the 2000 Charter of Fundamental Rights of the Union formally came under the Treaty framework and hence finally acquired a higher legal status (see Box 20.1). At the same time, new safeguard procedures could, in the future, strengthen member state control over their social security systems. Finally, there is now a horizontal 'social clause' stating that any EU policy must take into account 'requirements linked to the promotion of a high level of employment, the guarantee of adequate social protection, the fight against social exclusion, and a high level of education, training and protection of human health' (Article 9 TFEU).

KEY POINTS

- The Agreement on Social Policy in the Maastricht Treaty gave the Union more competences and allowed for more majority voting.

- On the basis of the Maastricht Social Protocol (the 'Social Chapter'), the UK had an opt-out that ended only after the Labour government took office in 1997.

- The Amsterdam Treaty transferred the Social Agreement's innovations into the main treaty, which is now binding for all.

- Although the Nice and Lisbon Treaties change only a few aspects of EU social policy, it is clear that formal competences have been extended over time to a very significant extent.

The development and scope of European social policy

There are a number of important subfields of social legislation, the most important of which are labour law, health and safety at the workplace, and anti-discrimination policy. The following sections outline when and how they were developed. During the early years of European integration, social policy consisted almost exclusively of efforts to secure the free movement of workers and in that sense was rather non-controversial. In a number of regulations, national social security systems were coordinated with a view to improving the status of internationally mobile workers and their families.

During the late 1960s, however, the political climate gradually became more favourable to a wider range of European social policy measures. At their 1972 Paris Summit, the Community heads of state and government declared that economic expansion should not be an end in itself, but should lead to improvements in more general living and working conditions. With relevant Community action in mind, they agreed a catalogue of social policy measures that were to be elaborated by the Commission. In the resulting Social Action Programme (that is, a list of intended legislative initiatives, covering a number of years) of 1974, the Council expressed its intention to adopt a series of social policy measures within two years.

That the Council stated that Community social policy should furthermore be conducted under Article 235 EEC (now 352 TFEU), which went beyond purely economic considerations, was a major development. This was confirmation that governments perceived social policy intervention as an integral part of European integration. As a consequence, the Treaty's subsidiary competence provisions were increasingly interpreted in a regulation-friendly manner in day-to-day policy-making. Originally, only issues that directly restricted the single market had qualified for harmonization (or 'approximation') under Article 100 EEC (now 26 TFEU). During the 1970s, a shift occurred. Henceforth, regulation was considered legitimate if it facilitated the practice of the free movement of production factors—that is, goods, services, labour, or capital. Several of the legislative measures proposed in the 1974 Social Action Programme were adopted by the Council in the years thereafter, and further such programmes followed the first one.

By 2011, there were more than eighty binding norms (regulations and directives), with more than ninety related amendments and geographical extensions, and more than 120 non-binding policy outputs. The slow, but rather steady, growth of binding rules has not been stopped by the emergence of the 'softer' modes of governance. The latter were particularly fashionable from the second half on the 1980s to 2003. Recent data shows a particularly large number of acts adapting or refining existing social standards, rather than setting fully innovative EU policies. (For detailed data until 2006, see Treib et al., 2009.)

There are three main fields of EU social regulation: health and safety; other working conditions; and equality at the workplace and beyond.

- With regard to *equality*, the European Court of Justice (ECJ) had become a major actor ever since it provided a broad interpretation of Article 119 EEC on domestic measures to ensure equal pay for both sexes, opening the way for action on the basis of the subsidiary competence provisions. Matters such as equal pay for work of equal value, the equal treatment of men and women regarding working conditions and social security, and even the issue of burden of proof in discrimination law suits were finally regulated at EU level (Hoskyns, 1996; Mazey, 1998). Since the Treaty of Amsterdam (Article 13 TFEU), a more general equality policy has been developed, targeting discrimination based on sex, racial or ethnic origin, religion or belief, disability, age, or sexual orientation.

- In the field of *working conditions*, a number of directives were adopted during the late 1970s, for example on the protection of workers in cases of collective redundancy, the transfer of undertakings, and employer insolvency. Many more directives followed during the 1990s and thereafter, including those on worker information, on conditions of work contracts, on the equal treatment of atypical (such as shift, temporary agency, or part-time) workers, and on parental leave.

- With regard to *health and safety at work*, the regulation was based on a number of specific action programmes. Directives include the protection of workers exposed to emissions (or pollutants) and responsible for heavy loads, as well as protection against risks of chemical, physical, and biological agents at work (such as lead or asbestos).

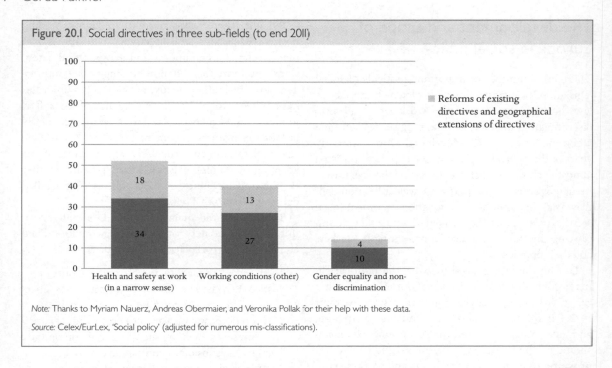

Figure 20.1 Social directives in three sub-fields (to end 2011)

■ Reforms of existing directives and geographical extensions of directives

Note: Thanks to Myriam Nauerz, Andreas Obermaier, and Veronika Pollak for their help with these data.

Source: Celex/EurLex, 'Social policy' (adjusted for numerous mis-classifications).

Figure 20.1 indicates the number of directives in these three subfields.

KEY POINTS

- The development of social legislation has increased since the late 1950s, with the 1990s being the most active decade.

- The introduction of soft modes of governance has not stopped the adoption of binding rules in this policy area.

- In addition to the issue of free movement of workers and equal treatment in national social security systems, the main areas of regulative European social policy are working conditions, anti-discrimination policy, and health and safety in the workplace.

The European Social Fund and the European Globalization Adjustment Fund

European Union policy is largely regulatory and this is particularly the case in the social field. However, as this and the following section will outline, the relative importance of regulation has declined in recent years, as both funding opportunities and 'soft' forms of governance have increased. In the case of funding, the Treaty of Rome provided for a 'European Social Fund' (ESF). Its goal was to simplify the employment of workers, to increase their geographical and occupational mobility within the Community, and to facilitate their adaptation to change, particularly through vocational training and retraining. Initially, the ESF reimbursed member states for some of the costs involved in introducing and implementing such measures. The Fund did not have any controlling capacity, however, because the transfer of money to the member states' employment services was quasi-automatic. And, in contrast to its original objective of rectifying specifically Italian problems after the opening up of market borders, it tended to be the best-funded and best-organized domestic labour market administrations that received most of the money (such as Germany). It was this anomaly in the system that prompted the first major reform of the ESF in 1971. This involved an agreement on the definition of target groups and the co-funding of only those domestic projects considered appropriate from a Community perspective. After a number of further reforms, the ESF now co-finances projects for young people seeking employment, for the long-term unemployed, for disadvantaged groups, and for promoting gender equality in the labour market. The

Table 20.1 European Globalization Adjustment Fund applications, 2007–10

Year	Number of applications	Total sum requested (€)	Total sum paid (€)
2007	10	57,704,150	18,610,698
2008	5	20,626,022	49,035,729
2009	30	166,581,220	52,349,047
2010	31	169,994,542	83,554,141
Total	**76**	**414,905,934**	**203,549,612**

Note: Thanks to Veronika Pollak for data research support.

Source: European Commission (2010b, 2009b, 2008b)

aim is to improve people's 'employability' through strategic long-term programmes (particularly in regions lagging behind), to upgrade and modernize workforce skills, and to foster entrepreneurial initiative. Over the period 2007–13, the ESF provides €76 billion in funding.

In addition to the ESF, other EU funds also seek to combat regional and social disparities, including: the European Regional Development Fund (ERDF); the European Agricultural Guidance and Guarantee Fund (EAGGF, Guidance Section); and the Financial Instrument for Fisheries Guidance (FIFG). Additionally, the Cohesion Fund finances environmental projects and trans-European infrastructure networks in member states with a gross domestic product (GDP) that is less than 90 per cent of the EU average. Finally, the European Globalization Adjustment Fund (EGF) aims to help workers made redundant as a result of changing global trade patterns to find another job as quickly as possible. Member states may receive up to 50 per cent of the cost of their relevant action plans (up to 65 per cent if the application was submitted between 1 May 2009 and 31 December 2011). The Fund became operational in 2007, with €500 million a year at its disposal. However, Table 20.1 shows that there are significantly fewer means distributed than originally expected, despite the fact that almost all projects ever submitted actually received funding (by 8 March 2012, a total of ninety-seven applications).

In sum, the EU's social dimension is less regulatory than is often assumed. In terms of the EU's overall Budget, it should be mentioned that, by 2011, the—admittedly broad—headings on cohesion and 'competitiveness for growth and employment' claimed 45 per cent of the EU Budget.

Finally, the steering effect of the EU's labour market policy—including the EGF—is much stronger than theses figures indicate, because they display only the EU's share of the overall project budgets. But the impact of the EU's criteria for project selection is greater than this, since national authorities also apply them with the prospect of European co-funding in mind. Moreover, the relative importance of EU funding has increased at a time of national spending cuts.

KEY POINTS

- The Treaty of Rome established a European Social Fund (ESF). Its aims are narrower than its name suggests, concerning only labour market policy and mostly targeting specific regions.

- The ESF co-funds projects and programmes in the member states. It has had, since 1971, its own priorities for funding, with a certain steering effect on national policies, because national governments want a share of the EU Budget to flow back into their countries.

- The EGF co-funds national support programmes for workers who have suffered redundancy as a result of globalization.

The open method of coordination

If the legislative or regulatory track of EU social policy seems to have comparatively less importance by now, this is not the result of any significant slowdown in legislative proposals, but because of a new (often called 'softer') style of intervention known as the open method of coordination (OMC) (see de la Porte and Pochet, 2002; see also Chapter 15). Thus the European Union has a novel role as a motor and, at the same time, as a constraint on national, social, and structural reform (see Goetschy, 2003).

The main features of the OMC were developed (initially without treaty basis) in the field of employment policy, as a follow-up to the Essen European Council of 1994. The Amsterdam Treaty's employment chapter later formalized it. Every year since, the EU has adopted employment policy guidelines. Their specification and implementation is left, however, to the national level, so that the domestic situation and party-political preferences can be taken into consideration. All the same, member states must present regular reports on how they have dealt with the guidelines and why they have chosen particular strategies in their 'national action plans' (NAPs). They have to defend their decisions at the European level in regular debates on the national employment policy. Thus peer pressure comes into play and has, at least potentially, a harmonizing effect on social policies in Europe.

The OMC has recently been extended to new fields, including pension reform, social inclusion, and education. To date, its success is hard to judge, because the lack of reliable data on its practical effects in the member states is only slowly being filled (but see Zeitlin et al., 2005; Kröger, 2008, 2009a). In any case, the net effect of this strategy may have been overstated in the early years of its existence, and it will always be difficult to measure since there is no counter-factual basis of comparison at the researcher's disposal (de la Porte and Pochet, 2004). It is plausible to expect that the joint policy learning (Sabatier and Jenkins-Smith, 1993) and mutual adaptation (DiMaggio and Powell, 1991) that result from this approach will have some beneficial effects, and that EU-level obligations, however loosely defined, will help governments to justify reforms domestically that they might otherwise not have dared to enforce for fear of electoral losses. Where national governments are not ready for policy change, however, the NAPs may do no more than either restate pre-existing domestic policies or perform a symbolic function (Scharpf, 2002). In such cases, the EU is helpless, since EU-level harmonization by means of more formal regulation (new laws) is explicitly ruled out under the OMC.

> ### KEY POINTS
>
> * The open method of coordination is a new EU-level approach that has been developed as an alternative to regulation.
>
> * It is based on European guidelines and national action plans (national reports using common indicators), and uses EU-level evaluations that feed into new policy guidelines.
>
> * The practical effects of the OMC have not, to date, been evaluated in a sufficiently systematic way and recent studies draw rather pessimistic conclusions.

Social partnership at European level

EU social policy-making is characterized by a style that some call 'Euro-corporatism' (Gorges, 1996). This involves intense cooperation between public and private actors in the European Union's social dimension. Corporatism is a way of making policy that includes not only public actors, but also interest groups as decisive co-actors (Streeck and Schmitter, 1991; see also Chapter 14). There is general agreement that EU social policy since Maastricht has been characterized by the entanglement of governmental negotiations in the EU Council and collective bargaining between the major economic interest group federations. As a consequence, the rather particular, closed, and stable policy network in EU social policy may be defined as a 'corporatist policy community' (Falkner, 1998).

The legislative procedure in EU social policy now works as follows. When the Commission consults on any planned social policy measure, European-level employer and labour groups may inform the Commission of their wish to initiate negotiations on the matter under discussion in order to reach a collective agreement. This process brings decision-making to a standstill for nine months. If a collective agreement is signed, it can, at the joint request of the signatories, be incorporated in a Council decision on the basis of a prior Commission proposal (see Chapter 15).

Since 1992, bargaining on social policy issues has therefore been pursued in two quite distinctive arenas, although the two are nevertheless interdependent. The traditional pattern of social policy-making is dominated by the EU Council and its working groups (see Chapter 11), although the adoption of a directive demands a Commission proposal and action by the

Table 20.2 EU-level social partner agreements (cross-sectoral)

Year	Agreements implemented by Council decision; monitored by the Commission	Autonomous agreements; implemented by the procedures and practices specific to management and labour and the member states; implementation and monitoring by the social partners
2010	Revision: parental leave	Inclusive labour markets
2007		Harassment and violence at work
2004		Work-related stress
2002		Telework
1999	Fixed-term work	
1997	Part-time work	
1995	Parental leave	

European Parliament (EP), depending on the specific procedure at stake. The interests represented by politicians and bureaucrats involved are predominantly territorial (in the EU Council) and party-political (in the EP). In this 'intergovernmental arena' for EU social policy, negotiations proceed according to the detailed rules about decision-taking that are specified in the Treaty. These are complemented by informal rules that have resulted from decades of negotiation practice.

A second, quite different, arena now surrounds negotiations between management and labour. Here, procedures are not prescribed in the Treaty, which contains only provisions about 'interface situations' in which the intergovernmental procedure and collective bargaining meet, notably specifying the rules on bringing to a standstill standard decision processes or initiating Council negotiations on implementation. Since the Maastricht Treaty did not even specify who 'labour and management' should be, this was decided informally. Moreover, the Commission and the Council did not designate the European interest groups as responsible for carrying out the collective negotiations, even if in practice they approved the special status of the then Union of Industrial and Employers' Confederations of Europe (UNICE, now the Confederation of European Business, or BUSINESS-EUROPE), the European Association for Public Sector Firms (CEEP), and the European Trade Union Congress (ETUC) as the responsible cross-sectoral social partners. These three groups, which wanted and received the leading role in 'negotiated legislation'

(Dølvik, 1997) on European social policy, had already participated in a 'social dialogue' with the Commission since the mid-1980s (see Chapter 14). When parental leave, the first issue to be discussed under the Social Agreement, was under consideration, the Commission stopped the standard legislative processes on the request of these groups and considered it appropriate to implement the Agreement, which resulted in a binding directive. Smaller interest groups, excluded from this process, complained about this, but the legal action taken by the European Association of Craft, Small and Medium Sized Enterprises (UEAPME) was rejected by the European Court of Justice (ECJ). Thereafter, both BUSINESSEUROPE and the ETUC have concluded cooperation agreements with smaller groups on the European Social Dialogue, while ultimately keeping their negotiation prerogatives intact.

Yet it is important to underline the point that the social partner negotiations on social policy issues are by no means entirely independent of the intergovernmental arena. There is intense contact and a large degree of interdependence amongst all relevant actors in social policy at the EU level—that is, amongst the EU Council, the social partners, the Commission, and, to a lesser extent, the European Parliament. To date, three legally binding, cross-sectoral collective agreements on labour law issues have been signed (see Table 20.2) and were implemented in directives (Falkner, 2000a): on parental leave (December 1995); on part-time work (June 1997); and on fixed-term work (March 1999).

A number of other negotiations failed to reach agreement, for example on the issue of temporary agency work, or were not initiated, such as on fighting sexual harassment, and on the informing and consultation of employees in national enterprises. Recently, further agreements were concluded or are being negotiated that the social partners (above all, industry) want to be non-binding and/or implemented in accordance with the procedures and practices specific to individual countries, rather than by a directive.

This can be interpreted as a move away from social partner agreements on effective minimum standards that are applicable throughout the EU. At the sectoral level, however, there are a couple of more recent agreements with subsequent binding directives, for example on working time in various industries (see Marginson and Keune, 2012).

> ### KEY POINTS
>
> - Since Maastricht, EU social policy has involved a 'corporatist policy community'.
>
> - The organized interests of labour and industry are free to agree social standards collectively, which are later made binding in Council directives.
>
> - On the cross-sectoral level, they have done so in three cases, but have failed or have settled for less binding recommendations in others.

Conclusion

This chapter has indicated that European social policy has been considerably extended and differentiated over time. Treaty bases have been revised several times to extend the range of competences. The European Social Fund has increased its resources and has had a practical impact on national employment promotion projects. The number of social directives has also increased over time, with the 1990s being the most active decade so far. The European Court of Justice has been influential on a number of social policy issues and, at times, has significantly increased the practical impact of EU social law. The equal treatment of women in the workplace and the protection of worker interests when enterprises change hands are two important examples (Liebfried and Pierson, 2000). Most recently, however, controversial cases such as Case C-438/05 *International Transport Workers' Federation and anor v Viking Line ABP* [2008] IRLR 143 and Case C-341/05 *Laval* [2007] ECR I-11767, have touched the borderlines between the market freedoms and basic social rights, such as union action (see Chapter 13).

When judging social policy developments at the EU level, at least four different evaluation criteria are worth considering (Falkner, 2000b). First, the closing of a number of gaps in labour law, introduced or widened by the single market programme, was a major task for EU social policy (Barnard, 2000: 62). Surprisingly, the EU performed better than most experts expected during the early 1990s and all major gaps are now closed.

Second, a somewhat more far-reaching criterion for judging EU social law is the differential between Commission proposals (which can be seen to be knowledge-based and common-goods-oriented approaches to the relevant problems) and Council legislation (sometimes seen as the lowest common denominator of self-interested country representatives). There was a huge gap during the late 1980s and early 1990s, which has been almost completely filled. Even some of the most controversial projects, on sexual harassment in the workplace and on employee consultation in the European Company Statute, have been adopted.

A third indicator of the scope of the EU's social dimension is action taken to prevent reductions in national social standards, potentially induced by the increased competitive pressures of the single market and economic and monetary union (sometimes called 'social dumping'). One possibility to prevent this from happening would have been to agree on fluctuation margins, which would have stopped any individual country from gaining competitive advantages through lowering social standards. However, such proposals were thought realistic in only a small number of member states, notably Belgium, France, and Germany (Busch, 1988; Dispersyn et al., 1990). At the level of the Social Affairs Council, there was little support.

Finally, a fourth evaluation criterion might be the rather small extent to which the EU has forged a truly supranational social order.

In any case, a full evaluation of the success of existing European social law is restricted by the lack of knowledge about its practical effects in the member states. One comparative study of ninety cases of domestic adaptation performance across a range of EU social directives (see Falkner et al., 2005) revealed that there are major implementation failures and that, to date, the European Commission has not been able to perform its control function adequately. While all countries are occasional non-compliers, some usually take their EU-related duties seriously. Others frequently privilege their domestic political concerns over the requirements of EU law. A further group of countries neglects these EU obligations almost as a matter of course. Extending this kind of analysis to new member states from Central and Eastern Europe shows that EU standards all too often remain a 'dead letter' (Falkner et al., 2008).

Finally, the enlargement of the European Union makes the adoption of joint regulation more difficult, because social policies and preferences differ even more widely in the enlarged EU than they did before. Clearly, a great disparity in social policy still persists between the member states and the cleavage may grow further as a result of the unequal state of crisis in individual countries. In Greece, 21 per cent of the population was officially unemployed in 2012, while the economy shrunk by 7.5 per cent during the third quarter of 2011 (*Agence Europe*, 13 March 2012: 10); the national minimum wage has been repeatedly cut

by law (in February 2012, from €751 a month gross to €586, and even €527 for those under the age of 25). It is therefore not surprising that the International Labour Organization (ILO) has warned that the impact on the Greek social model is dramatic (*Agence Europe*, 12 March 2012: 11). More worryingly, similar developments may occur in other EU countries soon.

Interestingly, faced with contracting economies and in the context of a European sovereign debt crisis, some countries have had to actively cut social standards in the frame of their austerity programmes. Yet the EU has regularly adopted ambitious programmes such as the 2000 Lisbon Agenda, followed by Europe 2020 in 2010, to coordinate efforts to make the EU the most competitive knowledge-based economy in the world, whilst (ideally) improving social cohesion and maintaining environmental sustainability. The European semester followed suit in 2011, to coordinate ex ante national budgetary and economic policies, in line with both the Stability and Growth Pact and the Europe 2020 strategy. However, it is doubtful whether these efforts will be effective, and whether they stand a chance of keeping up with the effects of major imbalances on the world's financial markets, on national budgets, and on social policies.

 ## QUESTIONS

1. Why did the evolution of a 'social dimension' lag behind the market integration aspects of European integration?

2. Why is the treaty base so important for European Union social law?

3. What are the main areas of EU social law?

4. To what extent is EU social policy a regulatory policy?

5. How does the European Social Fund influence national policy?

6. What is the 'open method of coordination' and what are its merits in the field of social policy?

7. To what extent is EU social policy corporatist?

8. Which criteria are best used for evaluating the development of the EU's social dimension?

 ## GUIDE TO FURTHER READING

Barbier, J.-C. (ed.) (2012) *EU Law, Governance and Social Policy*, European Integration online Papers (EIoP) special mini-issue I/16, available online at www.eiop.or.at   A timely collection that reviews recent developments in social policy in the European Union.

de Búrca, G., de Witte, B., and Ogertschnig, L. (eds) (2005) *Social Rights in Europe* (Oxford: Oxford University Press)   An excellent collection of essays on EU social policy.

Falkner, G., Treib, O., Hartlapp, M., and Leiber, S. (2005) *Complying with Europe: EU Minimum Harmonization and Soft Law in the Member States* (Cambridge: Cambridge University Press)   This book examines the implementation of six social directives (on, for example, working time, parental leave, and part-time work) in fifteen member states.

Falkner, G., Treib, O., Holzleithner, E., Causse, E., Furtlehner, P., Schulze M., and Wiedermann, C. (2008) *Compliance in the Enlarged European Union: Living Rights or Dead Letters?* (Aldershot: Ashgate)   This book studies the implementation of three EU social and anti-discrimination directives in Central and Eastern European countries.

Kröger, S. (ed.) (2009b) *What We Have Learnt: Advances, Pitfalls and Remaining Questions of OMC Research*, European Integration Online Papers (EIOP) special issue I/13, available online at http://www.eiop.or.at   An informative account of recent debates on the open method of coordination.

 ## WEBLINKS

http://ec.europa.eu/employment_social/social_dialogue/index_en.htm   The European Commission's Social Dialogue website.

http://ec.europa.eu/esf/home.jsp?langId=en   The website of the European Social Fund (ESF).

http://ec.europa.eu/social/   The website of the European Commission's Directorate-General for Employment and Social Affairs (DG Social) provides up-to-date information on all fields of European social law and policy.

http://ec.europa.eu/social/main.jsp?catId=326&langId=en   The website of the European Globalization Adjustment Fund (EGF).

http://www.eurofound.europa.eu/eiro/index.htm   The 'European Industrial Relations Observatory online' is an excellent source of information on all social dialogue issues, whether at national or EU level.

21

The Area of Freedom, Security, and Justice

Emek M. Uçarer

Chapter Contents

Reader's Guide

This chapter looks at one of the most recent European policies, Justice and Home Affairs (JHA), and its subsequent transformation into the Area of Freedom, Security, and Justice (AFSJ). The AFSJ comprises policy areas such as immigration and asylum, and police and judicial cooperation, some elements of which were found prior to the Lisbon Treaty in the EU's third pillar (see Chapters 3 and 4). The chapter focuses first on the early years of cooperation in this policy area and provides an introduction to the Schengen Agreement. It then reviews the procedural steps taken first by the Maastricht Treaty (1993), then at Amsterdam (1999), and subsequent institutional developments culminating in the Lisbon Treaty. The second half of the chapter concentrates on policy output, again looking at steps taken with Maastricht, Amsterdam, and Lisbon, but also in the landmark Tampere European Council meeting, the Hague Programme, and most recently the Stockholm Programme. It argues that, although some progress has already been made towards Europeanizing AFSJ policy, this field continues to be laced with intergovernmentalism. Moreover, given the inherent tensions in the policy, numerous challenges remain to be resolved.

Introduction

Cooperation in the Area of Freedom, Security, and Justice (AFSJ) has undergone a remarkable ascent from humble beginnings to a fully fledged and vibrant EU policy. One of the newest additions to the EU mandate, it seeks to engage the European Union in the fields of immigration and asylum policy, and police and judicial cooperation. Because of the sensitive nature of the issues involved, cooperation has been slow and difficult. However, it has resulted in a body of policies that apply across the EU's internal and external borders, and which have locked previously inward-looking national authorities into a multilateral process. This has involved significant political compromise, which led to the introduction of a complicated mix of Communitarized and intergovernmental institutional procedures peculiar to this field. The EU is now developing a complex immigration and asylum regime, and is also making progress on police and judicial cooperation. Particularly after the conclusion of the Amsterdam Treaty, the EU's capacity to reach collectively binding decisions in this field has improved considerably, creating momentum towards further cooperation and increasing concerns about the creation of a 'Fortress Europe' into which access is increasingly restricted.

Preludes to cooperation

If, in the late 1960s, government ministers responsible for home affairs and justice had been told that they would soon need to consult with fellow European ministers while formulating policies on immigration, asylum, judicial, and police matters, they would no doubt have found this a very unlikely and undesirable prospect. Yet, during the 1980s and 1990s, issues falling within their mandate have increasingly become of collective EU concern, provoking efforts to deal with them at the European, rather than exclusively at the national, level. Beginning in the mid-1970s and accelerating in the 1980s, these clusters were increasingly incorporated into the collective political agenda, leading to the creation of new, overlapping forums in which these issues could be discussed (see Box 21.1).

There were two broad sets of catalysts that drove this development. The first was the consequence of increased cross-border movements into and across Europe. After the Second World War, Western Europe became an area of immigration. Cross-border movements increased, straining border patrols and causing delays at points of entry. With this came growing concerns about transnational crime because of weak border controls and a lack of effective communication among European national law enforcement agencies. The second catalyst was the revitalization of the European integration agenda after the signing of the Single European Act (SEA) in 1986 (see Chapter 3). The removal of internal EU border controls was written into the 1957 Treaty of Rome, even though this had not been fully realized by the early 1980s. With this goal back on the agenda, attention turned to the need to create external Community borders, and to develop common and coherent rules on access.

BOX 21.1 Catalysts for early cooperation in Justice and Home Affairs (JHA) matters

Linked to immigration	Increase in cross-border movements between Western European countries
	Increase in labour and family unification migration into Western European countries
	Increase in applications for asylum
	Concerns about cross-border organized crime
Linked to the **European integration** project	Undesirable impacts of delays at borders on economic activities
	Desire to complete the creation of the **single market** by gradually removing controls at the Union's internal borders
	Recognition of the necessity to develop common measures to apply to the external borders before doing away with controls at the internal border

Early efforts targeted three groups: the citizens of the European Community, and then Union, whose freedom of movement within the EC/EU was to be secured; long-term EU residents of third countries—that is, non-EU citizens who had relocated to the EU and who held residence and work permits; and third-country nationals (TCNs), including labour migrants and refugees seeking to enter the collective territory of the EC/EU. Early efforts to cooperate were launched not by the EU, but by the Council of Europe (CoE), the membership of which comprised both Eastern and Western European countries. Judicial matters were raised often at CoE meetings. While the CoE's work was significant, the drawbacks of its processes, including slow and 'lowest common denominator' policy output, were also clear.

Cognizant of the shortcomings of the CoE, member states set up the 'Trevi Group' in 1975 as an informal assembly to deal with cross-border terrorism through closer cooperation among EC law enforcement authorities. Trevi was a loose network rather than an institution, and the meetings concluded in non-binding consultations on organized international crime, including drug and arms trafficking. Subsequently, several other groups were established, including the Judicial Cooperation Group, the Customs Mutual Assistance Group, and the Ad Hoc Groups on Immigration and Organized Crime. These groups spanned the four JHA policy clusters that were gradually becoming Europeanized: immigration policy; asylum policy; police cooperation; and judicial cooperation.

KEY POINTS

- Cooperation in Justice and Home Affairs was not foreseen in the Treaty of Rome.

- The Council of Europe (a non-EC institution) was the main forum for the discussion of JHA issues, but it worked slowly and its output was meagre.

- The Trevi Group was created in 1975 as a loose network within which terrorism might be discussed at the European level.

- The Trevi Group led to the setting up of similar groups in related areas.

The Schengen experiment

Perhaps the most ambitious project of these early years was Schengen. In 1985, a number of EC member states decided to do away with border controls. This was formalized in the 1985 Schengen Agreement and later the 1990 Schengen Implementation Convention. Belgium, the Netherlands, and Luxembourg (the 'Benelux' countries), Germany, France, and Italy created a new system that would connect their police forces and customs authorities. They also created the Schengen Information System (SIS), an innovative, shared database that stored important information (such as criminal records and asylum applications), and which was accessible by national law enforcement authorities. Schengen's primary objective was to develop policies for the Community's external borders that would eventually remove the EC's internal borders. This was an ambitious goal and the UK, Ireland, and Denmark remained extremely sceptical. Despite the fact that Schengen involved only some member states, it became a model for the EC (and later the Union) as a whole.

Within the Schengen framework, significant progress was made in each of the four emergent areas of cooperation. With respect to asylum, Schengen instituted a new system for assigning responsibility to review asylum claims to one state in order to stop multiple asylum applications and reduce the administrative costs of processing duplicate asylum claims. Schengen also provided the groundwork for an EU-wide visa policy through a common list of countries the citizens of which would need an entry visa, introducing also uniform Schengen visas. There was more modest output in judicial cooperation, with the easing of extradition procedures between member states. Finally, Schengen involved cooperation on law enforcement, particularly with regard to drug trafficking. However, since most of this work fell outside the EC decision-making structure, it was conducted away from the scrutiny of the general public and their elected representatives (see Box 21.2).

Maastricht and the 'third pillar'

Efforts were intensified in the early 1990s to shift the locus of decision-making towards the European institutions. With the implementation of the Treaty on

BOX 21.2 What is Schengen?

Named after the small Luxembourg border town where a subset of the member states of the then EC resolved to lift border controls, the Schengen system is considered a path-breaking initiative to provide for ease of travel between member states. In 1985, France, Germany, and the Benelux countries signed the first Schengen Agreement and were later joined by nine other EU members, bringing the total number of participating states to fifteen. The Schengen accords sought to remove controls on persons, including third-country nationals (TCNs), at their internal borders while allowing member states to reintroduce them only under limited circumstances. Member states agreed to develop common entry policies for their collective territory, to issue common entry visas, to designate a responsible state for reviewing asylum claims, and to combat transnational crime jointly. They also created a novel database—the Schengen Information System (SIS)—to exchange information between the member states on certain categories of individual and property. Because the original SIS was designed to interlink at most eighteen countries, a new version, SIS II, is being developed to launch in 2013, made necessary by the enlarged EU. The current twenty-six Schengen countries are: Austria; Belgium; Czech Republic; Denmark; Estonia; Finland; France; Germany; Greece; Hungary; Iceland; Italy; Latvia; Liechtenstein; Lithuania; Luxembourg; Malta; Netherlands; Norway; Poland; Portugal; Slovakia; Slovenia; Spain; Sweden; and Switzerland. Four of these countries (Iceland, Liechtenstein, Norway, and Switzerland) are not members of the EU. Two EU countries (the UK and Ireland) are not part of the Schengen system, although they have recently chosen to **opt in** on an issue-by-issue basis. Bulgaria, Cyprus, and Romania have opted in, but implementation is still pending.

KEY POINTS

- The 1985 Schengen Agreement was a commitment by a subset of EC member states to remove controls at their internal borders.

- Steps were taken by the Schengen members to agree on common rules on their external borders, for example with regard to visa policy.

- For those countries involved, Schengen allowed national civil servants in these fields to become accustomed to European-level cooperation.

European Union (TEU) in 1993, Justice and Home Affairs (JHA) was incorporated into the European Union, forming the third pillar of the Union. The TEU identified the following areas of 'common interest': asylum policy rules applicable to the crossing of the Union's external borders; immigration policy and the handling of third-country nationals (TCNs); combating drug addiction and drug trafficking; tackling international fraud; judicial cooperation in civil and criminal matters; customs cooperation; police cooperation to combat and prevent terrorism; and police cooperation in tackling international organized crime. The Treaty also created a new institutional home for the groups that had been set up in earlier decades and created a decision-making framework. However, this new JHA pillar was the product of an awkward inter-state compromise. In the run-up to Maastricht, while a majority of member states supported bringing JHA matters into the Union, they remained divided over how this should be done. Some argued that JHA should be handled within the first pillar, as a supranational policy; others preferred to keep this sensitive field as a largely intergovernmental dialogue.

Title VI TEU reflected the institutional consequences of this political compromise. With the third pillar, the Treaty established an intergovernmental negotiating sphere that marginalized the Community institutions, particularly the European Commission, within the JHA decision-making process. This third pillar set-up diverged significantly from standard decision-making in the EC. The key decision-taking body became the JHA Council. The European Commission's usual function as the initiator of European legislation (see Chapter 10) was diminished by its shared right of initiative in JHA and the role of the European Parliament did not extend beyond consultation, a situation that led to accusations that JHA exemplified the Union's democratic deficit (Geddes, 2008; Uçarer, 2009; Bache et al., 2011; see also Chapter 25). The European Court of Justice (ECJ), the body that might have enhanced the accountability and judicial oversight of policy, was excluded from jurisdiction in JHA matters (see Chapter 13).

Although bringing JHA into the EU was an important step, critics of the third pillar abounded. Two sets of interrelated criticisms were advanced. Critics lamented the lack of policy progress in the post-Maastricht period. The problem was that the post-Maastricht institutional arrangements were ill equipped to handle the projected, or indeed the existing, workload falling under JHA. The decision-making framework was cumbersome, with often non-binding policy instruments necessitating long-drawn-out (and potentially inconclusive) negotiations. All decisions in the third pillar had to be reached unanimously and this led to deadlock. When unanimity was reached, the result was often a lowest-common-denominator compromise that pleased few. Negotiations continued to be secretive and the European Parliament remained marginalized, particularly problematic at a time when the Union was trying hard to improve its image vis-à-vis its citizens.

> ### KEY POINTS
>
> - The Maastricht Treaty, which came into effect in 1993, created a 'third pillar' for Justice and Home Affairs.
>
> - The institutional framework put in place was intergovernmental and cumbersome.
>
> - The JHA framework was subject to much criticism in the mid-1990s.

Absorbing the third pillar: from Amsterdam to Lisbon

In the run-up to the 1999 Amsterdam Treaty, proposals for reforming Justice and Home Affairs (JHA) included: enhanced roles for the Commission, European Parliament (EP), and European Court of Justice (ECJ); the elimination of the unanimity rule; and the incorporation of the Schengen system into the European Union. As with Maastricht, there was a fierce political debate over these issues.

The challenge was to make the Union 'more relevant to its citizens and more responsive to their concerns', by creating an 'area of freedom, security and justice' (AFSJ) (Council of the European Union, 1996). Within such an area, barriers to the free movement of people across borders would be minimized without jeopardizing the safety, security, and human rights of EU citizens. The Amsterdam compromise led to three important changes. First, parts of the Maastricht third pillar were transferred to the first pillar, or 'Communitarized'. Second, the institutional framework for issues that remained within the third pillar was streamlined. And third, the Schengen framework was incorporated into the Union's *acquis communitaire*.

New first-pillar issues under Amsterdam

The Communitarization of parts of the erstwhile third pillar was the most significant development at Amsterdam with respect to JHA matters. These provisions, captured in Articles 61–4 of the Amsterdam Treaty, called for the Council to adopt policies (by 1 May 2004) to ensure the free movement of persons within the EU, whilst concurrently implementing security measures with respect to immigration, asylum, and external border controls. Article 67 specified new decision-making rules. For the first five years after the entry into force of the Amsterdam Treaty, a transition period was foreseen, during which unanimity was required in the JHA Council following consultations with the EP. The Council would act on a proposal from the Commission or a member state, the latter retaining its shared right of initiative. After five years, however, the Commission would gain an exclusive right of initiative. While the EP's access to the decision-making procedure would still be limited to consultation in most cases, an automatic shift to the co-decision procedure (now the ordinary legislative procedure, or OLP), which would give the EP much more of a say, was foreseen in the area of uniform visa rules and the procedures for issuing visas. The ECJ would receive a mandate for the first time, allowing it to interpret Title IV and to undertake preliminary rulings in policy areas falling within the first pillar in response to requests by national courts (see Chapter 13). Despite these improvements, the new Amsterdam architecture turned out to be a formidable maze created through masterful 'legal engineering' for political ends and opaque even for seasoned experts.

The left-over third pillar: cooperation in criminal matters

The Amsterdam reforms left criminal matters in the third pillar. The amended Title VI included combating crime, terrorism, trafficking in persons and offences against children, illicit drugs and arms trafficking, corruption, and fraud. The Treaty envisaged closer cooperation between police forces, customs, and judicial authorities, and with Europol (see 'Post-Maastricht developments in policy'), seeking an approximation of the criminal justice systems of the member states as necessary.

While the new Title VI essentially retained the intergovernmental framework created at Maastricht, the Commission obtained a shared right of initiative for the first time—an improvement over its pre-Amsterdam position. The EP gained the right to be consulted, but that was all. The Treaty constrained the ECJ in a similar fashion in that it recognized the jurisdiction of the Court to issue preliminary rulings (see Chapter 13) on the instruments adopted under Title VI, but importantly made this dependent on the assent of the member states. While the Commission, Parliament, and Court were to continue to struggle to play an active role in the third pillar, the Council retained its dominant decision-making function and unanimity remained the decision rule used in third pillar legislation.

Absorbing Schengen

After much debate, Schengen was incorporated into the EU by means of a protocol appended to the Amsterdam Treaty. The Protocol provided for the closer cooperation of the Schengen 13 (that is, the EU 15 minus Ireland and the UK) within the EU framework. With this development, cooperation on JHA matters became even more complicated, involving various overlapping groupings. There were those EU members that agreed to be bound by the Amsterdam changes (the EU 12); Denmark chose to opt out altogether, and the UK and Ireland would remain outside unless they chose to opt in. Moreover, there were actually fifteen signatories to the Schengen agreement (the Schengen 15), of which thirteen were EU members and two were not (Iceland and Norway). The two members of the EU that remained outside the Schengen system, the UK and Ireland, decided to take part in some elements of Schengen, including police and judicial cooperation. Of the twelve countries that subsequently joined the EU in 2004 and 2007, nine joined the Schengen area fully in 2007. Another non-EU country, Switzerland, partially joined Schengen in December 2008. This makes for quite a complex system: of the current twenty-six members, twenty-two are EU members and four (Iceland, Liechtenstein, Norway, and Switzerland) are not. As of 2012, three current EU members (Bulgaria, Romania, and Cyprus) are in line to join. Two current EU members (the UK and Ireland) remain outside the Schengen area and three non-EU microstates (Monaco, San Marino, and the Holy See)

are de facto Schengen members because they maintain open borders with their neighbours. One could argue that the incorporation of Schengen into the *acquis communautaire* did not result in desired simplification, but rather maintained, if not amplified, the convoluted system that emerged in the early 1990s. Not surprisingly, some now regard this particular aspect of AFSJ as the ultimate example of a multi-speed, or 'à la carte', Europe.

The Treaty of Nice made few substantial changes to these institutional developments, although it did extend the shared right of initiative for the Commission in the otherwise intergovernmental (residual) third pillar.

'Normalizing' AFSJ: the Constitutional Treaty and the Lisbon Treaty

The Convention on the Future of Europe and the 2003–04 intergovernmental conference (IGC), culminating in the October 2004 signing of the Constitutional Treaty (CT), marked the next stage in JHA reform. Leading up to this, a far-reaching overhaul of the JHA field was recommended by the Convention's working party on JHA, which proposed the 'normalization' of JHA by abolishing the pillar structure. Greater use of qualified majority voting (QMV) was proposed to overcome problems in decision-making, although unanimity would still need to be retained for judicial and police cooperation in criminal matters (JPCCM). The final text of the CT reflected many of these proposals and eliminated the pillar structure. It retained the shared right of initiative for the Commission and the member states in judicial cooperation in criminal matters, but foresaw proposals coming from coalitions composed of at least 25 per cent of the membership of the Union. While the Convention proposed an extension of the use of QMV in judicial cooperation, it qualified this with an additional mechanism through which a member state in significant opposition to the Council could suspend negotiations. These were all efforts to streamline the decision-making process whilst preserving a diminished capacity for member states to block decisions. The CT further provided for a role for national parliaments to monitor the implementation of JHA policies and for a judicial review of compliance by the ECJ. Finally, the Constitution retained the British and Irish opt-ins, and the Danish opt-out.

However, the CT was stalled when it was rejected in referenda in France and the Netherlands. The AFSJ provisions were later given a new life in the Lisbon Treaty, signed on 13 December 2007. The Lisbon Treaty contains all of the major innovations pertaining to AFSJ that were present in the CT, and underscores its salience by placing it ahead of economic and monetary union (EMU) and the Common Foreign and Security Policy (CFSP) in the Union's fundamental objectives. The Lisbon Treaty also incorporates the Prüm Convention (sometimes referred to as 'Schengen III') into the *acquis communautaire*. The Lisbon Treaty foresees jurisdiction for the ECJ to enforce all AFSJ decisions apart from provisions adopted under the post-Amsterdam third pillar. This is subject to limited jurisdiction for a transitional period of five years, after which jurisdiction is to extend to all prior legislation. The EP will operate with the ordinary legislative procedure (OLP, formerly co-decision) authority in almost all cases. However, the Lisbon Treaty's transformative provisions were also brought about by compromises. Opt-outs and opt-ins remain for Denmark, the UK, and Ireland (see Table 21.1). These concessions are criticized as moving further towards a multi-speed Europe. Nonetheless, the Lisbon Treaty represents the most significant reform of AFSJ poised to rectify vexing institutional problems that were created by Maastricht.

KEY POINTS

- The Amsterdam Treaty sought to address the shortcomings of the third pillar by bringing immigration and asylum, as well as judicial and police cooperation in civil matters, into the first pillar. The third pillar, cooperation in criminal matters (police and judicial cooperation), remained intergovernmental.

- Schengen was incorporated into the Treaty, but this did not result in simplification given the overlapping memberships involved in this agreement.

- The **Nice Treaty** added few changes to the Amsterdam set-up and extended a right of shared initiative to the Commission in the third pillar.

- The Lisbon Treaty is the most significant reform of Justice and Home Affairs to date. It makes important strides in normalizing this policy domain in the aftermath of the failed Constitutional Treaty.

Policy output: baby steps to bold agendas

There have been several spurts of policy since the beginnings of cooperation on Justice and Home Affairs (JHA), building on the early pre-Maastricht efforts, but gathering momentum after Maastricht and Amsterdam. More recently, in addition to making progress on the four main dossiers (immigration, asylum, police cooperation, and judicial cooperation), the European Union has acknowledged the importance of the external dimension of JHA and has embarked on attempts to export its emergent policies beyond the Union.

Post-Maastricht developments in policy

After Maastricht, member states first focused on rules to apply to third-country nationals (TCNs) entering the Union territory. The Council formulated common rules in this area for employment and education, and recommended common rules for the expulsion of TCNs. It also recommended a common format for 'bilateral readmission agreements' (which would allow for the deportation of TCNs) between member states and third countries. In 1997, an extradition convention was concluded among the EU member states. Agreement was also reached on the format of a uniform visa, as well as on a list of countries the nationals of which required a visa to enter EU territory. These relatively unambitious agreements sought to develop comparable procedural steps for the entry, sojourn, and expulsion of TCNs.

The most notable development in asylum was the conclusion of the 1990 Dublin Convention, an instrument of binding regional international law, which designated one member state as responsible for the handling of an asylum claim, resting on the concepts of safe countries of origin and transit into the EU, rejecting applications lodged by the nationals of countries deemed safe or by those who had passed through safe countries en route to EU territory. Refugee rights activists frowned upon these policies as dangerously restrictive and warned that such rules could potentially weaken refugee protection.

Work began on the European Dactyloscopy (EURODAC)—that is, fingerprinting—system, which would allow member states to keep track of asylum seekers, as well as on the negotiation of a common framework

Table 21.1 JHA/AFSJ cooperation: from Trevi to Lisbon

	Pre-Maastricht JHA	Post-Maastricht third pillar	Post-Amsterdam first pillar (Communitarized areas of former third pillar) Immigration; asylum; Police and Judicial Cooperation in Civil Matters	Post-Amsterdam third pillar Police and judicial cooperation in criminal matters	Lisbon Treaty
		Title VI TEU, Article K	Title IV TEC, Articles 61–69	Title VI TEU, Articles 29–42	Title IV TEC, Articles 61–69 Consolidated pillars
European Parliament	No role	Limited role, consultation	1999–2004 Consultation Post-2004 Codecision	Consultation	Ordinary legislative procedure
European Court of Justice	No jurisdiction	No jurisdiction	Referral for an obligatory first ruling for national last-instance courts	Preliminary rulings for framework decisions and decisions, conventions established under Title VI and measures implementing them	Jurisdiction to enforce all AFSJ decisions—post-Amsterdam third pillar subject to limited jurisdiction for a five-year transitional period Jurisdiction to extend to all prior legislation thereafter
Council	No direct role	Dominant actor	Dominant but Commission and EP ascendant Shared **power** position in decision-making	Dominant actor	Shared power position 'Enhanced cooperation' possible
Commission	Consultative Occasional observer at intergovernmental meetings	Shared right of initiative with member states except judicial and police cooperation (no right of initiative)	Shared right of initiative (member states asked the Commission to assume an exclusive right for asylum issues) Exclusive right of initiative	Shared right of initiative (previously impossible)	Exclusive right of initiative except in police and judicial cooperation (Commission shares right of initiative with a coalition of at least 25% of EU membership)
Decision-making mechanisms	Intergovernmental negotiations Non-binding decisions in the form of resolutions Binding decisions in the form of treaties	Unanimity rule on all issues	Council acts unanimously on proposals from Commission and member states *for the first five years* Move to QMV (except legal migration) Opt-in (UK, Ireland), opt-out (Denmark) Opt-in (UK, Ireland), opt-out (Denmark)	Council acts unanimously on proposals from Commission and member states	QMV for most decisions Opt-out (Denmark on judicial cooperation) Opt-ins (UK and Ireland)

Note: This covers asylum policy, the crossing of the external borders of the EU, immigration policy and the handling of third country nationals, combating drug addiction and trafficking, tackling international fraud, judicial cooperation in civil and criminal matters, customs cooperation, and police cooperation to combat and prevent terrorism and organized international crime.

Source: adapted and expanded from Uçarer 2010.

for the reception of individuals seeking temporary protection status in Union territory. The Maastricht Treaty also took earlier efforts to cooperate in customs, public safety, and cross-border matters further by embarking on the ambitious agenda to create a European Police Office (Europol) to enhance police cooperation and information exchange in combating terrorism and the trafficking of drugs and human beings. Based in The Hague, Europol became operational in October 1998. Ministers of the member states also signed an agreement to create a European Drugs Unit (EDU) to assist in criminal investigations. The Union thus sought to enlist the help of countries considered to be contributing to the supply of drugs, particularly those in the Caribbean and Latin America.

Amsterdam and Tampere

Following Amsterdam, progress accelerated, aided by a European Council dedicated exclusively to JHA. The goal of this summit, which was convened in Tampere (Finland) in October 1999, was to evaluate the impact of Amsterdam and to discuss the future direction of cooperation. Included in the 'Tampere milestones' were a reiterated commitment to the freedom of movement, development of common rules for the fair treatment of TCNs, including guidelines for dealing with racism and xenophobia, the convergence of judicial systems, and the fostering of transparency and democratic control. Among the more far-reaching goals were better controls on, and management of, migration and the deterrence of trafficking in human beings.

On matters of immigration and asylum, Tampere advocated a 'comprehensive approach', closely linked to the combating of poverty, and the removal of the political and economic conditions that compel individuals to leave their homes. At Tampere, it was argued that JHA/AFSJ policies should be linked closely to tools of foreign policy, including development cooperation and economic relations. This called for intensified cooperation between countries of origin and transit to address the causes of flight, empowering neighbouring countries to offer adequate protection to those in flight and speeding up the removal of illegal immigrants from Union territory.

EU member states committed themselves to creating a Common European Asylum System (CEAS), including standards for reviewing claims and caring for asylum applicants, and comparable rules for refugee recognition. The Commission was designated as the coordinator of policy proposals dealing with asylum and soon introduced numerous proposals, including on reception conditions for refugees, and a common set of minimum standards for the review of asylum claims, as well as common family reunification schemes for refugees. The Union also approved the creation of the European Refugee Fund, designed to aid EU recipient states during massive refugee influxes, such as those experienced during the fallout from Bosnia and Kosovo. By this point, the Dublin Convention had taken effect, and the EURODAC system was now functioning. The creation of the CEAS was in progress.

In matters of judicial and police cooperation, still third pillar issues, a European Judicial Area (EJA) was foreseen in which the mutual recognition of judicial decisions and cross-border information exchange for prosecutions, as well as minimum standards for civil procedural law, would be ensured.

Tampere also created the European Union's Judicial Cooperation Unit (Eurojust). Composed of national prosecutors, magistrates, and police officers, Eurojust would aid national prosecuting authorities in their criminal investigations of organized crime. A European Police College (CEPOL), which would also admit officers from the candidate countries, and a European Police Chiefs Task Force (PCTF) were also planned. Priorities were established for fighting money laundering, corruption, euro counterfeiting, drug trafficking, trafficking in human beings, the exploitation of women, the sexual exploitation of children, and high-tech and environmental crime, designating Europol as the lead agency in these efforts. Importantly, Tampere also established benchmarks and set deadlines for the accomplishment of its goals, which enlivened the policy process. Debate on the numerous items on the agenda after Tampere was protracted. Blame for the delays was variously attributed. While the member states (operating through the Council) blamed the Commission, critics noted that the Council was in no particular hurry to press forward with the adoption of these measures. The Commission tabled new and revised initiatives relating to asylum procedures: on reception conditions for asylum seekers; on the definition and status of refugees; and on a first-pillar instrument to replace the Dublin Convention. Nonetheless, the Presidency Conclusions issued at the end of the June 2002 Seville

European Council called emphatically for a 'speeding up' of work, suggesting continued frustration with the progress made since Tampere.

The Hague and Stockholm Programmes

In June 2004, the Commission published an assessment of the Tampere Programme, characterizing the previous five years as a time of progress hampered by the drawbacks in the decision-making rules (European Commission, 2004). The next phase of cooperation, the Commission argued, would involve creating an integrated border management system and visa policy, complete with a Visa Information System (VIS) database to store the biometric data of visa applicants, a common policy on the management of migration flows to meet economic and demographic needs, and the creation of the EJA. The Hague Programme that was subsequently adopted at the November 2004 Brussels European Council reiterated the call for the abolition of internal border controls soon after the projected launch of SIS II (see Box 21.3). The Hague Programme called for the implementation of the CEAS by 2010 and the gradual expansion of the European Refugee Fund. The Hague Programme further endorsed the Council Secretariat's Situation Centre (SitCen), which would provide strategic analyses of terrorist threats, and called for the creation of Frontex, the autonomous European Agency for the Management of Operational Cooperation at the External Borders of the Member States of the European Union. It invited greater coordination on the integration of existing migrants. As for the external dimension, the Hague Programme stressed partnership with countries of origin and/or transit, and the conclusion of further readmission agreements as necessary (see 'Extending JHA/AFSJ cooperation outwards'). The Hague Programme arguably gave policy-making a push, resulting in the adoption of hundreds of texts in 2007 alone.

The Hague Programme was followed by the Stockholm Programme to guide AFSJ cooperation for 2010–14, which echoes the political priorities of its predecessors: promoting European citizenship and fundamental rights; an internal security strategy to protect against organized crime and terrorism; integrated border management; a comprehensive Union migration policy; completing the CEAS by 2012 (a target that has been missed); and integrating these priorities into the external policies of the EU. It foresees an expansion of Europol, as well as several other measures in the police cooperation realm, and further empowers Frontex.

BOX 21.3   Strains on Schengen: the Arab Spring and domestic politics

Schengen is arguably the most important multilateral mechanism that jump-started the AFSJ. However, it has recently come under strain as a result of the 'Arab Spring' at a time when the EU is facing a significant crisis of the euro, its other most visible achievement. In May 2011, Schengen's provisions were temporarily suspended between Italy and France, and border checks were reinstated. The crisis was precipitated when Italy, not happy with the lackadaisical support that it received from the EU in the face of migrants arriving in Lampedusa and elsewhere to flee the upheaval in North Africa, issued about 22,000 travel documents to arrivals. Given the absence of border controls, these travel documents would allow arriving North Africans to travel onward, including to France. Despite the fact that Schengen is based on mutual recognition of entry and travel permits throughout the Schengen area, France refused to recognize the Italian documents as valid, reinstated border checks, and started sending individuals with these documents back to Italy. Unrelatedly, Denmark, citing a perceived increase in cross-border crime, also briefly reinstated controls at its Schengen borders. This was a concession to the anti-immigration Danish People's Party, on the cooperation of which the government relied in the legislative process. Meanwhile, while the initial stand-off deescalated between France and Italy, President Sarkozy announced in March 2012, from the campaign trail (a month before critical national elections in France), that France might pull out of Schengen unless the EU stemmed illegal migration. As with Denmark, this was in an effort to curry favour with nationalist, anti-immigration, and far-right electorate and political parties. Suddenly, it appeared that domestic politics and electoral cycles in these three EU member states, complicated by international developments, were poised to undermine Schengen and what it represented. Ultimately, no politician really wants to be blamed for the collapse of Schengen and the reinstatement of cumbersome border checks. That said, given the current political climate, Schengen is vulnerable and saving it might mean stalled progress on some of the more ambitious plans for a common EU immigration policy.

Extending JHA/AFSJ cooperation outwards

During the initial phases of cooperation in Justice and Home Affairs, the immediate goal was to lift barriers to the free movement of persons within the European Union. As the 1990s progressed, the planned enlargements projected the collective territory outwards, making it necessary to discuss JHA/AFSJ matters with the Union's *future* borders in mind. Member states began to involve certain third countries in some of their initiatives, attempting to solidify EU border controls by recruiting other countries to tighten their own controls (Lavenex and Uçarer, 2002). This involved entering into collective agreements with countries of origin and transit. These attempts to recruit neighbouring countries to adopt close variations of the EU's emergent border management regime were particularly pronounced in Central and Eastern Europe (CEE), the Maghreb, and the Mediterranean basin, because of the proximity of these areas to the EU.

EU policies began to radiate out to neighbouring countries, particularly those applying for membership. Schengen countries collectively signed agreements with Poland, Hungary, and the Czech Republic, in which the latter agreed to readmit individuals returned from EU territory. Most CEE countries were declared safe countries of origin and transit, compelling them to accept asylum seekers who had travelled through their territory to get to the EU. At the 1993

Copenhagen European Council, future membership was made conditional upon the rapid incorporation of the EU's JHA *acquis*, which, after Amsterdam, also included the Schengen *acquis*. The accession partnerships included an aid component, some of which was tied to the improvement of border controls. The EU assumed an advisory role for policy-making in CEE countries, with the aim of helping them to develop policies in line with those of the EU (Grabbe, 2006). Applicant countries began adopting the EU's JHA policies even if that meant implementing, often at the risk of souring relations, restrictive policies vis-à-vis countries the citizens of which had previously enjoyed, for example, visa-free access into their own territories. The 2004 and 2007 enlargements included the majority of these accession countries. Turkey and Croatia, which commenced accession negotiations on 3 October 2005, are required to make similar changes in preparation for membership (see Chapter 17). JHA's external dimension extends further than would-be member countries, however: the EU expects similar adjustments of countries that are not part of the enlargement process. These expectations are situated in the broader setting of the Union's external relations (see Chapters 16 and 18), and, more specifically, have become part of its aid and trade policies. Thus North African, Mediterranean, and African, Caribbean, and Pacific (ACP) countries are steered towards adopting some of the EU's deflective immigration and asylum policies to ease migratory pressures into the Union by including sending and transit countries in the screening process. To these ends, in addition to the readmission agreements negotiated by its member states, by 2011, the EU itself implemented readmission agreements with Albania, Bosnia and Herzegovina, the former Yugoslav Republic (FYR) of Macedonia, Hong Kong, Macao, Moldova, Montenegro, Russia, Serbia, Sri Lanka, and the Ukraine. The Commission has been authorized to negotiate similar agreements with Algeria, Cape Verde, China, Georgia, Morocco, Pakistan, and Turkey. The Hague and Stockholm Programmes further charged the EU to develop EU regional protection programmes in partnership with the third countries concerned. Developments in October 2005 in the Spanish enclaves of Ceuta and Melilla, where hundreds of sub-Saharan Africans attempted to jump razor-wire fences to gain access to Spanish territory and were subsequently expelled to Morocco, intensified calls to cooperate with third countries to secure Europe's borders.

The external dimension of the AFSJ is firmly rooted in the effort to develop compensatory measures, as the EU seeks to manage its collective borders. Yet the EU's efforts to extend its strict border controls outwards by assisting (and in some cases demanding) the adoption of stricter border control measures elsewhere involves an irony. While the EU attempts to liberalize the freedom of movement within its territory, it does so by applying potentially illiberal policies at its borders and by advocating such policies in its relations with third countries (Uçarer, 2001; see also Box 21.4). Frontex also plays a crucial role by engaging countries that are on EU's land borders in the southeast and the Western Balkans, and on its maritime borders in the Mediterranean. Frontex is capable of engaging perceived security threats through 'rapid border intervention teams' (RABITs), by dispatching aircraft, helicopters, and other patrol boats to hot spots. Such deployments, with operational names such as 'Hermes' and 'Poseidon', frequently occur in the Mediterranean, particularly near Malta and Italy, with their exposure to North Africa.

BOX 21.4 Fighting terrorism in the European Union

JHA/AFSJ cooperation owes its genesis partly to the efforts of the Trevi Group, the main goal of which was to establish cross-border cooperation in the fight against organized crime and terrorism. These matters were subsequently incorporated into the Union. Europol was created to facilitate the apprehension and prosecution of transborder criminals, and established jointly accessible databases to enhance police cooperation. The Commission began work in late 1999 to develop an instrument that would outline the Union's position on terrorism, covering terrorist acts directed against member states, the Union itself, and international terrorism.

Following the 11 September 2001 ('9/11') attacks, JHA ministers were immediately called to an extraordinary EU Council. During this and following meetings, EU politicians expressed solidarity with the US and supported military operations launched in Afghanistan. The events in the US prompted the EU to move speedily towards adopting anti-terrorist policies already in preparation. Terrorism was defined as 'offences intentionally committed by an individual or a group against one or more countries, their institutions or people, with the aim of intimidating them and seriously altering or destroying the political, economic, or social structures of a country' (European Commission, 2001b). In October 2001, the Council committed the Union to adopting a common definition of terrorist offences, a common decision on the freezing of assets with links to suspected terrorists, and establishing the **European arrest warrant (EAW)** designed to replace the protracted extradition procedures between EU member states with an automatic transfer of suspected persons from one EU country to another. The Council urged better co-ordination between Europol, Eurojust, intelligence units, police corps, and judicial authorities, and announced work on a list of terrorist organizations, which was adopted in 2001 and later updated. The Union called for increased vigilance for possible biological and chemical attacks, even though such attacks had never previously occurred in the EU. Finally, linking the fight against terrorism to effective border controls, the Council insisted on

the intensification of efforts to combat falsified and forged travel documents and visas (European Council, 2001). The Framework Decision on combating terrorism and the Framework Decision for the EAW (which included a list of thirty-two 'Euro-crimes') were adopted in June 2002.

The attention to anti-terrorism intensified yet further after the 11 March 2004 attacks in Madrid. While no stranger to terrorist attacks from separatist Basque militants, Spain's trauma sharpened the attention to terrorism, which quickly became the primary preoccupation. The EU and its member states subsequently negotiated a number of cross-border initiatives to enhance their collective capabilities to combat terrorism. Among these was the Prüm Convention, signed by Germany, Spain, France, Luxembourg, Netherlands, Austria, and Belgium on 27 May 2005, which enabled signatories to exchange DNA, fingerprint, and vehicle registration data to combat terrorism. The possibility that violent acts could be perpetrated by ill-integrated migrants—highlighted by the widely publicized murder of a prominent Dutch film director at the hands of a Muslim who held dual Dutch and Moroccan citizenship—rekindled the integration debate. Fears about 'home-grown' terrorism hit another high with the 7 July 2005 ('7/7') London bombings.

The Union is now working on improving its information exchange infrastructure to help with its anti-terrorism efforts. Along with a second-generation Schengen Information System (SIS II), a new EU Visa Information System (VIS) rolled out provisionally in 2011 in North African countries. Possessing interactive capabilities, SIS II will include additional information on 'violent troublemakers' (including football hooligans, but potentially also political protesters) and suspected terrorists, and will also store biometric information (digital pictures and fingerprints). In turn, the VIS will collect and store data from all visa applications in all member states, including biometric data in the form of digital photos and all ten fingerprints—something that is criticized for potentially falling afoul of data protection measures. While the attention directed towards anti-terrorist measures is warranted, the EU's efforts in this field have already attracted criticism from civil liberties and migrants' rights advocates (Statewatch, 2011). Activists caution against a possible backlash against migrants of Arab descent and argue against closing the EU's outer doors even more tightly. As in the post-9/11 US, European anti-terrorism measures have attracted sharp criticism from civil libertarians in Europe, who also re-main sceptical about closer anti-terrorism cooperation between the US and the EU for data protection reasons. The challenge in Europe is similar to that in the US: developing policy instruments that meet security needs while protecting the civil liberties of individuals residing in the EU territory. The events of 11 September, 11 March, and 7 July seem to have brought JHA cooperation full circle to its Trevi origins. It is certain that this dossier will remain very lively, if controversial, in the future.

KEY POINTS

- Ccooperation in the Area of Freedom, Security, and Justice has developed a significant external dimension, particularly vis-à-vis the EU's neighbours.

- The enlargement of the Union not only pushes its borders (and therefore the AFSJ) eastwards, but also commits ap-plicant countries to adopt JHA rules before their accession.

- AFSJ policy output also has an impact on countries that are not part of the enlargement process.

Conclusion

Cooperation in Justice and Home Affairs (JHA) has come a long way since its obscure beginnings in the 1970s. It currently occupies a prominent and perma-nent position in EU governance. The European Com-mission now has a more active role, facilitated by the creation within it of two new Directorates-General. The status of the European Parliament and the Eu-ropean Court of Justice has also improved since Am-sterdam, and they remain hopeful about the prospects for further institutional gains in the future. Matters discussed in this field continue to strain the sovereign sensibilities of the EU member states and the policy remains intrinsically intergovernmental. However, few believe that the European Union can achieve its **common market** goals without making significant progress in the Area of Freedom, Security, and Justice (AFSJ). As the events of 11 September 2001 in the US, and the attacks in Madrid and London, clearly dem-onstrate, the tackling of trans-border issues so typical of this dossier demands coordination and cooperation beyond the state. AFSJ is still a young field compared to the other more established **competences** of the EU.

The EU must contend with a number of important, and sometimes conflicting, challenges specific to AFSJ cooperation. In order to lift internal border controls on people moving within the EU, the Union must ar-ticulate and implement policies to manage its *external* borders. These policies should foster the freedom of movement of EU citizens and third-country nation-als within the Union. They should also spell out com-mon rules on the entry of TCNs. To demonstrate its commitment to basic human rights and democratic principles, the EU must protect TCNs against arbi-trary actions, uphold their civil liberties, and deter acts of violence against them. To maintain the rule of law, the Union must press forward with judicial and police cooperation, while ensuring the privacy and civil liberties of those living in the EU. To live up to its international obligations, the EU must keep its policies in line with its pre-existing treaty obligations, particularly in the field of refugee protection. To pro-tect its **legitimacy** and to improve its public image, the EU must take pains to address issues of transpar-ency and democratic deficit. Finally, it must undertake these endeavours without raising the spectre of an impenetrable 'Fortress Europe', which some argue al-ready exists. The challenges facing the policy remain substantial.

QUESTIONS

1. What are the catalysts that have led to the **Europeanization** of Justice and Home Affairs/Area of Freedom, Security, and Justice policy?

2. Fostering cooperation in JHA/AFSJ matters has not been a straightforward process. What have been the impediments to effective cooperation in this field?

3. The issues dealt with in JHA/AFSJ can also be addressed through unilateral decisions by individual countries, or by bilateral agreements concluded with interested parties. Why, then, is there such an effort to develop multilateral and collective responses in this field?

4. What are some of the lingering shortcomings of post-Amsterdam JHA/AFSJ cooperation?

5. What is meant by 'normalizing' JHA/AFSJ and how does the Lisbon Treaty contribute to such 'normalization'?

6. What are the negative consequences of closer cooperation in AFSJ matters?

7. How is the European Union extending the impact of its AFSJ policies beyond its borders?

8. To what extent was the European Council meeting held at Tampere a watershed in the evolution of JHA policy? How did the Hague and Stockholm Programmes build on Tampere?

 GUIDE TO FURTHER READING

Bache, I., George, S., and Bulmer, S. (eds) (2011) *Politics in the European Union*, 3rd edn (Oxford: Oxford University Press)   Bulmer's chapter on the Area of Freedom, Security, and Justice provides a current survey of most issues pertaining to this field.

Geddes, A. (2008) *Immigration and European Integration: Beyond Fortress Europe?*, 2nd edn (Manchester: Manchester University Press)   A very accessible and well-informed single-authored study of the EU's immigration regime.

Kaunert, C. (2011) *European Internal Security: Towards Supranational Governance in the Area of Freedom, Security, and Justice* (Manchester: Manchester University Press)   An comprehensive recent volume that assesses European internal security and integration.

Lavenex, S. and Uçarer, E. (eds) (2002) *Migration and the Externalities of European Integration* (Lanham, MD: Lexington Books)   An edited volume that focuses on the external dimension of EU migration policies.

Peers, S. 'Legislative updates', *European Journal of Migration and Law*—various issues (for example, (2010) 'Legislative update, EU immigration and asylum law 2010: extension of long-term residence rights and amending the law on trafficking in human beings', *European Journal of Migration and Law*, 13/2: 201–18)   These legislative updates capture the policy output, as well as providing insightful discussions of the decision-making process.

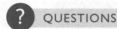 WEBLINKS

http://ec.europa.eu/policies/justice_citizens_rights_en.htm   The European Commission page on 'Justice and citizens' rights'.

http://www.consilium.europa.eu/policies/council-configurations/justice-et-affaires-interieures-%28jai%29?lang=en The Council of Ministers' Justice and Home Affairs (JHA) page.

http://www.europarl.europa.eu/committees/libe_home_en.htm   The page for the European Parliament's Committee on Civil Liberties, Justice and Home Affairs (LIBE).

http://www.migpolgroup.com   The Migration Policy Group website, including the monthly *Migration News Sheet.*

http://www.statewatch.org   Statewatch provides a critical approach to the role of AFSJ in the EU.

Similarly, the main agencies have their own websites, which are an excellent source of current developments.

http://www.cepol.europa.eu/   The website of the European Police College (CEPOL).

http://www.eurojust.europa.eu/Pages/home.aspx   The Eurojust website.

https://www.europol.europa.eu/   The Europol website.

http://www.frontex.europa.eu/   The Frontex website.

22

Economic and Monetary Union

Amy Verdun

Chapter Contents

Reader's Guide

This chapter provides an introduction to economic and monetary union (EMU). It describes the key components of EMU and what happens when countries join. EMU was the result of decades of collaboration and learning, which have been subdivided here into three periods: 1969–91, taking us from the European Council's first agreement to set up EMU to Maastricht, when the European Council included EMU in the Treaty on European Union (TEU); 1992–2002, from when plans for EMU were being developed to the irrevocable fixing of exchange rates; and 2002 onwards, once EMU had been established, and euro banknotes and coins were circulating in member states. Next, the chapter reviews various theoretical explanations, both economic and political, accounting for why EMU was created and looks at some criticisms of EMU. Finally, the chapter discusses how EMU has fared under the global financial crisis and the sovereign debt crisis, and at what we may expect of it in the years to come.

Introduction

Euro banknotes and coins were introduced on 1 January 2002. On that date, the euro became legal tender in twelve EU member states, among a total of more than 300 million people. All member states of the European Union, except Denmark, Sweden, and the UK, participated. It signalled the start of a new era in the history of the EU not least because, from this point on, the majority of EU citizens were, on a daily basis, in contact with a concrete symbol of European integration. What was the path that led to the euro?

Economic and monetary union (EMU) has been an integral part of European integration since the early 1970s, although those early plans were derailed. Once back on track in the late 1980s and 1990s, supporters of the idea of monetary union wanted to make sure that the process was done properly. Member states agreed that there should be economic and monetary convergence prior to starting EMU. But at the same time, some member states (such as the UK) did not want to join EMU.

What is economic and monetary policy?

Having a common currency is not unique to the European Union; the Roman Empire had a single currency. Belgium, France, Italy, Switzerland, and others were part of a Latin monetary union (LMU) from 1865 to 1927. They minted francs that were of equal value across their union. In 1872, the Danes, Norwegians, and Swedes launched a single currency, the Scandinavian krona, used until the outbreak of the First World War in 1914. Although the nineteenth-century European monetary unions were significant, the scale and scope of economic and monetary union (EMU) in the EU is further reaching, because these earlier unions only harmonized coinage and did not introduce a single monetary policy or a central bank. Thus EMU is without doubt the most spectacular and ambitious monetary union of all time.

The component parts of EMU

EMU, as we know it in the EU, refers to the union of participating countries, which have agreed to a single monetary policy, a single monetary authority, a single currency, and coordinated macroeconomic policies. Let us clarify these features.

First, what is monetary policy? Central banks formulate and implement monetary policy, in some cases in collaboration with the government—that is, with the ministry of finance and sometimes also with the economics ministry. Monetary policy aims at influencing the money supply and credit conditions. Central banks set a key interest rate. In EMU, monetary policy is no longer formulated at the national level, but decided upon at the European level by a single monetary authority: the European Central Bank (ECB).

In December 1991, at the Maastricht Summit, the European Council agreed to create a European System of Central Banks (ESCB). This consists of the ECB and the already existing national central banks, which, in EMU, are just 'branches' of the new ECB. The ECB Governing Council is responsible for formulation of the monetary policy for the 'eurozone' or 'euro area'. The ECB is responsible for the new single currency, sets a key short-term interest rate, and monitors the money supply. To facilitate coordination of economic and financial policies, an informal group has been set up. The so-called 'Eurogroup' consists of the ministers of finance, and sometimes economics, who get together to coordinate policies. The group typically meets before the meeting of the Economic and Financial Affairs Council (ECOFIN).

Strictly speaking, EMU could have been introduced without having a single currency. There were two alternatives: participating countries could have kept their national currencies and fixed their exchange rates irrevocably; or they could have introduced a common currency in parallel to the existing national currencies—something that the British government suggested in 1990 (the 'hard European currency unit (ecu)' proposal), but which did not receive support. While a parallel currency is introduced *alongside* existing national currencies, a single currency *replaces* them. A single currency would reduce the transactions costs that banks charge when currencies are exchanged. It was also politically more attractive because it would signal a full commitment to EMU.

Finally, in order to have a successful mix between fiscal and monetary policies, EMU envisages the coordination of economic policies (Article 121 TFEU, ex 99 EC). To secure the euro as a low-inflation currency, there are rules on public debts and budgetary deficits. Article 126 TFEU (ex 104 EC) states that member states must avoid budget deficits in excess of a reference value—set in a protocol annexed to the Treaty at 3 per cent of gross domestic product (GDP)—and general government debt should be at or below a reference value (60 per cent of GDP). Furthermore, monetary financing of the debts and deficits would not be permitted: countries could no longer use the printing press to create money to service their debt. This so-called 'no bailout clause' was put in place to reduce the likelihood of the ECB having to bail out member states should they be unable to pay their debts (Article 125 TFEU, ex 103 EC). Prior to EMU, a member state that ran high budget deficits with inflationary consequences would have been 'punished' by the market, because it would have needed to set higher short-term interest rates as a consequence.

The acronym 'EMU' consists of two components, 'economic' and 'monetary', with the latter the most prominent component. The term *economic and monetary union'* can be traced back to the discussions in the late 1960s and early 1970s. The policy-makers at the time were not sure how best to create EMU. To have fixed exchange rates—and ultimately a single currency—required some coordination of economic policies. Some countries—Belgium, Luxembourg, and France—thought that, by fixing the exchange rate, the necessary cooperation of the adjacent economic policies would naturally start to occur (the 'Monetarists'). Two other countries—West Germany and the Netherlands—held the opposite position. In their view, economic policies needed to be coordinated *before* fixing exchange rates or introducing a single currency (the 'Economists'). This debate is referred to as the debate between the 'Monetarists and the Economists'. (Note that the term 'Monetarists' used in this context does not have the same meaning as the term 'monetarists' referring to the followers of the ideas of Milton Friedman.)

The question of how to reach EMU had already been discussed in some detail by economic thinkers of the 1960s such as Bela Balassa and Jan Tinbergen. According to these and others, economic integration can be subdivided into a number of stages (see also Chapter 19). Originally, it was thought that these stages would be consecutive and that they would follow each other at a regular pace. More recently, this sequential order has been called into doubt: there is no clarity as to whether they should follow each other, or what the expected timing would be. Yet even though the framework may not be helpful as a predictive tool, it is still a useful analytical device.

The least far-reaching form of integration is a free trade area (FTA). In an FTA, participating members remove barriers to trade amongst themselves, but maintain the right to levy tariffs on third countries. The next stage of integration is a customs union. In addition to the free trade amongst members, a customs union has common external tariffs on goods and services from third countries. A common market—since 1985, renamed single market—is characterized by free movement of goods, services, labour, and capital among the participating states, and common rules, tariffs, and so on vis-à-vis third countries. An economic union implies not only a common/single market, but also a high degree of coordination of the most important areas of economic policy and market regulation, as well as monetary policies and income redistribution policies. A 'monetary union' contains a common/single market, but also further integration in the area of currency cooperation. However, this is not always the case: the Scandinavian monetary union did not contain a customs union. A monetary union either has irrevocably fixed exchange rates and full convertibility of currencies, or a common or single currency circulating within the monetary union. It also requires integration of budgetary and monetary policies. An economic and monetary union (EMU) combines the features of the economic union and the monetary union. This combination is what European leaders had in mind when they discussed EMU in 1969 and again in 1988. A full economic union (FEU) implies the complete unification of the economies of the participating member states and common policies for most economic matters. A full political union (FPU) is the term used when, in addition to the FEU, political governance and policy-making have moved to the supranational level. Effectively, political unification occurs when the final stage of integration has taken place and a new confederation or federation has been created.

The eventual institutional design of EMU in the 1980s and 1990s was an asymmetrical one (Verdun, 1996, 2000). It featured a relatively well-developed monetary union, but a much less developed economic union. Monetary policy was to be transferred to a new European supranational institution (the ECB), whereas in the area of economic policy-making decisions remained to be made by the national governments. To some extent, one observes here the difference between positive and negative integration. Positive integration refers to the creation of common rules, norms, and policies. Negative integration is all about taking away obstacles, and eliminating rules and procedures that are an obstruction to integration.

From The Hague to Maastricht (1969–91)

At the 1969 Hague Summit, the heads of state and government decided to explore a path to economic and monetary union. A group of experts, headed by Pierre Werner, prime minister and finance minister of Luxembourg, drafted the blueprint. The 1970 Werner Plan proposed three stages to reach EMU by 1980. On the institutional side, it recommended setting up two supranational bodies: a Community System for the Central Banks and a Centre of Decision for Economic Policy. The former would pursue monetary policies, while the latter would coordinate macroeconomic policies (including some tax policies). Most of the recommendations of the Werner Plan were adopted, but EMU did not take off in subsequent years.

There are two reasons why the creation of EMU stalled in the 1970s. First, there were substantial differences among the member states about how to get to EMU. Second, the international economic and monetary situation rapidly changed in the early 1970s, making for a totally different climate for cooperation. The so-called Bretton Woods agreement, which had facilitated stable exchange rates in Western Europe since 1945, ended in August 1971. Western European countries responded by setting up their own exchange rate mechanism (ERM), the so-called 'snake', which functioned with moderate success throughout the 1970s and in which not all member states participated, though several non-EEC members were involved.

Developments leading to the relaunch of EMU in the late 1980s

In 1979, the European Monetary System (EMS) was set up, in which all European Community (EC) member states were to participate. Not all were immediately part of its most important feature, the ERM—a system of fixed, but adjustable, exchange rates. The UK was not part of the ERM during the 1980s, but its currency was part of the European currency unit (ecu)—the unit of account at the heart of the EMS. In 1991, the British pound sterling did join the ERM, but it was forced to leave on 16 September 1992 ('Black Wednesday') following a period of intense selling of sterling in the financial markets, which the British government was unable to bring to a halt. Italy participated in the ERM from the outset, but was initially given more leeway. The rules stipulated that most currencies could not fluctuate more than ± 2.25 per cent from an agreed parity, whereas the bandwidth for those who needed more leeway (for example, Italy) was set at ± 6 per cent from the parity. If a currency threatened to move outside the agreed band, central banks would intervene by buying or selling currencies in order to keep the currency from leaving the band. If an imbalance were persistent, the so-called EC Monetary Committee (MC), an informal advisory body created by the Treaty of Rome to discuss monetary policy and exchange rate matters, would decide whether or not to adjust the parities. In 1999, the MC was renamed the Economic and Financial Committee (EFC).

The ERM needed some time to become successful. The first four years (1979–83) were learning years, with numerous exchange rates fluctuations and parity adjustments. The participating currencies became more stable in the interim period (1983–87), and thereafter, until summer 1992, the ERM witnessed no realignments. By this time, it had become an important 'symbol' of successful European integration. In the 1980s, the German currency, the Deutschmark, became the 'anchor currency'. Because it had been a strong currency, monetary authorities in ERM countries took German monetary policies as their point of reference, following the decisions of the German central bank (the *Bundesbank*) quite closely.

BOX 22.1 Three stages to economic and monetary union

First stage	I July 1990–31 December 1993	Free movement of capital among member states
		Closer coordination of economic policies
		Closer cooperation among central banks
Second stage	I January 1994–31 December 1998	Convergence of the economic and monetary policies of the member states (to ensure stability of prices and sound public finances)
Third stage	I January 1999–to date	Establishment of the European Central Bank
		Fixing of exchange rates
		Introduction of the single currency

BOX 22.2 The Maastricht convergence criteria

- Budget deficits should be no more than 3 per cent of gross domestic product (GDP).

- Accumulated public debt should be no more than 60 per cent of GDP.

- Exchange rates should have participated without devaluation or severe tensions in the exchange rate mechanism (ERM-2) for at least the previous two years.

- Inflation should not be more than 1.5 percentage points above the rate of the three best-performing member states.

- Long-term interest rates should be not more than 2 percentage points above the rate of the three best-performing member states.

Source: Article 140 TFEU and Protocol 12

A few other developments in the 1980s helped to relaunch the EMU process. The 1986 **Single European Act** (SEA) facilitated the completion of the single market and mentioned the need to relaunch EMU. The 1988 Hanover European Council mandated Commission President Jacques Delors to head a committee composed of the twelve central bank presidents, and one other Commissioner and a few experts, to draft a blueprint for EMU. Just as had the earlier Werner Report, the **Delors Report** (April 1989) proposed a road to EMU in three stages (see Box 22.1). It also envisaged the creation of a European System of Central Banks (ESCB). In contrast to the Werner Report, it did not find it necessary to set up a similar supranational institution in the economic sphere, but it had the same objectives: full freedom of goods, services, capital, and labour, and, if possible and if the political will was there, the introduction of a single currency. On the basis of the Delors Report, the June 1989 Madrid European Council adopted the EMU blueprint, with

the first stage of EMU (the **liberalization of capital markets**) starting on 1 July 1990. An **intergovernmental conference** (IGC) opened in Rome in October 1990 and closed in Maastricht in 1991 to discuss the next stages (see Chapter 3). One of the decisions taken during the IGC negotiations was that countries would have to meet certain criteria, dubbed 'convergence criteria', in order to be allowed to join EMU.

The Maastricht convergence criteria (see Box 22.2) referred to good performance in the area of inflation rates, interest rates, and exchange rates. Moreover, it was agreed that participating countries should not have excessive budgetary deficits or public debts. Finally, the national central bank needed to be made politically independent, and national monetary authorities could no longer use the printing press to reduce public debts and budgetary deficits (monetary financing). It is important to note that, right from the outset, there were 'escape clauses' built into the wording of the Maastricht Treaty. It was generally thought that the criteria would be applied generously with regard to the debt criterion, because it was believed that some countries, such as Belgium and Italy, would never be able to meet the reference value in less than a decade. As for the budgetary criteria, however, these *had* to be met.

It has been speculated that the creation of EMU was assisted by the fall of the Berlin Wall in 1989, and the end of communist regimes in Central and Eastern Europe (CEE) in 1990. The observant reader will have noted, however, that the Delors Report had already been completed by April 1989 and therefore preceded these turbulent political developments. Nevertheless, the political determination of German Chancellor Helmut Kohl to secure EMU was connected to his eagerness to move ahead quickly with German unification. The IGCs were completed in December 1991, and the European Council in Maastricht agreed to revise the Treaty of Rome and accept a new Treaty on European Union (TEU). It was signed on 7 February 1992 and came into force on 1 November 1993, after the national parliaments of all twelve member states ratified it (see 'From treaty to reality (1992–2002)').

KEY POINTS

- In the 1970s, EMU stalled because of differences among member states and changing international circumstances.

- The European Monetary System and the Single European Act contributed to the relaunch of EMU in the late 1980s.

- The Delors Report offered a blueprint for EMU.

- The treaty changes necessary for acceptance and implementation of EMU were negotiated in an intergovernmental conference, which was completed in Maastricht in 1991.

- Member states need to meet the 'Maastricht convergence criteria' to join EMU.

From treaty to reality (1992–2002)

The period from 1992 to 2002 posed numerous challenges for economic and monetary union, most notably over the ratification of the Maastricht Treaty, the issue of what would happen post-EMU, and the 'real' criteria for membership of the monetary union.

Ratification problems and the 'real' convergence criteria

The ratification process of the Maastricht Treaty turned out to be challenging. Only months after the Treaty was signed, on 2 June 1992, Danish citizens voted against it in a referendum. A razor-thin majority rejected the Treaty (50.7 per cent against; 49.3 per cent in favour). A French referendum was held on 20 September 1992. Against the background of major speculation in the financial markets, which had resulted in the British pound sterling and the Italian lira leaving the Exchange Rate Mechanism (ERM) days before the referendum, the French referendum resulted in a very slim majority in favour of the Treaty (51.05 per cent in favour; 48.95 per cent against). The result surprised most observers, because the French had overall been supporters of European integration. The period from late 1992 through early 1994 was characterized as one of continued exchange rate turbulence, placing the ERM under further pressure and casting a shadow on the run-up to EMU. In August 1993, the ERM exchange rate bands were widened from ± 2.25 per cent to ± 15 per cent. After the introduction of the euro, a new system, the ERM II, was set up to succeed the previous ERM. It maintained the ± 15 per cent bands.

In May 1998, the European Council decided that eleven countries would participate in EMU from 1 January 1999—the day on which exchange rates would be irrevocably fixed between the participating member states. However, Denmark, Sweden, and the UK did not want to join, whereas Greece was judged ready in June 2000 and joined the euro area as the twelfth member on 1 January 2001.

When eight Central and Eastern European (CEE) countries and two very small Mediterranean countries joined the EU on 1 May 2004, the accession treaty stipulated that these countries would eventually join EMU. However, they had to wait at least two years and fulfil the convergence criteria before they could adopt the euro. In 2007, Slovenia became the first new member state to join EMU. Two of the Baltic states, Estonia and Lithuania, were also very keen, although in May 2006 the assessment of the European Commission concluded that Lithuania met all of the convergence criteria except that of inflation. The assessment caused a public outcry because the Commission had adopted a very strict interpretation of the criterion. However, the two Baltic states decided subsequently to delay joining the euro area. In 2008, Cyprus and Malta joined; in 2009, Slovakia became the sixteenth member of the euro area; in 2011, Estonia, the seventeenth.

Managing EMU: the Stability and Growth Pact (SGP) before the sovereign debt crisis

In the mid-1990s, German Finance Minister Theo Waigel proposed rules for countries once in EMU. The Stability and Growth Pact (SGP) was put in place to ensure that no single member state, once it had become a member of EMU, could freeride, for example by incurring high debts and deficits. Under the SGP, member states that violate the rules to keep their public debt and budgetary deficit low can be penalized, and may have to pay a fine. The SGP was designed primarily to work as a deterrent.

The SGP involves multilateral budgetary surveillance (a 'preventive arm'), as well as specifying a deficit limit, the excessive deficit procedure (EDP) (a 'corrective arm') (see Box 22.3). When, on the basis of a Commission recommendation, the Council decides that an excessive deficit indeed exists, the member state concerned is obliged to reduce its deficit below the Treaty's reference value of 3 per cent of GDP;

otherwise financial sanctions can be levied against the member state in question.

In 2002, France, Germany, and Portugal were each, at different times, given an 'early warning' that they were in breach of the SGP. Portugal made the necessary corrections and hence the EDP was abrogated in 2004. But France and Germany failed to make the necessary adjustments to reduce their budgetary deficits. By November 2003, both were heading for the next step in the EDP (Article 126 TFEU, ex 104(9) EC) and thus were coming closer to the financial sanctions set out in the SGP. At a meeting of the Council of Economic and Financial Affairs Ministers (ECOFIN) on 25 November 2003, a proposal by the Commission to move France and Germany closer to the sanctions was defeated. The result was that the SGP was interrupted for the cases of France and Germany. Other member states, notably Austria, Finland, the Netherlands, and Spain, were outraged at the situation. Their judgement was that France and Germany had been exempted from the process because they were large enough to rally other member states around their cause. The four were particularly upset because they were convinced that if a smaller member state had faced the same situation, it would not have been able to

---

BOX 22.3 The Stability and Growth Pact

The Stability and Growth Pact aims to ensure that member states continue their budgetary discipline efforts after the introduction of the euro.

Dates	Decisions
The SGP comprised a European Council Resolution (adopted at Amsterdam on 17 June 1997) and Regulations of 7 July 1997.	The surveillance of budgetary positions and coordination of economic policies
The Council Regulations were revised on 27 June 2005.	Implementation of the excessive deficit procedure (EDP)
The rules were further strengthened in 2010 and 2011 ('six pack').	
Annually since 1999	Member states have undertaken to pursue the objective of a balanced, or nearly balanced, budget, and to present the Council and the Commission with a stability programme.
	Euro-outs (member states not taking part in the third stage of EMU) are also required to submit a convergence programme.
	Opening and closing (where appropriate) of an excessive deficit procedure for EU member states

obtain the same support. The crisis atmosphere that resulted from the 25 November 2003 Council decision prompted the European Commission to ask the European Court of Justice (ECJ) whether this Council decision was legal. In July 2004, the ECJ ruled that the November 2003 Council decision was, in fact, *illegal* because the Council had adopted its own text outside the context of the Treaty. But the ECJ did confirm that the Council has the right not to follow the recommendations of the Commission. The result of all of these developments was that the Commission felt that the SGP needed to be adjusted. By spring 2005, the SGP was revised so as to include more flexibility over the circumstances under which member states may temporarily run deficits in excess of the 3 per cent reference value, and small adjustments were made to the time schedule.

The preventive arm of the SGP was strengthened by a more differentiated medium-term orientation of the rules. The new provisions ensured that due attention was given to the fundamentals of fiscal sustainability when setting budgetary objectives. In future, the medium-term budgetary objective of a country is to be based on its debt ratio and potential growth. In practice, this means that countries with a combination of low debt and high potential growth are able to run a small deficit over the medium term, whereas a balanced budget or a surplus is required for countries with a combination of high debt and low potential growth. The preventive arm of the SGP was strengthened because member states committed to consolidate further their public finances when facing favourable economic conditions and accepted that the Commission is to give them 'policy advice' if this consolidation fails to occur. The new agreement was also more sensitive to the effects of efforts made by member states to make structural reforms. The SGP's corrective arm was also adjusted by allowing more room for economic judgements and leaving open the possibility that the one-year deadline for the correction of an excessive deficit could be increased to two years.

The first test of the new SGP came in the second half of 2008 when the global financial crisis upset markets and challenged the survival of the banking sector. Member state governments in the EU responded by guaranteeing the savings of consumers, buying out banks, and offering other stimulus packages. The rescue packages were so large that public finances were affected by them. The rules of the SGP still applied, however, even if, because of the economic crisis, these countries were allowed to overshoot the reference value for the duration of the downturn. Once growth returns, they need to satisfy the rules of a budgetary deficit of 3 per cent and there are stricter rules if member states have a public debt in excess of 60 per cent.

The global financial crisis, the economic recession, and the sovereign debt crisis changed the perceived importance of the role of the SGP in guiding EMU. Some of the rules were strengthened (see Chapter 27 and 'The global financial crisis and the sovereign debt crisis').

KEY POINTS

- The aftermath of the signing of the Maastricht Treaty posed challenges to creating economic and monetary union, including treaty ratification difficulties, the exchange rate mechanism crisis, and difficulties meeting the convergence criteria.

- Some member states have had difficulties avoiding excessive deficits.

- Difficulties implementing the Stability and Growth Pact led to a crisis, and subsequently to its revision.

- Government spending led to an increase in debts and deficits in the EU, which have to be addressed or the consequences of the SGP faced.

Explaining economic and monetary union

This section considers two ways in which economic and monetary union can be explained: first, from an economics perspective; and second, from a political science one.

An economics perspective

In the field of economics, there are two schools of thought that offer analytical tools with which to determine whether or not it made sense for the European Union to create EMU. The first argues that countries should create EMU only if they constitute a so-called 'optimum currency area' (OCA). Countries should adopt a single currency only when they are sufficiently integrated economically, when they have mechanisms in place that can deal with transfer payments if one part of the currency union is affected by an economic downturn and the other part is not, and when they no longer need the exchange rate instrument to make those adjustments. Most analysts claim that the EU is not an OCA, although a few think that a small number of its members come close to it. OCA theory states that if countries do not form an OCA, they should not give up their exchange rate instrument, but use it to make adjustments as the economic situation dictates. These analysts argue that the EU should not have moved to EMU. Others who judge that the EU does indeed constitute an OCA are less critical of this situation. They see the current group of countries as being well integrated. Furthermore, they use a broader definition of an OCA, claiming that original OCA theory is too rigid and pointing out that, following the original definition, no federation (including Canada, Germany, or the US) would constitute an OCA. Finally, some argue, following Frankel and Rose (1998), that once countries join EMU, they could become an OCA over time ('endogenous' OCA theory). Other developments that have influenced recent thinking about the role of exchange rates are the effects of financial markets on exchange rate policies—particularly on smaller open economies. Foreign exchange markets can create their own disturbances, which can be irrational. This effect is worse for smaller open economies than for larger established countries. However, the original OCA theorists did not take the destabilizing effects of exchange rate freedom into consideration.

A second school of thought focuses on central bank credibility. It argues that the EU witnessed long periods of collaboration in central banking prior to EMU. Central banks can be effective only if financial markets have confidence in their policies. In the case of the exchange rate mechanism, participating countries had to keep their exchange rates stable. They focused on the monetary policy of the strongest currency, the German Deutschmark. Many individual central banks, by choice, followed the policies of the leader (the *Bundesbank*). The most credible way in which to secure monetary policy is to commit firmly to it in a treaty. That is, in fact, what happened with Maastricht. A regime was set up that envisaged full central bank independence and gave the ECB a clear single mandate to maintain price stability.

A political science perspective

Political science has drawn on European integration theories (see Chapters 5–7) to explain EMU. It is noteworthy that scholars from opposing schools of thought have argued that EMU can be explained using different theoretical approaches. For reasons of simplicity, this section focuses on the two opposing schools in order to capture a larger set of arguments.

A neo-functionalist explanation (see Chapter 5) claims that EMU can best be explained as the result of spillover and incremental policy-making. The success of the exchange rate mechanism (ERM) and the completion of the single market necessitated further collaboration in the area of monetary integration. EMU was needed to maximize the benefits of these developments. Significant monetary policy convergence had occurred, arising out of the collaboration within the framework of the ERM and the tracking of German policies by other member states. Hence EMU could be seen as a natural step forward. Moreover, it is argued that supranational actors were instrumental in creating EMU—which is another characteristic of the neo-functionalist explanation of European integration. Not only were the Commission President and the services of the Commission (DG ECFIN) involved, but also various EC committees, such as the Monetary Committee—and they each proved influential.

An intergovernmentalist explanation (see Chapter 6) argues that EMU can best be understood by examining the interests and bargaining behaviour of the largest member states. This approach sees the European Council meetings as crucial for decisions such as the creation of EMU. By examining the interests of the largest member states, one is able to see why EMU happened. France was in favour of EMU as a way of containing German hegemony. Germany, in turn, was able to secure a monetary policy regime that was sufficiently close to its domestic regime. Some argue that Germany was in favour of EMU in the early 1990s to signal its full commitment to European integration, following German unification. The UK was not in favour of EMU, but was aware that it was likely to happen. The UK wanted to be involved in agenda-setting, in shaping the process, and in ensuring EMU would not create a more federal political union at the same time. It has also been argued that EMU served the economic interests of the business communities within these countries, which subsequently led governments to be more supportive of the project.

- Economists and political scientists have tried to explain economic and monetary union.
- Economists often use optimum currency area theory to assess EMU.
- Political scientists use theories of European integration to explain EMU.

Criticisms of economic and monetary union

Economic and monetary union is not without its critics, however. Criticisms may involve distinctive national perspectives, but can also rest on institutional grounds.

Countries outside the euro area

The Danes and Swedes are very proud of their political, social, and economic achievements, and many of them doubt that joining EMU will benefit their respective countries. A majority of their populations have been relatively sceptical about the EU and many see EMU as yet another example of unnecessary or undesirable European integration. In both countries, a referendum on EMU was held (in Denmark, in 2000; in Sweden, in 2003) and in both cases the majority of those who voted were against joining EMU. Denmark has an opt-out agreed at Maastricht and thus can choose to stay outside the euro area; although the Swedish government does not have an opt-out, it pursues policies that guarantee that it does not qualify for EMU. In the near future, the Danes might once again contemplate joining EMU.

The UK reflects an even more Eurosceptic population. A large segment of the UK population has had doubts about of European integration. A majority of British citizens, the media, and the Conservative Party seem deeply suspicious of policy-making in the rest of Europe, and fear they will have to make too many changes if they follow the lead of other European states. Another argument often heard is that citizens are unconvinced that there is a real need to create a single currency.

The global financial crisis, the economic recession, and the sovereign debt crisis have had varying effects on member state perception of EMU. Initially, in 2007 and 2008, the euro fared better than did most of the currencies of EU member states that had remained outside the euro area. Yet, in 2009, 2010, and 2011, some member state currencies strengthened against the euro. Others, the currencies of which weakened, pointed to the fact that a weaker currency is beneficial for the export sector and that this was a factor that assisted in speedier recovery following the economic downturn or recession after the onset of the financial crisis. All in all, support for the euro has been varied. In Denmark, some are now more interested than before in joining the euro. In the UK, by contrast, attitudes towards euro adoption still reflect the lack of interest by citizens and politicians alike.

The ten member states that joined the EU in 2004 have also had varying attitudes to euro adoption. The five that have joined to date (Slovenia, Cyprus, Malta, Slovakia, and Estonia) have been keen to do so. Those that have remained outside have done so for a variety of reasons. Some have a government and population that are reluctant (for example the Czech Republic); others are currently unable to join because they have suffered from the crisis and are very far removed from meeting the criteria for entry, which focus on inflation, deficit, debt, long-term interest rates, and participation in the exchange rate mechanism (for example Hungary or Latvia). Poland can be seen as a country in the middle, where the ruling government is more positively inclined towards euro adoption and most of the convergence criteria could be met. Here, the obstacles are more domestic. The government will need support from the opposition to change the Constitution to join EMU. Another difficulty would be having the Polish *zloty* be in the ERM for two years. In all cases, these countries have the formal requirement that they are obliged to join EMU once they meet the criteria. It should be noted that this is a formality, because countries, such as Sweden, that choose not to join the ERM can stay outside the euro area simply by having their currencies not enter the ERM.

Criticism of EMU's institutional design

EMU has also been criticized for its poor institutional design. Critics argue that the extreme independence of the European Central Bank (ECB) may lead to problems of legitimacy and accountability. The argument is developed in three steps. First, the ECB is more independent than any other central bank in the world. Its independence and its primary mandate (to secure price stability—in effect, low inflation) are firmly anchored in the Treaty. It also stipulates that no one is allowed to give instructions to the European Central Bank, nor should it take instruction from anyone. Second, it is difficult to change the ECB mandate, because it requires a treaty change, which means that all EU member states would have to sign and ratify the changed treaty. Third, there are very few checks and balances in place to ensure that the policies pursued by the ECB are those that the member states would have chosen—except for the one clear one, to secure price stability (low inflation). Even on that issue there is not much control: the ECB President gives quarterly reports to the European Parliament (EP), but the EP cannot give instructions to the ECB. Thus one has to trust that the ECB will pursue policies in accordance with its mandate and that the policy outcome will benefit the EU as a whole. Fourth, no supranational institution can pursue flanking policies that may correct imbalances occurring as a result of the policies pursued by the ECB.

Let us clarify this fourth issue a little further. Compared to mature federations, the institutional design of EMU is incomplete: there is a strong ECB that decides monetary policies for the entire euro area, yet there is no equivalent supranational economic institution that sets economic policies for that same area. Budgetary and fiscal policies remain in the hands of national governments. Although countries such as France argued strongly in favour of creating such a *gouvernement économique* ('economic government'), the choice was made not to go down that route.

What are the advantages and disadvantages of having a European economic government? The advantages would be that policies could then be pursued to correct imbalances throughout EMU that result from a strict monetary policy (one that focuses on combating inflation). However, an economic government would make sense only if a majority of the citizens of the euro area were to feel comfortable with it. If it were not to have that support, then a decision by such a body would be deemed illegitimate. The current situation in Europe is that most citizens feel most comfortable with their national government taking on the role of taxing and spending.

> ### KEY POINTS
>
> - Denmark, Sweden, and the UK have not wanted to participate in economic and monetary union.
> - There has been criticism of the institutional design of EMU.
> - Some concerns relate to the independence of the European Central Bank and how this raises questions about legitimacy and accountability.
> - The institutional design of EMU has also been criticized for being incomplete and falling short of 'an economic government'.

The global financial crisis and the sovereign debt crisis

In 2007–08, a major financial crisis hit the global economy. The crisis was caused by a series of problems, many of them originating in the US. However, the financial crisis and its aftermath affected the European Union even more than it did the US. After the collapse of investment bank Lehman Brothers in September 2008, stock exchanges dropped, credit dried up, and many banks were at risk of collapse. National governments responded by guaranteeing deposits, (partially) nationalizing banks, and by putting together rescue packages. In 2009, the real economy shrank. In the EU, almost all countries were showing negative growth or were in recession (defined as two successive quarters of negative growth). As the economic recession took hold of the EU, many member state governments chose to spend considerably more than they taxed, leaving them with high deficits and public debt. Some countries experienced problems in securing money in capital markets to refinance their debt (see Chapter 27). This situation posed immense challenges for the euro area, through pressures on financial markets, pressure on interest rates for governments to attract funds in capital markets, and vicious circles of lack of confidence in markets and government policies. The result was a major crisis in the EU and a need to create new institutions, such as the European Financial Stability Facility (EFSF), the forerunner of the European Stability Mechanism (ESM) that was to become operational in summer 2012, and changes to rules of the Stability and Growth Pact to ensure that governments will avoid excessive deficits and debt situations.

The changes to the Stability and Growth Pact (SGP) were substantial. On 11 December 2011, the reinforced SGP entered into force. The so-called 'six pack' (five regulations and one directive) includes rules that will kick in if member states fail to comply with the 3 per cent deficit and/or 60 per cent debt criteria. Some of the 'reinforced' rules include that the role of the debt is now taken to be as important as the deficit. In the past, the debt criterion was largely ignored. Another 'reinforced rule' is that it requires a qualified majority vote (QMV) to stop the sanctions (whereas before it required a QMV to impose sanctions on a member state that was facing financial sanctions). The changes to the SGP also provided the European Commission with a larger supervisory role in guiding member states through the fiscal year and ensuring sound policies

over the medium term. A new term, 'European semester', was introduced to capture this process of European Commission supervision of member state public finance over a six-month period.

KEY POINTS

- The global financial crisis posed major challenges to the euro area.

- Most countries in the EU faced recession following the global financial crisis.

- The EU's reaction to the crisis involved new institutions, changes to the Stability and Growth Pact which increased the supervisory role for the Commission.

Conclusion

It has taken more than thirty years to create economic and monetary union. It was a long and slow process that ultimately led to the creation of a single monetary policy, the European Central Bank, and rules on budgetary policies and public debts. The introduction of the euro was based on a lengthy and gradual process of learning about economic and monetary cooperation. Not only was it necessary for countries to have met the convergence criteria, but it was also crucial that member states maintain stable exchange rates and that they agree on common goals for EMU.

Economic and political motivations lay behind EMU. Although one can make a case for a purely economic rationale for monetary union, its ultimate creation cannot be understood without an appreciation of its political dimension. EMU is a new stage in European integration. It signals the capability of EU member states to take firm action together and it places the EU more clearly on the international map. Yet a number of issues remain unresolved. In discussing the asymmetrical EMU, the chapter has indicated how fragile the balance is between 'economic' and 'monetary' union. The sovereign debt crisis has also unearthed challenges in EMU institutional design. Thus it is not unthinkable that, in the future, further integration might be needed in the area of 'economic union' or that steps will have to be taken towards further political

unification, if only to redistribute more evenly the costs and benefits of EMU. At the same time, we have seen that European integration is a gradual process, which lacks legitimacy if pushed ahead too quickly (see Chapter 25).

What will the future of the EU be with EMU in place? The continuing presence of the euro may well give the EU a stronger position in world politics, if only because it might offer an alternative to the US dollar (but see Chapter 16 on this point). As such, the euro contributes to the symbolism of European integration. It offers a concrete token representing the rapid and far-reaching process of integration taking place in the EU.

The regional use of the euro has increased quite rapidly from being legal tender in eleven member states in 1999 to seventeen member states in 2012. Furthermore, it is conceivable that EU member states, such as Denmark, may want to join the euro area in the not-so-distant future, as will a number of Central and East European countries, thereby adding more to the euro's credibility and strength. Yet not all monetary unions in the past have lasted; EMU will survive only if it continues to be supported by the citizens, and by national and European politicians. Leaders will have to keep listening to the needs of their citizens. If they do so satisfactorily, the euro may well continue to have a very promising future.

QUESTIONS

1. Why was the term 'economic' and 'monetary' union used? What is an 'asymmetrical EMU'?

2. What are the various stages of economic integration from a free trade area to full political unification and what does each stage entail? Do all stages have to be passed in sequence?

3. What are the 'convergence criteria' and why were they invented?

4. Why has the Stability and Growth Pact been difficult to implement?

5. There are two opposing political science theories explaining why EMU happened. What are they? Do you agree that they are opposing theories or are they complementary?

6. What are the main criticisms of EMU?

7. Discuss how the creation of EMU was both an economic and politically driven process.

8. How have the global financial crisis, the economic recession that followed, and the sovereign debt crisis impacted EMU governance?

 GUIDE TO FURTHER READING

Dyson, K. and Featherstone, K. (1999) *The Road to Maastricht: Negotiating Economic and Monetary Union* (Oxford: Oxford University Press)   An influential political science volume, which examines the road to economic and monetary union based on hundreds of interviews.

Dyson, K. and Quaglia, L. (eds) (2010) *European Economic Governance and Policies: Volume I—Commentary on Key Historical and Institutional Documents*; (2011) *European Economic Governance and Policies: Volume II—Commentary on Key Policy Documents* (Oxford: Oxford University Press)   Two 800+-page volumes containing key documents, with annotations.

Heipertz, M. and Verdun. A. (2010) *Ruling Europe: The Politics of the Stability and Growth Pact* (Cambridge: Cambridge University Press)   A comprehensive account of the genesis of the Stability and Growth Pact, the 2003 crisis, and 2005 reform.

Hodson, D. (2011a) *Governing the Euro Area in Good Times and Bad* (Oxford: Oxford University Press)   A short book that offers an oversight into the past, present, and future of governance of the euro area, written in language accessible to the non-specialist.

Verdun, A. (2000) *European Responses to Globalization and Financial Market Integration: Perceptions of Economic and Monetary Union in Britain, France and Germany* (Basingstoke: Palgrave Macmillan)   A volume examining perceptions of EMU from the perspective of the member states and considering how actors use EMU to serve or frustrate their interests.

 WEBLINKS

http://ec.europa.eu/economy_finance/   The website of the European Commission (DG Ecfin).

http://www.consilium.europa.eu/policies/council-configurations/economic-and-financial-affairs?lang=en   The website of the Economic and Financial Affairs Council (ECOFIN).

http://www.ecb.int/   The official website of the European Central Bank.

http://www.euobserver.com   An online source of EU news and debates.

http://www.eurozone.europa.eu/?lang=en   The EU Council's eurozone portal.

23

The Common Agricultural Policy

Eve Fouilleux

Chapter Contents

Reader's Guide

This chapter examines one of the first European policies, the Common Agricultural Policy (CAP). It does so by focusing on the policy's objectives, instruments, actors, and debates. It looks at the way in which the CAP has evolved since the 1960s, and attempts to explain this evolution by asking and answering a number of important questions: why has the CAP been so problematic for European policy-makers? Why has it proven so resistant to change? And, given the constraints identified, how has reform come about? This chapter also looks at some of the challenges facing agricultural policy, as new debates emerge among citizens on the social, cultural, and environmental functions performed by agriculture.

Introduction

The Common Agricultural Policy (CAP) has long been of symbolic importance to the European integration process and has been subject to calls for reform since the 1960s. This chapter focuses on this reform process as a way of exploring not only the character of the 'old' CAP, but also the form that this controversial policy might take in the future. It begins with a brief introduction to the principles underpinning the CAP and then provides an explanation of why it has taken (or is taking) so long to reform this policy. In the following section, attention turns to the long reform process that has taken place step by step since 1992. Understanding the original policy and how it has progressively changed over time helps us to understand better contemporary debates on the CAP, as explained in the last section of this chapter.

The early days of the Common Agricultural Policy and the issue of CAP reform

This section presents the main principles and instruments of the early Common Agricultural Policy, and an overview of the CAP's brake mechanisms at national and European levels.

The early days of the policy

The objectives of the CAP, which came into force from 1962, were laid down in the Treaty of Rome in 1957 (Article 39) and subsequently at the Stresa Conference in July 1958. Three general principles underpinned the policy: market unity; Community preference; and financial solidarity. The initial move in establishing a European agricultural market (applying the so-called market unity principle) was the setting up of common market organizations (CMOs) for all agricultural products, most notably for wheat, barley, rye, corn, rice, sugar, dairy products, beef, pork, lamb, wine, and some fruits and vegetables. The idea was to allow free trade internally within the Community, but also to erect barriers to the outside world, to protect the income of European farmers.

The CMOs usually operated on the basis of three complementary policy tools: a guaranteed price; a public intervention system; and some variable levies at the Community's border. First, the notion of a guaranteed price is crucial to understanding how the CAP operated. The idea was that the specificities of the farming sector (dependence on climatic conditions and vulnerability to natural disasters) and the consequent structural instabilities of agricultural markets made some public intervention necessary to guarantee decent living conditions for farmers. This is why, instead of allowing the market to determine price levels, the prices that farmers received for their produce were institutional prices—that is, they were fixed centrally by Community

civil servants and politicians. Such a system had the objective of both supporting farmers' incomes and boosting agricultural production: the more farmers produced, the more money they earned. Indeed, with the food shortages of the post-1945 period and the security concerns of the Cold War in mind, the aim of self-sufficiency in foodstuffs was presented as one of the major objectives of the policy. In practice, the level of guaranteed prices was initially set on the basis of a political compromise between France and Germany. In the early 1960s, the Germans had a very inefficient cereal sector, but numerous politically powerful farmers, and asked for a high level of support for cereals. Although the French were more efficient and had a lower national price for cereals, they did not mind setting guaranteed prices higher under the CAP, as long as they did not have to pay for them. It is for this reason that Germany has ended up as the primary contributor to the CAP since 1962, while France has always been among the main financial beneficiaries.

Second, if the price began to fall owing, for example, to an excessive internal supply, which would have had the effect of depressing farmers' incomes, intervention agencies would step in when the price reached a certain level (the intervention price) to buy up the surplus and store it until the market was balanced again, thus keeping prices high.

Third, if the price fixed inside the Community was to be high enough to support farmers' incomes, it was imperative to prevent cheap imports from flooding the common market. Therefore, to achieve the second CAP principle (Community preference), a system of variable levies was set up for each product. Produce could generally only enter the common market if it was priced at or above the internal price; if not, the importer had to pay a tariff equalling the difference to the European Budget and thus had to sell their product at the European price. Moreover, a system of 'reimbursements' (refunds), similar to export subsidies, was also put in place, enabling European producers to sell their products on the world market at world prices without losing income. These subsidies covered the difference in cost between the world and the higher European prices.

Finally, to promote the principle of financial solidarity, a common fund was set up to cover the financing of the CAP. This fund, the European Agricultural Guidance and Guarantee Fund (EAGGF), comprised two parts: guidance and guarantee. While the guarantee section covered costs attached to the operation of the market system, such as the costs of intervention and export refunds, the much smaller guidance section was responsible for funding structural policies. The EAGGF originally comprised almost the entire EC Budget.

Problems arising and the first incremental reforms

Initially, this policy was very successful, in that it very quickly met its initial objectives of increasing productivity and of achieving European self-sufficiency. However, by the 1970s, *over*production had become a political issue, with the first surpluses having appeared in the form of the famous 'butter mountains' and 'wine lakes' of this period. These problems of overproduction, caused when the supply of agricultural produce outstrips demand, increased throughout the 1980s. As an ever-increasing volume of products surplus to internal requirements was being paid for at the guaranteed price, stored at high cost, and exported out of the Community, and with support from the agricultural budget compensating for lower prices on the world market, the CAP was becoming ever more costly to operate. It is far from surprising, therefore, that the CAP was frequently criticized during this time for being too expensive and for taking up too many EC resources, thereby preventing the development of other potentially important political priorities. As a consequence, agricultural policy began to be a major concern for European policy-makers and the issue of CAP reform appeared on the European political agenda.

The policy has proven very resistant to change, however. Some reforms took place from the late 1970s to the end of the 1980s, but these were marginal and incremental. The economic policy tools that were used during this first period of reform were mainly directed towards controlling the supply of produce by imposing quantitative restrictions on production. These took the form of 'guaranteed ceilings' for crops in 1981, milk quotas in 1984, and a regime imposing maximum guaranteed quantities (MGQs) for cereals in 1987–88, generalized to other commodities in 1988–89. Despite these changes, the principle of guaranteed prices for agricultural products remained the core element of the CAP.

Why is it so difficult to reform the CAP?

This modest change can be explained by institutional factors rooted in the workings of CAP decision-making. Beyond the formal rules of the process (see Box 23.1), decision-taking in this policy area is based on what might be termed an 'inflationist bargaining dynamic'. Because the CAP is a redistributive policy, each member state's minister of agriculture is under pressure to bring home the maximum that he or she can get from that part of the EU Budget dedicated to agriculture. As a consequence of the number of member states involved in the negotiations (all of them trying to increase their CAP budgetary return), the range

---

BOX 23.1 The formal CAP decision-making process

For much of the CAP's history, the main actors in the CAP decision-making process have been the European Commission, responsible for drafting legislation, and the Agricultural Council, responsible for taking decisions. The European Parliament (EP) has had only a very limited consultative role. CAP decision-making usually began with a proposal from the Commission, which might be made either on the basis of a broadly defined request from the **European Council**, or on a voluntary basis by the Commission. Once formulated, the Commission's proposal was then submitted to the EP for **consultation** and the Agricultural Council for decision. It was also transmitted to the Committee of Professional Agricultural Organizations (COPA), the main **interest group** representing European farmers, and to other institutions as appropriate, such as the **Committee of the Regions (CoR)**. The Agricultural Council might reject the Commission's proposal or ask for modifications. Alternatively,

it might begin to negotiate on the basis of what the Commission had proposed, resulting ultimately in a decision. Although the formal rule was **qualified majority voting (QMV)** within the Agricultural Council, more often than not a consensus was sought across all member states. This meant de facto that each member could veto any decision. Decision rules such as this have had important consequences for the CAP, especially with regard to the pace of reforms and their incremental nature.

However, in the past decade, two major changes have taken place with regard to CAP decision-making; these have fuelled a more vigorous reform process. First, after the **Nice Treaty** came into force in 2003, the Agricultural Council began to take decisions as a matter of course using the qualified majority rule. Second, since 2009, the EP has had ordinary legislative (OLP) powers in agricultural policy-making under the **Lisbon Treaty**.

of products involved, and the rules that have long governed the CAP, there is an inbuilt inflationary tendency. For example, each minister in the Council would agree to price increases in his or her neighbour's favoured products in order to get the increases that he or she wants himself or herself. As a consequence, decisions that would lead to a reduction in agricultural costs, or that would change the redistributive effects of the policy, are more than likely to be rejected by the Agricultural Council. This makes it very difficult for a body such as the Commission to propose reforms that cut costs. The CAP is also an excellent example of what happens when there is no real link between the EU institutions and the EU's citizens. In such circumstances, it is easy for governments to use the European Commission as a scapegoat for decisions that they really do not want to take. The Commission is restricted in what it can do when this happens and often ends up taking the blame for a policy that it would like to see reformed.

Second, the incremental character of CAP reform can also be explained by national political pressures, which are exported to the EC level through the agriculture ministers of each member state in the Agricultural Council. Owing to their ability to mobilize support in many European countries, farmers' organizations are able to exert pressure on governments to support their line on the CAP. Political influence of this kind was particularly intense in France and Germany in the 1970s and 1980s. In both countries, farmers were important in electoral terms, because public opinion, influenced by a deep-rooted affinity for rural life, viewed farmers' interests favourably. In the French case, close links were established from the late 1950s between the government and the main farmers' representative organizations, the *Fédération Nationale des Syndicats d'Exploitants Agricoles* (FNSEA, or 'National Federation of Farmers' Unions') and the *Centre National des Jeunes Agriculteurs* (CNJA, or 'Young Farmers' Association'). Thanks to their capacity for collective action, these organizations were able to impose their views on both right-wing governments (their traditional allies) and, after 1981, on successive socialist incumbents. Although the left-supporting farmers did manage to get organized during the 1980s with the establishment of the farming union *Confédération Paysanne* in 1987, which had a rather different position, they were still too weak to challenge the power of the right-leaning FNSEA. Consequently, over the course of the 1980s, the French position on the CAP remained very close to that of the FNSEA.

Farmers' opposition to CAP reform is usually explained simply with reference to their economic interests. However, the conservatism of farmers' associations has also had much to do with deep-rooted symbolic issues linked to the identity of the farming community. In the French case, for example, the FNSEA has vehemently refused to replace the guaranteed price system with direct payments, even if the latter were calculated to provide a higher income than the former for farmers. Such a position can be explained by certain ethical and professional values that have been inherited by CNJA and FNSEA leaders, arising out of their early experiences in the 1950s with the *Jeunesse Agricole Chrétienne* (JAC, or 'Young Christian Movement'). Farmers were considered to be individual entrepreneurs, actively working the land and selling the products that they had grown in order to earn their living. It is for this reason that they could not tolerate the idea of living and supporting their families on the back of direct income payments, which were viewed either as salaries or, even worse, as a form of social security/welfare payment. Another explanation relates directly to the nature of CAP instruments at that time. In upholding the idea that all farmers should get the same rewards, guaranteed prices symbolically have been feeding the myth of farmer unity. This is something of a paradox, because in practice they provided very different levels of support across the EU, across farmers, and across products. For example, the bigger a farmer, the more financial support available. In fact, guaranteed prices have always been used as a political tool by farming elites: in France, for example,

---

KEY POINTS

- The Common Agricultural Policy was based on three fundamental principles: market unity; Community preference; and financial solidarity.

- The original CAP comprised the institutional guaranteed price, a public intervention system, and variable levies at borders.

- The CAP began to pose problems in the 1970s: agricultural surpluses began to accumulate and the cost of the CAP increased dramatically, but an inflationary bias in decision-making prevented major reform.

- Farmers' reluctance to change is not only rooted in economic interests, but also reflects identity and symbolic dimensions.

they were fundamental to the FNSEA's monopoly in representing farmers. By mobilizing collective action to defend and promote the level of agricultural prices, farming elites were able to consolidate their own dominant position within the farming community.

After 1992: the long reform process

Despite the existence of a number of brake mechanisms, a first radical reform of the Common Agricultural Policy took place in 1992 as a reaction to international pressure. This opened the way for a long reform process, which is still ongoing.

Increasing external pressures and the MacSharry reform of 1992

World agricultural markets in the early 1980s were affected by massive instabilities. In 1982, member countries invited the Organisation for Economic Co-operation and Development (OECD) Secretariat-General to undertake a review of agricultural policies to analyse their effects on international trade. With the help of academic economists working in the field of welfare economics, the officials in charge constructed an economic model and tools that enabled estimates to be made of the impact of domestic policies on world prices and trade. These studies were initially used to classify the distorting effects of national policies, and later to rank policies, demonstrating which of them were in most serious need of reform. This process engendered a learning process within the international agricultural policy community and induced a profound change in the way in which agricultural policy issues were defined. Most notably, it was concluded that, to be less distorting, instruments used within an agricultural policy had to be 'decoupled' from agricultural production so that they would have no direct impact on the type and quantity of commodity produced by the farmer. This conclusion spoke directly to the CAP's price support system.

A very important concrete decision followed this international ideational shift. This was the end of the so-called 'agricultural exception' in international trade negotiations. In 1986, the Uruguay Round of the General Agreement on Tariffs and Trade (GATT) opened. For the first time, the negotiations included agriculture. As is often the case in GATT Rounds, the main players were the US and its allies, the Cairns

Group (a group of fourteen net exporters of agricultural produce, notably including Argentina, Australia, New Zealand, Uruguay, and Thailand). This group was on the offensive from the start, arguing strongly for a radical liberalization of international agricultural markets. The US denounced the CAP as a system that allowed European farmers to eschew competition with the rest of the world, thereby generating trade distortions for producers in third (or non-EU) countries. They called for an end to all trade-distorting domestic subsidies and tariff barriers on agricultural products. The EU, with traditionally more protectionist countries such as Norway and Japan, found itself on the defensive.

At the Heysel Ministerial Conference in December 1990, the US and EU positions were still at odds, leading to a stalemate in the negotiations and threatening the entire process. To put additional pressure on the Europeans, the Americans and their allies took the decision not to negotiate on any other aspect of the Round until the agricultural issue was resolved. Such a crisis in the GATT arena provided a window of opportunity for European reformers. A radical CAP reform was seen as the only solution. At this point, the Commission decided to launch a project that it had been preparing secretly for some months. Using its right of initiative (for the first time in the history of the CAP), the Commission delivered its radical CAP reform proposal to the Agricultural Council in February 1991. The spirit of the reform was in line with international requirements, in that it would partly replace the system of agricultural price support with a system of individual direct payments to farmers aimed at compensating their loss of income.

The political decision to implement such a radical shift in policy instruments, agreed by the Council in May 1992, was taken initially by Helmut Kohl and François Mitterrand, the then leaders of Germany and France. Both were very keen to conclude the Uruguay Round. Germany had important interests in the non-agricultural part of the negotiations and the German industrial policy community put intense pressure on the German government to resolve the impasse. In France, the pressures came—secretly—from the biggest cereal growers, who had a direct interest in the reform. Thanks to the agreed price decreases, they would be able to gain the upper hand in the European animal food market over US cereal substitutes. Such freeriding behaviour by the—very powerful—cereal lobby explains why the reform was immediately accepted by the French government, against the advice of the *Fédération Nationale des Syndicats d'Exploitants Agricoles* (FNSEA), which was totally opposed to it. In addition, in order to benefit from the reform at two levels, cereal growers (together with large landowners) lobbied actively for a full compensation of the price decreases for all (contrary to the Commission proposal of a sliding scale compensatory scheme dependent on the size of the farm). The negotiations on the Commission's proposal took place in the Agricultural Council over a period of eighteen months, resulting in the rewriting of the Commission's original proposal. At the end of this process, the outcome of the 1992 reform was not quite as innovative as it might have been. The deal that was finally concluded on 21 May 1992 (known as the 'MacSharry reform', deriving from the name of the agriculture commissioner at that time) was still regarded, however, as historic (see *Financial Times*, 22 May 1992).

An ongoing reform process

The MacSharry reform marked the point of departure of a much deeper CAP reform process. Even so, the reforms that followed that of 1992 were subject to similar budget-related concerns and pressures, interlinked international trade bargains and interests, free-riding strategies by specialized farmers' organizations, and brake mechanisms in the Agricultural Council.

The first post-MacSharry reform was agreed in March 1999 at the Berlin European Council and was incorporated into the Commission's Agenda 2000 plans. It was prepared and issued in the broader context of the Eastern enlargement of the EU (see Box 23.2). On the basis of this document, ten new regulations were adopted, which were to come into force from 2000. Alongside a number of subsidiarity/decentralization initiatives, the 1999 reform was remarkable in that it placed a new emphasis on the environment (see Box 23.4). Three possible options were presented to the member states. However, these were to be implemented on a voluntary basis. This was also the case for a proposal allowing the setting of maximum levels of direct aid received by farmers. Owing to national difficulties and conservative pressures, however, these optional measures were rarely implemented.

The Agenda 2000 reform also endorsed two important innovations that affected the policy discourse. First, the term 'multifunctionality' was introduced,

to signal that agriculture is not only about production, but also incorporated 'non-production' aspects of farming—that is, its social, cultural, territorial, and environmental dimensions. With this concept, European policy-makers were not only seeking new ways in which to legitimize the CAP within the EU, but also had the forthcoming World Trade Organization (WTO) Round in mind. When the Uruguay Round was concluded in 1994, the Agreement on Agriculture (AoA) defined three 'boxes' used to distinguish between support for agricultural policy programmes that directly stimulated production and consequently distorted trade, and those that were considered to have no direct effect on production and trade.

- Domestic measures with a direct effect on production were placed in the 'amber box': they had to be cut.

- Measures considered to be 'decoupled from production', with no linkage between the amount of payment and the production process, agricultural prices, or factors of production, were placed in the 'green box' and could be freely used.

- Payments linked to programmes aiming at limiting production went into the 'blue box' and did not need to be reduced, as long as certain conditions were met.

In the AoA, the post-1992 CAP compensatory payments were classified in the blue box—but, in view of the forthcoming WTO negotiations, their future was seen as uncertain. In that context, the strategy decided by the Agricultural Council in October 1999 involved 'securing' CAP payments in the blue box by arguing that the CAP could not be challenged because it pursued multifunctionality, meaning non-production, as well as production, goals.

The second discursive innovation of the Agenda 2000 reform was to distinguish between two 'pillars' of the CAP (not to be confused with the three EU pillars) (see Figure 23.1). In addition to a first pillar dedicated to market support, rural development became the 'second pillar' of the CAP. This was presented as a way of enhancing the 'multifunctionality' of European agriculture in line with a subsidiarity-based approach. However, Agenda 2000 was, in fact, only one small step in this direction, with a small percentage of total CAP expenditure allocated to the second pillar. Thirteen years later, actors involved in the policy still

BOX 23.2 Eastern enlargement and the CAP

A first crucial issue regarding EU enlargement and agriculture at the end of the 1990s was the extent to which the CAP was to be applied to the ten member states that were to join the EU in 2004, and whether the CAP instruments would have to be adapted. This raised questions about the economic consequences of applying CAP to the new members in respect of the general structure of farming. In addition, there were serious concerns about how the CAP would be financed in the future.

The European Commission presented its strategy for dealing with these questions at the beginning of 2002. Its proposal involved offering direct payments to farmers and introducing production quotas for new member countries after they joined. To ease transitional problems in rural areas and to encourage the restructuring of agricultural sectors, the Commission also proposed complementing its financial support with an enhanced rural development policy. Given that the immediate introduction of 100 per cent direct payments would have frozen existing structures and hampered modernization (not to mention bankrupted the EU), the Commission favoured its gradual introduction over a transition period of ten years, covering 25 per cent in 2004, 30 per cent in 2005, and 35 per cent in 2006, ultimately reaching 100 per cent in 2013.

For existing member states, the northern Europeans argued that the proposal was too costly, and that there should be no direct aid to the Central and East European (CEE) countries in the first few years after accession. The Dutch government pointed out that no direct aid for new members was assumed in the Agenda 2000 agreement in 1997. The Swedes argued that direct aid for the new member states would actually discourage much-needed agricultural restructuring. Germany was more concerned about predictions that its net contribution to the agricultural budget would grow after enlargement and that, as a result, its budgetary returns would decrease. France, always concerned to keep its own budgetary returns on CAP as high as possible, also expressed concern about the cost of the Commission's strategy, but firmly opposed the suggestion by some members that a more profound reform of the CAP was needed before enlargement.

For their part, most of the candidate countries reacted by saying that the Commission's proposal did not offer them enough and that they needed 100 per cent of direct aid paid from year one. This was not only for sectoral, but also for political, reasons, in order to convince their publics to agree to EU membership in the first place.

At the Brussels European Council on 25 October 2002, the EU heads of government and state finally adopted the main lines of the Commission's proposal on CAP and enlargement. In order to address some national concerns (from Germany in particular), they placed their decision in a framework of financial stability from 2007 to 2013. This meant that total annual expenditure on CAP direct payments and market-related expenditure for a Union of twenty-five members would not exceed the corresponding combined ceilings for 2006.

One important aspect of the 'CAP and EU enlargement' debate was the concern that CEE countries would not have the capacity to implement CAP legislation and control expenditures. Bulgaria and Romania were at the core of especially important debates in this respect in the years before their accession in 2007. In addition to more general concerns about their judicial systems and high-level corruption, the control of agricultural funds and food safety issues (animal disease control and bovine spongiform encephalopathy, or BSE, regulations, in particular) were seen as major areas of concern.

---

talk about the 'two pillars' of the CAP; however, the concept of multifunctionality has almost disappeared of their discourse. This may be explained by the much reduced pressure on CAP reform exerted in recent WTO negotiations.

A new CAP reform plan was issued by the European Commission in July 2002, one year after the opening of a new WTO Round, the so-called 'Doha Development Round' (see also Box 23.3). This plan was largely driven by the new WTO negotiations, within which the fate of the blue box became more and more uncertain, making it clear that the EU could secure CAP payments to European farmers only by transferring them to the green box, mean-

ing their further 'decoupling' from production. While initially supported by the UK, Germany, and other 'northern' governments, the new CAP reform proposal faced very strong French opposition. The French government refused to reduce its support for its larger cereal growers and wanted reform postponed until 2006. The Agricultural Council finally reached a compromise in June 2003. The 2003 'mid-term review' (MTR) of the CAP (so-called because it was foreseen in the 1999 Berlin Agreement as a simple reviewing exercise) is considered by some commentators as a second revolution in CAP reform (after the 'historic' 1992 reform). It introduced a new element, the Single Farm Payment (SFP), a unique

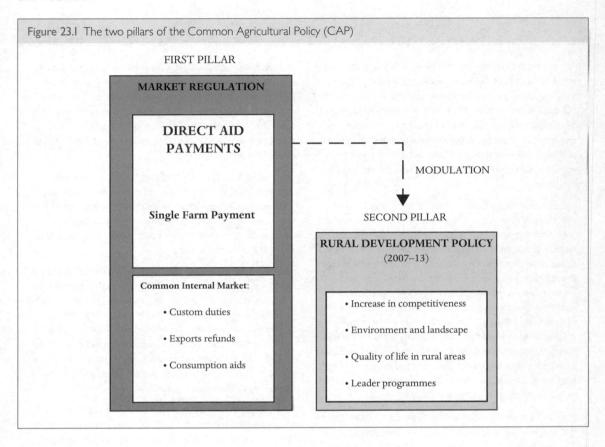

Figure 23.1 The two pillars of the Common Agricultural Policy (CAP)

CAP direct payment aimed at achieving a complete decoupling of support from production. Under this system, even a farmer who decides to grow nothing is eligible to receive the SFP, as long as he or she complies with EU environmental, food safety, animal welfare, and occupational safety standards. Finally, another important measure called 'modulation' was set up to transfer funds from the first CAP pillar (market support) to the second (rural development).

With no direct international pressure this time, a further reform (the so-called 'health check') was approved in November 2008. This was primarily concerned with budgets and efficiency. As usual, the Commission made ambitious initial proposals, which were considerably eroded in the negotiation process. For example, in the field of modulation, the Commission had asked for a basic rate of 13 per cent by 2013, rising to 23 per cent on individual payments over €100,000, 38 per cent above €200,000, and 58 per cent above €300,000. Owing to (among others) German pressure in the Council—since

reunification, Germany has had some very big farms—the final agreement included a much lower modulation scheme, with a basic rate of 10 per cent in 2013 and only an additional 4 per cent for individual payments above €300,000 (see Box 23.4).

In addition to the 1992, 1999, 2003, and 2008 global reforms of the CAP, further reforms have been decided on the same 'decoupling' model for various isolated products such as olive oil, cotton, and tobacco in 2003 and 2004, sugar in December 2005, fruits and vegetables in 2007, and wine in 2008.

More recently, after a public debate launched by the Commission in February 2010, which was seen as a success, Romanian Agriculture Commissioner Dacian Ciolos made some new reform proposals in 2010, using arguments and premises that were very different from those of his more liberal predecessor Mariann Fischer Boel. In November 2011, the Commission presented this reform in the form of seven legislative proposals. With the global objective one of building a new partnership between the CAP and society, the proposed reform comprised four main strands. First, it

Since the 1980s, the CAP has been often criticized for its effects on developing countries. Through its system of export refunds (payments given to the exporter to compensate for the difference between the European guaranteed price and the much lower world price), the EU was exporting agricultural products at prices much below their costs of production, contributing to the ruin of producers in the global south. For example, cans of Italian concentrated tomatoes, and millions of tons of frozen chicken and wheat from Northern Europe, regularly arrive on African markets at very low prices and cause local production to collapse.

Step by step, the 1992, 1999, 2003, and 2008 CAP reforms have reduced the level of internal prices and consequently phased out most export refunds (which now represent only 1 per cent of the CAP budget). This has reduced trade distortions considerably. However, although they are quantitatively less important, the CAP continues to produce negative effects on developing countries. Although most CAP payments have been shifted to the 'green' box of the WTO, many development non-governmental organizations (NGOs) argue that European products are highly subsidized and are thus exported below their costs of production. As such, they continue to compete unfairly with domestic products in less-developed countries. Others argue, however, that, under the present circumstances, the problem is not whether to support European agriculture or not, but whether to support less-developed countries' agriculture (through developing countries' national budgets or through cooperation policies, or even through tariffs in order to protect internal markets).

Another issue is formulated in terms of 'market access'. Some actors criticize the European Union for being too protectionist owing to its 'non-trade barriers' (such as EU environmental rules, animal welfare standards, and labelling legislation). However, these arguments tend to come from the minority of countries with large producers that export, or would like to export, their products to the EU.

Another controversial matter is the 'protein dependency' issue. Owing to the implementation of a zero import tariff on cereal substitutes (soy and corn gluten field) since 1967, Europe's production of meat, milk, and eggs has developed based on massive imports of soya from the US and, more recently, Latin America. In these regions, intensive industrial production of soya causes major social and environmental problems. The EU is highly dependent on these imports. In this context, the European Parliament has called on the Commission to support actively protein crops in the EU so as to give the Union greater autonomy (European Parliament, 2011b).

sought to 'ensure the competitiveness of all European farming, as a means to safeguard . . . food security' (Ciolos, 2011). This was to be based on a new direct payment system (with no historical reference), differentiated support based on objective needs, specific aid for young farmers, the option for coupled aid if justified, targeted support for less favoured areas, and a digressive payment scheme with a ceiling.

Second, the proposal aimed at 'laying down the foundations for a new competitiveness that is both environmentally and economically sustainable' (Ciolos, 2011), based on compulsory measures targeted at preserving natural balances, the doubling of funds for agronomic research, and incentives for farmers to organize themselves collectively in order to negotiate better with their powerful economic partners (food industry and retailers).

Third, the territorial dimension was emphasized as a crucial factor for competitiveness. Twenty measures were proposed relating to the rural development programmes for 2014–20.

Fourth and finally, it aimed 'to simplify the CAP'. At the time of writing, the negotiation process is ongoing with the European Parliament and the Agricultural Council. Based on this Commission proposal, no decision has yet been taken, but the final compromise is expected for the end of 2013.

The Commission's proposals have given rise to many comments and discussions by experts and bureaucrats (see, for example, Defra, 2011; d'Oultremont, 2011; Mahé, 2012). The farmers' organizations reacted to the proposal too. European farmers are represented in Brussels in two main organizations: the Committee of Professional Agricultural Organizations (COPA)–General Committee for Agricultural Cooperation in the European Union (COGECA) alliance, and European Coordination Via Campesina. These two organizations have developed very divergent visions of European agriculture and the CAP. The former, which represents mainly conventional farming and large and/or specialized agricultural enterprises, is the most powerful. It targets increased production and yields, and systematically argues that the ever-increasing

---

BOX 23.4 The content of key CAP reforms

The 1992 MacSharry reform	Price decrease: 30 per cent for crops (cereals and oilseeds); 15 per cent for beef
	Full 'compensation payments' based on cultivated area and historical yields (individual and/or regional) for each product
	Compulsory set-aside
	'Flanking measures' on agri-environment, early retirement, and forestry (very marginal budget)
The 1999 Agenda 2000 reform	Further price decrease: 15 per cent by 2006 for dairy products; 15 per cent for cereals; 20 per cent for beef
	Partial compensation payments
	Part of the direct payments become 'national envelopes' in order to target specific national and/or regional priorities, and member states are given the option to link direct payments to environmental criteria
The 2003 mid-term review reform	Further price decreases for cereals and for durum wheat, rice, dried fodder, protein crops, and nuts
	Introduction of the Single Farm Payment (SFP), calculated on the average total payments received in 2000, 2001, and 2002; regional calculations rather than individual (in order to redress imbalances between big and small farmers), except in France and the UK (owing to pressure from large-scale cereal growers and landowners)
	Modulation involving a transfer of 3 per cent of direct payments from the first to the second CAP pillar in 2005, 4 per cent in 2006, and 5 per cent from 2007
The 2008 'health check'	Milk quotas abolished (to be phased out progressively by 2015)
	Reform of some remaining intervention instruments
	Cancellation of compulsory set-aside
	All support switched to the SFP (except for sucker cows, goats, and sheep, for which a certain level of coupling is still allowed)
	Increased modulation: 10 per cent shifted from the first to the second CAP pillar, plus 4 per cent for payments above €300,000

---

world population and its growing needs in terms of food security issues justify the notion of the EU as a food-exporting power. The latter organization, which represents small agriculture and 'family farming', rejects industrial agriculture on economic, social, and environmental grounds. It emphasizes the need to develop local production and local markets, and argues for a stricter regulation of markets by public authorities. It also often adopts a common stance with environmental and development organizations over issues of sustainability and food sovereignty.

Both organizations were unhappy with the Commission's October 2011 reform proposals, but for different reasons. COPA–COGECA called for 're-inforcing the economic role of farmers and their cooperatives and making European agriculture a dynamic, innovative and more profitable sector' (COPA–COGECA, 2011); it also rejected the over-emphasis of the proposals on the environment by arguing that they 'will actually undermine the ability

of the agrifood sector to be competitive, efficient, and to achieve sustainable growth' (COPA–COGECA, 2011). By contrast, European Coordination Via Campesina, together with the European Movement for Food Sovereignty and another Common Agricultural Policy (FoodSovCAP), formed out of various national and European organizations, presented family farming, fair farm prices, the right to food of people in the global south, and preservation of natural resources as their main priorities, and deplored the fact that:

the measures . . . will not meet the environmental and social challenges faced by the CAP and they will not give enough legitimacy to EU subsidies on agriculture. The lack of regulation of markets and production will push the agricultural sector into even more serious crises, and intensify the current crisis of food prices.

(FoodSovCAP, 2012)

KEY POINTS

- The inclusion of agriculture in the Uruguay Round of the GATT in 1986 placed an important political constraint on European governments, which led to a radical CAP reform in 1992.

- Successive reforms took place, in 1999 in light of forthcoming enlargements, in 2003 to avoid a clash within the WTO, and in 2008 for budgetary reasons.

- In addition to the progressive replacement of institutional prices by direct payments to farmers ('decoupling'), these successive reforms have introduced various instrumental and discursive innovations, such as the concept of multifunctionality and the two pillars of the CAP, the Single Farm Payment system, and the modulation tool.

- A new reform was launched in November 2011, which will define a new CAP for the period 2014–20.

Past and present debates on the CAP and EU agriculture

For decades, the debate has been focused mainly on the budgetary, economic, and trade distortive effects of Common Agricultural Policy instruments, conducive to a radical shift of the policy in that matter. However, although they have not been the main engine for change, other important issues have emerged and have progressively found their way in the discussions; rural development, environment protection, and transparency fall into this category.

The long road to rural development

Since the early years of the CAP, the European Commission has tried to introduce a socio-economic dimension into the policy. The very first attempt of this kind was made by Dutch Agricultural Commissioner Sicco Mansholt in the late 1960s (European Economic Community, 1969). He proposed a radical revision of the CAP's market measures, together with an active structural agricultural policy at the European level, in order to help the restructuring of the sector. Strongly rejected by the Council, the proposal gave birth to a very timid structural policy in 1972, providing funds for such things as new technologies and equipment. Differing from other CAP measures, these structural measures were co-financed by member states through fixed, multi-annual budgetary 'envelopes'. Despite an increase in allocations since the mid-1980s, only an extremely small part of the European agricultural budget has ever been devoted to structural measures.

In the following decades, structural measures were replaced by efforts to create a rural development policy within the framework of the CAP, with social, forestry, and agri-environment measures supplementing structural goals. The European Commission has made various attempts to promote rural development as a parallel approach to agricultural policy since the beginning of the 1990s. Its Directorate-General for Agriculture was renamed 'Agriculture and Rural Development' at that time, and it published numerous documents promoting its 'sustainable rural development' strategy. An important event organized in this perspective was the European Conference on Rural Development (Cork, Ireland, November 1996), initially planned as a way of building an ambitious 'integrated' approach to the countryside within the CAP. The Cork Declaration invited European policy-makers to switch their public support from financing market measures to assisting rural development and agri-environmental programmes. The member states remained reluctant to adopt such an approach, however, and the Conference was seen as a failure.

Some progress was made in pursuing this agenda in 1999, with structural measures converted into the 'second pillar' of the CAP alongside agri-environmental measures. However, this new 'pillar' remained marginal from a budgetary point of view. Subsequently, some commentators expected the Eastern enlargement to provide an opportunity to reinforce rural development measures in the CAP, but this did not really happen (see Box 23.2). The 'modulation' measure, decided in 2003 and reinforced in 2008, was the first really concrete measure.

A new regulatory framework for rural development was adopted in September 2005, with three different themes: 'improving the competitiveness of the agricultural and forestry sector'; 'improving the environment and the countryside'; and 'improving the quality of life in rural areas and encouraging diversification of the rural economy'. Additional support was made available for so-called 'LEADER initiatives'—that is, highly specific projects designed and implemented by local partnership. Spreading funds between the four

Table 23.1 Agricultural expenditure, 2004–10

		2004	2005	2006	2007	2008	2009	2010
PILLAR I	Interventions in agricultural markets (%)	18	16	15	10	10	13	8
	Direct aids (%)	63	64	64	69	70	71	71
PILLAR II	Rural development (%)	18	19	20	20	20	16	21
Other (%)		1	1	1	1	<1	<1	<1
Total (%)		100	100	100	100	100	100	100
Total (€ m)		47,467.4	52,698.2	53,538.5	53,693.9	52,457.8	55,214	55,614.7

Source: Eur-Lex, General Budget of the EU for years 2006–10, Title 05

themes, ninety-four rural development programmes were approved for the 2007–13 period.

In sum, a major issue regarding EU rural development policy remains the persistent weakness of the second pillar, which is allocated only 21 per cent of the CAP budget, as compared with 79 per cent allocated to the first pillar in 2010 (see Table 23.1). Furthermore, EU rural development policy is often criticized as being too 'farming'-oriented. While agriculture is no longer the sole engine for rural development, it still consumes almost all available funds, with rural development actors outside the farming sector benefiting from only very scarce resources. In order to address this issue better, some commentators argue for a shift in rural development from the CAP to EU regional policy, a proposal strongly resisted by the agricultural policy community, who argue that the money must be 'really spent on the countryside, and not on large centres of population that call themselves rural'. To conclude, the most recent reform proposal covering 2014–20 seemed to put a renewed emphasis on rural development. In addition to a 'new form of governance based on partnership contracts between the Commission and the member states' (Ciolos, 2011), twenty 'more flexible and relevant' measures (Ciolos, 2011), with six clear priorities have been established—namely, competitiveness, innovation, risk management, ecosystems preservation, resource use efficiency, and social inclusion.

The environment as a core issue

The environment and, more broadly, issues of sustainable development have progressively found their way into the agricultural policy debate since the 1980s. The negative effects of modern farming were initially denounced by environmental groups. Problems identified included soil erosion in areas of intensive crop production, pollution by pesticides, water pollution caused by nitrate fertilizers in areas of intensive livestock production, and the homogenization of the rural landscape. Until the 1990s, however, owing to the opacity of the guaranteed price mechanism, it was not easy to explain to the public how the CAP affected the environment in rural areas by prompting farmers to intensify their practices, thereby exacerbating environmental degradation. With CAP support becoming gradually more transparent in 1992, 1999, 2003, and 2008, the situation became clearer and environmentalists could enter the agricultural policy debate more directly. Environmental organizations, such as the World Wildlife Fund for Nature (WWF), Friends of the Earth, and BirdLife have thus developed an increasing expertise and discursive capacity on agricultural issues, and they now contribute actively to the CAP debate (Ansaloni, 2012).

These organizations argue that farmers should, at the very least, comply with a minimum set of environmental requirements. They also call for a direct link to be set between the amount of subsidy provided to a farmer and the environmental performance of their farm, and/or the quantity of environmental public goods the they actually deliver. As BirdLife International puts it: 'We need to spend EU taxpayers' money more sensibly—let's support those farmers who maintain a healthy, thriving rural environment, and let's stop distributing unjustified and environmentally harmful subsidies' (BirdLife, 2008a).

Apart from environmentalists, 'alternative' farmers also try to have a voice in the debate. Without public support and in opposition to 'conventional' models of agriculture, these farmers have been proving that it is possible to farm differently. Organic farming is the best-known example, but there are others, all rejecting the conventional productivist model of agriculture, which is based on the trilogy of intensification–enlarging–investment. In contrast to this conventional model, alternative farmers have proved that farming can simultaneously be friendlier to the environment, can offer better working conditions and quality of life for the farmer, and can provide a similar or even better income. This sort of farming used to be denounced as old-fashioned and out of line with modernity and technical progress, but, thanks to an opening of the agricultural debate to incorporate environmental and sustainability issues, alternative farming is gaining much more attention at national, EU, and international levels. Organic farming is popular with consumers, and this model is more and more regarded by the scientific community as the way forward.

However, at the EU level, organic farming is mainly taken into consideration in regulatory terms (as in the harmonization of production norms or in certification rules) (Gibbon, 2008). In terms of support, alternative farming is considered only within the CAP's agri-environmental measures. In order to gain more influence over the CAP, the International Federation of Organic Agricultural Movements (IFOAM) regularly publishes position papers. Alternative farmers also increasingly make alliances with environmental groups (see BirdLife et al., 2009).

The new active participation of alternative farmers and environmentalist groups in the CAP debate does not, however, ensure that their views are taken into account in the final decisions. The 2008 reform, for example, has been denounced as highly disappointing by environmental organizations. According to a BirdLife representative in Brussels, the Agriculture Council's final compromise 'completely fails to address the new environmental challenges of the 21st Century . . . The patient is still ill and won't get any better with the prescribed treatment' (BirdLife, 2008b). In the more recent context of the preparation of the CAP reform post-2013, the EU environmentalists, together with the EU-IFOAM groups, have presented some very detailed policy proposals (BirdLife et al., 2009). The future will say whether or not these actors have been successful in extending their influence on the CAP.

On budgets and transparency: where does the money go?

The proportion of the EU Budget spent on agriculture and rural development has decreased substantially since the early 1980s, falling from 65.1 per cent of the total EC Budget in 1986 to 53.8 per cent in 2000, and 41 per cent in 2008. However, the debate on CAP expenditure is still very lively.

A first very general feature of the debate sets countries such as the UK, Sweden, and Denmark against countries such as France and Spain. The former ask why such a large proportion of EU funds (40.8 per cent in 2007) should go to agriculture instead of other sectors such as research and development (R&D—which benefits from only 3.5 per cent of the EU Budget in 2007), given that farmers represent such a small part of the population (see ECORYS, 2008). The latter argue that this is simply because the CAP is the only fully Europeanized policy, and that aggregate figures at national and EU levels show a very different picture, with R&D benefiting from 0.677 per cent of the European gross national product (GNP) against only 0.55 per cent for agriculture (Bertoncini, 2007). Behind these arguments for and against lies a crucial debate among member states, that of 'budgetary return'—namely, the benefits gained by a given country from the CAP *less* the contribution of that country via the EU Budget. This issue, which recalls Margaret Thatcher's demands for a Budget rebate for the UK back in 1984, continues to be present in all Agriculture Council negotiations.

Citizens have been left out of these debates. As a result of the opacity of the old guaranteed price system, the discussion was very much a technical one that was confined to the elite level. Under the reformed CAP and the direct payment system, CAP support became more understandable and the debate became public. As a consequence, demands for greater transparency about the beneficiaries of EU funds have become more frequent. Although data on individual payments were initially kept secret, since 2004 lists of the main beneficiaries of the CAP have been published in the member

Table 23.2 Distribution of total direct aid per tranche for select EU member states, financial year 2010

		UK	France	Denmark	Portugal	Ireland	Czech Republic	Poland
Total direct aids (€1,000)		3,313,025	8,080,217	956,402	636,693	1,268,911	563,477	1,847,301
Number of beneficiaries		180,880	379,350	55,150	194,090	125,020	24,610	1,387,510
Average amount per beneficiary (€)		18,316	21,300	17,342	3,280	10,150	22,896	1,331
Farmers paid less than €5,000	Share of beneficiaries	44.4%	31.1%	51.1%	89%	41.7%	64.9%	97.8%
	Share of expenditure	4.1%	2.4%	5.%	22.4%	9.8%	4.6%	64.2%
Farmers paid between €5,000 and €50,000	Share of beneficiaries	55.4%	58.2%	38.53%	10.9%	56.55%	25.72%	2.1%
	Share of expenditure	47.7%	58.3%	40%	41%	77.5%	16.8%	23.7%
Farmers paid between €50,000 and €200,000	Share of beneficiaries	0.1%	10.6%	10%	0.1%	1.7%	6.3%	0.1%
	Share of expenditure	43.2%	39.4%	53.1%	50.7%	22.1%	33.8%	72.1%
Farmers paid more than €200,000	Share of beneficiaries	0.5%	0.1%	0.4%	< 0.1%	< 0.1%	3.1%	< 0.1%
	Share of expenditure	9.1%	2.3%	7%	8.3%	0.4%	49.4%	4.2%

Source: Based on http://ec.europa.eu/agriculture/fin/directaid/2010/annexI_en.pdf

states. It came as a surprise when citizens discovered that huge CAP payments were made to the late Queen Mother in the UK, to Prince Rainier of Monaco, to big companies and food industries, and to members of governments (including EU Agriculture Commissioner Mariann Fischer Boel). In France, there was a scandal when it was revealed (see La Tribune, 3 November 2005: 2–3) that the first beneficiary on the list for 2004 was allocated more than (€850,000 to produce rice in the south of France, and the second, almost the same for 1,500 hectares of irrigated maize in south-west France (one of the less environmentally friendly crops in this area). Following an intense lobbying campaign by activists and journalists in favour of transparency (in particular those of farmsubsidy.org), the Council agreed to the full disclosure of all recipients of financial support under the CAP in October 2007, and decided that data would have to be made

publicly available in all member states by the end of 2008 for the second pillar and early in 2009 for the first.

In sum, the switch to direct payments has considerably reshaped the CAP debate. As Table 23.2 illustrates, although very different across different EU states, the distribution of CAP support is often very unequally spread. For example, 0.1 per cent of farmers receive 43 per cent of payments in the UK (with individual payments between €50,000 and €200,000) and 44.4 per cent of them receive only 4.1 per cent of the budget (with individual payments below €5,000). The sudden visibility of these inequalities has had important consequences for the farming community. It has created tensions within traditional farmers' unions, notably between the different kinds of producers—for example, intensive crop growers versus extensive cattle growers—and has considerably weakened them.

KEY POINTS

- Although advanced very early in the Common Agricultural Policy debate, the issue of rural development has faced important difficulties. The second pillar of the CAP now makes rural development policy within the CAP legitimate, but the budget allocated to it remains small.

- The environmental issue is gaining an ever-increasing importance in the CAP debate. The main argument is that direct payments should be more strictly linked to environmental performance.

- With the shift to direct payments, the distribution of CAP support suddenly became more visible. This turned social justice and transparency into core elements of the debate.

Conclusion

Originally intended to make Western Europe self-sufficient in food, the Common Agricultural Policy was equipped with 'productivist' instruments that led to an overproduction of agricultural produce and serious budgetary problems for the European Community. In the 1980s, the first reforms introduced supply control measures, such as quotas. At the beginning of the 1990s, as a consequence of international developments, new policy beliefs inspired the 'decoupling' of farm support from production. This provoked a radical reform of the CAP in 1992, which shifted policy instruments from market or price support to direct income support. This decreased centrally planned prices, compensating for these cuts through direct payments to farmers. This new path has continued in subsequent CAP reforms, with further 'decoupling' for an increasing number of products, and increasing attention paid to the environmental and social dimension of the CAP.

The evolution of the CAP since the 1990s is an excellent illustration of the complexity of the links that exist between national, European, and international political arenas. Inter-sectoral deals that are not easily understood at national level become even more complicated when various governments, coalitions of interests, and European and international institutions enter the game. Caught in the crossfire between national interest and international bargains, the EU's political system is complex, intricate, and competitive. The only way in which to deconstruct this complexity is by examining the actors involved in the policy process, the visions of agriculture and agricultural policy that they support, the nature of the political exchanges that take place amongst them, and the resources that they are able to invest to defend their position.

The CAP also provides a good example of how a reform can feed back into discussions about the very purpose of the policy. The shift from an opaque set of instruments (the guaranteed price mechanism) to a more transparent system of direct payment proved to have very direct impacts on the actors engaged in the process and the balance of power across member states, as well as on the substantive content of debates on the kind of agricultural policy that Europe ought to have.

? QUESTIONS

1. Why did the Common Agricultural Policy originally seek to maintain high prices for agricultural produce?

2. What were the negative consequences of the CAP's price support mechanism?

3. Why did the 1992 reform take place?

4. What do the 1992, 1999, 2003, and 2008 CAP reforms have in common?

5. To what extent does the current round of international trade negotiations pose a threat to the CAP?

6. Which new issues entered the agricultural policy debate from the late 1990s on and why?

7. How is the environmental issue taken into account in the CAP?

8. To what extent are developing countries affected by the CAP?

 GUIDE TO FURTHER READING

de Castro, P. (2010) *European Agriculture and New Global Challenges* (Rome: Donzelli Instant Book)   In this book, De Castro, professor of Agricultural Economics and former Italian Minister of Agriculture, provides an overview of the CAP and discusses its future.

Garzon, I. (2007) *Reforming the Common Agricultural Policy: History of a Paradigm Change* (Basingstoke: Palgrave Macmillan)   The book provides a comparison of the 1992, 1999, and 2003 CAP reforms, and argues that policy feedbacks of each reform led to a change in policy paradigm.

Greer, A. (2005) *Agricultural Policy in Europe* (Manchester: Manchester University Press)   This book provides a unique comparative analysis and shows that, despite the CAP, substantial agricultural policy variations exist across the EU.

Hill, B. and Davidova, S. (2011) *Understanding the Common Agricultural Policy* (London: Taylor and Francis, Earthscan)   The authors try to understand the CAP and its evolutions using economics as a basis for their exploration.

Jones, A. and Clark, J. (2001) *The Modalities of European Union Governance: New Institutionalist Explanations of Agri-environmental Policy* (Oxford: Oxford University Press)   An excellent study of the relationship between agricultural and environmental policy in the EU, exploring in the process many of the intricacies of the CAP.

 WEBLINKS

http://capreform.eu/   'Europe's common agricultural policy is broken—let's fix it!' is the slogan of this blog on CAP reform, which brings together researchers, activists, and analysts from across Europe.

http://commonagpolicy.blogspot.com/   Professor Wyn Grant's excellent blog on the CAP, regularly updated and featuring lots of useful information.

http://ec.europa.eu/agriculture/   The home page of the European Commission's Directorate-General for Agriculture and Rural Development.

http://ec.europa.eu/agriculture/organic/splash_en   A website that provides very rich and complete information on organic farming in the EU and a number of related issues (environment, animal welfare, agriculture and society, EU policy, etc.).

http://farmsubsidy.org/   An online database launched by a group of journalists and activists, featuring detailed data on who gets what from the CAP (on a country basis) and the EU Common Fisheries Policy (CFP).

24

Environmental Policy

David Benson and Andrew Jordan

Chapter Contents

Reader's Guide

Although an economically oriented organization dedicated to the liberalization of trade, the European Union has nonetheless developed an extensive array of policies and institutions dedicated to protecting and preserving the environment. Environmental concerns have consequently shifted from being a marginal aspect of the integration process to one that routinely grabs newspaper headlines and, unlike many other EU policy areas, generates strong political support amongst its citizens. Moreover, these policies have shown themselves to be remarkably resilient to economic and deregulatory pressures. This chapter documents and explores the reasons behind this relatively rapid and remarkably enduring transformation in the EU's governing capabilities, explores the main dynamics of policy-making in the environmental sector from different analytical perspectives, and identifies some future challenges.

Introduction

At its founding in 1957, the then **European Economic Community (EEC)** had no environmental policy, no environmental bureaucracy, and no environmental laws. The word 'environment' was not even mentioned in the **Treaty of Rome**. The EEC was primarily an **intergovernmental** agreement between six like-minded states to boost economic prosperity and repair political relations in war-torn Europe. More than fifty years later, EU environmental policy is 'broad in scope, extensive in detail and stringent in effect' (Weale et al., 2000: 1). It conforms to a set of guiding principles, has its own terminology, is the focus of significant activity amongst a dedicated network of environmental actors, is underpinned by a binding framework of environmental laws, and has an explicit basis in the founding treaties. In short, it has successfully evolved from a set of 'incidental measures' (Hildebrand, 2005: 16) to a mature system of multilevel environmental governance. Virtually all environmental policy in Europe is now made in, or in close association with, the European Union. And it is 'impossible to understand the environmental policy of any of the . . . Member States without understanding [EU] environmental policy' (Haigh, 1992: xi) because the two have become inextricably intertwined.

What is especially striking about this transformation is how quickly the EU assumed control over policy powers 'that in a federal state would have been ceded to the centre only grudgingly, if at all' (Sbragia, 1993: 337). Moreover, as a sector, environmental policy has consistently shown itself to be remarkably resilient to deregulatory pressures and/or declining public demands for ever higher standards. This chapter documents the reasons behind this rapid and remarkably enduring transformation (see Box 24.1), identifies the main dynamics of policy-making, and explores some future challenges.

The development of environmental policy: different perspectives

There are several ways in which to comprehend the evolution of EU environmental policy: one is to explore the content of the European Union's six environmental action programmes (EAPs) since 1973; a second is to examine the main policy outputs; a third is to scrutinize the periodic amendments to the founding treaties; and finally, the dynamic interplay between the main actors at the international, EU, and national levels can be examined. The remainder of this section is structured around these four perspectives.

The environmental action programmes

Six EAPs have been adopted by the Commission since the early 1970s. Initially, these were essentially 'wish lists' of new legislation, but they gradually became more comprehensive and programmatic. The first (1973–76), identified pressing priorities—namely, pollution and other threats to human health. Just as importantly, it also established several key principles

BOX 24.1	The evolution of EU environmental policy
1972	Heads of state and government, meeting in Paris, request the Commission to prepare an environmental strategy
1973	Commission adopts First Environmental Action Programme (EAP)
1981	Reorganization of Commission leads to creation of a dedicated Directorate-General for the environment
1987	Single European Act provides a more secure legal basis
1993	Maastricht Treaty enters into force and extends qualified majority voting (QMV) to almost all areas of environmental policy
1993	Publication of Fifth EAP: explores pursuit of a new goal—sustainable development
1997	Treaty of Amsterdam: makes promotion of sustainable development and environmental policy integration (EPI) central objectives
2002	The sixth, more binding, EAP is adopted
2008	EU adopts a comprehensive climate and energy package committing member states, inter alia, to 20 per cent reduction in greenhouse gas emissions by 2020
2010	The EU fails to achieve internal agreement on moving to new target of 30 per cent reduction in greenhouse gases by 2020
2011	After disappointing performance at an international meeting in Copenhagen in 2009, the EU reasserts its leadership on climate change issues at another meeting in Durban
2012	Conflicts erupt between the EU and its trading partners over the regulation of new energy sources such as biofuels and shale gas

(see Box 24.2), which were subsequently enshrined in the founding treaties (see 'The evolution of the treaties'). They were not particularly novel—many derived from national and/or Organisation for Economic Co-operation and Development (OECD) best practices—but they represented an innovative attempt to apply them together in a new supranational setting.

The second EAP (1977–81) followed the same approach, but emphasized the need for scientifically informed decision-making, through procedures such as environmental impact assessment (EIA) for proposed developments. Importantly, it also underlined the Commission's desire to become more involved in international-level policy-making activities (see 'Key items of policy').

By contrast, the third (1982–86) and fourth (1987–92) EAPs were more programmatic, setting out an overall strategy for protecting the environment *before* problems occurred. In contrast to the first programme, they were significantly more ambitious, identifying many more priority areas (Weale et al., 2000: 59). They also underscored the benefits of prevention by fitting the best available abatement technology to factories and vehicles.

The fifth (1993–2000) and sixth (2002–12) EAPs accelerated this shift to a more strategic and cross-cutting approach. The fifth introduced the notion of sustainable development, explored policy implementation through non-legislative instruments (known as 'new environmental policy instruments', or NEPIs), and identified new ways in which to embed greater environmental policy integration (see Box 24.2). The sixth developed this approach still further by initiating seven thematic strategies. Crucially, the sixth—and current—programme has greater legislative force, having been adopted by the European Parliament (EP) and the EU Council.

Key items of policy

Looking back at the content of all six EAPs, a steady trend is visible away from a rather ad hoc, reactive approach driven by the Commission, to a more strategic framework, co-developed by multiple stakeholders. A similar picture emerges from a cursory inspection of legal measures adopted annually (see Figure 24.1). In the 1960s and 1970s, legislative output was relatively slow, but then it rocketed in the 1980s

---

BOX 24.2 Key principles of EU environmental policy

Environmental management	Prevention (preventing problems is cheaper and fairer than paying to remedy them afterwards)
	Action at source (using the best available technology to minimize polluting emissions)
	Integrated pollution control (ensuring that, for example, attempts to remedy water pollution are not transformed into air or land pollution problems)
Specification of environmental standards	Resource conservation (environmental protection as a goal in its own right)
	High level of protection (aiming for the highest level of protection possible)
	Precaution (acting to protect the environment even when cause–effect relationships are not fully understood)
Allocation of authority	Appropriate level of action (acting at the 'right' level)
	Subsidiarity (only acting at EU level when problems cannot be tackled at national level)
Policy integration	Polluter pays (the polluter, rather than society as a whole, should pay to address problems)
	Environmental policy integration (integrating an environmental dimension into the development of new sectoral policies such as agriculture and transport)

Sources: Knill and Liefferink (2007: 28); Weale et al. (2000: 62–3)

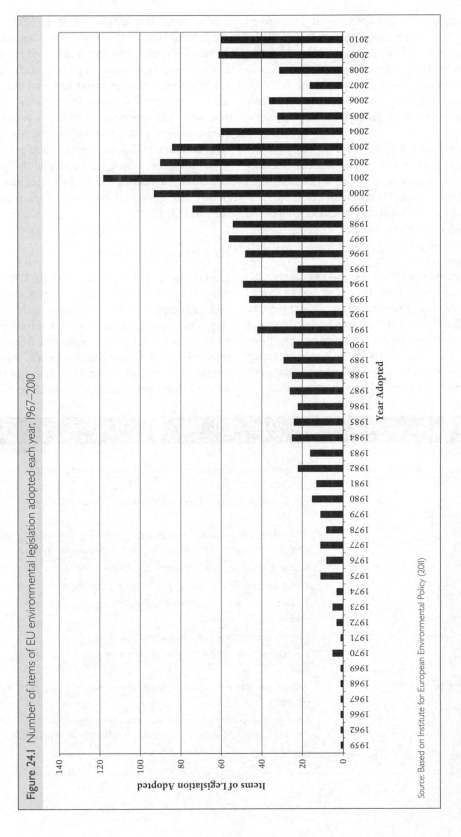

Figure 24.1 Number of items of EU environmental legislation adopted each year, 1967–2010

Source: Based on Institute for European Environmental Policy (2011)

and 1990s, tailing off again in the 2000s. By the late 1990s, more effort was being devoted to consolidating, streamlining, and reforming the environmental *acquis communautaire* via less prescriptive framework legislation, including directives on air quality (1996), water (2000), chemicals (2006), and marine issues (2008).

However, if we look at the purpose of these measures, a slightly different pattern emerges. Thus, the first environmental directives addressed traded products such as cars and chemicals. In the 1980s and particularly the 1990s, the EU began to diversify into new areas including access to environmental information, genetically modified organisms (GMOs), and even zoos, exemplifying the rising political demand for environmental protection 'for its own sake'. The overall pattern of policies therefore resembles more an inconsistent 'patchwork' (Héritier, 2002) than a comprehensive and carefully designed framework. It also nicely illustrates the fact that the EU is a 'regulatory state' (Majone, 1996) in the environmental sphere; non-legislative instruments are still rare at EU level.

The evolution of the treaties

Another way in which to comprehend environmental policy is to analyse the environmental provisions of the EU treaties. The legal codification of the environmental *acquis communautaire* has followed the same gradual, but ever increasing, pattern noted above. Thus the original Treaty of Rome contained no reference to environmental matters. New environmental measures consequently had to rely either on Article 100 EC (now 115 TFEU), relating to the internal market, or on Article 235 EC (now 352 TFEU), which allowed the EU to move into new policy areas to accomplish its goals. Arguments emerged as actors fought over the legal basis of environmental policies. For the Commission, Article 100 proved to be legally more secure and hence politically less contested than Article 235, hence the tendency (noted under 'Key items of policy') for early measures to target traded products.

In one sense, the Single European Act (SEA) established a more secure legal basis, with qualified majority voting (QMV) for issues with a single market dimension. This undoubtedly allowed the EU to enter new, and less 'obvious', areas such as access to environmental information and wildlife conservation—all somewhat removed from the internal market. In another sense, it simply codified the status quo: more than a hundred items of policy had already been adopted when it was

ratified in 1987 (Wurzel, 2008: 66). The Maastricht and Amsterdam Treaties introduced new policy principles (such as sustainable development, precaution, and environmental policy integration—see Box 24.2) into the founding treaties. Crucially, they also extended QMV to almost all areas and greatly increased the European Parliament's powers. By the late 1990s, most environmental policy therefore followed one decision-making route, QMV in the Council plus co-decision (now the ordinary legislative procedure, or OLP). Because the legal underpinnings of environmental policy were already embedded by these agreements, there was little need for new environmental content to be added to the following Nice (Jordan and Fairbrass, 2005) and Lisbon Treaties (Benson and Adelle, 2012).

Actor dynamics

The development of environmental policy has not, therefore, followed a single pattern. There have been periods of continuity and significant change. Furthermore, some aspects (for example, the action programmes) have evolved in a fairly gradual and systematic manner, whereas others (for example, the main types of policy) have emerged much more unpredictably and opportunistically. In order to understand these similarities and differences, we must look at the main actors and examine their motivations and the evolving constraints under which they operate.

The European Commission deserves the bulk of the credit for developing an EU environmental policy. Initially, it worked hard to establish a case for EU involvement. Undaunted by the absence of high-level political support (no Commission President has consistently championed environmental policy), a weak treaty basis, and limited administrative capacities (there was no designated environmental Directorate-General until 1981), the Commission quickly realized that it would have to be creative and flexible to thrive. Even so its DG Environment is still rather limited in size; it is dwarfed, for example, by its opposite number in the US, the federal Environmental Protection Agency (Sbragia, 1996: 244). The Commission is not, of course, monolithic; debates between the DGs responsible for environment, trade, and industry are often just as intense as those with external actors.

Given these limitations, DG Environment learnt to exploit opportunities and colonize institutional niches in the EU. This approach was the very essence of Monnet's neo-functionalist method of integrating 'by stealth', whereby incremental integration by the EU in key economic sectors creates so-called 'spillover' incentives for political integration in others (Weale, 2005; see also Chapter 5). In the environmental sector, the Monnet method succeeded brilliantly. But as the political and legal basis of EU policy became more secure, the Commission focused more efforts on managing and governing instead of expanding into new areas. This has coincided with a more open, inclusive, and less opportunistic modus operandi.

Until the 1980s, the chief policy-making body was the EU Council (see Chapter 11). The first meeting of the Environment Council took place in 1972. The participants—mostly national environment ministers—soon learnt that they could adopt policies in Brussels that were unattainable in their national governments. Pushed hard by a 'troika' of environmental 'leader' states comprising the Netherlands, Denmark, and West Germany, the Council began to adopt increasingly ambitious legislation in the 1980s. After 1982, West Germany emerged as a strong advocate of new policies, partly to address domestic political concerns, but also to boost its fledgling environmental technology industry (Sbragia, 1996: 241). Its underlying philosophy—that of 'ecological modernization'—now underpins all aspects of EU environmental policy, with advocates arguing that high levels of environmental protection are reconcilable with, and can even promote, economic growth. Less ambitious or 'laggard' states (typically from the Mediterranean region, but also including Ireland and the UK) were rather slow to recognize what was happening, adopting some policies almost 'absent-mindedly' (Weale et al., 2000: 359). Sbragia (1996: 237) has argued that the outcome of these actor constellations was a 'push–pull' dynamic: 'The internal politics of the . . . progressive States "pushes" the process in Brussels along . . . "pulling" most of the member states towards levels of environmental protection, which, left to their domestic devices, they most probably would not adopt.'

The stark division between 'leaders' and 'laggards' described by Sbragia had, however, begun to dissolve by the 2000s. New member states had entered the fray (for example, after 2004) and some existing participants (the UK, for example) had changed their preferences and bargaining tactics as a result of EU membership (Jordan, 2002). Consequently, new alliances began to evolve. These were often more strongly associated with how to achieve policy goals (for example, what policy instruments or style of enforcement should be applied), than whether to pitch standards at a higher or lower level (Sbragia, 2000: 295).

Two other things are important to note about the behaviour of states in the EU Council. First, given the right contextual conditions, the presidency of the EU Council matters a great deal (Wurzel, 2012). When a 'leader' state is in charge, there tends to be more substantive policy outputs than if a 'laggard' state is at the helm. Second, other than periodically issuing general, high-level affirmations, the European Council has never taken an active and sustained role in environmental policy-making. In the early years, this disengagement benefited environmental policy because it allowed the Monnet method to flourish below the political radar of many EU leaders (Wurzel, 2008: 83–4).

The European Parliament (see Chapter 12) is often described as the 'greenest' EU institution (Burns, 2012), although it did not actually establish its own dedicated environment body—a committee—until 1979. At first, it developed its influence indirectly by cultivating informal links with national actors and other EU institutions. During the 1970s and 1980s, it helped to draw attention to new environmental issues such as animal protection and policy implementation, which were subsequently taken up by actors within formal policy-making processes. With the appearance, first, of the cooperation and then later the co-decision/OLP procedures, its formal influence grew and its green ambitions remain essentially undiminished today. That said, its influence remains largely reactive in nature. It also struggles to hold the EU Council to account in environmentally important areas (such as agriculture, land use planning, energy, and taxation) in which unanimous voting remains the norm (Burns, 2012).

The European Court of Justice (ECJ) played a pivotal role in establishing the legal importance (and hence legitimacy) of EU environmental policy via rulings on the direct effect of directives (see Chapter 13). Although by no means an unqualified supporter of stronger environmental powers, during the 1970s and 1980s it was drawn into adjudicating on the legal basis of EU policy, often resolving them in favour of the Commission (Krämer, 2012). Earlier rulings also supported the Commission's right to participate in international environmental policy-making (Sbragia, 2005). As the legal basis of EU policy became simpler and more secure, the ECJ's focus shifted to resolving disputes over lax policy implementation.

Interest groups constitute the final type of policy actor. After the first EAP, national-level environmental pressure groups established (in 1974) a Europe-wide federation to coordinate their efforts in Brussels. The European Environment Bureau (EEB) now has more than 140 member organizations, ranging from large and very well-established national bodies to much smaller and more local ones. In the 1980s and 1990s, the number of environmental pressure groups lobbying directly in Brussels mushroomed—another indicator of how far European integration has proceeded in this sector. The EEB in turn belongs to the Green 10 (Adelle and Anderson, 2012); a looser coalition of the largest environmental pressure groups. Although all of these organizations are better organized than in the 1970s, they are comprehensively out-resourced by business interests that can hire the very best public relations (PR) firms to lobby EU policy-makers. Nonetheless, they are drawn to Brussels because they perceive that they can achieve things there that would be unattainable back home (see Chapter 14). They also lobby the EU to influence international-level policy dynamics, at which we look in the next section.

KEY POINTS

- At its inception in 1957, the European Union had no environmental policy. Environmental issues were not even explicitly mentioned in the Treaty of Rome.

- Nonetheless, over the last fifty years, the EU has developed a wide-ranging environmental *acquis communautaire*.

- Environmental policy development can be understood by examining, inter alia, the six Environmental Action Programmes, key policy outputs, EU treaty amendments;, and the interplay between policy actors at multiple levels.

- Several actors vie for influence within this system. Most notably, the Commission has been instrumental in driving policy development, often opportunistically and 'by stealth' (Weale, 2005). Other influential actors include the EU Council, the European Parliament, the European Court of Justice, and interest groups.

Linking different perspectives: the underlying dynamics of environmental policy

Having now introduced the main actors, policies, and legal frameworks, we are better placed to explore the underlying dynamics of EU policy-making. In the past, EU environmental policy could be explained through one main dynamic (for example, the regulatory competition between member states) and/or in rather binary terms (leaders vs laggards; EU institutions vs member states; industry vs environment). But as the sector has matured and become more deeply entangled with others, these analytical constructs no longer suffice (Lenschow, 2005); the nature of policy outputs and their differentiated outcomes on the ground seem too complex and contingent (Sbragia, 1996: 241) to fit into a single model or framework. To understand better how policy is made, analysts have therefore started to explore policy developments in particular sub-areas of environment policy using more governance-centred approaches (Lenschow, 2012). These studies have revealed the salience of three interacting dynamics: Europeanization; internationalization; and cross-sectoral policy integration.

Europeanization

Europeanization is the process through which EU-level policies affect domestic systems (see Chapter 9). As analysts started to investigate the domestic implications of the shift towards more multilevel environmental governance, the picture that emerged was one of differential Europeanization. Thus every state appears affected by EU membership, even those so-called leader states that worked hardest to shape EU policy. Moreover, they have been affected by the EU in different ways: the content of their policies has been more deeply affected than their style (for example, anticipatory or reactive, consensual or adversarial) or internal administrative structures. And while some aspects of national policy have become more similar, no long-term convergence towards a common 'European' model is apparent (Jordan and Liefferink, 2004). For now, national policies and policy systems appear too strongly rooted in national history to respond uniformly to EU policy demands. Growing multilevel environmental governance has therefore not yet created more universal environmental governance (Weale et al., 2000: 468).

Internationalization

International-level drivers are far more important in EU environmental policy than is sometimes assumed. After all, it was the 1972 UN Stockholm Conference that first gave EU actors an impetus to discuss their respective approaches, to build new institutions, and, eventually, to develop common policies. An internal–external dynamic has therefore been apparent since the very dawn of EU policy.

What does this particular dynamic entail? First and foremost, it involves different EU-level actors (chiefly the Commission and the presidency) working alongside the member states in international-level discussions. However, in practice, the point at which member state control ends and EU control begins varies from one issue area to the next. This has engendered highly complex and—it has to be said—rather introspective discussions about who should take the lead in a given issue area and according to what decision-making procedure. Over time, these internal relationships have changed. In the 1970s and 1980s, 'laggard' states in the European Union prevented the EU as a whole from developing a more progressive collective position in emerging global issue areas such as stratospheric ozone depletion (Sbragia, 2005). In the 1990s, changing internal political and legal conditions facilitated internal agreement, and this allowed the EU as a whole to adopt a more progressive position in areas such as global climate change, biodiversity protection, and sustainable development (Jordan et al., 2010). The EU has increasingly operated as a 'soft power' actor (see Nye, 2005) by promoting its environmental norms to third countries through its bilateral relations with other trading partners. Environmental policy has therefore assumed a greater role in the development of a broader EU foreign policy (see Chapter 16). However, the EU's position as self-styled environmental 'leader' (see Zito, 2005) was dented at the chaotic Copenhagen Conference on the United Nations Framework Convention on Climate Change (UNFCCC) in 2009, when EU negotiators were effectively sidelined by the US and China, and forced to accept a weakened deal on reducing global greenhouse gas emissions. At the next meeting, held in Durban in 2011, the EU restored its reputation for green leadership by building alliances with developing countries.

This takes us to the second dimension of internationalization: the drive to give the EU an external environmental face has, in turn, boomeranged back and affected internal EU policies via a process that is analogous to Europeanization. For example, the EU had to develop a suite of internal policies to control chemicals (such as chlorofluorocarbons, or CFCs) that deplete the ozone layer—a policy area originally formalized and transformed by two important UN agreements brokered in Vienna (1985) and Montreal (1987). As discussed under 'Policy dynamics in practice', the EU's participation in the UNFCCC Kyoto Protocol negotiations (1997) were subsequently to influence European and, in turn, national-level climate policy (Jordan et al., 2010). In the coming years, international climate commitments entered into at Copenhagen (2009), Cancun (2010), and Durban (2011) will similarly affect established areas of internal EU policy-making, such as agriculture, transport, and energy. Chief amongst these is the pledge to reduce EU-wide greenhouse gas emissions by 20 per cent by 2020.

Integration

Environmental policy integration is a long-standing goal of EU policy (see Box 24.2), linked to the achievement of more sustainable forms of development. In practice, integration means ensuring that economically powerful sectors, such as transport, agriculture, and energy, build an environmental dimension into their policy design and implementation processes. In the past, DG Environment approached integration from a somewhat weaker and more defensive position—that is, by issuing regulations to compel these non-environmental sectors to take environmental issues into account. The obvious benefit of this rather segmented approach was that a large amount of ambitious legislation could be adopted relatively quickly. The drawback was that a great deal of it was either watered down in the Council or systematically ignored by cognate sectors at the implementation stage.

In the 1990s, the environmental sector moved towards a more systematic form of integration via the Fifth and Sixth Environmental Action Programmes (EAPs), the post-1998 Cardiff Process of integrating environmental considerations into all policy sectors (Jordan and Schout, 2006), and the 2001 Sustainable Development Strategy. Moving out of the environmental 'policy ghetto' (Sbragia, 1993: 340) was always going to be fraught with difficulty, given the inherently (and perhaps even infinitely) expansive nature of environmental issues. But it seemed to offer the tantalizing prospect that the sectors might eventually bear more of the responsibility for adopting strong *and* implementable environmental policies. At the time, some environmentalists wondered whether this approach might, if pushed to its logical end point, eventually put environmental policy-makers out of their jobs. Other commentators, such as Liberatore (1993: 295), however, warned of the risks of 'policy dilution', under which sectors adopted and implemented new environmental measures, but in a greatly 'diluted and piecemeal' form. The next section examines which of these two predictions proved to be accurate.

Policy dynamics in practice

In the 2000s, the interplay between these three dynamics moved centre-stage. They certainly shaped the EU's response to climate change, which before 2000 comprised little more than an amalgam of national policies, but became *the* most dynamic and high-profile area not only of environmental policy, but of EU integration (Jordan et al., 2010). Thus, in a bid to achieve international leadership at the 1997 UN Kyoto Conference on climate change ('internationalization'), the EU took on the most far-reaching policy targets of any party (an 8 per cent reduction from 1990 levels by 2008–12). Sbragia and Damro (1999: 53) claim that this transformed the EU from a 'Vienna laggard' to the 'Kyoto leader'. The progressive and proactive stance adopted by the EU resulted from simultaneous pushing by greener member states and the Commission. However, the EU is struggling hard to implement this commitment within its borders ('Europeanization'), while at the same time still engaged in negotiating a new, 'post-Kyoto' agreement ('internationalization') after the Copenhagen meeting. Given that all sectors of the EU generate greenhouse gas emissions (and hence need to mitigate them) and/or stand to be affected by rising temperatures, it is apparent that, like sustainable development, climate change also requires unprecedented levels of cross-sectoral policy coordination ('integration'). In this respect, all three perspectives shed light on past environmental policy dynamics, but also hint at challenges to the sector's future development.

KEY POINTS

- EU environmental policy now exhibits a number of features that do not conform to a single analytical perspective. More governance-centred approaches have revealed the salience of three interacting dynamics: Europeanization; internationalization; and policy integration.

- Member states have been Europeanized by the EU in a non-uniform manner. There has been no long-term convergence towards a standard European mode of national policy.

- The EU has shaped, and in turn been shaped by, international-level environmental politics via a process known as 'internationalization'.

- The integration of the environment into sectoral policies has become a key EU objective, but its implementation remains patchy.

- One high-profile issue area in which these three interacting dynamics have been especially prominent is climate change.

Future challenges

In spite of the undoubted achievements, several hugely important challenges remain to be addressed in the environmental sector—namely improving integration, strengthening implementation, coping with enlargement, and expanding policy instrumentation.

Integration or consolidation?

In the late 1990s, greater integration leading to more sustainable forms of development was the 'big idea' in the environmental sector. Various strategic processes to embed integration were initiated (see 'Integration'), but the results thus far have been rather mixed. The institutional and cognitive barriers to better coordination in a complex, multilevel system such as the European Union are extremely daunting (Jordan and Schout, 2006). So it is hardly surprising to discover that non-environmental sectors did not willingly accept responsibility for 'greening' their own activities. On the contrary, they used some of the new integrating systems and structures to 'reverse integrate' economic and social factors into environmental policy-making in precisely the manner predicted by Liberatore (1993). However, the worsening economic climate in the 2000s and growing fears that Europe was falling behind emerging economic powers in Asia was what really blunted the Commission's enthusiasm for integration. The first Barroso Commission (2005–09) pointedly identified the delivery of the Lisbon Agenda of more 'jobs and growth' as its overriding strategic priority. The Cardiff Process of environmental policy integration (EPI) was disbanded, the thematic strategies envisaged in the Sixth Environmental Action Programme (EAP) were repeatedly delayed, and the 2001 Sustainable Development Strategy eviscerated of binding targets and implementing structures.

In the mid-to-late 2000s, environmental policy went 'back to basics'. Integration remained an objective, but this time it became organized around, and implemented through, binding climate change targets. The comprehensive new package of climate and energy policies adopted by the EU in late 2008 requires unprecedented degrees of coordination between the environment, transport, agriculture, and energy sectors. And the presence of a clear environmental threat (of runaway climate change) and strong international commitments (that is, Kyoto) appeared to be more forceful drivers of integration than the far broader (and hence politically weaker) legal commitments to integration and sustainable development contained in the Amsterdam Treaty.

Yet, in the post-2008 'age of austerity', with national fiscal capabilities under severe strain and the euro area in deep crisis, the temptation to backslide on integrating these environmental commitments may prove too much for both the EU and its member state governments. The EU's revised Lisbon Agenda issued in 2010, for example, was mainly predicated on stimulating job creation, while endorsing a weak 'green growth' interpretation of sustainable development. Before the climate conference in Durban, there was also little enthusiasm amongst EU national governments to go beyond the existing emission reduction target (of 20 per cent by 2020). In this context, ambitious integration objectives may take a back seat for a while.

Strengthening implementation

Agreeing upon and adopting integrated environmental policies is one thing, but implementing them is another entirely different challenge. Policy implementation was effectively a 'non-issue' until the Parliament politicized it in the 1980s (see Box 24.3). Poor implementation is, of course, an endemic problem in many EU policy areas. But in contrast to the competition and fisheries sectors, the Commission lacks inspection powers in relation to environmental issues, being reliant on other actors (for example, interest groups) to bring cases of non-compliance to its attention. Naturally, these groups have a vested interest in presenting failures in the worst possible light. The exact size of the EU implementation 'gap' remains a matter of intense academic and policy debate (Jordan and Tosun, 2012). But the continuing presence of poor implementation is undoubtedly a factor in the ongoing failure to arrest declining levels of environmental quality in Europe (European Environment Agency, 2007).

Three factors inhibit perfect implementation. First, despite measures introduced after the Seveso incident (see Box 24.3), monitoring and enforcement capabilities in the EU policy sector are still weaker than those at the national level. Second, despite pressure from interest groups and the European Parliament, member states remain fiercely opposed to strengthening the EU's enforcement powers or publicizing one another's failings. Finally, member states have largely accepted the development of EU environmental policy, although some have often only paid lip service to implementation for reasons of self-interest. While not a significant problem in the climate sector (to date, the EU has met its somewhat modest emissions reductions targets), if and when EU targets become more stringent, implementation could become a far more problematic issue (Jordan et al., 2010).

Coping with enlargement

EU environmental policy coped remarkably well with previous enlargements, but the 2004 and 2007 accessions were always expected to pose weightier problems for the policy process in Brussels, as well as in the new entrant states (see Chapter 17). The underlying problem was that their size, number (twelve in total), and relatively poor economic performance were unprecedented in the history of the EU. Prior to entry, they were granted financial assistance to upgrade their administrative and implementation structures, but it is still too early to determine whether this will prevent them from exacerbating the EU's ongoing implementation problems. What is abundantly clear, however, is that, in climate change policy-making (as opposed

---

BOX 24.3 Bridging the implementation 'gap'?

The implementation of EU environmental policy was not a live political issue in the 1970s. The Commission lacked the resources to enforce proper implementation, while some national governments perceived directives as statements of intent rather than legally binding obligations. Attitudes began to change in 1983 after hazardous dioxin waste from an industrial accident in Seveso in Italy was illegally dumped in France. This incident highlighted the poor implementation of EU directives and, when the European Parliament censured the Commission for its failings, this issue suddenly rose up the political agenda. The EU subsequently introduced measures to improve implementation, including expanding its legal enforcement section, producing annual implementation reports, increasing infringement actions against national governments, and establishing a Network for Implementation and Enforcement of Environmental Law (IMPEL) in 1992. However, some scholars continue to believe that implementation will always remain a policy problem 'without political solutions' (Jordan and Tosun, 2012).

to implementation), they are quite prepared to fight their corner in Brussels. During the adoption of the climate–energy package in late 2008, Poland led a group of eight Eastern European states that called for their relatively weak 'economic potential' to be taken into account at a time of 'serious financial difficulty' (ENDS Europe, 2008). This was the first occasion on which the new entrants had acted as a negotiating bloc in the environmental sector. But some did not join them, with France and Germany also active in demanding concessions. This event adds weight to the argument (outlined under 'Linking different perspectives: the underlying dynamics of environmental policy') that binary analytical categories are no longer as significant as they once were. The more immediate practical problem for the Commission, however, was that, having done it once and succeeded, the newer members may well be tempted to do it again, particularly if the economic crisis continues.

Future enlargements could also heap further pressure on EU environmental policy. As several states with a relatively low level of economic development queue up to join the EU, most prominently from the Balkans region, achieving the EU's high environmental objectives, including meeting current climate emissions reduction targets, may prove difficult in the coming years. Looking even further ahead, were Turkey to eventually join the EU, it would further complicate the process of allocating (or sharing) emissions reductions ('burdens'), because its per capita share is low at the moment, but is rising very sharply.

Enlarging the toolbox

In principle, the available toolbox of environmental policy instruments is relatively full. There has been an active technical debate over the (de)merits of 'new' instruments since the late 1960s (Jordan et al., 2005). These include voluntaristic instruments, including informal management standards, voluntary agreements (amongst polluters, but also between polluters and the state), and market-based instruments, such as environmental taxes and emissions trading. Nonetheless, despite significant learning and borrowing interactions between states, regulation remains the EU's instrument of choice (Jordan et al., 2005). The lack of a sound legal treaty base for fiscal measures has certainly played a part in retarding the use of environmental taxes, as has resistance from large polluters. Meanwhile, voluntary agreements have been trialled, but not extensively employed.

However, in the climate change domain, the international and scientific pressure to reduce emissions has encouraged the EU to dip deeper into its environmental toolbox, but with rather mixed success. The most prominent example of a voluntary agreement at EU level was supposed to reduce CO_2 emissions from new cars, but failed to meet expectations and has now been replaced by a (2010) regulation. In contrast, the EU has managed to pioneer an entirely new kind of instrument—emissions trading (see Box 24.4)—but it too has experienced serious implementation problems.

BOX 24.4 Emissions trading: a case of policy entrepreneurship?

In the 1990s, the EU tried—unsuccessfully—to adopt an EU-level carbon energy tax, but was thwarted by a blocking coalition of member states backed by business interests. However, EU influence over climate policy has grown since the late 1990s, resulting in large part from the emergence of the Emissions Trading Scheme (ETS). This scheme, based on the trading of greenhouse gas emissions allowances, is not a fiscal instrument and therefore did not fall foul of the unanimity requirement in the Council. Spotting a political opportunity to exploit this legal loophole in the treaties and noting that several member states had already adopted trading schemes, the Commission proposed an EU-wide emissions trading system. When this proposal was debated, the UK and Germany made it clear that they wanted a voluntary approach, whereas most other member states accepted the Commission's plan for a mandatory scheme (van Asselt, 2010). The Commission was nonetheless able to get its proposal accepted by offering concessions to the UK and Germany. An emissions trading directive was subsequently adopted with amazing speed, quickly becoming the keystone of the EU's new climate–energy package.

What does this tale reveal? First, that the opportunistic and unpredictable nature of EU policy-making—a hallmark of the 1970s and 1980s—has not entirely disappeared (Jordan et al., 2010): integration 'by stealth' (Weale, 2005) is still a powerful way of progressing EU environmental policy. Second, national governments retain strong control over events. Finally, internationalization is also a significant policy driver: emissions trading was originally suggested by the US government in the Kyoto Protocol negotiations.

Conclusion

Once a politically unimportant side project of EU integration, the environment has emerged as a key area of EU competence and a dynamic site of everyday politics. The focus of EU policy in this area has shifted over time from remedying problems to 'designing them out' of sectoral policies in accordance with the sustainability and environmental integration principles. But as the focus of environmental policy has become more diffuse, so the opportunities have grown for the sectors to 'reverse integrate' their concerns into environmental policy. Thinking about EU policy in terms of the outcome of intersecting processes of Europeanization, internationalization, and environmental policy integration helps to explain its current shape and functioning, while also pointing to a range of future challenges.

An active EU role in areas such as the environment is entirely unsurprising, as high levels of environmental quality are often held to be a luxury. Because the EU is comprised of very affluent states, it was obvious that this economically focused governance system would eventually be drawn into ensuring differing national standards did not disrupt free trade. Where problems span borders or involve a strong trade dimension, the 'value added' of EU involvement seems self-evident. Yet many issues now governed by the EU do not exhibit these characteristics: zoos, bathing and drinking water quality, waste water treatment, bird habitats, and renewable energy supplies, to name just a few. Nor does a functional–economic rationale completely explain why the EU, which is not a state, possesses such wide-ranging environmental powers, particularly when compared to other multilevel systems such as the US.

Putting aside these legal and administrative constraints, the underlying reason for this rapid transformation is probably political: once the basic idea had been accepted that the environment should be protected 'for its own sake, it was but a relatively short step to the regulation' of these and other apparently 'local' issues (Sbragia, 1996: 253). The absence of a fixed constitutional blueprint and relatively weak policy coordination structures, in addition to strong support from environmental interest groups and the public, allowed (and perhaps even tacitly encouraged) DG Environment to behave in an opportunistic and entrepreneurial manner in its environmental 'ghetto'.

Despite the current 'age of austerity', the tide of environmental policy shows no sign of receding. For sure, the 2000s witnessed a shift 'back to basics' centring on the production of new regulations that address climate change and energy security concerns. Environmental policy integration was also sidelined as national governments struggled to save both their own economies and the euro area. But the environmental *acquis communautaire* has endured, with limited evidence of significant dismantling. Moreover, many new policies continue to come on stream, for example on marine areas, emissions from aviation, and environmental crime.

To conclude, the political embedding of environmental policy and its continued popularity amongst ordinary citizens means that it may be considered one of the EU's greatest 'success stories'. However, important challenges remain, not least that of translating policy-making into tangible and enduring improvements in environmental quality 'on the ground', especially if the EU continues to expand eastwards. EU environmental policy has come a very long way in a short space of time, but it still remains a 'work in progress'.

QUESTIONS

1. Why did the EU first become involved in environmental policy-making in the late 1960s and what kinds of obstacles stood in its way in the early years?

2. What roles do the Council, the Commission, and the European Parliament play in environmental policy-making at EU level, and how have these changed over time?

3. In what ways does EU environmental policy interact with and affect national and international policies?

4. How 'effective' has EU environmental policy been?

5. How has the **Lisbon Treaty** affected the main dynamics of environmental policy?

6. How and to what extent has EU policy Europeanized national policy since the late 1960s?

7. Why is the full implementation of EU policy proving to be such a big challenge?

8. What challenges are EU environmental policy-makers likely to face in the future?

GUIDE TO FURTHER READING

Jordan, A. and Adelle, C. (eds) (2012) *Environmental Policy in the European Union*, 3rd edn (London: Routledge)   A textbook summarizing the main actors, institutions, and processes of environmental policy-making.

Jordan, A. and Liefferink, D. (eds) (2004) *Environmental Policy in Europe: The Europeanization of National Environmental Policy* (London: Routledge)   The first and most comprehensive analysis of the Europeanization of national environmental policy in different member states.

Jordan, A., Huitema, D., van Asselt, H., Rayner, T., and Berkhout, F. (eds) (2010) *Climate Change Policy in the European Union* (Cambridge: Cambridge University Press)   The first book-length account of policy-making in this rapidly evolving and politically salient area.

Knill, C. and Liefferink, D. (2007) *Environmental Politics in the European Union* (Manchester: Manchester University Press)   A concise analysis of the evolution of EU environmental politics.

Weale, A., Pridham, G., Cini, M., Konstadakopulos, D., Porter, M., and Flynn, B. (2000) *Environmental Governance in Europe* (Oxford: Oxford University Press)   A highly detailed empirical analysis of how and why the EU created such a complex and multilevel system of environmental governance.

WEBLINKS

http://ec.europa.eu/environment/index_en.htm   The home page of the European Commission's DG Environment.

http://www.eea.europa.eu/   The website of the European Environment Agency contains a wide-ranging database of statistics and reports on the state of the environment across the EU.

http://www.endseurope.com/   A private provider of daily environmental news in both print and electronic formats.

http://www.europeanenvironmentalpolicy.eu   An online manual summarizing every single item of environmental policy at EU level.

http://www.ieep.eu/   The Institute for European Environmental Policy (IEEP) is an independent body undertaking research and consultancy on policy across Europe.

PART 5

Issues and Debates

25

Democracy and Legitimacy in the European Union

Stijn Smismans

Chapter Contents

Reader's Guide

This chapter discusses the extent to which decision-making in the European Union can be considered democratic and legitimate. The chapter clarifies the concepts 'democracy' and 'legitimacy', and describes how, although initially the legitimacy of the European polity was not perceived as a problem, it became more problematic as the EU gained more competences. The European democratic deficit became an important issue of debate only during the 1990s after the Maastricht Treaty had transferred considerable powers to the EU. The main solution to the democratic deficit has been inspired by the parliamentary model of democracy and involves strengthening the European Parliament (EP), while also paying attention to the role of national parliaments and regional and local authorities. The chapter also shows how the governance debate at the start of the twenty-first century broadened the conceptual understanding of democracy in the EU, by addressing the complexity of European governance. By looking at different stages of policy-making and different modes of governance, while dealing with issues such as transparency and the role of civil society, the chapter discusses a wider range of issues associated with the democracy and legitimacy of the Union. It concludes by assessing the impact on EU democracy of the Constitutional Treaty and the Lisbon Treaty, and by warning that the current economic crisis is likely to amplify the EU's legitimacy problems.

Introduction

When one thinks about democracy, it is usually the political institutions of nation states that first come to mind. Yet the question can apply also to the case of the European Union. Addressing the question of democracy in the EU is particularly challenging because the European Union is a supranational polity: it is less than a state, but more than an international organization.

To help to address this question, we first need to distinguish between two terms: democracy and legitimacy. According to Bobbio (1987: 19), 'a "democratic regime" is . . . a set of procedural rules arriving at collective decisions in a way which accommodates and facilitates the fullest possible participation of interested parties'. Therefore democracy does not concern only states, but can also apply to any regime arriving at collective decisions. It can therefore also be applied to a supranational or multilevel polity such as the EU.

Whereas 'democracy' refers to a set of procedures guaranteeing the participation of the governed, 'legitimacy' refers to the generalized degree of trust that the governed have towards the political system. Broadly speaking, this generalized degree of trust can result from two elements. On the one hand, people might find a political system legitimate because they are sufficiently involved in the decision-making even if the outcome of those decisions is not always what they desire (input legitimacy). On the other hand, people might find a political system legitimate because they are satisfied with the policy outcomes produced by the political system (output legitimacy). The first aspect of legitimacy can be identified with the democratic process, whereas the second deals with performance and efficiency. Input and output legitimacy are normally combined, but one may be emphasized more than the other. For example, it is often argued that the EU has primarily been built on output legitimacy. However, as the EU has become involved in more and more policy areas, it has become increasingly difficult to base the legitimacy of the European polity on policy outputs alone.

From 'permissive consensus' to 'democratic deficit'

Back in 1957 when the European Economic Community (EEC) was first set up, democratic accountability was not high on the Community's agenda. At that time, the European Community could be considered a 'special purpose association' to which a limited number of well-defined functions were delegated. The democratic nature of the European Community was not a matter of serious concern and could, at this point, be guaranteed by the democratic credentials of the member states. The 'Monnet method', the sector-by-sector approach to European integration (see Chapter 5), was based on the idea of a strong (technical) European Commission, composed of independent Commissioners representing the general interest of the Community. The Commission held the exclusive right of initiative and played a central role as the executive body (see Chapter 10), while the Council of Ministers acted as the final decision-maker (see Chapter 11). The Parliamentary Assembly was only indirectly elected and had only consultative powers. As such, it had only as much importance as the advisory Economic and Social Committee (ESC), which was composed of representatives from national interest groups and stakeholders in the areas of EEC competence (see Chapter 12).

This functional approach to European integration was based on the idea of involving actors with particular expertise in the specific fields for which the EEC had been given competence. Functional expertise, rather than democratic participation, was the central issue of concern. The initial stages of European integration were thus said to be based on a 'permissive consensus' (Lindberg and Scheingold, 1970: 41). There was little popular interest in this elite-driven and technocratic project, and this coincided with a diffuse support for the idea of European integration—or, put differently, the legitimacy of the EEC was based on its output, without raising particular concerns about input legitimacy.

However, as the European Court of Justice (ECJ) defined more clearly the features of the European legal order, based on principles such as supremacy and direct effect (see Chapter 13), and with the Community acting in new policy areas, the daily impact of the European integration process became ever more evident and the functionalist approach became insufficient as a way of addressing the legitimacy of the European project. In this context, the concept of the 'democratic deficit' refers above all to the idea that the transfer of policy-making power from the national level to the EU has not been accompanied by sufficient democratic control at the European level. At the national level, European integration had strengthened the executive to the detriment of the parliament (Moravscik, 1994), because European policy issues are decided and debated by the government (represented at EU level in the Council) rather than by national parliaments. At the same time, the European Parliament was institutionally too weak to ensure democratic accountability at the European level.

Framed in these parliamentary terms, there were two possible solutions to the EU's democratic deficit. Either one could democratize European decision-making by increasing parliamentary representation at the European level by way of the European Parliament (the supranational or federal solution), or one could argue that democratic accountability can reside only in the national parliaments, in which case the priority had to be to limit the transfer of powers to the EU—and in as much as such transfer took place, national parliaments should have the means of ensuring the accountability of their minister in the Council (the intergovernmental solution).

As the EEC's influence grew during the 1970s and 1980s, political decision-makers opted for the first solution, and thus the further parliamentarization of the European level. In 1979, direct elections to the European Parliament (EP) were introduced to strengthen the direct democratic input at the European level. The Parliament subsequently received increasing powers in the budgetary and legislative process (see Chapter 12). In that way, the EU began to resemble a bicameral parliamentary democracy in which the legislative power is shared by two branches: one representing the population of the Union (the Parliament), and the other its member states (the Council).

However, democratizing the EU by strengthening the role of the EP faces two main difficulties. First, the parliamentary model of democracy—in which government is accountable to the will of the people expressed in a directly elected parliament—does not see the role of parliament only as that of a legislature, but also expects a parliament to have control over the executive through its involvement in the appointment of the government and/or its use of a vote of censure. While the EP has gained important legislative powers, its control over the Commission is more limited. Although the Treaty of Rome already allowed the Commission to be dismissed by the then Assembly, this possibility remained theoretical because the Parliament was deprived of any real power in the appointment of a new Commission. The Commission is appointed by the Council from candidates proposed

by the member states and thus tends to reflect the parliamentary majorities in power at the national level at the moment of appointment (see Chapters 10 and 12). As such, when European citizens vote in European elections, their opinion finds expression in parliamentary representation, but this does not automatically affect the composition of the 'executive'—that is, the Commission.

Second, the EU is neither a traditional international organization nor a state. It is a *sui generis* political system, which is best described as a supranational polity. Yet it has been repeatedly argued that this polity has no demos—that is, a 'people' with some common identity or shared values that might provide the basis for a parliamentary expression of democracy. The parliamentary model is based on the expression of the general will in parliament. The general will is (mostly) expressed by parliamentary decisions based on majority voting. In order to get these majoritarian decisions accepted by the minority, the governed represented in a parliament need to have a certain level of social unity, a common identity. However, it is argued that there is no such common identity in the EU, which, as Article 1 TEU states, is still based on a process of integration 'among the *peoples* of Europe'. Contrary to that, some have argued that there does exist a certain common cultural basis in Europe (Kaelble, 1994), that there is general acceptance of the 'idea of Europe' and 'a commitment to the shared values of the Union as expressed in its constituent documents' (Weiler, 1997: 270). This process could strengthen the loyalty of European citizens vis-à-vis the European polity in a similar way to that in which state action strengthens the loyalty of national citizens vis-à-vis the state, reinforcing the national demos. However, the shift in loyalty to the European level and the creation of some common identity seems to emerge very slowly (Risse, 2002). There is no European 'public sphere' in which citizens are informed on, and take part in, political discussions. There is no European media. Communication on European issues is nationally coloured and split into different languages. Although interest groups have started to lobby and organize at the European level, their activities in Brussels remain rather invisible to the wider public and do not create broader debate on European issues (see Chapter 14). European political parties are weak and European parliamentary elections are 'second-order elections', with turnout uneven and low. Hence, despite the increased legislative powers of the EP, the Parliament struggles to engage European citizens in a political debate that they can understand as the democratic expression of their concerns and interests.

- The democratic character of the European Economic Community was not a major issue of concern at its creation. As more competencies were transferred to the European Community, the democratic nature of the integration process became an issue of concern.

- The preferred solution to the European democratic deficit was to parliamentarize the European level, making the European Parliament directly elected and increasing its powers.

- Parliamentarization faces two problems: the absence of a European demos and a weak European public sphere means that European citizens do not participate in a shared debate about European politics; and there is no direct connection between voting preferences in the EP elections and the composition of the Commission.

Maastricht and the debate during the 1990s

The debate on the European Union's democratic deficit over the course of the 1990s continues to be inspired by the parliamentary model. While this remained the conceptual reference point used to frame democracy in the EU it also included an additional dimension with the introduction of 'European citizenship'. Potentially, this could encourage the development of a common European identity and partially address the 'no demos' problem.

The Maastricht Treaty strengthened the legislative power of the European Parliament by introducing the co-decision procedure (now the ordinary legislative procedure, or OLP); the Maastricht, Amsterdam, and Nice Treaties reinforced the European Parliament's control over the Commission, and attempted to create a better link between the EP election results and the composition of the Commission by ensuring that the Commission's term of office coincided with that of the Parliament. Moreover, although appointed by the Council (at the level of heads of state and government), both the Commission President and subsequently the entire Commission have to be approved by the EP. The latter has used this new power to question and

even oppose the appointment of new Commissioners (see Chapter 12). Parliamentary democracy at EU level has thus been strengthened both by increasing the EP's legislative power and by increasing the influence of the EP's elections over the composition of the Commission, although the latter is still far from a system in which the government is the direct expression of the political majority in parliament.

However, the Maastricht Treaty did not only strengthen parliamentarization at the European level, but also acknowledged the criticism of those arguing that democratic accountability is best guaranteed at the national level by introducing the principle of subsidiarity. This meant that, with the exception of areas for which it has exclusive competence, the EU can now act only if, and in so far as, the objectives of the proposed action cannot be sufficiently achieved by the member states. Moreover, the 1990s also saw attempts to strengthen the role of national parliaments in EU political decision-making. Member states tightened their domestic regulations to increase parliamentary control over their ministers in the Council, and the EU began to provide a better and more direct information flow to national parliaments so that they could fulfill this function effectively.

The Maastricht Treaty also addressed the role of regional and local authorities in European decision-making. While many European countries had witnessed a process of devolution of political power from the national to the regional level, the same regional and local authorities were seeing some of these newly acquired competences diluted as the EU began to operate in those policy areas. The member states agreed that regional and local actors also needed a place in European decision-making, and as such the Maastricht Treaty created an advisory Committee of the Regions (CoR), representing both regional and local authorities. It also allowed member states to be represented in the Council by a regional minister in policy areas for which the regions held legislative competence.

The initiatives to strengthen the role of the EP, national parliaments, and regional and local authorities in European decision-making all bear witness to the idea that democracy is, above all, about guaranteeing the control of political decision-making by a directly elected parliament, be it at the European, national, or sub-national level. Yet the Maastricht Treaty also introduced another dimension to framing democracy in the EU, through the concept of European citizenship (see Box 25.1).

BOX 25.1 European citizenship

According to Article 20 TFEU, 'every person holding the nationality of a Member State shall be a citizen of the Union. Citizenship of the Union shall be additional to and not replace national citizenship'.

European citizenship provides European citizens with extra rights that they would otherwise not possess if they were only citizens of their state. Article 20 TFEU sets out a list of such rights:

(a) the right to move and reside freely within the territory of the Member States;

(b) the right to vote and to stand as candidates in elections to the European Parliament and in municipal elections in their Member State of residence, under the same conditions as nationals of that State;

(c) the right to enjoy, in the territory of a third country in which the Member State of which they are nationals is not represented, the protection of the diplomatic and consular authorities of any Member State on the same conditions as the nationals of that State;

(d) the right to petition the European Parliament, to apply to the European Ombudsman, and to address the institutions and advisory bodies of the Union in any of the Treaty languages and to obtain a reply in the same language.

However, this list is not exhaustive. The narrow interpretation of the concept of European citizenship refers only to the rights mentioned in Article 20 TFEU, but that Article itself states that these are only examples of European citizenship rights. The broad interpretation of European citizenship thus refers to all of the rights and duties that the European citizens enjoy or to which they are subject as a result of the legal provisions of the European treaties and European legislation. The Court of Justice of the European Union (CJEU), for instance, has used the concept of European citizenship to ensure the respect of the principle of non-discrimination of a European citizen when residing in another member state.

Citizenship has traditionally been defined in the context of the nation state, and it is thought to be built on three elements: a set of rights and duties; participation; and identity. By introducing the concept of 'European citizenship', the Maastricht Treaty made it clear that the EU provides citizens with a set of rights and duties that means that they belong to the same community. They can participate democratically in this community by voting in the EP elections, for example, and through acquiring rights that they would not be able to exercise if they were only citizens of their state, such as the right to reside in another member state. European citizenship is therefore expected to strengthen the feeling of a common European identity and to provide some extra fuel to make parliamentary democracy at EU level work. However, the Maastricht Treaty and all subsequent treaties explicitly state that European citizenship is complementary to national citizenship, and is therefore not at odds with the idea that democratic legitimacy can reside at the same time in the European, national, or even subnational parliaments.

The debate on European citizenship, and in particular the question of how EU institutions use the concept, has mainly focused on the additional rights that citizens enjoy thanks to belonging to the EU. This is especially the case regarding the rights of citizens to move freely throughout the EU and reside in all of its member states. The expectation is that if citizens are better aware of all of the benefits that the EU provides, they will identify more with the Union. The citizenship debate thus has focused primarily on output legitimacy rather than on input legitimacy (although European citizenship also provides participatory rights) (Smismans, 2009; see Box 25.1).

This link between European rights and belonging to a European 'community' has also been exemplified in the debate at the end of the 1990s about the Charter of Fundamental Rights of the EU. With the adoption of the Charter, the EU wanted to make a clear statement of the fundamental rights and values for which it stands and with which its citizens can identify (Smismans, 2010). The way in which the Charter was drafted was also supposed to strengthen the sense of citizens' identification with the Union by making the drafting process more participatory. The drafting process took place in the first European Convention, which brought parliamentarians from the EP and national parliaments together with representatives from governments. Online consultations and debating activities made it not only a more parliamentary, but also a more open and participatory, process. However, the participatory process around the drafting of the Charter mainly reached an elite of informed and interested citizens, and failed to witness the involvement of the broader citizenry.

EU democracy and the governance debate

Despite all previous efforts to strengthen European democracy on the basis of the parliamentary model, the European Union was still not perceived as more legitimate by European citizens. Events, such as the resignation of the Santer Commission after it faced accusations of nepotism and financial management, made it ever more evident that democracy was not only about the role of parliament, but also about good governance and the parts played by other actors in policy-making (see Box 25.2). Thus, at the turn of the new century, the debate on democracy and legitimacy in the EU became more diversified.

Some scholars argued that the only way in which to resolve the EU's legitimacy problem was to strengthen the parliamentary model, further politicizing European decision-making. This could be achieved by creating a more direct link between the outcome of European parliamentary elections and the composition of the European Commission. European citizens could be offered a clear choice between different (ideological) policy positions, while at the same time the composition of the Commission could reflect the parliamentary majority and its ideological orientation. European citizens would therefore be able to elect their 'executive' on the basis of a European-wide public debate about policy choices. European decision-making would no longer be technocratic and ignored by European citizens.

This strategy was built on the assumption that if European elections were about clear ideological and political choices, reflected in the composition of the Commission, European citizens would engage more with the European debate and identify themselves as active participants in the EU polity. However, what if European political choices were still translated into purely national interpretations through national media? If this were to happen, the effect could be the further delegitimization of the EU, which would be depicted as imposing European-level policies at the national level. This could be particularly problematic where the national government had a different ideological orientation from the parliamentary majority in the European Parliament and the Commission. At the same time, this strategy would fundamentally change the role of the Commission from a motor driving European integration and representing 'the European interest' to an explicitly political body. If a European public sphere were not to emerge as a result of this strategy, such a supranational political body would be criticized on the basis of nationally defined interests and debates. As such, political leaders have been very reluctant to adopt such a radical approach.

Another argument is that framing EU democracy exclusively in terms of the role of parliament and parliamentary accountability is too much of a simplification and, to a certain extent, even misguided. First, when comparing the EU to a parliamentary democracy at the national level, the perfect functioning of the latter is too easily assumed. The EU is often criticized because the EP does not have the right of legislative initiative (which is the prerogative of the Commission), while assuming that this is always a central feature of parliamentary democracy. Yet, in many countries, legislative initiatives emerge de facto from the government.

Second, by focusing on representative democracy, the debate addresses only part of the problem and neglects other aspects of democratic accountability in European decision-making. The assumption is that democratic decision-making is guaranteed by means of parliamentary input, while the 'neutral' implementation of the parliamentary mandate is guaranteed by government and administration. However, this normative ideal has always been a fiction and is increasingly so in modern governance, in which the implementation of the parliamentary mandate is the result of the complex interaction of many actors deploying a multitude of policy instruments. If we want to conceptualize democratic accountability

BOX 25.2 Good governance according to the European Commission

The European Commission established its own concept of good governance in the White Paper on European Governance (WPEG). The WPEG was adopted in 2001 by the European Commission in order to improve both the efficiency and legitimacy of European governance. Five principles underpin good governance and the changes proposed: openness; participation;

accountability; effectiveness; and coherence. Each principle is important for establishing more democratic governance. The principles underpin democracy and the rule of law in the member states, but they apply to all levels of government—whether global, European, national, regional, or local.

Source: European Commission (2001a)

in modern governance, it is not enough to think in terms of parliamentary mandate; rather, we must address the question of who is involved in direct interaction with government and administration in the setting of the policy agenda and the drafting of new policy measures, as well as during the implementation process.

Third, there are multiple ways of conceptualizing democracy. While 'representative democracy' focuses on the electoral process and the representative role of parliament, theories of 'participatory democracy' stress the importance of more regular and direct citizen involvement in collective decision-making. This could involve referenda or more decentralized governance mechanisms. Theories of 'deliberative democracy' pay more attention to the quality of deliberative processes, rather than focus on who represents whom or ensuring direct citizen participation.

All of these arguments informed the debate on European governance that emerged at the end of the 1990s and the early twenty-first century. The so-called 'governance turn' in EU studies (see Chapter 8) argued, amongst other things, that European policy-making is not only about intergovernmental bargaining among member states and power struggles among the European institutions, but also involves many different actors at different stages and in different modes of policy-making. This governance debate resets in several ways the terms of the discussion about legitimacy and democracy in the EU. First, it is attentive to the different stages of policy-making. Democracy and legitimacy are not only about the legislative process and the power of parliament in legislative decision-making; what happens at the initial stage of policy-making, when the European Commission consults widely and interacts with many actors when drafting legislative proposals, matters too. Moreover,

once legislative acts have been adopted, the EU often adopts further regulatory measures by way of delegated legislation. If one wants to assess democracy and legitimacy in the EU, a closer look is required at this process as it affects the majority of EU decisions (see Box 25.3).

Second, the governance debate has made clear that there are different modes of European governance, and that democracy and legitimacy may be addressed differently for each of them. Traditionally, the legitimacy debate has focused on the 'Community method', based on legislative decision-making and a central role for the EP. However, many 'new modes of governance' (NMGs), such as the open method of coordination (OMC), hardly involve the European Parliament at all (see Chapter 15). The OMC was created in 2000 to allow the EU to coordinate the policies of the member states in particular policy fields, such as employment policy or macro-economic policy, but without adopting binding legislation at the European level. The OMC procedure is based on the adoption of European guidelines by the Council, on proposal of the Commission, addressed to the member states. While such guidelines are not binding, the member states have to adopt national action plans to explain how they intend to reach the targets set in the guidelines. They have to report to the European Commission on their initiatives, after which the Commission and Council can propose new guidelines and (for some policy areas) send recommendations to the member states. It has been argued that the legitimacy of the OMC resides in its participatory and decentralized character. Since the EU only adopts guidelines and not binding measures in the OMC, the absence of the EP is regarded as non-controversial. In the end, it is up to the member states to take decisions to implement such guidelines and, in that case, democratic

BOX 25.3   Delegated legislation

Delegated legislation is a common feature of modern govern-ance. Because adopting legislation often takes time, legislators may decide to delegate secondary or implementing decision-making to governments. While delegated legislation allows for speedier and more effective policy-making, it also takes decision-making out of the hands of the elected representa-tives in parliament; this may raise concerns about democratic accountability.

At the European level, delegated legislation is adopted through the so-called '**comitology**' procedure. The EU Council (and the European Parliament) delegate decision-making to the Commission. This does not mean that the Commission can act alone, however, because it needs to interact with a 'comitology committee' composed of representatives from the member states. Sometimes, the Commission only has to take into account the advice of the comitology committee; on other oc-casions, it can be overruled by it.

Comitology has often been criticized from a democratic point of view. It is a rather technocratic process driven by Com-mission officials and representatives from national administra-tions, normally without the involvement of elected politicians (although there are some exceptions to this rule under which there is some of involvement by the Council or the EP). More-over, comitology is a rather opaque process, with few knowing where, how, and why the decisions have been taken. However, some scholars have described comitology as 'deliberative **supranationalism**' (Joerges and Neyer, 1997) indicating that it is not simply a technocratic process, but a process that allows for informed deliberation at the EU level on the basis of expertise and representation of interests in the comitology committees. Over the last decade, the Commission has also taken some initiatives that are intended to make the system less opaque by providing online information on comitology.

The Lisbon Treaty sought to strengthen the democratic char-acter of delegated legislation. Legislative acts, which set out the most important provisions by way of the ordinary or special leg-islative procedures (thus involving the EP), have now two options to delegate to the Commission to take further action. The Com-mission is allowed to adopt either *delegated* **acts** or *implementing* acts. Delegated acts can set out provisions of a general scope, but cannot define the most important provisions, which can only be set out in legislation. The Commission can adopt delegated acts on its own, but given that they are still rather important provisions, the EP and the Council have the right to oppose such a decision, thus allowing some democratic control over the proc-ess by elected politicians. For the less generic and more technical provisions, the Commission can adopt implementing acts. Such acts are adopted through the comitology procedure, without involving the Council or the EP. Compared to the situation prior to the Lisbon Treaty, the new system of delegated legislation thus increases democratic control because of the new category of delegated acts. However, it can also be argued that, as far as the implementing acts are concerned, democratic control may actually have weakened, since neither the Council nor the EP can intervene anymore in comitology, in situations in which they occasionally had a role under the previous system.

accountability is guaranteed by national parlia-ments. Moreover, the drafting of European guide-lines and the national measures that implement them are said to be participatory, given the involve-ment of stakeholders. However, in reality, the stake-holder involvement is often patchy and national parliaments are not always well informed. By con-trast, European guidelines, despite the fact that they are not binding, may have a decisive influence on policy options. Although there remain doubts about the impact of the OMC, the democratic claims made in relation to this mode of governance need to be nuanced (Smismans, 2008).

Third, three concepts have been particularly cen-tral to the debate on the legitimacy of European governance—namely, 'participation', 'civil soci-ety', and 'transparency'. Democracy is not simply about participation in elections and representation through a parliament, but it is also about the partici-pation of multiple actors, such as interest groups, experts, representatives from national adminis-tration, and individual citizens. These actors are involved in many different stages of policy-making, from the drafting of a new legislative proposal to participation in the implementation of the OMC at national level.

Since the end of the 1990s, the EU institutions have often encouraged the participation of civil society in European governance. The Economic and Social Committee (ESC) has presented itself as the ideal insti-tutional form of representation for civil society, while the Commission has taken measures to ensure wider consultation at the initial stage of policy-making. The EU institutions have mainly sought the involvement of representatives from civil society organizations in policy-making, although the Commission has also taken initiatives to broaden general online consultations in which individual citizens can also participate. This has been referred to as 'participatory democracy' or 'participatory governance'.

The way in which the EU provides consultative processes at the initial stage of policy-making is often more extensive than in many of its member states. However, talk of civil society and online consultations do not ensure equality of access to European decision-making, because those with most resources and money are bound to be the most effective lobbyists (see Chapter 14). The debate on participation and civil society is therefore linked to that on transparency. One can distinguish *ex post* and *ex ante* dimensions of transparency when talking about EU legitimacy. Thus, by ensuring the transparency of the activities of the EU's institutions, one can ensure *ex post* democratic accountability. For example, this might involve the EP scrutinizing the Commission, national parliaments controlling the action of their ministers in the Council, or citizens voting for a particular party or group during EP elections. Many initiatives have been taken to increase transparency of this kind. For example, this has involved increasing the information sent by the Commission to both European and national parliaments, and by ensuring that Council meetings are public when dealing with legislative issues. Moreover, the EU institutions, and in particular the Commission, increasingly provide information during the drafting of policy measures. Such *ex ante* transparency allows for improved participation by civil society actors and stakeholders, and would thus also allow for better informed policy-making (and thus increased output legitimacy). Compared again with the transparency provided at the national level by many countries, even within the EU, the EU's initiatives on transparency are relatively far-reaching. However, the EU governance system is so complex and remote that it remains the preserve of an informed elite. With the European Transparency Initiative (ETI), introduced by the Commission in 2005 to increase openness, transparency, and accountability of European governance, the EU also aims to shed some light on this elite when they participate in European policy-making. It does this by providing for a Transparency Register that contains information on interest groups' lobbying of the EU institutions (see Chapter 14).

> ### KEY POINTS
>
> • At the turn of the century, the debate on democracy and legitimacy in the European Union became more diversified.
>
> • Further parliamentarization and a politicization of the European Commission may not be a suitable or practicable response to the EU's democratic deficit.
>
> • The governance debate broadened the conceptualization of democracy and legitimacy in the EU beyond the legislative process, the electoral process, and the power games that persist among the EU's institutions. It did this by looking at the complexity of European decision-making at multiple levels of governance and at different stages of decision-making.
>
> • Participation by multiple actors and civil society, as well as transparency, are key elements in the conceptualization of democracy.

The Constitutional Treaty and the Treaty of Lisbon

The debate surrounding the Constitutional Treaty (CT) between 2001 and 2005 added another layer to the conceptualization of EU democracy. This concerned the question of the 'constituent power' necessary to create and revise the constitutional rules of the European Union. Democracy is not only about participation in European governance, but also raises questions about the initial design of the institutional framework. Before the CT, the constitutional rules of the European polity had always been drafted behind the closed doors of diplomatic meetings at intergovernmental conferences (IGCs), leading to treaty reform. The European Convention charged with drafting the CT aimed at a more open and participatory debate on the constitutional design of the EU by also involving European and national parliamentarians, by using online consultations, and by hosting broader debating events. However, the French and Dutch 'no' votes in referenda on the proposed CT in 2005, which led to the demise of the CT, illustrate the difficulties involved in building the EU's legitimacy on the basis of a constitutional document.

Although not as innovative in democratic terms as the CT, the Lisbon Treaty subsequently provides some new ideas on EU democracy and legitimacy. First, and for the first time, the Treaty includes an explicit title, 'Provisions on democratic principles'. In it, Article 10 clearly states that the Union 'shall be founded on representative democracy', indicating the representative role of the European Parliament, stating that the Council and the European Council are accountable to the national parliaments, and mentioning the role of political parties. By contrast, Article 11 stresses elements that can be described as 'participatory democracy' (although the concept is not explicitly used)—namely, the importance of dialogue with citizens and civil society organizations (CSOs).

Second, the Treaty introduces the 'citizens' initiative' as a new democratic instrument and form of direct participatory democracy (Article 11(4) TEU). This allows European citizens to gather a million signatures to ask the Commission to draft a proposal on an issue on which they consider European action is required (as long as it falls within the competences of the EU) (see Box 25.4). The Citizens' Initiative is likely to stir up the European debate, and make the EU both more visible and bottom-up. However, it also entails risks if EU action does not live up to the expectations of those taking the initiative.

Third, the Lisbon Treaty has strengthened the principle of subsidiarity by giving national parliaments a way of controlling whether new proposals made by the Commission respect this principle. The new procedure allows control *ex ante*, before a decision is taken, which is more efficient than *ex post* control by the European Court of Justice (ECJ) on whether a decision already taken respects subsidiarity. This is because the Court is reluctant to contradict a value judgement made by the European institutions. However, the success of this new procedure depends on whether national parliaments manage to collaborate within the short time span in which the procedure allows them to act.

Finally, the Lisbon Treaty has further strengthened the role of the EP by turning the co-decision procedure into the ordinary legislative procedure (OLP) and by giving the EP a controlling role over the adoption of a new type of delegated acts. The Lisbon Treaty also contributes to further parliamentarization of EU decision-making by strengthening the links between EP elections and the Commission's composition: Article 17(7) TEU now requires the European Council to take into account the outcome of the EP elections before nominating a candidate for Commission President (see Chapter 12).

KEY POINTS

- The debate on the Constitutional Treaty raised the question of who holds the constituent power to design the constitutional rules of the European Union. It failed, however, to create a broad participatory debate on the constitutional setting of the Union.

- The Lisbon Treaty has, for the first time, explicitly defined the democratic principles of the EU.

- The Lisbon Treaty strengthens both the representative and participatory dimensions of democracy in the EU.

BOX 25.4   The European Citizens' Initiative

A European Citizens' Initiative is an invitation to the European Commission to propose legislation on matters in which the EU has competence to legislate. In order to launch a citizens' initiative, citizens must form a 'citizens' committee' composed of at least seven EU citizens being resident in at least seven different member states. The members of the committee must be EU citizens old enough to vote in the EP elections

The citizens' committee must register its initiative before starting to collect statements of support from citizens. Once the registration is confirmed, organizers have one year in which to collect signatures.

The Commission will carefully examine the initiative. Within three months of receiving the initiative: Commission representatives will meet the organizers, so that they can explain the issues raised in their initiative; the organizers will have the opportunity to present their initiative at a public hearing in the EP; and the Commission will adopt a formal response spelling out what action it will propose in response to the citizens' initiative, if any, and the reasons for doing or not doing so. The response, which will take the form of a Communication, will be formally adopted by the College of Commissioners and published in all official EU languages. The Commission is not obliged to propose legislation as a result of an initiative. If the Commission decides to put forward a legislative proposal, the normal legislative procedure is initiated.

Source: European Citizens' Initiative (2012)

EU democracy and the economic crisis

The austerity policies adopted in Europe in reaction to the 2007–08 banking and subsequent sovereign debt crises put democracy under pressure in all European countries (see Chapter 27), but the economic crisis constitutes a particular challenge for the legitimacy of the European Union. As social inequalities and unemployment rise and people experience a worsening of their economic situation, the political system may lose legitimacy and social unrest may emerge. People are likely to feel increased dissatisfaction with the choices made by their political leaders and the failure of the political elite to address the crisis, and may choose a more radical expression of their dissent or turn to populist alternatives.

The economic crisis and the way in which the EU has reacted to it have amplified in an unprecedented fashion all of the main features of the EU's democratic deficit. First, the economic crisis constitutes a real blow to the EU's output legitimacy. The EU's prolonged inaction, and its patchy and delayed policy response to the crisis, have illustrated the Union's shortcomings in the delivery of effective policies. Although the origins of the economic crisis do not lie in the European integration process, but in the lending and speculative practices of the banking sector and the lack of regulation of global financial transactions, economic and monetary union (EMU) now appears for many to be the problem rather than the solution to the economic crisis. Even if the euro survives, European citizens are more likely to be more sceptical from now on towards further steps in European integration and political decision-makers will need a convincing narrative if they are to continue to advocate integration.

Second, the reaction to the economic crisis exemplifies the lack of a European demos and the deficient nature of the European public sphere. The adoption of a common European response to the economic crisis has proved difficult because solidarity among European countries cannot be taken for granted, and political decision-makers tend to communicate with their own national electorate and media in terms of defending their national interest.

Third, the solution finally adopted—that is, giving the EU increased power to keep national budgets under control—appears only to exacerbate the European democratic deficit, because it involves a further transfer of sovereignty from the member states to the EU, while the latter fails to provide sufficient democratic accountability for its new policy-making powers.

The 'six pack'—that is, the six pieces of legislation on economic governance adopted in autumn 2011—and the Treaty on Stability, Coordination and Governance in the Economic and Monetary Union adopted on 2 March 2012 constitute the most important transfer of sovereignty to the EU since the Maastricht Treaty. These new fiscal policy rules further limit the member states' sovereignty to decide on their own budget (even for non-eurozone countries, as far as the 'six pack' is concerned). Decisions on a state's budget are amongst the most important political decisions that a government can make, and, as such, they should be open to democratic input and control. However, while the new rules state that the national parliaments retain sovereignty to decide over their national budgets, this is in fact strongly limited by the margins of budgetary deficit accepted by the EU and the strong policy guidance on budgetary choices. Although national parliaments retain their formal role in adopting the national budget, the budgetary margins and policy options set out in the budget will increasingly be drafted at the European level. The European Commission takes the lead in this regard, with no intervention by either the European Parliament or the national parliaments, and with the Council acting only as a potential (intergovernmental) blocking authority. Finally, by giving the Commission (and the European Court of Justice) increased controlling powers over national budgets, the member states are likely to use the EU as a scapegoat for their austerity policies; this too puts at risk the legitimacy of the EU.

KEY POINTS

- Times of economic crisis are very challenging for democratic systems.
- The European Union's output legitimacy has been called into question as a consequence of its slow reaction to the crisis.
- The solutions to the crisis have amplified the EU's democratic deficit, because it has involved a transfer of sovereignty from the member states to the EU with little democratic accountability; and the absence of a role for the European Parliament or national parliaments.

Conclusion

As the European Union became involved in a broader range of policy areas, its legitimacy could no longer be taken for granted. Policy output (output legitimacy) alone was no longer enough. However, organizing democratic participation and accountability (input legitimacy) in a supranational polity is challenging, owing to the EU's distance from European citizens and the Union's complexity. The institutional set-up of the EU provides for some of the most important elements needed to ensure democracy—namely, that the EU is based on a division of powers guaranteed through respect for the rule of law. In a democracy, decision-making cannot be in the hands of a single authority, but has to be shared by several bodies in a system of checks and balances. Although the EU does not have a strict separation of powers across its legislative, executive, and judicial powers, it is based on a system of 'institutional balance' in which the Commission represents the Community interests, the Council, the member state interest, and the European Parliament, the European citizens' (Lenaerts and Verhoeven, 2002).

Respect for this institutional balance is guaranteed by the European Court of Justice, so that none of the EU institutions can act beyond the powers that they have been given by the treaties. Within this institutional set-up, the body most directly representing Europe's citizens, the European Parliament, has gradually been given more powers. The EU has also tried to strengthen its democratic credentials by providing other checks and balances through the principle of subsidiarity, by keeping up with more modern understandings of democracy, and by ensuring transparency and by institutionalizing consultation and participation. These initiatives have shortcomings.

Yet the main challenge for EU democracy remains the difficulty of linking European decision-making to a broad public debate across the member states, because national politicians and media either ignore European issues or address them from a particular national angle, while turnout in EP elections is in decline. Some therefore argue that the EU can never be democratic and that decision-making should remain national. However, such argumentation often builds on inaccurate assumptions. First, comparing the EU to an idealized idea of democracy at the national level is misinformed, since many of the difficulties of democracy in the EU are not unique to the European level, but are equally present at the national level.

Second, the fact that decision-making does not take place at the European level does not imply that it will 'return' to the national level. In today's globalized world, many issues, such as environmental protection or the regulation of new technologies, require decision-making beyond national borders, while the working of the global market has undermined the capacity of national governments to act on their own. From that perspective, the alternative to European decision-making does not look particularly more democratic, because decisions may simply be taken in less democratic settings such as the World Trade Organization (WTO), or by big corporations acting on the global market.

?   QUESTIONS

1. Why was the democratic nature of the European Economic Community not an issue of concern at its creation?

2. Why does the European Union still suffer from a democratic deficit despite the gradual increase in the powers of the European Parliament?

3. Are national parliaments the real source for legitimacy in the EU?

4. How did the governance debate change our understanding of democracy and legitimacy in the EU?

5. Can you identify elements of 'participatory democracy' in the EU?

6. Has the Lisbon Treaty strengthened democracy in the EU?

7. Why does the economic crisis constitute a strong challenge to the legitimacy of the EU?

8. Would decision-making be more democratic if it were not taking place at the European level, but at the national or international level?

GUIDE TO FURTHER READING

Bellamy, R., Castiglione, D., and Shaw, J. (eds) (2006) *Making European Citizens: Civic Inclusion in a Transnational Context* (Basingstoke: Palgrave)   This book examines the development of transnational citizenship in Europe.

Harlow, C. (2002) *Accountability in the European Union* (Oxford: Oxford University Press)   Based on an analysis of the differing understandings of the concept of accountability in the member states, this book studies the mechanisms through which the EU attempts to hold policy-makers to account.

Kohler-Koch, B. and Rittberger, B. (eds) (2007) *Debating the Democratic Legitimacy of the European Union* (Lanham, MD: Rowman & Littlefield)   This edited book discusses the role of parliamentary representation, the public sphere, participation, and deliberation in the EU.

Kröger, S. and Friedrich, D. (eds) (2012) *The Challenge of Democratic Representation in the European Union* (Basingstoke: Palgrave)   This book provides an analysis of the concept of democratic representation and its different meanings in the context of the EU.

Smismans, S. (ed) (2006b) *Civil Society and Legitimate European Governance* (Cheltenham: Edward Elgar)   This study provides both theoretical analysis and empirical assessment of the role of civil society and interest groups in European governance, addressing the potential and challenges in relation to the legitimacy of European decision-making.

WEBLINKS

http://europeangovernance.livingreviews.org/   *Living Reviews in European Governance* is an e-journal, publishing solicited state-of-the-art articles in the field of European democracy and research.

http://ec.europa.eu/citizens-initiative/public/welcome   The home page of the European Citizen's Initiative.

http://ec.europa.eu/transparency/civil_society   The European Commission explains its relations with civil society organizations.

http://www.eui.eu/RSCAS/Research/EUDO   The European Union Democracy Observatory (EUDO) at the European University in Florence produces a permanent and periodic assessment of democratic practices within the EU.

http://www.reconproject.eu/projectweb/portalproject/RECONWorkingPapers.html   The RECON Online Working Paper Series publishes current research on democracy and the democratization of the political order in Europe.

26

Public Opinion and the European Union

Lauren M. McLaren and Simona Guerra

Chapter Contents

Reader's Guide

This chapter provides an overview of trends in public opinion toward the European Union. The chapter also discusses the key factors thought to explain differences in mass opinion regarding the EU. These include rational utilitarianism (opinions stemming from calculations about the costs and benefits of the EU), perceptions of the national government (domestic proxies), elite discussion of the EU, political psychology factors such as cognitive mobilization (attentiveness to politics) and concerns about the loss of national identity, and finally the role of the mass media in driving opinions regarding the EU.

Introduction

The European Union began primarily as an elite-driven process. The early days of agreements and negotiations were seen as too complicated for the ordinary citizen and so most decisions were taken outside of the public limelight. Hence early observers of public opinion toward the European project remarked on what was perceived as a 'permissive consensus' of public opinion (Lindberg and Schein-gold, 1970), whereby citizens generally held neutral opinions regarding what their governments were doing in Brussels, giving these governments considerable leeway to pursue policies outside of the purview of an attentive public. It was only after the addition of Eurosceptic member states (particularly the UK and Denmark) in the first enlargement (1973) that the European Community (EC) began to consult with mass publics on issues related to European integration (see Box 26.1). Even then, such consultation tended to be limited and was primarily focused around referenda campaigns. In general, through the mid-1980s, EU member governments and bureaucrats were interested in limited public involvement in the integration process. The Single European Act (SEA) seems to have marked a turning point in this regard, as member state governments began selling their varying visions of a renewed European project that would contribute to further economic development of the member states. It is also at this point that more EU policies began to impinge upon national policy-making because of increased economic coordination within the European Community/EU.

Nowadays, it would be difficult to argue that mass European publics are providing a 'permissive consensus' for EU-level policy-making. Referenda since the 1990s have come very close to putting the brakes on European integration. The 2005 referenda in France and the Netherlands on the Constitutional Treaty (CT) and the subsequent rejection of the revised treaty, the Lisbon Treaty, in Ireland in 2008

(see Box 26.2) highlight the important role that the mass public now plays in the integration project. Moreover, it is clear that public opinion is important in constraining integration outside of referenda settings as well. This chapter outlines the leading explanations for differences of opinion regarding the EU. It begins, however, with an overview of general trends in the European public's opinions toward the EU.

General perceptions of the European Union

Since the early 1970s, the European Commission has sponsored regular opinion polls that monitor public support for various aspects of the European project (along with a whole host of other topics). The reports—known as 'Eurobarometer' polls—are published by the Commission and are freely available online (see http://ec.europa.eu/public_opinion/index_en.htm). One of the key questions that has been used to determine levels of support for European integration is: 'Generally speaking, do you think that [*our country's*] membership of the European Union is a good thing, a bad thing, or neither good nor bad?' (See Table 26.1.)

BOX 26.1 Euroscepticism

The term 'Euroscepticism' was first used in 1986 to describe the position of British Prime Minister Margaret Thatcher (*The Times*, 30 June 1986) and later was used in the 26 December 1992 issue of *The Economist* with regard to the increasingly negative German public opinion on European integration after Germany was ordered to adjust its rules on beer purity to conform with the internal market (Hooghe and Marks, 2007). In academic discourse, the term has tended to refer to 'doubt and distrust on the subject of European integration' (Flood, 2002: 73). The terms 'hard Euroscepticism' and 'soft Euroscepticism' have been used to describe the varying types and degrees of Euroscepticism.

- *Hard Euroscepticism* exists where there is a principled opposition to the EU and European integration. It is therefore associated with parties who believe that their countries should withdraw from EU membership, or whose policies towards the EU are tantamount to opposition to the entire project of European integration.

- *Soft Euroscepticism* arises when there is not a principled objection to European integration or EU membership, but rather concerns on one (or a number) of policy areas, leading to the expression of *qualified* opposition to the EU, or a sense that the 'national interest' is at odds with the EU's trajectory (Taggart and Szczerbiak, 2002: 7).

Kopecky and Mudde (2002) develop a four-part typology to describe public opinion on the EU: 'Eurorejects' are those who oppose the ideal of integration and the reality of the EU; 'Euroenthusisasts' support both the EU and the ideal of ever-closer union; 'Europragmatists' do not support integration, but view the EU as useful; and 'Eurosceptics' support the idea of integration, but not its realization through the current EU. As Ray (2007) indicates, although this conceptualization has the theoretical appeal of separating out Europe from the EU, it is not clear whether this distinction is reflected in political debate. Thus, for the most part, experts on the topic tend to assume a range of negative opinions on European integration, including outright opposition to the EU, when using the term 'Eurosceptic' (Hooghe and Marks, 2007).

Table 26.1 Public opinion on EU membership, 1991 and 2011

	EU membership a good thing			EU membership a bad thing			EU membership neither good nor bad			N	
	1991	2011	Diff	1991	2011	Diff	1991	2011	Diff	1991	2011
France	73%	46%	−27%	8%	20%	13%	19%	34%	15%	963	998
Belgium	79%	67%	−12%	4%	11%	7%	17%	22%	5%	1,019	1,009
Netherlands	91%	69%	−22%	2%	12%	10%	7%	19%	12%	1,014	1,004
West Germany	74%	59%	−15%	8%	15%	7%	18%	26%	7%	1,009	972
Italy	83%	43%	−40%	3%	18%	16%	14%	38%	24%	953	985
Luxembourg	86%	75%	−11%	3%	12%	9%	10%	13%	2%	491	490
Denmark	63%	55%	−8%	18%	17%	−1%	19%	28%	9%	979	998
Ireland	80%	67%	−13%	6%	14%	8%	14%	19%	5%	971	954
UK	60%	29%	−31%	13%	33%	20%	27%	38%	11%	1,282	1,234
Greece	80%	37%	−43%	7%	35%	28%	13%	28%	15%	947	991
Spain	82%	58%	−24%	4%	19%	15%	14%	23%	9%	949	947
Portugal	83%	41%	−42%	3%	29%	25%	14%	31%	17%	951	991
East Germany	83%	49%	−34%	1%	18%	17%	16%	33%	17%	1,019	507
Finland	—	45%	—	—	22%	—	—	33%	—	—	990
Sweden	—	57%	—	—	18%	—	—	26%	—	—	1,029
Austria	—	37%	—	—	26%	—	—	36%	—	—	995
Cyprus (Republic)	—	38%	—	—	26%	—	—	36%	—	—	493
Czech Republic	—	31%	—	—	19%	—	—	50%	—	—	1,001
Estonia	—	47%	—	—	10%	—	—	43%	—	—	983
Hungary	—	32%	—	—	23%	—	—	45%	—	—	991
Latvia	—	26%	—	—	21%	—	—	53%	—	—	977
Lithuania	—	52%	—	—	16%	—	—	32%	—	—	984
Malta	—	42%	—	—	21%	—	—	38%	—	—	481
Poland	—	54%	—	—	10%	—	—	36%	—	—	958
Slovakia	—	52%	—	—	10%	—	—	38%	—	—	1,004
Slovenia	—	38%	—	—	21%	—	—	40%	—	—	1,005
Bulgaria	—	49%	—	—	11%	—	—	40%	—	—	953
Romania	—	59%	—	—	11%	—	—	30%	—	—	985
Average	78%	48%	−30%	6%	19%	12%	16%	33%	17%	12,547	25,909

Sources: Eurobarometer 35, Spring 1991; Eurobarometer 75(3), Spring 2011; data downloaded from http://zacat.gesis.org/webview/index.jsp

In the period leading up to the Maastricht Treaty ratification, there was a marked increase in levels of Euroenthusiasm (see McLaren, 2006; see also Chapter 3). By 1991, over 70 per cent of Europeans (on average across the European Community) were claiming that their country's membership of the Community was a good thing. In general, Europeans were enthusiastic about the EC in 1991 (see Table 26.1). The only countries in which less than two-thirds of the public thought their country's membership of the EC was a good thing were the UK and Denmark, and even in these countries an overwhelming majority still thought that EC membership was a good thing.

Since the early 1990s, Europeans have been markedly less enthusiastic about the EU and, not surprisingly, the eurozone crisis (see Chapter 27) has produced some recent fluctuations in attitudes toward the European Union (see Table 26.1). Indeed, by 2011, only in Ireland, Belgium, Luxembourg, and the Netherlands do we find at least two-thirds of the public saying that their country's membership of the EU has been a good thing. In many other countries in 2011, we do still find a clear majority who think their country's membership of the EU is positive, in spite of the eurozone crisis; this includes Denmark, Spain, Germany, Sweden, Finland, Poland, Slovakia, and Romania. Based on respondents who say that EU membership has been a good thing, the decline in support between 1991 and 2011 is quite substantial in Greece, Portugal, Italy, the eastern regions of Germany, the UK, and France. The shift in responses has not all been toward thinking EU membership has been a bad thing; some have moved toward having mixed feelings about the EU. However, not surprisingly in Greece, the change in percentages saying the EU membership is a bad thing is fairly large, as is the case in Portugal. In addition, in several of the newer member states, particularly Latvia, the Czech Republic, and Hungary, support for EU membership appears to be quite low. The British public also remains amongst the most Eurosceptic and public support for EU membership in the UK has clearly declined since 1991.

Perhaps most surprisingly, public opinion regarding the EU amongst the member states that joined the EU in May 2004 and January 2007 is fairly lukewarm (see McLaren, 2006; see also Chapter 17). The cross-time trends in the Central and East European (CEE) Candidate Barometers—that is, polls conducted by the European Commission prior to the entry of these countries into the EU—indicated that, even in the early 1990s, the image of the EU in the CEE countries was not all that positive. Moreover, amongst many of the CEE candidates, citizens became less and less positive toward the EU through the mid-1990s, presumably as a result of the EU's initially hesitant response to the prospect of a CEE enlargement. It was only after the EU finally opened accession talks with these countries in 1997 that its image was bolstered amongst their mass publics. However, levels of enthusiasm for the EU amongst the CEE countries are nowhere near the level of enthusiasm seen in the member states in 1991 (see Table 26.1).

KEY POINTS

- Trends in public opinion toward the European Union are collected through regular opinion surveys known as 'Eurobarometer' polls.

- Enthusiasm for the European integration project was generally on the rise until 1991.

- Enthusiasm for European integration was considerably reduced by 2011.

- Public opinion on the EU in Central and Eastern Europe has been relatively lukewarm.

Explaining public attitudes towards European integration

Ever since the rejection of the 'permissive consensus' on the part of European publics, theories have been developed to try to explain why some Europeans tend to be more positive about the European integration process, while others tend to be more negative. These theories generally fall into the following groups: political economy and rationality; attitudes to the national government (domestic proxies); the influence of political elites; political psychology (including cognitive mobilization and identity); and media effects. We discuss each of these in turn.

Political economy and rationality

In the mid-1980s, the discipline of political science was becoming heavily influenced by rational, utilitarian approaches to the study of politics. More specifically, models of political behaviour were being developed around the assumption that individuals rationally pursue their self-interests. This approach has had a considerable impact on the study of attitudes to European integration. Some of these theories have been *egocentric* in nature—that is, individuals support or oppose the integration project because they have personally benefited (or will benefit) from it or have been harmed (or will be harmed) by it. Other approaches that would fit within this context are more *sociotropic* in nature: citizens of some of the EU member states are said to be more supportive of the European project because their *countries* have benefited from the European project.

With regard to the egocentric utilitarian theories, the contention is that individuals from certain socio-economic backgrounds are doing far better economically than individuals of other backgrounds as a result of European integration. In particular, the opening up of the single market and the introduction of the common currency are thought to benefit top-level business executives the most, who no longer face trade barriers and exchange rate differences across most of the EU. Similarly, individuals with higher levels of education will be more likely than those with little education to feel that their knowledge and skills will serve them well in a wider EU market. Furthermore, those with higher incomes are argued to be more favourable towards European integration because of freed capital markets and monetary union, which makes it more possible for such individuals to move capital across the EU to earn better interest rates. On the other hand, those with poor job skills, educations, and incomes are expected to be the most fearful of a common market and monetary integration (see Gabel, 1998).

These theories are generally supported empirically. For example, *Eurobarometer 71(3)*, conducted in summer 2009, reported that while 71 per cent of professionals and executives claim that their country's membership of the EU has been a good thing, only 51 per cent of skilled manual workers and 40 per cent of unskilled manual workers say the same; similarly, only 43 per cent of the unemployed across the EU think that their country's membership of the EU has been a good thing. In addition, while 39 per cent of those with lower levels of education are happy about their country's membership of the EU, an overwhelming 65 per cent of those with higher levels of education claim that their country's EU membership is good. There are almost identical percentages for income. It must be noted, however, that the lack of positive attitudes towards the EU does not necessarily translate into negativity; in general,

those who are not thought to do very well from an expanded market lean towards neutral responses more heavily than groups such as professionals and executives. Thus the potential losers of EU integration do not appear to perceive themselves as such and instead tend to be generally neutral about the project. Although it might have been expected that these relationships would be reversed in the newer member states because workers and those with lower education and skills levels would eventually benefit from the free movement of labour within the EU, it appears that even in this group of countries it is the educated professional class that is generally most positive about the EU (Tilley and Garry, 2007; Guerra, 2013).

In addition to proposing the notion of egocentric utilitarianism, rational approaches have also focused upon the sociotropic costs and benefits that the EU brings. The EU can provide economic benefits to member states in two realms—namely, trade and budgetary outlays (see Eichenberg and Dalton, 1993). Analyses indicate that, at least up until the 2004 enlargement of the EU, these factors explain attitudes to integration fairly consistently. A country's EU Budget balance in particular had a strong impact on the percentage in the country saying that EU membership is a good thing (see McLaren, 2006; see also Chapter 3). For example, key net contributors to the EU Budget—the UK and Germany—contained the smallest percentage of citizens claiming that their country's EU membership is good (at about 30 per cent in the UK and 40 per cent in Germany). On the other hand, citizens in countries that had been the largest beneficiaries of the EU Budget—particularly Spain and Ireland—were far more positive about their country's membership of the EU, with approximately 65 per cent in Spain and 75 per cent in Ireland claiming to feel positively about EU membership. The trend for trade benefits was not quite as clear, however (McLaren, 2006). Moreover, based on post-2004 enlargement estimates of Budget contributions and benefits, it appears that nowadays being a net recipient of EU funds has little bearing on whether citizens of a country think their country's membership of the EU has been a good thing—that is, the goodwill 'purchased' with EU funds in countries such as Spain and Ireland does not appear to be working in the same way in the newer member states. It is also important to note that, despite the current economic crisis, there remains a high level of positive feeling about the EU in these two countries, although people in the other traditional recipient countries, Greece, Italy, and Portugal, have become less enthusiastic about the European Union in recent years.

Domestic proxies and attitudes to the national government

The arguments presented under 'Political economy and rationality' assume that EU citizens are able to consider rationally the impact of economic costs and benefits of EU membership on their own personal lives or on their countries. The approaches discussed in this section and the next argue that support for or opposition to integration may have very little to do with perceived economic gains or losses. This is because it is unlikely that most Europeans are able to calculate whether they have indeed benefited or not from European integration: the egocentric utilitarian models demand a great deal of knowledge of both the integration process and the economy, and for the ordinary European to come to any conclusion about whether he or she is going to be harmed by the process is likely to be extraordinarily difficult. Thus many researchers have argued that, because of the complexity of the integration process (and the EU institutions), the EU is often perceived in terms of *national* issues rather than European-level ones. This effect is seen most clearly in the context of referenda on European issues (Franklin et al., 1994) in that referenda often turn into a vote on the national government's popularity. For example, the French nearly voted against the Maastricht Treaty in 1992, not because of opposition to the components of that treaty (for example, monetary integration), but because of unhappiness with the government of the day (see Box 26.2). Further, it is likely that the French and Dutch votes in the 2005 Constitutional Treaty referenda were also driven to some extent by unhappiness with the government of the day. Moreover, European elections are generally fought on national issues rather than European-level issues (van der Eijk and Franklin, 1996).

Even outside of the context of referenda and elections, general feelings about the EU are also driven in part by feelings about the national government. As argued by Christopher Anderson (1998), survey after survey shows that few Europeans know much about the details of the European project; so they must be formulating their opinions toward this project from something other than their own knowledge and experience. Anderson's contention is that such attitudes

are in part projections of feelings about the national government—that is, hostility to the national government is projected onto the EU level, while positive feelings about one's national government also translate into positive feelings about the EU.

On the other hand, and somewhat confusingly, other research has argued the opposite. Specifically, when the national political system is functioning well, particularly when there is little corruption, a strong rule of law, and a well-developed welfare state, individuals are less positive about the EU than when they live in countries in which there is a high level of corruption, weak enforcement of the rule of law, and a weak welfare state. In the case of the former, it is thought that some individuals may see little need for an additional level of government when the national government is functioning so well, while in the case of the latter, individuals may look to the EU to counterbalance the weak national political institutions.

Mass publics and political elites

Another approach examines the mass–elite linkages. These linkages can mainly be structured in two forms:

- *political elites* can be instrumental in helping to determine citizens' attitudes in a top-down approach, which views the cueing process as a form of information flowing from elites to citizens (see Zaller, 1992);

- *mass opinion* can also cue elites, in that elites can assume a position on European integration that reflects citizens' views in a bottom-up manner (Carubba, 2001).

Both of these approaches have been found to be correct, but the former has been more widely examined and supported (Franklin et al., 1994; Ray 2003a, 2003b). For example, early research shows that negative attitudes in countries such as the UK, Norway, and Denmark follow the negative connotation of discourse about the EU emerging from the political elites in these countries (Slater, 1982). Some research suggests that there might be different outcomes in the top-down approach, depending on which political parties are doing the cueing and which political party a citizen generally supports (Wildgen and Feld, 1976). Other evidence indicates that, when political parties are united in their position on the EU (as in Siune and Svensson, 1993), they can further strengthen their influence on

BOX 26.2 The constitutional referenda in France and the Netherlands, and the Irish rejection of the Lisbon Treaty

In 2001, EU member states established a **European convention** for the purpose of drafting a Constitutional Treaty (CT) for the EU. The creation of a 'European Constitution' was to be both symbolically and substantively important, and implied a further move toward **supranational governance** in the EU. While the majority of EU member states ratified the CT, in 2005 French and Dutch voters put a brake on the process by voting 'no' in referenda held 29 May 2005 and 1 June 2005, respectively. Why?

While the French are not overly Eurosceptic, trends in support for the EU indicate that positive feelings about the EU have been in decline since the early 1990s (see McLaren, 2006). Thus, in considerable contrast to the Netherlands (as we shall see), the French 'no' vote was perhaps less of a surprise. Indeed, previous experience indicates that even when feelings about the EU are generally positive, votes in EU referenda in France can be very close indeed. This was the case with the vote on the Maastricht Treaty on European Union, in which a bare majority of 51.05 per cent voted to support the Treaty. While there was some discussion that the vote in the French referendum on the CT was really a vote on Turkey's eventual membership of the EU, in fact the 'no' vote in France appears to be the product of two key issues: the state of the French economy; and opposition to the incumbent government. Concerns about France's economic outlook came to light during the referendum campaign. Amongst these were general worries about unemployment in France, fears about the relocation of French business and the decline of the small business sector, and anxiety about undermining of the French 'social model', in conjunction with the failure of the CT to address the issue of 'social Europe'. The latter were predominantly concerns amongst the French Left. At the same time, the government—and French President Jacques Chirac in particular—was becoming increasingly unpopular, so that for many French voters the referendum became a confidence vote. Thus, on 29 May 2005, 54.7 per cent voted against the CT (with 70 per cent voter turnout).

While referenda in France are relatively common nowadays, they are far less so in the Netherlands. In fact, the constitutional referendum held on 1 June 2005 was the first such referendum in modern Dutch history. The Dutch are generally amongst the most enthusiastic EU supporters, and so it was widely predicted that they would provide resounding support for the CT. However, with a relatively high turnout of 62 per cent, 61.8 per cent voted against it. While the referendum was to be consultative only, most major parties had pledged to respect the voters' wishes, whatever the outcome.

Given the widespread support for the EU and European integration in the Netherlands, the big question posed with regard to the referendum result was why the vote went the way it did. One of the key explanations seems to be that Dutch citizens were unclear as to what they were being asked to approve. The referendum campaign had got off to a very slow start, and media and politicians

had struggled to find ways in which to frame the debate about the Treaty. Moreover, in the absence of clear information as to what that CT meant for the EU and for the Netherlands, many Dutch citizens relied on the sorts of cues discussed in this chapter—especially opposition to the government. There may have been some EU-related reasons for the 'no' vote as well, however. One of these relates to the Budget contribution made by the Netherlands; another is connected to unhappiness with the way in which the Dutch government had adopted the euro, because many commentators at the time had argued that it had led to the Dutch guilder being devalued against the euro. It was also perceived that the introduction of the euro had led to an increase in prices. The prospect of Turkish membership of the EU contributed in part to the 'no' vote too, both because of the threat of cheap labour and because of the perceived threat to Dutch culture. Finally, as the EU has continued to expand, two fears have subsequently developed: one is whether this small (original) member state can continue to wield influence in the new Europe; the other is whether Dutch interests can still be protected within the EU. Ultimately, however, the 'no' vote may have been in great part a result simply of the disorganization of the 'yes' campaign.

Since their entry into the EU, the Irish have been, like the Dutch, among the most enthusiastic supporters of the EU. This is in great part a result of the large-scale economic development of the country shortly after it became a full EU member state, with many Irish citizens attributing this development specifically to the EU. Thus Irish votes against EU projects tend to come as fairly major surprises. The most recent of these occurred on 12 June 2008 when the revised CT, named the Lisbon Treaty, was rejected by 53.4 per cent of Irish voters (with a turnout of 53.1 per cent).

Although Irish enthusiasm for the EU might have been expected to guarantee a 'yes' vote, events in previous years provided clues that a 'yes' was far from secure. In 2001, Ireland voted against the **Nice Treaty**, which was primarily stipulating rules on voting and the functioning of EU institutions in preparation for the 2004 enlargement. At that time, the 'no' vote was mainly a result of issues of Irish neutrality, prompted by revised provisions within the Nice Treaty on the EU's Common Foreign and Security Policy (CFSP). The Irish eventually supported a revised treaty that took these concerns into consideration.

Why did the Irish vote 'no' again in 2008? The answer seems to mirror the events in the Netherlands from 2005—namely, the Irish vote appears to be a result of the failure of the 'yes' campaign to inform and mobilize. In the absence of a coordinated 'yes' campaign, the 'no' camp was able to spread fears about the impact of the treaty on Irish neutrality, as well as on abortion laws, taxation laws, and workers' rights. At least some portion of the negative vote also appears to be connected to dissatisfaction with the government. Ultimately, ordinary citizens were—yet again—able to put the brakes on EU plans on institutional reform.

mass publics. Thus consensus across political parties emerges as an important factor explaining public support or opposition to European integration.

Moving away from this top-down approach, Marco Steenbergen and his colleagues (2007) show that both the top-down and bottom-up approaches seem to be correct: political parties are responsive to mass opinions, and mass opinions are shaped also by parties' cues. However, public opinion can cue parties in systems that use proportional representation (PR), but not in plurality systems, while in the run-up to national elections, political parties may be less responsive towards the masses on the EU issue. Finally, leadership is a significant factor (Ray, 2003a): mainstream parties seem to have less mobilizing ability than parties on the fringes of the political system, and there is a stronger disconnection between citizens and mainstream parties with regard to the EU issue. This means that the electorate is more likely to be mobilized by protest parties that frame the EU in Eurosceptic terms.

Political parties may have a weak mobilizing force in post-communist countries, where trust toward political parties is often very low (Klingemann et al., 2006). The EU is highly salient in these countries (Tilley and Garry, 2007), but because of the deep distrust of political parties, the latter tend to be less credible on international issues related to the EU. As a consequence, there tends to be far less top-down elite cueing of citizens on the issue of European integration in these countries.

Political psychology: cognitive mobilization and identity

Early studies of attitudes to European integration conceptualized the project in terms of 'cosmopolitanism' and contended that those who were more 'cognitively mobilized', specifically those who think about and discuss political issues, would gravitate toward the new supranational organization. It was also contended that differences in opinion regarding the European Community were likely to stem from familiarity with the project itself—that is, the more people knew about it, the less fearful, and thus the more supportive, they would be of it. Evidence indicates that those who talk about politics with their friends and family—the 'cognitively mobilized'—are indeed more supportive of the European integration project (see Inglehart, 1970). Moreover, knowledge of the EU appears to have positive implications for public opinion: those who are

able to pass a 'knowledge quiz' about the history and institutions of the EU are, on the whole, more enthusiastic about the project than those who know very little about the EU (see Karp et al., 2003).

The quest for rational explanations of individual-level feelings toward the EU was motivated by the assumption that the European project was mostly economic in nature. Such an assumption is not unreasonable, in that much of the integration that has occurred has indeed been in various sectors of the economy. However, the overriding goal of such integration has always been political—namely, the prevention of war on the European continent. Because the most recent of these large-scale wars, the Second World War, is often perceived as having been motivated in part by nationalist expansion, one of the phenomena to be thwarted was therefore to be the roots of such expansion. While the project as a whole has mostly been sold to Europeans as an economic one, particularly through the 1980s and 1990s, some are likely to perceive it not in economic terms, but instead in terms of threat to one of their key identities.

The body of work known as 'social identity theory' leads us to the firm conclusion that identities are extremely important for people and that protectiveness of 'in-groups' (social groups to which an individual belongs and with which he or she identifies) can develop even in the context of seemingly meaningless laboratory experiments and even when individuals expect no material gain for themselves by maintaining such an identity (Tajfel, 1970). The reasons for this behaviour are still not entirely clear, but the major explanations are that many people use in-group identity and protectiveness to bolster their self-esteem, while others use identity to help them to simplify and understand the world (Turner, 1985).

European integration may be perceived by Europeans as a potential threat to a basic identity that they have used for either (or both) of these purposes—namely, their *national* identities. A Eurobarometer poll conducted in May 2011 asked Europeans about a range of possible problems that they worry might result from European integration. In Cyprus, 24 per cent mentioned that they worry about the loss of national identity resulting from European integration, with 20 per cent in both the UK and Greece also perceiving this as a problem of European integration. In non-member states Iceland and Croatia, 24–25 per cent also mention this. On average, though, only approximately 12 per cent across Europe mention this as a potential result of European integration. Generally, then, it appears only to be a minority in all EU member states who report being concerned about this.

As argued by Liesbet Hooghe and Gary Marks (2004), however, what may be important is the *exclusiveness* of national identity. Thus the important distinction may be between those who hold multiple territorial identities and those who feel themselves to identify only with their nationality. In fact, exclusively national identity seems to vary widely across the EU. In the original six member states, as well as Spain and Ireland, fewer than half of those surveyed by Eurobarometer tend to see themselves in exclusively national terms, while clear majorities of the samples in the UK, Lithuania, Hungary, and Estonia claim to identify exclusively as nationals. Evidence also indicates that this factor is important in explaining general feelings about the EU.

The media: framing the EU

Research on how sources of information can influence mass publics is a relatively recent field of analysis in the realm of public opinion regarding the EU. In the 1980s, it was found that negative or positive media coverage can impact citizens' attitudes, but only when citizens can identify with the views being expressed in the media (Dalton and Duval, 1986)—that is, mass media cannot affect public opinion unless the messages ring true to a great extent. In the realm of public opinion on European integration, news clearly matters (de Vreese and Semetko, 2004) and, as an analysis of the British media stresses (Carey and Burton, 2004), readers of pro-EU newspapers have different views from readers of the Eurosceptic media.

Debate on the role of the media in public opinion has further developed around questions about the competency of the ordinary citizen, and whether such a citizen can take decisions on a rational and informed basis. Citizens can fill their gaps in information through two main channels: first, through education, cognitive skills, and the socialization process, which includes family, peers, and social networks; and second, from lifetime learning through the media. However, the role of the media in filling gaps in knowledge may vary according to the type of source, and the amount and duration of the exposure, as well as the prominence and tone of the media coverage. Further, research shows that 'people with higher education . . . learn at a faster rate' and are also the key individuals seeking more information (Norris, 2010: 3–4). Citizens with higher levels of knowledge are also

more aware and tend to be clearer in their views, ideology, and beliefs, limiting the effect of the media and other potential cues; mass publics that are less aware are likely to rely more on such cues for information.

Day-to-day reporting of the EU in particular has a generally low profile, and can be described as a sort of 'dog who never barks'. Controversy and scandal can increase the prominence of EU debates, however. In the past decade, there are three key areas that have produced controversy about the EU and which the media has covered: the EU has increased its size, and its population is now more heterogeneous, with a higher number of pro-EU, but also Eurosceptic European citizens; there are more opportunities for Euroscepticism to become visible, particularly after the French (2005), Dutch (2005), and Irish (2008) referenda, and the economic crisis; and finally enlargements have provided further opportunities for political elites to enter a Eurosceptic discourse and channel citizens' discontent towards such a perceived distant project as European integration (Taggart and Szczerbiak, 2005). Thus Euroscepticism becomes embedded within the EU integration process and can find an outlet in the media. This is because the media tend to publish or broadcast heated disputes and controversies; this tendency can, in turn, have an impact on the information received by mass publics about the EU.

'Framing' is also an important component of how the media can (be used to) affect public opinion. A frame is 'an emphasis in salience of certain aspects of a topic' (de Vreese, 2002; de Vreese et al., 2011) and, before accession to the EU, in Central and Eastern Europe (CEE) the EU tended to be framed in contradictory ways: it was 'democracy' and 'good Europe', but it was also 'demon Europe' (Horolets, 2006: 171–6). In Poland, newspaper articles used titles such as 'Europhobia', forecasting a future in which foreigners would buy up Polish land while the Polish farmers would starve. The debate became more controversial, particularly during the accession referendum in 2003 (Szczerbiak and Taggart, 2004: 575), and people's preferences became more strongly defined as the media campaign progressed.

Evidence suggests that political communication (mass publics–political party linkage and the media) explain much of the variation in public attitudes towards European integration compared to other theoretical explanations. Further variations can be explained by contextual differences, such as elections, or political and media systems, a field of research that is currently growing.

BOX 26.3 News coverage during European Parliament elections

Media coverage of the EU or European integration is generally limited in EU member states. It might be expected that such coverage would increase during European Parliament elections; however, studies of the 1999 European Parliament (EP) election media campaigns indicated that even when citizens are being mobilized to vote in elections that one would expect to be about European issues, media coverage of the EU is still relatively low and the main actors and debates during these elections are national.

Analysis of the news coverage of the 2004 EP elections (de Vreese et al., 2006) found evidence that there were different patterns across the EU member states. The visibility of EU news in television newscasts and on newspaper front pages had increased since the 1999 EP elections in half of the EU15. Nevertheless, the average news visibility on the newspapers' front pages decreased between these elections (from 6.2 to 5.6 per cent) and, despite the increase in media attention, the main actors of the electoral campaigns were still predominantly national political actors. Old and new member states also showed

a mixed pattern with regard to the *tone* of the news, with a more negative coverage in the old member states and more positive evaluative coverage in the broadsheet press and television news of newer member states, albeit with rather negative coverage in the tabloid press across these newer member states (de Vreese et al., 2006).

In 2009, media campaigns during the EP elections focused on European issues only in the campaigns of the Eurosceptic far-right and far-left parties. The mainstream parties were more reluctant to focus on European issues, unless they had agreed on common campaigns at the transnational level (Davidson-Schmich and Vladescu, 2010).

Overall, news matters, but news on the EU rarely appears on the front of the page and is mainly debated by domestic political actors. In the political parties' campaigns, Europe is most relevant in the Eurosceptic far-right and far-left parties. With turnout at EP elections very low, it appears that the combined effect of Eurosceptic news and no news leads to an absence of EU enthusiasm.

KEY POINTS

- *Egocentric utilitarianism* explains support for the European Union in terms of the economic costs and benefits of the European project to the individual, while *sociotropic utilitarianism* explains support for the EU in terms of the benefits that the EU has brought to the country.

- Political elites can cue mass attitudes, in a top-down approach, and mass publics can cue elites, in a bottom-up approach. Consensus across political parties on European integration, ideological closeness, and leadership influence are all important for top-down elite cueing to occur, while elites who are divided on the issue of European integration decrease political parties' influence on this issue, and intra-party dissent favours a bottom-up approach.

- Cognitively mobilized Europeans are amongst the strongest supporters of the European project. Exclusiveness of national identity may be more important than concern about the loss of identity in explaining hostility to the EU.

- The framing of the EU by the media or elites (via the media) can have a substantial impact on how citizens come to view the EU.

The perceived poverty of the European Union

Since the 1970s, levels of trust towards national institutions and political parties have been eroding, first in the UK and then across Western Europe more generally. Similarly, EU institutions have also suffered from declining levels of trust.

Generally, EU citizens trust the European Parliament more than any other institution, while the Council is ranked as last after the European Commission and the European Central Bank (ECB). In September 2006, *Eurobarometer 65* reported that 52 per cent of EU citizens trusted the European Parliament; after six years, only 41 per cent trusted the EP and only one citizen out of three (32 per cent) trusted the Council. A steady decrease in trust in the European Commission and ECB has also occurred (*Eurobarometer*, 2011c).

As discussed under 'Domestic proxies and attitudes to the national government', research on levels of trust at the aggregate level shows that high levels of distrust for the political elites and negative perceptions of the domestic situation generally correlate with higher levels of public support for the EU (Sánchez-Cuenca, 2000). Those countries in which citizens perceive that their national institutions perform poorly, for example in Mediterranean countries, usually have higher levels of trust for the EU, because joining the EU could improve the domestic situation. Nonetheless, Anderson (1998) found that, at the individual level, satisfaction with democracy and support for the government had a positive impact on support for the EU. His results are more significant in Denmark, but less so in Italy or Ireland. This shows that, again, the domestic context affects patterns of support for EU integration and opposition to it. Anderson's model does not work well for Spain, but the explanation proposed by Sánchez-Cuenca does. Looking at the data on the evaluation of the economic situation at the domestic level, Nordic countries—that is, Sweden (86 per cent), Finland (65 per cent), and Denmark (43 per cent)—have a high percentage answering that the economic situation is 'good', while Italy (9 per cent), Spain (4 per cent), and Ireland (3 per cent) have very low percentages of positive answers (*Eurobarometer*, 2011c). That could explain why Anderson's model is less significant in Italy or Ireland, where citizens perceive a negative economic situation. Nonetheless, data on trust towards the EU

shows that it gains more positive support (34 per cent) compared to national institutions, such as the parliament (27 per cent) and the government (24 per cent) (*Eurobarometer*, 2011c). Overall, although levels of trust towards the EU institutions have decreased, and the alleged democratic deficit of the EU and its legitimacy in tackling the economic crisis (see Chapter 25) are still debated, the EU is still judged a more effective and trustworthy actor compared to national institutions.

KEY POINTS

- Trust in the European Union institutions has declined in the first decade of the twenty-first century.

- Trust in the EU institutions is, on average, higher than trust in national institutions.

- For many countries, trust in EU institutions may be lower because national institutions work relatively well, making a shift to supranational governance unnecessary.

- Many EU citizens are said to trust the EU's institutions because their own national institutions function poorly.

Conclusion

The analyses discussed in this chapter point to several conclusions. The first is that feelings about the European Union seem to range from ambivalence to support. Only very small numbers across the EU are openly hostile to it. However, these proportions do vary by country, and hostility is far greater in countries such as the UK and Latvia than in the rest of the EU. It was also noted that, despite the current economic crisis in the EU, high numbers of EU citizens remain relatively positive about the EU.

This chapter also outlined the explanations for differences of opinion regarding the EU. First, some of this difference in opinion was argued to be *utilitarian* in nature. There were said to be two components to this utilitarian approach: egocentric and sociotropic. Egocentric utilitarians support the EU because it has brought them economic benefits or is likely to bring them such benefits; others in this category are ambivalent toward the project because they have not received any benefits themselves. Sociotropic utilitarians support or oppose the project because of the budgetary outlays that they have received

from the EU, which have presumably increased economic development and growth, or because of the large amount that their country contributes to the EU Budget.

Second, some of the differences in attitudes to the EU are thought to be related to perceptions of the national government—that is, some individuals project their feelings about their own government onto the EU level: when they feel positively about the national government, the EU gets an extra boost of support, but when they feel negatively about the national government, the EU is punished.

Third, the chapter introduced two political psychology explanations for differences in opinion regarding the EU: cognitive mobilization and identity. With regard to cognitive mobilization, it was argued that higher levels of political discussion (or cognitive mobilization) and greater knowledge of the EU both appear to lead to more positive opinions about the EU. Those who do not talk politics much with friends and family, and who do not know much about the EU, tend to be far more ambivalent about the European project. In addition, some portion of public opinion toward the EU is argued to be driven by concerns regarding the loss of national identity. More specifically, individuals who identify exclusively in national terms (vis-à-vis Europe) are either more hostile or, in some cases, more ambivalent to the EU.

Fourth, an analysis of the mass–elite linkages shows that it can take two forms: political elites can cue mass attitudes in a top-down approach; and mass publics can cue elites, in a bottom-up approach. Elites and the domestic context matter, but dissent across political parties and within a political party can favour a bottom-up approach. Increasing levels of distrust towards political parties further undermine their possible influence on citizens.

Finally, recent research on the role of the media finds that news matters and becomes the strongest factor impacting on citizens' attitudes when compared to the other theoretical frameworks. That can assume further normative connotations, because news coverage can be framed strategically, with implications for what information citizens receive regarding the EU.

Overall, then, we have a fairly good idea as to why some individuals are positive about the EU, some are negative, and many others are simply ambivalent. Still, even when we take all of the factors that we have considered in this chapter into account, it is also clear that there is room for improvement in our explanations. Thus it is highly likely that research in this field will continue to develop further alternative theories in the near future.

? QUESTIONS

1. What is 'Euroscepticism'?

2. What explains votes against EU treaties in countries in which citizens are generally positive about the European Union, such as France, the Netherlands, and Ireland?

3. To what extent are European citizens utilitarian in their approach to the EU?

4. How can cognitive mobilization contribute to positive feelings about the EU?

5. What role does identity play in public opinion regarding the EU?

6. Do political parties cue citizens on Europe, or can citizens influence political parties' attitude on EU integration?

7. How can the media shape citizens' attitudes towards the EU?

8. How can trust towards national institutions impact on public support for the EU?

GUIDE TO FURTHER READING

Checkel, J. T. and Katzenstein, P. J. (eds) (2009) *European Identity* (Cambridge: Cambridge University Press)   This book examines European identity after the latest EU enlargement and the challenges ahead for the European political process.

Hooghe, L. and Marks, G. (eds) (2007) *Acta Politica*, 42/2–3 (special issue entitled 'Sources of Euroscepticism')   This special issue examines economic interest and identity as sources of Euroscepticism among Europe's citizens, and how public opinion is cued by the media and political parties.

Leconte, C. (2010) *Understanding Euroscepticism* (Basingstoke: Palgrave Macmillan)   This book examines the process of European integration, and how different actors can engage with the process and oppose it.

Sanders, D. Magalhaes, P., and Toka, G. (eds) (2012) *Citizens and the European Polity: Mass Attitudes towards the European and National Politics* (Oxford: Oxford University Press)   This book presents an overview of mass attitudes in the European Union from 1970s.

Taggart, P. and Szczerbiak, A. (eds) (2008) *Opposing Europe? The Comparative Party Politics of Euroscepticism, Vols I and II* (Oxford: Oxford University Press)   This two-volume analysis of Euroscepticism offers both a theoretical and empirical investigation of patterns of opposition towards EU integration, with case studies and country surveys in the first volume.

http://ec.europa.eu/public_opinion/index_en.htm   The Public Opinion Unit of the European Commission writes regular reports on Eurobarometer and Candidate Barometer Polls.

http://www.europeanelectionstudies.net/   The European Election Studies group has led the way in studying voting behaviour in European elections since 1979.

http://www.gesis.org/en/home/   The German Social Sciences Infrastructure Services is the key European archive for Eurobarometer data, and offers online access to codebooks and data.

http://www.piredeu.eu/   The Providing an Infrastructure for Research on Electoral Democracy in the European Union (PIREDEU) project (2008–11) starts from the previous studies undergone by the European Election Studies group, and provides data and documents on the 2009 European Parliament elections.

http://www.sussex.ac.uk/sei/research/europeanpartieselectionsreferendumsnetwork   The website of the European Parties Elections and Referendums Network (EPERN), coordinated by the Sussex European Institute.

27

The European Union and the Economic Crisis

Dermot Hodson and Uwe Puetter

Reader's Guide

This chapter discusses the European Union's response to the economic crisis that began in mid-2007. The chapter covers the period up to the middle of 2012. It identifies what challenges this crisis poses to the existing institutional set-up of economic and monetary union (EMU) and the EU as a whole. A timeline of the crisis thus far is provided and the main changes to the institutional framework of European economic governance are reviewed. It is considered whether the crisis can be understood as a catalyst for further integration or rather uncertainty over the fate of the euro constitutes an existential threat to the process of European integration itself. Mention is also made here of the potential impact of the crisis on relations between euro area members and the rest of the EU, and on the Union's role as an actor in the international arena. The chapter concludes by discussing how the crisis might unfold and what further responses it may trigger.

Introduction

Looking back on the history of European integration, it is difficult to remember a time when the European Union or its predecessors were not facing a crisis of one sort or another. The 1950s were marred by the political fallout from the failure of the European Defence Community Treaty, just as the 'empty chair' crisis came to dominate the 1960s (see Chapter 2). The 1970s, meanwhile, saw initial plans for economic and monetary union (EMU) abandoned following the collapse of the Bretton Woods system and the first oil shock. The side effects of this economic turmoil lingered on in several member states in the 1980s, with the 1990s witnessing exchange rate crises, as well as a crisis of legitimacy for European integration after Denmark's 'no' vote against the Maastricht Treaty. Concerns over the EU's legitimacy merely intensified in the 2000s, with plans for a Constitutional Treaty rejected by voters in France and the Netherlands, and the Lisbon Treaty passed only after a second referendum in Ireland (see Chapters 3, 4, 23, and 25).

In spite of these successive crises, the process of European integration has evolved, with the EU of the Lisbon Treaty an altogether different animal from the European Economic Community (EEC) of the Rome Treaty. Indeed, major advances in European integration have often followed periods of profound crisis, with the single market programme coming after a period of economic malaise in the early 1980s and progress towards EMU in the 1990s intensifying after a series of crises in the functioning of the European Monetary System (EMS). Some commentators even see crises as the principal opportunity for further cooperation between member states, with Jean Monnet famously arguing that 'Europe will be forged in crises, and will be the sum of the solutions adopted for those crises' (Monnet, 1976: 488).

Mid-2007 saw the beginning of the worst economic crisis in the history of the EU, with the collapse of the subprime mortgage market in the United States (US) sowing the seeds for the biggest banking crisis in Europe for a century, the steepest recession endured by its member states in memory, and a sovereign debt crisis that threatened (and, at the time of writing, continues to threaten) to tear the euro area apart. Whether this crisis is merely the next term in a sixty-year sequence of disruption and advancements in the integration process or the end point of the EU as we know it is not yet clear. What is apparent is that the economic crisis has laid bare severe shortcomings in the way in which EU policies and governance mechanisms work. The crisis also gave rise to a number of ideas on how to change the functioning of the single currency and the EU more generally—some more far-reaching than others.

The way in which the EU has reacted to the economic crisis is extraordinary too. The heads of state and government have never met so frequently as during the crisis, with summits taking place on average every two months between mid-2007 and the end of

2011, and finance ministers meeting more often still. Few of these meetings have dealt decisively with the crisis, but the decisions taken have been momentous nonetheless. In addition to a far-reaching reform of euro area governance, EU leaders have pledged up to €2 trillion to revive European banks and around €1 trillion to contain the fiscal crisis in Greece, Ireland, Portugal, Spain, and other euro area members.

Financial support to member states has not been offered lightly, with Greece, Ireland, and Portugal forced to accept swingeing budgetary cuts and emergency revenue-raising measures, as well as unprecedented surveillance of their economic policies by the EU and International Monetary Fund (IMF). These policies have proved hugely unpopular with the three countries concerned, with the governing parties in both Ireland and Portugal thrown out in general elections in 2011. Greece, meanwhile, has been the site of mass protests and street violence, with the resignation of Prime Minister George Papandreou in November 2011 followed by the appointment of a temporary, caretaker government led by former European Central Bank (ECB) Vice President Lucas Papademos. Italy too resorted in November 2011 to a temporary caretaker government led by former European Commissioner Mario Monti, after financial markets lost faith in Prime Minister Silvio Berlusconi's ability to keep the country's public finances under control.

Political tensions have also been inflamed in those member states forced to provide emergency financial support to their EU peers. Germany, the largest contributor to these funds by virtue of its size, has been a reluctant rescuer. Facing criticism at home for supporting seemingly profligate member states as well as challenges before the *Bundesverfassungsgericht* (Federal Constitutional Court) over the legality of such measures, Chancellor Angela Merkel has been insistent that institutional reforms at the EU level concentrate on stronger fiscal discipline and stringent conditionality mechanisms linked to the provision of financial support.

The crisis has already triggered two initiatives to change the Lisbon Treaty so as to reform European economic governance. Both initiatives were strongly influenced by German demands. The first of these changes, which was agreed by EU leaders in December 2010, provided for the creation of a permanent, legally incontrovertible financial rescue fund. On this basis, the European Stability Mechanism (ESM) was created. The second was a new Treaty on Stability, Coordination and Governance, also referred to as the 'Fiscal Compact', which provided for closer economic policy coordination and a binding commitment to fiscal discipline in national law. Whereas the first of these changes was based on a small-scale revision to the Lisbon Treaty, the second was concluded in the form of an intergovernmental treaty because of the refusal of the United Kingdom (UK) to agree to these measures at a European Council meeting in December 2011.

The Fiscal Compact was signed by twenty-five of the twenty-seven EU member states in March 2012. This treaty required ratification by all member states, with Ireland the sole country to commit to a referendum. Even if the Fiscal Compact is ratified by most or all of its initial signatories, there is no guarantee that the changes will leave the EU any better placed to bring fiscal respite to Greece, Ireland, Portugal, and Spain or to prevent the fiscal storm from spreading to other euro area members. This leaves EU policy-makers facing an uncomfortable choice between ever-more-extraordinary policy responses to the unfolding crisis, on the one hand, and the possibility that the single currency will not survive the economic crisis in its current form or at all, on the other. For some, the crisis could pave the way for a further centralization of policy-making powers at the EU level and the creation of fiscal union. This may include the collective issuing of debt in the form of so-called 'euro bonds' or fiscal transfers through an enlarged EU Budget. For others, member states' unwillingness to cede sovereignty in this sensitive domain leaves the euro area dependent on an essentially intergovernmental approach to decision-making, for better or worse.

This chapter explores how the economic crisis has shaped EU politics and how the EU has responded to the economic crisis. It begins with a timeline of the crisis, before going on to discuss its consequences for decision-making in the euro area and in the EU more generally. The penultimate section asks how the economic crisis is likely to impact the EU's standing as an international actor and the conclusion considers the fate of the EU with or without a functioning monetary union.

The story of the economic crisis (so far)

The economic crisis, by some reckonings, struck the EU on 9 August 2007. The first sign of trouble was a press release from French financial institution BNP Paribas, which suspended trading on three investment funds as a result of difficulties in the US subprime mortgage market. Trouble had been brewing in this market for months, with the second biggest provider of subprime mortgages in the US (that is, home loans offered to individuals with poor credit ratings) filing for bankruptcy in February 2007. Such difficulties were related, in turn, to a sharp slowdown in the US housing market in 2006, leaving many subprime mortgage holders unable to make their loan repayments. This turmoil soon spread to the country's financial sector at large, with US investment bank Bear Stearns announcing large subprime-related losses in July 2007.

Within weeks of BNP Paribas's press release, it was clear that several European banks had been irreparably damaged by the subprime crisis. In Germany in August 2007, Sachsen Landesbank was hastily bought by Landesbank Baden-Wuerttemberg after an Irish-based subsidiary of the former had incurred large subprime-related losses. In the UK, Northern Rock fell victim to the first run on a bank in Britain for 150 years after struggling to meet its own borrowing needs in increasingly nervous financial markets.

In March 2008, the US Federal Reserve negotiated the sale of Bear Sterns to another US investment bank, JP Morgan, after the former had incurred in excess of US$3 billion in subprime-related losses. No such solution could be found for Lehman Brothers, another troubled US investment bank, forcing this financial institution into bankruptcy in September 2008. Sensible though this decision may have seemed to some at the time, given that Lehman Brothers gambled and lost by investing in risky mortgages and commercial real estate activity, it caused an intensification of the economic crisis not only in the US, but worldwide.

EU member states' initial responses to the collapse of Lehman Brothers were ineffective and uncoordinated. A case in point was Ireland's unexpected decision in September 2008 to guarantee Irish banks. This move seriously destabilized the UK financial system as British savers switched to Irish bank accounts on the understanding that their savings would be safer. Fearful of such 'beggar thy neighbour' policies, several EU member states moved quickly to guarantee bank deposits, ignoring calls for a more coordinated approach. A coordinated response from EU member states eventually materialized in October 2008, however, with the European Council agreeing to inject up to €2 trillion into European banks—a move that brought an end to the banking crisis in the short term (see Box 27.1).

BOX 27.1   Explaining the economic crisis

Economists are divided as to the precise causes of the economic crisis, but most emphasize excessive risk-taking in financial markets in the early 2000s (see FSA, 2009). Symptomatic of such risk-taking is the increasing importance of **securitization** since the mid-1980s. 'Securitization' refers here to a financial practice that allows banks to sell on the risks associated with loans to other financial institutions. Initially, it was hoped that securitization would diversify risk should borrowers fail to meet repayments on these loans. In the event, it served only to amplify risk by imposing worldwide losses when US house prices started to fall in 2006.

Many economists also see a link between the economic crisis and the problem of **global imbalances** (Obstfeld and Rogoff, 2009). This problem refers to the accumulation of large **current account surpluses** in Asia and in oil-exporting countries since the mid-1990s, mirrored by the largest **current account deficit** in the history of the US. The causes of these imbalances are complex, with commentators focusing on high levels of savings in Asian countries, high oil prices, the reluctance of the US to reduce consumption, and the tendency of some surplus countries to peg their currencies to the dollar. The consequences of global imbalances are easier to discern, with the savings glut in Asia and in the oil-exporting countries fuelling low **interest rates** in the US and among other developing countries. These low interest rates were a key factor behind the US **housing bubble**, which burst to such spectacular effect in 2006.

The euro area had a current account position of 'close to balance' or 'in surplus' during the first decade of the single currency and so was only indirectly exposed to the problem of global imbalances. The euro area did suffer from its own problem of internal balances, however, with the fall in interest rates experienced by some member states upon joining the single currency fuelling **credit booms** and housing bubbles. Portugal was an early victim of these imbalances, experiencing an inflationary boom between 1999 and 2002, followed by a prolonged period of low growth. The Portuguese economy's failure to recover from this prior shock is one reason why it proved so vulnerable once the economic crisis struck. Ireland, Spain, and Greece, on the other hand, saw credit booms and housing bubbles cut short by the economic crisis—facts that might explain why the **fiscal hangover** from the economic crisis was so strong in these countries.

Falling interest rates associated with joining a single currency is only one source of macroeconomic imbalances in the euro area; another is the failure of these countries to monitor excessive risk-taking by banks through a robust system of financial supervision. Such failures were acute in Ireland, with the Central Bank of Ireland and the Financial Regulator singularly failing to sound the alarm over excessive risk-taking by borrowers and lenders alike. Problematic too was the failure of some peripheral euro area countries to prevent sustained losses of competitiveness during the first decade of EMU. This situation was particularly problematic in Portugal, which saw its unit labour costs relative to other euro area countries continue to rise even after economic conditions slowed in 2002. For some economists, this situation was simply the corollary of developments in Germany, which experienced a sustained fall in relative unit labour costs after 1999 in an effort to restore competitiveness and to shake off a decade of economic underperformance following the country's unification in 1990.

The economic crisis had taken its toll on the real economy even before the banking crisis of autumn 2008 struck, with real gross domestic product (GDP) falling for the first time on record in the first quarter of the year. The causes of this recession were both foreign and domestic, with euro area exporters suffering from the worst outlook for global trade since the Second World War, and euro area consumers and businesses spending less as banks grew more reluctant to lend. In an attempt to counteract these developments, EU leaders agreed in December 2008 on a fiscal stimulus package, with member states committing themselves to tax cuts and expenditure increases valued at 1.5 per cent of GDP.

This fiscal stimulus package provided a valuable lifeline to consumers and businesses, contributing towards a resumption of real GDP growth in the third quarter of 2009. Although the euro area had by now exited recession, concerns over the state of public finances in the euro area intensified after all members experienced a sharp increase in government borrowing. Those countries that had witnessed an end to prolonged housing booms at the outset of the economic crisis were particularly hard hit, with Spain and Ireland posting budget deficits in excess of 10 per cent of GDP in 2009, as the stamp duties associated with buoyant housing sales evaporated and the effects of a very steep recession hit.

Greece was a more treacherous case. Whereas Ireland and Spain began the economic crisis with levels of government debt below 40 per cent of GDP, government debt was in excess of 100 per cent for Greece. This debt level alone provided grounds for pessimism about the state of Greek public finances once the recession hit. Matters were made considerably worse, however, when new Prime Minister George Papandreou announced in October 2009 that previous administrations had concealed the true scale of government borrowing. As a result of this announcement, Greece's budget deficit was revised from 3.7 per cent of GDP to 12.5 per cent, leading to a sudden loss of faith by financial markets in the country's ability to repay its national debt without outside assistance.

Had Greece not been a member of the euro area, then it would presumably have been offered assistance without delay; an EU–IMF financial support package was, after all, agreed with three non-euro area EU members, Hungary, Latvia, and Romania, in late 2008 and early 2009 with a minimum of fuss. That Greece was a member of the euro area complicated matters both legally and politically. Legally, the EU could not offer the same type of financial assistance to Greece as that which it offered to Hungary, Latvia, and Romania, since the latter was carried out under Article 143 TFEU, which applies only to non-euro area members. Politically, member states were divided on the decision to involve the IMF in the affairs of a euro area country. Those in favour of such a move saw the Fund as an external constraint, with IMF officials expected to take a hard line on the economic reforms needed in euro area members. Those against feared that that the Commission, European Central Bank (ECB), and the Eurogroup would be forced to make policy concessions to the IMF in return for financial

support, thus undermining the EU's autonomy over the governance of EMU.

After several long months of procrastination—a period in which Greece's fiscal problems went from bad to worse—the heads of state or government finally agreed, in May 2010, on a €100 billion financial support package for Greece. The EU contribution to this package took place outside the Treaty, with individual member states putting up €80 billion in bilateral loans to Greece. In exchange for this financial support, Greece signed up to a detailed programme of economic policies designed to get its public finances under control. A troika of representatives from the Commission, ECB, and IMF assumed responsibility for negotiating this programme and monitoring its implementation, thus ensuring that key decisions over Greece's economy would, in principle, be jointly decided by the EU and IMF (see Box 27.2).

By May 2010, financial market concern about the sustainability of public finances in other euro area members was intensified. In response, euro area leaders pledged €60 billion via a newly created European Financial Stabilization Mechanism (EFSM) and €440 billion via a new European Financial Stability Facility (EFSF) to provide financial support to any euro area member state that might need it. Ireland became the first member state

---

BOX 27.2 The ECB and the economic crisis

The European Central Bank (ECB) has responded to the economic crisis and its after effects with a combination of decisiveness and caution. When it comes to providing **liquidity** to European banks, the ECB has generally acted decisively. A case in point was the Bank's decision to allocate €94 billion in overnight loans on the day on which BNP Paribas sounded the alarm over problems in the US subprime market. More recent is the ECB's decision to provide low-cost three-year loans to European banks, with more than €500 billion allocated between December 2011 and March 2012. The ECB has been altogether hesitant about cutting interest rates, waiting until November 2008 to reduce the cost of borrowing in the euro area. The US Federal Reserve, in contrast, had embarked on a similar course of action in September 2008.

Between November 2008 and May 2009, the ECB's **base rate** fell from 3.75 per cent to 1.0 per cent. Fearful that these historically low interest rates would be insufficient to prevent the threat of deflation—sustained falls in the overall level of prices—the Bank launched a new 'covered bond scheme' in June 2009. This scheme committed the Bank to spend €60 billion on bonds issued

by private banks. This was a relatively small sum compared to the US Federal Reserve's mortgage-backed securities (MBSs) purchase programme, which saw the US monetary authority spend a staggering US$1.25 trillion between January 2009 and March 2010 on bonds issued by private and public institutions alike.

With the launch of its **European Securities Markets Programme (SMP)** in May 2010, the ECB finally agreed to purchase bonds issued by euro area governments, albeit from investors who have purchased government bonds rather than directly from the governments themselves. This programme remains a relatively modest affair, with the Bank allocating around €220 billion for the purpose as of March 2012. By comparison, the US Federal Reserve spent US$600 billion on US government bonds between November 2010 and June 2011 under its second **quantitative easing** programme (better known as 'QE2'). In September 2012 the ECB eventually announced an unlimited government bond-buying plan under which it can purchase the bonds of countries which have formally requested financial assistance from the ESM and which are subject to a so-called structural adjustment programme.

to access these funds in November 2010. Portugal was next in line, securing €78 billion in loans from the EU and IMF in May 2011. In December 2010, agreement was reached on a permanent successor to the transitory EFSF in the form of the ESM (see Box 27.3).

The euro area sovereign debt crisis entered a new and uncertain phase in late 2011 as Greece was gripped by social unrest and financial markets grew increasingly concerned about Italy. Italy's public finances have long been in a perilous state: the country entered EMU in 1999 with debt in excess of 100 per cent of GDP in 1999 and it remained above this threshold for the next decade, a situation that became increasingly untenable as the euro crisis wore on. Problematic here was not only financial market incredulity over Prime Minister Silvio Berlusconi's inability to get government borrowing under control, but also the fact that the EFSF was considered too small to support a member state of the size of Italy. While Greece, Ireland, and Portugal each account for less than 2 per cent of total euro area GDP, this figure was around 16 per cent for Italy.

In Greece, the appointment in November 2011 of a caretaker government led by Lucas Papademos helped to reassure financial markets in the short term. So too did the agreement in February 2012 on a second EU–IMF financial support package worth €130 billion, alongside a deal that saw a vast majority of Greek bondholders accept a 75 per cent reduction of the value of their loans. Even with these additional measures, however, Greece's fiscal crisis remains dire, with the chances of its debt reaching manageable levels by 2020 remaining slim. The country's political crisis further deepened when national elections in May 2012 failed to produce a stable majority. A new round of elections a month later brought former Conservative Prime Minister Antonis Samaras back to power. Although Samaras won the election on the promise to keep the country in the euro, the government's capacity to implement the reforms demanded by the EU and the IMF was questioned from the beginning. In the case of Italy, the appointment in November 2011 of a caretaker government led by Mario Monti also brought short-term respite, although it

---

BOX 27.3   The EFSM, EFSF, and ESM

Article 122 TFEU allows the Council to grant financial assistance to a member state that 'is in difficulties or is seriously threatened with severe difficulties caused by natural disasters or exceptional occurrences beyond its control'. Whether the drafters of the Treaty thought that an economic crisis could count as such an occurrence is unclear. The fact that the Article was located within the Treaty's Title on EMU suggested that they might well have done. The use of this Article as the **legal basis** for a financial assistance mechanism proved controversial nonetheless. A reluctance to empower the Commission was almost certainly at play here, since Article 122 can be activated only on the basis of a proposal from that institution. The fact that all EU member states contribute to financial assistance granted under this Article was also politically problematic, with the UK government, in particular, facing criticisms at home for supporting the euro area.

As a result, two parallel instruments were created. The smaller European Financial Stabilization Mechanism (EFSM), which is guaranteed through the EU Budget, resembles financial assistance instruments used by the Commission in other contexts. The much larger European Financial Stability Facility (EFSF) keeps the Commission at arm's length. The body does not have a basis in the Lisbon Treaty, but instead has the status of a public limited company (plc) registered in Luxembourg and owned by the member states that share the single currency. The EFSF is managed by a chief executive, Klaus Regling, and its

operations are overseen by a board that includes representatives of each euro area member state. The Commission and the ECB are represented at meetings of the EFSF board, but only as observers, which means that this body remains firmly under the control of the member states.

The decision to establish the ESM can be seen as an attempt to create a permanent successor to both the EFSM and EFSF. Anxious to ensure that emergency financial support for euro area members was fully compatible with the Treaty, German Chancellor Angela Merkel convinced the European Council in December 2010 to accept a limited revision to Article 136 TFEU to allow for the activation of a stability mechanism 'if indispensable to safeguard the stability of the euro area as a whole'. This was followed in July 2011 by the signature of a new intergovernmental treaty setting out the statues of the ESM and authorizing it to lend up to €500 billion to euro area members. Amid mounting concerns that this amount would be insufficient to provide financial support to larger euro area economies such as Italy and Spain, the Eurogroup decided in March 2012 that the ESM and EFSF could run in parallel for one year once the former enters into force. The ratification of the ESM was completed in September 2012 after legal challenges in Estonia, Germany, and Ireland had been rejected. EFSF chief executive Klaus Regling was selected to also become the first ESM managing director.

remains to be seen how he will succeed where his predecessors have persistently fallen short.

Following the turmoil over Italy and Greece in late 2011, pressure mounted on EU leaders to consider a more radical set of policy responses to the ongoing economic crisis. Under the new Fiscal Compact, all EU member states except the Czech Republic and the UK have agreed to codify their commitment to the pursuit of balanced budgets in national law, and to agree to a closer coordination of economic policies in other areas. These commitments can be seen as an attempt to ease Germany's concerns about providing financial support to countries that are perceived as fiscally profligate, but they proved controversial with other member states. Ireland, having initially sought to ratify the Fiscal Compact via Parliament, opted to hold a referendum in May 2012. Concerns over a repeat of the 'no' vote against the Nice Treaty in 2001 and the Lisbon Treaty in 2007 proved unfounded, with just over 60 per cent of voters supporting the changes to the Irish Constitution required to codify the Fiscal Compact. A second banana skin was avoided when new Socialist French president François Hollande, who took office in May 2012, chose not to reopen negotiations about the Fiscal Compact, opting instead to increase pressure on Germany to agree growth-enhancing measures and an expansion of the EU's stabilization instruments, so as to reduce borrowing costs for struggling member states. With the final agreement in July 2012 to provide up to €100 billion of EFSF support to help the recapitalization of Spain's crisis-plagued banking sector, the first of the bigger EU economies started to receive financial assistance.

KEY POINTS

- Problems in the US subprime mortgage market in mid-2007 triggered severe liquidity shortages and a banking crisis in the European Union.

- The financial crisis in turn paved the way for a steep recession, fiscal turmoil, and political instability.

- The EU's stop–start response to the economic crisis included a coordinated rescue of banks, a modest fiscal stimulus package, and, in cooperation with the International Monetary Fund, emergency loans for member states.

- The provision of financial support to euro area member states has proved politically contentious, with Germany insisting on treaty reforms to ensure the legality of this aid and to prevent future fiscal crises.

EU institutions and governance in the light of the economic crisis

For those who posit a link between crises and European integration, the economic crisis should have provided the perfect opportunity for a further transfer of powers to the supranational level, but the evidence thus far suggests that this is far from proving to be the case. Although there has been no shortage of institutional reforms in response to the economic crisis, the changes implemented have confirmed the essentially intergovernmental character of economic decision-making under EMU. This section provides an overview of these reforms, discussing the emergence of Euro summits as a significant new feature of euro area governance, before discussing the new responsibilities entrusted to the European Commission. This is followed by an examination of the potential implications of these reforms for relations between euro area members and other EU member states.

The presidentialization of euro area governance

Prior to the economic crisis, the Eurogroup was the key forum for economic discussion and decision-making under EMU. This meeting of euro area finance ministers, which was created by the European Council in December 1997, assumed an increasingly important role during its first decade of EMU, with the Economic and Financial Affairs Council (ECOFIN) devoting less and less time to EMU matters and the European Council rarely involved in day-to-day euro area business. When it came to the reform of the Stability and Growth Pact (SGP) in March 2005, for example, it was the Eurogroup that took the lead on negotiations. ECOFIN and the European Council merely signed off on the results of these negotiations (see Chapter 22).

The Eurogroup has been busier than ever in response to the economic crisis. It was, for example, euro area finance ministers who negotiated the allocation of capital and loan guarantees to the EFSF and agreed on the statutes of the ESM. The Eurogroup was also put in charge of assessing compliance by Greece, Ireland, and Portugal with the economic policy programmes accompanying the EU–IMF financial support packages. These important functions notwithstanding, a striking feature of the economic crisis has been the extent to which the heads of state or government have come to play a more hands on role in relation to EMU business.

An early indication of this presidentialization of economic decision-making under EMU occurred in October 2008 with the decision by euro area heads of state or government to hold an emergency summit in Paris to discuss the unfolding banking crisis. This was the first time that the member states sharing the single currency had met at the level of heads of state or government. It was the first of several such ad hoc gatherings in response to the crisis. Euro area leaders met, for example, at the Bibliothèque Solvay in Brussels in March 2010 to discuss the unfolding sovereign debt crisis in Greece. Another euro area summit took place in March 2011 to discuss plans for the Euro Plus Pact—an initiative designed to foster closer economic policy coordination between euro area members, Bulgaria, Denmark, Latvia, Lithuania, Poland, and Romania—as well as the financing of the ESM.

Far from being a temporary phenomenon driven by the exigencies of crisis management, meetings of euro area heads of state or government are set to become a permanent feature of EMU's governance architecture. Under the Fiscal Compact signed in March 2010, it was agreed that the heads of state or government would meet informally at least twice a year to discuss issues related to EMU and to provide 'strategic orientations for the conduct of economic policies'. Euro summits, it was further agreed, would be chaired by a president of the Euro summit, who would be elected by simple majority for a two-and-a-half-year term of office.

That the new Euro summit will reign supreme over the Eurogroup is clear from an agreement reached by euro area leaders in October 2011, which states that the president of the Euro summit should both be consulted on the agenda for Eurogroup meetings and have the right to convene meetings of euro area finance ministers to discuss specific policy issues. For some, the presidentialization of euro area governance can be viewed as a retrograde step, with the heads of state or government ill-suited to technical discussions about the functioning of EMU. The failure of successive Euro summits to formulate a decisive response to the sovereign debt crisis certainly speaks to this point. That euro area heads of state or government continued to meet in this setting in spite of their lack of progress, however, shows an unprecedented determination to act collectively even in cases of severe disagreement. One might therefore say that the crisis gave rise to a new deliberative intergovernmentalism among euro area leaders (Puetter, 2012).

The role of the Commission

Prior to the crisis, the Commission's role in relation to euro area governance was that of a watchdog, with responsibility for barking when member states failed to meet their commitment to coordinate economic policies under the Treaty. This role applied both to the Broad Economic Policy Guidelines, non-binding recommendations on member states' economic policies drawn up by the Commission and endorsed by ECOFIN, and the Stability and Growth Pact, which commits member states to run budgets that are in balance or surplus over the medium term and deficits below 3 per cent of GDP. Having raised the alarm in cases of non-compliance with these instruments, the Commission was ultimately dependent on ECOFIN to take matters further. This left EU finance ministers responsible for endorsing non-binding recommendations against member states that breached the Guidelines and for imposing financial penalties against member states that persistently violated the SGP.

A recurring theme during EMU's first decade was ECOFIN's reluctance to play the role of sanctioner, with EU finance ministers showing little inclination to criticize member states for breaching the Guidelines and failing to impose financial penalties under the SGP when it counted (Hodson, 2011a). The most egregious example of the former occurred in November 2003, when the Commission saw its recommendations against France and Germany fail to reach the required qualified majority of support in ECOFIN. Legislative reforms to euro area governance in the light of the crisis, which came into effect in November 2011 as part of the so-called 'six pack' sought to prevent similar situations from arising by introducing a new principle of reverse voting (see Box 27.4).

Member states' reluctance to empower the Commission in this sensitive policy domain is discernible in relation to the other reforms adopted in the light of the crisis. The creation of the ESM would have been the perfect opportunity to give the Commission a central role in the provision of financial support to member states that lose control of their public finances. Instead, the ESM will be a largely intergovernmental body. The board of governors of

BOX 27.4 The 'six pack'

In September 2010, the Commission presented a set of six legislative proposals for reforming euro area governance. These proposals called, among other things, for:

- greater emphasis on government debt in EU fiscal surveillance, with member states posting debt-to-GDP ratios in excess of 60 per cent required to take specific steps to get government borrowing under control;

- more frequent use of pecuniary sanctions so as to allow for financial penalties sooner rather than later under the excessive deficit procedure, and against member states that fail to keep government debt and medium-term government borrowing within agreed limits;

- a new principle of 'reverse voting' according to which Commission recommendations for corrective action in relation to the SGP will take effect unless they are opposed by a qualified majority of finance ministers;

- the creation of an excessive imbalance procedure so as to prevent and, if necessary, correct potentially destabilizing macroeconomic imbalances between member states; and

- changes to national budgetary rules so as to establish agreed minimum standards for, inter alia, public accounting and statistics, forecasts, and fiscal rules.

Following several long months of negotiation between the Council and the European Parliament, agreement was reached in September 2011, allowing the legislative proposals to enter into force two months later. The fact that the Parliament was involved in these negotiations was the result of a change in the Lisbon Treaty, which extended the **ordinary legislative procedure (OLP)** to **regulations** governing the conduct of multilateral surveillance (Article 121(6) TFEU).

the ESM will comprise representatives of euro area members, with the Commission invited to participate in meetings of this forum, but not to be a full participant.

Relations between euro area members

The crisis also revealed specific patterns of interaction between different euro area member states that advocate diverging policy ideas as regards the reform of euro area economic governance. The original institutional design of EMU is considered to reflect a compromise between Germany and France, in which the former insisted on price stability and fiscal discipline in exchange for giving up its national currency, while the latter emphasized a key role for national governments in jointly controlling all key aspects of economic governance and thus providing a political counterweight to the independent ECB (see Moravcsik, 1998; Dyson and Featherstone, 1999). The institutional reform of euro area governance implemented in the light of the crisis has proceeded along similar lines, with Germany seeing the Fiscal Compact as a means of strengthening member states' commitments to fiscal discipline through the introduction of stringent budgetary rules embedded in national law. That the Fiscal Compact also includes a commitment to close coordination among national governments through the formalization of

Euro summits can be seen as a concession to France, albeit one that stops short of its long-standing goal of controlling the ECB.

Smaller euro area member states also influenced the EU's response to the economic crisis. Finland has emerged as a staunch defender of fiscal discipline, and a reluctant contributor to financial support for Greece and other member states. The country's stellar track record of compliance under the SGP may be one reason for this hawkish line. Another is the strong showing of the True Finns, a nationalist, Eurosceptic party that experienced a five-fold increase in support in the 2011 parliamentary elections after campaigning against the financial rescue of euro area members. The Netherlands was another vocal advocate of the Fiscal Compact. Though the Dutch government also faced political difficulties in adopting a fiscal austerity package in April 2011, the euro policy of Prime Minister Mark Rutte received support in the general election of September 2012.

Relations between euro area members and other EU member states

Although the reforms enacted in the light of the crisis do not entail a significant transfer of sovereignty to the supranational level, they do entail considerably closer cooperation between euro area members. For this reason, the crisis has reignited long-standing fears that the single currency might pave the way for a two-speed Europe in which euro area members press ahead with plans for integration at the expense of other EU member states (Tuytschaever, 2000). These concerns came to a head in December 2011, with British Prime Minister David Cameron's refusal to support plans for further changes to the Lisbon Treaty to facilitate closer cooperation between the euro area and other willing member states. The result was that all EU member states, with the exception of the UK and the Czech Republic, decided to press ahead with their own intergovernmental treaty, the Fiscal Compact.

Relations between the euro area and other EU member states are further complicated by the fact that the EU is not clearly divided into two camps, but rather into several groups. Member states such as Poland, which envisages joining the euro area, called for closer involvement in euro area decision-making, so as to avoid decisions that will affect it in the future being taken without it. This criticism has been raised since the beginning of the crisis. Eventually, provisions were included in the Fiscal Compact requiring the involvement of non-euro area members who are signatories to the new treaty to be involved in Euro summits when institutional issues are discussed. Finally, Denmark and Sweden advocated closer EU economic governance throughout the crisis despite their reluctance to join the single currency.

KEY POINTS

- While some commentators see the economic crisis as the perfect opportunity for a further transfer of powers to the supranational level, there are few signs that this has happened.

- Euro area heads of state or government have played a lead role in the European Union's response to the economic crisis and this role will be formalized under the Fiscal Compact, which provides for regular Euro summits.

- The Commission has been given new responsibilities under reforms agreed in the light of the economic crisis, but it has been granted few new powers because of member states' reluctance to cede sovereignty in this sensitive domain.

- These reforms reflect familiar Franco-German compromises about the institutional design of economic and monetary union, as well as the influence of smaller, fiscally conservative member states.

The crisis and Europe's place in the world

Prior to the economic crisis, there was much discussion among economists about the euro's emergence as an international currency that might one day challenge the US dollar. The single currency certainly put in a strong international showing during its first decade, accounting in 2007 for around 20 per cent of daily foreign exchange rate transactions worldwide, as well as serving as a reference currency in the exchange rate policies of more than forty countries in Europe and beyond (Papaioannou and Portes, 2008). Some scholars still remained sceptical about the euro area's international role, seeing euro area member states' reluctance to speak with one voice in international financial fora as being among the most serious obstacles to the single currency's international rise (see, however, Cohen, 2008).

An irony of the economic crisis is that it has provided euro area members with an opportunity like never before to speak with one voice in international financial institutions and fora (see Hodson, 2011b). EU member states put up a relatively united front at the landmark G20 leaders' summits in London and Pittsburgh in 2009. The representatives of EU member states within the IMF's Executive Board, meanwhile, spoke with one voice on the provision of financial support for Hungary, Latvia, and Romania, and did the same for Greece once EU heads of state or government had settled their differences on this issue.

In spite of these developments, the euro's international standing is likely to be diminished as a result of the economic crisis. First, the member states' failure to find a workable solution to the euro area's sovereign debt crisis has hit confidence in the single currency. Indeed, a sizeable number of central banks worldwide have already taken steps to reduce their exposure to the euro. Second, the fact that the euro area and the United States were so hard hit by the economic crisis has triggered a debate about whether there might be a viable alternative to the euro and dollar as international currencies. Significant in this respect was the suggestion by Governor of the People's Bank of China Zhou Xiaochuan in 2009 that special drawing rights (SDRs)—an international reserve asset created by the IMF and viewed by some economists as an embryonic global currency—could assume a greater role internationally.

If the economic crisis has tarnished the euro's image as an international currency, then it has also sullied the EU's wider ambitions to be a global actor. This can be seen most starkly in the area of EU development policy. At a United Nations summit in Monterrey in 2002, the (then) EU15 states agreed, along with other developed economies, to raise national expenditure on overseas development assistance (ODA) to 0.7 per cent of gross national income (GNI) by 2015. Prior to the economic crisis, member states made fairly good progress towards meeting this goal, but development budgets are now under strain as national governments attempt to get their borrowing under control. According to the latest forecasts, member states are likely to spend only 0.48 per cent

on ODA on average by 2015, an outcome that would severely dent the EU's claims to be the world's most generous development donor.

KEY POINTS

• The economic crisis has seen euro area members speak with one voice on a range of international issues.

• The euro area's international standing has nonetheless been undermined by the crisis.

• There are now doubts as to the single currency's standing as the world's second most important currency.

• The EU's ambitions to be a global actor have also been dealt a blow by the economic crisis, with member states' expenditure on overseas development aid already in decline.

Conclusion

To say that the European Union has been hard hit by the economic crisis would be a serious understatement. What began as a localized problem in the US subprime mortgage market in mid-2007 brought Europe's banking system to the brink of collapse, triggered a recession of unusual severity, and sparked a sovereign debt crisis in the euro area that continues to rage. Desperate times have brought forth desperate measures from EU leaders, who agreed a coordinated package to stabilize the banks and eventually provided unprecedented financial support to euro area members at risk of defaulting on their government debt.

Did the crisis leave the euro area and the EU at the brink of collapse, or did it provide the trigger for a big leap forward in the integration process? The evidence surveyed in this chapter suggests that neither outcome has materialized. Thus far—and it is impossible to know what the future holds in store—the crisis has neither caused the EU to collapse nor triggered a radical departure from the existing model of decentralized economic governance within which member states are the main decision-makers, even if they have submitted themselves to new common rules and stricter coordination procedures.

This conclusion holds in spite of an unprecedented degree of collective action in response to the economic crisis, with euro area members agreeing on a long list of institutional reforms and new policy instruments. These reforms include an overhaul of the SGP, an amendment of the Lisbon Treaty to allow for the creation of a permanent crisis resolution mechanism, the ESM, and the Fiscal Compact, a new intergovernmental treaty with far-reaching consequences for how the EU will operate in the future. Economic and monetary union, in short, remains an experiment in policy-making in which member states have pooled sovereignty in the area of monetary policy, but retained control of their economic policies.

With little end to the economic crisis in sight as this chapter goes to press in 2012, member states could yet consider more centralized approaches to decision-making. Member states have agreed to take forward plans for a banking union and there has been much talk thus far about the creation of a genuine fiscal union in which a centralized budget would provide assistance to member states facing asymmetric economic disturbances. Another recurring proposal is that of euro bonds, which would allow for the joint issuance of government debt by euro area members. Such proposals would, if implemented, have profound implications for the EU's already contested legitimacy in so far as they would place new demands on European taxpayers. This raises the question of whether more direct forms of political representation at the EU level are required (see Chapter 25). However, member states remain reluctant to countenance measures that would further weaken the grip of national governments and parliaments.

Whether the reforms enacted to date go far enough or even in the right direction is a matter of debate, with doubts remaining as to whether the single currency will survive the economic crisis in its current form. The most optimistic scenario at the present juncture sees Ireland, Portugal, and Greece muddling through several years of low growth and painful austerity measures, before finally breaking free of the EU–IMF financial support packages. Scenarios at the other end of the spectrum include a disorderly default by Greece that triggers a second systemic banking crisis in Europe and causes the sovereign debt crisis to spread to larger euro area members.

The controversy surrounding the Fiscal Compact shows that, whatever reform steps are taken, they are subject to contestation and political debate. Whereas questions of burden-sharing, solidarity, and the right economic reform strategy are central to the debates among euro area countries, the issue of institutional reform needs to be considered in the wider EU context. The division of the EU into euro area countries, aspiring euro area members, proponents of closer EU27 economic policy coordination, and Eurosceptics further contributes to the challenges the EU is facing and raises the stakes in political decision-making.

For some, even the question of how the EU might survive without the single currency is no longer only a hypothetical one. Suggestions by US economist Martin Feldstein (1997: 72) that the break-up of EMU 'could reinforce long-standing animosities based on history, nationality, and religion' are speculative at best, but a disorderly return to national currencies could see the temporary reintroduction of border controls to prevent large movements of money between former euro area members, as well as protracted legal disputes over contracts previously denominated in euro. What impact such disputes might have on the course of European integration more generally is impossible to say.

? QUESTIONS

1. What are the key characteristics of the European Union's response to the economic crisis?

2. Why and how are the heads of state and government seeking closer control over EU economic governance in view of the economic crisis?

3. Did the Commission acquire new powers as a result of the economic crisis?

4. What is the difference between the European Financial Stabilization Mechanism, European Financial Stability Facility, and European Stability Mechanism?

5. To what extent does the EU develop through crises?

6. Why did the economic crisis affect euro area member states differently?

7. How has the economic crisis affected the relationship between euro area members and other EU member states?

8. In what way does the Fiscal Compact change EU economic governance? Why was it concluded outside the EU Treaty?

GUIDE TO FURTHER READING

Financial Services Authority (FSA) (2009) *The Turner Review: A Regulatory Response to the Global Banking Crisis* (London: HMSO)   An accessible account of how the economic crisis arose, written before the euro area sovereign debt difficulties began.

Helleiner, E., Pagliari, E., and Zimmermann, H. (eds) (2010) *Global Finance in Crisis* (London: Routledge)   This edited book discusses the regulatory causes and consequences of the economic crisis, and includes some of the leading scholars in the field of international political economy.

Hodson, D. (2011a) *Governing the Euro Area in Good Times and Bad* (Oxford: Oxford University Press)   This book discusses the evolution of euro area governance, from the launch of the single currency in 1999 to the beginning of the sovereign debt crisis in 2010.

Puetter, U. (2012) 'Europe's deliberative intergovernmentalism: the role of the Council and European Council in EU economic governance', *Journal of European Public Policy*, 19/2: 161–78   This article explores intergovernmental responses to the economic crisis and the emerging role of euro area heads of state in the governance of economic and monetary union.

Tsoukalis, L. (2011) 'The JCMS Annual Review Lecture: the shattering of illusions—and what next?', *Journal of Common Market Studies*, 49/1: 19–44   This article provides an analysis of the economic crisis in the context of the wider European integration process.

 ## WEBLINKS

http://blogs.ft.com/brusselsblog/   The *Financial Times* Brussels Blog provides up-to-date news on the unfolding economic crisis and other EU issues.

http://ec.europa.eu/economy_finance/economic_governance/index_en.htm   The European Commission's DG EC-FIN offers online access to key legal and political documents on the new economic governance framework.

http://www.ecb.eu/ecb/html/crisis.en.html   A timeline of the economic crisis from the European Central Bank.

http://www.european-council.europa.eu/eurozone-governance/keyevents   A summary of key events within a timeline and relevant documents on euro area governance from the European Council.

http://www.voxeu.org   VOXEU provides a commentary on the economic crisis and other issues from leading economists.

Glossary

1992 Programme The Commission's programme and timetable for implementation of the internal market. In its 1985 White Paper, the Commission listed some 300 legislative measures to be taken to implement the single market programme. These included the elimination of physical, technical, and tax frontiers. *See* single market (programme); Single European Act.

à la carte A non-uniform method of integration that would allow member states to select policies as if from a menu.

accession treaty An international agreement concluded between the EU member states and the acceding country. It defines the accession conditions of the new member state, and the subsequent adaptations and adjustments of the EU Treaty.

accession The process of joining the EU.

accountability The requirement for representatives to answer to the represented on how they have performed their duties and powers, and for them to act upon criticisms and accept responsibility for failure, incompetence, or deceit.

acquis communautaire A French term that refers literally to the Community patrimony. It is the cumulative body of the objectives, substantive rules, policies, and, in particular, the primary and secondary legislation and case law—all of which form part of the legal order of the EU. It includes the content of the treaties, legislation, judgements by the courts, and international agreements. All member states are bound to comply with the *acquis communautaire*.

advocacy coalition (or advocacy network) A network of institutional and non-institutional actors that interact together to defend a common cause.

African, Caribbean, and Pacific (ACP) countries Those developing countries in Sub-Saharan Africa, the Caribbean, and the Pacific that have entered into partnership with the EU through the Lomé and Cotonou Conventions.

Agenda 2000 An influential action programme adopted by the Commission on 15 July 1987, which set out the reforms needed for the EU to enlarge in 2004 and in 2007.

agenda-setting The process by which an issue or problem emerges onto the political scene and is framed for subsequent debate.

Altiero Spinelli An important federalist thinker and politician (1907–86), responsible for the influential Ventotene Manifesto of 1941 and for the European Parliament's Draft Treaty on European Union (1984), which helped to shape the European political agenda of the late 1980s.

amending treaty *See* reform treaty.

Amsterdam Treaty Signed in October 1997 and in force from 1 May 1999, the Treaty amended certain provisions of the Treaty on European Union (TEU) and the European Community treaties.

assent Introduced by the Single European Act (1986), the assent procedure requires the EU Council to obtain the European Parliament's approval before certain important decisions are taken. The assent principle is based on a single reading. Parliament may accept or reject a proposal, but cannot amend it. If Parliament does not give its assent, the act in question cannot be adopted. This procedure applies mainly to the accession of new member states, association agreements, and other fundamental agreements with third countries.

association agreement An agreement between the EU and a third country that creates a framework for cooperation in several policy fields such as trade, socio-economic issues, and security, as well as the creation of joint institutional structures.

avis A French term that literally means 'opinion'. In the context of EU enlargement, once a country has formally submitted an application for membership to the Council of the European Union, the Commission is invited to submit its so-called *avis* (or opinion) to the Council. In its *avis*, the Commission presents recommendations about the process, including any conditions for immediate accession talks.

barrier to trade One of the protectionist technical and fiscal rules, and physical constraints, that carve up or prevent the creation of the internal market.

base rate The rate of interest used by banks as a basis on which to make loans to their customers.

benchmarking One of the mechanisms of the open method of coordination (OMC) that allows for the comparison and adjustment of the policies of member states on the basis of common objectives.

benign elitism The neo-functionalist characteristic tendency to assume the tacit support of the European peoples upon which experts and executives rely when pushing for further European integration.

best practice exchange One of the OMC mechanisms to encourage member states to pool information, to compare themselves to one another, and to reassess policies against their relative performance.

bicameral Involving two chambers. Usually refers to parliaments divided into an upper and lower house.

bipolarity The understanding of the international system before the end of the Cold War as being structured around the two major superpowers—namely, the United States and the Soviet Union.

Bolkestein Directive Directive 2006/123/EC on Services in the Internal Market, which aims to break down barriers to trade in services across the EU. It was controversial because while some believe that it will boost European competitiveness, critics feel that it promotes social dumping.

Bologna Process A series of reforms aimed to make European higher education more compatible and comparable, more competitive, and more attractive for Europeans, and for students and scholars from other continents. It was agreed in the Bologna Declaration of June 1999 by the ministers responsible for higher education in the member states.

brake clause One of a number of clauses that have been created in order to enable the ordinary legislative procedure (OLP) to be applied to the measures for coordinating social security systems for migrant workers, judicial cooperation in criminal matters, and the establishment of common rules for certain criminal offences. The OLP is restrained by a braking mechanism: a member state may submit an appeal to the European Council if it considers that the fundamental principles of its social security system or its criminal justice system are threatened by the draft legislation being proposed.

Bretton Woods agreement Signed by forty-four countries in July 1944, this agreement was set up to support an international monetary system of stable exchange rates. Its aim was to make national currencies convertible on current account, to encourage multilateral world trade, and to avoid disruptive devaluations and financial crashes. The Bretton Woods system itself collapsed in 1971, when President Richard Nixon severed the link between the dollar and gold. By 1973, most major world economies had allowed their currencies to float freely against the dollar.

Broad Economic Policy Guidelines (BEPGs) The 1993 Treaty of Maastricht first introduced a system for coordinating the economic policies of EU member states. Article 121 TFEU states: 'Member States shall regard their economic policies as a matter of common concern and shall co-ordinate them within the Council.' The BEPGs are adopted by the Council as a reference document guiding the conduct of the whole range of economic policies in the member states. They play a central role in the system of economic policy coordination, setting out economic policy recommendations that give a basis for economic policy in both the member states and the EU as a whole in the current year, and which take into account the particular circumstances of each member state and the different degree of urgency of measures.

Budget rebate (or British rebate) The refund that the UK receives on its contribution to the EU Budget, which was negotiated by UK Prime Minister Margaret Thatcher in 1984. The main reason for the rebate is that a high proportion of the EU Budget is spent on the Common Agricultural Policy (CAP), which benefits the UK much less than other countries.

budgetary deficit A governmental shortfall of current revenue over current expenditure.

bureau-shaping An approach to public sector organization, which originates in the work of Patrick Dunleavy. The approach contends that public officials have preferences for the type of work that they handle, and thus they will develop individual and collective strategies to pursue these preferences. Collective bureau-shaping strategies are likely to be pursued to shape organizations by a variety of means.

cabotage In road haulage, the transport of loads that have both their origin and their destination in a foreign country.

candidate countries Countries that have applied for membership of the EU and whose application has been accepted by the European Council.

capabilities catalogue A document listing the military capabilities necessary to carry out the Petersberg Tasks.

Cecchini Report One of the reports published in 1988 in response to the European Commission's 1985 White Paper Completing the Internal Market. The report was drafted by a group of experts, chaired by Paolo Cecchini. The report examined the benefits and costs of creating a single market in Europe. According to the report, the single market would lead to lower trade costs and greater economies of scale, as firms exploited increased opportunities; it was also expected that there would be greater production efficiency achieved through market enlargement, intensified competition, and industrial restructuring.

central bank A national bank that provides services for the country's government and commercial banking system. It manages public debt, controls the money supply, and regulates the monetary and credit system.

Charles de Gaulle President of France 1959–69, de Gaulle was responsible for keeping the UK out of the EEC in the 1960s and for the 'empty chair' crisis, which is said to have slowed down the European integration process after 1966. *See* 'empty chair' crisis.

Charter of Fundamental Rights of the European Union The first formal EU document to combine and declare all of the values and fundamental rights (economic and social, as well as civil and political) to which EU citizens should be entitled. The text of the Charter does not establish new rights, but assembles existing rights that were previously scattered over a range of international sources. It was drafted through a convention and proclaimed at the 2000 Nice European Council. It became binding in December 2009 when the Lisbon Treaty entered into force.

checks and balances The system of building safety mechanisms into government that stems from the idea that no one branch of government should be able do something without another branch of government reviewing that action and, if necessary, halting it.

citizens' initiative One of the new democratic instruments incorporated into the Lisbon Treaty to enhance democracy and transparency in the EU. The initiative allows 1 million EU citizens to participate directly in the development of EU policies, by calling on the European Commission to make a legislative proposal. The first initiative was registered on 9 May 2012.

civil society An intermediate realm between the state and the individual or family; a particular type of political society rooted in principles of citizenship.

closer cooperation *See* enhanced cooperation procedure.

co-decision *See* ordinary legislative procedure (OLP).

co-determination The process by which employees participate in company decision-making through, for example, works councils.

cognitive mobilization The ability of voters to deal with the complexities of politics and to make their own political decisions thanks to the advance of education and the information explosion through the mass media.

cohesion A principle that favours the reduction of regional and social disparities across the EU.

Cohesion Fund An EU fund aimed at member states with a gross national income per inhabitant that is less than 90 per cent of the EU average. It aims to reduce their economic and social shortfall, as well as to stabilize their economies. It is now subject to the same rules of programming, management, and monitoring as the European Social Fund (ESF) and the European Regional Development Fund (ERDF).

collective agreement An agreement reached through collective bargaining between an employer and one or more trade unions, or between employers' associations and trade union confederations. It is normal to divide collective agreements into *procedural agreements*, which regulate the relationships between the parties and the treatment of individual workers (such as disciplinary procedures), and *substantive agreements*, which cover the wages and conditions of the workers affected, although in practice the distinction between the two is not always clear-cut.

collective bargaining The process of negotiating an agreement on pay or on the working conditions of employees between trade unions and employers or employer associations.

collective good A shared good that cannot be withheld from those who have not paid for its use (such as 'clean air').

collegiality A principle that implies that decisions taken by one are the collective responsibility of all.

comitology (or 'committee procedure') The procedure under which the European Commission executes its implementing powers delegated to it by the legislative branch—that is, the European Parliament and the Council of the European Union—with the assistance of so called 'comitology committees' consisting of member state representatives. This delegation of power is now based on Article 290 TFEU.

Committee of Permanent Representatives (Coreper) Committee responsible for preparing the work of the Council of the European Union. It consists of the member states' ambassadors to the European Union ('permanent representatives') and is chaired by the member state that holds the EU Council presidency.

Committee of the Regions (CoR) A Committee set up by the Maastricht Treaty as an advisory body composed of nominated representatives of Europe's regional and local authorities, to ensure that regional and local identities and interests are respected within the EU.

Common Commercial Policy (CCP) The set of principles, procedures, and rules that govern the EU's involvement in international trade and commercial negotiations.

common external tariff A central element of any customs union: a set of common tariffs, agreed by all members, imposed on goods coming into the union from outside its borders.

common market An economic agreement that extends cooperation beyond a customs union, to provide for the free movement of goods, services, capital, and labour.

common market organization (CMO) An organization operating for individual items of agricultural produce that involves public intervention, a price guaranteed for farmers, and levies at the EU's borders.

common strategy Overall policy guidelines for EU activities within individual non-member countries.

Communitarization The shift of policy activity from the intergovernmental pillars to the Community pillar.

Community method The use of the 'established' process of decision-making, which involves a Commission legislative initiative being agreed by the Council, and now usually the European Parliament. It also implies that the European Court of Justice will have jurisdiction over any decision taken.

Community preference The preference and price advantage from which EU agricultural products benefit in comparison with imported products.

competence The legal capacity to deal with a matter.

compulsory spending (Formerly) That part of the EU's Budget on which only the EU Council could make a decision. The Lisbon Treaty has done away with the distinction between compulsory and non-compulsory spending. In the post-Lisbon context, the European Parliament and the EU Council decide together on the whole EU Budget. The underlying principle and the amount are legally determined by the treaties, secondary legislation, conventions, international treaties, or private contracts. In addition, the Lisbon Treaty simplifies the decision-taking procedure and makes the long-term Budget plan, or financial perspectives, legally binding.

conciliation (procedure) The third stage of the ordinary legislative procedure (OLP), at which point an equal number of representatives of the Parliament and Council get together to try to work out an agreement acceptable to all. The conciliation procedure always applies if the EU Council does not approve all of the amendments of the European Parliament adopted at its second reading.

conciliation committee A committee that, as part of the conciliation procedure, brings together equal numbers of representatives from the European Parliament and the EU Council to broker an inter-institutional agreement on outstanding problems with the proposed legislation. The committee has to be convened within six weeks (which may be extended by two weeks on the initiative of either institution) after the Council's second reading. The Committee has six (or eight) weeks in which to draw up a 'joint text' from the date of its first meeting. Within a period of six (or eight) weeks, the joint text is submitted by the presidents of the Parliament and Council delegations for approval, without any possibility of amendment. If the conciliation committee does not reach an agreement or if the 'joint text' is not approved by the Parliament or the Council, the act is deemed not to have been adopted.

conditionality (EU enlargement) The principle that applicant states must meet certain conditions before they can become EU member states; (EU external relations) provisions that make the granting of EU aid conditional on good governance, observance of human rights, and the introduction of market economics.

confederation A political model that involves a loose grouping of states, characterized by the fact that the centre has fewer powers than the states or regions.

consensual (decision-making) A type of decision-making that involves the agreement of all, even where this is not formally a requirement.

consolidated treaty A treaty that incorporates all of the amendments made since the original Treaty of Rome.

Constitutional Convention *See* Convention (on the Future of Europe).

Constitutional Treaty Sometimes known as the 'EU Constitution', a treaty signed on 24 October 2004. It was not ratified due to negative referenda in France and the Netherlands in 2005.

constitutionalization The formalization of the rules of the game, which, in an EU context, might involve a process whereby the treaties become over time—de jure or only de facto—a constitution.

constructive abstention A provision that allows member states to abstain in the Council on Common Foreign and Security Policy (CFSP) decisions, without blocking a unanimous agreement.

constructivism A theoretical approach that claims that politics is affected as much by ideas as by power. It argues that the fundamental structures of political life are social rather than material.

consultation (procedure) A special legislative procedure, under Article 289 TFEU, whereby the European Parliament is asked for its opinion on proposed legislation before the Council adopts it. The Parliament may approve or reject a legislative proposal, or propose amendments to it. The Council is not legally obliged to take account of Parliament's opinion, but in line with the case law of the European Court of Justice, it must not take a decision without having received it.

Convention (on the Future of Europe) A body set up in 2002 to debate alternative models and visions of the EU, and to prepare a draft constitution that could be used as the basis of discussion in the intergovernmental conference of 2004.

convergence criteria The rules that member states have to meet before they can join economic and monetary union (EMU) in 1999.

convertibility (of currencies) The extent to which one currency is freely exchangeable into other currencies.

cooperation Usually implies government-to-government relations (with little supranational involvement).

cooperation procedure A legislative procedure introduced in the Single European Act (Article 252, ex 198c EC), which allowed the European Parliament a second reading of draft legislation. Since Amsterdam, it had been hardly used, because most policies originally falling under cooperation came under the then co-decision procedure (now ordinary legislative procedure, or OLP); the Lisbon Treaty repealed the cooperation procedure.

Copenhagen criteria The criteria that applicant states have to meet in order to join the EU. It was agreed at the Copenhagen European Council meeting in 1993.

core Europe (or 'hard core') The idea that a small group of countries able and willing to enter into closer cooperation with one another might 'leave behind' the less enthusiastically integrationist members of the EU.

co-regulation The mechanism whereby an EU legal act entrusts the attainment of the objectives defined by the legislative authority to parties that are recognized in the field, such as economic operators, the social partners, non-governmental organizations (NGOs), or associations. It is one of the modes of governance developed in the context of the Lisbon Strategy to simplify and improve regulation in the EU.

corporatism A system of interest representation in which the constituent units are organized into a limited number of singular, compulsory, non-competitive, hierarchically ordered, and functionally differentiated categories, recognized or licensed (if not created) by the state and granted a deliberate representational monopoly within their respective categories, in exchange for observing certain controls on their selection of leaders and articulation of demands and supports.

cosmopolitanism The idea that citizens are 'citizens of the world'.

Council of Europe A European political organization founded on 5 May 1949 by ten countries and distinct from the EU. The Council of Europe, based in Strasbourg, has forty-seven member countries. It seeks to develop throughout Europe common and democratic principles based on the European Convention on Human Rights (ECHR) and other reference texts on the protection of individuals.

covered bond scheme Under such a scheme, bonds are issued to free up cash, tied up in assets such as mortgages, for on-lending. Covered bonds allow the issuing bank to raise funds at a lower cost. They are generally fixed-interest instruments, thus the interest rate risk for the issuing bank is known and can be suitably managed.

credit boom Part of the credit boom–bust cycle, an episode characterized by a sustained increase in several economic indicators usually followed by a sharp and rapid contraction.

credit condition One of the criteria used for the grant of credit by banks.

critical juncture A period of institutional flux within the historical institutionalist model of institutional development. This literature assumes a dual model characterized by relatively long periods of path-dependent institutional stability and reproduction that are punctuated occasionally by brief phases of institutional flux (the 'critical junctures'), during which more dramatic change is possible. Junctures are critical because they place institutional arrangements on paths or trajectories that are then very difficult to alter.

cueing A form of information flowing from elites to citizens to illustrate mass–elite linkages. These linkages can mainly be structured in two forms. Political elites can be instrumental in helping to determine citizens' attitudes in a top-down approach, or elites can assume a position on European integration that reflects citizens' views, in a bottom-up manner.

current account deficit A negative difference between a country's savings and its investment.

current account surplus A positive difference between a country's savings and its investment.

customs union An economic association of states based on an agreement to eliminate tariffs and other obstacles to trade, and which also includes a common trade policy vis-à-vis third countries, usually by establishing a common external tariff on goods imported into the union.

Davignon Report A document issued by EC foreign ministers in 1970, outlining how the Community might develop its own foreign policy and setting out some initial steps to that end.

decoupling The divorcing of the grant of direct aid to farmers from production in the context of the Common Agricultural Policy (CAP).

deepening An intensification of integration processes and structures.

delegated act A new category of legal act created under the Treaty of Lisbon in which the legislator delegates the power to adopt acts amending non-essential elements of a legislative act to the Commission. Delegated acts may specify certain technical details or they may consist of a subsequent amendment to certain elements of a legislative act. The legislator can therefore concentrate on policy direction and objectives without entering into overly technical debates.

delegated legislation Legislation made usually by executive bodies on behalf of legislatures. It often involves the making of administrative rules and the filling in of gaps in existing legislation.

delegation The handing over of powers by a legitimate political institution to a body that then acts on its behalf.

deliberative intergovernmentalism A version of contemporary EU intergovernmentalism that stresses the relevance of policy deliberation. It refers to two different dimensions regarding the analysis of intergovernmentalism; the first concerns the question of what makes intergovernmental relations dependent on deliberative processes; the second relates to the question of under what conditions we should expect policy deliberation to flourish in an intergovernmental context and what would this imply.

Delors Report The report drafted by central bankers in 1989, which later formed the basis of the monetary union section of the Treaty on European Union. The Committee that produced the report was chaired by Jacques Delors, then Commission President.

democratic deficit The loss of democracy caused by the transfer of powers to the European institutions and to member state executives arising out of European integration. It implies that representative institutions (parliaments) lose out in this process.

demos The people of a nation as a political unit; a politically defined public community.

dependent variable The object of study; the phenomenon that one is trying to explain.

derogation A temporary exception to legislation.

Die Linke Literally, 'The Left', a democratic socialist political party in Germany, founded in 2007.

differentiated integration *See* differentiation.

differentiation The idea that subsets of member states might engage in European integration projects that do not involve all existing members; contrasts with the notion of the EU as a uniform Community.

diffuse interest group A type of interest group that is characterized by its broad scope and lack of clear membership. These include, for example, religious, social, human rights, consumer, and environmental groups.

direct action A case brought directly before the European courts.

direct effect A principle of EU law by which provisions of EU law are to be enforced in national courts, and which imposes obligations on those against whom they are enforced.

direct implementation The putting into effect of European legislation by the European institutions rather than by national governments.

direct support In the context of the Common Agricultural Policy (CAP), the agricultural subsidies given directly to farmers, decoupled from production.

directive A legislative instrument that lays down certain end results that must be achieved in every member state. National authorities have to adapt their laws to meet these goals, but are free to decide how to do so. Directives may concern one or more member states, or all of them.

dirigiste *See* interventionist.

Doha Development Round The latest round of trade negotiations among the World Trade Organization (WTO) membership, aiming to achieve major reform of the international trading system through the introduction of lower trade barriers and revised trade rules. The work programme covers some twenty areas of trade and its agenda is fundamentally to improve the trading prospects of developing countries.

domestic proxy A representative or an agent authorized to act on behalf of others. In the political context, a national government is authorized to act on behalf of citizens.

Dooge Committee A committee set up after the Fontainebleau European Council in 1984 to discuss the institutional reforms required to complete the internal market and to solve the paralysis provoked by the excessive use of unanimity in the Council. It submitted its final report to the European Council in March 1985, which identified a number of priority objectives necessary to deepen integration, such as restricting the use of unanimity in the Council, strengthening the legislative role of the European Parliament, and giving more executive power to the Commission. The Committee conclusions paved the way to the Single European Act.

dual majority (or double majority) (system of voting) A voting system that takes into consideration the number of votes and population necessary to achieve a majority. The Treaty of Lisbon simplifies the system with a view to improving its efficiency. It abolishes the weighting of votes and establishes a dual majority system for adopting decisions. Thus a qualified majority is achieved if it covers at least 55 per cent of member states representing at least 65 per cent of the population of the EU. Where the Council does not act on a proposal from the Commission, the qualified majority should cover at least 72 per cent of member states representing at least 65 per cent of the population. The Treaty of Lisbon also provides for a blocking minority composed of at least four member states representing over 35 per cent of the EU population. This new system of qualified majority voting (QMV) will apply with effect from 1 November 2014. However, until 31 March 2017, any member state may request, on a case-by-case basis, that a decision is taken in accordance with the rules in force before 1 November 2014 (that is, in accordance with the qualified majority, as defined by the Treaty of Nice).

dumping Selling at below cost, often to force competition out of the market.

economic and monetary union (EMU) A form of integration that combines the features of the economic union (which implies the existence of a single market, but also a high degree of coordination of the most important areas of economic policy and market regulation, as well as monetary policies and income redistribution policies) and the monetary union, which implies further integration in the area of currency cooperation. The process involves three stages and the fulfilment of the so-called 'convergence criteria' by all participating countries.

economic union A form of integration that implies the existence of a single market (and therefore free movement of goods, services, labour, and capital among the participating states and common rules, tariffs, and so on, vis-à-vis third countries), but also a high degree of coordination of the most important areas of economic policy and market regulation, as well as monetary policies and income redistribution policies.

Economist An advocate of one of the possible economic strategies with which to achieve economic and monetary union (EMU); in the 1960s and 1970s, the Economist camp postulated that economic policies needed to be coordinated before fixing exchange rates or introducing a single currency. *Cf.* Monetarist

efficiency The ratio of output to input of any system.

elite pluralism A system of interest mediation in which access to the EU consultative institutions is open, but competitive, resulting in biased access patterns.

elite socialization Closely related to the neo-functionalist idea of political spillover, this theory posits that European integration promotes shifts of loyalty among civil servants and other elite actors; thus members of the European Parliament (MEPs) will tend to become more European in their outlook, although this may be disputed empirically.

elitist A characteristic describing the tendency of neo-functionalists to see European integration as driven by functional and technocratic needs. Although not apolitical, it sees little role for democratic and accountable governance.

embedded liberalism A term introduced by John Ruggie to describe the policy orientation of the interwar international economic order and to explain the social conditions upon which it rested. This order was based on two doctrines: the first is that states should cooperate in devising and implementing international economic institutions to facilitate international market integration and to preserve international economic stability; the second is that states should retain sufficient autonomy to pursue economic and social objectives domestically.

emergency brake *See* brake clause.

'empty chair' crisis The crisis that affected the European Community after July 1965 when France boycotted the meetings of the Council in opposition to Commission proposals addressing the financing of the Common Agricultural Policy (CAP). France insisted on a political agreement that would clarify the role of the Commission and majority voting if it were to participate again. This crisis was resolved in the Luxembourg Compromise in January 1966. *See* Luxembourg Compromise.

enforcement The process of ensuring that EU rules are implemented. It may involve taking action in the European courts.

engrenage The enmeshing of EU elites, which may arise out of a process of socialization in Brussels.

enhanced cooperation (procedure) Initially established by the Amsterdam Treaty as 'closer cooperation' and renamed 'enhanced cooperation', a procedure that allows groups of member states that wish to integrate further than provided for in the treaties to do so, with the exception of areas of exclusive Union competence. The Commission will assess the request and it may submit a proposal to the Council in this respect. If the Commission decides not to present a proposal, it will explain its reasons to the member states concerned.

enlargement The process of expanding the EU geographically to include new member states.

Environmental Action Programme (EAP) Since 1973, a document defining the future orientation of EU policy in the environmental field and suggesting specific proposals that the Commission intends to put forward over the coming years.

epistemic community A network of knowledge-based experts or groups with an authoritative claim to policy-relevant knowledge within the domain of their expertise.

epistemology The theory of knowledge, which accounts for the way in which knowledge about the world is acquired.

Erasmus The European Commission's flagship programme for higher education students, teachers, and institutions, intending to encourage student and staff mobility for work and study, and promoting transnational cooperation projects among universities across Europe.

euro area (or eurozone) The economic area that covers those countries that have so far joined the EU's single currency.

euro bond A government bond issued in euros jointly by all of the euro area member states. This is a debt investment whereby an investor loans a certain amount of money, for a certain amount of time, with a certain interest rate, to the eurozone as a whole, which then forwards the money to individual governments. Euro bonds have been suggested as an effective way in which to tackle the sovereign debt crisis, although they remain controversial.

Euro Plus Pact As agreed by the euro area heads of state or government, and joined by Bulgaria, Denmark, Latvia, Lithuania, Poland, and Romania, this agreement further strengthens the economic pillar of economic and monetary union (EMU) and achieves a new quality of economic policy coordination, with the objective of improving competitiveness and thereby leading to a higher degree of convergence, reinforcing the EU's social market economy. The Pact remains open for other member states to join. The Pact fully respects the integrity of the single market.

Euro summit Under the Fiscal Compact signed in March 2010, it was agreed that the heads of state or government would meet informally at least twice a year to discuss issues related to economic and monetary union (EMU) and to provide 'strategic orientations for the conduct of economic policies'. Euro summits, it was further agreed, would be chaired by a president, who would be elected by simple majority for a two-and-a-half-year term of office. The new Euro summits will reign supreme over the Eurogroup.

Eurobarometer A European Commission publication and website monitoring and analysing public opinion in the member states since 1973.

Eurogroup An informal group comprising those member states of ECOFIN that are members of the single currency; (also) an interest group operating at the EU level, typically organized as a federation of national interest groups.

Europe 2020 The EU's growth strategy for the coming decade. It has five objectives on employment, innovation, education, social inclusion, and climate/energy to be reached by 2020. Each member state has adopted its own national targets in each of these areas. Concrete actions at EU and national levels underpin the strategy.

Europe agreement One of the agreements that constituted the legal framework of relations between the EU and the Central and Eastern European (CEE) countries, adapted to the specific situation of each partner state while setting common political, economic, and commercial objectives. In the context of accession to the EU, they formed the framework for implementation of the accession process.

European (or EU) citizenship A status conferred directly on every EU citizen under the Treaty on the Functioning of the European Union (TFEU)—that is, any person who holds the nationality of an EU country is automatically also an EU citizen. EU citizenship is additional to, and does not replace, national citizenship.

European Agency for the Management of Operational Cooperation at the External Borders of the Member States of the European Union (Frontex) Set up in 2004 to reinforce and streamline cooperation between national border authorities, Frontex has several operational areas of activity, including training, risk analysis, research, and rapid response capability via the European Border Guard Teams (EBGT). It also helps member states in joint return operations involving foreign nationals staying illegally, and provides information systems and an information-sharing environment regarding the current state of affairs at the external borders.

European Agricultural Guidance and Guarantee Fund (EAGGF) One of the funds supporting the Common Agricultural Policy (CAP). The EAGGF is composed of two sections, the guidance section and the guarantee section. Within the framework of European economic and social cohesion policy, the EAGGF supports rural development and the improvement of agricultural structures.

European arrest warrant (EAW) A system that replaces the lengthier extradition procedures amongst EU member states, simplifying the arrest and return of suspected criminals across the Union; introduced after the terrorist attacks on the US of 11 September 2001 ('9/11').

European Atomic Energy Community (Euratom, or EAEC) The Euratom Treaty was signed on 25 March 1957 by six states—namely, Belgium, France, Italy, Luxembourg, the Netherlands, and West Germany—to coordinate their research programmes for the peaceful use of nuclear energy. The Treaty today helps in the pooling of knowledge, infrastructure, and funding of nuclear energy. It ensures the security of atomic energy supply within the framework of a centralized monitoring system.

European Central Bank (ECB) Established in Frankfurt in 1999, the central bank is responsible for the single monetary policy of the euro area.

European Coal and Steel Community (ECSC) Established by six states in April 1951 by the Treaty of Paris, the ECSC allowed for the pooling of authority over coal and steel industries. Because it was based on a fifty-year treaty, the ECSC ceased to exist on 23 July 2002.

European Committee for Electrotechnical Standardization (CENELEC) The body responsible for standardization in the electro-technical engineering field, it prepares voluntary standards, which help to facilitate trade between countries, to create new markets, to cut compliance costs, and to support the development of a single European market.

European Committee for Standardization (CEN) Officially created as an international non-profit association based in Brussels on 30 October 1975, CEN is a business facilitator in Europe, removing trade barriers for European industry and consumers. Its mission is to foster the European economy in global trading, and the welfare of European citizens and the environment. It provides a platform for the development of European standards and other technical specifications.

European Company Statute A statute that refers to a regulatory framework aiming to create a 'European company' with its own legislative framework, which will allow companies incorporated in different member states to merge or to form a holding company or joint subsidiary, while avoiding the legal and practical constraints arising from the existence of different legal systems. This legislative framework also provides for the involvement of employees in European companies, giving due recognition to their place and role in the business.

European Convention *See* Convention (on the Future of Europe).

European Convention on Human Rights (ECHR) An international treaty to protect human rights and fundamental freedoms in Europe. Drafted in 1950 by the then newly formed Council of Europe, the Convention entered into force on 3 September 1953. All Council of Europe member states are party to the Convention and new members are expected to ratify the Convention at the earliest opportunity. The Convention established the European Court of Human Rights (ECtHR).

European Council A body that defines the general political direction and priorities of the EU. With the entry into force of the Treaty of Lisbon on 1 December 2009, it became an institution, with its own president.

European Council of Economics and Finance Ministers (ECOFIN) Composed of the economics and finance ministers of the member states, as well as budget ministers when budgetary issues are discussed,

ECOFIN meets once a month to discuss EU policy in a number of areas, including economic policy coordination, economic surveillance, monitoring of member states' budgetary policy and public finances, the euro (legal, practical, and international aspects), financial markets and capital movements, and economic relations with third countries. ECOFIN also prepares and adopts every year, together with the European Parliament, the Budget of the European Union. *See* Eurogroup.

European Court of Auditors (ECA) Established by the Treaty of Brussels of 1975, the Court carries out the audit of EU finances. Thus it assesses the collection and spending of EU funds, it examines whether financial operations have been properly recorded and disclosed, and legally and regularly executed and managed, and it assists the European Parliament and the EU Council in overseeing the implementation of the EU Budget.

European Court of Human Rights (ECtHR) An international court set up in 1959, which rules on individual or state applications alleging violations of the civil and political rights set out in the European Convention on Human Rights (ECHR). Since 1998, it has sat as a full-time court and individuals can apply to it directly.

European currency unit (ecu) The unit of account under the European Monetary System (EMS), composed of a 'basket of currencies'; replaced by the euro.

European Economic and Social Committee (EESC) A tripartite advisory body composed of individual members, who are nominated by the EU member states and who represent employers, workers, and other interests, such as environmental organizations or farmers.

European Economic Community (EEC) A body created by the 1957 Treaty of Rome, its aim being to bring about economic integration, including a common market, among its six founding members: Belgium, France, Germany, Italy, Luxembourg, and the Netherlands.

European Employment Strategy (EES) A 'soft' law mechanism designed to coordinate the employment policies of the EU member states. While the objectives, priorities, and targets are agreed at EU level, the national governments are fully responsible for formulating and implementing the necessary policies.

European External Action Service (EEAS) A body formed to assist the High Representative, comprising staff from the European Commission, the General Secretariat of the Council (GSC), and the diplomatic services of EU member states.

European Financial Stability Facility (EFSF) A facility created by the euro area member states following the decisions taken on 9 May 2010 within the framework of ECOFIN, with a mandate to safeguard financial stability in Europe by providing financial assistance to the euro area. The EFSF is a part of the wider safety net, alongside the European Financial Stability Mechanism (EFSM). The EFSM and the EFSF can be activated only after a request for financial assistance has been made by the concerned member state and a macroeconomic adjustment programme, incorporating strict conditionality, has been agreed with the Commission, in liaison with the European Central Bank (ECB).

European Financial Stability Mechanism (EFSM) This mechanism provides financial assistance to EU member states in financial difficulties. The EFSM reproduces for the EU27 the basic mechanics of the existing balance-of-payments regulation for non-euro area member states. The EFSM is a part of the wider safety net alongside the European Financial Stability Facility (EFSF). The EFSM and the EFSF can be activated only after a request for financial assistance has been made by the concerned member state and a macroeconomic adjustment programme, incorporating strict conditionality, has been agreed with the Commission, in liaison with the European Central Bank (ECB).

European Free Trade Association (EFTA) An international organization set up in 1960 to promote free trade amongst its members. Most of its original members have since joined the European Union.

European Globalization Adjustment Fund (EGF) A financial tool aiming towards the effective re-entry into the labour market of those workers who have lost their jobs. The EGF provides individual support for a limited period of time to workers who are affected by trade-adjustment redundancies. All member states can apply for support according to specific criteria.

European integration The process of political and economic (and possibly also cultural and social) integration of the states of Europe into a unified bloc.

European Investment Bank (EIB) Created by the Treaty of Rome in 1958 as the long-term lending bank of the EU, its task is to contribute towards the integration, balanced development, and economic and social cohesion of the EU member states.

European Monetary System (EMS) A regulated exchange rate system established in the EC in 1979 after failures to set up economic and monetary union earlier in the decade, the EMS aimed to promote monetary cooperation and exchange rate stability.

European Neighbourhood Policy (ENP) Developed in 2004 by the European Commission to frame the bilateral policy between the EU and each partner country, the policy aims to avoid the emergence of new dividing lines between the enlarged EU and its neighbours, and to strengthen prosperity, stability, and security.

European Ombudsman An independent body that investigates complaints about maladministration in the institutions and bodies of the European Union.

European partnership Within the framework of the stabilization and association process with the countries of the Western Balkans, the European Union has set up such partnerships with Albania, Bosnia and Herzegovina, the former Yugoslav Republic (FYR) of Macedonia, Montenegro and Serbia, including Kosovo, as defined by United Nations Security Council Resolution 1244 of 10 June 1999. The partnership establishes a framework of priority action and a financial structure to improve the stability and prosperity of the country, with a view to greater integration with the EU, because the state is recognized as a potential candidate for membership.

European Police Office (Europol) The European law enforcement agency, which aims to make Europe safer by assisting EU member states in their fight against serious international crime and terrorism.

European political cooperation (EPC) A form of foreign policy cooperation prior to Maastricht, set up after 1970 and formalized by the Single European Act.

European Regional Development Fund (ERDF) A fund that aims to strengthen economic and social cohesion in the EU by correcting imbalances between its regions. The ERDF finances: direct aid to investments in companies (in particular small and medium-sized enterprises, or SMEs) to create sustainable jobs; infrastructures linked notably to research and innovation, telecommunications, environment, energy, and transport; financial instruments to support regional and local development, and to foster cooperation between towns and regions; and technical assistance measures. The ERDF can intervene in the three objectives of regional policy—namely, convergence, regional competitiveness and employment, and European territorial cooperation.

European Securities Markets Programme (SMP) One of the programmes of the European Central Bank (ECB) that correspond to the strategies that it pursues on a temporary basis to deal with specific monetary problems, often concerned with liquidity shortages in the inter-banking market and their negative impact on the transmission of monetary policy. Through the SMP, the ECB purchases government bonds, in secondary markets, in order to provide liquidity to alleviate pressures from sovereign debt risk.

European semester A cycle of economic policy coordination, this is an additional instrument for the EU's preventive surveillance of the economic and fiscal policies of its member states. The main new aspect is that the enforcement of economic policy coordination is now extended right through to the budgetary process of every member state. The European semester is based on a coordination process lasting several months, with fixed calendar deadlines.

European Social Dialogue A joint consultation procedure involving social partners at EU level, aiming to discuss and negotiate agreements where relevant.

European Social Fund (ESF) Set up in 1957, a fund that aims to sustain and improve mobility in the European labour market through education and requalification initiatives for workers in areas experiencing industrial decline.

European Stability Mechanism (ESM) A permanent rescue funding programme to succeed the temporary European Financial Stability Facility (EFSF) and European Financial Stabilization Mechanism. It is foreseen that the new European Stability Mechanism (ESM) will enter into force on 1 July 2013, following an amendment to the Treaty on the Functioning of the European Union (TFEU) and the signing of an ESM Treaty by the euro area countries.

European System of Central Banks (ESCB) A system that brings together the national central banks, together with the European Central Bank (ECB).

European Telecommunications Standards Institute (ETSI) Recognized as an official European standards organization by the EU, a body that produces globally applicable standards for information and communications technology (ICT).

European Working Time Directive (EWTD) A directive aiming to protect the health and safety of workers in the European Union. It lays down minimum requirements in relation to working hours, rest periods, annual leave, and working arrangements for night workers.

Europeanization The process of European integration itself, or a shorthand for the incorporation of European characteristics into domestic institutions, politics, and identities (see Chapter 9).

Eurosceptic Someone who is opposed to European integration, or is sceptical about the EU and its aims.

Eurosclerosis A word used to characterize the period of EC history between 1966 and the early 1980s, during which the process of integration appeared to have slowed down and the common market objective was not implemented.

Eurostat Established in 1953, the statistical office of the European Union. Its task is to provide the EU with statistics at the European level that enable comparisons between countries and regions.

eurozone *See* euro area.

excessive deficit procedure (EDP) The procedure under monetary union (EMU) that can be used to sanction those member states who fail to control their budget deficits.

Exchange Rate Mechanism (ERM) The main element of the European monetary system, a mechanism that aimed to create a zone of monetary stability within Western Europe.

exclusive competence One of the specific areas in which only the EU is able to legislate and adopt legally binding acts. The member states may intervene in the areas concerned only if empowered to do so by the Union or in order to implement Union acts (*cf.* shared competence).

executive The branch of government responsible for implementing laws taken by parliament; the administration.

extraordinary rendition The handing over or surrender of a fugitive from one state to another, in contravention of national and international law, such as when a suspect is handed over without the permission of a judicial authority or, after the transfer, that person is tortured or held in breach of his or her human rights.

falsifiable hypothesis A hypothesis that can be tested and which may thus be proven false. As Popper pointed out, it is relatively easy to gather evidence for just about any idea, but a hypothesis is essentially worthless unless it makes predictions that could contradict it.

Federal Reserve (the Fed) The United States' central bank.

federalism An ideological position that suggests that everyone can be satisfied by combining national and regional/territorial interests in a complex web of checks and balances between a central government and a multiplicity of regional governments. In an EU context, it tends to imply an ideological approach that advocates the creation of a federal state in Europe.

federation A way of organizing a political system, which involves the constitutionally defined sharing of functions between a federal centre and the states. A federation will usually have a bicameral parliament, a constitutional court, and a constitution.

finalité politique The EU's final constitutional settlement.

Financial Instrument for Fisheries Guidance (FIFG) An instrument that aims to contribute to achieving the objectives of the Common Fisheries Policy (CFP). It supports structural measures in fisheries, aquaculture, and the processing and marketing of fishery and aquaculture products. It aims to promote the restructuring of the sector by putting in place the right conditions for its development and modernization.

financial perspective The EU's multi-annual spending (budget) plan.

financial solidarity The sharing of financial burdens across the EU members.

Fiscal Compact *See* Treaty on Stability, Coordination and Governance in the Economic and Monetary Union.

fiscal crisis An inability of the state to raise enough tax revenue to pay for its expenditure.

fiscal discipline A notion dealing with the specific externalities associated to the adverse spillover effects of excessive deficits leading to potentially unsustainable debt accumulation in member countries. Among economists and policy-makers, there is not much disagreement either on the risk that irresponsible fiscal behaviour creates for monetary union, or on the need for common rules or mechanisms that ensure fiscal discipline. There is, however, disagreement on the proper design of those rules and mechanisms. Hence, the discussion focuses on issues of design rather than of principle.

fiscal hangover An expression referring to the end of the happy days of economic and monetary union (EMU) and how the financial crisis has to change the rules of the game regarding financial transactions, the regulation of banks, and how states manage their debts.

fiscal policy The means by which a government adjusts its levels of spending in order to monitor and influence a nation's economy.

fiscal stimulus package An energizing plan that provides tax rebates directly to taxpayers.

fiscal transfer A financial transfer from a central authority to a subsidiary in a federal system, or to a member of a fiscal union. *See* fiscal union.

fiscal union The integration of the fiscal policy of nations or states, under which decisions about the collection and expenditure of taxes are taken by common institutions and shared by the participating governments.

flexibility One of the mechanisms, first introduced in the Amsterdam Treaty, which allows the EU to pursue differentiated integration. The Lisbon Treaty incorporates changes to its application under the

enhanced cooperation procedure. *See* enhanced cooperation procedure.

fonctionnaire A French term that means 'civil servant'. In the EU context, this term is used to refer to the civil servants working for the EU institutions.

'Fortress Europe' In the context of the EU, the strengthening of the EU's external borders to promote the territorial integrity and security of the Union, and the effect that it has on limiting the access of migrants into the EU.

Fouchet Plan A plan proposed in 1961 and pushed by the French government, which would have led to the creation of a European intergovernmental defence organization, but which was rejected by the EC's member states.

founding fathers The principal architects of European integration following the end of the Second World War, including Konrad Adenauer, Winston Churchill, Alcide de Gasperi, Walter Hallstein, Jean Monnet, Robert Schuman, Paul Henri Spaak, and Altiero Spinelli.

framework directive Incorporated into the 2001 White Paper on European Governance (WPEG) as part of the Commission's strategy for better and faster regulation, these are less heavy-handed legal instruments that offer more flexible implementation, and which tend to be agreed more quickly by the EU Council and the European Parliament.

framework-type legislation Legislation that does not involve legally enforceable rules, but which rests on mechanisms such as sharing ideas, benchmarking, and naming and shaming.

framing An important component of how the media can affect public opinion. A frame is an emphasis in salience of certain aspects of a topic.

Franco-German axis The relationship between France and Germany that is often said to lie at the heart of the European integration process.

free trade area (FTA) A group of countries that agree progressively to reduce barriers to trade, such as quotas and tariffs, which are often imposed at borders.

freeriding Reaping the benefits of a collective agreement without having participated in efforts to forge the agreement or to implement it. *See* collective good.

Friends of the Constitution In January 2007, the Spanish and Luxembourg governments convened a ministerial-level meeting of member states that had ratified the Constitution to discuss how the EU might proceed on the basis of the 2004 Constitution.

Front National A French far-right political party.

full economic union (FEU) The complete unification of the economies of the participating member states and common policies for most economic matters.

full political union (FPU) The term used when, in addition to full economic union (FEU), political governance and policy-making have moved to the supranational level. Effectively, political union occurs when the final stage of integration has taken place and a new confederation or federation has been created.

functional 'spillover' The knock-on effect of integration in one sector, which is said by neo-functionalists to provoke integration in neighbouring sectors.

G20 The group of twenty leading industrialized nations.

game theory An interdisciplinary rational approach to the study of human behaviour in which 'games' are a metaphor for a wide range of human interactions. It analyses the strategic interaction among a group of rational players (or agents) who behave strategically. A strategy of a player is the predetermined rule by which a player decides his or her course of action during the game. Each player tries to maximize his or her pay-off irrespective of what other players are doing.

General Agreement on Tariffs and Trade (GATT) First signed in 1947, the agreement was designed to provide an international forum that encouraged free trade between member states by regulating and reducing tariffs on traded goods, and by providing a common mechanism for resolving trade disputes. It lasted until the creation of the World Trade Organization (WTO) on 1 January 1995.

geo-political A characteristic referring to the relationship between geography, politics, and international relations.

global imbalance A situation in which there are large trade deficits and large trade surpluses in different parts of the world, which is perceived to be unsustainable and in need of rebalancing.

globalization A contested concept that usually refers to the growing economic interdependence of states and non-state actors worldwide. Often associated with increased capital mobility and the spread of neoliberal ideas, it implies that market authority is enhanced at the cost of formal political authority.

good governance A concept that encompasses the role of public authorities in establishing the environment in which economic operators function and in determining the distribution of benefits, as well as the relationship between the ruler and the ruled. It is typically defined in terms of the mechanisms thought to be needed to promote it. Thus governance is associated with democracy and civil rights, with transparency, with the rule of law, and with efficient public services.

governance The intentional regulation of social relationships and the underlying conflicts by reliable and durable means and institutions, instead of the direct use of power and violence.

governance turn The shift in interest in EU studies that included the increased application of theories of governance, comparative politics, and public policy, as well as the study of the EU as a political system in its own right.

grand theory A theory that tries to explain the entirety of a political process, such as European integration.

gross domestic product (GDP) The market value of all officially recognized final goods and services produced within a country in a given period.

gross national product (GNP) A measure of the country's total economic activity.

guarantee price (or intervention price) In the context of the Common Agricultural Policy (CAP), the (agricultural) price at which member states intervene in the market to buy up produce.

hard ecu proposal One of the alternatives to introduce a single currency into the EU, this proposal foresaw the introduction of a common currency in parallel to the existing national currencies. This suggestion was not implemented.

hard law Another way of saying 'the law', emphasizing its enforceability (*cf.* soft law).

harmonization The act of setting common European standards from which states are unable to deviate (either upwards or downwards).

headline goal Initially, a political commitment agreed at the Helsinki European Council in 1999 to deploy, by 2003, 50,000–60,000 troops in sixty days, sustainable for a year (a 'Rapid Reaction Force') to meet the requirements of the Petersberg Tasks. It has since been superseded by a new headline goal.

health check A review of the Common Agricultural Policy (CAP) as part of the overall review of the EU Budget. The reason for doing this in parallel is that the CAP forms a significant part of the EU Budget and, without looking at this policy, there is significantly less scope for reforms in the overall Budget.

hegemony Power, control, or influence exercised by a leading state over other states.

High Authority The original name given to the (now) European Commission in the 1950 Schumann Declaration and subsequently incorporated into the European Coal and Steel Community (ECSC) Treaty.

High Representative The Amsterdam Treaty created the post of 'High Representative for the Common Foreign and Security Policy'; the Lisbon Treaty renames the position the 'High Representative of the Union for Foreign Affairs and Security Policy' and extends his or her responsibilities by assigning the High Representative the functions of Council presidency in matters of foreign affairs, of Commissioner responsible for External Relations, and of High Representative for the Common Foreign and Security Policy (CFSP). The High Representative is one of the five vice-presidents of the European Commission and presides over the Foreign Affairs Council (FAC).

housing bubble An increase in housing prices fuelled by demand and speculation. The bubble is said to burst when demand decreases or stagnates while supply increases, resulting in a sharp drop in prices.

independent variable A factor contributing to an explanation of a phenomenon (a dependent variable).

individual direct payment An agricultural subsidy paid directly to individual farmers.

infringement proceedings An action for breach of European law that may result in a court case.

input legitimacy One part of a concept that follows Scharpf's distinction between input-oriented and output-oriented legitimacy. On the input side, democratic legitimacy requires mechanisms or procedures to link political decisions with citizens' preferences. In modern democracies, these mechanisms are reflected in representative institutions in which political decision-makers can be held accountable by the means of elections. *See* legitimacy; output legitimacy.

institutional balance In the EU context, a concept meaning that each institution has to act in accordance with the powers conferred on it by the treaties.

institutional isomorphism A term used by DiMaggio and Powell (1991) to denote the tendency for institutions within a similar environment to come to resemble each other.

institutionalist *See* new institutionalism.

integration The combination of parts of a unified whole—that is, a dynamic process of change. European integration is usually associated with the intensely institutionalized form of cooperation found in Europe after 1951.

integration theory Sometimes used generally as a shorthand for all theoretical and conceptual approaches that discuss European integration; otherwise it refers more specifically to supranational (especially neo-functionalist) theories of European integration.

interdependence The extent to which the actions of one state impact upon others.

interest group Any group of individuals or associations that is organized, with shared political interests and informality, and which does not aspire to public office or to compete in elections, but rather to the pursuit of goals through frequent informal interactions with politicians and bureaucrats.

interest intermediation The process of translating interests into policy, through the medium of interest organizations.

interest rate The rate of return on savings, or the rate paid on borrowings.

intergovernmental (cooperation) Cooperation that involves sovereign states and which occurs on a government-to-government basis, without the extensive involvement of supranational actors.

intergovernmental conference (IGC) A structured negotiation among the EU's member states, which usually leads to treaty revision. *See* simplified revision procedure.

intergovernmental treaty A treaty that formally sits outside of the EU framework (in other words, not an EU Treaty), such as the Treaty on Stability, Coordination and Governance, signed by twenty-five of the twenty-seven member states.

intergovernmentalism A theory of European integration that privileges the role of states. When conceptualizing decision-making mechanisms in the context of the EU, this refers to decisions being made by the member states only, without involvement of the supranational institutions.

International Monetary Fund (IMF) Conceived in 1994, an organization of 188 countries, working to foster global monetary cooperation, to secure financial stability, to facilitate international trade, to promote high employment and sustainable economic growth, and to reduce poverty around the world. *See* Bretton Woods agreement.

interpretivism A tradition that developed largely as a criticism of the dominant theory of positivism. Interpretivists argue that the positivist idea of a chain of causation is quite logical in the natural world, where a particular stimulus consistently produces a given effect, but does not apply in the social world. People do not merely react to stimuli; rather, they actively interpret the situations in which they find themselves and act on the basis of these interpretations.

intervening variable A variable that explains the relationships between independent and dependent variables.

intervention price *See* guarantee price.

interventionism The concept that governments involve themselves in the regulation of markets, through policy, rather than leave markets to regulate themselves.

Ioannina Compromise A negotiated compromise that takes its name from an informal meeting of foreign ministers in the Greek city of Ioannina on 29 March 1994. The resulting compromise lays down that if members of the Council representing between twenty-three votes (the old blocking minority threshold) and twenty-six votes (the new threshold) express

their intention of opposing the taking of a decision by the Council by qualified majority, the Council will do all within its power, within a reasonable space of time, to reach a satisfactory solution that can be adopted by at least sixty-eight votes out of eighty-seven. The Lisbon Treaty (Article 16 TEU) introduces a new definition of the rule of qualified majority that shall apply from 1 November 2014 onwards. *See* dual majority (voting); qualified majority voting.

Jean Monnet One of the founders of the European integration project. The driving force behind the 1950 Schuman Plan, which led to the establishment of the European Coal and Steel Community (ECSC), Monnet became the first head of the ECSC's High Authority. He continued to play an active role in European integration throughout his life, although often behind the scenes.

joint action Coordinated action by member states to commit resources for an agreed (foreign policy) objective.

joint-decision trap The idea promoted by Fritz Scharpf in 1988 that while it might be increasingly difficult in future for further integration to take place, it will also be impossible for states to go back on agreements already made; as such, states are 'trapped' within the European integration process.

judicial activism In the context of the Court of Justice of the European Union (CJEU), this refers to the way in which the Court exploits the gaps and vagueness existing in areas of EU law so as to expand its powers and role. The Court has been criticized on the basis that its activism exceeds its judicial powers and falls into the area of policy-making.

judicial review The right of a court to review a law or other act for constitutionality or its violation of some fundamental principle.

Keynesian A position that supports J. M. Keynes's economic theory and which has as its starting point the assumption that state finances should be used to counteract cyclical economic downturns. The argument implies that governments should focus on issues of employment and economic growth, rather on variables such as inflation.

Konrad Adenauer The first Chancellor of the Federal Republic of German after the end of the Second World War, Adenauer held office for fourteen years and was responsible for overseeing the reconstruction of Germany in the 1950s, particularly in the context of European integration, of which he was a key supporter.

laissez-faire An economic position that argues that the state (governments) should play only a minimal regulatory role in economic affairs, with decisions left mainly to the market.

LEADER This EU programme is designed to support local businesses, farmers, foresters, community groups, those involved in tourism, and a range of rural enterprises. The fund can cover 50 per cent of the cost of a project. If the project is a farm diversification, the programme may be able to offer a grant covering up to 100 per cent of costs.

League of Nations An international organization set up in 1922 that had as its rationale the maintenance of peace in Europe.

legal basis *See* treaty base.

legitimacy The extent to which a regime's procedures for making and enforcing laws are acceptable to all of its subjects; the right to rule. *See* input legitimacy; output legitimacy.

liberal intergovernmentalism Andrew Moravcsik's update on classical intergovernmentalism (*see* Chapter 6).

liberal-democratic A system of representative government that is characterized by universal adult suffrage, political equality, majority rule, and a constitutional check on the power of rulers.

liberalization of capital markets The removal of exchange controls by states, allowing capital to flow freely across state borders.

liberalization of services The removal of barriers to the establishment and provision of services across state borders.

liquidity The ability to convert an asset to cash quickly.

Lisbon Agenda (or Lisbon Process, or Lisbon Strategy) The EU strategy intended to turn the Union into the most competitive and dynamic economy in the world by 2010.

Lisbon Treaty Revising the Nice version of the TEU, the Lisbon Treaty was signed in 2007 and entered into force in December 2009 after a protracted ratification. *See* Treaty on the European Union (TEU); Treaty on the Functioning of the EU (TFEU).

list system A method of voting for several electoral candidates, usually members of the same political party, with one mark of the ballot. Electors vote for one of several lists of candidates usually prepared by the political parties.

lock-out A situation in which employers lock employees out of their place of work as a consequence of a labour dispute.

Luxembourg Compromise An intergovernmental agreement arrived at in January 1966 between the member states that solved the 'empty chair' crisis. It states that when vital interests of one or more countries are at stake, members of the Council will endeavour to reach solutions that can be adopted by all, while respecting their mutual interests.

Maastricht Treaty *See* Treaty on the European Union (TEU).

Maastricht Treaty ratification The process that lead to the approval—in both national parliaments and in some cases in referenda—of the Treaty on the European Union (TEU), which came into force in 1993.

macro-economic imbalance (procedure) A new tool that helps to detect and correct risky economic developments as part of the 'macro-economic surveillance' leg of the EU's new rules on economic governance (the so-called 'six pack'). *See* 'six pack'.

macro-economic policy An economic policy that deals with aggregates such as national income and investment in the economy.

majoritarian Characterized by the application of majority rule; the principle that the majority should be allowed to rule the minority.

market citizenship The concept introduced to the EC in the 1950s whereby citizens of member states became endowed with certain rights as workers within the European Community.

market integration The breaking down of barriers to trade amongst the EU's member states, plus any regulation necessary to ensure the smooth running of the single market. It does not involve an explicitly political dimension.

market unity The removal of protection across the Union, allowing agricultural produce to move freely across borders.

market-making measure A measure that involves the prohibition of certain types of market behaviour.

market-shaping measure A measure that lays down an institutional model that shapes market behaviour.

middle-range theory A theory that aims to explain only part of a political process and which does not have totalizing ambitions.

modulation The transfer of agricultural subsidies to agri-environmental and other rural development projects.

modus operandi A Latin expression meaning 'method of operating or proceeding'.

Monetarist An advocate of one of the possible economic strategies with which to achieve economic and monetary union (EMU); in the 1960s and 1970s, the Monetarist camp postulated that, by fixing the exchange rate, the necessary cooperation of the adjacent economic policies would naturally start to occur (cf. Economist).

monetary union A form of integration that usually contains a single market (and therefore free movement of goods, services, labour, and capital among the participating states and common rules, tariffs, and so on, vis-à-vis third countries) and has further integration in the area of currency cooperation. A monetary union either has irrevocably fixed exchange rates and full convertibility of currencies, or a common or single currency circulating within the monetary union. It also requires integration of budgetary and monetary policies.

money supply The stock of liquid assets in an economy that can be freely exchanged for goods and services.

Monnet method See Community method.

Monti Report On the invitation of Commission President Barroso, Mario Monti delivered on 9 May 2010 a report concluding that the economic crisis had opened a window of opportunity for Europe to become more pragmatic and in which it could relaunch the single market.

multifunctionality The notion in agricultural policy that the policy can be used to serve a range of functions, including environmental protection and rural development.

multilateral budgetary surveillance Against the background of the Stability and Growth Pact (SGP), a monitoring mechanism that aims to ensure that national economic policy is broadly consistent with the SGP and thus with the proper functioning of economic and monetary union (EMU).

multilevel governance An approach to the study of EU politics that emphasizes the interaction of the many different actors who influence European policy outcomes.

multi-speed (Europe/EU) A characteristic of differentiated integration whereby common objectives are pursued by a group of member states able and willing to advance further than others in the integration process.

mutual recognition The principle that an economic product sold in one member state should not be prohibited from sale anywhere in the EU. This was upheld in the famous Cassis de Dijon (1979) case brought to the European Court of Justice. Exceptions can be made in cases of public health and safety, however.

n = 1 problem The situation in which the object under scholarly scrutiny cannot be compared to other cases. This renders generalization beyond the case impossible (because there are no other instances of what is being studied).

national action plan (NAP) A key element of the European Employment Strategy, an annual report supplied by each member state to the Commission and the Council on the principal measures taken to implement its employment policy in the light of the guidelines for employment drawn up each year by the Council under Article 148 (3) TFEU.

national envelope In the context of the Common Agricultural Policy (CAP), a de facto national allocation paid to a member state from the EU Budget, and which each state can distribute to its farmers to target specific national and/or regional priorities.

national sovereignty The doctrine that sovereignty belongs to and derives from the nation, an abstract entity normally linked to a physical territory, and its past, present, and future citizens.

negative integration A form of integration that involves the removal of barriers between the member states.

negotiating directive A directive that sets out the terms on which the Commission negotiates in international trade and other contexts, and establishing the boundaries of the negotiating mandate and providing for monitoring of the negotiations and their outcomes.

neo-corporatism A model of policy-making that links producer interests to the state and in which interest organizations are incorporated into the system. The 'neo-' prefix was added in the 1970s to distinguish this from corporatism in the past—particularly in the fascist era.

neo-functionalism A theory of European integration that views integration as an incremental process, involving the spillover of integration in one sector to others, ultimately leading to some kind of political community.

neoliberalism An economic school that advocates the reduction of state influence in the market, the liberalization of the economy, the privatization of state-owned firms, and the tight control of money supply, and which supports a general trend towards deregulation.

neo-realism An international relations theory, associated with the work of Kenneth Waltz, which claims that the international state system is anarchic and that, as such, state uncertainty is a given. States will want to maintain their independence and survival will be their primary objective, but they may nonetheless engage in European integration if this serves their ends.

net contributor A country that receives less from the EU Budget than it contributes.

net recipient A country that receives more from the EU Budget than it contributes.

new approach A novel approach to regulating internal market rules, as established in the Commission's White Paper on Completing the Internal Market (1985) in which legislative acts would set out only the main objectives and detailed rules would be adopted through private standardization bodies.

new institutionalism A conceptual approach to the study of politics that restates the importance of institutional factors in political life. It takes a number of very different forms, from rational institutionalism and historical institutionalism, to sociological institutionalism.

new mode of governance (NMG) In contrast to the traditional Community method, which relies on the proposal, adoption, and implementation of legislation by the EU's main institutions, the policy goals of an NMG are achieved through a novel mechanism that involves explicit, but not legally binding, commitments from the member states. In a formalized process, each government commits itself to certain goals in areas such as education policy, innovation, or labour market reform. The European Commission is involved both in the design stage of specific policies and in a monitoring function overseeing subsequent implementation.

Nice Treaty A treaty revision agreed at Nice in December 2000, signed in February 2001, and ratified in 2002. It introduced a number of institutional reforms that paved the way for the enlargement of the Union in 2004 and afterwards.

non-compulsory spending See compulsory spending.

non-majoritarian (institution) A governmental entity that possesses and exercises specialized public authority, separate from that of other institutions, but is neither directly elected by the people nor directly managed by elected officials.

non-state actor Usually, any actor that is not a national government; often refers to transnational actors, such as interest groups (rather than to international organizations).

non-tariff barriers See barrier to trade.

normative Of value judgements—that is, 'what ought to be', as opposed to positive statements about 'what is'.

Ombudsman See European Ombudsman.

ontology An underlying conception of the world—that is, of the nature of being; that which is being presupposed by a theory.

open method of coordination (OMC) An approach to EU policy-making that is an alternative to regulation and which involves more informal means of encouraging compliance than 'hard' legislation.

opportunity structure See political opportunity structure.

opt in The practice whereby one or more member states, having opted out of a particular policy area, decide at a later date to cooperate with those other member states that have proceeded despite the earlier opt-out(s) (*cf.* opt out).

opt out The practice whereby one or more member states refuse to cooperate in a particular policy area despite the fact that majority of member states wish to commit themselves to do so. To allow for progress among those who wish to proceed, the reluctant member states may 'opt out', which usually occurs in the context of a treaty revision. Member states that opt out may opt in at a later stage (*cf.* opt in).

optimum currency area (OCA) A theoretical notion that implies that monetary union will work effectively only when the states participating are economically very similar.

orange card system According to Protocols 1 and 2 of the Treaty of Lisbon, if one third (or one quarter in relation to freedom, security, and justice) of national parliaments feel that draft legislation could be better achieved by domestic legislation, the Commission must review the proposed act.

ordinary legislative procedure (OLP) The main procedure for adopting legislation in the European Union, known before the Lisbon Treaty entered into force as 'co-decision'. The OLP makes the Parliament an equal co-legislative partner with the Council. Whilst agreement is normally concluded at first reading following informal negotiations, under the OLP the EP has the right to hold up to three readings of legislation, to reject the legislation, and to hold conciliation meetings with the Council to negotiate a compromise agreement (Article 294 TFEU).

Organisation for Economic Co-operation and Development (OECD) Established in 1961 and based in Paris, the mission of this body is to promote policies that will improve the economic and social well-being of people around the world.

original six The original signatories of the Treaty of Rome—namely, France, Germany, Italy, Belgium, Luxembourg, and the Netherlands.

output legitimacy Following Scharpf democratic legitimacy is a two-dimensional concept, which refers to both the inputs as well as the outputs of a political system. Scharpf argues that democracy would be an empty ritual if the democratic procedure were not able to produce effective outcomes—that is, to achieve the goals about which citizens care collectively. *See* legitimacy; input legitimacy.

package deal The exchange of loss in some issues for benefits in others, resulting in mutual overall gain between actors with different interests. EU decision-making presents legislators with multiple issues for consideration, and their repeated interactions in the EU legislative process create opportunities for package deals and exchange of support.

parity Equality in amount, status, or character.

parsimony The characteristic of a theory that provides an extremely simplified depiction of reality.

partial theory A theory that only purports to address or explain an aspect of a specific political phenomenon.

participatory democracy A theory of democracy that stresses the importance of more regular and direct citizen involvement in collective decision-making, such as via referenda or via more decentralized governance mechanisms.

Passerelle clause A clause that allows for derogation from the legislative procedures initially specified under the treaties. Specifically, and under certain conditions, a Passerelle clause makes it possible to switch from the special legislative procedure to the ordinary legislative procedure (OLP) in order to adopt an act, and to switch from voting by unanimity to qualified majority voting (QMV) in a given policy area. Activating a Passerelle clause depends on a decision being adopted unanimously by the Council or by the European Council.

path-dependence The idea that decisions taken in the past limit the scope of decisions in the present (and future).

permanent representation The diplomatic delegation of any member state vis-à-vis the EU in Brussels.

permanent structured cooperation According to Article 42 TEU, the cooperation that must be established within the Union framework by those member states with military capabilities that fulfil higher criteria and which have made more binding commitments to one another in this area.

permissive consensus The political context that allowed elites in the post-1945 period to engage in European integration, without involving Europe's citizens.

pillars Prior to the Treaty of Lisbon, the structure of the European Union was akin to a Greek temple consisting of three pillars—namely Pillar 1, Pillar 2, and Pillar 3. With the entry into force of the Treaty of Lisbon on 1 December 2009, the pillars disappeared. *Pillar 1* comprised the original communities and was typically supranational. *Pillar 2* comprised intergovernmental cooperation in foreign and security policy. *Pillar 3* comprised intergovernmental cooperation in police and judicial cooperation in criminal matters (PJCCM).

Plan 'D' Commissioner Margot Wallstrom's communication strategy, emphasizing democracy, dialogue, and debate.

pluralism A general approach that implies that organized groups play an important role in the political process.

plurality system A type of electoral system that awards the seat to the candidate who receives the most votes regardless of whether the candidate receives a majority of votes.

policy convergence The tendency for policies (in different countries) to begin to take on similar forms over time.

policy network A set of actors who are linked by relatively stable relationships of a non-hierarchical and interdependent nature. These actors share common interests with regard to a policy and exchange resources to pursue these shared interests, acknowledging that cooperation is the best way in which to achieve common goals.

policy style A set of characteristics that describe different ways of policy-making (for example, in a particular sector or across a particular country).

policy transfer The replication of policies pursued in one context (country, sector) to others.

political codetermination A political model of codetermination in which a complex set of legal and social institutions shape employee participation in company decision-making through works councils and representation in the supervisory boards of large firms.

political opportunity structure The various characteristics of a political system, such as political institutions, political culture, and the structure of opponents and allies, which influence elements within it, such as social movements, organizational forms, and the way in which political actors behave.

polity A politically organized society.

positive integration A form of integration that involves the construction of policies and/or institutions.

positive-sum outcome An outcome that constitutes more than the sum of its parts. It is often talked of in EU terms as an 'upgrading of the common interest'.

post-national A form of governance beyond the nation state.

power The ability to control outcomes; the capacity of A to force B to do something in A's interest.

Praesidium In the context of the 2002 Convention on the Future of Europe, the Praesidium was the steering group responsible for setting the Convention's agenda and overseeing its progress. *See* Convention on the Future of Europe.

preliminary ruling (procedure) An judgment of the European Court of Justice that arises as a response to a question of European law posed in a domestic court.

presidency of the EU Council A leadership position that is held on a six-monthly basis by member states in rotation. Since the Lisbon Treaty entered into force, the European Council has its own appointed President.

price support The system of agricultural support that involves keeping food prices higher than the market price, to give farmers a higher and more stable income.

primus inter pares A Latin expression meaning 'first amongst equals'.

primus super pares A Latin expression that means 'first above equals'.

proportional representation (PR) A form of electoral system that attempts to match the proportion of seats won by a political party with the proportion of the total vote for that party.

proportionality A principle that implies that the means should not exceed the ends; applies to decision-making and the legislative process.

public debt The amount of money owed by the state.

public goods theory A branch of economics that studies, from the perspective of economic theory, how voters, politicians, and government officials behave.

public sphere A space or arena for broad public deliberation, discussion, and engagement in societal issues. According to Habermas, the democratic deficit can be eliminated only if a European public sphere comes into existence in which the democratic process is incorporated.

qualified majority voting (QMV) A system of voting based on the qualified majority, which is the number of votes required in the Council for a decision to be adopted when issues are being debated on the basis of Article 16 TEU and Article 238 TFEU. Under the ordinary legislative procedure (OLP), the Council acts by qualified majority in combination with the European Parliament. With the entry into force of the Treaty of Lisbon, a new system known as 'double majority' was introduced. It will enter into force on 1 November 2014. *See* dual majority; ordinary legislative procedure (OLP).

quantitative easing The process whereby, when lower interest rates have been used to encourage people to spend, not save, and interest rates can go no lower, a central bank pumps money into the economy directly, by buying assets or simply by printing money.

Rapid Reaction Force A transnational military force managed by the European Union.

Rapporteur A member of the European Parliament (MEP) responsible for drafting legislative opinions.

ratification crisis (1992) The crisis provoked by the Danish 'no' vote in their 1992 referendum on the Maastricht Treaty.

ratification Formal approval. In the EU context, it implies approval of Treaty revisions by national parliaments and sometimes also by popular referendum.

rational choice *See* rationalism.

rational utilitarianism The idea that opinions stem from calculations involving the weighing up of costs and benefits.

rationalism A theory that assumes that individuals (or states) are able to rank options in order of preference and to choose the best available preference.

realism A rationalist theory of international relations.

recession A temporary depression in economic activity or prosperity, which is, specifically, three consecutive quarters of negative growth.

redistributive The characteristic of a policy that transfers wealth from one group to another.

reference *See* Preliminary ruling.

reference currency A tool for settling trade transactions.

reference value A baseline measure against which economic progress can be assessed.

reflection group A group established prior to an intergovernmental conference (ICG) to prepare preliminary papers on relevant issues.

reflectivism A perspective that centres on ontological and epistemological questions not answered to a satisfactory degree by the rationalist, behaviourist, or positivist perspectives, such as the nature of knowledge, its objectivity or subjectivity, and the nature of international politics. Reflectivism questions the existence of objective truth and our ability to discover such truths.

reform treaty A Treaty that amends the provisions of existing EU treaties. The difference between a reform treaty (operating within the framework of existing treaties) and a constitution (which would consolidate all of the rules governing the EU and give rise to a new set of legal principles) shaped the debates over the ratification of the Lisbon Treaty and member states' justification not to hold referenda.

regime The framework of principles, norms, rules, and decision-making procedures around which actors' expectations occur. An international regime is usually considered to take the form of an international organization. It is a concept associated with neo-realism.

regulation The rules or legislation made in order to provoke certain policy outcomes; one of the legislative instruments used by the EU. EU regulations are directly effective, spelling out not only the aims of legislation, but also what must be done and how (*cf.* directive).

regulatory competition A situation in which a country tries to offer a regulatory environment that will attract business from abroad. This may involve deregulation.

regulatory impact assessment (RIA) An evaluation intended to provide a detailed and systematic appraisal of the potential impacts of a new regulation in order to assess whether the regulation is likely to achieve the desired objectives.

regulatory state The expansion in the use of rule-making, monitoring. and enforcement techniques and institutions by the state, and a parallel change in the way in which its positive functions in society are being carried out.

representation The principle by which delegates are chosen to act for a particular constituency (group of electors).

res public composita A composite union comprising diverse publics.

right of association The democratic right of people to form groups such as trades unions.

Robert Schuman Former French Foreign Minister and one of the 'founding fathers' of the European Coal and Steel Community (ECSC), through his Schuman Plan of 1950.

run on a bank Crisis that occurs when a large number of customers withdraw their deposits from a financial institution and either demand cash, or transfer those funds into government bonds or a safer institution, because they believe that financial institution is, or might become, insolvent.

rural development policy The EU's common rural development policy aims to address the challenges faced by rural areas and to unlock their potential. Rural development addresses three key areas: improving the competitiveness of the agricultural and forestry sector; improving the environment and the countryside; and improving the quality of life in rural areas and encouraging diversification of the rural economy.

safeguard clause An economic safeguard clause is a traditional trade liberalization safeguard measure.

Schengen Agreement An agreement to create a border-free European Community. It was originally outside the treaties, but was incorporated at Amsterdam.

Schengen Information System (SIS) In Europe, the largest shared database on maintaining public security,

supporting police and judicial cooperation, and managing external border control. Participating states provide entries ('alerts') on wanted and missing persons, lost and stolen property, and entry bans. It is immediately and directly accessible to all police officers at street level, and other law enforcement officials and authorities who need the information to carry out their roles in protecting law and order and fighting crime.

Schuman Plan Signed on 9 May 1950, it led to the setting up of the European Coal and Steel Community (ECSC).

secession The act of withdrawing from an organization, union, or a political entity.

sectoral integration A description of, or strategy for, integration that involves an incremental sector-by-sector approach. *See* spillover.

securitization The financial practice of pooling various types of contractual debt, such as residential mortgages, commercial mortgages, auto loans, or credit card debt obligations, and selling that consolidated debt as bonds to various investors.

separation of powers A condition of democratic political systems under which the executive, legislature, and judiciary are separate, providing a system of checks and balances that serve to prevent abuses of power.

set-aside A characteristic of land, which farmers are not allowed to use for any agricultural purpose. It was introduced by the EU in 1992 as part of a package of reforms of the Common Agricultural Policy (CAP) to prevent over-production. It applies only to farmers growing crops.

shared competence A specific area in which the member states and the EU have powers to legislate and adopt legally binding acts. The member states exercise their powers in so far as the Union has not exercised, or has decided to stop exercising, its competence. Most of the EU's competences fall into this category (*cf.* exclusive competence).

simplified revision procedure The Treaty of Lisbon creates a simplified procedure for the amendment of policies and internal actions of the EU. The government of any member state, the Commission, or the European Parliament can submit proposals for amendments to the European Council. The European Council then adopts a decision laying down the amendments made to the treaties. The European Council acts by unanimity after consulting the Commission, the Parliament, and the European Central Bank (ECB) if the amendment concerns monetary matters. New provisions of the treaties enter into force only after they have been ratified by all member states pursuant to their respective constitutional requirements. This procedure avoids the convening of a convention and an IGC. However, the competences of the EU may not be extended by means of a simplified revision procedure.

Single European Act (SEA) The first of the large-scale Treaty revisions, signed in 1986. It came into force in 1987 and served as a 'vehicle' for the single market programme.

single European market *See* single market (programme).

Single Farm Payment (SFP) A unique direct payment under the Common Agricultural Policy (CAP), aimed at achieving a complete decoupling of support and production. Under this system, even a farmer who decides to grow nothing is eligible to receive this payment, as long as he or she complies with environmental, food safety, animal welfare, and occupational safety standards.

single market (programme) The goal of one unified internal EU market, free of (national) barriers to trade. While the idea was included in the Treaty of Rome, the single market is usually associated with the revitalization of the Community from the mid-1980s.

Single Market Act Adopted by the European Commission in April 2011, the act aims to deliver twelve instruments to relaunch the single market for 2012. These twelve instruments of growth, competitiveness, and social progress range from worker mobility, to small and medium-sized enterprise (SME) finance and consumer protection, via digital content, taxation, and trans-European networks.

single monetary policy Common monetary policy across the euro area. *See* economic and monetary union (EMU).

Sinn Féin An Irish Republican party seeking to end British rule in Northern Ireland.

'six pack' The five regulations and one directive that entered into force on 13 December 2011. It applies to all member states with some specific rules for euro area member states, especially regarding financial sanctions. Not only does it cover fiscal surveillance, but it also includes macro-economic surveillance under the new macro-economic imbalance procedure.

'snake' A system aimed to stabilize exchange rates within the EC in the 1970s.

Social Chapter Agreed at Maastricht, the Social Chapter establishes minimum social conditions within the EU.

social constructivism *See* constructivism.

social dumping The undercutting of social standards in order to improve competitiveness.

social partnership The partnership of labour (the unions) and capital (employers) acting together and enjoying a privileged position in the EU policy process.

social spillover A recent neo-functionalist concept that divorces social from political spillover in order to explain the learning and socialization processes that help to drive the European integration process.

soft law Those documents that are not formally or legally binding, but which may still produce political effects (*cf.* hard law).

sovereign debt crisis A crisis that arises when national governments are unable to guarantee repayment of debt that they have issued—even though sovereign debt is theoretically considered to be risk-free, because the government can employ different measures to guarantee repayment, by increasing taxes or printing money.

sovereignty The supremacy of a state, which is not subject to any higher authority; supreme, unrestricted power (of a state).

Spaak Report Following the Messina Conference, Belgian socialist politician Paul-Henri Spaak was appointed to prepare a report on the creation of a common European market. The 1956 Spaak Report recommended greater economic union and the union of nuclear energy production.

spillback A mechanism indentified by neo-functionalist theorists. According to Schmitter, spillback occurs in regional integration when, in response to tensions, actors withdraw from their original objective, downgrading their commitment to mutual cooperation. *See* spillover.

spillover A mechanism identified by neo-functionalist theorists who claimed that sectoral integration in one area would have knock-on effects in others and would 'spill over', thereby increasing the scope of European integration.

Spinelli Report On 14 February 1984, the European Parliament adopted a draft Treaty on European Union (TEU), also known as the 'Spinelli Report' because it was written by Altiero Spinelli. The aim of the report was to bring about a reform of the Community institutions. The report was soon buried by the governments of the member states, but it provided an impetus for the negotiations that led to the Single European Act and the Maastricht Treaty. *See* Altiero Spinelli.

Stability and Growth Pact (SGP) An agreement of the EU member states concerning conduct over their fiscal policy, which aimed to ensure that the constraints on member states prior to the introduction of the single currency would continue after economic and monetary union (EMU) was in place.

stabilization and association agreement (SAA) A framework for the implementation of the stabilization and association process between the EU and the Western Balkan countries. Each agreement is adapted to the specific situation of each partner country, while establishing common political, economic, and commercial objectives and encouraging regional cooperation. *See* Stabilization and Association Process (SAP).

Stabilization and Association Process (SAP) The main framework for EU relations with the Western Balkan region (Albania, Bosnia and Herzegovina, Croatia, FYR Macedonia, Montenegro, Serbia, and Kosovo under UN Security Council Resolution 1244). In addition to the political, economic, and institutional criteria established at the Copenhagen European Council in 1993, the SAP added five further specific criteria for the Western Balkans: full cooperation with the International Criminal Tribunal for the former Yugoslavia (ICTY), respect for human and minority rights, the creation of real opportunities for refugees and internally displaced persons to return, and a visible commitment to regional cooperation.

stakeholder A person, group, organization, member, or system who affects or can be affected by an organization's actions.

state-centrism A conceptual approach to understanding European integration that gives primacy to the role of state actors within the process.

statehood The condition of being a state. *See* stateness.

stateness The quality of being a state—that is, a legal territorial entity with a stable population and a government.

strong currency A situation arising out of relative levels of exchange rate whereby the value of national money is increased. This has the effect of lowering the price of imports (making imported goods cheaper), but also of increasing the price of exports, making exports less competitive in international markets.

Structural Fund A financial instrument aimed at fostering economic and social cohesion in the EU by part-financing regional and horizontal operations in the member states. There are four types of Structural Fund: the European Regional Development Fund (ERDF); the European Social Fund (ESF); the European Agricultural Guidance and Guarantee Fund (EAGGF) Guidance section; and the Financial Instrument for Fisheries Guidance (FIFG).

structural policy The EU's framework to maintain a sufficient level of economic and social cohesion amongst member states. It incorporates a number of programmes and financial instruments, including the Structural Fund, with which to achieve its aims.

subprime mortgage market The market comprising mortgage loans to people who were perceived to be at high risk of defaulting on the repayment schedule. These loans are characterized by higher interest rates and less favourable terms in order to compensate for the higher credit risk. The subprime mortgage crisis arose in the US as a result of the bundling together of subprime and regular mortgages.

subsidiarity The principle that tries to ensure that decisions are taken as close as possible to the citizen. *See* orange card system.

superstate A political term that implies that the aim of supporters of European integration is to turn the EU into a state, with connotations of the detachment of elites and the European institutions from ordinary citizens.

supranational governance A theory of European integration proposed by Wayne Sandholtz and Alec Stone Sweet, which draws on neo-functionalism and provides an alternative approach to Moravcsik's liberal intergovernmentalism.

supranational institution An institution in the EU system of governance to which the member states have delegated sovereignty, such as the European Commission, the European Parliament, the European Central Bank (ECB), or the courts of the European Union.

supranational Above the national level. It may refer to institutions, policies, or a particular 'type' of cooperation/integration.

supranationalism An approach to the study of the EU that emphasizes the autonomy of the European institutions and the importance of common European policies.

sustainability (or 'sustainable development') The ability to meet the needs of the present without compromising the needs of future generations.

Tampere A city in Finland at which a summit meeting in 1999 agreed to create an 'area of freedom, security and justice' (AFSJ) in Europe.

teleological In the context of the EU's legal doctrine, the characteristic of an arguments drawn from the objectives that EU law establishes either implicitly or explicitly. A typical teleological argument is the reference to the need to achieve a single European market.

third-country national (TCN) A citizen of a country outside the European Union.

transaction costs The costs related to the exchange of money.

transfer payment A payment not made in return for any contribution to current output. Usually refers to agricultural subsidies.

transparency Used in the EU to refer to the extent of openness within the EU institutions.

transposition The translation of European law into domestic law.

treaty base The treaty provision that underpins a particular piece of European legislation.

treaty base game The act of selecting a treaty base (in a 'grey area') for political ends.

Treaty establishing the European Stability Mechanism A treaty signed by euro area member states on 2 February 2012. The European Stability Mechanism (ESM) is constituted as an international financial institution based in Luxembourg. Its purpose is to provide financial assistance to euro area member states experiencing or being threatened by severe financing problems. *See* European Stability Mechanism (ESM).

Treaty of Brussels Signed on 17 March 1948 between Belgium, France, Luxembourg, the Netherlands, and the UK, the Treaty of Brussels (or 'Brussels Pact') aimed to set out terms for economic, social, and cultural cooperation, and especially collective self-defence. It provided for the establishment of an international organization that led to the creation of the Western European Union (WEU). *See* Western European Union (WEU).

Treaty of Dunkirk A treaty signed on 4 March 1947, between France and the UK in Dunkirk (France), as a treaty of alliance and mutual assistance against a possible German attack.

Treaty of Rome Signed in 1957, the Rome Treaty formally established the European Economic Community (EEC) and the European Atomic Energy Community (Euratom, or EAEC).

Treaty on Stability, Coordination and Governance in the Economic and Monetary Union (or the Fiscal Compact) Agreed on 30 January 2012 by the informal European Council, the only really substantive binding provision of this treaty is that the member states undertake to adopt, at the national level, rules that limit their structural deficit to 0.5 per cent of gross domestic product (GDP). This should be done 'preferably at the constitutional level'.

Treaty on the European Union (TEU) (or Maastricht Treaty) The Lisbon Treaty amends the EU's two core treaties, this and the Treaty establishing the European Community (TEC). The TEU established the European Union, prepared for economic and monetary union (EMU), and introduced elements of a political union (citizenship, and common foreign and internal affairs policy).

Treaty on the Functioning of the European Union (TFEU) The Lisbon Treaty amends the EU's two core treaties, the Treaty on European Union (TEU) and the Treaty establishing the European Community (TEC), renaming the latter as the TFEU. The TEU organizes the functioning of the Union and determines the areas of, delimitation of, and arrangements for exercising its competences.

Trevi (Group) A forum for internal security cooperation, which operated from the mid-1970s until 1993.

troika (i) The country holding the presidency of the EU Council together with the previous presidency and the forthcoming presidency; (ii) in Common Foreign and Security Policy (CFSP), it traditionally referred to the presidency of the EU Council, the High Representative for CFSP, and the Commission, but since the Lisbon Treaty entered into force, the High Representative of the Union for Foreign Affairs and Security Policy functions as Council President in matters of foreign affairs, as Commissioner for External Relations, and as High Representative for the Common Foreign and Security Policy. *See* High Representative.

unanimity The principle that all member states must vote in favour for an agreement to be reached. It implies that each member state holds a potential veto.

Uruguay Round The eighth round of multilateral trade negotiations (MTN) conducted within the framework of the General Agreement on Tariffs and Trade (GATT), spanning from 1986 to 1994 and embracing 123 countries. The Round transformed the GATT into the World Trade Organization (WTO). The Uruguay Round Agreement on Agriculture provides for converting quantitative restrictions to tariffs and for a phased reduction of tariffs. The agreement also imposes rules and disciplines on agricultural export subsidies, domestic subsidies, and sanitary and phytosanitary measures.

utilitarian theory A theory that relates to choosing the greatest good for the greatest number of people.

variable geometry An image of the European Union that foresees the breakdown of a unified form of co-operation, and the introduction of a 'pick and choose' approach to further integration.

variable levy In the context of the Common Agricultural Policy (CAP), a levy raised on produce before it enters the common market, so that it is priced at or above the internal price. A system of 'reimbursements'

(refunds) enables European producers to sell their products on the world market at world prices without losing income.

veto player According to Tsebelis, for policy change to occur, a certain number of individual or collective actors (veto players) have to agree to the proposed change.

voluntary agreement An agreement resulting from the autonomous European Social Dialogue, which proceeds without the initiative or participation of the Commission and, as such, its implementation is not subject to legal enforcement. *See* European Social Dialogue.

Walter Hallstein The first president of the European Commission from 1958 to 1969, a committed European, and a decisive proponent of European integration. In his opinion, the most important prerequisite for a successful political integration of Europe was the creation of common economic institutions. As president of the European Commission, Hallstein worked towards a rapid realization of the common market.

Warsaw Pact Signed on 14 May 1955 by the USSR, Poland, East Germany, Czechoslovakia, Hungary, Romania, Bulgaria, and Albania, the 'Warsaw Treaty of Friendship, Cooperation, and Mutual Assistance' aimed to ensure the close integration of military, economic, and cultural policy between these communist nations. The democratic revolutions of 1989 in Eastern Europe heralded the end of the Warsaw Pact and the Cold War between East and West.

Werner Plan This 1970 blueprint for economic and monetary union (EMU) proposed three stages with which to reach EMU by 1980. On the institutional side, it recommended setting up two supranational bodies: 'a Community System for the Central Banks' and a 'Centre of Decision for Economic Policy'. The former would pursue monetary policies, whereas the latter would coordinate macroeconomic policies (including some tax policies). Most of the recommendations of the Werner Plan were adopted.

Western European Union (WEU) A collaborative defence agreement and extension of the 1948 Treaty of Brussels, signed in 1955. It was designed to allow for the rearmament of West Germany. It was revitalized in the 1980s, and subsequently served as a bridge between the North Atlantic Treaty Organization (NATO) and the EU. Its functions have lately been subsumed within the European Union. *See* Treaty of Brussels.

widening Generally refers to the enlargement of the EU, but may also be used to denote the increasing scope of Community or Union competences.

Working Time Directive *See* European Working Time Directive.

World Trade Organization (WTO) An international organization that oversees the global trade in goods and services.

yellow card If a draft legislative act's compliance with the subsidiarity principle is contested by a third of the votes allocated to national parliaments (the yellow card), the Commission has to review the proposal and decide to maintain, amend, or withdraw the act, also motivating its decision. This threshold is a quarter in the case of a draft submitted on the basis of

Article 76 TFEU on the Area of Freedom, Security, and Justice (AFSJ). *See* Subsidiarity.

Yugoslavia A country in the Western Balkans that existed during most of the twentieth century. In 1963, it was renamed the Socialist Federal Republic of Yugoslavia, which included six republics—namely, Bosnia and Herzegovina, Croatia, SR Macedonia, Montenegro, Slovenia, and Serbia—and two autonomous provinces (Vojvodina and Kosovo). After the 1991 Balkan Wars, which followed the secession of most of the country's constituent entities, the Federal Republic of Yugoslavia existed until 2003, when it was renamed Serbia and Montenegro. On the basis of a referendum held on 21 May 2006, Montenegro declared independence on 3 June of that year.

zero-sum game A game played (by states) in which the victory of one group implies the loss of another.

Zollverein A customs union between German states in the eighteenth century under Bismarck; the economic basis for German unification.

References

Aalberts, T. A. (2004) 'The future of sovereignty in multilevel governance in Europe: a constructivist reading', *Journal of Common Market Studies*, 42/1: 23–46.

Achen, C. H. (2006) 'Evaluating political decision-making models' in R. Thomson, F. N. Stokman, C. H. Achen, and T. Koenig (eds) *The European Union Decides* (Cambridge: Cambridge University Press), pp. 264–98.

Adelle, C. and Anderson, J. (2012) 'Lobby groups' in A. Jordan and C. Adelle (eds) *Environmental Policy in the European Union*, 3rd edn (London: Routledge), pp. 152–69.

Alter, K. (2001) *Establishing the Supremacy of European Law* (Oxford: Oxford University Press).

Andersen, M. S. and Liefferink, D. (eds) (1997) *European Environmental Policy: The Pioneers* (Manchester: Manchester University Press).

Anderson, C. J. (1998) 'When in doubt, use proxies: attitudes toward domestic politics and support for European integration', *Comparative Political Studies*, 31/5: 569–601.

Anderson, G. (ed.) (2012) *Internal Markets and Multilevel Governance: The Experience of the European Union, Australia, Canada, Switzerland, and the United States* (Oxford: Oxford University Press).

Anderson, J. J. (1995) 'The state of the (European) Union: from the single market to Maastricht, from singular events to general theories', *World Politics*, 47/2: 441–65.

Ansaloni, M. (2012) *Configuration des Débats Politiques et Diversité de l'Action Publique en Europe: La Politique Agricole Commune et l'Environnement en France, en Hongrie et au Royaume-Uni*, PhD thesis, University of Montpellier 1.

Armstrong, K. and Bulmer, S. (1998) *The Governance of the Single European Market* (Manchester: Manchester University Press).

Arnull, A. (2006) *The European Union and its Court of Justice*, 2nd edn (Oxford: Oxford University Press).

Arnull, A. and Wincott, D. (eds) (2002) *Accountability and Legitimacy in the European Union* (Oxford: Oxford University Press).

Aron, R. and Lerner, D. (1957) *France Defeats EDC* (London: Thames and Hudson).

Aspinwall, M. and Greenwood, J. (1998) 'Conceptualising collective action in the European Union: an introduction' in J. Greenwood and M. Aspinwall (eds) *Collective Action in the European Union: Interests and the New Politics of Associability* (London: Routledge), pp. 1–30.

Aspinwall, M. and Schneider, G. (2001) 'Institutional research on the European Union: mapping the field' in M. Aspinwall and G. Schneider (eds) *The Rules of Integration: Institutionalist Approaches to the Study of Europe* (Manchester: Manchester University Press), pp. 1–18.

Axelrod, R. (1984) *The Evolution of Co-operation* (New York: Basic Books).

Bache, I. (2008) *Europeanization and Multilevel Governance: Cohesion Policy in the European Union and Britain* (London: Rowman & Littlefield).

Bache, I., George, S., and Bulmer, S. (eds) (2011) *Politics in the European Union*, 3rd edn (Oxford: Oxford University Press).

Balme, R. and Chabanet, D. (eds) (2008) *European Governance and Democracy: Power and Protest in the EU* (Lanham, MD: Rowman & Littlefield).

Barber, L. (1995) 'The men who run Europe', *Financial Times*, 11–12 March, section 2: 1–2.

Barbier, J.-C. (ed.) (2012) 'EU law, governance and social policy', *European Integration online Papers (EIoP)*, 16/1.

Barents, R. (2010) 'The Court of Justice after the Treaty of Lisbon' *Common Market Law Review*, 47/3: 709–28.

Barnard, C. (2000) 'Regulating competitive federalism in the European Union? The case of EC social policy' in J. Shaw (ed.) *Social Law and Policy in an Evolving European Union* (Oxford: Hart), pp. 49–69.

Baumgartner, F. and Leech, B. (1998) *Basic Interests: The Importance of Groups in Politics and Political Science* (Princeton, NJ: Princeton University Press).

Bayliss, J., Smith, S., and Owens, P. (2010) *The Globalization of World Politics*, 5th edn (Oxford: Oxford University Press).

Bellamy, A. (2002) *Kosovo and the International Society* (New York: Palgrave).

Bellamy, R. and Attuci, C. (2009) 'Normative theory and the EU: between contract and community' in A. Wiener and T. Diez (eds) *European Integration Theory*, 2nd edn (Oxford: Oxford University Press), pp. 198–220.

Bellamy, R. and Castiglione, D. (2011) 'Democracy by delegation? Who represents whom and how in European governance', *Government and Opposition*, 46/1: 101–25.

Bellamy, R., Castiglione, D., and Shaw, J. (eds) (2006) *Making European Citizens: Civic Inclusion in a Transnational Context* (Basingstoke: Palgrave).

Benson, D. and Adelle, C. (2012) 'Re-assessing European Union environmental policy after the Lisbon Treaty' in A. Jordan and C. Adelle (eds) *Environmental Policy in the European Union*, 3rd edn (London: Routledge), pp. 32–48.

Benz, A. (1998) 'Politikverflechtung ohne Politikverflechtungsfalle: Koordination und Strukturdynamik im europäischen Mehrebenensystem', *Politische Vierteljahresschrift*, 39/4: 558–89.

Benz, A. and Eberlein, B. (1999) 'The Europeanization of regional policies: patterns of multi-level governance', *Journal of European Public Policy*, 6/2: 329–48.

Berger, S. and Dore, R. (1996) *National Diversity and Global Capitalism* (Ithaca, NY: Cornell University Press).

Berkhout, J. and Lowery, D. (2008) 'Counting organized interests in the European Union: a comparison of data sources', *Journal of European Public Policy*, 15/4: 489–513.

Bertoncini, Y. (2007) 'The EU Budget as an instrument to finance collective goods: key points for the debate', Paper presented at the Notre Europe seminar 'The EU Budget: What For?', 19 April, Brussels.

Bertrand, R. (1956) 'The European common market proposal', *International Organization*, 10/4: 559–74.

Best, E., Christiansen, T., and Settembri, P. (eds) (2008) *The Institutions of the Enlarged European Union: Continuity and Change* (Cheltenham: Edward Elgar).

Beyers, J. (2002) 'Gaining and seeking access: the European adaptation of domestic interest associations', *European Journal of Political Research*, 41/5: 585–612.

Beyers, J. and Dierrickx, G. (1998) 'The working groups of the Council of the European Union: supranational or intergovernmental negotiations?', *Journal of Common Market Studies*, 36/3: 289–317.

Beyers, J., Eising, R., and Maloney, W. (eds) (2008) *West European Politics*, 31/6 (special issue entitled 'The politics of organised interests in Europe: lessons from EU studies and comparative politics').

BirdLife (2008a) 'Europe's farmland birds continue to suffer from agricultural policy', 2 December, available online at http://www.birdlife.org/news/news/2008/12/monitoring.html

BirdLife (2008b) 'CAP Health Check: the environment gets a placebo treatment', 20 November, available online at http://www.birdlife.org/news/extra/europe/health_check.html

BirdLife, European Environmental Bureau (EEB), European Forum on Nature Conservation and Pastoralism (EFNCP), International Federation of Organic Agriculture Movements (IFOAM), and World Wildlife Fund for Nature (WWF) (2009) *Proposal for a New EU Common Agricultural Policy*, available online at http://www.eeb.org/EEB/?LinkServID=2ED32A72-ED91-1F04-34B8AB7D239E5BA5

Blavoukos, S. and Pagoulatos, G. (2008) 'Enlargement waves and interest group participation in the EU policymaking system: establishing a framework of analysis', *West European Politics*, 31/6: 1147–65.

Blom-Hansen, J. (2011) 'The EU comitology system: taking stock before the new Lisbon regime', *Journal of European Public Policy*, 18/4: 607–17.

Bobbio, N. (1987) *The Future of Democracy* (Cambridge: Polity Press).

Bond, M. (2011) *The Council of Europe* (London: Routledge).

Borrás, S. and Jacobsson, K. (2004) 'The open method of co-ordination and new governance patterns', *Journal of European Public Policy*, 11/2: 185–203.

Borrás, S. and Radaelli, C. M. (2010) *Recalibrating the Open Method of Coordination: Towards Diverse and More Effective Usages* (Stockholm: Swedish Institute for European Policy Studies).

Borrás, S. and Radaelli, C. M. (eds) (2011) *Journal of European Public Policy*, 18/4 (special issue entitled 'The politics of the Lisbon Agenda: governance architectures and domestic usages of Europe').

Börzel, T. A. (1997) 'What's so special about policy networks? An exploration of the concept and its usefulness in studying European governance', *European Integration online Papers (EIoP)*, 16/1.

Börzel, T. A. (2002) 'Pace-setting, foot-dragging and fence-sitting: member state responses to Europeanisation', *Journal of Common Market Studies*, 40/2: 193–214.

Börzel, T. A. (2003) *Environmental Leaders and Laggards in the European Union: Why There is (not) a Southern Problem* (London: Ashgate).

Börzel, T. A. (ed.) (2006) *The Disparity of European Integration: Revisiting Neofunctionalism in Honor of Ernst Haas* (London: Routledge).

Börzel, T. A. and Risse, T. (2000) 'When Europe hits home: Europeanization and domestic change', *European Integration online Papers (EIoP)*, 15/4.

Börzel, T. A. and Risse, T. (2007) 'Europeanization: the domestic impact of EU politics', in K. E. Jorgensen, M. A. Pollack, and B. Rosamond (eds) *Handbook of European Union Politics* (London: Sage), pp. 483–504.

Börzel, T. A., Hofmann, T., Panke, D., and Sprungk, C. (2010) 'Obstinate and inefficient: why member states do not comply with European law', *Comparative Political Studies*, 43/11: 1363–90.

Bossong, R. (2012) *Assessing the EU's Added Value in the Area of Terrorism Prevention and Radicalisation*, Economics of Security Working Paper 60, available online at http://www.economics-of-security.eu/sites/default/files/WP60_Bossong_Assessing_Added_Value.pdf

Bulkeley, H. Davies, A., Evans, B., Gibbs, D., Kern, K., and Theobald, K. (2003) 'Environmental governance and transnational municipal networks in Europe', *Journal of Environmental Policy and Planning*, 5/3: 235–54.

Bulmer, S. (1983) 'Domestic politics and European Community policy-making', *Journal of Common Market Studies*, 21/4: 349–63.

Burley, A. M. and Mattli, W. (1993) 'Europe before the court: a political theory of legal integration', *International Organization*, 47/1: 41–76.

Burns, C. (2012) 'The European Parliament' in A. Jordan and C. Adelle (eds) *Environmental Policy in the European Union*, 3rd edn (London: Routledge), pp. 132–51.

Burns, C., Carter, N., and Worsfold, N. (2012) 'Enlargement and the environment: the changing behaviour of the European Parliament', *Journal of Common Market Studies*, 50/1: 54–70.

Busch, K. (1988) *The Corridor Model: A Concept for Further Development of an EU Social Policy* (Brussels: European Trade Union Institute).

Busuioc, M., Groenleer, M., and Trondal, J. (2012) (eds) *The Agency Phenomenon in the European Union* (Manchester: Manchester University Press).

Cameron, D. (1992) 'The 1992 initiative: causes and consequences' in A. Sbragia (ed.) *Europolitics: Insitutions and Policy-making in the 'New' European Community* (Washington DC: Brookings), pp. 23–74.

Cameron, F. (2012) *An Introduction to European Foreign Policy* (London: Routledge).

Caporaso, J. A. (1996) 'The European Union and forms of state: Westphalian, regulatory or post-modern?', *Journal of Common Market Studies*, 34/1: 29–52.

Caporaso, J. A. and Jupille, J. (2001) 'The Europeanization of gender equality policy and domestic structural change' in M. G. Cowles, J. A. Caporaso, and T. Risse (eds) *Transforming Europe: Europeanization and Domestic Change* (Ithaca, NY: Cornell University Press), pp. 21–43.

Caporaso, J. A. and Tarrow, S. (2009) 'Polanyi in Brussels: supranational institutions and the transnational embedding of markets', *International Organization*, 63/4: 593–620.

Carey, S. and Burton, J. (2004) 'Research note: the influence of the press in shaping public opinion towards the European Union in Britain', *Political Studies*, 53/3: 623–40.

Carubba, C. J. (2001) 'The electoral connection in European Union politics', *Journal of Politics*, 63/1: 141–58.

Chalmers, D. and Tomkins, A. (2007) *European Union Public Law* (Cambridge: Cambridge University Press).

Checkel, J. T. (2001) 'A constructivist research programme in EU studies', *European Union Politics*, 2/2: 219–49.

Checkel, J. T. (2007) 'Constructivism and EU politics' in K. E. Jørgensen, M. A. Pollack, and B. Rosamond (eds) *Handbook of European Union Politics* (London: Sage), pp. 57–76.

Checkel, J. T. and Katzenstein, P. J. (eds) *European Identity* (Cambridge: Cambridge University Press).

Choi, Y. J. and Caporaso, J. (2002) 'Comparative regional integration' in W. Carlsnaes, T. Risse, and B. Simmons (eds) Handbook of International Relations (London: Sage), pp. 480–99

Christiansen, T. (1997) 'Reconstructing European space: from territorial politics to multi-level governance' in K. E. Jørgensen (ed.) *Reflective Approaches to European Governance* (London: Macmillan), pp. 51–68.

Christiansen, T. and Kirchner, E. (eds) (2000) *Committee Governance in the European Union* (Manchester: Manchester University Press).

Christiansen, T. and Larsson, T. (eds) (2007) *The Role of Committees in the Policy Process of the European Union* (Cheltenham: Edward Elgar).

Christiansen, T. and Piattoni, S. (eds) (2004) *Informal Governance in the European Union* (Cheltenham: Edward Elgar).

Christiansen, T. and Polak, J. (2009) 'Comitology between political decision-making and technocratic governance: regulating GMOs in the European Union', *EIPASCOPE*, 1: 5–11.

Christiansen, T., Jørgensen, K. E., and Wiener, A. (eds) (2001) *The Social Construction of Europe* (London: Sage).

Chryssochoou, D. N. (2009) *Theorizing European Integration*, 2nd edn (London and New York: Routledge).

Church, C. H. (1996) *European Integration Theory in the 1990s*, European Dossier Series (London: University of North London).

Church, C. H. and Phinnemore, D. (2002) *The Penguin Guide to the European Treaties: From Rome to Maastricht, Amsterdam, Nice and Beyond* (London: Penguin).

Church, C. H. and Phinnemore, D. (2006) *Understanding the European Constitution: An Introduction to the EU Constitutional Treaty* (London: Routledge).

Cini, M. (2007) *From Integration to Integrity: Administrative Ethics and Reform in the European Commission* (Manchester: Manchester University Press).

Cini, M. and Bourne, A. K. (eds) (2006) *Palgrave Advances in European Union Studies* (Basingstoke: Palgrave Macmillan).

Ciolos, D. (2011) 'A new partnership between Europe and its farmers', Speech presenting the legislative proposals on the reform of the common agricultural policy to the European Parliament, SPEECH/11/653, 12 October, Brussels.

Cocks, P. (1980) 'Towards a Marxist theory of European integration', *International Organization*, 34/1: 1–40.

Coen, D. (2009) 'Business lobbying in the European Union', in D. Coen and J. Richardson (eds) *Lobbying the European Union: Institutions, Actors, and Issues* (New York: Oxford University Press), pp. 145–68.

Coen, D. and Richardson, J. (eds) (2009) *Lobbying the European Union: Institutions, Actors, and Issues* (New York: Oxford University Press).

Coen, D. and Thatcher, M. (2007) 'Network governance and multi-level delegation: European networks of regulatory agencies', *Journal of Public Policy*, 28/1: 49–71.

Cohen, B. J. (1971) *The Future of Sterling as an International Currency* (London: Macmillan).

Cohen, B. (2008) 'The euro in a global context: challenges and capacities', in K. Dyson (ed.) *The Euro at 10: Europeanization, Power, and Convergence* (Oxford: Oxford University Press), pp. 37–53.

Conant, L. J. (2002) *Justice Contained: Law And Politics in the European Union* (Ithaca, NY: Cornell University Press).

Conzelmann, T. (1998) '"Europeanization" of regional development policies? Linking the multi-level approach with theories of policy learning and policy change', *European Integration online Papers (EIoP)*, 4/2.

Coombes, D. (1970) *Politics and Bureaucracy in the European Community: A Portrait of the Commission of the EEC* (London: George Allen & Unwin).

Committee of Professional Agricultural Organizations–General Committee for Agricultural Cooperation in the European Union (COPA–COGECA) (2011) *The Future of the CAP after 2013: The Reaction of EU Farmers and Agri-cooperatives to the Commission's Legislative Proposals*, PAC(11)7038, Brussels.

Corbett, R. (1998) *The European Parliament's Role in Closer EU Integration* (London: Macmillan).

Corbett, R., Jacobs, F., and Shackleton, M. (2011) *The European Parliament*, 8th edn (London: John Harper).

Council of the European Union (1996) *The European Union Today and Tomorrow: Adapting the European Union for the Benefit of its Peoples and Preparing it for the Future—A General Outline for a Draft Revision of the Treaties* (Brussels: EU Council).

Council of the European Union (2007) 'Accession of Bulgaria and Romania: EU appointments and changes to Council procedures', Press release 5002/07, available online at http://www.consilium. europa.eu/ueDocs/cms_Data/docs/pressData/en/misc/92310.pdf

Council of the European Union (2008) *Brussels European Council: Presidency Conclusions*, 14 February, Brussels, available online at http://www.consilium. europa.eu/ueDocs/cms_Data/docs/pressData/en/ec/97669.pdf

Council of the European Union (2009) *Council Conclusions on a Strategic Framework for European Cooperation in Education and Training* ('ET 2020'), 12 May, Brussels.

Council of the European Union (2010) *Lisbon European Council: Presidency Conclusions*, 23–24 March, Lisbon, available online at http://ue.eu.int/ueDocs/cms_Data/docs/pressData/en/ec/00100-r1.en0.htm

Council of the European Union (2011) *Financial Activity Report 2010: Section II—European Council and Council*, 30 June, Brussels, available online at http://www.consilium.europa.eu/media/1250609/st11598.en11.pdf

Cowles, M. G. (1995) 'Seizing the agenda for the new Europe: the ERT and EC 1992', *Journal of Common Market Studies*, 33/4: 501–26.

Cowles, M. G. (1997) 'Organizing industrial coalitions: a challenge for the future?' in H. Wallace and A. R. Young (eds) *Participation and Policy-making in the European Union* (Oxford: Clarendon Press), pp. 116–40.

Cowles, M. G., Caporaso, J. A., and Risse, T. (eds) (2001) *Transforming Europe: Europeanization and Domestic Change* (Ithaca, NY: Cornell University Press).

Cox, R. (1981) 'Social forces, states and world orders: beyond international relations theory', *Millennium: Journal of International Studies*, 10/2: 126–55.

Craig, P. (2010) *The Lisbon Treaty: Law, Politics, and Treaty Reform* (Oxford: Oxford University Press).

Craig, P. and de Búrca, G. (2011) *EU Law: Text, Cases and Materials*, 5th edn (Oxford: Oxford University Press).

Crespy, A. and Gajewska, K. (2010) 'New Parliament, new cleavages after the Eastern enlargement? The conflict over the Services Directive as an opposition between the liberals and the regulators', *Journal of Common Market Studies*, 48/5: 1185–208.

Curtin, D. (1993) 'The constitutional structure of the Union: a Europe of bits and pieces', *Common Market Law Review*, 30/1: 17–69.

d'Oultremont, C. (2011) 'The CAP post-2013: more equitable, green and market oriented?', *European Policy Brief*, 5, available online at http://www.egmontinstitute.be/papers/11/eur/EPB5.pdf

da Conceição-Heldt, E. (2004) *The Common Fisheries Policy of the European Union: A Study of Integrative and Distributive Bargaining* (London: Routledge).

da Conceição-Heldt, E. (2006) 'Taking actors' preferences and the institutional setting seriously: the EU Common Fisheries Policy', *Journal of Public Policy*, 26/3: 279–99.

Dalton, R. J. and Duval, R. (1986) 'The political environment and foreign policy opinions: British attitudes toward European integration, 1972–1979', *British Journal of Political Science*, 16/1: 623–40.

Damro, C. (2012) 'Market power Europe', *Journal of European Public Policy*, 19/5: 682–99.

Dashwood, A. (1983) 'Hastening slowly the Community's path towards harmonisation' in H. Wallace, W. Wallace, and C. Webb (eds) *Policy-making in the European Community*, 2nd edn (Chichester: John Wiley), pp. 273–99.

Dashwood, A., Dougan, M., Rodger, B., Spaventa, E., and Wyatt, D. (2011) *Wyatt and Dashwood's European Union law*, 6th edn, (Oxford: Hart Publishing).

Davidson-Scmich, L. K. and Vladescu, E. (2010) 'The 2009 European Parliament campaigns: national, Eurosceptic, or simply lacklustre?', Paper for Panel Session I.1: 'Media coverage and its effects in the European Parliament elections', PIREDEU User Community Conference, 18–19 November, Brussels.

Davies, A. C. L. (2008) 'One step forward, two steps back? The *Viking* and *Laval* cases in the ECJ', *Industrial Law Journal*, 37/2: 126–48.

de Búrca, G., de Witte, B., and Ogertschnig, L. (eds) (2005) *Social Rights in Europe* (Oxford: Oxford University Press).

de Castro, P. (2010) *European Agriculture and New Global Challenges* (Rome: Donzelli Instant Book).

de Grieco, J. M. (1995) 'The Maastricht Treaty, economic and monetary union and the neo-realist research programme', *Review of International Studies*, 21/1: 21–40.

de Grieco, J. M. (1996) 'State interests and international rule trajectories: a neorealist interpretation of the Maastricht Treaty and European economic and monetary union', *Security Studies*, 5/2: 176–222.

de la Porte, C. and Pochet, P. (2002) *Building Social Europe through the Open Method of Co-Ordination* (Berlin: PIE Peter Lang).

de la Porte, C. and Pochet, P. (2004) 'The European employment strategy: existing research and remaining questions', European briefing, *Journal of European Social Policy*, 14/1: 71–8.

de Schoutheete, P. (2011) 'Decision-making in the Union', Policy Brief No 24 (Paris: Notre Europe).

de Vreese, C. H. (2002) *Framing Europe: Television News and European Integration* (Amsterdam: Aksant Academic).

de Vreese, C. H. and Semetko, H. A. (2004) 'News matters: influences on the vote in the Danish 2000 euro referendum campaign', *European Journal of Political Research*, 43/5: 699–722.

de Vreese, C. H, Banducci, S. A., Semetko, H. A., and Boomgaarden, H. G. (2006) 'The news coverage of the 2004 European Parliamentary election campaign in 25 countries', *European Union Politics*, 7/4: 479–506.

de Vreese, C. H., Boomgaarden, H. G., and Semetko, H. A. (2011) '(In)direct framing effects: the effects of news media framing on public support for Turkish membership in the European Union', *Communication Research*, 38/2: 179–205.

Dedman, M. (2009) *The Origins and Development of the European Union: A History of European Integration* (London: Routledge).

Dehousse, R., Boussaguet, L., and Jacquot, S. (2010) 'Change and continuity in European governance', *Les Cahiers Européens de Sciences Po.*, 6, available online at http://www.cee.sciences-po.fr/erpa/docs/wp_2010_6.pdf

Delgado, J. (2006) 'Single market trails home bias', *Bruegel Policy Brief*, 5, 7 October, Brussels.

Department for Environment, Food and Rural Affairs (Defra) (2011) *CAP Reform Post 2013: DEFRA Discussion Paper on the Impact in England of EU Commission Regulatory Proposals for Common Agricultural Policy Reform, Post 2013*, available online at http://www.defra.gov.uk/consult/2011/12/12/cap-reform-1112/

DG Enlargement (2006) *Twinning: A Tested Experience in a Broader European Context* (Brussels: European Commission), available online at http://ec.europa.eu/enlargement/archives/pdf/press_corner/publications/twinning_en.pdf

Diebold, W., Jr (1959) *The Schuman Plan: A Study in Economic Cooperation, 1950–1959* (New York: Praeger).

Diez, T. (1999) '"Speaking Europe": the politics of integration discourse', *Journal of European Public Policy*, 6/4: 598–613.

DiMaggio, P. and Powell, W. (1991) 'The iron cage revisited: institutional isomorphism and collective rationality in organizational fields' in P. DiMaggio and W. Powell (eds) *The New Institutionalism in Organizational Analysis* (Chicago, IL: University of Chicago Press), pp. 63–82.

Dinan, D. (2004) *Europe Recast* (Basingstoke: Palgrave).

Dinan, D. (2009) 'Institutions and governance: a new treaty, a newly elected parliament and a new Commission', *Journal of Common Market Studies Annual Review*, 48: 95–118.

Dinan, D. (2011) 'Governance and institutions: implementing the Lisbon Treaty in the shadow of the euro crisis', *Journal of Common Market Studies Annual Review*, 49: 103–21.

Dispersyn, M., Vandervorst, P., de Falleur, M., and Meulders, D. (1990) 'La construction d'un serpent social européen', *Revue Belge de Sécurité Sociale*, 12: 889–979.

Dod's (2011) *European Public Affairs Directory (EPAD) 2011* (London: Dod's Parliamentary Communications).

Dølvik, J. E. (1997) *Redrawing Boundaries of Solidarity? ETUC, Social Dialogue and the Europeanization of Trade Unions in the 1990s*, ARENA Report No. 5, Oslo.

Dover, R. (2007) 'For Queen and company: the role of intelligence in the UK arms trade', *Political Studies*, 55/4: 683–708.

Dowding, K. (2000) 'Institutional research on the European Union: a critical review', *European Union Politics*, 1/1: 125–44.

Dunne, T. and Schmidt, B. C. (2011) 'Realism', in J. Baylis and S. Smith (eds) *The Globalization of World Politics*, 2nd edn, (Oxford: Oxford University Press), pp. 162–83.

Dyson, K. and Featherstone, K. (1999) *The Road to Maastricht: Negotiating Economic and Monetary Union* (Oxford: Oxford University Press).

Dyson, K. and Quaglia, L. (eds) (2010) *European Economic Governance and Policies, Vol. I: Commentary on Key Historical and Institutional Documents* (Oxford: Oxford University Press).

Dyson, K. and Quaglia, L. (eds) (2011) *European Economic Governance and Policies, Vol. II: Commentary on Key Policy Documents* (Oxford: Oxford University Press).

Easton, D. (1965) *A Systems Analysis of Political Life* (New York: John Wiley & Sons).

Eberlein, B. and Grande, W. (2005) 'Beyond delegation: transnational regulatory regimes and the EU regulatory state', *Journal of European Public Policy*, 12/1: 89–112.

Eberlein, B. and Kerwer, D. (2002) 'Theorising the new modes of European Union governance', *European Integration Online Papers (EIoP)*, 6/5: 1–21.

Eberlein, B. and Kerwer, D. (2004) 'New governance in the European Union: a theoretical perspective', *Journal of Common Market Studies*, 42/1: 121–42.

ECORYS (2008) *Progress on EU Sustainable Development Strategy: Final Report* (Rotterdam: ECORYS).

Eeckhout, P. (2004) *External Relations of the European Union: Legal and Constitutional Foundations* (Oxford: Oxford University Press).

Egan, M. (2001) *Constructing a European Market: Standards, Regulation and Governance* (Oxford: Oxford University Press).

Egan, M. (2012) 'Single market' in E. Jones, A. Menon, and S. Weatherill (eds) *Handbook of the European Union* (Oxford: Oxford University Press).

Egan, M. and Guimaries, M. H. (2011) 'Compliance in the single market', Paper prepared for the EUSA Biennial Conference, 3–5 March, Boston, available online at http://euce.org/eusa/2011/papers/2e_guimaraes.pdf

Egeberg, M. (2006a) 'Executive politics as usual: role behaviour and conflict dimensions in the college of European commissioners', *Journal of European Public Policy*, 13/1: 1–15.

Egeberg, M. (ed.) (2006b) *Multilevel Union Administration: The Transformation of Executive Politics in Europe* (Basingstoke: Palgrave).

Egeberg, M. and Heskestad, A. (2010) 'The denationalisation of *cabinets* in the European Commission', *Journal of Common Market Studies*, 48/4: 775–86.

Egeberg, M., Schaefer, G. F., and Trondal, J. (2003) 'The many faces of EU committee governance', *West European Politics*, 26/3: 19–40.

Eichenberg, R. C. and Dalton, R. J. (1993) 'Europeans and the European Community: the dynamics of public support for European integration', *International Organization*, 47/4: 507–34.

Eising, R. (2004) 'Multi-level governance and business interests in the European Union', *Governance*, 17/2: 211–46.

Eising, R. (2007) 'The access of business interests to EU institutions: towards elite pluralism?', *Journal of European Public Policy*, 14/3: 384–403.

Eising, R. (2009) *The Political Economy of State–Business Relations in Europe: Capitalism, Interest Intermediation, and EU Policy-making* (London: Routledge).

Eising, R. and Kohler-Koch, B. (eds) (1999) *The Transformation of Governance in the European Union* (London: Routledge).

Elgström, O. and Jönsson, C. (2000) 'Negotiating in the European Union: bargaining or problem-solving?', *Journal of European Public Policy*, 7/5: 684–704.

ENDS Europe (2008) 'EU climate change plans survive summit test', 16 October.

Eriksen, E. O. (2011) 'Governance between expertise and democracy: the case of European security', *Journal of European Public Policy*, 18/8: 1169–89.

Eriksen, E. O and Fossum, J. E. (eds) (2012) *Rethinking Democracy and the European Union* (London: Routledge).

Eriksen, E. O., Fossum, J. E., and Menéndez, A. J. (eds) (2005) *Developing a Constitution for Europe* (London: Routledge).

Eurobarometer (2011a) *Eurobarometer 74: Public Opinion in the European Union*, available online at http://ec.europa.eu/public_opinion/archives/eb/eb74/eb74_publ_en.pdf

Eurobarometer (2011b) *Eurobarometer 75: Public Opinion in the European Union*, available online at http://ec.europa.eu/public_opinion/archives/eb/eb75/eb75_en.htm

Eurobarometer (2011c) *Eurobarometer 76: Public Opinion in the European Union*, available online at http://ec.europa.eu/public_opinion/archives/eb/eb76/eb76_en.htm

European Citizens Initiative (2012) 'Basic facts', available online at http://ec.europa.eu/citizens-initiative/public/basic-facts

European Commission (1992a) *The Internal Market after 1992: Meeting the Challenge*, SEC(92)2044, October, Brussels.

European Commission (1992b) *An Open and Structured Dialogue between the Commission and Special Interest Groups*, SEC(92)2272 final, December, Brussels.

European Commission (2001a) *European Governance: A White Paper*, COM(2001)428 final, July, Brussels.

European Commission (2001b) *Proposal for a Council Framework Decision on Combating Terrorism*, COM(2001)521 final, February, Brussels.

European Commission (2002a) *Towards a Reinforced Culture of Consultation and Dialogue: General Principles and Minimum Standards for Consultation of Interested Parties by the Commission*, COM(2002)704 final, December, Brussels.

European Commission (2002b) *The Mid-Term Review of the Common Agricultural Policy*, COM(2002)294 final, March, Brussels.

European Commission (2002c) *A Project for the European Union*, COM(2002)394 final, July, Brussels.

European Commission (2004) *Area of Freedom, Security and Justice: Assessment of the Tampere Programme and Future Orientations*, COM(2004) 4002 final, June, Brussels.

European Commission (2005a) 'European Roadmap towards a Zero Victim Target: The EC Mine Action Strategy and Multiannual Indicative Programming 2005–2007', available online at http://eeas.europa.eu/anti_landmines/docs/strategy_0507_en.pdf

European Commission (2006) *Green Paper: European Transparency Initiative*, COM(2006)194 final, May, Brussels.

European Commission (2008a) *European Transparency Initiative: A Framework for Relations with Interest Representatives (Register and Code of Conduct)*, COM(2008)323 final, May, Brussels.

European Commission (2008b) *'Education & Training 2010': Main Policy Initiatives and Outputs in Education and Training since the Year 2000*, February, Brussels, available online at http://ec.europa.eu/education/policies/2010/doc/compendium05_en.pdf

European Commission (2008c) *Report from the Commission to the European Parliament and the Council on the Activities of the European Globalisation Adjustment Fund in 2007*, COM(2008)421 final, July, Brussels.

European Commission (2009a) *Five Years of an Enlarged EU: Economic Achievements and Challenges*, February, Brussels, available online at http://ec.europa.eu/economy_finance/publications/publication14078_en.pdf

European Commission (2009b) *Report from the Commission to the European Parliament and the Council on the Activities of the European Globalisation Adjustment Fund in 2008*, COM(2009)394 final, July, Brussels.

European Commission (2010a) *The CAP towards 2020: Meeting the Food, Natural Resources and Territorial Challenges of the Future*, COM(2010)672 final, November, Brussels.

European Commission (2010b) *Report from the Commission to the European Parliament and the Council on the Activities of the European Globalisation Adjustment Fund in 2009*, COM(2010) 464 final, Brussels.

European Commission (2011) *Communication from the Commission to the European Parliament and the Council: Enlargement Strategy and Main Challenges 2011–2012*, COM(2011)666 final, October, Brussels.

European Commission (2008c) *An Updated Strategic Framework for European Cooperation in Education and Training*, COM(2008)865 final, December, Brussels.

European Commission/Organisation for Economic Co-operation and Development (OECD) (2010) *EU Donor Atlas, Vol. 1*, January, available online at http://ec.europa.eu./development/index.en.cfmp

European Council (2001) *Declaration by the Heads of State and Government of the European Union and the President of the Commission: Follow-up to the September 11 Attacks and the Fight against Terrorism*, SN 4296/2/01, October, Brussels.

European Council (2012) *Conclusions of the European Council (1–2 March)*, EUCO 4/3/12 REV 3, 8 May, Brussels.

European Economic and Social Committee (EESC) (2004) *Final Report of the Ad Hoc Group on Structured Cooperation with European Civil Society Organisations and Networks*, CESE 1498/2003, February, Brussels.

European Economic Community (1969) *Le Plan Mansholt: Un Memorandum de la Commission sur la Réforme de l'Agriculture de la CEE* (Paris: SECLAF).

European Environment Agency (EEA) (2007) *Europe's Environment: The Fourth Assessment* (Copenhagen: EEA).

European Movement for Food Sovereignty and another Common Agricultural Policy (FoodSovCAP) (2012) *FoodSocCAP Position on CAP Reform*, March, Brussels, available online at http://www.eurovia.org/IMG/article_PDF_article_a560.pdf

European Parliament (2001) *EP Resolution on the Commission White Paper on European Governance*, C5-0454/2001, available online at http://www.europarl.europa.eu/sides/getDoc.do?pubRef=-//EP//TEXT+REPORT+A5-2001-0399+0+DOC+XML+V0//EN

European Parliament (2011a) *Agreement between the European Parliament and the European Commission on the Establishment of a Transparency Register for Organisations and Self-Employed Individuals Engaged in EU Policy-making and Policy Implementation*, OJ L 191/29, 22.7.2011, available online at http://eur-lex.europa.eu/LexUriServ/LexUriServ.do?uri=OJ:L:2011:191:0029:0038:EN:PDF

European Parliament (2011b) *The EU Protein Deficit: What Solution for a Long-standing Problem?*, A7-0026/2011, available online at http://www.europarl.europa.eu/sides/getDoc.do?type=REPORT&reference=A7-2011-0026&language=EN

Faleg, G. (2012) 'Between knowledge and power: epistemic communities and the emergence of security sector reform in the EU security architecture', *European Security*, 21: 1–24.

Falkner, G. (1998) *EU Social Policy in the 1990s: Towards a Corporatist Policy Community* (London: Routledge).

Falkner, G. (2000a) 'The Council or the social partners? EC social policy between diplomacy and collective bargaining', *Journal of European Public Policy*, 7/5: 705–24.

Falkner, G. (2000b) 'EG-Sozialpolitik nach Verflechtungsfalle und Entscheidungslücke: Bewertungsmaßstäbe und Entwicklungstrends', *Politische Vierteljahresschrift*, 41/2: 279–301.

Falkner, G., Hartlapp, M., Leiber, S., and Treib, O. (2004) 'Non-compliance with EU directives in the member states: opposition through the backdoor?', *West European Politics*, 27/1: 2–73.

Falkner, G., Treib, O., Hartlapp, M., and Leiber, S. (2005) *Complying with Europe: EU Minimum Harmonisation and Soft Law in the Member States* (Cambridge: Cambridge University Press).

Falkner, G., Treib, O., Holzleithner, E., Causse, E., Furtlehner, P., Schulze, M., and Wiedermann, C. (2008) *Compliance in the Enlarged European Union: Living Rights or Dead Letters?* (Aldershot: Ashgate).

Featherstone, K. and Radaelli, C. (eds) (2003) *The Politics of Europeanisation* (Oxford: Oxford University Press).

Feldstein, M. (1997) 'EMU and international conflict', *Foreign Affairs*, 76/6: 60–74.

Fennelly, N. (1998) 'Preserving the legal coherence within the new treaty: the ECJ after the Treaty of Amsterdam', *Maastricht Journal of European and Comparative Law*, 5/2: 185–99.

Financial Services Authority (FSA) (2009) *The Turner Review: A Regulatory Response to the Global Banking Crisis* (London: HMSO).

Finke, D. (2009) 'Challenges to intergovernmentalism: an empirical analysis of EU treaty negotiations since Maastricht', *West European Politics*, 32/3: 466–95.

Flood, C. (2002) 'The challenge of Euroscepticism' in J. Gower (ed.) *The European Union Handbook*, 2nd edn (London: Fitzroy Dearborn), pp. 73–84.

Føllesdal, A. (2007) 'Normative political theory and the European Union' in K. E. Jørgensen, M. A. Pollack, and B. Rosamond (eds) *Handbook of European Union Politics* (London: Sage), pp. 317–35.

Føllesdal, A. and Hix, S. (2006) 'Why there is a democratic deficit in the EU: a response to Majone and Moravcsik', *Journal of Common Market Studies*, 44/3: 533–62.

FoodSovCAP (2012) *See* European Movement for Food Sovereignty and another Common Agricultural Policy

Forster, A. (1998) 'Britain and the negotiation of the Maastricht Treaty: a critique of liberal intergovernmentalism', *Journal of Common Market Studies*, 36/2: 347–68.

Frankel, J. A. and Rose, A. K. (1998) 'The endogeneity of the optimum currency area criteria', *Economic Journal*, 108/499: 1009–25.

Franklin, M. N., Marsh, M., and McLaren, L. M. (1994) 'The European question: opposition to unification in the wake of Maastricht', *Journal of Common Market Studies*, 32/4: 455–72.

Friis, L. and Murphy, A. (2001) 'Enlargement of the European Union: impacts on the EU, the candidates and the "next neighbours"', *The ECSA Review*, 14/1.

Fusacchia, A. (2009) 'Selection, appointment, and redeployment of senior Commission officials', PhD thesis, European University Institute, Florence.

Gabel, M. J. (1998) *Interests and Integration: Market Liberalization, Public Opinion, and European Union* (Ann Arbor, MI: University of Michigan Press).

Galloway, D. (2001) *The Treaty of Nice and Beyond* (Sheffield: Sheffield Academic Press).

Garman, J. and Hilditch, L. (1998) 'Behind the scenes: an examination of the informal processes at work in conciliation', *Journal of European Public Policy*, 5/2: 271–84.

Garrett, G. (1992) 'International cooperation and institutional choice: the European Community's internal market', *International Organization*, 46/2: 533–60.

Garrett, G. and Tsebelis, G. (1996) 'An institutional critique of intergovernmentalism', *International Organization*, 50/2: 269–99.

Garzon, I. (2007) *Reforming the Common Agricultural Policy: History of a Paradigm Change* (Basingstoke: Palgrave Macmillan).

Geddes, A. (2008) *Immigration and European Integration: Beyond Fortress Europe?*, 2nd edn (Manchester: Manchester University Press).

George, S. (1998) *An Awkward Partner: Britain in the European Community*, 3rd edn (Oxford: Oxford University Press).

George, S. and Bache, I. (2011) *Politics in the European Union* (Oxford: Oxford University Press).

Gibbon, P. (2008) 'An analysis of standards-based regulation in the EU organic sector, 1991–2007', *Journal of Agrarian Change*, 8/4: 553–82.

Gilbert, M. F. (2003) *Surpassing Realism: The Politics of European Integration since 1945* (Lanham, MD: Rowman & Littlefield).

Gilbert, M. F. (2011) *European Integration: A Concise History* (Lanham MD: AltaMira Press).

Gill, S. (1998) 'European governance and new constitutionalism: economic and monetary union and alternatives to disciplinary neoliberalism in Europe', *New Political Economy*, 3/1: 5–26.

Gillingham, J. (2003) *European Integration 1950–2003: Superstate or New Market Economy* (Cambridge: Cambridge University Press).

Goetschy, J. (2003) 'The European employment strategy, multi-level governance and policy coordination: past, present and future' in J. Zeitlin and D. Trubek (eds) *Governing Work and Welfare in a New Economy: European and American Experiments* (Oxford: Oxford University Press), pp. 59–87.

Gorges, M. J. (1996) *Euro-corporatism? Interest Intermediation in the European Community* (London: University Press of America).

Grabbe, H. (2001) 'How does Europeanization affect CEE governance? Conditionality, diffusion and diversity', *Journal of European Public Policy*, 8/6: 1013–31.

Grabbe, H. (2006) *The EU's Transformative Power: Europeanization through Conditionality in Central and Eastern Europe* (Basingstoke: Palgrave Macmillan).

Grande, E. (1994), Vom Nationalstaat zur europaischen Politikverflechtung: Expansion und Transformation moderner Staatlichkeit—undersucht am Beispiel der Forschungs—und Technologiepolitik', PhD thesis, Universität Konstanz.

Greenwood, J. (2011) *Interest Representation in the European Union*, 3rd edn (New York: Palgrave Macmillan).

Greer, A. (2005) *Agricultural Policy in Europe* (Manchester: Manchester University Press).

Grin G. (2003) *Battle of the Single European Market: Achievements And Economic Thought 1985–2000* (London: Kegan Paul).

Groenleer, M., Kaeding, M., and Versluis, E. (2010) 'Regulatory governance through agencies of the European Union? The role of the European agencies for maritime and aviation safety in the implementation of European transport legislation', *Journal of European Public Policy*, 17/8: 1212–30.

Grote, J. R. and Lang, A. (2003) 'Europeanization and organizational change in national trade associations: an organizational ecology perspective' in K. Featherstone and C. M. Radaelli (eds) *The Politics of Europeanization* (Oxford: Oxford University Press), pp. 225–54.

Guay, T. R. (1996) 'Integration and Europe's defence industry: a "reactive spillover" approach', *Political Studies Journal*, 24/3: 404–16.

Guerra, S. (2013) *Central and Eastern European Attitudes in the Face of the Union: A Comparative Perspective* (Basingstoke: Palgrave Macmillan).

Haas, E. B. (1958) *The Uniting of Europe: Political, Social and Economic Forces, 1950–1957* (Stanford, CA: Stanford University Press).

Haas, E. B. (1970) 'The study of regional integration: reflections on the joy and anguish of pretheorizing', *International Organization*, 24/4: 607–46.

Haas, E. B. (1975) *The Obsolescence of Regional Integration Theory*, Research Studies 25 (Berkeley, CA: Institute of International Studies).

Haas, E. B. (1976) 'Turbulent fields and the theory of regional integration', *International Organization*, 30/2: 173–212.

Haas, E. B. (2001) 'Does constructivism subsume neofunctionalism?' in T. Christiansen, K. E. Jørgensen, and A. Wiener (eds) *The Social Construction of Europe* (London: Sage), pp. 22–31.

Haas, E. B. (2004) 'Introduction: institutionalism or constructivism?' in E. B. Haas, *The Uniting of Europe: Political, Social and Economic Forces, 1950–1957*, 3rd edn (Notre Dame, IN: University of Notre Dame Press), pp. xii–lvi.

Haas, E. B. and Schmitter, P. C. (1964) 'Economic and differential patterns of political integration: projections about unity in Latin America', *International Organization*, 18/3: 705–38.

Haas, P. M. and Haas, E. B. (2002) 'Pragmatic constructivism and the study of international institutions', *Millennium: Journal of International Studies*, 31/3: 573–601.

Hacker, B. and van Treeck, T. (2010) *What Influence for European Governance?* (Berlin: Friedrich Ebert Stiftung).

Haigh, N. (ed.) (1992) *Manual of Environmental Policy* (London: Longman).

Hall, P. (1986) *Governing the Economy: The Politics of State Intervention In Britain and France* (Cambridge: Polity Press).

Hall, P. A. and Taylor, R. C. R. (1996) 'Political science and the three institutionalisms', *Political Studies*, 44/5: 936–57.

Hall, P. and Soskice, D. (2001) *Varieties of Capitalism* (Oxford: Oxford University Press).

Hamilton, D. and Quinlan, J. (eds) (2005) *Deep Integration: How Transatlantic Markets are Leading to Globalization* (Brussels: Centre for Transatlantic Relations/Centre for European Policy Studies).

Harlow, C. (2002) *Accountability in the European Union* (Oxford: Oxford University Press).

Hartley, T. (2007) *The Foundations of European Community Law*, 6th edn (Oxford: Oxford University Press).

Harvey, B. (1993) 'Lobbying in Europe: the experience of voluntary organizations' in S. Mazey and J. R. Richardson (eds) *Lobbying in the European Community* (Oxford: Oxford University Press), pp. 188–200.

Hayes-Renshaw, F. (2009) 'Least accessible but not inaccessible: lobbying the Council' in D. Coen and J. R. Richardson (eds) *Lobbying the European Union: Institutions, Actors, and Issues* (New York: Oxford University Press), pp. 70–88.

Hayes-Renshaw, F. and Wallace, H. (2006) *The Council of Ministers*, 2nd edn (New York: St Martin's Press).

Heipertz, M. and Verdun, A. (2010) *Ruling Europe: The Politics of the Stability and Growth Pact* (Cambridge: Cambridge University Press).

Helferrich, B. and Kolb, F. (2001) 'Multilevel action coordination in European contentious politics: the case of the European Women's Lobby' in D. Imig and S. Tarrow (eds) *Contentious Europeans: Protest and Politics in an Emerging Polity* (Lanham, MD: Rowman & Littlefield), pp. 143–62.

Helleiner, E., Pagliari, S., and Zimmerman, H. (eds) (2010) *Global Finance in Crisis* (London: Routledge).

Héritier, A. (1996) 'The accommodation of diversity in European policy-making and its outcomes: regulatory policy as patchwork', *Journal of European Public Policy*, 3/2: 149–67.

Héritier, A. (2002) 'The accommodation of diversity in European policy-making and its outcomes', in A. Jordan (ed.) *Environmental Policy in the European Union* (London: Earthscan), pp. 180–97.

Héritier, A., Kerwer, D., Knill, C., Lehmkuhl, D., Teutsch, M., and Douillet, A.-C. (2001) *Differential Europe: The European Union Impact on National Policymaking* (Lanham, MD: Rowman & Littlefield).

Hertz, R. and Leuffen, D. (2011) 'Too big to run? Analysing the impact of enlargement on the speed of EU decision-making', *European Union Politics*, 12/2: 193–215.

Hildebrand, P. M. (2005) 'The European Community's environmental policy, 1957 to 1992' in A. Jordan (ed.) *Environmental Policy in the European Union*, 2nd edn (London: Earthscan), pp. 19–41.

Hill, B. and Davidova, S. (2011) *Understanding the Common Agricultural Policy* (London: Taylor and Francis, Earthscan).

Hill, C. and Smith, M. (eds) (2011) *International Relations and the European Union*, 2nd edn (Oxford: Oxford University Press).

Hillion, C. (2010) *The Creeping Nationalisation of the EU Enlargement Policy*, SIEPS Report 6 (Stockholm: Swedish Institute for European Policy Studies).

Hingel, A. J. (2001) 'Education policies and European governance: contribution to the interservice groups on European governance', *European Journal for Education Law and Policy*, 5/1–2: 7–16.

Hirst, P. and Thompson, G. (1996) *Globalization in Question: The International Economy and the Possibilities of Governance* (Cambridge: Polity Press).

Hix, S. (1994) 'The study of the European Union: the challenge to comparative politics', *West European Politics*, 17/1: 1–30.

Hix, S. (1998) 'The study of the European Union II: the "new governance" agenda and its rival', *Journal of European Integration*, 5/1: 38–65.

Hix, S. (2005) *The Political System of the European Union* (Basingstoke: Palgrave).

Hix, S. (2007) 'The EU as a polity (I)' in K. E. Jørgensen, M. A. Pollack, and B. Rosamond (eds) *Handbook of European Union Politics* (London: Sage), pp. 141–58.

Hix, S. and Høyland, B. (2011) *The Political System of the European Union*, 3rd edn (Basingstoke: Palgrave Macmillan).

Hix, S., Noury, A. G., and Roland, G. (2007) *Democratic Politics in the European Parliament* (Cambridge: Cambridge University Press).

Hix, S., Scully, R., and Farrell, D. (2011) 'National or European parliamentarians? Evidence from a new survey of the members of the European Parliament', available online at http://www2.lse.ac.uk/government/research/resgroups/EPRG/pdf/Hix-Scully-Farrell.pdf

Hodson, D. (2011a) *Governing the Euro Area in Good Times and Bad* (Oxford: Oxford University Press).

Hodson, D. (2011b) 'The EU economy: the eurozone in 2010', *Annual Review of the European Union, Journal of Common Market Studies*, 49/1: 231–50.

Hoffmann, S. (1966) 'Obstinate or obsolete? The fate of the nation-state and the case of Western Europe', *Daedalus*, 95/3: 862–915.

Hoffmann, S. (1989) 'The European Community and 1992', *Foreign Affairs*, 68/4: 27–47.

Hoffmann, S. (1995) 'Introduction' in S. Hoffmann (ed.) *The European Sisyphus: Essays on Europe 1964–94* (Oxford: Westview), pp. 1–5.

Hoffmann, S. (ed.) *The European Sisyphus: Essays on Europe 1964–94* (Oxford: Westview).

Hogan, M. J. (1987) *The Marshall Plan, Britain and the Reconstruction of Western Europe, 1947–1952* (Cambridge: Cambridge University Press).

Holland, M. and Doidge, M. (2012) *Development Policy of the European Union* (Basingstoke: Palgrave Macmillan).

Hooghe, L. (2001) *The European Commission and the Integration of Europe: Images of Governance* (Cambridge: Cambridge University Press).

Hooghe, L. (2012) 'Images of Europe: how Commission officials conceive their institution's role', *Journal of Common Market Studies*, 50/1: 87–111.

Hooghe, L. and Marks, G. (1997) 'The making of a polity: the struggle over European integration', *European integration online Papers (EIoP)*, 1/4.

Hooghe, L. and Marks, G. (2001a) *Multi-level Governance and European Integration* (Lanham, MD: Rowman & Littlefield).

Hooghe, L. and Marks, G. (2001b) 'Types of multi-level governance', *European Integration online Papers (EIoP)*, 5/11.

Hooghe, L. and Marks, G. (2004) 'Does identity or economic rationality drive public opinion on European integration?', *Political Science*, 37/3: 415–20.

Hooghe, L. and Marks, G. (eds) (2007) *Acta Politica*, 42/2–3 (special issue entitled 'Sources of Euroscepticism')

Hooghe, L. and Marks, G. (2009) 'A postfunctionalist theory of European integration: from permissive consensus to constraining dissensus', *British Journal of Political Science*, 39/1: 1–23.

Horkheimer, M. (1982) [1937] *Critical Theory* (New York: Seabury Press).

Horolets, A. (2006) *Obrazy Europy w Polskim Dyskursie Publicznym* [*Representations of Europe in Polish Public Discourse*] (Krakow: Universitas Publishing House).

Hoskyns, C. (1996) *Integrating Gender* (London: Verso).

Hout, W. (2010) 'Governance and development: changing EU policies', *Third World Quarterly*, 31/1: 1–12.

Howarth, J. (2000) 'Britain, NATO, CESDP: fixed strategies, changing tactics', *European Foreign Affairs Review*, 16/3: 1–2.

Hudson, J. and Lowe, S. (2004) *Understanding the Policy Process* (Bristol: Policy Press).

Hurrell, A. and Menon, A. (1996) 'Politics like any other? Comparative politics, international relations and the study of the EC', *West European Politics*, 19/2: 386–402.

Imig, D. and Tarrow, S. (eds) (2001) *Contentious Europeans: Protest and Politics in an Emerging Polity* (Lanham, MD: Rowan & Littlefield).

Inglehart, R. (1970) 'Cognitive mobilization and European identity', *Comparative Politics*, 3/1: 45–70.

Institute for European Environmental Policy (2011) *Manual of European Environmental Policy*, available online at http://www.europeanenvironmentalpolicy.eu/view/meep/MEEP_0109.xml#MEEP_0109F1

Jabko, N. (2006) *Playing the Market: A Political Strategy for Uniting Europe, 1985–2005* (Ithaca, NY: Cornell University Press).

Jachtenfuchs, M. (1997) 'Conceptualizing European governance' in K. E. Jørgensen (ed.) *Reflective Approaches to European Governance* (Basingstoke: Macmillan), pp. 39–50.

Jachtenfuchs, M. (2001) 'The governance approach to European integration', *Journal of Common Market Studies*, 39/2: 245–64.

Jachtenfuchs, M. (2007) 'The EU as a polity (II)', in K. E. Jørgensen, M. A. Pollack, and B. Rosamond (eds) *Handbook of European Union Politics* (London: Sage), pp. 159–73.

Jackson, P. T. (2011) *The Conduct of Inquiry in International Relations* (London: Routledge).

Jacoby, W. (2004) *The Enlargement of the EU and NATO: Ordering from the Menu in Central Europe* (Cambridge: Cambridge University Press).

Jacqué, J. P. (2011) 'The accession of the European Union to the European Convention on Human Rights and Fundamental Freedoms', *Common Market Law Review*, 48/4: 995–1023.

Jensen, C. S. (2000) 'Neofunctionalist theories and the development of European social and labour market policy', *Journal of Common Market Studies*, 38/1: 71–92.

Joerges, C. and Neyer, J. (1997) 'From intergovernmental bargaining to deliberative political processes: the constitutionalisation of comitology', *European Law Journal*, 3/3: 273–99.

Jones, A. and Clarke, J. (2001) *The Modalities of European Union Governance: New Institutionalist Explanations of Agri-Environmental Policy* (Oxford: Oxford University Press).

Jordan, A. (2002) *The Europeanization of British Environmental Policy* (Basingstoke: Palgrave).

Jordan, A. and Adelle, C. (eds) (2012) *Environmental Policy in the European Union*, 3rd edn (London: Routledge).

Jordan, A. and Fairbrass, J. (2005) 'European Union environmental policy after the Nice Summit' in A. Jordan (ed.) *Environmental Policy in the European Union*, 2nd edn (London: Earthscan), pp. 42–6.

Jordan, A. and Liefferink, D. (eds) (2004) *Environmental Policy on Europe: The Europeanization of National Environmental Policy* (London: Routledge).

Jordan, A. and Schout, A. (2006) *The Coordination of the European Union* (Oxford: Oxford University Press).

Jordan, A. and Tosun, J. (2012) 'Policy implementation' in A. Jordan and C. Adelle (eds) *Environmental Policy in the European Union*, 3rd edn (London: Routledge).

Jordan, A., Huitema, D., van Asselt, H., Rayner, T., and Berkhout, F. (eds) (2010) *Climate Change Policy in the European Union* (Cambridge: Cambridge University Press).

Jordan, A., Wurzel, R., Zito, A., and Brückner, L. (2005) 'European governance and the transfer of "new" environmental policy instruments in the EU' in A. Jordan (ed.) *Environmental Policy in the European Union*, 2nd edn (London: Earthscan), pp. 317–35.

Jørgensen, K. E., Pollack, M., and Rosamond, B. (eds) (2007) *Handbook of European Union Politics* (London: Sage).

Journal of European Public Policy (2005) 'Special issue: the disparity of European integration—revisiting neo-functionalism in honour of Ernst Haas', 12/2.

Judge, D. and Earnshaw, D. (2009) *The European Parliament*, 2nd edn (Basingstoke: Palgrave).

Kaelble, H. (1994) 'L'Europe "vécue" et l'Europe "pensée" aux XXe siècle: les spécificités sociales de L'Europe' in R. Girault (ed.) *Identité et Conscience Européennes aux XXe Siècle* (Paris: Hachette), pp. 27–45.

Kaiser, R. and Prange, H. (2002) 'A new concept of deepening European integration? The European research area and the emerging role of policy coordination in a multi-level governance system', *European Integration online Papers (EIoP)*, 18.

Kallas, S. (2005) 'The need for a European transparency initiative', SPEECH/05/130, 3 March, European Foundation for Management, Nottingham Business School, Nottingham.

Karp J. A., Banducci, S. A., and Bowler, S. (2003) 'To know it is to love it? Satisfaction with democracy in the European Union', *Comparative Political Studies*, 36/3: 271–92.

Karppi, I. (2005) 'Good governance and prospects for local institutional stability in the enlarged European Union', *Journal of East–West Business*, 11/1–2: 93–117.

Kassim, H., Peterson, J., Bauer, M. W., Dehousse, R., Hooghe, L., and Thompson, A. (2012) *The European Commission of the 21st Century: Administration of the Past or Future?* (Oxford: Oxford University Press).

Katzenstein, P. J. (1996) *The Culture of National Security: Norms and Identity in World Politics* (Boulder, CO: Westview).

Katzenstein, P. J. (ed.) (1997) *Tamed Power: Germany in Europe* (Ithaca, NY: Cornell University Press).

Katzenstein, P. J., Keohane, R. O., and Krasner, S. (1998b) 'International organization and the study of world politics', *International Organization*, 52/4: 645–85.

Kaunert, C. (2011) *European Internal Security: Towards Supranational Governance in the Area of Freedom, Security, and Justice* (Manchester: Manchester University Press).

Keane, R. (2004) 'The Solana process in Serbia and Montenegro: coherence in EU foreign policy', *International Peacekeeping*, 11/3: 491–507.

Keohane, R. O. (1988) 'International institutions: two approaches', *International Studies Quarterly*, 32/4: 379–96.

Keohane, R. O. (1989) *International Institutions and State Power: Essays in International Relations Theory* (Boulder, CO: Westview).

Keohane, R. O. and Hoffmann, S. (eds) (1991) *The New European Community: Decision Making and Institutional Change* (Boulder, CO: Westview).

Keohane, R. O. and Nye, J. (1975) 'International interdependence and integration', in F. Greenstein and N. Polsby (eds) *Handbook of Political Science* (Andover, MA: Addison-Wesley).

Keohane, R. O. and Nye, J. (1976) *Power and Interdependence: World Politics in Transition* (Boston, MA: Little, Brown).

Klingemann, H. D., Fuchs, D., and Zielonka, J. (eds) (2006) *Democracy and Political Culture in Eastern Europe* (London: Routledge).

Knill, C. and Liefferink, D. (2007) *Environmental Politics in the European Union* (Manchester: Manchester University Press).

Knill, C. and Tosun, J. (2009) 'Hierarchy, networks, or markets: how does the EU shape environmental policy adoptions within and beyond its borders?', *Journal of European Public Policy*, 16/6: 873–94.

Knio, K. (2010) 'Investigating the two faces of governance: the case of the Euro–Mediterranean Development Bank', *Third World Quarterly*, 31/1: 105–21.

Knodt, M., Greenwood, J., and Quittkat, C. (eds) (2011) *Journal of European Integration*, 33/4 (issue entitled 'Territorial and functional interest representation in EU governance').

Kohler-Koch, B. (1999) 'The evolution and transformation of European governance' in B. Kohler-Koch and R. Eising (eds) *The Transformation of Governance in the European Union* (London: Routledge), pp. 14–35.

Kohler-Koch, B. (2010) 'Civil society and EU democracy: "Astroturf" representation?', *Journal of European Public Policy*, 17/1: 100–16.

Kohler-Koch, B. and Eising, R. (eds) (1999) *The Transformation of Governance in the European Union* (London: Routledge).

Kohler-Koch, B. and Rittberger, B. (2006) 'Review article: the "governance turn" in EU studies', *Journal of Common Market Studies*, 44/1: 27–49.

Kohler-Koch, B. and Rittberger, B. (eds) (2007) *Debating the Democratic Legitimacy of the European Union* (Lanham, MD: Rowman & Littlefield).

Kohler-Koch, B. and Rittberger, B. (2009) 'A futile quest for coherence: the many frames of EU governance' in B. Kohler-Koch and F. Larat (eds) *European Multi-Level Governance: Contrasting Images in National Research* (Cheltenham: Edward Elgar), pp. 3–18.

Kopecky, P. and Mudde, C. (2002) 'Two sides of Euroscepticism: party positions on European integration in East Central Europe', *European Union Politics*, 3/3: 297–326.

Krahmann, E. (2003) 'Conceptualising security governance', *Cooperation and Conflict*, 38/1: 5–26.

Krämer, L. (2012) 'The European Court of Justice', in A. Jordan and C. Adelle (eds) *Environmental Policy in the European Union*, 3rd edn (London: Earthscan), pp. 113–31.

Kröger, S. (2008) 'The open method of coordination: nine years later and so little wiser', Paper presented at the workshop *The OMC within the Lisbon Strategy: Empirical Assessments and Theoretical Implications*, 28–29 November, Institute for European Integration Research, Vienna.

Kröger, S. (2009a) 'The open method of coordination: part of the problem or part of the solution?', Paper presented at the workshop *'Nouveaux' Modes de Gouvernance et Action Publique Européenne*, 23 January, Section d'études européennes de l'AFSP, PACTE/IEP de Grenoble, Grenoble.

Kröger, S. (ed.) (2009b) 'What we have learnt: advances, pitfalls and remaining questions of OMC research', *European Integration Online Papers (EIoP)*, 13/1.

Kröger, S. and Friedrich, D. (eds) (2012) *The Challenge of Democratic Representation in the European Union* (Basingstoke: Palgrave).

Kronsell, A. (2005) 'Gender, power and European integration theory', *Journal of European Public Policy*, 12/6: 1022–40.

Kurpas, S., Grøn, C., and Kaczynski, P. M. (2008) *The European Commission after Enlargement: Does More Add up to Less?*, CEPS Special Report (Brussels: Centre for European Policy Studies).

Ladrech, R. (1994) 'Europeanization of domestic politics and institutions: the case of France', *Journal of Common Market Studies*, 32/1: 69–88.

Laffan, B. and Shaw, C. (2006) *Classifying and Mapping OMC in Different Policy Areas*, Report for NEWGOV, 02/D09, available online at http://www.eu-newgov.org/database/DELIV/D02D09_Classifying_and_Mapping_OMC.pdf

Lanaerts, K. and Van Nuffel, P. (2011) *European Union Law*, 3rd edn (London: Sweet and Maxwell).

Landmarks (2007) *The European Public Affairs Directory (EPAD)* (Brussels: Landmarks sa/nv).

Laurent, P. H. (1970) 'Paul-Henri Spaak and the diplomatic origins of the common market, 1955–56', *Political Science Quarterly*, 85/3: 373–96.

Laursen, F. (ed.) (2006) *The Treaty of Nice: Actor Preferences, Bargaining and Institutional Choice* (Leiden: Martinus Nijhoff).

Laursen, F. (ed.) (2012) *The Making of the EU's Lisbon Treaty: The Role of Member States* (Bern: Peter Lang).

Lavenex, S. (2001) 'The Europeanization of refugee policy: normative challenges and institutional legacies', *Journal of Common Market Studies*, 39/5: 825–50.

Lavenex, S. (2004) 'EU external governance in "wider Europe"', *Journal of European Public Policy*, 11/4: 680–700.

Lavenex, S. and Uçarer, E. M. (eds) (2002) *Migration and the Externalities of European Integration* (Lanham, MD: Lexington Books).

Leconte, C. (2010) *Understanding Euroscepticism* (Basingstoke: Palgrave Macmillan).

Leinen, J. and Méndez de Vigo, I. (2001) *Report on the Laeken European Council and the Future of the Union*, A5-0368/2001, October, Brussels.

Lenaerts, K. and Verhoeven, A. (2002) 'Institutional balance as a guarantee for democracy in EU governance' in C. Joerges and R. Dehousse (eds) *Good Governance in Europe's Integrated Market* (Oxford: Oxford University Press), pp. 35–88.

Lenschow, A. (1999) 'Transformation in European environmental governance' in B. Kohler-Koch (ed.) *The Transformation of Governance in the European Union* (London: Routledge), pp. 39–60.

Lenschow, A. (2005) 'Environmental policy' in H. Wallace, W. Wallace, and M. Pollack (eds) *Policy-making in the European Union*, 5th edn (Oxford: Oxford University Press), pp. 305–72.

Lenschow, A. (2012) 'Studying EU environmental policy' in A. Jordan and C. Adelle (eds) *Environmental Policy in the European Union*, 3rd edn (London: Routledge), pp. 49–72.

Lewis, J. (2003) 'Institutional environments and everyday EU decision making: rationalist or constructivist?' *Comparative Political Studies*, 36/1: 97–124.

Lewis, J. (2005a) 'Is the Council becoming an upper house?' in C. Parsons and N. Jabko (eds) *With US or against US? The State of the European Union, Vol. 7* (Oxford: Oxford University Press), pp. 143–71.

Lewis, J. (2005b) 'The Janus face of Brussels: socialization and everyday decision making in the European Union', *International Organization*, 59/4: 937–71.

Liberatore, A. (1993) 'Problems of transnational policy making: environmental policy in the EC', *European Journal of Political Research*, 19/2–3: 281–305.

Liebfried, S. and Pierson, P. (eds) (1995) 'Semi-sovereign welfare states: social policy in a multi-tiered Europe' in S. Liebfried and P. Pierson (eds) *European Social Policy: Between Fragmentation and Integration* (Washington DC: Brookings Institution), pp. 43–77.

Liebfried, S. and Pierson, P. (2000) 'Social policy: left to court and markets?' in H. Wallace and W. Wallace (eds) *Policy-making in the European Union*, 4th edn (Oxford: Oxford University Press), pp. 267–92.

Liefferink, D. and Andersen, M. S. (1998) 'Strategies of the "green" member states in EU environmental policy-making', *Journal of European Public Policy*, 5/2: 254–70.

Lindberg, L. N. (1963) *The Political Dynamics of European Economic Integration* (Stanford, CA: Stanford University Press).

Lindberg, L. N. and Scheingold, S. A. (1970) *Europe's Would-be Polity: Patterns of Change in the European Community* (Princeton, NJ: Prentice-Hall).

Lindberg, L. N. and Scheingold, S. A. (eds) (1971) *Regional Integration: Theory and Research* (Cambridge, MA: Harvard University Press).

Locher, B. and Prügl, E. (2009) 'Gender and European integration' in A. Wiener and T. Diez (eds) *European Integration Theory*, 2nd edn (Oxford: Oxford University Press), pp. 181–97.

Ludlow, P. (2007) 'A view on Brussels: the Lisbon Council of October 2007—wrapping up the treaty and debating globalisation', *Eurocomment Briefing Note*, 5/6, Brussels.

Lynch, P. N., Neuwahl, N. W., and Rees, N. (eds) (2000) *Reforming the European Union from Maastricht to Amsterdam* (London: Longman).

Macmillan, C. (2009) 'The application of neofunctionalism to the enlargement process: the case of Turkey', *Journal of Common Market Studies*, 47/4: 789–809.

Mahé, L.-P. (2012) 'Do the proposals for the CAP after 2013 herald a "major" reform?', Policy Paper No. 53, Notre Europe, March.

Maher, I., Billiet, S., and Hodson, D. (2009) 'The principal–agent approach to EU studies: apply liberally but handle with care', *Comparative European Politics*, 7/4: 409–13.

Mahoney, C. and Beckstrand, M. (2011) 'Following the money: EU funding of civil society groups', *Journal of Common Market Studies*, 49/6: 1339–61.

Majone, G. (1994) 'The rise of the regulatory state in Europe', *West European Politics*, 17/3: 77–101.

Majone, G. (1995) 'The development of social regulation in the European Community: policy externalities, transaction costs, motivational factors', EUI Working Paper, Florence.

Majone, G. (ed.) (1996) *Regulating Europe* (London: Routledge).

Majone, G. (1999) 'The regulatory state and its legitimacy problems', *West European Politics*, 22/1: 1–24.

Majone, G. (2009) *Europe as the Would-be World Power: The EU at 50* (Cambridge: Cambridge University Press).

Mandel, E. (1970) *Europe versus America: Contradictions of Imperialism* (London: New Left Books).

Mandelkern Group (2001) *Mandelkern Group on Better Regulation Final Report*, November, Brussels, available online at http://ec.europa.eu/governance/better_regulation/documents/mandelkern_report.pdf

Manners, I. (2007) 'Another Europe is possible: critical perspectives on European Union politics' in K. E. Jørgensen, M. A. Pollack, and B. Rosamond (eds) *Handbook of European Union Politics* (London: Sage), pp. 77–95.

March, J. G. and Olsen, J. P. (1989) *Rediscovering Institutions: The Organizational Basics of Politics* (New York: Free Press).

Marginson, P. and Keune, M. (2012) 'European social dialogue as multi-level governance: towards more autonomy and new dependencies' in J.-C. Barbier (ed.) 'EU law, governance and social policy', *European Integration Online Papers* (EIoP) special mini-issue 16/4, available online at http://eiop.or.at/eiop/texte/2012-004a.htm

Marks, G. (1992) 'Structural policy in the European Community' in A. Sbragia (ed.) *Europolitics: Institutions and Policy-making in the 'New' European Community* (Washington DC: Brookings Institute), pp. 191–224.

Marks, G. (1993) 'Structural policy and multi-level governance in the EC', in A. Sbragia (ed.) *The Euro-Polity* (Boulder CO: Lynne Rienner), pp. 391–411.

Marks, G. and Hooghe, L. (2001) *Multi-level Governance and European Integration* (Lanham, MD: Rowman & Littlefield).

Marks, G., Hooghe, L., and Blank, K. (1996) 'European integration from the 1980s: state-centric v. multi-level governance', *Journal of Common Market Studies*, 34/3: 341–78.

Marks, G., Neilsen, F., Ray, L., and Salk, J. E. (1996) 'Competencies, cracks, and conflicts: regional mobilization in the European Union', *Comparative Political Studies*, 29/2: 164–92.

Marks, G., Scharpf, F. W., Schmitter, P. C., and Streeck, W. (1996) *Governance in the European Union* (London: Sage).

Marsh, D. (2009) *The Euro* (New Haven, CT: Yale University Press).

Marshall, T. H. (1975) *Social Policy* (London: Hutchinson).

Mattila, M. (2008) 'Voting and coalitions in the Council after the enlargement' in D. Naurin and H. Wallace (eds) *Unveiling the Council of the European Union: Games Governments Play in Brussels* (Basingstoke: Palgrave MacMillan), pp. 23–36.

Mazey, S. (1998) 'The European Union and women's rights: from the Europeanisation of national agendas to the nationalisation of a European agenda?' in D. Hine and H. Kassim (eds) *Beyond the Market: The EU and National Social Policy* (London: Routledge), pp. 134–56.

Mazey, S. and Richardson, J. R. (2002) 'Pluralisme ouvert ou restreint? Les groupes d'interêt dans l'Union européenne', in R. Balme, D. Chabanet, and V. Wright (eds) *L'Action Collective en Europe [Collective Action in Europe]* (Paris: Presses de Science Po.), pp. 123–61.

McGowan, F. and Wallace, H. (1996) 'Towards a European regulatory state', *Journal of European Public Policy*, 3/4: 560–76.

McGowan, L. (2007) 'Theorising European integration: revisiting neofunctionalism and testing its suitability explaining the development of EC competition policy', *European Integration online Papers (EIoP)*, 11/3: 1–17.

McGuire, S. and Smith, M. (2008) *The European Union and the United States: Competition and Convergence in the Global Arena* (Basingstoke: Palgrave).

McLaren, L. N. (2006) *Identity, Interests and Attitudes to European Integration* (Basingstoke: Palgrave).

Mearsheimer J. J. (1990) 'Back to the future: instability in Europe after the Cold War', *International Security*, 15/1: 5–56.

Menon, A. (2011) 'European defence policy: from Lisbon to Libya', *Survival*, 53/3: 75–90.

Menon, A. and Sedelmeier, U. (2010) 'Instruments and intentionality: civilian crisis management and enlargement conditionality in EU security policy', *West European Politics*, 33/1: 75–92.

Mérand, F., Foucault, M., and Irondelle, B. (2012) *European Security since the Fall of the Berlin Wall* (Toronto: University of Toronto Press).

Messerlin, P. (2001) *Measuring the Costs of Protection in Europe* (Washington DC: IIE).

Milward, A. S. (1992) *The European Rescue of the Nation State* (London: Routledge).

Molitor, B. (1995) *Report of the Group of Independent Experts on Legislation and Administrative Simplification*, COM(95)288 final, May, Brussels.

Monar, J. and Wessels, W. (eds) (2001) *The European Union after the Treaty of Amsterdam* (London: Continuum).

Monnet, J. (1976) *Mémoires* (Paris: Fayard).

Monti, M. (2010) 'A new strategy for the single market: at the service of Europe's economy and society', available online at http://ec.europa.eu/bepa/pdf/monti_report_final_10_05_2010_en.pdf

Moran, M. (2002) 'Review article: understanding the regulatory state', *British Journal of Political Science*, 32/2: 391–413.

Moravscik, A. (1991) 'Negotiating the Single European Act: national interests and conventional statecraft in the European Community', *International Organization*, 45/1: 19–56.

Moravcsik, A. (1993) 'Preferences and power in the European Community: a liberal intergovernmentalist approach', *Journal of Common Market Studies*, 34/4: 473–524.

Moravscik, A. (1994) *Why the European Community Strengthens the State: Domestic Politics and International Cooperation*, Harvard University Center for European Studies Working Paper Series No. 52, available online at http://www.ces.fas.harvard.edu/publications/docs/pdfs/Moravcsik52.pdf

Moravcsik, A. (1998) *The Choice for Europe: Social Purpose and State Power from Messina to Maastricht* (Ithaca, NY: Cornell University Press).

Moravcsik, A. (2001) 'A constructivist research programme for EU studies', *European Union Politics*, 2/2: 219–49.

Moravcsik, A. (2002) 'Reassessing legitimacy in the European Union', *Journal of Common Market Studies*, 40/4: 603–24.

Moravcsik, A. (2005) 'The European constitutional compromise and the neofunctionalist legacy', *Journal of European Public Policy*, 12/2: 349–86.

Moravcsik, A. and Schimmelfennig, F. (2009) 'Liberal intergovernmentalism' in A. Wiener and T. Diez (eds) *European Integration Theory* (Oxford: Oxford University Press), pp. 67–87.

Morgenthau, H. (1985) *Politics among Nations: The Struggle for Power and Peace*, 6th edn (New York: Knopf).

Mügge, D. (2011) 'From pragmatism to dogmatism: European Union governance, policy paradigms and financial meltdown', *New Political Economy*, 16/2: 185–206.

Naurin, D. (2007) 'Backstage behavior: lobbyists in public and private settings in Sweden and the European Union', *Comparative Politics*, 29/2: 209–28.

Naurin, D. and Wallace, H. (eds) (2008) *Unveiling the Council of the European Union: Games Governments Play in Brussels* (London and New York: Palgrave Macmillan).

Newman, A. L. (2008) 'Building transnational civil liberties: transgovernmental entrepreneurs and the European Data Privacy Directive', *International Organization*, 62/1: 103–30.

Neyer, J. and Wiener, A. (2011) *Political Theory of the European Union* (Oxford: Oxford University Press).

Nicolaïdis, K. and Schmidt, S. (2007) 'Mutual recognition on trial: the long road to services liberalization', *Journal of European Public Policy*, 14/5: 717–34.

Nicolson F. and East, R. (1987) *From Six to Twelve: The Enlargement of the European Communities* (Harlow: Longman).

Niemann, A. (2006) *Explaining Decisions in the European Union* (Cambridge: Cambridge University Press).

Niemann, A. and Schmitter, P. C. (2009) 'Neofunctionalism' in A. Wiener and T. Diez (eds) *European Integration Theory* (Oxford: Oxford University Press), pp. 45–66.

Norris, P. (2010) 'To them that hath: news media and knowledge gaps', Paper for panel session II.1: 'Political knowledge and information', PIREDEU User Community Conference, 18–19 November, Brussels.

Noutcheva, G. (2012) *European Foreign Policy and the Challenges of Balkan Accession: Conditionality, Legitimacy and Compliance* (London: Routledge).

Nugent, N. (2010) *The Government and Politics of the European Union*, 4th edn (Basingstoke: Macmillan).

Nye, J. (2005) *Soft Power* (New York: PublicAffairs).

Nye, J. S. (1971) 'Comparing common markets: a revised neo-functionalist model' in L. N. Lindberg and S. A. Scheingold (eds) *Regional Integration: Theory and Research* (Harvard: Harvard University Press), pp. 192–231.

O'Neill, M. (1996) *The Politics of European Integration: A Reader* (London: Routledge).

O'Toole, L. J. and Hanf, K. I. (2003) 'Multi-level governance networks and the use of policy instruments in the European Union' in T. Bressers and W. Rosenbaum (eds) *Achieving Sustainable Development: The Challenge of Governance across Social Scales* (Westport, CT: Praeger), pp. 257–79.

Obermaier, A. J. (2008) 'The national judiciary: sword of European Court of Justice rulings—the example of the *Kohll/Decker* jurisprudence', *European Law Journal*, 14/6: 735–52.

Obstfeld, M. and Rogoff, K. (2009) 'Global imbalances and the financial crisis: products of common causes', Paper prepared for the Federal Reserve Bank of San Francisco Asia Economic Policy Conference, 18–20 October, Santa Barbara, CA, available online at http://elsa.berkeley.edu/~obstfeld/santabarbara.pdf

Olson, M. (1965) *The Logic of Collective Action: Public Goods and the Theory of Groups* (Cambridge, MA: Harvard University Press).

Padoa-Schioppa, T., Emerson, M., King, M., Milleron, J. C., Paelinck, J. H. P., Papademos, L. D., Pastor, A., and Scharpf, F. W. (1987) *Efficiency, Stability, Equity* (Oxford: Oxford University Press).

Palayret, J.-M., Wallace, H., and Winand, P. (2006) *Vision, Votes, and Vetoes. The Empty Chair Crisis and the Luxembourg Compromise Forty Years on* (Brussels: PIE-Peter Lang).

Panke, D. (2006) 'More arguing than bargaining? The institutional designs of the European convention and intergovernmental conferences compared', *Journal of European Integration*, 28/4: 357–79.

Panke, D. (2010) *Small States in the European Union: Coping with Structural Disadvantages* (Aldershot: Ashgate).

Panke, D. (2011) 'Microstates in negotiations beyond the nation-state: Malta, Cyprus and Luxembourg as active and successful policy shapers?', *International Negotiation*, 16/2: 297–317.

Papaionnou, E. and Portes, R. (2008) *The International Role of the Euro: A Status Report*, European Economy Economic Papers 317, April, available online at http://ec.europa.eu/economy_finance/publications/publication12409_en.pdf

Parker, O. (2012) 'The ethics of an ambiguous "cosmopolitics": citizens and entrepreneurs in the European project', *International Theory*, 4/2: 198–232.

Pearce, J. and Sutton, J. (1983) *Protection and Industrial Policy in Europe* (London: Routledge).

Peers, S. (various) 'Legislative updates', *European Journal of Migration and Law*—various issues.

Pelkmans, J. (1997) *European Integration, Methods and Economic Analysis* (London: Longman).

Pelkmans, J. (2010) 'Required: a bold follow-up to Monti', *CEPS Commentary 22*, July, Brussels, available online at http://www.ceps.eu/ceps/download/3624

Pelkmans, J. and Winters, A. (1988) *Europe's Domestic Market* (London: Royal Institute of International Affairs).

Pelkmans, J., Hanf, D., and Chang, M. (2008) *The EU Internal Market in Comparative Perspective, Economic, Political and Legal Analyses, Vol. 8* (Berlin: Peter Lang Publishers).

Pérez-Solórzano Borragán, N. and Smismans, S. (2012) 'The EU and institutional change in industrial relations in the new member states' in Stijn Smismans (ed.) *The European Union and Industrial Relations* (Manchester, Manchester University Press), pp. 116–38.

Peterson, J. (1995) 'Decision making in the European Union: towards a framework for analysis', *Journal of European Public Policy*, 2/1: 69–93.

Peterson, J. (2008) 'Enlargement, reform and the European Commission: weathering a perfect storm?', *Journal of European Public Policy*, 15/5: 761–80.

Peterson, J. and Bomberg, E. (2009) *Decision-making in the European Union* (Basingstoke: Palgrave Macmillan).

Phelan, W. (2011) 'Why do the EU member states accept the supremacy of European law? Explaining supremacy as an alternative to bilateral reciprocity', *Journal of European Public Policy*, 18/5: 766–77.

Phinnemore, D. and Warleigh-Lack, A. (eds) (2009) *Reflections on European Integration* (Basingstoke: Palgrave).

Piattoni, S. (2009) 'Multi-level governance: a historical and conceptual analysis', *Journal of European Integration*, 31/2: 163–80.

Pierson, P. (1998) 'The path to European integration: a historical institutionalist analysis' in W. Sandholtz and A. Stone Sweet (eds) *European Integration and Supranational Governance* (Oxford: Oxford University Press), pp. 27–59.

Pierson, P. (2004) *Politics in Time: History, Institutions, and Social Analysis* (Princeton, NJ: Princeton University Press).

Piris, J.-C. (2010) *The Lisbon Treaty: A Legal and Political Analysis* (Cambridge: Cambridge University Press).

Poidevin, R. and Spierenberg, D. (1994) *History of the High Authority of the European Coal and Steel Community* (London: Weidenfeld and Nicolson).

Polanyi, K. (2001; 1957) *The Great Transformation* (Boston, MA: Beacon Press).

Pollack, M. A. (1997) 'Representing diffuse interests in the European Union', *Journal of European Public Policy*, 4/4: 572–90.

Pollack, M. A. (2002) *The Engines of Integration: Delegation, Agencies and Agenda-setting in the EU* (Oxford: Oxford University Press).

Pollack, M. A. (2005) 'Theorizing the European Union: international organization, domestic polity, or experiment in new governance?', *Annual Review of Political Science*, 8/1: 357–98.

Pollack, M. A. (2007) 'Rational choice and EU politics' in K. E. Jørgensen, M. A. Pollack, and B. Rosamond (eds) *Handbook of European Union Politics* (London: Sage), pp. 31–55.

Pollack, M. A. (2009) 'The new institutionalisms and European integration' in A. Wiener and T. Diez (eds) *European Integration Theory*, 2nd edn (Oxford: Oxford University Press), pp. 125–43.

Pollack, M. A. (2012) 'Theorizing the European Union: realist, intergovernmentalist and institutionalist approaches' in E. Jones, A. Menon, and S. Weatherill (eds) *The Oxford Handbook of the European Union* (Oxford: Oxford University Press).

Poloni-Staudinger, L. (2008) 'The domestic opportunity structure and supranational activity: an explanation of environmental group activity at European Union level', *European Union Politics*, 9/4: 531–58.

Presidency of the EU (2009) *Declaration by the Presidency on the Western Balkans*, Gymnich Meeting with the Western Balkans, Hluboká nad Vltavou, 28 March.

Puchala, D. J. (1971) *International Politics Today* (New York: Dodd Mead).

Puchala, D. J. (1999) 'Institutionalism, intergovernmentalism and European integration: a review article', *Journal of Common Market Studies*, 37/2: 317–31.

Puetter, U. (2006) *The Eurogroup: How a Secretive Group of Finance Ministers Shape European Economic Governance* (Manchester: Manchester University Press).

Puetter, U. (2012) 'Europe's deliberative intergovernmentalism: the role of the Council and European Council in EU economic governance', *Journal of European Public Policy*, 19/2: 161–78.

Putnam, R. (1988) 'Diplomacy and domestic politics: the logic of two-level games', *International Organization*, 42/3: 427–60.

Quittkat, C. and Kohler-Koch, B. (2011) 'Die Öffnung der europäischen Politik für die Zivilgesellschaft: das Konsultationsregime der Europäischen Kommission' in B. Kohler-Koch and C. Quittkat (eds) *Die Entzauberung partizipativer Demokratie: Zur Rolle der Zivilgesellschaft bei der Demokratisierung von EU-Governance* (Frankfurt aM: Campus), pp. 74–97.

Radaelli, C. M. (1998) *Governing European Regulation: The Challenge Ahead*, RSC Policy Paper No. 98/3, European University Institute, Florence, available online at http://www.eui.eu/RSCAS/WP-Texts/RSCPP98_03.html

Radaelli, C. M. (2003) *The Open Method of Coordination: A New Governance Architecture for the European Union?*, SIEPS Report 2003/1, Swedish Institute for European Policy Studies, Stockholm, available online at http://eucenter.wisc.edu/OMC/Papers/radaelli.pdf

Ray, L. (2003a) 'Reconsidering the link between incumbent support and pro-EU opinion', *European Union Politics*, 4/3: 259–79.

Ray, L. (2003b) 'When parties matter: the conditional influence of party positions on voter opinions about European integration', *Journal of Politics*, 65/4: 978–94.

Ray, L. (2007) 'Mainstream Euroskepticism: trend or oxymoron?', *Acta Politica*, 42: 153–72.

Rees, W. (2011) *The US–EU Security Relationship: Tensions between a European and a Global Agenda* (Basingstoke: Palgrave Macmillan).

Reif, K. and Schmitt, H. (1980) 'Nine second-order national elections: a conceptual framework for the analysis of European election results', *European Journal of Political Research*, 8/1: 3–44.

Reilly, A. (2004) '"Governance": agreement and divergence in responses to the EU White Paper', *Regional and Federal Studies*, 14/1: 136–56.

Reinalda, B. and Verbeek, B. (2004) 'Patterns of decision making within international organizations', in B. Reinalda and B. Verbeek (eds) *Decision Making within International Organizations* (London: Routledge), pp. 231–46.

Rhodes, M. (1995) 'A regulatory conundrum: industrial relations and the "social dimension"' in S. Leibfried and P. Pierson (eds) *Fragmented Social Policy: The European Union's Social Dimension in Comparative Perspective* (Washington DC: Brookings Institution), pp. 78–122.

Rhodes, M. and van Apeldoorn, B. (1998) 'Capital unbound? The transformation of European corporate governance', *Journal of European Public Policy*, 5/3: 407–28.

Rhodes, R. A. W. (1996) 'The new governance: governing without government', *Political Studies*, 44/4: 652–67.

Risse, T. (2000) '"Let's argue!" Communicative action in international relations', *International Organization*, 54/1: 1–39.

Risse, T. (2002) 'Nationalism and collective identities: Europe versus the nation-state?' in P. Heywood, E. Jones, and M. Rhodes (eds) *Developments in Western European Politics*, (Basingstoke: Palgrave), pp. 77–93.

Risse, T. (2005) 'Nationalism, European identity and the puzzles of European integration', *Journal of European Public Policy*, 12/2: 291–309.

Risse, T. (2009) 'Social constructivism and European integration' in A. Wiener and T. Diez (eds) *European Integration Theory* (Oxford: Oxford University Press), pp. 144–60.

Risse-Kappen, T. (1996) 'Exploring the nature of the beast: international relations theory and comparative policy analysis meet the European Union', *Journal of Common Market Studies*, 34/1: 54–81.

Rittberger, B. (2005) *Building Europe's Parliament: Democratic Representation beyond the Nation State* (Oxford: Oxford University Press).

Rosamond, B. (2000) *Theories of European Integration* (Basingstoke: Palgrave).

Rosamond, B. (2005) 'The uniting of Europe and the foundations of EU studies: revisiting the neofunctionalism of Ernst B. Haas', *Journal of European Public Policy*, 12/2: 237–54.

Rosamond, B. (2007) 'European integration and the social science of EU studies: the disciplinary politics of a sub-field', *International Affairs*, 83/2: 231–52.

Rosenau, J. N. and Czempiel, E.-O. (1992) *Governance without Government: Order and Change in World Politics* (Cambridge: Cambridge University Press).

Rosenau, J. N. and Durfee, M. (1995) *Thinking Theory Thoroughly: Coherent Approaches in an Incoherent World* (Boulder, CO: Westview).

Ross, G. (1995) 'Assessing the Delors era and social policy' in S. Leibfried and P. Pierson (eds) *European Social Policy: Between Fragmentation and Integration* (Washington DC: Brookings Institution), pp. 357–88.

Rozbicka, P. (2011) 'Myths and reality of EU policy processes and interest-group participation: why are interest groups not as successful as they would like to be?', PhD thesis, European University Institute, Florence.

Ruggie, J. G. (1982) 'International regimes, transactions and change: embedded liberalism in the postwar economic order', *International Organization*, 36/2: 379–416.

Ruggie, J. G. (1998) *Constructing the World Polity: Essays on International Institutionalisation* (London: Routledge).

Ruggie, J. G., Katzenstein, P. J., Keohane, R. O., and Schmitter, P. C. (2005) 'Transformation in world politics: the intellectual contribution of Ernst B. Haas', *Annual Review of Political Science*, 8/1: 271–96.

Rutten, M. (2002) *From Saint-Malo to Nice: European Defence—Core Documents* (Paris: Institute for Security Studies).

Sabatier, P. A. and Jenkins-Smith, H. C. (eds) (1993) *Policy Change and Learning: An Advocacy Coalition Approach* (Boulder, CO: Westview).

Sánchez-Cuenca, I. (2000) 'The political basis of support for European integration', *European Union Politics*, 1/2: 147–71.

Sanders, D. and Bellucci, P. (eds) (2012) *The Europeanization of National Polities? Citizenship and Support in a Post-enlargement Union* (Oxford: Oxford University Press).

Sanders, D., Magalhaes, P., and Toka, G. (eds) (2012) *Citizens and the European Polity: Mass Attitudes Towards the European and National Politics* (Oxford: Oxford University Press).

Sandholtz, W. (1998) 'The emergence of a supranational telecommunications regime' in W. Sandholtz and A. Stone Sweet (eds) *European Integration and Supranational Governance* (Oxford: Oxford University Press), pp. 134–63.

Sandholtz, W. and Stone Sweet, A. (1997) 'European integration and supranational governance', *Journal of European Public Policy*, 4/3: 297–317.

Sandholtz, W. and Stone Sweet, A. (eds) (1998) *European Integration and Supranational Governance* (Oxford: Oxford University Press).

Sandholtz, W. and Stone Sweet, A. (1999) 'European integration and supranational governance revisited: rejoinder to Branch and Ohrgaard', *Journal of European Public Policy*, 6/1: 37–41.

Sandholtz, W. and Zysman, J. (1989) '1992: recasting the European bargain', *World Politics*, 42/1: 95–128.

Sbragia, A. M. (1993) 'EC environmental policy' in A. W. Cafruny and G. G. Rosenthal (eds) *The State of the European Community* (Boulder, CO: Lynne Rienner), pp. 337–52.

Sbragia, A. M. (1996) 'Environmental policy: the "push–pull" of policy-making' in H. Wallace and W. Wallace (eds) *Policy-making in the European Union*, 3rd edn (Oxford: Oxford University Press), pp. 235–55.

Sbragia, A. M. (2000) 'Environmental policy' in H. Wallace and W. Wallace (eds) *Policy-making in the European Union*, 4th edn (Oxford: Oxford University Press), pp. 293–316.

Sbragia, A. M. (2005) 'Institution building from below and above: the European Community in global environmental politics' in A. Jordan (ed.) *Environmental Policy in the European Union*, 2nd edn (London: Earthscan), pp. 201–24.

Sbragia, A. M. and Damro, C. (1999) 'The changing role of the European Union in international environmental politics', *Environment and Planning C*, 17/1: 53–68.

Scharpf, F. W. (1988) 'The joint-decision trap: lessons from German federalism and European integration', *Public Administration*, 66/3: 239–78.

Scharpf, F. W. (1997) *Games Real Actors Play: Actor-Centered Institutionalism in Policy Research* (Boulder, CO: Westview).

Scharpf, F. W. (1999) *Governing in Europe: Effective and Democratic?* (Oxford: Oxford University Press).

Scharpf, F. W. (2002) 'The European social model: coping with the challenges of diversity', *Journal of Common Market Studies*, 40/4: 645–70.

Scharpf, F. W. (2010) 'The asymmetry of European integration, or why the EU cannot be a "social market economy"', *Socio-Economic Review*, 8/2: 211–50.

Schimmelfennig, F. (2001) 'The Community trap: liberal norms, rhetorical action, and the Eastern enlargement of the European Union', *International Organization*, 55/1: 47–80.

Schimmelfennig, F. and Sedelmeier, U. (2002) 'Theorizing EU enlargement: research focus, hypotheses, and the state of research', *Journal of European Public Policy*, 9/4: 500–28.

Schimmelfennig, F. and Sedelmeier, U. (2004) 'Governance by conditionality: EU rule transfer to the candidate countries of Central and Eastern Europe', *Journal of European Public Policy*, 11/4: 661–79.

Schimmelfennig, F. and Sedelmeier, U. (2005a) *The Europeanization of Central and Eastern Europe* (Ithaca, NY: Cornell University Press).

Schimmelfennig, F. and Sedelmeier, U. (eds) (2005b) *The Politics of European Union Enlargement. Theoretical Approaches* (London: Routledge).

Schimmelfennig, F. and Wagner, W. (2004) 'Preface: external governance in the European Union', *Journal of European Public Policy*, 11/4: 657–60.

Schimmelfennig, F., Engert, S., and Knobel, H. (2006) *International Socialization in Europe: European Organizations, Political Conditionality and Democratic Change* (Basingstoke: Palgrave).

Schmidt, S. K. (2007) 'Mutual recognition as a new mode of governance', *Journal of European Public Policy*, 14/5: 667–81.

Schmidt, V. A. (2006) *Democracy in Europe: The EU and National Polities* (Oxford: Oxford University Press).

Schmitter, P. (1969) 'Three neofunctional hypotheses about international integration', *International Organization*, 23/1: 161–6.

Schmitter, P. C. (2004) 'Neo-functionalism' in A. Wiener and T. Diez (eds) *European Integration Theory* (Oxford: Oxford University Press), pp. 45–74.

Schneider, G., Steunenberg, B., and Widgren, M. (2006) 'Evidence with insight: what models contribute to EU research' in R. Thomson, F. N. Stokman, C. H. Achen, and T. Koenig (eds) *The European Union Decides* (Cambridge: Cambridge University Press), pp. 299–316.

Schultze, C. J. (2003) 'Cities and EU governance: policy-takers or policy-makers?', *Regional and Federal Studies*, 12/1: 121–47.

Scott, J. and Trubek, D. M. (2002) 'Mind the gap: law and new approaches to governance in the European Union', *European Law Journal*, 8/1: 1–18.

Scully, R. (2005) *Becoming Europeans? Attitudes, Behaviour and Socialisation in the European Parliament* (Oxford: Oxford University Press).

Shackleton, M. (2012) 'The European Parliament', in J. Peterson and M. Shackleton (eds) *The Institutions of the European Union*, 3rd edn (Oxford: Oxford University Press), pp. 124–47.

Shapiro, M. (1992) 'The European Court of Justice' in A. M. Sbragia (ed.) *Europolitics* (Washington DC: Brookings Institution), pp. 123–51.

Shore, C. (2011) 'European governance or governmentality? The European Commission and the future of democratic government', *European Law Journal*, 17/3: 287–303.

Simonian, H. (1985) *The Privileged Partnership: Franco-German Relations in the European Community, 1969–84* (Oxford: Clarendon).

Siune, K. and Svensson, P. (1993) 'The Danes and the Maastricht Treaty: The Danish EC referendum of June 1992', *Electoral Studies*, 12/2: 99–111.

Skelcher, C. (2005) 'Jurisdictional integrity, polycentrism, and the design of democratic governance', *Governance*, 18/1: 89–110.

Skogstad, G. (2003) 'Legitimacy and/or policy effectiveness? Network governance and GMO regulation in the European Union', *Journal of European Public Policy*, 10/3: 321–38.

Slater, M. (1982) 'Political elites, popular indifference, and community building', *Journal of Common Market Studies*, 21/1–2: 67–87.

Smismans, S. (2004) *Law, Legitimacy, and European Governance: Functional Participation in Social Regulation* (Oxford: Oxford University Press).

Smismans, S. (2006a) 'New modes of governance and the participatory myth', *European Governance Papers*, 6/1: 1–23.

Smismans, S. (ed.) (2006b) *Civil Society and Legitimate European Governance* (Cheltenham: Edward Elgar).

Smismans, S. (2008) 'New modes of governance and the participatory myth', *West European Politics*, 31/5: 874–95.

Smismans, S. (2009) 'European civil society and citizenship: complementary or exclusionary concepts?', *Policy & Society*, 27/4: 59–70.

Smismans, S. (2010) 'The European Union's fundamental rights myth', *Journal of Common Market Studies*, 48/1: 45–66.

Smith, M. (2001) 'The Common Foreign and Security Policy' in S. Bromley (ed.) *Governing the European Union* (London: Sage), pp. 255–86.

Smith, M. (2004) 'Toward a theory of EU foreign policy-making: multi-level governance, domestic politics, and national adaptation to Europe's Common Foreign and Security Policy', *Journal of European Public Policy*, 11/4: 740–58.

Smith, M. E. (2008) *Europe's Foreign and Security Policy: The Institutionalisation of Cooperation* (Cambridge University Press: Cambridge).

Smith, S. (2001) 'Reflectivist and constructivist approaches to international theory' in J. Baylis and S. Smith (eds) *The Globalization of World Politics: An Introduction to International Relations*, 2nd edn (Oxford: Oxford University Press), pp. 224–49.

Spaak, P.-H. (1956) *The Brussels Report on the General Common Market*, June, Brussels.

Spence, D. and Edwards, G. (eds) (2006) *The European Commission* (London: John Harper Publishing).

Stasavage, D. (2004). 'Open-door or closed door? Transparency in domestic and international bargaining', *International Organization*, 58/2: 667–703.

Statewatch (2011) *The Effects of Security Policies on Rights and Liberties in the European Union, and their Export beyond the EU's Borders*, Statewatch Analysis No. 11/11, available online at http://www.statewatch.org/analyses/no-128-sec-lib-eu.pdf

Steenbergen, M. R, Edwards, E. E., and de Vries, C. E. (2007) 'Who's cueing whom? Mass–elite linkages and the future of European integration', *European Union Politics*, 8/1: 13–35.

Steffek, J., Kissling, C., and Nanz, P. (eds) (2007) *Civil Society Participation in European and Global Governance: A Cure for the Democratic Deficit?* (Basingstoke: Palgrave Macmillan).

Stephenson, P. (2010) 'Let's get physical: the European Commission and cultivated spillover in completing the single market's transport infrastructure', *Journal of European Public Policy*, 17/7: 1039–105.

Stoker, G. (1998) 'Governance as theory: five propositions', *International Social Science Journal*, 50/155: 17–28.

Stone Sweet, A. (2004) *The Judicial Construction of Europe* (Oxford: Oxford University Press).

Stone Sweet, A. (2010) 'The European Court of Justice and the judicialization of EU governance', *Living Reviews in European Governance*, 5/2: 5–50.

Stone Sweet, A. and Brunell, T. L. (1998) 'Constructing a supranational constitution: dispute resolution and governance in the European Community', *American Political Science Review*, 92/1: 63–81.

Stone Sweet, A. and Brunell, T. L. (2004) 'Constructing a supranational constitution' in A. Stone Sweet (ed.) *The Judicial Construction of Europe* (Oxford: Oxford University Press).

Stone Sweet, A. and Caporaso, J. (1998) 'From free trade to supranational polity: the European Court and integration' in W. Sandholtz and A. Stone Sweet (eds) *European Integration and Supranational Governance* (Oxford: Oxford University Press), pp. 92–134.

Streeck, W. and Schmitter, P. C. (1991) 'From national corporatism to transnational pluralism: organized interests in the single European market', *Politics and Society*, 19/2: 133–65.

Sun, J. M. and Pelkmans, J. (1995) 'Regulatory competition in the single market', *Journal of Common Market Studies*, 33/1: 67–89.

Sutcliffe, J. B. (2000) 'The 1999 reform of the structural regulations: multi-level governance or renationalization?', *Journal of European Public Policy*, 7/2: 290–309.

Suvarierol, S. (2008) 'Beyond the myth of nationality: analysing networks within the European Commission', *West European Politics*, 31/4: 701–24.

Szczerbiak, A. and Taggart, P. (2004) 'The politics of European referendum outcomes and turnout: two models', *West European Politics*, 27/4: 557–83.

Taggart, P. and Szczerbiak, A. (2002) 'Europeanization, Euroscepticism and party systems: party-based Euroscepticism in the candidate states of Central and Eastern Europe', *Perspectives on European Politics and Society*, 3/1: 23–41.

Taggart, P. and Szczerbiak, A. (2005) 'Three patterns of party competition over Europe', Paper presented at the conference 'Euroskepticism: causes and consequences', 1–2 July, Amsterdam.

Taggart, P. and Szczerbiak, A. (eds) (2008) *Opposing Europe? The Comparative Party Politics of Euroscepticism, Vols I and II* (Oxford: Oxford University Press).

Tajfel, H. (1970) 'Experiments in intergroup discrimination', *Scientific American*, 223/2: 96–102.

Tallberg, J. (2006) *Leadership and Negotiation in the European Union* (Cambridge: Cambridge University Press).

Taylor, P. (1975) 'The politics of the European Communities: the confederal phase', *World Politics*, 27/3: 335–60.

Taylor, P. (1993) *International Organization in the Modern World: The Regional and the Global Process* (New York: Pinter).

Taylor, P. (1996) *The European Union in the 1990s* (Oxford: Oxford University Press).

Thielemann, E. (1998) 'Policy networks and European governance: the Europeanisation of regional policy-making in Germany', *Regional and Industrial Research Paper Series*, 27: 1–39.

Thomson, R. (2009) 'Actor alignments in the European Union before and after enlargement', *European Journal of Political Research*, 48/6: 756–81.

Thomson, R. (2011) *Resolving Controversy in the European Union: Legislative Decision-making before and after Enlargement* (Cambridge: Cambridge University Press).

Thomson, R. and Hosli, M. O. (2006) 'Explaining legislative decision-making in the European Union', in R. Thomson, F. N. Stokman, C. H. Achen, and T. Koenig (eds) *The European Union Decides* (Cambridge: Cambridge University Press), pp. 1–24.

Thomson, R., Stokman, F. N., Achen, C. H., and Koenig, T. (eds) (2006) *The European Union Decides* (Cambridge: Cambridge University Press).

Tilley, J. and Garry, J. (2007) 'Public support for integration in the newly enlarged EU: exploring differences between former communist countries and established member states' in M. Marsh, S. Mikhaylov, and H. Schmitt (eds) *European Elections after Eastern Enlargement*, CONNEX Report Series No. 1 (Mannheim: MZES Mannheim Centre for European Social Research, University of Mannheim), pp. 181–203.

Toal, G. (2005) 'Being geopolitical', *Political Geography*, 24/3: 365–72.

Tömmel, I. and Verdun, A. (eds) (2008) *Innovative Governance in the European Union* (Boulder, CO: Lynne Rienner).

Tranholm-Mikkelsen, J. (1991) 'Neo-functionalism: obstinate or obsolete? A reappraisal in the light of the new dynamism of the EC', *Millennium: Journal of International Studies*, 20/1: 1–22.

Treib, O., Bähr, H., and Falkner, G. (2009) 'Social policy and environmental policy: comparing modes of governance' in U. Diedrichs and W. Wessels (eds) *The Dynamics of Change in EU Governance: Policy-making and System Evolution* (Cheltenham: Edward Elgar), pp. 103–31.

Trondal, J. (2010) *An Emergent European Executive Order* (Oxford: Oxford University Press).

Trondal, J. and Jeppesen, L. (2008) 'Images of agency governance in the European Union', *West European Politics*, 31/3: 417–41.

Trondal, J., van der Berg, C., and Suvarierol, S. (2008) 'The compound machinery of government: the case of seconded officials in the European Commission', *Governance*, 21/2: 253–74.

Truman, D. B. (1951) *The Governmental Process: Political Interests and Public Opinion* (New York: Alfred A. Knopf).

Tsebelis, G. (1990) *Nested Games: Rational Choice in Comparative Politics* (Berkeley, CA: University of California Press).

Tsebelis, G. (1994) 'The power of the European Parliament as conditional agenda-setter', *American Political Science Review*, 88/1, 128–42.

Tsebelis, G. and Garrett, G. (1997) 'Agenda setting, vetoes and the European Union's co-decision procedure', *Journal of Legislative Studies*, 3/3: 74–92.

Tsoukalis, L. (1997) *The New European Economy Revisited* (Oxford: Oxford University Press).

Tsoukalis, L. (2011) 'The JCMS annual review lecture: the shattering of illusions—and what next?', *Journal of Common Market Studies*, 49/1: 19–44.

Turner, J. C. (1985) 'Social categorization and the self-concept: a social cognitive theory of group behavior', *Advances in Group Processes*, 2: 77–122.

Tuytschaever, F. (2000) 'EMU and the catch-22 of EU constitution-making' in G. de Búrca and J. Scott (eds) *Constitutional Change in the EU: From Uniformity to Flexibility* (Oxford: Hart Publishing), pp. 173–96.

Uçarer, E. M. (2001) 'Managing asylum and European integration: expanding spheres of exclusion?', *International Studies Perspectives*, 2/3: 291–307.

Uçarer, E. M. (2009) 'Safeguarding asylum as a human right: NGOs and the European Union' in J. Joachim and B. Locher (eds) *Transnational Activism in the UN and the EU* (New York: Routledge), pp. 121–39.

Uçarer, E. M. (2010) 'Justice and Home Affairs' in M. Cini and N. Pérez-Solórzano Borragán (eds) *European Union Politic*, 3rd edn (Oxford: Oxford University Press), pp. 306–23.

Urwin, D. W. (1995) *The Community of Europe* (London: Longman).

Vachudova, M. A. (2005) *Europe Undivided: Democracy, Leverage and Integration after Communism* (Oxford: Oxford University Press).

van Apeldoorn, B. (1992) *Transnational Capitalism and the Struggle over European Integration* (London and New York: Routledge).

van Asselt, H. (2010) 'Emissions trading: the enthusiastic adoption of an alien instrument?', in A. Jordan, D. Huitema, H. van Asselt, T. Rayner, and F. Berkhout (eds) *Climate Change Policy in the European Union* (Cambridge: Cambridge University Press), pp. 125–44.

van der Eijk, C. and Franklin, M. (eds) (1996) *Choosing Europe? The European Electorate and National Politics in the Face of Union* (Ann Arbor, MI: University of Michigan Press).

van Keulen, M. (1999) *Going Europe or Going Dutch: How the Dutch Government Shapes European Policy* (Amsterdam: Amsterdam University Press).

Verdun, A. (1996) 'An "asymmetrical" economic and monetary union in the EU: perceptions of monetary authorities and social partners', *Journal of European Integration*, 20/1: 59–81.

Verdun, A. (2000) *European Responses to Globalization and Financial Market Integration: Perceptions of Economic and Monetary Union in Belgium, France and Germany* (Basingstoke: Palgrave Macmillan).

Verdun, A. (2002) *The Euro: European Integration Theory and Economic and Monetary Union* (Lanham, MD: Rowman & Littlefield).

Versluis, E., van Keulen, M., and Stephenson, P. (2011) *Analysing the European Union Policy Process* (Basingstoke: Palgrave).

von Homeyer, I. (2004) 'Differential effects of enlargement on EU environmental governance', *Environmental Politics*, 13/1: 52–76.

Votewatch (2011) *Voting in the 2009–2014 European Parliament: How Do MEPs Vote after Lisbon? Third Report*, available online at http://www.votewatch.eu/blog/wp-content/uploads/2011/01/votewatch_report_voting_behavior_26_january_beta.pdf

Wæver, O. (2009) 'Discursive approaches' in T. Diez and A. Wiener (eds) *European Integration Theory* (Oxford: Oxford University Press), pp. 163–80.

Wallace, H. (2002) 'The Council: an institutional chameleon', *Governance*, 15/3: 325–44.

Wallace, H. (2010) 'An institutional anatomy and five policy modes', in H. Wallace, M. A. Pollack, and A. R. Young (eds) *Policy-making in the European Union* (Oxford: Oxford University Press), pp. 69–104.

Wallace, W. (1982) 'European as a confederation: the Community and the nation-state', *Journal of Common Market Studies*, 21/1: 57–68.

Walters, W. (2004) 'The frontiers of the European Union: a geostrategic perspective', *Geopolitics*, 9/2: 674–98.

Waltz, K. (1979) *Theory of International Politics* (New York: McGraw Hill).

Warleigh, A. (2000) 'The hustle: citizenship practice, NGOs and policy coalitions in the European Union—the cases of auto oil, drinking water and unit pricing', *Journal of European Public Policy*, 7/2: 229–43.

Warleigh, A. (2001) 'Europeanizing civil society: NGOs as agents of political socialization', *Journal of Common Market Studies*, 39/4: 619–39.

Warleigh, A. (2003) *Democracy in the European Union: Theory, Practice and Reform* (London: Sage).

Warleigh-Lack, A. (2006) 'Towards a conceptual framework for regionalization: bridging "new regionalism" and "integration theory"', *Review of International Political Economy*, 13/5: 750–71.

Warleigh-Lack, A. and Drachenberg, R. (2011) 'Spillover in a soft policy era? Evidence from the open method of co-ordination in education and training', *Journal of European Public Policy*, 18/7: 999–1015.

Warleigh-Lack, A. and Rosamond, B. (2010) 'Across the EU studies–new regionalism frontier: an invitation to dialogue', *Journal of Common Market Studies*, 48/4: 993–1013.

Weale, A. (2005) 'European environmental policy by stealth' in A. Jordan (ed.) *Environmental policy in the European Union*, 2nd edn (London: Earthscan), pp. 336–54.

Weale, A., Pridham, G., Cini, M., Konstadakopulos, D., Porter, M., and Flynn, B. (2000) *Environmental Governance in Europe* (Oxford: Oxford University Press).

Weiler, J. H. H. (1997) 'Legitimacy and democracy of Union governance' in G. Edwards and A. Pijpers (eds) *The Politics of European Treaty Reform* (London: Pinter), pp. 249–87.

Wendt, A. (1999) *Social Theory of International Politics* (Cambridge: Cambridge University Press).

Wessels, W. (1997) 'Ever closer fusion? A dynamic macro-political view on integration processes', *Journal of Common Market Studies*, 35/2: 267–99.

Wessels, W. (1998) 'Comitology: fusion in action—politico-administrative trends in the EU system', *Journal of European Public Policy*, 5/2: 209–34.

Wessels, W. and Rometsch, D. (1996) 'Conclusion: European Union and national institutions' in D. Rometsch and W. Wessels (eds) *The European Union and Member States: Towards Institutional Fusion?* (Manchester: Manchester University Press), pp. 328–65.

Widgren, M. (1994) 'Voting power in the EC decision making and consequences of the different enlargements', *European Economic Review*, 38/4: 1153–70.

Wiener, A. (2006) 'Constructivism and sociological institutionalism' in M. Cini and A. K. Bourne (eds) *Palgrave Advances in European Union Studies* (Basingstoke: Palgrave), pp. 35–55.

Wiener, A. and Diez, T. (eds) (2009) *European Integration Theory*, 2nd edn (Oxford: Oxford University Press).

Wildgen, J. K. and Feld, W. J. (1976) 'Evaluative and cognitive factors in the prediction of European unification', *Comparative Political Studies*, 9/3: 309–34.

Wincott, D. (1995) 'Institutional interaction and European integration: towards an everyday critique of liberal intergovernmentalism', *Journal of Common Market Studies*, 33/4: 597–609.

Wong, R. and Hill, C. (eds) (2011) *National and European Foreign Policy: Towards Europeanization* (London: Routledge).

Wonka, A. (2008) 'Decision-making dynamics in the European Commission: partisan, national or sectoral?', *Journal of European Public Policy*, 15/8: 1145–63.

Wonka, A. and Rittberger, B. (2011) 'Perspectives on EU governance: an empirical assessment of the political attitudes of EU agency professionals', *Journal of European Public Policy*, 18/6: 888–908.

Wurzel, R. K. W. (2008) 'Environmental policy' in J. Hayward (ed.) *Leaderless Europe* (Oxford: Oxford University Press), pp. 66–88.

Wurzel, R. K. W. (2012) 'The Council of Ministers' in A. Jordan and C. Adelle (eds) *Environmental Policy in the European Union*, 3rd edn (London: Routledge), pp. 75–94.

Young, A. (2006) 'The politics of regulation and the single market', in K. E. Jørgensen, M. A. Pollack, and B. Rosamond (eds) *Handbook of European Union Politics* (London: Sage), pp. 373–94.

Young, A. R. (1997) 'Consumption without representation? Consumers in the single market' in H. Wallace and A. R. Young (eds) *Participation and Policy-making in the European Union* (Oxford: Clarendon Press), pp. 206–34.

Zaller, J. (1992) *The Nature and Origins of Mass Opinion* (Cambridge: Cambridge University Press).

Zeitlin, J., Pochet, P., and Magnusson, L. (eds) (2005) *The Open Method of Co-Ordination in Action: The European Employment and Social Inclusion Strategies* (Brussels: PIE Peter Lang).

Zito, A. R. (2001) 'Epistemic communities, collective entrepreneurship and European integration', *Journal of European Public Policy*, 8/4: 585–603.

Zito, A. R. (2005) 'The European Union as an environmental leader in a global environment', *Globalizations*, 2/3: 363–75.

Zysman, J. (1994) 'How institutions create historically rooted trajectories of growth', *Industrial and Corporate Change*, 3/1: 243–83.

Index